HUMAN RIGHTS ACT 1998:
A PRACTITIONER'S GUIDE

AUSTRALIA
LBC Information Services
Sydney

CANADA AND USA
Carswell
Toronto

NEW ZEALAND
Brooker's
Auckland

SINGAPORE AND MALAYSIA
Thomson Information (S.E. Asia)
Singapore

HUMAN RIGHTS ACT 1998:
A PRACTITIONER'S GUIDE

General Editor

CHRISTOPHER BAKER

LONDON • SWEET & MAXWELL • 1998

Published in 1998 by
Sweet & Maxwell Limited
100 Avenue Road
London NW3 3PF
(http://www.smlawpub.co.uk)

Typeset by Dataword Services Limited of Chilcompton
Printed and bound in Great Britain by Bell & Bain, Glasgow

No natural forests were destroyed
to make this product, only farmed
timber was used and re-planted.

ISBN 0752 00606 1

A C.I.P. catalogue record for this book
is available from the British Library

Christopher Baker (Chaps 1 & 2); David Carter (Chap. 13); Judith Carter (Chap. 5);
Iain Colville (Chap. 8); Leon Daniel (Chap. 4 — Pt II); Andrew Dymond (Chap. 7);
Francis Fitzpatrick (Chap. 14); John Friel (Chap. 11); Deborah Hay (Chap. 11);
Josephine Henderson (Chap. 6); David Hewitt (Chap. 10); Caroline Hunter (Chap. 7);
Alyson Kilpatrick (Chap. 3); Jonathan Manning (Chap. 3); Jonathan Peacock (Chap. 14);
Nigel Richardson (Chap. 4 — Pt I); Prof. Robin C. A. White (Chap 12); Tim Wright (Chap.
9).
1998

Preface

Until the Human Rights Act 1998, most legal practitioners in this country will have had a very limited (if any) sense of need to become familiar with the law of the European Convention for the Protection of Human Rights and Fundamental Freedoms. This book seeks to address the fundamental and wide-ranging change which the Act makes in giving formal effect to certain aspects of the Convention in domestic law. At a stroke, it will be necessary for all advocates and advisers to be conversant not only with the Convention itself and its Protocols, but also with around 40 years' worth of accumulated jurisprudence

Accordingly, although this book is a guide to the provisions of the Act itself, considering their meaning and effect, it is also a guide to the relevant parts of Convention law. Without pretending to present encyclopedic coverage of all the latter material, it is the intention to present the essential elements of this considerable body of law in a practical and accessible manner. Because the Convention provides in many ways a very different system of law, and because the Act allows and envisages scope for national courts and tribunals to adapt and apply Convention law (by having regard to it, without being bound by it), the future development of domestic law is — to a considerable extent — unclear. This book accordingly looks at some of the ways in which this development may be affected, in terms of practical issues.

Chapters 1 and 2 provide an outline of the Act and Convention law generally. At a time of increasing professional specialisation, and so as to provide a convenient guide to the impact of the Act and Convention law in different areas of domestic law and practice, Chapters 3 to 14 then go on to examine the Act and the Convention in the context of particular fields of practice. In this way, the practitioner has access both to the general principles and to a sense of their application.

I thank the contributors of the 12 specialist chapters, whose work accounts for the large majority of the text. By reason of production schedules, they have endeavoured to state the law as at September 1998, in readiness for Royal Assent. I also want to express my gratitude to Ruth, Jonathan and Rosy, whose understanding and patience helped to make this book possible; and also in particular to Susan Marshall, at Sweet and Maxwell, for all her support and assistance.

Christopher Baker
Arden Chambers
London
November 1998

General Note on References for Strasbourg Cases and Convention Provisions

Case references

The current official series of reports of judgments and decisions of the Strasbourg authorities ("R.J.D.") is published by Carl Heymanns Verlag, in English and French. The series began in 1996. References to these reports in this book are given in this manner: *Benham v. U.K.*, R.J.D. 1996–III 738, para. 10 — *i.e.* the case name, the year and volume reference, the page number, and (where relevant) the particular numbered paragraph in the judgment.

Until 1996, the previous official series of reports of judgments of the European Court of Human Rights was published by Carl Heymanns Verlag, in English and French. Series A of these reports contains the judgments of the Court, and from 1984 it also contains extracts from the Commission report. Series B (which is not up-to-date) contains pleadings, arguments and documents. References to these reports in this book are given in this manner: *Golder v. U.K.* (1975) Series A, No. 18, para. 6 — *i.e.* the case name, the year in which the judgment was given, the volume number for the report, and (where relevant) the particular numbered paragraph in the judgment. Where it is the Commission report, rather than the Court judgment, to which reference is made, this is indicated.

Beween 1975 and 1995, the previous series of Decisions and Reports of the European Commission of Human Rights was published by the Council of Europe, in English and French. It is a selection of cases including admissibility decisions, and reports on the merits of cases which are not referred to the Court. References to these reports in this book are given in this manner: *S v. U.K.* (1986) 47 D.R. 274 — *i.e.* the case name, the year of the decision, the volume number of the series, and the page number of that volume. From volume 76, the series was published in two parts (*e.g.* 76–A and 76–B), with volume A containing the report in the original language of the case, and the B volume following later with the translation.

From 1959 to 1974, the precursor to the Decisions and Reports series was the Collection of Decisions of the European Commission of Human Rights, also published by the Council of Europe in English and French. References to these reports in this book are given in this manner: *X v. U.K.* (1967) 25 C.D. 76 — *i.e.* case name, year of decision, volume number, page number.

Foremost among the "unofficial" series of reports is Sweet and Maxwell's European Human Rights Reports (E.H.R.R.), which includes Court judgments and some Commission reports and decisions. From 1993, there is a separate Commission Supplement (E.H.R.R. C.D.), containing summaries and extracts of Commission decisions. References to these reports in this book are given in this manner: *Lithgow v. U.K.* (1986) 8 E.H.R.R. 329 — *i.e.* case name, year of publication, volume number, page number.

Since most practitioners tend to use and have readier access to the E.H.R.R. reports, where possible both the official and the E.H.R.R. references are given in this book. In such cases, the reference appears as *Lithgow v. U.K.* (1986) Series A, No. 102; 8 E.H.R.R. 329, para. 105 — *i.e.* combining the references, but omitting the year of publication for the E.H.R.R. report.

Some reports can also be found in the Digest of Strasbourg Case-Law Relating to the European Convention on Human Rights, published by Carl Heymanns Verlag from 1984, and in the Yearbook of the European Convention on Human Rights.

Each petition to the Commission is given an official reference number, *e.g.* 9006/80. These reference numbers are not reproduced in this book where a case report is cited.

The internet site for the Court can be found at: www.dhcour.coe.fr/

Convention references

References in the text to Convention provisions take into account the changes in substance and numbering made by the Eleventh Protocol. Where the previous Convention provisions are referred to they are indicated by an asterisk.

DISCLAIMER

The views expressed in this book are solely those of the authors and do not represent those of any institution.

Contents

CHAPTER 5: IMMIGRATION AND ASYLUM............. 5–01

Judith Carter

CHAPTER 6: FAMILY AND CHILD LAW 6–01

Josephine Henderson

Table of U.K. Cases

Table of Statutes

Table of Statutory Instruments

Table of Cases before the
European Court of Human Rights

Table of Cases before the European Commission of Human Rights

Table of E.C. Cases

Table of International Legislation

ERRATUM

p. 432: Section 7. – (9)(a) should read "in relation to proceedings before a court or tribunal outside Scotland...."

Section 7. – (9)(b) should read "in relation to proceedings before a court or tribunal in Scotland...."

After section 7. – (9)(c)(ii) and before "and includes provision made...." should be inserted "rules made by a Northern Ireland department for those purposes,"

p. 439: Section **21**. – (f)(i) should read "made in exercise of Her Majesty's Royal Prerogative,"

E.C. Secondary Legislation

CHAPTER 1

The Act in Outline

Christopher Baker (Barrister, Arden Chambers)

A. THE HISTORICAL AND POLITICAL CONTEXT

1–01 It is often said that the United Kingdom does not have a written constitution. While in one sense this is true, such a statement is apt to conceal the fact that there is indeed a significant amount of legal material, in the form of legislation, which has provided some written definition to domestic constitutional arrangements (in their widest sense). Along with such materials as the Magna Carta, the Bill of Rights 1689, the Act of Settlement 1700, the Acts of Union, the Parliament Acts 1911 and 1949, the Crown Proceedings Act 1947, and the European Communities Act 1972, the Human Rights Act 1998 (referred to throughout this book as "the Act") has assumed an important place in this incomplete and idiosyncratic patchwork.

1. The disparity between domestic and international law

1–02 The Act is the response to a growing sense of unease, discomfort and astonishment, particularly in political and legal circles, that the United Kingdom can have played such a major part, over more than half a century, in assuring fundamental rights and freedoms in other states without having achieved the same within its own jurisdiction. Perhaps nowhere has this strange imbalance been more marked than in respect of the United Kingdom's position, internationally and internally, with regard to the European Convention for the Protection of Human Rights and Fundamental Freedoms (Cmnd 8969, referred to throughout in this book as "the Convention") The U.K. government was heavily involved in the drafting of the Convention, was one of the first to sign it in 1950, and was the first to ratify it in 1951. Since 1966 the United Kingdom has also accepted the right of individuals to petition the Strasbourg authorities in respect of alleged breaches of the Convention. Yet the rights and freedoms guaranteed by the state as obligations in international law were not themselves part of, or actionable within, the domestic legal system.

2. A change in perception

1–03 The attitude of the various governments of the day had been that the Convention, as a manifestation of a Bill of Rights, was really needed by the people of other states and not by the people of the United Kingdom. The view repeatedly stated was to the effect that the government, "have at present no reason to suppose that there is a conflict between any of the provisions of the Convention and the law of the United Kingdom or the general rules governing administrative practice in this country" (written answer in the House of Lords on March 23, 1978 by the Minister of State, Home Office).

Perhaps two factors above all contributed to a widespread sense that this was not a sufficient or satisfactory response. First, there grew to be a significant (though not perhaps disproportionate) number of cases, often receiving considerable publicity, in which domestic law or legal practice was held by the Strasbourg authorities to be in violation of the Convention. The results of such decisions have included important legislative changes, including the Contempt of Court Act 1981 and the Interception of Communications Act 1985; new Prison Rules and practices; changes in the Immigration Rules; and (in one case) the making of a derogation from the terms of the Convention. Secondly, a sense of disquiet developed about an average delay of five years and an average cost of around £30,000 involved in taking a case to Strasbourg. Substantial momentum grew behind the view that there was much to be gained from giving domestic courts the jurisdiction, and state authorities the obligation, to give effect to the Convention. Indeed, the very fact that the various governments of the day did not take this action possibly helped to create (ironically) the expectation that much would be changed if the Convention became part of domestic law.

3. Previous attempts at change

1-04   As long ago as 1977, a modern Bill of Rights was introduced in the House of Lords by Lord Wade. This measure would have given the Convention and its existing Protocols the immediate and unreserved force of law within the United Kingdom, enforceable by action in the ordinary courts. In the event of any conflict between the Convention provisions and any prior or subsequent legislation, the Convention provisions would have prevailed unless (in the case of subsequent legislation) otherwise explicitly provided. That Bill led to a Select Committee of the House of Lords, which reported on the matter in 1978 (1977–78 H.L. 176). The Committee was almost evenly divided about the wisdom of a Bill of Rights, though it was agreed that any Bill should be based on the Convention. Other attempts at incorporation of the Convention have included (in the House of Commons) those made by Sir Edward Gardiner Q.C. (in 1987) and (in the House of Lords) by Lord Lester of Herne Hill (in 1994 and again in 1996).

4. The 1997 General Election, and White Paper

1-05   In its manifesto for the 1997 General Election, the Labour Party made a commitment to incorporate the Convention. After success in the election, the government then issued the Human Rights Bill simultaneously with a White Paper entitled "Rights Brought Home: The Human Rights Bill" (1997 C.M. 3782). The theme, bringing rights home, was practical, yet of potentially great significance. It was stated in this way:

"1.18 We therefore believe that the time has come to enable people to enforce their Convention rights against the State in the British courts . . ."

"1.19 Our aim is a straightforward one. It is to make more directly accessible the rights which the British people already enjoy under the Convention. In other words, to bring those rights home."

The White Paper referred to the delay and expense involved in taking a case to the European Human Rights Commission and Court in Strasbourg, observing that this might deter some people altogether from pursuing their rights. The government also expressed the hope that, by having direct jurisdiction over the application of the Convention, domestic courts could also help to influence the jurisprudence in Strasbourg, because domestic court judgments would make the Court more familiar with domestic law and custom.

5. The Human Rights Bill

1–06 Although the White Paper was prepared by the Home Office, the Bill was introduced as a House of Lords' measure. When moving the Second Reading, the Lord Chancellor (Lord Irvine of Lairg) stated the reasoning in these terms:

"The traditional freedom of the individual under an unwritten constitution to do himself that which is not prohibited by law gives no protection from misuse of power by the state, nor any protection from acts or omissions of public bodies . . . incompatible with . . . human rights under the Convention." (*Hansard*, H.L., November 3, 1997, col. 1228)

He referred to the failure of the legal system to provide protection in 50 cases in which the European Court had found a violation of the Convention by the United Kingdom, half of these being since 1990. In numerical terms, this was second only to Italy. He was also forceful in saying that one had to "reject as absurd the proposition that because we have liberty, we have no need of human rights" (*ibid.*). This remark was a rebuff to the traditional view, substantially influenced by Dicey (*The Law of the Constitution*), that the common law provided for individual liberty through the principle that each person is free to do as they wish unless expressly prohibited by law (see, *e.g. Entick v. Carrington* (1765) 19 St Tr. 1030).

1–07 When he subsequently introduced the Bill into the House of Commons, the Home Secretary (Jack Straw) commented:

"This is the first major Bill on human rights for more than 300 years. It will strengthen representative and democratic government. It does so by enabling citizens to challenge more easily actions of the state if they fail to match the standards set by the European Convention." (*Hansard*, H.C., February 16, 1998, col. 769)

He emphasised that the Bill did not remove any existing freedoms. But, he said, "those freedoms alone are not enough: they need to be complemented by positive rights that individuals can assert when they believe that they have been treated unfairly by the state, or that the state and its institutions have failed properly to protect them." (*ibid.*)

In other words, the Bill would establish a minimum "floor" of civil and political rights by giving effect to the Convention.

Although the general framework of the Bill survived its passage through Parliament intact, two particular developments deserve mention here. In its original form, the Bill made no specific provision in relation to either the freedom of expression (with particular relevance for the press), or in relation to the freedom of thought, conscience and religion (with particular relevance for churches and religious groups). Both of these aspects were contentious. First, the press were concerned that, at a time particularly of great public debate about the need for curbs on some of the excesses of (especially) the "popular" press, and about the perceived need for some development of greater protection for personal privacy, there was a danger that the courts would use Article 8 (right to respect for private and family life) as a means of developing a right to privacy to the detriment of free speech and journalistic investigation. Secondly, religious groups were concerned that the application of the Act to religious bodies would embroil them in litigation, and involve challenges to the application of religious practice and teaching in contexts such as employment and schooling. In the result, sections 12 and 13 (which were introduced as government amendments during the Committee stage in the House of Commons) now make specific provision in relation to both these areas (see further, paragraphs 1–67—1–71 below).

6. Hansard references

1–08 *Hansard*, H.L.: November 3, 1997, cols. 1227–1312 (Second Reading); November 18, 1997 cols. 466–481, 490–527, 533–562 (Committee); January 19, 1998 cols. 1252–1311, 1317–1368, and January 29, 1998 cols. 381–422 (Report); February 5, 1998 cols. 747–842 (Third Reading). *Hansard*, H.C.: February 16, 1998 cols. 769–868 (Second Reading); May 20, 1998 cols. 975–1074; June 3, 1998 cols. 388–475; June 17, 1998 cols. 391–434; June 24, 1998 cols. 1054–1143; July 2, 1998 cols. 534–575 (Committee); October 21, 1998 cols. 1293–1368 (Third Reading). *Hansard*, H.L.; October 29, 1998 cols. 2084–2119 (consideration of Commons amendments).

B. THE LEGAL CONTEXT

1–09 The background to the Bill needs to be explained in relation to the legal theory which, for over 40 years, created the position that the law of the Convention, though binding on the U.K. government at Strasbourg, did not have effect within national boundaries (or, at least, not directly). An understanding of this is important to an appreciation of the effect of the Act.

1. Parliamentary supremacy

1–10 In the traditions of British constitutional law, parliament is supreme and sovereign (see Dicey, *op cit.*) For more detailed explanation and criticism of the theory and practice of this, see, *e.g.* Bradley and Ewing, *Constitutional and Administrative Law* (Longman, 12th ed., Chap. 4); Hunt, *Using Human Rights Law in English Courts* (Hart). By this is meant that Parliament is omnicompetent, and has the exclusive right to change the law. There is a number of components and consequences to this. First, the courts must uphold parliamentary legislation, and cannot hold it to be unlawful or invalid (see, *e.g.* *Pickin v. British Railways Board* [1974] A.C. 765). The respectful distance which the courts are expected to keep from the affairs of parliament is further exemplified by Article 9 of the Bill of Rights 1689, which provides that "the freedom of speech and debates or proceedings in Parliament ought not to be impeached or questioned in any court or place out of Parliament".

Next, and central to questions relating to the Convention, domestic courts will not fail to uphold and apply parliamentary legislation on grounds that it conflicts with international law or a treaty obligation of the United Kingdom (*Mortensen v. Peters* (1906) 8 F.(J.) 93; *Rustomjee v. The Queen* (1876) 2 Q.B.D. 69; *Blackburn v. Att. Gen.* [1971] 1 W.L.R. 1037) An international treaty obligation is not "justiciable" by domestic courts unless and until it has been incorporated into domestic law by Parliament (*J. H. Rayner (Mincing Lane) Ltd v. Department of Trade and Industry* [1990] 2 A.C. 418). It is in this sense that our system of law is said to be "dualist", *i.e.* operating separately in the planes of international and domestic law. This may be compared to other, "monist" systems in which this dichotomy is not (or not so rigidly) recognised.

2. The Convention and the common law

1–11 The received view, as regards the standing of the Convention in domestic law, was expressed in *R. v. Home Secretary, ex p. Brind* [1991] 1 A.C. 696, 747 *per* Lord Bridge:

> "It is accepted, of course, by the applicants that, like any other treaty obligations which have not been embodied in the law by statute, the Convention is not part of the domestic law, that the courts accordingly have no power to enforce Convention rights directly and that, if domestic legislation conflicts with the Convention, the courts must nevertheless enforce it."

Considered, therefore, in the context of these constitutional practices, the introduction of Convention law into domestic law by Act of Parliament carries tremendous significance.

1–12 However, the somewhat fundamentalist attitude explained above has not been universal in its application, and certainly not to the extent of denying all possible relevance to the Convention in domestic law terms. The common law has shown a willingness to have regard to customary international law, and to adopt the latter's rules where these are not inconsistent with existing legislation or case law (see *Chung Chi Cheung v. The King* [1939] A.C. 160, 168 *per* Lord Atkin). In *Att.-Gen. v. BBC* [1993] A.C. 534, Lord Fraser suggested that the courts should have regard to the Convention and Convention law where "domestic law is not firmly settled" (see also *R v. Mid-Glamorgan Family Health Services, ex p. Martin* [1995] 1 W.L.R. 110, at 118–119). It is also accepted that the Convention can be an aid to interpretation in the case of statutory ambiguity or uncertainty (see, *e.g. Brind*, above), allied to which is a working presumption that Parliament is taken as having intended to comply with international treaty obligations (see, *e.g. Re Lonrho plc* [1990] 2 A.C. 154, 208 in respect of legislation passed in consequence of Convention case law).

Moreover, there have been respects in which the courts have been prepared to entertain the idea that consideration of the exercise of various discretions also requires recourse to the Convention. In *R. v. Khan* [1996] 1 W.L.R. 162 the House of Lords indicated that breach of Convention rights in obtaining evidence may be relevant to the exercise of discretion as to the admissibility of that evidence in criminal proceedings, pursuant to section 78 of the Police and Criminal Evidence Act 1984. In *R. v. Secretary of State for Transport, ex p. Richmond upon Thames LBC* [1996] 1 W.L.R. 1460 the Court of Appeal considered that ministers were to be presumed to have intended to comply with the requirements of the Convention in the exercise of statutory powers, unless a clear, contrary legislative intent was shown. Where the standards of the Convention are in step with the common law, and influence European law, the view has also been expressed that it would be unreal and potentially unjust to develop public law without regard to them (see *R. v. Secretary of State for the Home Department, ex p. McQuillan* [1995] 4 All E.R. 400).

In general terms it can be said that, prior to the Act, an increasing tension developed between regard for the apparent orthodoxy of *ex. p. Brind* and a desire that the common law should neither stand still nor develop in isolation from — or, worse, conflict with — the Convention. (For an extensive analysis and critique of the recent case law see Hunt, *op. cit*).

3. The Convention and European law

1–13   European law was introduced into and formally takes effect within the domestic legal order by the European Communities Act 1972. There may also now be an argument for saying that, apart from the E.C. Act, European law may influence the common law through the latter's recognition of international treaty obligations (see Hunt, *op, cit*, Chapters 2, 3 and 7) and by the identification of common standards (see *McQuillan* above). By reason of the regard which, through the jurisprudence of the ECJ, European law holds for fundamental rights and treaty obligations such as the Convention, this provides a route by which Convention rights may be given effect in domestic law (for discussion of the position in European law see paragraphs 2–05—2–06).

4. Human rights generally under English law

1–14   Before the Act, civil and political rights under English law could be described as being residual — unless restrained by the law, persons are free to do as they like (see paragraph 1–06 above, and *Att.-Gen. v. Observer Ltd* [1990] 1

A.C. 109, at 178 and 660). Much of the language of the law in this respect was not couched in terms of rights, though the courts have more recently shown a willingness to express themselves in this way (*e.g. Derbyshire County Council v. Times Newspapers Ltd* [1993] A.C. 534 — right of free speech).

Various human rights, accorded through the Convention, can be said to have been recognised in English law before the Act. The right to life (*e.g. Airedale NHS Trust v. Bland* [1993] A.C. 789; Abortion Act 1967), freedom from ill-treatment (*e.g.* Offences Against the Person Act 1861; personal injury torts), right to personal liberty (*e.g. Khawaja v. Secretary of State for the Home Department* [1984] A.C. 74), freedom from arbitrary search and seizure (*e.g. Entick v. Carrington* (1765) 19 State Tr. 1029, *Marcel v. Metropolitan Police Commissioner* [1992] Ch. 225), freedom of expression (*e.g. Derbyshire County Council v. Times Newspapers Ltd*, above), freedom of conscience and religion (*e.g. Wheeler v. Leicester City Council* [1985] 1 A.C. 1054), freedom of association and assembly (*e.g. Chertsey UDC v. Mixnam's Properties Ltd* [1965] A.C. 735; Trade Union and Labour Relations (Consolidation) Act 1992), the protection of personal property (*e.g. Prest v. Secretary of State for Wales* (1982) 81 L.G.R. 193; Theft Acts; property torts), the right to education (see the Education Acts; *Meade v. Haringey London Borough Council* [1979] 1 W.L.R. 637), and the right to vote and stand for election (*e.g.* Representation of the People Act 1983), all have recognition in English law.

In some respects, domestic law can clearly be seen to go further than the Convention as to the nature and extent of rights which are protected (*e.g.* the right to housing, under Part VII of the Housing Act 1996, see Chapter 7). This is particularly because the Convention is primarily concerned with civil and political rights, rather than social and economic rights. In other respects, it is evident that domestic law has failed to secure rights in the manner and to the extent required by the Convention (see paragraph 1–06 above).

C. GENERAL STRUCTURE AND APPROACH

1–15 Although the Labour Party's election commitment was to introduce legislation to "incorporate" the Convention into domestic law, the long title to the Act speaks more accurately in terms of giving "further effect" to the Convention rights. As was made apparent during the Committee stage of the Bill in the House of Lords, there is an important distinction between making the Convention provisions part of domestic law (as under Lord Wade's Bill), and the scheme adopted under the Act. In reply to an amendment proposed by Lord Simon of Glaisdale, the Lord Chancellor said of the scheme adopted by the Act:

"The convention rights will not . . . in themselves become part of our substantive domestic law." (*Hansard*, H.L., November 18, 1997, col. 508.)

The consequence is that the Convention rights are not directly justiciable and enforceable by domestic courts (*Hansard*, H.L., January 29, 1998, cols. 421–422). Instead, two particular methods have been used to secure the Convention rights within domestic law, as explained below. These methods are notably distinguishable from the manner in which European Community law has been given effect in domestic law: section 2(1) of the European Communities Act 1972 gave general effect to the Community treaties in domestic law, and section 3(1) required domestic courts — when determining questions arising under Community law provisions — to do so in accordance with decisions and principles of the ECJ.

Article 1 requires the contracting parties to "secure to everyone within their jurisdiction" the rights and freedoms defined in section I of the Convention. As explained below (see paragraph 2–07), the manner in which each state chooses to do this is a matter for that state to decide, and Article 1 does not require the incorporation of the Convention into domestic law. However, to the extent that domestic law, including the Act, fails to secure all the necessary rights, there will be a violation of the Convention which may be the subject of complaint to Strasbourg (see further, paragraph 1–72).

As is self-evident from the subject-matter, the Act binds the Crown (section 22(5)).

1. Statutory interpretation

1–16 By section 3(1) all legislation must, so far as possible, be read and given effect in a way which is compatible with the Convention rights (see further, paragraph 1–31 and following below), so making it generally necessary to test statutory provisions against these standards. Although this provision will chiefly be significant in terms of statutory construction by the courts, it is applicable generally and thus relevant to all those involved in the application of legislation. The new method of interpretation carries a very significant leaning in favour of compatibility, and could well result in a different construction from that which otherwise might follow. This approach goes much wider in its use of the Convention that the previous common law approach (see above paragraphs 1–11—1–12). Furthermore, if a compatible construction cannot be arrived at, some courts have the jurisdiction to make formal orders of incompatibility (see further, paragraphs 1–40—1–41 below). A remedial order may in consequence be made by a Minister in order to amend incompatible legislation (see paragraph 1–44 below).

Allied to the interpretative provision are new requirements in relation to parliamentary procedure, designed to focus attention on the requirements of the Convention rights during the passage of legislation through Parliament (see further, paragraph 1–45 below).

As regards the legislative activity of Parliament, the general approach of the Act is accordingly limited in the extent to which the Convention is given effect. In legal terms, it does not impinge upon the supremacy of Parliament, which remains free as a matter of domestic law to act contrary to the requirements of the Convention. The Act also maintains that supremacy in terms of the relationship of the courts and Parliament, since the courts are not given the power to annul any legislation. A declaration of incompatibility does no more, but no less, than provide a formal order about the existence of a conflict between the two systems of law.

2. Public authorities

1–17 By section 6(1) it is generally unlawful for any public authority to act in a way which is incompatible with a Convention right (see further, paragraph 1–46 and following below). This complements the interpretative mechanism under section 3 by imposing a direct, positive obligation on most organs of the state to observe these rights. Consequently, the day to day affairs of the state are rendered generally subject, in domestic law, to these rights. This obligation extends to the courts themselves, so that the processes of litigation also fall to be examined by those standards. However, although general, the obligation is not unlimited, and it is important to consider both the scope of the term "public authority" and the nature of the conduct which falls within the ambit of the statutory duty. Those advising both public authorities, and others dealing with public authorities, will thus need to become familiar with the principles of law applicable under the Act and the Convention.

3. Forensic application of the Convention and Convention law

1–18 When any court or tribunal is determining a question which has arisen in connection with a Convention right, it is not only the terms of the Convention provisions which fall to be considered. By section 2(1) a court or tribunal determining any question which has arisen in connection with a Convention right must take into account other sources of Convention law where relevant to the proceedings. The institutions creating these legal materials are: the European Court of Human Rights (referred to throughout this book as "the Court"); the European Commission of Human Rights (referred to throughout this book as "the Commission"); and the Committee of Ministers. The materials are:

(a) any judgment, decision, declaration or advisory opinion of the Court;

(b) opinions of the Commission in a report to the Committee of Ministers under *Article 31 (i.e. on whether or not there has been a violation);

(c) decisions of the Commission in connection with *Articles 26 or 27(2) (i.e. admissibility of petitions); and

(d) decisions of the Committee of Ministers under Article 46.

(Throughout this book, Convention Articles marked * are referred to as unamended by the Eleventh Protocol — see paragraph 2–13 below.)

Where the legal materials referred to above are to be relied on, they must be evidenced in such manner as may be provided for by any rules (section 2(2)).

1–19 The obligation of the court or tribunal is only to take these materials into account: they are not binding. The Strasbourg authorities themselves do not have a doctrine of *stare decisis*, though they do generally follow their own previous decisions. Moreover, the only decisions which are binding under the Convention on the United Kingdom are those to which the United Kingdom is itself a party (Article 46(1)). Under the Act it will be for domestic courts to consider the extent to which Convention case law is relevant to any particular issue, and how that case law should be applied. Once there is a decision of a domestic court on a particular point, the doctrine of precedent can then apply to it in the usual way, subject to consideration of any subsequent developments at Strasbourg. This creates the opportunity for domestic courts to develop an indigenous body of human rights law, influenced by Strasbourg but built upon the existing foundations of English law. In opposition to a proposed amendment which would have made sources of law emanating from the Court binding upon domestic courts, the Lord Chancellor referred to the need for the courts to have "flexibility and discretion" in "developing human rights law"; and gave as an example the possibility of Strasbourg decisions becoming outdated. As drafted, section 2(1) would allow the courts to use their "common sense" (*Hansard*, H.L., January 19, 1998, col. 1271).

The Convention rights, of course, are drafted in very general terms. This represents a challenge in itself for the English law common law tradition, which has tended to proceed on the basis of the incremental and deductive development of general principles applied to the facts presented by particular cases. It may well take some while before judges, tribunals and advisers become familiar with dealing in the broad statements of rights and freedoms used in the Convention. Furthermore, the approach of the Strasbourg authorities tends to be different, generally being described as inductive — *i.e.* inferring general principles from the observation of particular factual situations. Some of the concepts used and developed by Strasbourg are also distinct: margin of appreciation, proportionality, and manifest unreasonableness are examples of approaches which — to varying extents — have existing parallels or application in domestic law. (For the general principles of Convention law see Chapter 2.) The challenge for domestic law will lie in becoming much more immediately familiar with these principles and examples of their application, and in weaving these into existing structures. Given the very substantial increase in recent years in the number of petitions being made to Strasbourg from the United Kingdom (itself the product of greater familiarity among advisers and the public with Convention law), and in turn the increasing frequency with which violations have been found, it can certainly be anticipated that significant developments will occur, whether in form, method or substance.

1–20 It will undoubtedly take some time for the general outlines of this new domestic jurisprudence to emerge. However, one of the central tenets of the Act is that, in "bringing rights home" (in the words of the White Paper), issues arising in relation to the Convention rights can be dealt with as they arise in the course of ordinary proceedings. Although the general level of familiarity among advisers and the public may take a while to reach the point where these issues begin to be taken as a matter of course, the opportunity for doing so will be immediate once the Act is in force. In comparison to the delay inherent in the Strasbourg machinery, involving not only the time taken by the Strasbourg authorities but also the requirement to exhaust all domestic remedies first, this will provide a welcome contrast.

4. The Convention rights

1–21   For obvious reasons, the Act does not give effect to those parts of the Convention which deal with procedural and institutional matters relevant to the Strasbourg authorities, and it is the majority of section I of the Convention (Rights and Freedoms), together with the substantive parts of the First and Sixth Protocols, with which the Act is most immediately concerned. Throughout the Act there is reference to Convention rights. By section 1(1) this is defined to mean the rights and fundamental freedoms set out in Articles 2 to 12 and Article 14 of the Convention, together with Articles 1 to 3 of the First Protocol and Articles 1 and 2 of the Sixth Protocol, and as these are to be read with Articles 16 to 18 of the Convention. These provisions are set out in Schedule 1 to the Act, the whole of which is reproduced at Appendix 1.

The Articles set out in Schedule 1 are reproduced with the convenient headings they have been given under the amendments made by the Eleventh Protocol, which also replaces the procedural and institutional provisions in section II of the Convention. The numbering of several Articles, whose substance remains the same, is thus altered. Some of the references in the Act to particular Articles relate to the new numbering (*e.g.* section 7(7) — victims), whereas others refer to the old numbering (*e.g.* section 2(1) — sources of Convention law). (See further, section 21(2)–(4).)

It will immediately be apparent from the above that all of section I of the Convention is given effect under the Act, except for Articles 1, 13 and 15. While the omission of Article 1 (the general obligation on states to secure the Convention rights) and Article 15 (the right of derogation) is self-evident, the omission of Article 13 is curious. This latter provision (which is reproduced in Appendix 2) requires the state to provide an "effective remedy" for violations of the guaranteed rights and freedoms. Such a remedy is to be before a "national authority", and should exist even where the violation has been committed by those "acting in an official capacity". At first sight, the exclusion of Article 13 from the scope of the Act seems both bizarre and paradoxical.

1–22   Responding to questions about the omission, on the Second Reading in the House of Lords, the Under-Secretary of State (Lord Williams of Mostyn) replied: "Our view is, quite unambiguously, that Article 13 is met by the passage of the Bill. The answer to the question is as plain and simple as that." (*Hansard,* H.L., November 3, 1997, col. 1308.) This was amplified during the Committee stage when the Lord Chancellor stated that the Bill gave effect to Article 13 by enabling Convention rights to be raised before domestic courts (*Hansard,* H.L., November 18, 1997, col. 475). He added that,

> "to incorporate expressly Article 13 may lead to the courts fashioning remedies about which we know nothing other than the [section] 8 remedies which we regard as sufficient and clear." (*ibid.,* col. 477)

However, Lord Lester of Herne Hill raised the question whether, nonetheless, it was the government's intention that the courts should be entitled to have regard to Article 13 and the case law upon it, where otherwise it would be relevant. The Lord Chancellor responded by saying that the courts might have regard to Article 13, in particular when considering "the very ample provisions" of section 8(1) (judicial remedies for unlawful action by public authorities). In relation to the case law, the Lord Chancellor referred to section 2(1) (the obligation to consider the various sources of Convention law) and stated: "That means what it says. The court must take into account such material." (*ibid.* cols. 476–477.) When these matters came to be debated in Committee in the House of Commons (*Hansard*, H.C., May 20, 1998, cols. 975–987, particularly at 980–981), the remarks of the Lord Chancellor gave rise to some uncertainty and confusion and it is not clear what the position will be with regard to the case law under Article 13.

1–23 Amendments to section 1 or Schedule 1 can be made by the Secretary of State pursuant to section 1(4). This can be done in order "to reflect the effect, in relation to the United Kingdom, of a protocol". This power will be relevant where the government ratifies new or existing protocols in the future. For example, the government has stated that it intends to sign and ratify the Seventh Protocol (reproduced at Appendix 2) once legislation can be passed so as to render some provisions of domestic law compatible with the Protocol.

As the result of a government amendment, the Act refers — in connection with the requirement of compatibility — to "a Convention right" in section 4(1) and section 6(1). The Bill as originally drafted had referred to "one or more Convention rights". The change was introduced so as to prevent confusion in the situation where particular rights in different Articles were required to be balanced against one another. This balancing exercise is now to be carried out in the context of the particular Article on which the claim of incompatibility is based (*Hansard*, H.L., January 19, 1998, cols. 1295–1298 and 1300–1301).

5. Derogations and reservations

1–24 Under Article 15 contracting states are permitted in certain circumstances to take measures derogating from some of the Convention rights. Under Article 57 contracting states are also permitted, upon signature or ratification, to make reservations of a specific nature in respect of any Convention provision. A reservation is a statement that domestic law is not in conformity with that provision.

Section 1(2) provides that the Articles setting out the Convention rights are to have effect for the purposes of the Act subject to any designated derogation or reservation. Section 14 makes provision in respect of derogations. At present, the United Kingdom has one derogation, the text of which is set out in Part I of Schedule 3, and which is designated by section 14(1)(a). This relates to Article 5(3) (right to liberty and security), and was made in response to *Brogan v. U.K.* (1988) Series A, No. 145–B; 11 E.H.R.R. 117, as regards the length of periods of detention under counter-terrorist legislation. The validity of the derogation was upheld in *Brannigan and McBride v. U.K.* (1993) Series A, No. 258–B; 17 E.H.R.R. 594. Further derogations may be designated by the Secretary of State under section 14(1)(b). This may even be done in anticipation of the United Kingdom making a proposed derogation (section 14(6)). Designations only have effect until the derogation is withdrawn or (if not) for a period of five years, subject to extension for a further five years (section 16(1) and (2)). They also come to an end if the derogation is amended or replaced (section 14(3)). There is an obligation on the Secretary of State to review existing derogations before the end of the period of designation (section 17).

1–25 Reservations are dealt with under section 15. At present, the United Kingdom has one reservation, the text of which is set out in Part II of Schedule 3, and which is designated by section 15(1)(a). This relates to Article 2 of the First Protocol (right to education), and more particularly with respect to the principle that (in exercising any functions in relation to education and teaching) the state must respect the right of parents to ensure conformity with their own religious and philosophical convictions. The reservation accepts this principle only so far as it is compatible with the provision of efficient instruction and training, and with the avoidance of unreasonable public expenditure. Further reservations may be designated by the Secretary of State under section 15(1)(b). There is no maximum period of validity for a reservation, and no requirement for review, as is the case for derogations. The complete or partial withdrawal of a reservation brings the designation to an end, but the Secretary of State has the power to make a further designation (section 15(3) and (4))

The Secretary of State is under a duty to make appropriate amendments to Schedule 3 (in respect of designations) and the Act generally (in respect of reservations) in order to reflect the making of new designations, or the cessation of existing ones (sections 14(5) and 15(5)). The withdrawal of a designated derogation by the United Kingdom requires the Secretary of State to make appropriate amendments to the Act (section 16(7)). These powers are exercisable by statutory instrument (section 20(1)).

6. Effect on existing rights and freedoms

1–26 It is expressed by section 11(a) that reliance upon a Convention right does not restrict other existing rights or freedoms. Such other rights must have been conferred on that person "by or under any law having effect in any part of the United Kingdom". By section 11(b), the existing right of a person to make a claim or bring proceedings is also unaffected by sections 7 to 9 (unlawfulness by public authorities). The intention is that Convention rights provide a "floor" of rights, and that the Act "only gives and does not take away" (*Hansard*, H.L., November 18, 1997, col. 510).

7. Implied repeal

1–27 The doctrine of implied repeal (whereby the later of two inconsistent Acts is taken, in the absence of express provision, to replace the earlier legislation) is intended to have no application to the Act (*Hansard*, H.L., November 18, 1997, col. 509; January 19, 1998, col. 1294). Section 3 is designed not so as to conflict with earlier Acts, but so as to require them to be interpreted in a particular way. The existence of court powers to make merely a declaration of incompatibility reinforces this view.

8. Convention rights and private law

1–28 The Convention primarily has regard to the legal relations between private persons and the state. In certain respects, it can also be said to affect the relations between private persons. (For an extensive critique of the latter see *Human Rights in the Private Sphere* (Clapham, 1993)). However, the manner in which the Convention is given effect under the Act reinforces the essential emphasis upon the actions of the state. The Lord Chancellor made this plain in closing the Third Reading in the House of Lords:

> "we have not provided for the convention rights to be directly justiciable in actions between private individuals. We have sought to protect the human rights of individuals against the abuse of power by the state, broadly defined, rather than to protect them against each other." (*Hansard*, H.L., February 5, 1998, col. 840)

So, for example, a private individual (A) cannot bring an action against a neighbour (B) alleging a breach by B of rights under Article 8. But A might be able to bring proceedings against a local authority which failed to exercise powers to protect A's rights; and might be able to complain if a court hearing the dispute between A and B acted in a way which was incompatible with those rights.

9. Territorial application

1–29 In addition to England and Wales, and Scotland, the Act also extends to Northern Ireland (section 22(6)). But no extension has been made to cover the Channel Islands and the Isle of Man. The U.K. government consulted the island governments who asked that the Act not be extended to them. Instead, the island authorities have each announced their intentions to introduce legislation to incorporate the Convention into their law (*Hansard*, H.L., January 19, 1998, cols. 1307–1308; *Hansard*, H.C., June 3, 1998, col. 472).

10. Commencement

1–30 Apart from sections 18, 20 and 21(5) (which take effect on the passing of the Act), commencement is to take place by order of the Secretary of State. It is expected that commencement of the main provisions will not happen until the year 2000 onwards.

D. INTERPRETATION OF LEGISLATION

1–31 The law-making activity of Parliament, the Crown and other bodies is rendered, pursuant to section 3, subject to a device whereby the meaning of legislative provisions is to be ascertained and heavily influenced by a test of compatibility with Convention rights. In addition, the higher courts can mark any failure of the legislation to satisfy this test by granting declaratory relief to that effect.

1. Which legislation?

1–32 The interpretative rule under section 3(1) applies to all primary and subordinate legislation, whenever passed (sections (2)(a)). In consequence, the Act looks backwards as well as forwards in this respect, and for this reason questions of statutory construction already decided by the courts may have to be reconsidered, and could be decided differently.

Primary legislation is defined by section 21(1) to mean any public general Act, local and personal Act, private Act, Measure of the Church Assembly, Measure of the General Synod of the Church of England, Order in Council made under section 38(1)(a) of the Northern Ireland Constitution Act 1973 or corresponding provision of the Northern Ireland Act 1996, and any Order in Council made in exercise of the Royal Prerogative or which amends those Acts themselves defined as primary legislation. The term also includes (save in relation to the devolved powers in Wales and Scotland) any order or instrument made under primary legislation to the extent that it brings such provisions into force or amends any primary legislation.

Subordinate legislation is defined by section 21(1) to cover any other Order in Council, any other instruments made under primary legislation, Acts of the Northern Ireland and Scottish Parliaments, Acts and Measures of the Northern Ireland Assembly, instruments made under primary legislation which are not themselves defined as primary legislation, together with Scottish and Northern Ireland instruments.

2. "Read and given effect"

1–33 Section 3(1) provides that legislation "must be read and given effect" so as to be compatible with the Convention rights. Unlike section 2(1) which is specifically directed at courts and tribunals, this obligation is general and not expressly directed at any particular person or body. Though this provision (sandwiched — as it were — between the exclusively forensic obligation in section 2(1), and the forensic discretion in section 4(2)) is clearly concerned primarily with the jurisdiction and functions of the courts, it would seem also to be directed at public authorities. The Lord Chancellor appeared to suggest this was the case:

> "Having decided to adopt that interpretative approach [*i.e.* section 3(1)] it is of course helpful to the courts (*and other public authorities*) for the Bill to signal what the position is intended to be where a compatible construction is impossible." (*Hansard,* H.L., November 18, 1997, col. 521. Emphasis supplied.)

1–34 However, if the obligation is extended beyond the courts themselves, it could be said to affect questions which may not also fall within the scope of section 6 (the obligation of public authorities to act compatibly with Convention rights). This might be so because the definition of legislation extends to local and private Acts which can relate to persons other than public authorities. It could thus be that activity in purported pursuance of statute might not fall within section 6, but might be said to be in breach of section 3(1), in so far as it was based upon a misconstruction or misapplication of the legislation. In turn this could give rise to the question whether, apart from construing the legislation in question, the courts ought to provide other remedies (such as damages) if Convention rights have been violated.

It would seem that the answer to this is twofold. First, it is clearly not intended that the Convention rights should be directly justiciable in respect of the activities of private persons, even though the courts may be called upon to interpret legislation applicable to (and in the context of) an entirely private law dispute between private individuals. In addition, the omission of Article 13 from the list of Convention rights given effect under the Act, and the confinement of the remedies provided by the Act to those in section 8, would indicate that a private law cause of action for damages or other relief is not intended to follow in every circumstance where legislation has been misconstrued or misapplied.

Secondly, so far as public authorities are concerned, section 3(1) not only complements the duty under section 6 to act in a manner compatible with the Convention, but also clearly adds to the grounds on which judicial review may be sought (see further, Chapter 3).

3. Compatibility

1–35   In its ordinary use, "compatible" means "to be consistent with", and it is the latter term which has been used in the corresponding provision in the New Zealand Bill of Rights 1990 (see below, paragraph 1–36). Compatibility is a test known to the Convention and Convention law: Article 35(3) provides that incompatibility with the provisions of the Convention is one of the grounds of inadmissibility of an application, and it is a term used both by the Court and the Commission. In E.C. law there is also familiarity with the need for domestic measures to be compatible with European law. In some instances, even before the Act, domestic courts compared Convention law with domestic law, using terms such as "consistency" or "no conflict or discrepancy" to express the lack of difference on questions of principle, even if the language used in each legal system was distinct (*e.g. Att.-Gen. v. Guardian Newspapers (No. 2)* [1990] 1 A.C. 109; *Derbyshire CC v. Times Newspapers Ltd* [1993] A.C. 534; *Re D (Minors) (Adoption Reports: Confidentiality)* [1996] A.C. 593; *John v. MGN Ltd* [1997] Q.B. 586).

Compatibility involves the coincidence of the particular legislation with the particular Convention right relied on. This may well involve a balancing exercise between different interests, and between different Convention provisions, which may be affected by any number of factors, whether general or particular (see paragraph 1–23). It is an assessment which may change over time, in accordance not only with changes of approach by the Court in Strasbourg, but also in accordance with changed perceptions domestically.

4. "So far as possible"

1–36   The intention underlying section 3(1) was expressed by the Lord Chancellor as follows:

"We want the courts to strive to find an interpretation of legislation which is consistent with convention rights so far as the language of the legislation allows and only in the last resort to conclude that the legislation is simply incompatible with them." (*Hansard*, H.L., November 18, 1997, col. 535. See also the Home Secretary, *Hansard*, H.C., June 3, 1998, cols. 421–422.)

While the sub-section prescribes the result which those concerned are entreated to achieve, the method by which this is to be done is not stated. The courts will be left to apply and develop workable approaches, using existing techniques but possibly also needing to acquire some new ones. In this exercise, some of the general principles of the Court in the interpretation of the Convention itself may well come into play, so as to determine which interpretations are possible and which are not.

Section 6 of the New Zealand Bill of Rights 1990 has some similarity to section 3(1) while adopting a different formulation. The former provides: "Wherever an enactment can be given a meaning that is consistent with [this Bill of Rights], that meaning shall be preferred to any other meaning". (See further Joseph (1996) 7 Public Law Review 162.)

1–37   In practice, the ordinary meaning of most statutory provisions may well not prove problematic. And only in rare cases is it presently contemplated that there would be actual incompatibility. In between these states of clarity, however, may exist a range of less certain situations, including (but not confined to) cases of ambiguous meaning. By reason of section 3(1), the search for a compatible interpretation does not depend on ambiguity — it is to be achieved simply for its own sake. But it can only be achieved within the bounds of possibility, and on the actual wording of the legislation. As the Home Secretary sought to make clear:

"I do not think the courts will need to apply themselves to the words that I am about to use, but, for the avoidance of doubt, I will say that it is not our intention that the courts, in applying [section 3], should contort the meaning of words to produce implausible or incredible meanings." (*Hansard*, H.C., June 3, 1998, col. 422.)

The limits of a compatible interpretation would presumably be reached in the face of clear contrary wording in the legislation in question. They might also be reached where the only compatible interpretation(s) necessarily involved some serious conflict with other provisions, or produced an unworkable or absurd result. The formulation adopted under section 3(1), however, leaves it open to a court to determine that a compatible construction is possible provided that certain consequences (otherwise construable, but not necessary under the legislation) are avoided. In this way, the provision is "read and given effect" in a compatible way.

1–38   It is not clear how the approach under section 3(1) affects the use of parliamentary materials as an aid to statutory construction pursuant to *Pepper v. Hart* [1993] A.C. 593. Under that decision, such materials may be used only where the legislation is ambiguous or obscure, or where the literal meaning leads to an absurdity. In requiring the courts to strive for a compatible meaning, in a manner independent of questions of ambiguity, it would seem that in this respect parliamentary materials are unlikely to be admissible (though contrast the position where it is unclear which of two or more compatible constructions should be adopted). Where the courts reach the conclusion that the legislation is incompatible, it will usually be on the basis of wording that could not be said to be unclear. Nor would it ordinarily be said that incompatibility in itself was an absurdity. It would seem therefore that the admission and reliance upon Ministerial statements under section 19 of the compatibility (or otherwise) of legislation will be very limited, unless the courts now adopt a different approach (though see further, paragraph 1–45).

5. Effect of the obligation under section 3(1)

1–39   It is a cardinal principle of the Act that, maintaining the supremacy of Parliament, primary legislation continues to have effect even to the extent that it is incompatible with the Convention rights. In parallel with the limited effect of a declaration of incompatibility (see below paragraph 1–43), the interpretative obligation under section 3(1) does not affect the validity, continuing operation or enforcement of any incompatible primary legislation (section 3(2)(b)). For subordinate legislation, however, a similar saving only exists in so far as primary legislation prevents removal of the incompatibility (section 3(2)(c)). So if statute permits it, incompatible subordinate legislation may be disregarded.

6. Declaration of incompatibility

1–40   The government expressed the opinion that it would be only in rare cases that any incompatibility would be found (*Hansard*, H.L., February 16, 1998, col. 773). Where this does happen, certain courts have the discretion (but not the obligation) to make a declaration of incompatibility under section 4. In debate, the Lord Chancellor said that he "certainly would expect" the courts generally to make such declarations where the situation arose, but that "there may be reasons peculiar to the particular case" why this should not be done (*Hansard*, H.L., November 18, 1997, col. 546). As an example he cited the possible existence of an alternative statutory or other remedy which it might be thought the applicant should follow first.

Only certain courts are given the power to make a declaration, namely the House of Lords, the Privy Council, the Courts-Martial Appeal Court, the Court of Appeal and the High Court (section 4(5)). Most notably, therefore, the Crown Court — even though it is part of the Supreme Court — cannot make a declaration. The reasoning given for this limitation was that

> "we do not believe that trials should be upset, or potentially upset, by declarations of incompatibility that may go to the very foundations of the prosecution" (*Hansard*, H.L., November 18, 1997, col. 551).

Since the Crown Court will nonetheless have the obligation of interpreting any applicable legislation upon which a prosecution may be founded, which may include reaching a conclusion that the legislation is incompatible, this reasoning is not particularly persuasive, particularly when civil trials and hearings in the High Court will not suffer the same limitation.

1–41   The courts' power will be exercisable in respect of primary legislation in any proceedings where the question of compatibility arises and the court is satisfied that the incompatibility exists (section 4(1) and (2)). For subordinate legislation, the courts' power arises where the provision was made in the exercise of a power conferred by primary legislation, and only where the court is satisfied that (disregarding any possibility of revocation) the primary legislation prevents removal of the incompatibility (section 4(3) and (4)).

Under the Act, there is no limitation or guidance as to the persons who may be entitled to ask the court to make a declaration, or (save for one matter, see below paragraph 1–42) as to the procedure.

7. The Crown's right to intervene

1–42   Where the court is considering whether to make a declaration, the Crown is entitled to notification of this, in accordance with rules of court (section 5(1)). The purpose of this is to allow the Crown to consider whether a Minister, or someone nominated by a Minister, should give notice to be joined as a party to the proceedings (section 5(2)). If notification is given on behalf of the Crown, in accordance with rules of court, that person is entitled — without more — to be joined. Subject to the rules of court which may be made, it is possible that in proceedings where this arises there may need to be an adjournment, because the necessity for notifying the Crown may not emerge until a fairly late stage. It is, however, expressly provided that the application to be joined may be made at any time during the proceedings (section 5(3)).

No express provision is made in the Act as to the costs of the Crown, which are left to the general discretion of the court to be exercised in accordance with all the circumstances of the case (*Hansard,* H.L., November 18, 1997, cols. 557–561). Relevant factors may include the substantive merits of the applicant's case, the applicant's financial position and the existence of any broader public interest in the alleged incompatibility.

Specific provision is made in criminal cases so as to allow the person joined under section 5 to appeal against the making of a declaration of incompatibility (section 5(4)). This would arise in those cases where the Crown was not itself the prosecutor (*e.g.* local authority or private prosecutions). The need for this provision arises because the general rights of appeal in criminal cases from those courts which have the power to make declarations (the Court of Appeal, the Courts-Martial Appeal Court, and the Divisional Court) are limited to the prosecutor and the defendant. Under section 5(4), the person joined as a party under this section may appeal to the House of Lords against any declaration made in the proceedings, but only with the leave of the court making the declaration or the House of Lords (section 5(4) and (5)). This might present a curious situation in a case where the court held that there was an incompatibility but, in the exercise of discretion, decided not to make a declaration. If such a situation arose, the Crown would not be able to appeal because there would be no order against which to appeal, but the ruling on the incompatibility would be binding on other courts as a matter of precedent. It is perhaps conceivable that such a situation might arise only in the case of legislation which was in the process anyway of repeal or amendment.

8. Effect of declaration

1–43   A declaration of incompatibility has no real *legal* effect. By section 4(6) the order does not affect the validity, continuing operation or enforcement of the legislation, and nor is it binding on the parties to the proceedings in which it is made. The purpose of it is to put pressure on the government to take consequential action to remove the incompatibility (see below).

9. Remedial action

1–44   Under the provisions of section 10 and Schedule 2, Ministers (or Her Majesty in Council, in cases concerning an Order in Council) are empowered in certain cases to amend legislation by a "remedial order" so as to render the legislation compatible with the Convention. Section 10 applies in three situations: (1) where a declaration of incompatibility has been made under section 4, subject to rights of appeal (section 10(1)(a)); (2) where the Minister (or Her Majesty in Council) considers that legislation has become incompatible with an obligation of the United Kingdom arising under the Convention after a decision of the Court in proceedings against the United Kingdom (section 10(1)(b)); and (3) where a provision of subordinate legislation has been quashed or declared invalid by reason of incompatibility, and the Minister proposes to use the urgency procedure in Schedule 2, paragraph 2(b) (section 10(4)). However, before the power is exercised, the Minister must consider that there are compelling reasons for proceeding under section 10 (section 10(2) and (3)(b)).

Schedule 2 makes detailed provision as to the orders which may be made, and the procedure to be followed. The procedure includes the provision of required information (*ibid.*, paragraphs 3(1)(a) and 4(1)), which must include an explanation of the incompatibility together with a statement of reasons for proceeding under section 10 and for the terms of the order (*ibid.*, paragraph 5). Although remedial orders can have retrospective effect (Schedule 2, paragraph 1(1)(b)), no person is to be guilty of an offence solely as a result of that effect (*ibid.*, paragraph 1(4)).

E. PARLIAMENTARY PROCEDURE

1–45   In two respects, the Act introduces specific requirements for the procedure to be followed in Parliament. In addition to the procedures relating to remedial orders (see above), a Minister in charge of a Bill in either House must make a written statement before the Second Reading. The statement will either be to the effect that, in the Minister's view, the provisions of the Bill are compatible with the Convention rights, or to the effect that the Minister is unable to make a statement of compatibility but the government still wishes to proceed (section 19(1)). The Minister has discretion as to the manner in which the statement is published (section 19(2)). Inability to make a statement of incompatibility will signal a potential conflict between primary legislation and the Convention rights, but the Act itself does not require the Minister to set out what the conflict might be. It is clearly expected that such matters will emerge from existing parliamentary processes, and it is possible that subsequent statements in Parliament by the Minister may become relevant under *Pepper v. Hart* [1993] A.C. 593.

F. ACTS OF PUBLIC AUTHORITIES

1–46 The second, and complementary, approach of the Act is the obligation cast on public authorities under section 6 to act in a way which is compatible with the Convention rights. This aspect is considered in greater detail in Chapter 3, in relation to general issues of administrative law and the impact upon judicial review. In many ways, the duty under section 6, and the remedies which might follow from breach of it, are likely to be of more widespread practical significance than the new approach to the interpretation of legislation. This is because of the very wide range of persons and bodies, and the diverse situations, in respect of which section 6 will be relevant and be capable of being raised and litigated. The imposition of this legal liability is also generally free from the complications of parliamentary supremacy which have restricted the effect of the Act in relation to legislation.

1. Definition of a public authority

1–47 A very broad definition of "public authority" has been deliberately adopted (*Hansard*, H.L., January 19, 1998, col. 1262). By section 6(3) it includes first any court or tribunal, and secondly "any person certain of whose functions are functions of a public nature". On this latter basis, however, a person is not — on this count alone — to be a public body in respect of acts of a private nature (section 6(5)). The only wholesale exclusion is for the two Houses of Parliament, and for persons exercising functions in connection with proceedings in Parliament (section 6(3)). This exclusion does not exempt the judicial committee of the House of Lords (section 6(4)). Amendments introduced during the passage of the Bill in the House of Lords, against the wishes of the government, added exclusions for ecclesiastical courts and — in general terms — for acts done by or on behalf of religious bodies in spiritual matters. These amendments were removed during the Committee stages of the Bill in the House of Commons (see further, paragraphs 1–70—1–71 below).

The Home Secretary explained during Committee (*Hansard*, H.C., June 17, 1998, col. 406 and following) the government's intention behind the definition of public authority, and that it should go beyond the narrow category of central and local government and the police. He said (*ibid*, col. 406):

"The principle of bringing rights home suggested that liability in domestic proceedings should lie with bodies in respect of whose actions the United Kingdom government were answerable in Strasbourg. The idea was that if someone could get a remedy in Strasbourg, he or she should be able to get a remedy at home."

(The position as to state liability under the Convention is considered at paragraph 2–21, below.)

1–48   The Home Secretary referred to the creation of three categories under section 6: first, "obvious" public authorities — such as government departments, local authorities, and the police; secondly, organisations with a mix of public and private functions — such as Railtrack, Group 4 and water companies; and thirdly, organisations with no public functions. The third category will fall outside section 6 altogether. In the first category, it seems to be the position that every act is intended to fall within section 6 (*Hansard*, H.C., June 17, 1998 cols. 409–410). As for the second category, the government was anxious not to catch the commercial activities of such organisations (such as property development) which were nothing to do with the exercise of public functions, and so liability is excluded in respect of private acts for this category. The Home Secretary referred to two possible approaches of definition, whether to define a public authority and a public function by reference to the substance and nature of the act, or by the form and legal personality of the institution. In summary, he said (*ibid.*, col. 433):

"As we are dealing with public functions and with an evolving situation, we believe that the test must relate to the substance and nature of the act, not to the form and legal personality".

It is left to the courts to determine whether an organisation exercises public functions, in respect of which it will be relevant to consider the jurisprudence on judicial review (see further, paragraph 3–15 and following below; and see also Arrowsmith, *Civil Liability and Public Authorities* (1992)), together with the factors and circumstances as to which acts will fall within section 6. The government believed that the BBC and the Press Complaints Commission would be regarded as exercising public functions (*Hansard*, H.C., June 17, 1998, col. 411), though not the press (*ibid.*, col. 414). The Home Secretary also accepted that bodies regulating the professions would be public bodies for the purpose of that regulation (*ibid.*, col. 412), and stated his belief that the British Board of Film Classification also exercised public functions (*ibid.*, col. 413).

1–49   A public authority can be said to be a person or administrative body entrusted with functions to perform for the benefit of the public and not for private profit or gain (*Att.-Gen. v. Margate Pier and Harbour (Company of Proprietors)* [1900] 1 Ch. 749, *Parker v. LCC* [1904] 2 K.B. 501, *Lyles v. Southend-on-Sea Corporation* [1905] 2 K.B. 1, *Welch v. Bank of England* [1955] Ch. 508 at 541, decisions under the Public Authorities Protection Act 1893; *DPP v. Manners* [1978] A.C. 43, approving *R. v. Joy and Emmony* (1974) 60 Cr.App.R. 132, under the Prevention of Corruption Act 1916). In *Foster v. British Gas plc* [1991] 1 Q.B. 405, paragraph 20, the ECJ held that a body, whatever its legal form, which has been made responsible, pursuant to a measure adopted by the state, for providing a public service under the control of the state and has for that purpose special powers beyond those which result from the normal rules applicable in relations between individuals, is included among the bodies against which the provisions of a Directive capable of having direct effect may be relied upon. Following the decision of the ECJ, the House of Lords held ([1991] 2 A.C. 306) that a Directive could be enforced against the nationalised British Gas Corporation as an emanation of the state. (See also Directive 80/723, Art. 2, as amended by Directives 85/413 and 93/84, as to public authorities and public undertakings.) The term "public authority" is also used in Civil Evidence Act 1995, s.9, where it is defined by subsection (4) to include any public or statutory undertaking, any government department and any person holding office under Her Majesty.

2. Acts of a public authority

1–50   For the purposes of section 6, an act includes a failure to act (subsection (6)), but not every act or omission is caught. Excluded from the scope of the section are:

- conduct where the authority could not have acted differently by reason of primary legislation (section 6(2)(a));

- conduct where the authority was acting so as to give effect to, or enforce, provisions contained in or made under primary legislation, and the provisions cannot be read or given effect in a way which is compatible with the Convention rights (section 6(2)(b)); and

- any failure to move proposals in Parliament for legislation, to make primary legislation or to make any remedial order (section 6(6)).

These exclusions constitute further recognition of the supremacy of Parliament.

1–51   The acts of a public authority for these purposes will presumably include conduct for which, under general principles, the authority would be liable. Bodies such as local authorities can act only by their servants and agents, and vicarious liability attaches where there is a sufficient degree of control over the activity. However, the principle of vicarious liability does not itself assist in this context, since it is now generally held to rest on the theory that if the subordinate is liable, the superior also carries liability. Under the Act, the subordinate will not carry any liability, unless that person also happens to be a public authority. Consequently, it would seem that liability under section 6 in respect of the conduct of third parties will exist where that conduct has been authorised or adopted — expressly or impliedly — by the public authority.

Activity for these purposes would not seem to be confined to executive, or operational, matters. Decision-making may amount to an act, whether or not put into effect. Thus policies drawn up by public authorities should in themselves be justiciable under section 6, as much as their implementation.

The effect of section 6(2)(b) would seem to exclude from liability under section 6 situations where a public authority can demonstrate that it was acting pursuant to some statutory authorisation (see generally *Clerk and Lindsell on Torts*, (17th ed.,) paras 3–64 *et seq.* and 18–115 *et seq.*). Thus it would seem that the intention of section 6 is not to abrogate the general defence in tort of statutory authorisation, though any relevant statutory provision will need to be tested for compatibility with Convention rights under section 3.

3. Incompatibility

1–52 Although the parliamentary draughtsman has chosen to use "incompatibility" to define the test which is to be applied to both the interpretation of legislative provisions and the conduct of public authorities, the application of this in each of these two contexts is obviously different. In the first, it relates to the meaning and consequence of the language of the legislation; in the second, it relates to the quality and effect of the conduct. In both cases, it is necessary to consider whether any Convention rights apply, and — if there has been an interference with a right — whether that interference can be justified. Unlike the new approach to legislative interpretation, there is no statutory leaning in favour of a conclusion of compatibility in the case of public authorities. In a civil case, the onus must be on an applicant to establish that the conduct is incompatible. In a criminal case, if issues of incompatible conduct are raised, the onus will ordinarily be on the prosecution to establish compatibility.

4. Unlawfulness

1–53 The effect of section 6(1) is to render incompatible conduct unlawful. However, nothing in the Act creates a criminal offence (section 7(8)). Unlawful conduct may give rise not only to an applicant's entitlement to bring proceedings for a remedy under section 8 (whether civil or administrative in nature), but also to grounds for defending proceedings brought by a public authority (whether civil or criminal) and having any appropriate orders made (sections 7(1) and 8(1)) — see further below. It is not entirely clear whether the legal consequences of such unlawfulness go wider than the scope of the judicial remedies provided under section 8 (see paragraphs 1–58—1–59 below). Subject to any rules of court, it is unclear for example whether the jurisdiction of the Commissioner for Local Administration (the local government ombudsman) under Part III of the Local Government Act 1974 has been enlarged so as to encompass possible maladministration related to violations of Convention rights. However, a public authority which failed to avoid or rectify a violation of Convention rights may find that, even in the absence of a direct challenge under the Act, the resulting unlawfulness could have some collateral or evidential effect.

G. PROCEEDINGS INVOLVING PUBLIC AUTHORITIES

1–54 Sections 7 to 9 create the legal framework within which conduct made unlawful by section 6(1) can be litigated, an understanding of which is clearly crucial for the adviser. The general intention is that, as with questions of legislative interpretation under the Act, issues concerning the legality of the conduct of public authorities should be capable of being litigated as and when they arise within the context of ordinary proceedings.

1. Sword and shield

1–55   Section 7(1) enables a litigant alleging unlawfulness under section 6(1) either to bring proceedings under the Act, or to rely on the relevant Convention right(s) in any legal proceedings. For the latter purpose, the term "legal proceedings" includes any proceedings brought by or at the instigation of a public authority, and an appeal against the decision of a court or tribunal (section 7(6)). The Act accordingly creates rights of action, defences, and grounds of appeal. In a context such as that in *Wandsworth LBC v. Winder* [1985] A.C. 461, the litigant should be able to set up a defence relying on Convention rights in whatever forum the point arises, although the ability to raise a counterclaim or third party claim will depend upon compliance with any rules of court (see section 7(2)).

Protection is afforded not only against actual unlawful conduct, but also against any such proposed conduct (section 7(1)). There is consequently express statutory authorisation for the bringing of pre-emptive legal proceedings in order to prevent a violation of Convention rights from occurring.

2. Standing and victims

1–56   One of the most significant practical limitations of the Act is the requirement that — whether for the purposes of bringing or defending proceedings, or appealing — a person must be a "victim" of the unlawful act in order to be able to rely on section 6(1) in any of the permitted ways (section 7(1)). It is specifically provided that, where the proceedings are brought by way of judicial review, the applicant is to be taken to have a sufficient interest (as required under section 31(3) Supreme Court Act 1981 and RSC, Ord. 53, r.3(7)) only where that person is a victim of the act in question (section 7(3)). In the case of proposed unlawful acts, victim status is apparently to be judged in relation to the state of affairs were the act to be carried out (section 7(1) and (3)). For the purposes of section 7, the test under Article 34 is to be used (pursuant to section 7(7)) in determining whether or not a person is a victim (see paragraphs 2–15 and following).

In resisting calls for the Act to adopt the existing approach to *locus standi* used in judicial review proceedings, the Lord Chancellor stated the intention "to mirror the approach taken by the Strasbourg court in interpreting convention rights" (*Hansard,* H.L., February 5, 1998, col. 810). He acknowledged that "as a consequence, and despite the flexibility of the Strasbourg test, a narrower test will apply . . ." (*ibid.*), but referred to the possibility of public interest groups giving assistance and providing representation for victims, or to file *amicus* briefs (which has been a feature of the procedure in Strasbourg). (See also *Hansard,* H.C., June 24, 1998, cols. 1083–1086.) Many will nonetheless see this narrower approach as unwelcome or unnecessary.

3. Appropriate court or tribunal

1–57   The appropriate court or tribunal in which proceedings should be brought against a public authority is to be defined by rules, either rules of court or rules to be made by the Secretary of State or the Lord Chancellor (section

7(2) and (9)). In making rules, regard must be had to section 9 (judicial acts) (section 7(10)).

During the passage of the Bill in the House of Lords, it was specifically observed that the jurisdiction of a special adjudicator hearing asylum appeals under the Asylum and Immigration Appeals Act 1993 was restricted and would not extend to Convention issues under the Act. So as to enable tribunals of limited jurisdiction to determine such issues, and grant appropriate remedies, the government introduced an amendment so as to permit Ministers to make rules giving tribunals jurisdiction where necessary, but without prejudice to any existing tribunal powers under which Convention rights might be raised (section 7(11); *Hansard,* H.L., January 19, 1998, cols. 1360–1362; *Hansard,* H.C., June 24, 1998 cols. 1109–1111).

4. Remedies

1–58   Where a court finds an act to be unlawful, it may grant any relief or remedy, or make any order, which it considers "just and appropriate", provided this is within its powers (section 8(1)). This latter limitation will be relevant, for example, in terms of the inability of the county court to make orders of *certiorari, mandamus* or prohibition (see County Courts Act 1984, s.38(3)), and the limited jurisdiction of criminal courts. Though the forms of available relief under the Act include an award of damages, only those courts having the power to award damages or compensation in civil proceedings can grant such a remedy (section 8(2)). The Minister with power to make rules may by order augment the powers of a tribunal as to both the grounds and the nature of any relief which may be granted (section 7(11) — see paragraph 1–57 above).

The power to award damages is also confined by the requirement for the court to satisfy itself that "the award is necessary to afford just satisfaction to the person in whose favour it is made" (section 8(3)). This mirrors and refers to the position under Article 41 as to the jurisdiction of the Court under the Convention (see paragraphs 2–25 and following). No award of damages may be made unless the court has duly satisfied itself in this respect, taking account of all the circumstances of the case. Specifically, the court must consider (in respect of the particular unlawful act) any other remedy or order which has been granted or made, and the consequences of any court decision. The remedies and decisions to be considered here include those of any court, and not just the court faced with the claim for damages (section 8(3)(a) and (b)). The effect of this is to require the court to consider the totality and completeness of the reparation which the applicant has already received. The apparent reason for requiring the court to take into account the consequences of any court decision is to mirror the practice of the Court, which often determines that the finding of a violation of a Convention right in itself constitutes sufficient satisfaction. The exercise of the jurisdiction to award damages is subject, both as to the fact and quantum of the award, to a general requirement to have regard to the principles of the Court under Article 41. Under the Convention, the Court has taken a largely conservative approach to the award of compensation.

1–59   Subject to questions of jurisdiction and just satisfaction, the courts have been given a very wide discretion under section 8(1). It will undoubtedly be one of the most important consequences of the Act to see how the courts develop and apply these powers, albeit without the inclusion of Article 13 among the Convention rights (see paragraphs 1-21—1-22).

The general provisions as to contribution between liable parties (under the Civil Liability (Contribution) Act 1978) are made to apply for the purposes of an award under section 8 (section 8(5)).

5. Judicial acts

1-60 Since the courts are themselves subject to the obligation under section 6(1) not to act in an incompatible manner, the question arises as to the way in which any alleged breach of Convention rights by the courts should be litigated. Section 9(1) provides that such proceedings in respect of a judicial act may be brought only,

- by exercising a right of appeal;

- on an application for judicial review; or

- in any forum which may be prescribed by rules.

This provision does not create new rights to judicial review over the courts (section 9(2)). A challenge to a decision of the Crown Court in a matter relating to trial on indictment will accordingly still need to be made by way of appeal.

1-61 A "judicial act" means a judicial act of a court, including an act done on the instructions or on behalf of a judge; and for these purposes "judge" includes a member of a tribunal, a justice of the peace, and a clerk or other officer entitled to exercise the jurisdiction of a court (section 9(5)). The administrative acts of court staff, such as listing, are accordingly not covered by section 9(1); but such acts would nonetheless be actionable under section 7(1).

The reasoning behind section 9 was revealed when the government moved amendments on Report in the House of Lords (*Hansard*, H.L., January 29, 1998, cols. 388–391). The Lord Chancellor explained that there were two overall purposes behind the form of section 9: to provide an enforceable right to compensation for breaches of Article 5 (right to liberty and security), and to preserve judicial immunity generally (see, *e.g.* Bradley and Ewing, *Constitutional and Administrative Law*, (12th ed., 1997), pp. 425–426). Hence, section 9(3) enables a court to award damages in respect of a judicial act done in good faith, but only to the extent required by Article 5(5) (which provides that every person who has been the victim of arrest or detention in contravention of Article 5 shall have an enforceable right to compensation). A person wrongfully detained by an order of a court in breach of Article 5 but in good faith will thus be entitled to claim damages. Judicial acts committed otherwise than in good faith and in breach of Convention rights will also be actionable, and could give rise to an award of damages under section 8. Otherwise, no claim for damages in respect of judicial acts is maintainable. Other relief, including the right of appeal, is not affected.

Where an award of damages is permitted by section 9(3), it is to be made against the Crown, and not against the individual judge (section 9(4)). No award can be made unless the Minister responsible for the particular court, or his nominee, is joined as a party to the proceedings (*ibid.*, and section 9(5)).

6. Commencement and application of section 7(1)

1–62 The entitlement of a person to rely on Convention rights in any legal proceedings brought by or at the instigation of a public authority under section 7(1)(b) applies whenever the allegedly unlawful act took place, whether before or after commencement of the Act (section 22(4)). Otherwise, section 7(1) does not apply to an act taking place before the commencement of section 7 (*ibid.*).

7. Limitation

1–63 Proceedings under section 7(1)(a) are subject to special limitation provisions. Subject to any stricter rule (see below), the basic period is one year beginning with the date on which the act took place (section 7(5)(a)). The court or tribunal has discretion under section 7(5)(b) to extend the basic period to such longer period as it considers equitable, having regard to all the circumstances (reminiscent of the court's power in personal injury cases under Limitation Act 1980, s.33, though the government deliberately avoided the use of any list of factors under section 7 which the court is to take into account — see *Hansard*, H.C. June 24, 1998, cols. 1096–1097). The use of a special limitation period in relation to public authorities is not new: until it was repealed in 1954, the Public Authorities Protection Act 1893 prescribed a particularly short limitation period (originally six months, extended to 12 months by section 21(1) of the Limitation Act 1939) for

> "any action, prosecution or other proceeding . . . against any person for any act done in pursuance, or execution, or intended execution of any Act of Parliament, or of any public duty or authority, or in respect of any alleged neglect or default in the execution of any such Act, duty or authority . . ."

The period allowed by section 7(5), however, is subject to any stricter time limit which is applicable. The obvious case is judicial review, or a procedure analogous to it under any new rules of court.

It is important to note that the limitation period under section 7(5) applies only to proceedings brought under section 7(1)(a). If a victim were to bring proceedings under an existing cause of action, relying on Convention rights as an additional argument, the limitation period would be that applicable to that cause of action (see *Hansard*, H.C., June 24, 1998, col. 1094).

8. Significance for the common law

1–64 It will be crucial to see how the courts make use in practice of the Convention rights in relation to their own decision-making, as a matter of common law. Provisions such as Article 6 (the right to a fair trial) have a direct impact upon the way in which justice is administered (though in the case of Article 6, the principles it embodies are already well-recognised in domestic law). But all of the Convention rights have relevance to the way in which the state, through the courts, defines and determines disputes which are before it. In dealing with disputes between private persons and public authorities, the courts will clearly operate the Convention rights directly within the scope of the Act itself, so that there may be little need for the common law to develop significantly in this regard. In contrast, private persons will not be able to rely directly on the Convention rights in disputes between them (in the same way that they might, say, rely on the law of tort or contract), but they will be entitled to expect that the court in resolving such disputes will shape and apply domestic law in a way which is compatible with any relevant Convention rights. The common law will thus need to march in step with Convention law, at least in the latter respect, if the courts are to avoid the possibility of decisions being reached which are incompatible with the Convention rights.

This raises some potentially intricate questions about the doctrine of precedent. What, for example, is the status of decisions made before the commencement of the Act which are otherwise binding but which (if applied) would lead to results incompatible with Convention rights? The answer would seem to be that the Act has generally abrogated the binding effect of such decisions, in favour of the principle of compatibility; otherwise the common law doctrine of precedent would override the express statutory obligation on the courts. The effect of statute on questions of precedent generally depends on the extent to which the common law has been altered or revoked (see generally Cross and Harris, *Precedent in English Law*, (4th ed., 1991) pp. 173–177), and it is difficult to conceive of few statutes which have had as substantial an effect as this Act.

1–65 Another question is: how does the doctrine of precedent apply to decisions of domestic courts under the Act which are superseded by decisions of the Court in Strasbourg? The courts are bound under section 2(1) to take decisions from Strasbourg into account when determining any question which has arisen under the Act in connection with a Convention right. This obligation, however, does not help to determine how the domestic court may use or apply a later Strasbourg decision. If the domestic court came to the conclusion that a failure to apply the Strasbourg decision would result in the court acting in a manner incompatible with Convention rights, it would seem to follow that the court should give precedence to the Strasbourg decision, even at the cost of not following an otherwise binding domestic ruling.

The context and application of this problem with regard to E.C. law is probably sufficiently different to prevent effective comparison (see pp.182–185 *ibid.* as to the position in E.C. law).

9. Nature of liability under section 6

1–66 The liability which arises under section 6 is difficult to classify in terms of existing legal categories (see paragraph 3–28). While the operation of Convention rights under section 6 is confined (broadly speaking) to public law, the liability which may arise under section 6 possesses characteristics of a private law cause of action. How the liability comes to be viewed is likely to depend substantially on the procedural rules which are to be made under section 7. It seems probable, however, that it is to be regarded as a *sui generis* form of statutory liability.

H. FREEDOM OF EXPRESSION

1–67 The application of the Act to the press was one of the most contentious aspects during the passage of the Bill (see above paragraph 1–07). On the Second Reading in the House of Commons, the Home Secretary signalled the government's intention to introduce specific amendments to the Bill in relation to the press (*Hansard,* H.C., February 16, 1998, cols. 775–779), in order to assuage anxieties that — notwithstanding the government's confidence that the Act would not erode press freedoms — the legislation would lead to developments of the common law which would inhibit legitimate investigation into matters of public interest. Of particular concern in the press was that the courts might use Article 8 as a basis for further development of the law on privacy (see *Halsbury's Laws of England,* (4th ed.), vol. 8(2), para. 110, as to the existence and extent of such a right previously under domestic law). The amendments were subsequently made in Committee (*Hansard,* H.C. July 2, 1998 cols. 534–563), and are to be found in section 12.

It is important to note that the application of section 12 is confined neither to cases where a public authority is a party to proceedings, nor to cases involving the press (see subsection (1)). It applies to anyone whose right to freedom of expression may be affected (*Hansard,* H.C., July 2, 1998, col. 536). The section accordingly has a broader effect than would arise from merely giving effect to Article 10 in domestic law. The section does not relate to criminal proceedings (subsection (5)), but does apply in relation to tribunals (*ibid.*). Thus judges wanting to impose reporting restrictions in criminal cases will not be bound by these provisions, although courts as public authorities will still be bound by the general obligation to act compatibly with Convention rights (including Article 10).

1–68 Subsection (2) is concerned with *ex parte* injunctions to restrain publication, and requires an applicant to show that all practicable steps have been taken to notify the respondent, unless compelling reasons for no notification can be demonstrated. The Home Secretary indicated an expectation that the exemption for compelling reasons would not often be used (though they might arise in cases involving national security), and that even *inter partes* injunctions would continue to be rare (*ibid.*). Subsection (3) sets a high threshold for interlocutory injunctions, by requiring the court to be satisfied that the applicant is likely to establish at trial that publication should not be allowed.

Subsection (4) emphasises the importance of the freedom of expression under Article 10, by requiring the court to have particular regard to it, thus giving the right protected by Article 10 special prominence in domestic law. Additionally, where the proceedings relate to journalistic, literary or artistic material, the court must also have regard to actual or imminent publication (including potentially in a foreign country), and to the public interest in publication. Journalistic, literary or artistic material is not defined; nor are the matters to which the courts should have regard in determining the public interest. In section 13 of the Police and

Criminal Act 1984, journalistic material is defined to mean material acquired or created for the purposes of journalism. The terms literary and artistic work are defined in sections 3 and 4 of the Copyright, Designs and Patents Act 1988. The public interest is a matter which the courts are well-versed in determining, for example in defamation proceedings (see generally *Gatley on Libel and Slander*, (9th ed.), paragraph 12.27 *et seq.*). Under the Convention, Article 10(2) also imports a test of the public interest in determining whether an interference with the freedom of expression can be justified.

1–69 Where subsection (4) applies, the courts must also have regard to any relevant privacy code. It is not obligatory for any publication to have — or be party to — a privacy code, but if there is no such code the publication cannot take advantage of section 12(4)(b). The Press Complaints Commission Code (ratified November 26, 1997), to which national and many regional newspapers are members, provides that everyone is entitled to respect for private and family life, home, health and correspondence, and that a publication will be expected to justify intrusions into any individual's private life without consent (clause 3). The use of long lens photography to take pictures of people in private places without their consent is unacceptable, such places being defined as those (whether public or private) where there is a reasonable expectation of privacy (*ibid.*). However, clause 3 of the Code is expressly subject to exceptions where these can be demonstrated to be in the public interest, including the detection or exposing of crime or serious misdemeanour, protecting public health and safety, and preventing the public from being misled by a statement or action. In cases involving children, editors are required to demonstrate an exceptional public interest to override the normally paramount interests of the child. Compliance with, or breach of, a relevant privacy code will be relevant to a court's determination under section 12.

The importance of the freedom of expression under Convention law has been emphasised in many cases (see paragraphs 2–97—2–98). Its significance, as one of the most important freedoms, has also been emphasised in domestic law (*e.g. Derbyshire County Council v. Times Newspapers Ltd* [1993] A.C. 534, 551; *Att.-Gen. v. Observer Ltd* [1990] 1 A.C. 109, 283–284). On a number of notable occasions, however, domestic law has been held to be in conflict with the Convention in relation to Article 10 (see *Sunday Times v. U.K.* (1979) Series A, No. 30; 2 E.H.R.R. 245 — the thalidomide case, which in part led to the Contempt of Court Act 1981; *Observer and Guardian v. U.K.* (1991) Series A, No. 216; 14 E.H.R.R. 153 — the "Spycatcher" case; *Tolstoy Miloslavsky v. U.K.* (1995) Series A, No. 316–B; 20 E.H.R.R. 442 — concerning quantum of damages for defamation, an area subsequently reappraised by the Court of Appeal in *John v. MGN Ltd* [1997] Q.B. 586; and *Goodwin v. U.K.* (1996) 22 E.H.R.R. 123 — concerning an order for disclosure of journalistic sources made in *X Ltd v. Morgan Grampian (Publishers) Ltd* [1991] 1 A.C. 1).

I. FREEDOM OF RELIGION

1–70 By amendments carried at the Third Reading in the House of Lords (*Hansard*, H.L., February 5, 1998, cols. 747–842), and following earlier extensive debate on the issue (*Hansard*, H.L., January 19, 1998, cols. 1319–1351), various significant changes were made to the Bill, against the wishes of the government, which would have had the effect of making specific provision in relation to religious bodies and excluding them from aspects of the legislation. On the Second Reading in the House of Commons (*Hansard*, H.C., February 16, 1998, cols. 779–780), the Home Secretary announced his intention to consult on those amendments. In the result (see the extensive debate subsequently on this in Committee — *Hansard*, H.C., May 20, 1998, cols. 1013–1070), the government decided to remove all the amendments, and to replace them with a single provision, which is to be found in section 13.

The formula adopted by the government in section 13(1) is similar to that in relation to the freedom of expression, namely to require a court or tribunal to have particular regard to the importance of the right under Article 9 (freedom of thought, conscience and religion). However, in this instance, the application of the section is confined solely to questions which arise under the Act, with the effect of narrowing the ambit of this provision in comparison to section 12. By section 13(1), Article 9 is given special prominence amongst Convention rights.

1–71 Religious organisations (which are undefined) are thus not excluded from being public authorities under section 6, though some of them will not *per se* be public authorities (*e.g.* charities), and much of their conduct is essentially private in nature and thus not within the scope of possible liability (*e.g.* admission to membership and priesthood, worship, and running of a church). While this leaves religious organisations at risk generally of having to defend proceedings brought under section 7 (whether meritorious or not), section 13(1) does mean that other rights which may be relied on by litigants (such as under Articles 8, 12 and 14) will have to be considered to be subordinate to Article 9, notwithstanding the respect shown under the Convention in relation to religious matters (*e.g. Gay News Ltd and Lemon v. U.K.* (1982) 28 D.R. 77; 5 E.H.R.R. 123, C.D. — and see paragraph 2–94). The Churches' concerns related particularly to the employment of suitable persons within religious organisations such as schools (in terms of the prospective employee's personal belief), requirements for religious marriages (*e.g.* in relation to divorced people), and in relation to the authority and tenets of ecclesiastical courts. The government considered that these concerns were generally unjustified (see *Hansard*, H.L., January 19, 1998, cols. 1345–1347), while agreeing to exclude Measures of the Church Assembly and the General Synod of the Church of England from the ambit of Ministerial power to amend legislation by remedial order under section 10 (see subsection (6)). The two areas in which the Act may particularly affect the Churches are the provision of education in religious schools, and marriage. The Convention, however, provides neither a right to employment, nor a right to enjoy any particular form of marriage ceremony. In response to issues about staffing in religious schools, the government tabled amendments to the School Standards and Framework Bill so as to meet concerns about recruitment and selection (*Hansard*, H.C., May 20, 1998, col. 1024).

As recognition of the limits of Article 9, in *R. v. Bow Street Magistrates' Court ex p. Choudhury* [1991] 1 Q.B. 429 (the "Satanic Verses" case), the Divisional Court held that the absence of a law protecting religions other than Christianity, akin to blasphemy, was not a breach of Article 9, a decision subsequently endorsed by the Commission (*Choudhury v. U.K.* (1991) 12 H.R.L.J. 172).

J. STRASBOURG'S ROLE IN FUTURE

1–72 It will be appreciated that one of the primary purposes of the Act is to reduce the necessity for applicants to take complaints about violations of Convention rights to the Strasbourg authorities. Furthermore, because an application to the Strasbourg authorities under the Convention is inadmissible where domestic remedies have not been exhausted (Article 35(1)), the Act will in fact require Convention points to be taken where possible before domestic courts and tribunals. For this reason, if for no other, domestic courts and tribunals are likely to be faced with Convention points raised by would-be applicants anxious to be able to demonstrate (should the need arise) that they have indeed availed themselves of such protection and assistance as domestic law allows.

It would, however, be mistaken to believe that recourse to the Strasbourg authorities will diminish to a *de minimis* level. Apart from the indisputable increase in the number and variety of Convention points likely to be taken and the consequent generation of issues within domestic proceedings capable of finding their way to Strasbourg as a tribunal of last resort, the effect of Convention rights within domestic law remains limited under the Act. Thus, however it may occur, the failure of the state to secure the rights and freedoms under the Convention for individual and bodies will continue (subject to the pre-existing requirement for exhaustion of domestic remedies) to be capable of complaint to the Strasbourg authorities. It is the government's hope, though, that deficiences in terms of the relations between the state (in all its forms) and those subject to the power of the state will, to a large extent, be identified and dealt with by domestic legal procedures. To the extent that the courts are unwilling or unable to assist in the protection of rights under the Convention, and/or to the extent that Parliament acts contrary to those rights, recourse to Strasbourg will remain important.

CHAPTER 2

Introduction to Convention Law

Christopher Baker (Barrister, Arden Chambers)

2–01   The essential elements of Convention law are the rights and freedoms contained in the Convention, the general principles and approaches which are used in applying it, the accumulated application of the Convention in the case law, and the legal machinery. The specialist chapters which follow will consider in more detail the Convention law in particular areas, and its impact under the Act. Although the machinery of the Convention itself is not included within the scope of the Act, some understanding of it is necessary in order to appreciate how Convention law works, and procedure can have an impact on substantive law   so it is included here so far as relevant. This chapter is approached in two parts: first the general aspects of the Convention, and second the specific provisions concerning the rights and freedoms guaranteed.

PART I — GENERAL

A. THE CONVENTION IN CONTEXT

2–02   It is helpful to understand the origins of the Convention, and the international context within which it operates. In particular, this provides assistance in explaining not only the strengths but also the limitations of Convention law.

1. Origins

2–03   After the second world war, there was widespread concern within Europe to prevent both the repetition of the atrocities associated particularly with Nazi Germany and with the war generally, and the spread of communism. In consequence, an international organisation known as the Council of Europe ("the Council") was formed by the Statute of the Council of Europe 1949. Article 3 of the Statute required every member to "accept the principles of the rule of law and of the enjoyment by all persons within its jurisdiction of human rights and fundamental freedoms". The Council's general purpose was to promote European unity, to protect human rights and to encourage economic and social development.

The Council drafted the Convention during 1949 and 1950, as a statement of common principles, in which the United Kingdom was a leading force. The Convention was signed at Rome on November 4, 1950, and the U.K. government was the first to ratify the Convention, which it did on March 8, 1951. The Convention came into force on September 3, 1953.

The Council is an entirely separate entity from the institutions of the European Union, and should not be confused with them. Council members are European states, and include those states which are also members of the European Union; but the institutions of the Union are not themselves members of the Council. The Council's headquarters and institutions are in Strasbourg, and consist of the Committee of Ministers, the Parliamentary Assembly, and the Congress of Local and Regional Authorities of Europe.

2. The international context

2–04   The Convention is but one of a number of international systems for the protection of human rights, and can legitimately claim to be one of the most successful. It was preceded by the Universal Declaration of Human Rights 1948, which provided the foundation for much of the Council's drafting. The Convention is concerned principally with civil and political rights, although it does also cover matters falling within the area of economic and rights. (In *Airey v. Ireland* (1979) Series A, No. 32; 2 E.H.R.R. 305, para. 26, the Court stated that there is no "watertight division" separating Convention rights from these other rights.) Other treaties cover different areas, or have different emphases. The European Social Charter ("ECS") was drafted by the Council and came into force in 1965. It is concerned with social rights (such as work-related rights, training, health, social security, and welfare). The U.K. government — having signed the ECS in 1961 — has not, however, accepted a number of its provisions. The Council has also drafted the European Convention for the Prevention of Torture and Inhuman or Degrading Treatment of Punishment, which came into force in 1989, and to which the U.K. government is a signatory. Its function is self-explanatory. Most Convention states are also parties to the International Covenant on Civil and Political Rights 1966 ("ICCPR"), and the International Covenant on Economic, Social and Cultural Rights 1966 ("ICESCR"), which have originated through the United Nations. Comparison with the ICCPR, in particular, is instructive, as an indication of the scope and limitation of the Convention.

3. The Convention and the European Union

2–05   The European Union is not a party to the Convention, and the European Court of Justice ("ECJ") has concluded that the Union cannot accede to the Convention without a change to the E.C. Treaty (The Treaty of Rome, 1957): Opinion 2/94 [1996] E.C.R. I–1759. Applications under the Convention against the European Union have been rejected (*CFDT v. European Communities* (1978) 13 D.R. 231; *D v. Belgium and the European Communities* [1987] 2 C.M.L.R. 57). Furthermore, the E.C. Treaty is not in itself a source of fundamental rights and freedoms. The Treaty on European Union 1992 (The Maastricht Treaty), on the other hand, does contain explicit provision in relation to fundamental rights. In addition to the preamble, Article F(2) provides:

"The Union shall respect fundamental rights, as guaranteed by the European Convention for the Protection of Human Rights and Fundamental Freedoms . . . and as they result from the constitutional traditions common to the Member States, as general principles of Community law."

Article K2(1) also refers to compliance with the Convention in the context of various matters concerning justice and home affairs. However, neither Article is justiciable, by reason of Article L of the Treaty on European Union, which prevents the ECJ from passing judgment on them.

2–06 Although initially somewhat reluctant in this regard, the ECJ developed a jurisprudence that recognised the existence of fundamental rights relevant to European law (see, *e.g. Stauder v. City of Ulm* [1969] E.C.R. 419; [1970] C.M.L.R. 112). Thus, while Convention law is not in itself part of European law, it is clear that fundamental rights nevertheless form an integral part of the general principles of law whose observance the Court ensures (*Nold* [1974] E.C.R. 491). For this purpose, the ECJ "draws inspiration" from the constitutional traditions common to Member States, and from international treaties for the protection of human rights in which Member States have participated. In this context, the Convention has been held to have special significance (the *ERT case* [1991] E.C.R. I–2925, para. 41).

However, an issue must fall within the scope of European law in order for it to become subject to treatment in this way (see for example *R. v. MAFF, ex p. Bostock* [1994] 3 C.M.L.R. 547 as to landlord and tenant relations); and the ECJ accordingly cannot give interpretative guidance for determining whether national legislation is in conformity with the Convention where that legislation does not fall within the scope of European law (see *Kremzow v. Austria* [1997] E.C.R. I–2629). It is unclear what might happen if European law were to be in conflict with Convention law.

4. The Convention and domestic law of other contracting states

2–07 Article 1 of the Convention requires each contracting party to "secure to everyone within their jurisdiction the rights and freedoms defined in Section I of this Convention". (Section I contains Articles 2 to 18, which are discussed individually below.) This obligation, however, has been held consistently not to require a state to incorporate the Convention into domestic law (see *Swedish Engine Drivers' Union v. Sweden* (1976) Series A, No. 20; 1 E.H.R.R. 617; *Ireland v. U.K.* (1978) Series A, No. 25; 2 E.H.R.R. 25; *Observer and Guardian v. U.K.* (1991) Series A, No. 216; 14 E.H.R.R. 153). A state may satisfy Article 1 by ensuring that its legal system guarantees Convention rights in such manner as the state may decide.

Different states, and their legal systems, have accordingly adopted different methods of approach. This is not the place to consider the comparative differences between national systems, but they may at least be relevant in determining the context within which issues arise for consideration in Strasbourg.

B. THE CONVENTION IN OPERATION

2–08 The Convention as originally drafted has since been amplified by a number of additions, or "protocols". To date there have been 11, four of which are substantive (the First, Fourth, Sixth and Seventh Protocols). Of the substantive protocols, the U.K. government has to date ratified only the First, though it has proposed to ratify the Seventh (see the White Paper, Rights Brought Home: The Human Rights Bill (1997 C.M. 3782), para. 4.15), and now also the Sixth (abolition of death penalty). The protocols are, where so provided, to be read as additional Articles of the Convention: these provisions accordingly do not replace or reduce the scope of existing provisions (*Abdulaziz, Cabales and Balkandali v. U.K.* (1985) Series A, No. 94; 7 E.H.R.R. 471, para. 60; *Burghartz v. Switzerland* (1994) Series A, No. 280–B; 18 E.H.R.R. 101, para. 23).

Article 15 permits a contracting party to derogate from certain Articles in certain circumstances (see further below "Derogations") The United Kingdom has one derogation, in respect of Article 5(3). This relates to legislation concerning the prevention of terrorism. The text is annexed to the Act at Schedule 3, Part I (see further Chapter 1, above). Article 64 also permits a contracting party to enter a reservation when domestic law does not conform with the Convention (see further below "Reservations") The United Kingdom has one reservation in respect of Article 2, First Protocol. This relates to legislation concerning state education. The text is annexed to the Act at Schedule 3, Part II (see further Chapter 1, above).

The number of contracting states has grown very significantly since the early 1950s, and has now reached 40. This diversity of national traditions and circumstances, and degrees of legal and democratic maturity, not only gives rise to some fairly obvious consequences (such as a tendency to locate a lowest common denominator), but has also given rise to some concern about the qualification and experience of some of those appointed to the Convention machinery.

1. Reform of the Convention's legal machinery

2–09   The success of the Convention, evidenced particularly by the growth of contracting parties and case work, has produced its own problems and shown up weaknesses in the legal machinery. Most seriously, it was taking an average of more than five years for cases to be finally determined. The case for reform became compelling. In consequence, the Eleventh Protocol was drafted so as to replace the original Articles 19 to 56 of the Convention, which dealt with the establishment and operation of the Commission and the Court (see further below), by effectively merging the two institutions. There are also some minor and consequential changes to the remainder of the Convention. The Eleventh Protocol was opened for signature on May 11, 1994, and enters into force on November 1, 1998. The Act reproduces the Convention as amended by the Eleventh Protocol, and references below to Convention provisions also anticipate these amendments — save where otherwise indicated by an asterisk. The original as well as the amended provisions are discussed below, so that the reader can appreciate the separate roles of the Commission and the Court.

2. Petitions

2–10   One of the strengths of the Convention has been the relative ease with which the legal machinery can be invoked by individuals; and this — as opposed to the inter-state jurisdiction of the Court — has provided the main driving-force behind Convention law. Although, prior to the Eleventh Protocol, the right of non-governmental petition has depended upon the discretionary recognition of such right by each contracting party (*Article 25(1)), acceptance of this right became a political norm among contracting states. While not the first to do so, the U.K. government recognised the right in 1966. The exercise of the right depends upon establishing standing as a "victim" (see Victims, below).

3. The European Commission on Human Rights ("the Commission")

2–11   The seat of the Commission has been in Strasbourg. Its main functions have been to receive all applications, to reject those which it considered it should not deal with or were inadmissible, to investigate those petitions which were accepted, to try and secure a "friendly settlement", to report to the Committee of Ministers on petitions which have been accepted, and to bring cases before the Court (*Articles 25 to 31, and 48).

There were a number of restrictions upon the competence of the Commission. It could receive non-governmental petitions only from a person, non-governmental orgainsation or group of individuals claiming to be the "victim" of a violation of a Convention right by a contracting party (*Article 25). It could only deal with a matter after all domestic remedies had been exhausted, and within a period of six months from the date on which the final decision was taken ("Article 26), and any petition which the Commission considered to be inadmissible under *Article 26 had to be rejected (*Article 27(3)). The Commission has also been precluded from dealing with certain other petitions (*Article 27(1)). Any petition which the Commission considered to be either "incompatible" with the Convention, or "manifestly ill-founded", or "an abuse of the right of petition", was to be considered inadmissible (*Article 27(2)). So far as relevant to this outline, these matters for the Commission are considered below.

4. The European Court of Human Rights ("the Court")

2–12   The seat of the Court has been and will continue to be in Strasbourg. Its jurisdiction has extended to all cases concerning the interpretation and application of the Convention which the contracting parties or the Commission refer to it. It has been for the Court to consider whether, on the facts, there has been any violation of the obligations arising from the Convention. If domestic law allowed only partial reparation for the consequences of such violation, the Court has been required, if necessary, to afford "just satisfaction" to the injured party (*Article 50).

5. The new machinery (the Eleventh Protocol)

2–13   Under the new machinery, the Commission and the Court are, in effect, merged. There is a full-time Court, comprising a registry and the plenary Court (Articles 19, 25 and 26). The judges sit in committees (of three), in Chambers (of seven), and in a Grand Chamber (of 17) (Article 27(1)).

The jurisdiction of the Court extends to all matters concerning the interpretation and application of the Convention and the protocols which are referred to it (Article 32(1)). In addition to inter-state cases (Article 33), the right of individual application by a "victim" remains (Article 34 — see "Victims", below, and "Petitions", above). The right of individual application largely ceases to be optional for the contracting parties (*ibid.*); and the inter-state jurisdiction remains mandatory (Article 33). The jurisdiction of the Court to provide the Committee of Ministers with advisory opinions continues (Article 47), but this power has yet to be invoked.

The essential framework of the original provisions stays in place. In addition to the question of the standing of a victim, the admissibility criteria remain (now in Article 35), together with provisions relating to striking out (Article 37), investigation (Article 38(1)(a)) and the securing of friendly settlements (Articles 38(1)(b) and 39). The power to afford just satisfaction also continues (Article 41).

6. State jurisdiction

2–14 Under the Convention, the concept central to the responsibility of states, and to the competence *ratione loci* of the Commission, is that of domestic "jurisdiction" (Article 1). A state's jurisdiction is not confined to the national territory — otherwise the acts of the state committed abroad would be immune. The reasoning for this is the control exercised by the state over persons, property, and (possibly) territory abroad (*Loizidou v. Turkey* (1995) Series A, No. 310; 20 E.H.R.R. 99; see also *Cyprus v. Turkey* (1997) 23 E.H.R.R. 244). Hence, the state can be responsible for the acts of authorised agents (*e.g.* armed forces) which have effect beyond national boundaries (*Cyprus v. Turkey* (1975) 2 D.R. 125). But conversely, a person resident in the United Kingdom was not able to complain about the government's failure to intervene abroad to protect the delivery of mail against alleged non-delivery by Soviet postal authorities (*Bertrand Russell Peace Foundation Ltd v. U.K.* (1978) 14 D.R. 117). However, there may be some scope for state responsibility as regards protection of diplomatic staff while abroad (*X v. U.K.* (1977) 12 D.R. 73).

If a state makes a declaration under Article 56, the application of the Convention may also be extended over dependent territories. Thus the U.K. government has given effect to the Convention in Guernsey, Jersey and the Isle of Man, among other dependencies (see *Tyrer v. U.K.* (1978) Series A, No. 26; 2 E.H.R.R. 1 — Isle of Man; *Gillow v. U.K.* (1986) Series A, No. 109; 11 E.H.R.R. 335 — Guernsey). The Commission held that it had no competence in respect of the repatriation of Vietnamese "boat people" from Hong Kong, the United Kingdom having made no relevant Article 56 declaration (*Bui Van Thanh v. U.K.* (1990) 65 D.R. 330).

7. Victims, and *ratione personae*

2–15 Under this heading it is convenient to consider the three main elements, pursuant to Article 34, of the competence of the Strasbourg authorities in relation to individual applications (competence *ratione personae*). First, the applicant must be a person, non-governmental organisation or group of individuals. Secondly, they must claim to be the victim of a violation of a Convention right. Thirdly, the violation must be alleged against a contracting party.

The classification of an applicant as a "victim" is one of the keystones of the Convention, because it controls access to the legal machinery (see *Klass v. FRG* (1978) Series A, No. 28; 2 E.H.R.R. 214, para. 34). The Court and the Commission have built up a very large amount of case law on this question, concerned with assessing whether an applicant is sufficiently affected by the violation in issue. This has some similarity with the approach in domestic law to the question of standing (or *locus standi*) for the purposes of judicial review (see further Chapters 1 and 3).

2–16 The categories of applicant, although broad, have been held not to include local government institutions or semi-state bodies (see *Rothenthurm Commune v. Switzerland* (1988) 59 D.R. 251; *Ayuntamiento de M v. Spain* (1991) 68 D.R. 209). Those falling within the categories have included not only individuals, but also companies (*Pine Valley Developments Ltd v. Ireland* (1991) Series A, No. 222; 14 E.H.R.R. 319, paras 40–43), trade unions (*CCSU v. U.K.* (1987) 50 D.R. 228; 10 E.H.R.R. 269), churches (*Church of Scientology v. Sweden* (1980) 21 D.R. 109), professional associations (*Asociación de Aviadores de la Republica v. Spain* (1988) 41 D.R. 211), and political parties (*United Communist Party of Turkey v. Turkey* (1998) 26 E.H.R.R. 121; *Liberal Party v. U.K.* (1980) 21 D.R. 211; 4 E.H.R.R. 106).

There is no requirement of nationality, or residence. Indeed, more residents may be an insufficient basis for complaint (see *Bertrand Russell Peace Foundation Ltd v. U.K.*, above). Rather, the effective requirement is one of presence within the state's jurisdiction. Thus, aliens arriving within the jurisdiction of a contracting party are entitled to invoke the Convention machinery (see further, Chapter 5).

2–17 It is clear that, by the requirement for the applicant to be a victim, the Convention does not permit *actio popularis* (*i.e.* general interest litigation) or, to put it another way, complaints of hypothetical breaches. Hence, a person cannot complain about legal measures unless able to show that they have had (or are likely to have had) some personal effect. In *Amuur v. France* (1996) 22 E.H.R.R. 533 the Court held that "victim" denoted a person directly affected by the act or omission in issue. There has been some diversity of approach on this, and it is clear that there is inherently some degree of flexibility. In *Klass* the existence of legislation authorising secret surveillance was held to be capable of complaint, without the necessity for the applicants to allege that such measures had actually been applied to them. The Court spoke of the need for the system of individual applications to be "efficacious", which can be understood where secrecy inhibits investigation. However, in *Hilton v. U.K.* (1988) 57 D.R. 108 (concerning a security check by the secret service) the Commission distinguished *Klass*, and considered that it was necessary for the applicant to show a reasonable likelihood that personal information had been compiled and retained — otherwise anyone in the United Kingdom could claim to be a victim. In *Halford v. U.K.* R.J.D. 1997–III 1004; (1997) 24 E.H.R.R. 523, the Court similarly proceeded on the basis that there was a reasonable likelihood that the applicant's telephone calls had been intercepted.

There may be both direct and indirect consequences of a Convention violation. Relatives of a person who has died (*Wolfgram v. FRG* (1986) 46 D.R.

213; 9 E.H.R.R. 548), or of a person who has been refused a residence permit (*Abdulaziz, Cabales and Balkandali v. U.K.* (1985) Series A, No. 94; 7 E.H.R.R. 471) can pursue complaints in their own right. In *Sadik v. Greece* (1997) 24 E.H.R.R. 323, the widow and children of the applicant were held entitled to continue the proceedings before the Court, having a legitimate moral interest in challenging his conviction for a criminal offence, and a definite pecuniary interest in respect of the fine paid by the applicant (see also *Andersson v. Sweden* R.J.D. 1997–IV 1407; (1998) 25 E.H.R.R. 727). In *Paton v. U.K.* (1980) 19 D.R. 244; 3 E.H.R.R. 408, a prospective father was held to be a victim as regarded a right to life claim in respect of the termination of his wife's pregnancy.

2–18 It is not necessary for actual detriment to have occurred. In a number of cases it has been held that a risk of being directly affected can be sufficient. In *Campbell and Cosans v. U.K.* (1982) Series A, No. 48; 4 E.H.R.R. 293, pupils' attendance in a school where corporal punishment was used was held to be sufficient risk of degrading treatment. Similarly, the application of legislation has been held to give rise to such a risk: *Marckx v. Belgium* (1979) Series A, No. 31; 2 E.H.R.R. 330 and *Johnston v. Ireland* (1986) Series A, No. 112; 9 E.H.R.R. 203 (rules on succession concerning children born out of wedlock); *Dudgeon v. U.K.* (1981) Series A, No. 45; 4 E.H.R.R. 149 and *Norris v. Ireland* (1988) Series A, No. 142; 13 E.H.R.R. 186 (laws proscribing homosexual acts). Immigration cases display the possibility of a complaint being made before an alleged violation takes place, where otherwise the harm may be irremediable (*Soering v. U.K.* (1989) Series A, No. 161; 11 E.H.R.R. 439). But in *Vijayanathan and Pusparajah v. France* (1992) Series A, No. 241–B; 15 E.H.R.R. 62 the Court rejected an application concerning a deportation order because actual expulsion had not yet become sufficiently imminent.

The Court has taken the view that prejudice or detriment is relevant to questions of just satisfaction rather than status as a victim, and that the latter question here is one of personal affect (*e.g. Eckle v. FRG* (1982) Series A, No. 51; 5 E.H.R.R. 1; *Lüdi v. Switzerland* (1992) Series A, No. 238; 15 E.H.R.R. 173). Thus, the abandonment of legal proceedings, or mitigation of penalty, by the state in respect of the matter complained of will not necessarily deprive the applicant of standing (*Eckle*). The Court considered that if national authorities acknowledged the violation, at least in substance, and afforded redress, the applicant would, however, lose victim status (*ibid.; Lüdi*, above; see also *Amuur*, above). The Commission has held that, even without recognition by the state of a violation, legislation introduced mid-way through child custody proceedings which improved the legal position of the applicant father was sufficient to deprive him of standing (*X v. Denmark* (1978) 15 D.R. 128).

2–19 A great deal inevitably turns on the nature of the right, and the circumstances of the alleged violation. Rights to vote or in respect of elections (under Article 3 of the First Protocol) are obviously capable of broader application by the population. Similarly, in *Open Door Counselling Ltd and Dublin Well Woman Centre Ltd v. Ireland* (1992) Series A, No. 246; 15 E.H.R.R. 244, women of child-bearing age were considered to be sufficiently affected by an injunction on the provision of information about abortion services, on the basis of belonging to a class. In *Brüggermann and Scheuten v. FRG* (1978) 10 D.R. 100 the Commission accepted that women — without any necessity for them to be pregnant or to have been refused an abortion — were victims of new restrictions on abortion; but applications by a pressure group and its male chairman were rejected. In *Leigh, Guardian Newspapers Ltd and Observer Ltd v. United Kingdom* (1984) 38 D.R. 74, the Commission would not extend the category to cover every journalist who might be affected by a legal ruling as to journalistic access to and use of documents which had been involved in court proceedings. The detriment was considered to be too indirect and remote. Vagueness in the law, though, may affect a wider class and be capable of complaint more generally (see *Times Newspapers Ltd v. U.K.* (1990) 65 D.R. 307).

2-20 It is inherent in the nature of some of the Convention rights (such as the right to life, or to private life) that they will not be applicable to non-natural persons such as companies. Majority shareholders in a company have been considered entitled to complain where they were conducting their business through the company (see *Yarrow v. U.K.* (1983) 30 D.R. 155; 5 E.H.R.R. 498). However, in *Agrotexim v. Greece* (1995) Series A, No. 330; 21 E.H.R.R. 250 the Court declined to follow the Commission's approach which had adopted the fall in value of shares as a criterion for according victim status. The company still existed (although in liquidation), and the possibility remained of it making its own application. The position in relation to minority shareholders has also given rise to differing results (*Neves e Silva v. Portugal* (1989) Series A, No. 153; 13 E.H.R.R. 576 — minority shareholder able to complain; *Yarrow*, above — insufficient personal interest, effects too indirect, and interests protected by possibility of company making application.)

2-21 Violations are capable of complaint only where alleged against the state, or state institutions. There is thus a distinction between the activities of the state, and activities of private individuals and bodies. However, there may well be an overlap between the general responsibility of the state, and the immediate responsibility of a private person. Where the state has positive obligations (see below), a failure to have adequately protected the rights of private persons in their dealings with one another may give rise to a complaint against the state. Hence, in *Costello-Roberts v. U.K.* (1993) Series A, No. 247–C; 19 E.H.R.R. 192 the Court held that the state was responsible for corporal punishment in private schools because the state had a positive obligation under Article 2 of the First Protocol (the right to education) which could not be delegated.

The distinction between state responsibility and private action is not always easy to draw, yet is one of the essential features of Convention law. For example, in *Nielsen v. Denmark* (1988) Series A, No. 144; 11 E.H.R.R. 175 the Commission found that a decision to admit a child to a state psychiatric unit was taken by the doctor, but the majority of the Court viewed it as the exercise of custodial rights by the child's mother. Moreover, at a time when state functions are increasingly the subject of privatisation, contracting out, and public-private partnership, the division of responsibility between different bodies is likely to become more complex. There are unresolved questions as to the state's position in relation to the BBC (*Hilton v. U.K.* (1988) 57 D.R. 108) and British Rail (*Young, James and Webster v. U.K.* (1981) Series A, No. 44; 4 E.H.R.R. 38).

8. Incompatibility

2–22   The Strasbourg authorities are able to entertain complaints falling within the scope of the rights and freedoms contained in the Convention and protocols. Applications which concern legal subject-matter falling outside those areas will, however, be rejected as being incompatible *ratione materiae*. The Convention has been held not to cover areas such as rights of entry, residence and acquisition of nationality (*K and W v. Netherlands* (1985) 43 D.R. 216; 8 E.H.R.R. 95), the right to work (*X v. Denmark* (1975) 3 D.R. 153) or state financial assistance (*Andersson and Kullman v. Sweden* (1986) 46 D.R. 251).

On this reasoning, the Strasbourg authorities also reject applications which effectively assert that a domestic court has made an error of fact or law (*e.g. X v. FRG* (1957) 1 Y.B. 150). The Convention machinery will not be engaged as a court of further appeal (the so-called "fourth instance" doctrine, below).

9. Manifestly ill-founded

2–23   This test for admissibility under *Article 27(2) requires the Strasbourg authorities to look at the merits of an application and decide whether a *prima facie* or arguable case has been established (*Boyle and Rice v. U.K.* (1988) Series A, No. 131; 10 E.H.R.R. 425). In *Klass v. FRG* (1974) 1 D.R. 20 the Commission stated that applications raising complex questions of law, and which are of general interest, cannot be rejected under this test; but subsequent cases have demonstrated a more critical, and possibly over-critical approach.

10. Factual issues

2–24   The investigation of the facts has, in general, been a matter for the Commission. In the *Greek case* (1969) 12 Y.B. 1, for example, the Commission heard 58 witnesses together with medical experts concerning allegations of torture and ill-treatment following the military *coup*. It has been truly exceptional for the Court to hear witnesses (but see *Brozicek v. Italy* (1989) Series A, No. 167; 12 E.H.R.R. 371 and *Young, James and Webster v. U.K.* (1981) Series A, No. 44; 4 E.H.R.R. 38). The Court was not, however, bound by the Commission's findings (see, *e.g. Cruz Varas v. Sweden* (1991) Series A, No. 201; 14 E.H.R.R. 1). Where findings of fact have been made by a domestic court, the Court will — as a general rule — rely on these, while retaining the power to depart from them in appropriate cases (*Ribitsch v. Austria* (1996) Series A, No. 336; 21 E.H.R.R. 573).

The concept of a burden of proof has achieved only a limited role in resolving factual issues. At the initial stage, when the admissibility of a petition is considered, the applicant needs to present a "beginning of proof" (or *commencement de preuve*) in order to satisfy the Strasbourg authorities that the complaint is not manifestly ill-founded. Thereafter, all parties have a duty to co-operate with the investigation by the Strasbourg authorities. Apart from this, there is no burden on the applicant, because it is the function of the Strasbourg authorities to establish the facts (Article 38). The Court has generally avoided any burden of proof. In *Ireland v. U.K.* (1978) Series A, No. 25; 2 E.H.R.R. 25 the Court indicated a preference simply to examine all the available or required material. However, the state has effectively been required to show that it was not responsible for injuries sustained during detention, in order to rebut the inference of responsibility (*Tomasi v. France* (1992) Series A, No. 241-A; 15 E.H.R.R. 1). The Court has also tended to approach the necessary standard of proof with flexibility.

11. Remedies: "just satisfaction"

2–25 Where a violation has been found, and domestic law does not allow full reparation to be made, Article 41 requires the Court, where necessary, to afford "just satisfaction" to the injured party. This discretion, however, extends only to an award of pecuniary compensation. The Court has no power to annul domestic judgments or criminal convictions, or to make other consequential orders. In many instances, the Court has determined that the finding of a violation was in itself sufficient satisfaction, particularly if the violation may seem technical rather than substantial, and where the applicant has suffered no worse than a feeling of injustice. e.g. *Robins v. U.K.*, R.J.D. 1997 V 181 (unreasonable delay in costs proceedings); *Saunders v. U.K.*, R.J.D. 1996 VI 2004; (1997) 23 E.H.R.R. 313 (infringement of right against self-incrimination); *Chalal v. U.K.*, R.J.D. 1996–V 1831; (1997) 23 E.H.R.R. 413 (challenge against deportation order and lack of effective judicial control and remedies); *Campbell v. U.K.* (1992) Series A, No. 233–A; 15 E.H.R.R. 137 (opening prisoner's correspondence); *Modinos v. Cyprus* (1993) Series A, No. 259; 16 E.H.R.R. 485 (criminalisation of homosexual conduct).

The Court's discretion is exercised in a broad way, according to the circumstances in each case, and damages are often said to be assessed on an equitable basis. The case law does not provide much indication of the principles on which this is done, though the Court clearly considers the nature and effect of the violation (*Scott v. Spain* R.J.D. 1996–VI 2382; (1997) 24 E.H.R.R. 391 — subsequent conviction for murder overtook complaint regarding previous detention), and sometimes other factors such as the conduct of the applicant (*A v. Denmark* R.J.D. 1996–I 85; (1996) 22 E.H.R.R. 458).

2–26 Awards are made under two heads: pecuniary and non-pecuniary loss; and costs and expenses. Pecuniary loss includes loss of income, past and future (*Young, James and Webster v. U.K.* (1982) Series A, No. 55; 5 E.H.R.R. 201, *Open Door Counselling Ltd and Dublin Well Woman Centre Ltd v. Ireland* (1992) Series A, No. 246; 15 E.H.R.R. 244); diminution in value of property (*Sporrong and Lönnroth v. Sweden* (1984) Series A, No. 88; 7 E.H.R.R. 256, *Pine Valley Developments Ltd v. Ireland* (1991) Series A, No. 222; 14 E.H.R.R. 319, *Hentrich v. France* (1996) Series A, No. 322; 21 E.H.R.R. 199); and impositions such as taxes and fines (*Darby v. Sweden* (1990) Series A, No. 187; 13 E.H.R.R. 774; *Jersild v. Denmark* (1994) Series A, No. 298; 19 E.H.R.R. 1).

Non-pecuniary loss (also referred to as moral damage) includes pain and suffering, distress, anxiety, feelings of injustice and frustration, and damage to way of life. Aggravated or exemplary damages have not been awarded. In *Aydin v. Turkey* R.J.D. 1997–VI 1866; (1998) 25 E.H.R.R. 251, the Court awarded £25,000 (of £90,000 claimed) in respect of the rape and humiliation of a prisoner. In *Halford v. U.K.* R.J.D. 1997–III 1004; (1997) 24 E.H.R.R. 523, the applicant was awarded £10,000 compensation for intrusion into privacy caused by the tapping of telephone calls at work. In *Quinn v. France* (1995) Series A, No. 311; 21 E.H.R.R. 529, the applicant was awarded 10,000FF for a delay of 11 hours in releasing him from custody, and 50,000FF for a period of excessively lengthy detention. In *Andersson v. Sweden* (1992) Series A, No. 226; 14 E.H.R.R. 615, a mother and son were each awarded 50,000 Skr for anxiety and distress after the son was taken into care and contact between them was restricted. In *Olsson v. Sweden* (1988) Series A, No. 130; 11 E.H.R.R. 259, parents of children taken into care were awarded 200,000 Skr when contact was restricted. In *O v. U.K.* (1988) Series A, No. 136–A; 13 E.H.R.R. 578, amounts between £5,000 and £12,000 were awarded for loss of opportunities, and feelings of distress and frustration to parents whose children had been taken into care.

2–27   Causation must be established between the violation and the loss (*e.g. Kampanis v. Greece* (1995) Series A, No. 325; 21 E.H.R.R. 43). This may be difficult to achieve, for example where the Court is unable to determine (and will not speculate upon) what the outcome would have been had domestic legal proceedings been properly conducted in accordance with Convention standards (*Coyne v. U.K.* R.J.D. 1997–V 1842; *Findlay v. U.K.*, R.J.D. 1997–I 263; (1997) 24 E.H.R.R. 221; *Saunders v. U.K.* R.J.D. 1996–VI 2044; (1997) 23 E.H.R.R. 313; *Umlauft v. Austria* (1996) Series A, No. 328–B; 22 E.H.R.R. 76; *Ruiz-Mateos v. Spain* (1993) Series A, No. 262; 16 E.H.R.R. 505; see also *Langborger v. Sweden* (1989) Series A, No. 155; 12 E.H.R.R. 416).

Quantification may also be a problem. The Court, however, has developed a concept of loss of opportunities, which is used where quantification of damage is difficult. Thus in *Sporrong and Lönnroth* (above) attempts were made to measure the effect on market value of a planning restriction by technical formulae, but the Court ultimately approached the lost opportunity in the round. In *Weeks v. U.K.* (1988) Series A, No. 143–A; 13 E.H.R.R. 435 the consequence of the applicant's detention was considered in terms of a loss of practical benefit. Awards will be made to reflect any *ex gratia* payment which has been made (*A v. Denmark* R.J.D. 1996–I 85; (1996) 22 E.H.R.R. 458).

The Court will award interest in appropriate cases (*Pine Valley*, above; *Stran Greek Refineries and Stratis Andreadis v. Greece* (1994) Series A, No. 301-B; *Schuler-Zgraggen v. Switzerland* (1995) Series A, No. 305–A; 21 E.H.R.R. 404).

C. GENERAL APPROACHES TO INTERPRETATION AND APPLICATION

2–28   This section considers a number of elements of general application in relation to the interpretation and application of the substantive Convention provisions. In particular, the Convention was designed to maintain and promote the ideals and values of a democratic society; and not only is democracy a fundamental feature of the European public order, but it is the only political model compatible with the Convention (*United Communist Party of Turkey v. Turkey* (1998) 26 E.H.R.R. 121).

1. General interpretation of treaties

2–29 The interpretation of international treaties is governed by rules of international law, and these are set out in the Vienna Convention on the Law of Treaties 1969, Cmnd 7964. The Vienna Convention has accordingly been used in the interpretation of the Convention. By Article 31(1) of the Vienna Convention, a treaty

> "shall be interpreted in good faith in accordance with the ordinary meaning to be given to the terms of the treaty in their context and in the light of its object and purposes".

The context of a treaty comprises — in addition to the text, its preamble and annexes — related agreements and instruments of the contracting parties (Vienna Convention, Article 31(2)). Other elements of interpretation include subsequent agreements and practices of the parties, and any relevant rules of international law (Article 31(3) *ibid.*).

2–30 Recourse may be had to "supplementary means of interpretation". These include the preparatory work (or *travaux préparatoires*) of a treaty and the circumstances of its conclusion. These sources can be used so as to confirm the meaning resulting from Article 31 (*ibid.*), or to determine the meaning when such interpretation leaves the meaning ambiguous or obscure, or when it leads to a result that is manifestly absurd or unreasonable (Article 32 *ibid.*). The *travaux préparatoires* of the Convention are published in *Collected Edition of the Travaux Préparatoires of the European Convention on Human Rights*. It has not happened often that these sources have been consulted by the Court, and there may be a tendency now to do so even less. In *Johnston v. Ireland* (1986) Series A, No. 112; 9 E.H.R.R. 203 the Court considered (at paragraph 52) the origins of Article 12 (the right to marry) which lay in Article 16 of the Universal Declaration of Human Rights 1948, together with the account given in the *travaux préparatoires* as to why, in a material respect, there was a difference between them. In *Lithgow v. U.K.* (1986) Series A, No. 102; 8 E.H.R.R. 329, the Court considered the *travaux préparatoires* in connection with Article 1 of the First Protocol and the requirement to pay compensation for expropriation.

The English and French versions of the Convention are the two, equally authentic versions of it (see generally Article 33(1) and (2) of the Vienna Convention). The terms of a treaty are presumed to have the same meaning in each authentic text (Article 33(3) *ibid.*). Should the two versions be found to differ in their meaning, they would need to be interpreted so as to find the meaning "which best reconciles the texts, having regard to the object and purpose of the treaty" (Article 33(4) *ibid.*; see also *Wemhoff v. FRG* (1968) Series A, No. 7; 1 E.H.R.R. 55).

2. Purposive approach

2–31   Pursuant to the Vienna Convention, the Strasbourg authorities attach substantial weight to the object and purpose of the Convention. This approach may be termed "teleological". In *Wemhoff v. FRG* (1968) Series A, No. 7; 1 E.H.R.R. 55 para. 8 the Court stated that it was necessary,

> "to seek the interpretation that is most appropriate in order to realise the aim and achieve the object of the treaty, and not that which would restrict to the greatest possible degree the obligations undertaken by the parties."

The preamble to the Convention refers to the "achievement of greater unity" between members of the Council of Europe, and states that "one of the methods by which that aim is to be pursued is the maintenance and further realisation of human rights and fundamental freedoms". It also recites belief in fundamental freedoms as the foundation of "justice and peace", and the maintenance of these by "an effective political democracy" and by "a common understanding and observance of the Human Rights upon which they depend". These elements have been reflected in the case law, referring to the protection of individual human rights (*Soering v. U.K.* (1989) Series A, No. 161; 11 E.H.R.R. 439), and democracy (*Handyside v. U.K.* (1976) Series A, No. 24; 1 E.H.R.R. 737).

Allied to the purposive approach is the insistence of the Strasbourg authorities that the Convention should be "effective". In *Artico v. Italy* (1980) Series A, No. 37; 3 E.H.R.R. 7 para. 33, the Court emphasised that "the Convention is intended to guarantee not rights that are theoretical or illusory but rights that are practical and effective". This insistence has found expression particularly in the development of positive obligations (see below). There are necessarily limits to the meaning and scope of Convention provisions. The Court has observed, for example, that the ordinary meaning of the words "right to marry" in Article 12 is clear and refused to construe them so as to include a right to divorce (*Johnston v. Ireland* (1986) Series A, No. 112; 9 E.H.R.R. 203). The Court has also emphasised on a number of occasions that, in identifying the scope of particular provisions, the Convention and the protocols are to be read as whole, and not in isolation (*e.g.* the *Belgian Linguistic* case (1968) Series A, No. 6; 1 E.H.R.R. 252 para. I B 1), and with a view to achieving harmony between the individual provisions (*e.g. Soering v. U.K.*, above at paragraph 103).

3. Consensual approach

2–32   The preamble to the Convention refers to the contracting parties having resolved to "take the first steps for the collective enforcement of certain of the rights stated in the Universal Declaration". This finds an echo in the Court's search for common standards, or consensus, applicable across the breadth of the contracting parties. This is particularly so in relation to the development of case law in new areas (see below at paragraph 2–33).

There is, of course, considerable diversity of law and practice across the range of states which have submitted to the jurisdiction of the Court. As a matter of practicality as well as theory, the Court recognises a "margin of appreciation" (or area of discretion) as to the manner in which the contracting parties comply with their obligations under the Convention (see below). Hence, where actual consensus does not exist, there is a tendency to look for a lowest common denominator in order to locate the area of co-incidence between the approaches and attitudes in different states; and the Court will pay substantial regard to existing practices so long as these can be justified. In *B. v. France* (1992) Series A, No. 232–C; 16 E.H.R.R. 1 para. 48, for example, in respect of the rights of transsexuals, the Court observed that there was "no sufficiently broad consensus" in order to persuade the Court to depart from earlier judgments (see also *X, Y and Z v. U.K.* R.J.D. 1997–II 619; (1997) 24 E.H.R.R. 143).

Where the law or practice of a state is considered to be out of line with the general picture across other states, the weight of opinion is likely to be influential. In *Tyrer v. U.K.* (1978) Series A, No. 26; 2 E.H.R.R. 1, para. 31 (the Isle of Man birching case), it was held that

> "the Court cannot but be influenced by the developments and commonly accepted standards in the penal policy of the member States of the Council of Europe in this field".

The U.K. government sought to rely on public opinion on the Island itself, but the Court was dismissive of this. Similarly, the relative readiness of some states (particularly Sweden) to permit or encourage intervention by the authorities in matters concerning the protection of children, and to the detriment of parental rights, has given rise to adverse findings by the Court (*Andersson v. Sweden* (1991) 212–B; 14 E.H.R.R. 615; *Olsson v. Sweden* (1988) Series A, No. 130; 11 E.H.R.R. 259).

4. Evolutionary approach

2–33   It is not surprising that, after nearly 50 years, the Convention now begins to look somewhat dated, and this despite the addition of its protocols. However, the approach of the Court seeks to ensure the continuing relevancy and review of Convention law. The Court refers to the Convention as a "living instrument" which is to be "interpreted in the light of present day conditions" (*Tyrer v. U.K.* (1978) Series A, No. 26; 2 E.H.R.R. 1, para. 31). Changing circumstances, practices and attitudes thus all find their expression in questions of interpretation. On matters relating to the death penalty (*Soering v. U.K.* (1989) Series A, No. 161; 11 E.H.R.R. 439), illegitimacy (*Marckx v. Belgium* (1979) Series A, No. 31; 2 E.H.R.R. 330), and homosexuality (*Dudgeon v. U.K.* (1981) Series A, No. 45; 4 E.H.R.R. 149), the Court has reflected what it perceived to be changes in circumstances. In *B v. France* (above) paragraph 48, the Court noted that, since earlier decisions in relation to transsexuals, it was "undeniable that attitudes have changed, science has progressed and increasing importance is attached to the problem of transsexualism". Nonetheless, these changes were not sufficiently uniform across the contracting parties to persuade the Court to depart from those earlier decisions.

5. Precedent

2–34   Strasbourg judgments are binding only between the parties to the application. Convention law does not have a doctrine of *stare decisis*, and the

Court has reversed earlier rulings. In *Cossey v. U.K.* (1990) Series A, No. 184; 13 E.H.R.R. 622, para. 35 the Court observed that it "usually follows and applies its own precedents, such a course being in the interest of legal certainty and the orderly development of the Convention case law". As the Court explained, where "cogent reasons" exist, it is free to depart from an earlier judgment. This may happen where it is necessary to "ensure that the interpretation of the Convention reflects societal changes and remains in line with present day conditions".

There is also no differentiation between *ratio decidendi* and *obiter dicta* in respect of the judgments of the Strasbourg authorities, although the context and manner of expression may affect the weight to be attached to a particular statement.

6. Positive and negative obligations

2–35   An important element of the Convention is the inclusion of — and distinction between — so-called positive and negative obligations. Article 1 requires a state to "secure" the rights and freedoms set out in the Convention. In combination with the particular Articles defining the substantive rights, the Strasbourg authorities have construed this to mean not only that the state is prohibited from certain activity so as to avoid interference with rights (negative obligations), but also that it is required to undertake certain activity for the protection of rights (positive obligations).

The wording of the Convention itself incorporates a number of self-evidently positive obligations. Examples include the protection by law of the right to life (Article 2(1)), the various duties in relation to detained persons under Article 5(2)–(5) and in relation to fair trials, and the right to free elections (Article 3 of the First Protocol).

The extrapolation of positive obligations has been further developed by the Court, particularly in relation to Article 8 (respect for private and family life). In a number of cases following *Marckx v. Belgium* (1979) Series A, No. 31; 2 E.H.R.R. 330, the Court has stated and elaborated upon the duty imposed upon states. In *Marckx* (at paragraph 31) it was held that although the essential object of Article 8 is to protect the individual against arbitrary interference by public authorities, "there may in addition be positive obligations inherent in an effective 'respect' for family life". As Belgian family law did not encompass a child born out of wedlock, it failed to secure "a normal family life" for the mother and child. Other cases following this line in connection with Article 8 have included *Airey v. Ireland* (1979) Series A, No. 32; 2 E.H.R.R. 305 (where there was held to be a requirement for effective access to a court for an order of judicial separation so as to relieve spouses from the duty to live together, which was obstructed by the level of legal costs and lack of legal aid), and *Johnston v. Ireland* (1986) Series A, No. 112; 9 E.H.R.R. 203 (where the obligation was held not to extend as far as requiring the state to introduce measures permitting divorce and remarriage).

2–36   One consequence of the existence of positive obligations is that state responsibility may effectively (but secondarily) be engaged in respect of the relations between private persons, as well as between such persons and the state (see generally, Clapham, *Human Rights in the Private Sphere*, 1993). This is sometimes — though not entirely appositely — termed *drittwirkung* (horizontal effect), after the German law concept of the same name. In *X and Y v. Netherlands* (1985) Series A, No. 91; 8 E.H.R.R. 235 (a case concerning laws which effectively prevented a criminal charge being brought for the rape or indecent assault of a mentally disabled girl), the Court again considered Article 8, and observed that the inherent positive obligations "may involve the adoption of measures designed to secure respect for private life even in the sphere of the relations of individuals between themselves" (paragraph 23). This approach had been foreshadowed in *Young, James and Webster v. U.K.* (1981) Series A, No. 44; 4 E.H.R.R. 38, and was subsequently used in *Platform "Ärzte für das Leben" v Austria* (1988) Series A, No. 139; 13 E.H.R.R. 204, both cases concerning Article 11 (freedom of assembly and association). In the latter case, it was held that the state was under an obligation to take "reasonable and appropriate measures" to provide protection against the disruption of demonstrations.

2–37 It is unclear how the incidence of positive obligations will be developed, in terms of the extent of particular obligations and the interaction of different Convention provisions. In *Costello Roberts v U.K.* (1993) Series A, No. 247–C; 19 E.H.R.R. 112, the Court would not apply Article 8 in respect of a complaint about corporal punishment in a private boarding school, but instead approached it as a case falling within Article 2 of the First Protocol (the right to education). In that light, it held that the state could not absolve itself from responsibility to secure a Convention right by delegating its obligations to private bodies or individuals. This approach may clearly be relevant to the privatisation or contracting out of state functions.

In *Abdulaziz, Cabales & Balkandali v. U.K.* (1985) Series A, No. 94; 7 E.H.R.R. 471, para. 67, the Court repeated its observation that the notion of respect in Article 8, especially in relation to positive obligations, was not clear-cut:

" . . . having regard to the diversity of the practices followed and the situations obtaining in the Contracting States, the notion's requirements will vary considerably from case to case. Accordingly, this is an area in which the Contracting Parties enjoy a wide margin of appreciation in determining the steps to be taken to ensure compliance with the Convention with due regard to the needs and resources of the community and of individuals . . ."

Partly for this reason, the extent of positive obligations is somewhat vague; and even where a positive obligation exists the Court may well find that a state has not violated the Convention because an increased level of state intervention cannot be imposed.

7. Priorities and balances

2–38 Formally speaking, all the rights and freedoms guaranteed in the Convention have equal standing. However, while under most of the Articles the contracting parties enjoy rights of derogation (or exemption) pursuant to Article

15(1) (see further below), a few of the Convention obligations are non-derogable and thereby — in effect — entrenched. Thus, Article 3 (prohibition of torture), Article 4(1) (prohibition of slavery), and Article 7 (no punishment without law) are not derogable (see, *e.g. Ireland v. U.K.* (1978) Series A, No. 25; 2 E.H.R.R. 25; *Ahmed v. Austria* (1997) 24 E.H.R.R. 278). Article 2 (right to life) is not derogable except in respect of deaths resulting from lawful acts of war (see also Sixth Protocol).

The Strasbourg authorities also give particular emphasis to some of the rights and freedoms. In *Lingens v. Austria* (1986) Series A, No. 103; 8 E.H.R.R. 407, para. 41 the Court recalled that freedom of expression (Article 10(1)) "constitutes one of the essential foundations of a democratic society and one of the basic conditions for its progress and for each individual's self-fulfilment". Moreover, it observed (paragraph 42):

> "Freedom of the press furthermore affords the public one of the best means of discovering and forming an opinion of the ideas and attitudes of political leaders. More generally, freedom of political debate is at the very core of the concept of a democratic society which prevails throughout the Convention."

The balancing of interests is an inherent part of the Convention, just as for any system of law (see further below, Margin of Appreciation, and Proportionality). Several Articles individually provide for balances to be struck in determining their operation. Articles 8 to 11 in particular make provision for there to be limitations to the rights and freedoms, provided that these are in accordance with or prescribed by law, and that they are "necessary in a democratic society" in pursuit of a legitimate aim. It can also be necessary to balance rights and freedoms against one another, as in the case of Article 8 (respect for private and family life) and Article 10 (freedom of expression) in relation to press intrusion, as well as to read the whole of the Convention and the protocols together as one (see paragraph 2–31 above). Moreover, Article 17 — as explained by the Court in *Lawless v. Ireland* (1961) Series A, No. 3; 1 E.H.R.R. 15 — is intended by way of general provision to make it impossible for individuals to rely on a Convention right so as to subvert the enjoyment of rights by others.

8. Autonomous meanings

2–39   Under Article 31 of the Vienna Convention, the "ordinary meaning" is to be given to the terms of a treaty, unless it is established that the parties intended there to be a special meaning. Under the Convention, the particular meanings which are carried by terms in domestic law are not generally relied upon by the Strasbourg authorities. Instead, it is established that Convention terms carry an "autonomous" (or independent) meaning. In *Adolf v. Austria* (1982) Series A, No. 49; 4 E.H.R.R. 313, the Court had to consider whether there was a criminal charge against the applicant, or whether he was charged with a criminal offence, for the purposes of Article 6. The Court observed (paragraph 30):

"These expressions are to be interpreted as having an 'autonomous' meaning in the context of the Convention and not on the basis of their meaning in domestic law. The legislation of the State concerned is certainly relevant, but it provides no more than a starting-point . . ."

In some instances, terms carry a meaning which relates both to Convention and domestic law. In *Winterwerp v. Netherlands* (1979) Series A, No. 33; 2 E.H.R.R. 387, the Court considered the meaning of "lawful" for the purposes of detention under Article 5(1)(e). It held that the term presupposed conformity with domestic law in the first place, but also with the requirements of Convention law, and that the detention was not arbitrary. Similarly in *Sunday Times v. U.K.* (1979) Series A, No. 30; 2 E.H.R.R. 245, the Court approached the meaning of "law" for the purposes of Article 10 (freedom of expression) as being autonomous. For a rule to be "law" the Court prescribed two requirements additional to domestic criteria (paragraph 49):

"Firstly, the law must be adequately accessible: the citizen must be able to have an indication that is adequate in the circumstances of the legal rules applicable to a given case. Secondly, a norm cannot be regarded as a 'law' unless it is formulated with sufficient precision to enable the citizen to regulate his conduct."

9. The fourth instance doctrine

2–40 The Strasbourg authorities will not act as a court of further appeal (*quatrième instance*, or fourth instance) on questions of national law. Hence, in *X and Y v. Netherlands* (1985) Series A, No. 91; 8 E.H.R.R. 235, para. 29 the Court stated:

"It is in no way the task of the European Court of Human Rights to take the place of the competent national courts in the interpretation of domestic law . . ."

(See also *Sunday Times v. U.K.* (1979) Series A, No. 30; 2 E.H.R.R. 245, para. 65.) Similarly, it is primarily for national courts to determine the admissibility of evidence (*Schenck v. Switzerland* (1991) Series A, No. 140; 13 E.H.R.R. 242). However, under Article 6 it is for the Court to satisfy itself that proceedings as a whole were fair (*Miailhe v. France (No. 2)* (1997) Series A, No. 256–C; 23 E.H.R.R. 491). Furthermore, where compliance with national law is itself a component of Convention law (as in the case of lawful arrest, under Article 5(1)), the Strasbourg authorities do have jurisdiction to consider whether national law was properly observed (though in practice considerable deference is shown to national courts' expertise).

10. Margin of appreciation

2–41 A central element of the Court's jurisprudence, as regards its relationship with national authorities, has been the principle of a "margin of appreciation", which means the range of discretion open to public authorities without violating Convention provisions. In *Handyside v. U.K.* (1976) Series A, No. 24; 1 E.H.R.R. 737 (the "Little Red Schoolbook" case), the Court explained this principle in the context of Article 10(2) (the limitations on the freedom of expression).

> "48. The Court points out that the machinery of protection established by the Convention is subsidiary to the national systems safeguarding human rights . . . The Convention leaves to each Contracting State, in the first place, the task of securing the rights and freedoms it enshrines.
> . . . By reason of their direct and continuous contact with the vital forces of their countries, State authorities are in principle in a better position than the international judge to give an opinion on the exact content of [the requirements of morals] . . . [I]t is for the national authorities to make the initial assessment . . .
> Consequently, Article 10(2) leaves to the Contracting States a margin of appreciation. This margin is given both to the domestic legislator . . . and to the bodies, judicial amongst others, that are called upon to interpret and apply the laws in force.
> . . .
> 50. It follows from this that it is in no way the Court's task to take the place of the competent national courts but rather to review under Article 10 the decisions they delivered in the exercise of their power of appreciation . . ."

2–42 This principle has come to be applied in a considerable variety of situations. Under Article 5 (right to liberty and security), it has been held that each state is competent to organise its own system of military discipline and in this enjoys a certain margin of appreciation (*Engel v. Netherlands* (1976) Series A, No. 22; 1 E.H.R.R. 647). Under Article 8 (respect for private and family life) there is a wide margin as to the requirements of effective "respect" (*Abdulaziz, Cabales and Balkandali v. U.K.* (1985) Series A, No. 94; 7 E.H.R.R. 471). Under Article 14 (prohibition of discrimination), a certain margin has been also held to apply in assessing whether and to what extent differences in otherwise similar situations justify a different treatment in law (*Rasmussen v. Denmark* (1984) Series A, No. 87; 7 E.H.R.R. 371). And under Article 1 of the First Protocol, it has been held that national authorities enjoy a wide margin as to the implementation of social and economic policies in the context of leasehold reform (*James v. U.K.* (1986) Series A, No. 98; 8 E.H.R.R. 123).

There is not a uniform margin of appreciation across the varying contexts in which it comes to be applied, and its scope may be difficult to predict in advance. The Court has recognised that the scope of the margin will vary according to the circumstances, the subject matter and its background; and that one of the relevant factors may be the existence (or otherwise) of common ground between the laws of the contracting parties (*Rasmussen*, above). Article 15(1) (derogations) has given rise to considerable discretion in circumstances of public emergency (see *Ireland v. U.K.* (1978) Series A, No. 25; 2 E.H.R.R. 25, a case concerning anti-terrorism and the IRA). Similarly, the protection of national security has sometimes justified a wider margin (*Leander v. Sweden* (1987) Series A, No. 116; 9 E.H.R.R. 433). A wider margin exists in respect of matters concerning religion, morals or personal beliefs than in those concerning politics or the public interest (*Handyside*, above; *Wingrove v. U.K.* R.J.D. 1996–V 1937; (1997) 24 E.H.R.R. 1). The refusal to allow a transsexual to be registered as the "father" of a child has been held to attract a wide margin, given the complex scientific, legal, moral and social issues involved, and the absence of any generally shared approach among states (*X, Y and Z v. U.K.* R.J.D. 1997–II 619; (1997) 24 E.H.R.R. 143).

2–43   As regards the authority and impartiality of the judiciary, the Court has taken a narrower approach. In *Sunday Times v. U.K.* (1979) Series A, No. 30; 2 E.H.R.R. 245, para. 59 it was held:

> "The domestic law and practice of the Contracting States reveal a fairly substantial measure of common ground in this area. This is reflected in a number of provisions of the Convention, including Article 6, which have no equivalent as far as 'morals' are concerned. Accordingly, here a more extensive European supervision corresponds to a less discretionary power of appreciation."

A similarly narrow view was expressed in *Dudgeon v. U.K.* (1981) Series A, No. 45, 4 E.H.R.R. 149 concerning law rendering criminal certain homosexual acts in private between consenting adults. The government sought to rely on *Handyside* (above) and the wider approach in connection with the protection of morals, but the Court took a different approach saying (at paragraph 52):

> ". . . not only the nature of the aim of the restriction [upon a right] but also the nature of the activities involved will affect the scope of the margin of appreciation. The present case concerns a most intimate aspect of private life. Accordingly, there must exist particularly serious reasons before interferences on the part of the public authorities can be legitimate for the purposes of paragraph 2 of Article 8."

11. Proportionality

2–44   The principle of proportionality is a companion to the margin of appreciation, and provides a means whereby the Strasbourg authorities limit and test the extent and exercise of the discretion given to national authorities. It has been applied in a number of contexts under the Convention where it becomes necessary to determine whether state activity can be justified.

In *Handyside v. U.K.* (1976) Series A, No. 24; 1 E.H.R.R. 737, the Court considered the principle in the context of the margin of appreciation for the state to interfere with freedom of expression, pursuant to the various mechanisms in Article 10(2).

> "49. . . . Article 10(2) does not give the Contracting states an unlimited power of appreciation. The Court, which, with the Commission, is responsible for ensuring the observance of those States' engagements (Article 19), is empowered to give the final ruling on whether a 'restriction' or 'penalty' is reconcilable with freedom of expression as protected by

Article 10. The domestic margin of appreciation thus goes hand in hand with a European supervision. Such supervision concerns both the aim of the measure challenged and its 'necessity'; it covers not only the basic legislation but also the decision applying it, even one given by an independent court

. . .

The Court's supervisory functions oblige it to pay the utmost attention to the principles characterising a 'democratic society' . . . This means, amongst other things, that every 'formality', 'condition', 'restriction' or 'penalty' imposed in this sphere must be proportionate to the legitimate aim pursued."

Other cases in which this approach has subsequently been taken under Article 10 include *Observer and Guardian v. U.K.* (1991) Series A, No. 216; 14 E.H.R.R. 153 (the "Spycatcher" case), and *Lingens v. Austria* (1986) Series A, No. 103; 8 E.H.R.R. 407.

2–45   In *Dudgeon v. U.K.* (1981) Series A, No. 45; 4 E.H.R.R. 149 the Court applied the principle in the context of Article 8 (respect for private and family life) and the criminalisation of certain homosexual conduct. It held (at paragraph 60):

". . . such justifications as there are for retaining the law in force unamended are outweighed by the detrimental effects which the very existence of the legislative provisions in question can have on the life of a person of homosexual orientation like the applicant. Although members of the public who regard homosexuality as immoral may be shocked, offended or disturbed by the commission by others of private homosexual acts, this cannot on its own warrant the application of penal sanctions when it is consenting adults alone who are involved."

Other Article 8 cases include *Gillow v. U.K.* (1986) Series A, No. 109; 11 E.H.R.R. 335, and *Buckley v. U.K.* R.J.D. 1996–IV 1271; (1997) 23 E.H.R.R. 101.

Proportionality between the means employed and the aim sought to be realised has also arisen in the context of Article 6 (right to a fair trial): see *Fayed v. U.K.* (1994) Series A, No. 294–B; 18 E.H.R.R. 393, concerning the enquiry into the takeover of the House of Fraser; and *Stubbings v. U.K.* R.J.D. 1996–IV 1487; (1997) 23 E.H.R.R. 213, concerning the limitation period for an action in trespass, following the House of Lords' ruling in *Stubbings v. Webb* [1993] A.C. 498. Further examples of applying proportionality include cases under Article 14 (prohibition on discrimination): *Rasmussen v. Denmark* (1984) Series A, No. 87; 7 E.H.R.R. 371; *Abdulaziz, Cabales and Balkandali v. U.K.* (1985) Series A, No. 94; 7 E.H.R.R. 471; and *Gaygusuz v. Austria* R.J.D. 1996–IV 1129; (1997) 23 E.H.R.R. 364).

2–46   In several cases under Article 1 of the First Protocol (protection of property), the Court has considered the balance of interests which accompanies the test of proportionality. In *Sporrong and Lönnroth v. Sweden* (1982) Series A,

No. 52; 5 E.H.R.R. 35 the test was expressed by the notion of the "fair balance" that must be struck between the demands of the general interest of the community and the requirements of the protection of the individual's fundamental rights. The requisite balance is not found if the person concerned has had to bear "an individual and excessive burden". In *James v. U.K.* (1986) Series A, No. 98; 8 E.H.R.R. 123 the Court reiterated that the search for this balance was reflected in the structure of Article 1 of the First Protocol as a whole, and held that a measure must be both appropriate for achieving its aim and not disproportionate thereto.

In *Pressos Compania Naviera SA v. Belgium* (1995) Series A, No. 332; 21 E.H.R.R. 301, retrospective legislation was passed which deprived the plaintiff of claims for compensation in respect of a maritime collision alleged to have been caused by the negligence of Belgian pilots. While observing that national authorities were allowed a wide margin of appreciation in determining what was in the public interest, the Court held that the taking of property (*i.e.* the tortious claims for compensation) without the payment of any amount reasonably related to its value would amount to a disproportionate interference and justifiable only in exceptional circumstances. In this case, financial reasons relied on by the government were found not to be sufficient to justify the extinction of very large claims for damages.

12. Derogations

2–47   Article 15 affords a limited right to contracting states to derogate from some of their responsibilities under the Convention in circumstances of public emergency. The United Kingdom presently has one derogation, for the purposes of Article 5(3), which was made in response to the decision in *Brogan v. U.K.* (1988) Series A, No. 145–B; 11 E.H.R.R. 117. The validity of the derogation was upheld in *Brannigan v. U.K.* (1993) Series A, No. 258–B; 17 E.H.R.R. 539. The derogation is reproduced at Schedule 3 to the Act.

13. Reservations

2–48   Article 57 (formerly *Article 64) permits contracting states to make a reservation to the extent that any provision of domestic law does not conform with any provision of the Convention. General reservations are not permitted. The United Kingdom presently has one reservation, made on signing the First Protocol in 1952, with the effect that the right of parents for respect for their religious and philosophical beliefs in the education of their children has been accepted only in so far as this is compatible with the provision of efficient instruction and training, and the avoidance of unreasonable public expenditure (see further Chapter 11). The reservation is reproduced at Schedule 3 to the Act.

14. Article 16 — Restrictions on political activity of aliens

2–49   Article 16 affords contracting states considerable latitude to restrict the political activities of aliens by disapplying Articles 10 (freedom of expression), 11 (freedom of association and assembly) and 14 (prohibition of discrimination) in this respect. It appears to be the position that the disapplication of Article 14 here is not confined to its operation in conjunction with Articles 10 and 11, but also covers other Convention rights. Article 16 was considered by the Court in *Piermont v. France* (1995) Series A, No. 314; 20 E.H.R.R. 301, where it rejected the claim of the government under Article 16 in a case where a German MEP took part in a demonstration in French Polynesia. The Court held that although (at the time) citizenship of the E.C. was not recognised by the E.C. Treaty, nonetheless possession of the nationality of an E.U. state, together with status as an MEP, did not allow Article 16 to be used against her.

15. Article 17 — Prohibition on abuse of rights

2–50 Article 17 is designed to prevent reliance on Convention rights as a means to destroy any Convention right (see *Lawless v. Ireland* (1961) Series A, No. 3; 1 E.H.R.R. 15), or to curtail those rights beyond the prescribed limits. This provision applies to states, groups and individuals. It has rarely been the subject of consideration in respect of states by the Commission, and never by the Court. In *Glimmerveen and Hagenback v. Netherlands* (1979) 18 D.R. 187; 4 E.H.R.R. 260, the Commission recalled that "the general purpose of Article 17 is to prevent totalitarian groups from exploiting in their own interests the principles enunciated by the Convention". The Court approved that decision in *Jersild v. Denmark* (1994) Series A, No. 298; 19 E.H.R.R. 1, without itself finding it necessary to consider Article 17 there.

16. Article 18 — Limitation on use of restrictions on rights

2–51 Article 18 is concerned to prevent the use of restrictions of rights by the state for improper purposes. Its operation is akin to that of Article 14, in that it can only be applied in conjunction with other Convention provisions. It does not apply where the Convention right in question is not itself subject to restrictions (*Kamma v. Netherlands* (1974) 1 D.R. 4). In practical terms, attempts to rely on Article 18 have foundered on difficulties of proof (*e.g. Engel v. Netherlands* (1976) Series A, No. 22; 1 E.H.R.R. 706), and on an unwillingness of the Court to consider them.

17. Implied limitations

2–52 Some of the Convention rights are subject to express limitations within their own provisions. States have also argued that further limitations are to be implied. In some respects, the Strasbourg authorities have agreed (*e.g. Golder v. U.K.* (1975) Series A, No. 18; 1 E.H.R.R. 524, paras 37–40 in respect of Article 6; see also *Mathieu-Mohin and Clerfat v. Belgium* (1987) Series A, No. 113; 10 E.H.R.R. 1 in respect of Article 3 of the First Protocol). However, the Strasbourg authorities have drawn a line where the wording of the Convention makes it clear that the express terms are exhaustive (*Golder*, above, paragraph 44 in relation to Article 8).

18. Waiver of Convention rights

2–53 Although it is generally accepted that Convention rights can be waived, the Court has been reluctant to accede to submissions of this sort by states, and has not set out general principles to be applied in such cases. Some rights have been considered to be too fundamental to permit any waiver (*De Wilde, Ooms and Versyp v. Belgium (the "Vagrancy" cases)* (1971) Series A, No. 12; 1 E.H.R.R. 373, para. 65 — in respect of Article 5; see also *Albert and Le Compte v. Belgium* (1983) Series A, No. 58; 5 E.H.R.R. 533, para. 35).

In *Deweer v. Belgium* (1980) Series A, No. 35; 2 E.H.R.R. 439, the Court held that while the right of access to a tribunal under Article 6 was capable of being waived, one of the conditions for an effective waiver was an absence of pressure (at paragraph 49). The effective waiver of a procedural right also requires "minimum guarantees commensurate to its importance" (*Pfeiffer and Plankl v. Austria* (1992) Series A, No. 227; 14 E.H.R.R. 692, at paragraph 37). A succession of cases has furthermore laid down the requirement for any waiver to be established in "an unequivocal manner" (*e.g. Albert and Le Compte*, above, paragraph 35; *Colozza and Rubinat v. Italy* (1985) Series A, No. 89; 7 E.H.R.R. 516, para. 28; *Barberà, Messegué and Jabardo v. Spain* (1988) Series A, No. 146; 11 E.H.R.R. 360, para. 82; *Oberschlick v. Austria* (1991) Series A, No. 204; 19 E.H.R.R. 389, para. 51).

2–54   In *Le Compte, Van Leuven and De Meyere v. Belgium* (1981) Series A, No. 43; 4 E.H.R.R. 1, para. 59, the Court held that nothing in Article 6 prevented the waiver of the right to a public hearing of the applicants' "own free will, whether expressly or tacitly". In *Håkansson and Sturesson v. Sweden* (1990) Series A, No. 171; 13 E.H.R.R. 1, paras 66–67, and *Schuler-Sgraggen v. Switzerland* (1993) Series A, No. 263; 16 E.H.R.R. 405, para. 58, the Court added that, as well as being unequivocal, such a waiver "must not run counter to the public interest". In *Pauger v. Austria* R.J.D. 1997–III 881; (1998) 25 E.H.R.R. 105, the applicant — a professor of law, who was familiar with court procedure — never requested the Constitutional Court to conduct a public hearing, which was not usually held unless a request was made. In these circumstances, it was held that he had tacitly waived the right to a public hearing. Furthermore, because of an earlier ruling of the Constitutional Court in another case on point, it was held that this case did not raise a matter of public interest which warranted a public hearing.

Tacit waivers of other rights are regarded particularly critically. In *MS v. Sweden* R.J.D. 1997–IV 1437; (1997) 3 B.H.R.C. 248, the Court held that it could not be inferred from an application for compensation from the Social Insurance Office (SIO) in respect of an accident at work that the applicant had unequivocally waived her rights under Article 8 with regard to her medical records. The records had been obtained by the SIO from the applicant's clinic. (See also Chapter 13 as to the position in relation to rights in employment; and *Van der Mussele v. Belgium* (1983) Series A, No. 70; 6 E.H.R.R. 163, paragraphs 36–39 in relation to consent for the purposes of Article 4).

PART II — THE RIGHTS AND FREEDOMS GUARANTEED

D. ARTICLE 2 — RIGHT TO LIFE

2–55   The right to life is the most fundamental of all. The precedence given to this right is emphasised by the inability of states to derogate from it under

Article 15(1), except in respect of deaths resulting from lawful acts of war (Article 15(2)). In contrast to its importance, Article 2 has produced relatively little case law. It imposes, first, a positive obligation on the state to protect by law the right to life of every natural person. It also prohibits the intentional deprivation of life, except in four prescribed circumstances.

1. When does life begin?

2–56   In distinction to other human rights systems, the Convention does not make provision for when life is to be taken as beginning. The case law has left the point uncertain. A number of cases on abortion have potentially raised the issue, without providing clear guidance. In *Paton v. U.K.* (1980) 19 D.R. 244; 3 E.H.R.R. 409 the Commission hinted that the unborn foetus would not be protected; while in *H. v. Norway* (1992) No. 17004/90, unreported, the Commission did not exclude the possibility of protection in some circumstances, without stating what these might be. (See further Chapter 9.)

2. The extent of protection

2–57   The positive obligation to protect the right to life by law requires states to make a sufficient degree of provision for this in their legal systems, both in respect of the acts of private individuals as well as the acts of state agents. How this is to be done (for example by criminal penalty or civil liability), is primarily left to the state to decide, in accordance with the margin of appreciation.

The duty also extends to the investigation of suspicious deaths and the effective enforcement of law (*McCann*, below), but it does not go so far as to exclude any possible violence (*W v. U.K.* (1983) 32 D.R. 190; 5 E.H.R.R. 504; see also *X v. Ireland* (1973) 16 Y.B. 388). In a case concerned with a vaccination scheme, the Commission said that the positive duty was to take "appropriate steps to safeguard life" (*X v. U.K.* (1978) 14 D.R. 31; see also *LCB v. U.K., The Times*, June 15, 1998). The Commission left open the question whether the state was required to impose a legal duty on the public to give assistance to others in medical emergencies (*Hughes v. U.K.* (1986) 48 D.R. 258).

3. Prohibition against deprivation of life

2–58   In *McCann v. U.K.* (1995) Series A, No. 324; 21 E.H.R.R. 97 (the Gibraltar IRA shooting case), the Court confirmed that Article 2 requires a strict interpretation by reason of its fundamental nature. Thus the exceptions to the general prohibition against the taking of life are both exhaustive and narrowly confined. The prohibition affects the agents of the state, such as soldiers, police and prison officers, but does not make the state responsible for the acts of private persons.

4. Capital punishment

2–59   The first exception to the general rule under Article 2(1) concerns the right of the state to use the death penalty. However, this exception has been overtaken by the Sixth Protocol (see below para. 2–138), which abolishes the death penalty in peacetime for those states which are party to it. In view of the effect given to the Sixth Protocol under the Act (see above para. 1–21), nothing further need be said here about the death penalty.

5. Permitted use of force

2–60   Apart from the death penalty, there are three situations when the use of force resulting in death is permitted. All of these require the force to be "no more than absolutely necessary", and this imports a stricter and more compelling test of necessity than is used elsewhere in the Convention, for example under Article 8(2) (*McCann*, above). This imports a proportionality test, to which is relevant the degree of care exercised by the authorities. In *McCann*, the state was found to have violated Article 2 by reason of a lack of proper care and control in the organisation and execution of the security operation. In *Stewart v. U.K.* (1984) 39 D.R. 162, the Commission considered the test to mean that the use of force had to be "strictly proportionate to the achievement of the permitted purpose", having regard to the nature of the aim pursued, the dangers to life and limb inherent in the situation and the degree of risk that the force used might result in the loss of life.

The circumstances in which such force may be used are: (a) the defence of any person from unlawful violence; (b) in order to effect a lawful arrest or to prevent the escape of a person lawfully detained; or (c) in action lawfully taken for the purpose of quelling a riot or insurrection. The first of these does not extend to the defence of property.

E. ARTICLE 3 — PROHIBITION OF TORTURE

2–61   Article 3 is not capable of derogation by contracting states, and is not qualified. Its importance is underlined by an insistence that "ill-treatment must attain a minimum level of severity if it is to fall within the scope of Article 3" (*Ireland v. U.K.* (1978) Series A, No. 25; 2 E.H.R.R. 25, para. 162). The assessment of this minimum is relative, depending on all the circumstances of the case (see also *Tyrer v. U.K.* (1978) Series A, No. 26; 2 E.H.R.R. 1, para. 30, as to degrading treatment or punishment).

The difference between torture and ill-treatment derives principally from a difference of the intensity of the suffering inflicted, and torture connotes "deliberate inhuman treatment causing very serious and cruel suffering" (*Ireland v. U.K.*, above, para. 167). In the *Ireland* case, the Court held that interrogation techniques used on IRA suspects, which caused some psychiatric symptoms, did not cross the threshold between ill-treatment and torture. In the *Greek* case (12 Y.B. 1 (Commission), C.M. Res. D.H. (70) 1 (Committee of Ministers)), findings of torture were made in respect of severe beatings (see also *Aydin v. Turkey* R.J.D. 1997–VI 1866; (1998) 25 E.H.R.R. 251, where the rape and humiliation of a prisoner violated Article 3).

In *Tyrer*, above, the Court considered that the use of birching on bare buttocks as a judicial punishment, while not inhuman, was degrading. Reliance on local public support, efficacy as a deterrent, administration of the punishment in private, lack of lasting injury, and use for crimes of violence, were all rejected by the Court as justifications for the practice. The use of corporal punishment with a gym shoe, with the pupil wearing shorts, as a disciplinary measure in an independent school was distinguished from *Tyrer* in *Costello-Roberts v. U.K.* (1993) Series A, No. 247–C; 19 E.H.R.R. 112, albeit by a bare majority and with some misgivings (*cf. Campbell and Cosans v. U.K.* (1982) Series A, No. 48; 4 E.H.R.R. 293).

2–62 Article 3 has been applied (though on the facts often unsuccessfully) in a variety of contexts, amongst them being conditions of detention (*McFeeley v. U.K.* (1980) 20 D.R. 44 — IRA "dirty" protest, *B v. U.K.* (1981) 32 D.R. 5 — conditions at Broadmoor); extradition cases (*Soering v. U.K.* (1989) Series A, No. 161; 11 E.H.R.R. 439, where the applicant's return to the United States would have left him facing the "death row" phenomenon, in breach of Article 3 — see further Chapter 5, but compare *Ahmed v. Austria* R.J.D. 1996–VI 2195; (1997) 24 E.H.R.R. 278, and *HLR v. France* R.J.D. 1997–III 745; (1998) 26 E.H.R.R. 29); and medical treatment (*Hurtado v. Switzerland* (1994) Series A, No. 280–A — failure to provide treatment to a detainee was a breach, *Herczegfalvy v. Austria* (1992) Series A, No. 244; 15 E.H.R.R. 437 — forcible administration of food and drugs to mental patient, see further Chapters 9 and 10).

F. ARTICLE 4 — PROHIBITION OF SLAVERY AND FORCED LABOUR

2–63 There is little case law on Article 4. In *Van Droogenbroeck v. Belgium* (1982) Series A, No. 50; 4 E.H.R.R. 443 the Court held that there was no breach of Article 4(1), when a court ordered that after serving his sentence the applicant should be "placed at the Government's disposal" for 10 years. In *Van der Mussele v. Belgium* (1983) Series A, No. 70; 6 E.H.R.R. 163 a requirement for pupil lawyers to undertake *pro bono* work was found to be capable of engaging responsibility under Article 4(2), although no breach was made out because there was both prior consent by the applicant (by entry into the profession with knowledge of the requirement), and the burden thus imposed was not excessive or disproportionate in all the circumstances and in view of the underlying purposes of the Article.

Some types of work or service are excluded from Article 4 by Article 4(3), including military service and work connected with lawful detention.

G. ARTICLE 5 — RIGHT TO LIBERTY AND SECURITY

2–64 This provision is considered extensively in Chapter 4 (Criminal Justice) and Chapter 10 (Mental Health).

H. ARTICLE 6 — RIGHT TO A FAIR TRIAL

2–65 This provision is considered in several of the specialist chapters, below, but by reason of its scope and importance, and the frequency of its use, a general outline of it is called for.

Article 6(1) provides for the right to a fair and public hearing, within a reasonable time, and before an independent and impartial tribunal established by law. This right arises in respect of the determination of a person's civil rights and obligations, or of any criminal charge. Article 6(2) embodies the presumption of innocence in criminal cases, and Article 6(3) provides for certain other minimum rights for those charged with criminal offences (as to which see particularly Chapter 4).

2–66 As the Court has repeatedly stated, the right to a fair trial is one of the "fundamental principles of any democratic society within the meaning of the Convention" (*e.g. Sutter v. Switzerland* (1984) Series A, No. 74; 6 E.H.R.R. 272, para. 26), and it is not to be interpreted restrictively. At the same time, the Strasbourg authorities have maintained observance of the "*quatrième instance*" doctrine (see paragraph 2–40 above), which has helped to restrain the effect and application of Article 6 and prevent the Court from becoming a forum for further appeal. Moreover, the scope of Article 6 has been confined, particularly in respect of administrative decision-making, by the Court's view that the due process guarantees are not violated where an adjudicatory body — which of itself has not satisfied the requirements under Article 6(1) — is subject to subsequent control by a judicial body that has full jurisdiction and does provide the guarantees (*Albert and Le Compte v. Belgium* (1983) Series A, No. 58; 5 E.H.R.R. 533, para. 29; *Bryan v. U.K.* (1995) 335–A; 21 E.H.R.R. 342, para. 40) — see further, paragraph 2–79 below.

Article 6 has been the most frequently-cited basis of complaint under the Convention, yet in relation to the United Kingdom there have been comparatively few violations and of limited scope. The requirements of Article 6 will not seem strange to a common lawyer, but they will now provide a touchstone against which the activities of courts and other decision-makers will need to be judged.

1. Civil rights and obligations

2–67 In its interpretation of the concept of civil rights and obligations, the Court has held that this has an autonomous meaning, so that while the classification in domestic law may be influential it is not decisive (*e.g. Feldebrugge v. The Netherlands* (1986) Series A, No. 99; 8 E.H.R.R. 425, para. 26). Apart from the difference between criminal charges (see below) and civil matters, the principal distinction which the Court has attempted to draw is that between public and private law. The effect of this has been that Article 6 has been held to apply only to rights and obligations which arise in private law (*König v. FRG* (1978) Series A, No. 27; 2 E.H.R.R. 170, para. 95), although more recent cases have witnessed an apparently greater willingness to classify issues within the private law sphere.

The Court has not developed a general definition, but has approached the question on a case-by-case basis. In doing so, the Court looks to the nature, or "character", of the right or obligation, rather than the manner in which it is determined. The legal relations between private persons in various fields of law have not proved to be problematic in this regard. Thus in *Rasmussen v. Denmark*

(1984) Series A, No. 87; 7 E.H.R.R. 371, para. 32, a paternity suit was held to be civil in nature despite an element of public interest.

2–68   It is with regard to the relations between a private person and the state that the characterisation of the issue becomes more difficult. In *Stran Greek Refineries and Stratis Andreadis v. Greece* (1994) Series A, No. 301–B; 19 E.H.R.R. 293, para. 39, the Court summarised the position in this way:

> "Article 6(1) applies irrespective of the status of the parties, of the nature of the legislation which governs the manner in which the dispute is to be determined and of the character of the authority which has jurisdiction in the matter; it is enough that the outcome of the proceedings should be decisive for private rights and obligations".

In approaching this, the Court will have regard to the existence of any "common standard pointing to a uniform European notion" (see *Feldbrugge*, above, para. 29).

Several areas in which the state has relations with private persons have been held to give rise to civil rights and obligations. These include the right to practice a profession (*H v. Belgium* (1987) Series A, No. 127; 10 E.H.R.R. 339), a system of regulation of milk quotas (*Procola v. Luxembourg* (1995) Series A, No. 326; 22 E.H.R.R. 193), the refusal to issue a licence for an industrial installation (*Benthem v Netherlands* (1985) Series A, No. 97; 8 E.H.R.R. 1), withdrawal of a liquor licence (*Tre Traktörer Aktiebolag v Sweden* (1989) Series A, No. 159; 13 E.H.R.R. 309), refusal of permission to occupy residential premises (*Gillow v. U.K.* (1986) Series A, No. 109; 11 E.H.R.R. 335), expropriation of land (*Sporrong and Lönnroth v. Sweden* (1982) Series A, No. 52; 5 E.H.R.R. 35), rights to compensation (*Editions Périscope v. France* (1992) Series A, No. 234–B; 14 E.H.R.R. 597; *Stran Greek Refineries* above), and decision-making about child care issues (*Olsson v. Sweden (No2)* (1992) Series A, No. 250; 17 E.H.R.R. 134; *Keegan v. Ireland* (1994) Series A, No. 290; 18 E.H.R.R. 342). The Court has gone as far as recognising certain social security rights within this category (see Chapter 12).

On the other side of a somewhat uncertain line, immigration (see Chapter 5), tax issues (see Chapter 14), the right to stand for election (*Pierre-Bloch v. France* (1998) 26 E.H.R.R. 202), and certain questions in relation to public sector office and employment (*e.g. X v. U.K.* (1980) 21 D.R. 168 — police officer; *cf. Darnell v. U.K.* (1993) Series A, No. 272; 18 E.H.R.R. 205 — NHS employee) are among those matters which the Strasbourg authorities have held to be more of a public nature.

2. Criminal charges

2–69   As with the interpretation of civil rights and obligations, the Strasbourg authorities have approached the concept of a "criminal charge" as carrying an autonomous meaning (*e.g. Adolf v. Austria* (1982) Series A, No. 49; 4 E.H.R.R. 313, para. 30). However, if domestic law classifies the matter as criminal, then this is decisive. Beyond this, it is necessary to consider the nature of the offence, and the nature and severity of the possible penalty (see *Engel v. Netherlands*

(1976) Series A, No. 22; 1 E.H.R.R. 706; *Oztürk v. FRG* (1984) Series A, No. 73; 6 E.H.R.R. 409; *Campbell and Fell v. U.K.* (1984) Series A, No. 80; 7 E.H.R.R. 165).

The Court has been called upon in a number of cases to consider whether disciplinary offences are criminal in nature. Offences which have the nature of internal regulation are in principle disciplinary. Where the possible punishment, however, is deprivation of liberty, this will be criminal unless the effect of it is not "appreciably detrimental". Thus, matters of military discipline have been held to fall within the ambit (*Engel*, above); as have aspects of prison discipline (*Campbell and Fell*, above). So too have regulatory offences (*Oztürk*, above), breaching the requirement of confidentiality in legal proceedings (*Weber v. Switzerland* (1990) Series A, No. 177; 12 E.H.R.R. 508), breaching parliamentary privilege (*Demicola v. Malta* (1991) Series A, No. 210; 14 E.H.R.R. 47), and the assessment of tax surcharges (*Bendenoun v. France* (1994) Series A, No. 284; 18 E.H.R.R. 54). In *Benham v. U.K.* R.J.D. 1996–III 738; (1996) 22 E.H.R.R. 293, the Court held that although proceedings for committal to prison in respect of non-payment of community charge were civil, the nature and severity of the sentence meant that the applicant was facing a criminal charge for the purposes of Article 6.

The concept of a "charge" carries an autonomous meaning, for which it is necessary to look at substance rather than form, and determine whether the person has been substantially affected by the steps taken (*Deweer v. Belgium* (1980) Series A, No. 35; 2 E.H.R.R. 439). In English law, this will usually be at the time of arrest (*X v. U.K.* (1979) 17 D.R. 122) or being charged by the police (*Ewing v. U.K.* (1986) 45 D.R. 269; 10 E.H.R.R. 141). The application of Article 6 continues until the charge is finally determined, including sentence and appeal (*Delcourt v. Belgium* (1970) Series A, No. 11; 1 E.H.R.R. 355).

For further discussion, see Chapter 4.

3. Determinations

2–70 The application of Article 6(1) requires there to be a dispute which is the subject-matter of a determination. The necessity for a dispute is clearer from the French text of the Convention, which refers to "*contestations sur . . . droits et obligations de caractère civil*". In *James v. U.K.* (1986) Series A, No. 98; 8 E.H.R.R. 123, para. 81, this aspect of Article 6(1) was explained in the following way:

> "Article 6(1) extends only to '*contestations*' (disputes) over (civil) 'rights and obligations' which can be said, at least on arguable grounds, to be recognised under domestic law: it does not in itself guarantee any particular content for (civil) 'rights and obligations' in the substantive law of the Contracting States".

It is accordingly necessary for an applicant to have identified at least an arguable claim under domestic law. The limiting effect of this can be demonstrated by reference to *Powell and Rayner v. U.K.* (1990) Series A, No. 172; 12 E.H.R.R. 355, where the applicants complained about excessive noise levels suffered in their properties near Heathrow Airport. The Court held that there was no jurisdiction to entertain a complaint under Article 6(1) because the essence of the grievance was directed against the limitation of domestic liability under the Civil Aviation Act 1982. It reasoned (paragraph 36):

". . . the effect of [the statutory provisions] is to exclude liability in nuisance with regard to the flight of aircraft in certain circumstances, with the result that the applicants cannot claim to have a substantive right under English law to obtain relief for exposure to aircraft noise in those circumstances. To this extent there is no "civil right" recognised under domestic law to attract the application of Article 6(1)."

2–71   In *Dyer v. U.K.* (1984) 39 D.R. 246; 7 E.H.R.R. 469, the Commission considered the admissibility of a complaint under Article 6 where the applicant had been precluded from suing the Crown in negligence because of its immunity from liability under the Crown Proceedings Act 1947. The Commission held the application to be inadmissible because the statutory immunity prevented any dispute from arising in domestic law.

The Court has held, however, that the state does not enjoy unlimited scope to remove issues of civil liability from the jursidiction of the courts (see further, "Right of access to a court", below). In *Fayed v. U.K.* (1994) Series A, No. 294–B; 18 E.H.R.R. 393, the applicants' reputations had been adversely affected by the report of a government inquiry (concerning the House of Fraser takeover). They alleged that the defence of qualified or absolute privilege (which would have been a successful defence to proceedings for defamation) amounted to a violation of Article 6(1). The Court observed (paragraph 65):

"Whether a person has an actionable domestic claim may depend not only on the substantive content, properly speaking, of the relevant civil right as defined under national law but also on the existence of procedural bars preventing or limiting the possibilities of bringing potential claims to court. In the latter kind of case Article 6(1) may have a degree of applicability. Certainly the Convention enforcement bodies may not create by way of interpretation of Article 6(1) a substantive civil right which has no legal basis in the State concerned. However, it would not be consistent with the rule of law in a democratic society or with the basic principle underlying Article 6(1) — namely that civil claims must be capable of being submitted to a judge for adjudication — if, for example, a State could, without restraint or control by the Convention enforcement bodies, remove from the jurisdiction of the courts a whole range of civil claims or confer immunities from civil liability on large groups or categories of persons."

The requirement for a dispute has not been applied in a strict way, and has been approached substantively rather than formally. A dispute may involve questions of fact as well as law, and may concern not only the existence of a right but also its scope and manner of enjoyment. The dispute must, however, be genuine and of a serious nature (*Benthem v. Netherlands* (1985) Series A, No. 97; 8 E.H.R.R. 1, para. 32). As in the case of criminal charges, Article 6(1) applies through the stages of legal determination, from first to last. Pre-trial stages may be included (*e.g. Golder v. U.K.*, below). Costs proceedings which may be regarded as a continuation of the substantive litigation are also included (*Robins v. U.K.* R.J.D. 1997–V 181).

The application of Article 6(1) to administrative determinations is considered in Chapter 3.

4. Right of access to a court

2–72 One of the ways in which the Court has developed an effective and purposive interpretation of Article 6(1) is by the guarantee of a right of access to a court. In *Golder v. U.K.* (1975) Series A, No. 18; 1 E.H.R.R. 524 the applicant — a serving prisoner — was denied permission to correspond with a solicitor about the commencement of defamation proceedings against a prison officer. The Court held that the right of access to a court (in this case requiring access through a solicitor) was to be inferred from the Convention. This approach was adopted in *Airey v. Ireland* (1979) Series A, No. 32; 2 E.H.R.R. 305 where the Court held that the applicant had effectively been denied access to a court for the purpose of obtaining a judicial separation, because legal representation was required and the applicant could neither afford it nor obtain legal aid. This decision does not, however, establish a general right to legal aid, comparable to that required under Article 6(3)(c) in relation to criminal cases (see, *e.g. Tham v. U.K.* (1996) 22 E.H.R.R. C.D. 100 — regarding legal aid for bankruptcy proceedings). Various factors are relevant, including the ability of the person to put their case effectively, the relative importance of the issues raised, other opportunities to have the issues determined, the existence of reasonable prospects of success, and the extent to which legal representation is compulsory.

The Court summarised the principles in *Lithgow v. U.K.* (1986) Series A, No. 102; 8 E.H.R.R. 329, para. 194 in this way:

> "(a) The right of access to the courts secured by Article 6(1) is not absolute but may be subject to limitations; these are permitted by implication since the right of access 'by its very nature calls for regulation by the State, regulation which may vary in time and in place according to the needs and resources of the comunity and of individuals'.
> (b) In laying down such regulation, the Contracting States enjoy a certain margin of appreciation, but the final decision as to observance of the Convention's requirements rests with the Court. It must be satisfied that the limitations applied do not restrict or reduce the access left to the individual in such a way or to such an extent that the very essence of the right is impaired.
> (c) Furthermore, a limitation will not be compatible with Article 6(1) if it does not pursue a legitimate aim and if there is not a reasonable relationship of proportionality between the means employed and the aim soughht to be achieved."

2–73 Applying these principles in the *Fayed* case, the Court found that the system of investigation pursued legitimate aims with regard to the public interest in the proper conduct of the affairs of public companies whose owners benefit from limited liability, and that the underlying objective in according the inspectors freedom to report was legitimate. Notwithstanding its acceptance that judicial review would not have provided the applicants with a remedy whereby they could have argued before a court that the inspectors' findings of fact were erroneous, the Court held that there were sufficient safeguards to ensure a fair procedure and the reliability of findings of fact.

In *Stubbings v. U.K.* R.J.D. 1996–IV 1487; (1997) 23 E.H.R.R. 213, the applicant complained about the limitation period of six years under Limitation Act 1980, s.2, which, pursuant to the decision of the House of Lords in *Stubbings v. Webb* [1993] A.C. 498, had been held to bar the bringing of an action for the deliberate infliction of sexual abuse outside that period. The Court, however, held that the restriction on the right of access to a court had not breached Article 6(1), because the limitation pursued a legitimate objective, was proportionate and did not remove the essence of the right. This last requirement was explained in *Ashingdane v. U.K.* (1985) Series A, No. 93; 7 E.H.R.R. 528, para. 57 and means that any restriction cannot be such that "the very essence of the right is impaired".

5. Fair hearing

2–74   While the aspects of a fair trial are common to both criminal and civil disputes, the Court has indicated that states have a greater latitude in the conduct of civil cases than they do in respect of criminal trials (*Dombo Beheer v. Netherlands* (1993) Series A, No. 274; 18 E.H.R.R. 213, para. 32). Most of the cases have concerned criminal proceedings (which are discussed in Chapter 4), but some elements are applicable to civil litigation. The requirements of a fair hearing are not set in stone, and need to be considered in terms of the overall fairness of the proceedings rather than in isolation. This aspect of Article 6 complements the other, more specific guarantees contained in it (see generally para. 12–14 and following, below). Several elements have been held to be inherent to the concept of a fair hearing, foremost among these being the notion of "equality of arms", *i.e.* a fair balance between the parties. In *Dombo Beheer*, paragraph 33, this was held to imply that in civil litigation involving opposing interests

> "each party must be afforded a reasonable opportunity to present his case — including his evidence — under conditions that do not place him at a substantial disadvantage *vis-à-vis* his opponent".

This was held to have been breached where one side had been allowed to call one of the parties to an agreement, but the other side had not been allowed to call the other party (see also *Ruiz-Mateos v. Spain* (1993) Series A, No. 262; 16 E.H.R.R. 505 — applicants not allowed to respond to written submissions; and *Stran Greek Refineries v. Greece* (1994) Series A, No. 301–B; 19 E.H.R.R. 293 — passing of legislation by the government to defeat the applicants' civil claim against the government).

Other elements of a fair hearing include a requirement to give reasoned decisions, sufficient so that for example a party can effectively exercise any right of appeal (*Hadjianastassiou v. Greece* (1992) Series A, No. 252; 16 E.H.R.R. 219). This does not mean that every point has to be covered, but it does mean that crucial submissions need to be addressed (*Hiro Balani v. Spain* (1994) Series A, No. 303–B; 19 E.H.R.R. 565). Also under the consideration of fairness, the Strasbourg authorities have looked at the relevant rules and admission of evidence in the proceedings, giving states a considerable margin in this respect even in criminal proceedings (*Schenk v. Switzerland* (1988) Series A, No. 140; 13 E.H.R.R. 242; *cf. Lüdi v. Switzerland* (1992) Series A, No. 238; 15 E.H.R.R. 173).

6. Public hearing and judgment

2–75   Article 6(1) requires judgment to be pronounced publicly, and for the hearing to be conducted generally in public. As to the latter, the Convention itself provides for the exclusion of the press and public in certain circumstances which are capable of covering a wide range of circumstances: namely, the interests of morals, public order or national security in a democratic society; where the interests of juveniles or the private life of the parties so require; or to the extent strictly necessary in the opinion of the court in special circumstances where publicity would prejudice the interest of justice. Thus, in *Campbell and Fell v. U.K.* (1984) Series A, No. 80; 7 E.H.R.R. 165 the Court held that prison disciplinary proceedings could be held in private on grounds of public order and security. The right to a public hearing may also be waived in appropriate circumstances (*Håkansson v. Sweden* (1990) Series A, No. 171; 13 E.H.R.R. 1).

7. Prompt adjudication

2–76   Article 6(1) requires a hearing within a "reasonable time". This has generated a very considerable number of applications to the Strasbourg authorities. Delay undermines the effectiveness and credibility of justice (*H v. France* (1989) Series A, No. 162; 12 E.H.R.R. 74). In civil proceedings, the time generally is taken to run from the commencement of the proceedings, and continues until enforcement. In *Robins v. U.K.*, R.J.D. 1997–V 181, the resolution of costs proceedings took over four years, and there was held to have been responsibility on the part of the authorities for about half of that period.

While the state is not held responsible for delay caused by the applicant, it is responsible both for delay in particular instances, and structurally. States have an obligation "to organise their legal systems so as to allow the courts to comply with the requirements of Article 6(1)" (*Zimmerman and Steiner v. Switzerland* (1983) Series A, No. 66; 6 E.H.R.R. 17, para. 29). Thus a failure to allocate adequate resources in response to a backlog of cases, and to deal with structural deficiencies, may engage state liability (*e.g. Guincho v. Portugal* (1984) Series A, No. 81; 7 E.H.R.R. 223). The position is different where delays result from circumstances which were not reasonably foreseeable, and the state takes reasonably prompt remedial action (*Buchholz v. FRG* (1981) Series A, No. 42; 3 E.H.R.R. 597, para. 51).

2–77   The reasonableness of the period depends on all the circumstances, and there is no absolute period. Relevant factors include the complexity of the factual or legal issues, the conduct of the applicant and the authorities, and what was at stake for the applicant (*Zimmerman*, above). The state will be expected to show "particular diligence" in cases which are critical to the applicant and have a "particular quality of irreversibility" (*H v. U.K.* (1987) Series A, No. 120; 10 E.H.R.R. 95). Examples have been held to include cases concerning the family (*ibid.*) and employment (*Buchholz*, above). In *X v. France* (1992) Series A, No. 234–C; 14 E.H.R.R. 483 the applicant claimed compensation through the French administrative courts for negligence by the authorities after he contracted HIV and developed AIDS from infected blood transfusions. The Court held that the applicant's state of health demanded exceptional diligence (see also *Vallée v. France* (1994) Series A, No. 289–A; 18 E.H.R.R. 549, and *A. v. Denmark* R.J.D. 1996–I 85; (1996) 22 E.H.R.R. 458).

8. Independent and impartial tribunal, established by law

2–78 A "tribunal" denotes a judicial function, whose decisions have the force of law (*Benthem v. Netherlands* (1985) Series A, No. 97; 8 E.H.R.R. 1, para. 40). A body which also possesses administrative functions may nonetheless be a tribunal for these purposes (*Campbell and Fell v. U.K.* (1984) Series A, No. 80; 7 E.H.R.R. 165, paras 33 and 81, in relation to the Board of Visitors in prisons). Article 6(1) requires that the tribunal be established by law, as opposed to depending on the discretion of the executive (*Zand v. Switzerland* (1978) 15 D.R. 70, 80; see also below as to independence).

The independence of a tribunal refers to independence from the executive and the parties. In *Campbell and Fell*, above at paragraph 78, the Court referred to the following factors: the manner and duration of appointment of the tribunal members; the existence of guarantees against outside pressures; and whether the body presents the appearance of independence. In *Findlay v. U.K.* R.J.D. 1997–I 263; (1997) 24 E.H.R.R. 227 and *Coyne v. U.K.* R.J.D. 1997–V 1842, the courts martial system was found not to afford and independent an impartial tribunal because of the various roles of the convening officer. In *Findlay*, the convening officer brought the charges, selected the member of the court, chose the officers for the prosecution and defence, ensured witnesses attended, and ratified the court's decision.

2–79 The requirement for impartiality has a clear connection with independence, but goes further. It normally denotes the "absence of prejudice or bias" (*Piersack v. Belgium* (1982) Series A, No. 53; 5 E.H.R.R. 169, para. 30). In testing for this, the Court has approved and distinguished a subjective test (*i.e.* endeavouring to ascertain the personal conviction of a given judge in a given case) and an objective test (*i.e.* determining whether the judge offered guarantees sufficient to exclude any legitimate doubt in this respect): see *ibid.*, paragraph 30, and *Hauschildt v. Denmark* (1989) Series A, No. 154; 12 E.H.R.R. 266, para. 46. Impartiality is presumed (*Le Compte, Van Leuven and De Meyere v. Belgium* (1981) Series A, No. 43; 4 E.H.R.R. 1, para. 58), and the evidential burden of proving subjective bias has been very difficult to surmount. The objective test, based as it is on a "legitimate doubt", has been much easier for applicants to satisfy (e.g. *Piersack*, above, *Langborger v. Sweden* (1989) Series A, No. 155; 12 E.H.R.R. 416, and *Demicola v. Malta* (1991) Series A, No. 210; 14 E.H.R.R. 47).

Even if a particular tribunal lacks any of the elements required by Article 6(1), it is sufficient if the applicant has access to an independent judicial body with full jurisdictional control over the prior procedure, and which itself provides the Article 6(1) guarantees (*Bryan v. U.K.* (1995) Series A, No. 335-A; 21 E.H.R.R. 342, para. 40; see also *Crabtree v. U.K.* (1997) 23 E.H.R.R. C.D. 202 in relation to an unsuccessful claim in respect of a fostering panel). Thus the availability of judicial review and other remedies may well be sufficient to cure any original deficiency, though whether this is so requires consideration of the applicant's complaints and the context (see generally *Albert and Le Compte v. Belgium* (1983) Series A, No. 58; 5 E.H.R.R. 533; *W v. U.K.* (1987) Series A, No. 121; 10 E.H.R.R. 29; *Zumtobel v. Austria* (1993) Series A, No. 268-A; 17 E.H.R.R. 116).

I. ARTICLE 7 — NO PUNISHMENT WITHOUT LAW

2–80   Article 7 is considered at paragraphs 4–112—4–113.

J. ARTICLE 8 — RIGHT TO RESPECT FOR PRIVATE AND FAMILY LIFE

2–81   Article 8 covers a wide range of rights: respect for private and family life, home and correspondence. Aspects of these are considered in detail below particularly in Chapters 5 to 8. This section will focus on aspects of private life and correspondence, and some general issues. Together with Articles 9 to 11, Article 8 creates not only a complex matrix of rights, but also some extremely intricate problems, and difficult and unpredictable solutions. The scope of these rights is extended by the existence of positive obligations on states, as well as negative obligations (see generally at paragraphs 2–35—2–37). There is a clear relationship, and sometimes conflict, between (on the one hand) Article 8, and (on the other) Articles 9 and 10, and Articles 1 and 2 of the First Protocol. The general structure of Articles 8 to 11 is identical, by first defining the right, and then setting out the conditions justifying an interference with that right. The Court has held that the wording of Article 8(2) leaves no room for the concept of implied limitations on the right (*Golder v. U.K.* (1975) Series A, No. 18; 1 E.H.R.R. 524, para. 44).

1. Private life

2–82   The concept of private life is much broader than that of privacy, although its ambit is imprecise. In *Niemitz v. Germany* (1992) Series A, No. 251-B; 16 E.H.R.R. 97, para. 29 it was said:

> "The Court does not consider it possible or necessary to attempt an exhaustive definition of the notion of 'private life'. However, it would be too restrictive to limit the notion to an 'inner circle' in which the individual may live his own personal life as he chooses and to exclude therefrom entirely the outside world not encompassed within that circle. Respect for

private life must also comprise to a certain degree the right to establish and develop relationships with other human beings."

In that case it was held that the search of a lawyer's office gave rise to protection under Article 8 (see also *Kopp v. Switzerland* (1998) Legal Action, July at 21). It has also been held to include questions of personal identity (*B v. France* (1992) Series A, No. 232; 16 E.H.R.R. 1 — sexual identity; *Burghartz v. Switzerland* (1994) Series A, No. 280–B; 18 E.H.R.R. 101 — names); personal information (*Leander v. Sweden* (1987) Series A, No. 116; 9 E.H.R.R. 433, *Gaskin v. U.K.* (1989) Series A, No. 160; 12 E.H.R.R. 36); telephone calls from business premises (*Halford v. U.K.* (1997) 24 E.H.R.R. 523); health and injury (see Chapter 9); and sexual activity (*Dudgeon v. U.K.* (1981) Series A, No. 45; 4 E.H.R.R. 149).

2. Correspondence

2–83   Correspondence includes not only mail (*Golder v. U.K.* (1975) Series A, No. 18; 1 E.H.R.R. 524; *Silver v. U.K.* (1983) Series A, No. 61; 5 E.H.R.R. 347) but also telephone communications (*Halford v. U.K.*, above).

3. Respect

2–84   Article 8 is unusual in the way it is expressed. It protects no particular action, instead referring to the right to "respect" for the areas covered by the Article (see also the second sentence of Article 2, of the First Protocol). This is to be contrasted with the first draft, reflecting Article 12 of the Universal Declaration of Human Rights, the latter providing:

"No one shall be subjected to arbitrary interference with his privacy, family, home or correspondence, nor to attacks upon his honour and reputation. Everyone has the right to the protection of the law against such interference or attacks."

The scope of Article 8 is both limited in comparison, allowing a particular margin of appreciation for states to determine what ought to be protected by the notion of respect, but also extended by the impact of positive obligations. The protection for individual autonomy, while significant in some aspects, is neither general nor complete. It is apparent that not every state activity affecting interests covered by Article 8 will engage responsibility under Article 8(1).

2–85   In *Johnston v. Ireland* (1986) Series A, No. 112; 9 E.H.R.R. 203, para. 55, the Court summarised the purpose of Article 8, in the context of family life, by saying:

"Although the essential object of Article 8 is to protect the individual against arbitrary interference by the public authorities, there may in addition be positive obligations inherent in an effective 'respect' for family life. However, especially as far as those positive obligations are concerned, the notion of 'respect' is not clear-cut . . ."

In determining the scope of the right under Article 8(1), the Court has required the state to have regard to

> "the fair balance that has to be struck between the general interest of the community and the interests of the individual, the search for which is inherent in the whole Convention" (*Cossey v. U.K.* (1990) Series A, No. 184; 13 E.H.R.R. 622, para. 37).

On this approach, in *Ahmut v. Netherlands* R.J.D. 1996–VI 2017; (1997) 24 E.H.R.R. 62, the Court held that the extent of a state's obligation to grant admittance to relatives of settled immigrants varied according to the particular circumstances of the individuals involved and the general interest, but that Article 8 did not guarantee a right to choose the most suitable place to develop family life. In *Stubbings v. U.K.* R.J.D. 1996–IV 1487; (1997) 23 E.H.R.R. 213, although Article 8 was held to impose an obligation on the state to protect an individual's right to respect for private life in the context of sexual abuse suffered by a child, that obligation was discharged by the provision of criminal sanctions and did not require that the applicant be able to bring civil proceedings outside the limitation period of six years. Respect may entail state responsibility for relations between private parties, as well as directly between the state and individuals (e.g. *Airey v. Ireland* (1979) Series A, No. 32; 2 E.H.R.R. 305).

4. Interference

2–86 The applicant effectively carries an onus of establishing the fact of an interference with the right under Article 8(1). This issue may become conflated and linked with the question of victim status (see paragraph 2–15 and following above). Where the applicant cannot actually show that any particular interference has occurred, the test can involve a fairly simple finding of factual likelihood, as in *Campbell v. U.K.* (1992) Series A, No. 233–A; 15 E.H.R.R. 137 (interference with prisoner's correspondence, adjudged to exist on the basis of the prison régime without the necessity for proving that any particular letter had been opened), and *Halford v. U.K.* R.J.D. 1997–III 1004; (1997) 24 E.H.R.R. 523 (telephone-tapping, there being a reasonable likelihood of interception at work but not at home). Determining the existence of an interference may also be more subtle, through the mere existence of legislation affecting the individual (as in *Dudgeon v. U.K.* (1981) Series A, No. 45, 4 E.H.R.R. 149 and *Norris v. Ireland* (1988) Series A, No. 142; 13 E.H.R.R. 186 — legislation proscribing homosexual conduct; and *Klass v. FRG* (1978) Series A, No. 28; 2 E.H.R.R. 214 — secret surveillance).

5. Justification

2–87 It is effectively for the state to establish that any interference with the right under Article 8(1) is justified under Article 8(2). Interference is justified where it is in accordance with the law, in pursuit of a legitimate aim, and is necessary in a democratic society. Article 8(2), because it provides for an exception to a right guaranteed by the Convention, is to be narrowly interpreted (*Klass v. FRG* (1978) Series A, No. 28; 2 E.H.R.R. 214, para. 42). The essence of these requirements is to prevent and control arbitrary discretion and abuse of power.

(a) In accordance with the law

2–88   The words "in accordance with the law" in Article 8(2), and the words "prescribed by law" in Articles 9(2)–11(2), are to be read in the same way (*Sunday Times v. U.K.* (1979) Series A, No. 30; 2 E.H.R.R. 245, para. 48; *Silver v. U.K.* (1983) Series A, No. 61; 5 E.H.R.R. 347, para. 85; *Malone v. U.K.* (1984) Series A, No. 82; 7 E.H.R.R. 14, para. 66). It is a necessary component of this test that the particular interference must have some basis in domestic law (*Sunday Times* paragraph 47). "Law" carries an autonomous meaning here (*ibid.*, paragraph 49), and may be drawn from a variety of sources, including international law (*Groppera Radio AG v. Switzerland* (1990) Series A, No. 173; 12 E.H.R.R. 321, para. 68), case law (*Sunday Times*, paragraph 49), and subordinate legislation (*Golder v. U.K.* (1975) Series A, No. 18; 1 E.H.R.R. 524, para. 45). Furthermore, in order to satisfy the test of "law" for these purposes, there are two additional criteria to be applied to any rule. First, "the law must be adequately accessible: the citizen must be able to have an indication that is adequate, in the circumstances, of the legal rules applicable to a given case"; and secondly, "a norm cannot be regarded as 'law' unless it is formulated with sufficient precision to enable the citizen to regulate his conduct: he must be able — if need be with appropriate advice — to foresee, to a degree that is reasonable in the circumstances, the consequences which a given action may entail" (*Sunday Times*, paragraph 49).

In *Silver*, orders and instructions issued by the Home Office to prison governors, but not published and not having or purporting to have the force of law, were held not to be part of the law for these purposes, though the Court nonetheless considered that these materials were to be taken into account in determining the question of foreseeability to the extent that they had been made known (paragraphs 26, and 86–88). The Court rejected the applicant's contentions that the conditions and procedures governing interferences with correspondence had to be contained in the substantive law itself, and that necessary safeguards against abuse must be enshrined within the very text which authorises the imposition of restrictions. Instead, the Court considered that the question of safeguards was linked with the availability of effective remedies for the purposes of Article 13 (paragraphs 89–90).

2–89   The requirement of foreseeability is not applied in the same way in all cases, nor is it easy to define. In *Malone v. U.K.* (1984) Series A, No. 82; 7 E.H.R.R. 14 the Court held that this requirement could not be the same in the context of secret controls of staff concerned with national security, as in many other fields (see also *Leander v. Sweden* (1987) Series A, No. 116; 9 E.H.R.R. 433). In the former context, it could not mean the individual being enabled to foresee precisely what checks would be made: rather it meant having an adequate indication as to the circumstances in which, and the conditions on which, the public authorities could resort to interference (paragraph 67). In cases involving secret measures, the law itself (as opposed to administrative practice —

evidenced for example by practice manuals) must indicate the scope of the discretion with a sufficient degree of clarity (paragraph 68). The Court held that the accumulation of legislation and administrative practice did not amount to a sufficient basis of law. The government's response was to introduce the Interception of Communications Act 1985, which the Commission held to be a sufficient legal basis in *Christie v. U.K.* (1994) 78-A D.R. 119; although in *Halford v. U.K.* R.J.D. 1997–III 1004; (1997) 24 E.H.R.R. 523 the limitations of that Act were demonstrated because it did not apply to calls made from the applicant's office, and the Court held that in the absence of any other regulation the interception was not in accordance with law. In *Kruslin v. France* (1990) Series A, No. 176-A; 12 E.H.R.R. 547 the Court rejected the government's assertion that French case law laid down piecemeal over a period of time (mainly after the interference), together with extrapolation from legislative provision and case law, satisfied the requirement of foreseeability in a telephone-tapping case.

The Court has acknowledged that degrees of precision and accessibility exist within the foreseeability test, depending particularly upon the subject-matter, content, and the persons affected. Restraint of trade (*Barthold v. FRG* (1985) Series A, No. 90; 7 E.H.R.R. 383, para. 47) and obscenity (*Müller v. Switzerland* (1988) Series A, No. 133; 13 E.H.R.R. 212, para. 29) have been acknowledged as areas where absolute precision in the framing of laws is not possible. The Court has also been minded to apply a higher threshold of accessibility in relation to highly technical and complex material intended primarily for specialists, who could be expected to inform themselves (*Groppera Radio v. Switzerland* (1990) Series A, No. 173; 12 E.H.R.R. 321).

(b) Legitimate aim

2–90 To be justified under Article 8(2), an interference must pursue an aim recognised by the Convention: national security, public safety, the economic well-being of the country, the prevention of disorder or crime, the protection of health or morals, or the protection of the rights and freedoms of others. It is for the state to identify and establish the objective(s). In practical terms, where an applicant challenges the reason given by the state as not being the real reason, the Strasbourg authorities have been slow to find against states on this basis. Doubtless also because the prescribed purposes are broadly defined, the Court has consistently found in favour of states where there has been issue about the true purpose.

(c) Necessary in a democratic society

2–91 The word necessary is neither synonymous with indispensable, nor does it have the flexibility of expressions such as admissible, ordinary, useful, reasonable, or desirable (*Handyside v. U.K.* (1976) Series A, No. 24; 1 E.H.R.R. 737, para. 48; *Silver v. U.K.* (1983) Series A, No. 61; 5 E.H.R.R. 347, para. 97). Under this test, to be compatible with the Convention, the interference must *inter alia* correspond to a "pressing social need" and also be "proportionate to the legitimate aim pursued" (*ibid.* paragraphs 48–49 and 97 respectively; and as to proportionality see generally paragraphs 2–44—2–46). The state enjoys a certain but not unlimited margin of appreciation (see generally paragraphs

2–41—2–43) when it comes to the imposition of restrictions, and it is for the state to make the initial assessment, but it is for the Court to give the final ruling as a court of review rather than by way of full appeal (*ibid.* paragraphs 48 and 50, and 97 respectively). It is for the state to demonstrate the pressing social need relied on. Examples of cases where these issues have arisen include: prisoners' correspondence (*Golder v. U.K.* (1976) Series A, No. 18; 1 E.H.R.R. 524, *Silver* above, *Campbell v. U.K.* (1992) Series A, No. 233; 15 E.H.R.R. 137 — see generally Chapter 4); immigration decisions (*Berrehab v. Netherlands* (1988) Series A, No. 138; 11 E.H.R.R. 322, *Moustaquim v. Belgium* (1991) Series A, No. 193; 13 E.H.R.R. 802, *Beldjoudi v. France* (1992) Series A, No. 234–A; 14 E.H.R.R. 801 — see generally Chapter 5); child care functions (*W v. U.K.* (1987) Series A, No. 121; 10 E.H.R.R. 29, *Olsson v. Sweden (No. 1)* (1988) Series A, No. 130; 11 E.H.R.R. 259, and *No 2* (1992) Series A, No. 250; 17 E.H.R.R. 134 — see generally Chapter 6); housing policy and practice (*Gillow v. U.K.* (1986) Series A, No. 109; 11 E.H.R.R. 335 — see generally Chapter 7); and disclosure of medical information (*MS v. Sweden* R.J.D. 1997–IV 1437; (1997) 3 B.H.R.C. 248, *Z v. Finland* R.J.D. 1997–I 223; (1998) 25 E.H.R.R. 371 — see further Chapter 9).

2–92 The test can be particularly difficult to operate or anticipate, although certain aspects of the approach of the Strasbourg authorities have provided a framework. The starting point is the particular nature or aspect of the Convention right in question. Special emphasis is placed upon certain aspects of the rights covered by Article 8(1), such as the private enjoyment of sexual relations (*Dudgeon v. U.K.* (1981) Series A, No. 45; 4 E.H.R.R. 149, para. 52), relations and correspondence with legal advisers (*Niemitz v. Germany* (1992) Series A, No. 251–B; 16 E.H.R.R. 97, para. 37; *Campbell v. U.K.*, above, paragraphs 46–48), and the protection of personal data (*MS v. Sweden* and *Z v. Finland*, above). Similarly, the nature of the interests of the state is to be considered, affecting as it does the scope of the margin of appreciation enjoyed by the national authorities (see *Gillow v. U.K.*, above, paragraph 55). Cases of national security have thus unsurprisingly been held to give states a wide margin (*e.g. Leander v. Sweden* (1987) Series A, No. 116; 9 E.H.R.R. 433, para. 59), though in such a case the Court requires to be satisfied that adequate and effective guarantees against abuse are in place (*ibid.* paragraph 60; *Klass v FRG* (1978) Series A, No. 28; 2 E.H.R.R. 214 paragraphs 49–50). In *Funke v. France* (1993) Series A, No. 256–A; 16 E.H.R.R. 297, the Court recognised that the state encounters serious difficulties in preventing outflow of capital and tax evasion, owing to the scale and complexity of banking systems and financial channels, and the immense scope for international investment (paragraph 56). These difficulties were held to justify recourse to measures such as house searches and seizures, although the safeguards in that case were held to be too lax and full of loopholes (paragraph 57).

Cases of justification on other grounds include *Laskey v. U.K.* R.J.D. 1997–I 120; (1997) 24 E.H.R.R. 250, where the use of the criminal law to prosecute and convict an organised group of gay men for engaging in sado-masochistic practices was held to be justified on the grounds of the protection of health. In *Chappell v. U.K.* (1989) Series A, No. 152; 12 E.H.R.R. 1, the Court considered that the execution at the applicant's premises of an Anton Piller order in legal proceedings between private persons could be justified under Article 8(2), since it was for the protection of the rights of others, *i.e.* the plaintiffs' claim for breach of copyright in respect of "pirate" video-copying.

2–93 Among the fundamental characteristics of a democratic society, in the context of which necessity is to be judged, is the rule of law. In *Klass* (paragraph 55), the Court observed that this implied

> "*inter alia* that an interference by the executive authorities with an individual's rights should be subject to an effective control which should normally be assured by the judiciary, at least in the last resort, judicial control offering the best guarantees of independence, impartiality and a proper procedure."

Other characteristics which have been identified as important include "tolerance and broad-mindedness" (*Dudgeon v. U.K.* (1981) Series A, No. 45; 4 E.H.R.R. 149, para. 53). The search for such characteristics is conducted by the Strasbourg authorities across the national boundaries of contracting states, though this is by no means a straightforward exercise

K. ARTICLE 9 — FREEDOM OF THOUGHT, CONSCIENCE AND RELIGION

2–94 Although it has produced relatively little case law, the right to freedom of thought, conscience and religion as enshrined in Article 9 has been described by the Court as one of the foundations of a democratic society: "The pluralism indissociable from a democratic society, which has been dearly won over the centuries, depends on it" (*Kokkinakis v. Greece* (1993) Series A, No. 260–A; 17 E.H.R.R. 397, para. 31). The right protected by Article 9 includes not only the freedom to believe, but also the freedom to manifest and change one's religion or belief (Article 9(1)). A state may, however, impose restrictions only on the freedom to manifest religion or belief (Article 9(2)), so that the protection given by the Article is extensive.

The rights protected here may often need to be considered in conjunction with other Convention rights (both in combination and opposition), in particular Article 10 (freedom of expression) and Article 2 of the First Protocol (right to education). Where a more apposite Convention provision applies in a particular case, the Court is likely not to rely on Article 9 (*e.g. Johnston v. Ireland* (1986) Series A, No. 112; 9 E.H.R.R. 203, paras 62–63; *Valsamis v. Greece* (1997) 24 E.H.R.R. 294). However, where Article 9 is in point, it may have the effect of providing a greater and overriding degree of protection than Article 10 (*e.g. Wingrove, Otto-Preminger-Institut* and *Gay News*, below).

1. Scope of Article 9

2–95 It is not clear what limits may be placed on the scope of thought, conscience and religion for these purposes (*cf.* "religious and philosophical convictions" in Article 2 of the First Protocol — see Chapter 11). The Court has not defined these terms. In *Arrowsmith v. U.K.* (1978) 19 D.R. 5; 3 E.H.R.R. 218, the Commission accepted that pacificism was included, because it was a philosophy. In *Gay News Ltd and Lemon v. U.K.* (1982) 28 D.R. 77; 5 E.H.R.R. 123, the Commission was not persuaded that the publication of a sexually explicit poem involving Christ constituted the exercise of a religious or other belief (paragraph 13 — see further *R. v. Lemon* [1979] A.C. 617). In *C v. U.K.* (1983) 37 D.R. 142; 6 E.H.R.R. 587, the Commission considered that the objection of a Quaker to the use of taxes for military purposes did not fall within the scope of Article 9, because the general nature of the obligation to pay tax and the political nature of the decisions as to the use of public expenditure took the matter beyond the essentially personal ambit of the Article. In *X and Church of Scientology v. Sweden* (1979) 16 D.R. 68, the Commission decided that an advertisement by the Church was commercial in nature, and thus not a manifestation of religion.

It is unclear to what extent Article 9 may comprise positive obligations (see generally paragraphs 2–35—2–37) to enable individuals to exercise their beliefs. In *Kokkinakis*, above, the Court seemed to accept that "improper proselytism" (see further at paragraph 2–96 below) was not compatible with respect for the freedoms of others (paragraph 48 — but without defining where the line was to be drawn between this and true evangelism). The question of controlling the relations between individuals was taken up again in *Otto-Preminger-Institut v. Austria* (1994) Series A, No. 295–A; 19 E.H.R.R. 34 where the Court observed:

> "the manner in which religious beliefs and doctrines are opposed or denied is a matter which may engage the responsibility of the State, notably its responsibility to ensure the peaceful enjoyment of the right guaranteed under Article 9 to the holders of those beliefs and doctrines. Indeed, in extreme cases the effect of particular methods of opposing or denying religious beliefs can be such as to inhibit those who hold such beliefs from exercising their freedom to hold and express them" (paragraph 47).

However, in *Choudhury v. U.K.* (1991) 12 H.R.L.J. 172 (the "Satanic Verses" case), the Commission rejected the applicant's complaint under Article 9 about the lack of any criminal sanction akin to blasphemy for offence caused to non-Christian religions (see also *R. v. Bow Street Magistrates' Court, ex p. Choudhury* [1991] Q.B. 429). The aim of blasphemy laws, though, is in accordance with Article 9, and legitimate (*Wingrove v. U.K.* R.J.D. 1996–V 1937; (1997) 24 E.H.R.R. 1). In *Johnston v. Ireland* (1986) Series A, No. 112; 9 E.H.R.R. 203 the Court also held that Article 9 could not be taken to extend to the non-availability of divorce under Irish law.

2. Interference and justification

2–96   The general observations made above in relation to Article 8 (paragraphs 2–86—2–93) are also applicable in relation to Article 9, though there are some differences in the detail of paragraph (2) in each Article. The capacity of the state to place restrictions on the exercise of the freedom under

Article 9 is limited to outward manifestations of religion and belief (Article 9(2)). In *Manoussakis v. Greece* R.J.D. 1996–IV 1346; (1997) 23 E.H.R.R. 387, a requirement to obtain prior authorisation to use premises as a place of worship was held not to be justified, and the applicants' conviction for using the premises without authorisation was disproportionate. As the Court noted, the Greek legal system allowed far-reaching interference by the authorities with the exercise of the freedom of religion, and evidence before the Court showed that these powers had been used — to the point of prohibition — against religious movements, particularly Jehovah's Witnesses to which the applicants belonged. In *Kokkinakis*, above, the Court was concerned with Greece's unusual laws against proselytism. While the state was held to be entitled to frame criminal laws in this area with a degree of looseness, without the measure ceasing to be prescribed by law for the purposes of Article 9(2) (applying *Müller v. Switzerland* (1988) Series A, No. 133; 13 E.H.R.R. 212), the Court decided that the national authorities had failed to spell out why the applicant's conduct was considered to be improper. Accordingly, no pressing social need had been demonstrated for the applicant's criminal conviction.

L. ARTICLE 10 — FREEDOM OF EXPRESSION

2–97 The freedom of expression, enshrined in Article 10, has been consistently regarded as one of the fundamental elements of the Convention, and is consequently held by the Strasbourg authorities to have a special prominence. Thus, in *Handyside v. U.K.* (1976) Series A, No. 24; 1 E.H.R.R. 737, para. 49, it was stated:

"The Court's supervisory functions oblige it to pay the utmost attention to the principles characterising a 'democratic society'. Freedom of expression constitutes one of the essential foundations of such a society, one of the basic conditions for its progress and for the development of every man."

In this context, the safeguards to be afforded to the press are of particular importance (*Lingens v. Austria* (1986) Series A, No. 103; 8 E.H.R.R. 407, para. 41; *Observer and Guardian v. U.K.* (1991) Series A, No. 216; 14 E.H.R.R. 153, para. 59 (the "Spycatcher" case); *Castells v. Spain* (1992) Series A, No. 236; 14 E.H.R.R. 445, para. 43; *Jersild v. Denmark* (1994) Series A, No. 298; 19 E.H.R.R. 1, para. 31). While the press must not overstep the bounds set, it is incumbent on it to impart information and ideas on political matters as in other areas of public interest; the freedom of the press also affords one of the best means of discovering and forming an opinion of the ideas and attitudes of political leaders; and freedom of political debate "is at the very core of the concept of a democratic society" (*Lingens*, above, paragraphs 41 and 42). As well as being important to the press, the Court has held that the principles embodied in Article 10 are equally applicable to the administration of justice, "which serves the interests of the community at large and requires the co-operation of an enlightened public" (*Sunday Times v. U.K.* (1979) Series A, No. 30; 2 E.H.R.R. 245, para. 65).

2–98   The prominence and pervasiveness of the freedom of expression give rise especially to a heightened level of scrutiny by the Strasbourg authorities, and also to questions about its application in conjunction with other, overlapping and conflicting rights. When faced with a state's arguments for the justification of interference with the freedom of expression, the Court has been concerned both not to abdicate its responsibility under Article 19 to ensure the observance of state obligations under the Convention (*Open Door Counselling Ltd and Dublin Well Woman Centre Ltd v. Ireland* (1992) Series A, No. 246–A; 15 E.H.R.R. 244, para. 69), and that its supervision should not prove "illusory" (*Handyside*, above, para. 50). While it has been emphasised that the Court does not take the place of the competent national authorities in the exercise of their power of appreciation, nonetheless the Court will review on the basis of all the circumstances and arguments as a whole whether the reasons given by the national authorities to justify an interference are relevant and sufficient under Article 10(2) (*ibid.*). One aspect of this review involves consideration of the relationship of Article 10 to other Convention rights, some of which have elements in common with Article 10 (such as the freedom of assembly — *e.g. Vogt v. Germany* (1995) Series A, No. 323; 21 E.H.R.R. 205; *Plattform "Ärzte für das leben" v. Austria* (1988) Series A, No. 139; Commission at 15–32, para. 2), but which may often be in conflict with it (such as the right to respect for private life, the right to freedom of thought, and the right to a fair trial — see, *e.g. Lingens v. Austria* (1986) Series A, No. 103; 8 E.H.R.R. 407, paras 37–38; *Otto-Preminger-Institut v. Austria* (1994) Series A, No. 295–A; 19 E.H.R.R. 34; *Sunday Times v. U.K.* (1979) Series A, No. 30; 2 E.H.R.R. 245). Where there is a conflict between Convention rights, a balancing exercise ensues (*e.g. Chorherr v. Austria* (1993) Series A, No. 266–B; 17 E.H.R.R. 358, in which the state justified interference under Article 10 through its positive obligations under Article 11). Where cases can be considered in the context of another Convention right, the Strasbourg authorities often do so (*e.g. Sigurjónsson v. Iceland* (1993) Series A, No. 264; 16 E.H.R.R. 462 — decided under Article 11).

1. Scope of Article 10

2–99   Attempts to try and confine the meaning of "expression" have not been successful, whether in terms of content, medium or intended audience; and it is clear that Article 10 has a wide scope. In *Müller v. Switzerland* (1988) Series A, No. 133; 13 E.H.R.R. 212, the Court noted that Article 10 does not distinguish between the various forms of expression, and held that it includes freedom of artistic expression "which affords the opportunity to take part in the public exchange of cultural, political and social information and ideas of all kinds" (paragraph 27). In *markt intern Verlag and Beermann v. FRG* (1989) Series A, No. 165; 12 E.H.R.R. 161, the Court rejected the state's argument that an article of a commercial nature in a trade publication should be excluded from the scope of Article 10 on the grounds that the Convention did not protect a freedom to conduct business and engage in competition. The Court held that Article 10 did not apply solely to certain types of information or ideas of forms of expression (paragraph 26). In *Groppera Radio AG v. Switzerland* (1990) Series A, No. 173; 12 E.H.R.R. 321, the Court declined to give a precise definition of what is meant by "information" or "ideas", but considered that the broadcasting of light music and commercials was covered (paragraphs 54–55) (see also *Autronic AG v. Switzerland* (1983) Series A, No. 178; 12 E.H.R.R. 485). Even expressions which may be regarded contemptuously nonetheless have been held to fall within the ambit of Article 10, although they are likely to receive little in the way of protection (*e.g. Otto-Preminger-Institut v. Austria*, above, paragraph 49, giving as an example gratuitously offensive remarks about the religions of others; see also *Jersild v. Denmark* (1994) Series A, No. 298; 19 E.H.R.R. 1, dissemination of racist insults). In extreme cases, it might be the case that Article 17 would be relied on to limit the ambit of Article 10. However, the Court has repeatedly emphasised that Article 10 is applicable not only to information or ideas which are welcomed or found to be inoffensive or to which there is indifference, but also

"to those that shock, offend or disturb the State or any sector of the population. Such are the demands of that pluralism, tolerance and broadmindedness without which there is no 'democratic society' (*Handyside v. U.K.* (1976) Series A, No. 24; 1 E.H.R.R. 737, para. 49).

2–100   The forms of expression covered by Article 10 are similarly wide, comprehending paintings (*Müller*, above) and (in some circumstances) dress (*Stevens v. U.K.* (1986) 46 D.R. 245), in addition to spoken and written words. A wide range of media are also covered, including: television and radio broadcasting (*Autronic, Groppera Radio*, above); film (*Otto-Preminger-Institut*, above, *Wingrove v. U.K.* R.J.D. 1996–V 1937; (1996) 24 E.H.R.R. 1); and print (*Lingens*, above). In *Bowman v. U.K.* (1998) 26 E.H.R.R. 1, Article 10 was applied to the distribution of election leaflets. While a difference of treatment by the state between the various forms of expression may be permissible, this could fall foul of Article 14 (prohibition of discrimination): see *Casado Coca v. Spain* (1994) Series A, No. 285–A; 18 E.H.R.R. 1, para. 35.

The freedom of expression includes protection against being compelled by the state to disclose information (*Goodwin v. U.K.* R.J.D. 1996–II 483; (1996) 22 E.H.R.R. 123 — concerning an order requiring a journalist to disclose his sources, affirmed by the House of Lords at [1991] 1 A.C. 1; but contrast *BBC v. U.K.* (1996) 84 D.R. 129; 21 E.H.R.R. C.D. 93, regarding the order to produce material in relation to the P.C. Keith Blakelock killing at Broadwater Farm), and against self-incrimination (*K v. Austria* (1993) Series A, No. 255–B; Commission decision at paragraphs 45 and 49). Attempts to rely on Article 10 in order to obtain access to information from the state have been unsuccessful. In *Leander v. Sweden* (1987) Series A, No. 116; 9 E.H.R.R. 433, the Court held, in respect of the compilation of a secret file on security personnel, that Article 10 did not confer on the individual a right of access to the file, nor did it embody an obligation on the government to impart the information to the individual (paragraph 74). Rather, "the right to freedom to receive information basically prohibits a Government from restricting a person from receiving information that others wish or may be willing to impart to him" (*ibid.*). Similarly, in *Gaskin v. U.K.* (1989) Series A, No. 160; 12 E.H.R.R. 36, para. 52, the Court held that Article 10 did not embody an obligation on the state to disclose social services records to a foster child (although such an obligation was there held to exist under Article 8 — contrast *McGinley v. U.K., The Times,* June 15, 1998). However, it does seem clear that some positive obligations (see generally paragraphs 2–35—2–37) are capable of arising under Article 10, even though they have yet to be spelt out (*cf Plattform "Ärzte für das leben" v. Austria* (1988) Series A, No. 139; 13 E.H.R.R. 204, para. 32, where the Court held that Article 11 "sometimes requires positive measures to be taken, even in the sphere of relations between individuals, if need be").

2. Interference

2–101   Interferences with the right to freedom of expression are not confined to instances of prior censorship. Thus criminal and civil sanctions following publication fall within Article 10, bearing in mind their effect upon the future exercise of the right (*e.g. Lingens v. Austria* (1986) Series A, No. 103; 8 E.H.R.R. 407, para. 44; *Tolstoy Miloslavsky v. U.K.* (1995) Series A, No. 316–B; 20 E.H.R.R. 442). The seizure and forfeiture of material can also amount to an interference (*Otto-Preminger-Institut v. Austria* (1994) Series A, No. 295–A; 19 E.H.R.R. 34; *Müller v. Switzerland* (1988) Series A, No. 133; 13 E.H.R.R. 212). The manner and effect of the particular interference is likely to have an impact on the assessment of any justification for the interference, since they form part of the overall picture to which the Court has regard when carrying out its review. Prior censorship, particularly of perishable news, and sanctions which would seriously hamper the contribution of the press to discussion of matters of public interest, require strong reasons for their justification (see, *e.g. Observer and Guardian v. U.K.* (1991) Series A, No. 216; 14 E.H.R.R. 153; *Jersild v. Denmark* (1994) Series A, No. 298; 19 E.H.R.R. 1, para. 35).

The third sentence of Article 10(1) refers specifically to the right of states to require the licensing of broadcasting, television or cinema enterprises. In *Groppera Radio AG v. Switzerland* (1990) Series A, No. 173; 12 E.H.R.R. 321, para. 61, the Court concluded that the purpose of this sentence

> "is to make it clear that States are permitted to control by a licensing system the way in which broadcasting is organised in their territories, particularly in its technical aspects. It does not, however, provide that licensing measures shall not otherwise be subject to the requirements of paragraph 2, for that would lead to a result contrary to the object and purpose of Article 10 taken as a whole".

The Court thus held that any licensing requirements themselves had to satisfy the test of justification under Article 10(2), even though the power to impose them is contained in Article 10(1). Subsequently, in *Informationsverein Lentia v. Austria* (1993) Series A, No. 276; 17 E.H.R.R. 93 the applicant successfully challenged the Austrian broadcasting monopoly under Article 10(2) (see also *Radio ABC v. Austria* (1998) 25 E.H.R.R. 185). The Court clarified the basis upon which conditions might be imposed on broadcast licences, holding that it was not only technical considerations which might apply but also matters such as the nature and objectives of a proposed station, its potential audience, the rights and needs of a specific audience, and the obligations deriving from international legal instruments. This may thus extend the range of legitimate aims beyond those applicable under Article 10(2), while leaving any interference subject still to be justified under the other requirements of Article 10(2).

2–102 The existence of issues concerning expression, though necessary to the applicability of Article 10, may not be sufficient to ensure its application. In *Glasenapp v. FRG* (1986) Series A, No. 104; 9 E.H.R.R. 25, concerning the dismissal of a teacher by reason of her political opinions, the Court held that the heart of the issue was the question of access to the civil service, which the *travaux préparatoires* showed had been deliberately excluded from the scope of the Convention. Although the applicant was not deprived of the protection afforded by Article 10 as a civil servant, there was no interference with the exercise of her rights (see also *Kosiek v. FRG* (1986) Series A, No. 105; 9 E.H.R.R. 328). The Court's approach is open to criticism, and in *Vogt v. Germany* (1995) Series A, No. 323; 21 E.H.R.R. 205, the Court (by a bare majority) distinguished *Glasenapp*, on the basis that access to public service was not considered to lie at the heart of the matter.

3. Justification

2–103 The general principles and observations set out in paragraphs 2–87— 2–94 above in relation to Article 8 also apply in relation to the right to freedom of expression, though there are differences of detail between paragraph (2) of each Article. Article 10(2) permits the state to impose formalities, conditions, restrictions or penalties upon the exercise of the right to freedom of expression, but only so far as these can be justified.

(a) Duties and responsibilities

2–104 Article 10(2), uniquely, makes reference to "duties and responsibilities" inherent in the exercise of the right, and in a manner which could be thought to suggest more extensive or more readily-justified interference. The significance of these words, while not minimal, however, has not been great. In *Handyside v. U.K.* (1976) Series A, No. 24; 1 E.H.R.R. 737, para. 49, the Court said that the scope of these obligations depends on the situation of the person exercising the freedom of expression, and on the technical means used. In *Otto-Preminger-Institut v. Austria* (1994) Series A, No. 295–A; 19 E.H.R.R. 34, para. 49, the Court observed that amongst these obligations, in the context of religious opinions and beliefs, might properly be included a duty "to avoid as far as possible expressions that are gratuitously offensive to others and thus an infringement of their rights, and which therefore do not contribute to any form of public debate capable of furthering progress in human affairs". In *Jersild v Denmark* (1994) Series A, No. 298; 19 E.H.R.R. 1, para. 31, the Court said that an important factor in relation to journalism was the potential impact of the medium being used, so that those using audiovisual media may have greater responsibility — according to the often-acknowledged, increased and more immediate impact of this form of expression. The thoroughness of a journalist's research was observed in *De Haes v. Belgium* R.J.D. 1997–I 198; (1998) 25 E.H.R.R. 1 as a ground for saying that his professional obligations had been discharged.

(b) Legitimate aims

2–105   The legitimate aims of an interference by the state with the right to freedom of expression are: (a) the interests of national security, territorial integrity or public safety (*e.g. Observer and Guardian v. U.K.* (1991) Series A, No. 216; 14 E.H.R.R. 153; *Vereniging Weekblad "Bluf" v. Netherlands* (1995) Series A, No. 306–A; 20 E.H.R.R. 189), (b) the prevention of disorder or crime (*e.g. Groppera Radio AG v. Switzerland* (1990) Series A, No. 173; 12 E.H.R.R. 321), (c) the protection of health or morals (*e.g. Handyside v. U.K.* (1976) Series A, No. 24; 1 E.H.R.R. 737), (d) the protection of the reputation or rights of others (*e.g. De Haes v. Belgium*, above, reputation; *Otto-Preminger-Institut v. Austria* (1994) Series A, No. 295–A; 19 E.H.R.R. 34, right to respect for others' religious feelings; *Bowman v. U.K.* (1998) 26 E.H.R.R. 1, rights of electoral candidates and the electorate), (e) preventing the disclosure of information received in confidence (*e.g. Goodwin v. U.K.* R.J.D. 1996–II 483; (1996) 22 E.H.R.R. 123), or (f) maintaining the authority and impartiality of the judiciary (*e.g. Sunday Times v. U.K.* (1979) Series A, No. 30; 2 E.H.R.R. 245; *Barfod v. Denmark* (1989) Series A, No. 149; 13 E.H.R.R. 493). As mentioned below, different levels of justification may apply in respect of each of these aims, depending upon the circumstances of each case.

(c) Necessary in a democratic society

2–106   The requirement for the state to demonstrate the necessity for the particular interference has given rise to much of the case law under Article 10. Given the wide range of matters and circumstances to which Article 10 may apply, and the scope of the matters which the Court takes into account, the outcome of this exercise can be difficult to predict, and the facts of each case need to be considered with care.

The function of the Court is cast in terms of a supervisory review of the measures undertaken by the state, leaving it to the state to make the initial assessment as to what is necessary. But that review is active, considering all the circumstances of the case, and not just the decision taken in isolation. The Court's review is not limited to ascertaining whether the state exercised its discretion reasonably, carefully and in good faith (see *Olsson v. Sweden* (1988) Series A, No. 130; 11 E.H.R.R. 259, para. 68). Within the state's margin of appreciation (see generally at paragraphs 2–41—2.43), the Court will not interefere. But the scope of that margin, and the intensity of the Court's review, are not fixed — they depend upon the particular features of the case. In *Otto-Preminger-Institut v. Austria* (1994) Series A, No. 295–A; 19 E.H.R.R. 34, para. 50, the Court summarised the nature of the review under Article 10:

> " 'The authorities' margin of appreciation, however, is not unlimited. It goes hand in hand with Convention supervision, the scope of which will vary according to the circumstances. In cases such as the present one, where there has been an interference with the exercise of the freedoms guaranteed in paragraph 1 of Article 10, the supervision must be strict because of the importance of the freedoms in question. The necessity for any restriction must be convincingly established . . ."

2–107   Although the Court has afforded states a fairly wide margin in areas where there is diversity of national practice, such as in relation to moral questions, the width of this margin still varies as between different contexts, and is affected not only by the nature of the aim of the restriction but also by the nature of the activities involved (*Dudgeon v. U.K.* (1981) Series A, No. 45; 4 E.H.R.R. 149). In comparison to moral issues, the Court has discerned a fairly substantial measure of common ground between states with regard to maintaining the authority of the judiciary, and in this area "a more extensive European supervision corresponds to a less discretionary power of appreciation" (*Sunday Times v. U.K.* (1979) Series A, No. 30; 2 E.H.R.R. 245, para. 59). In *Casado Coca v. Spain* (1994) Series A, No. 285–A; 18 E.H.R.R. 1, relating to disciplinary proceedings brought against a member of the Spanish Bar for advertising his services, the Court decided that the national authorities were much better placed to decide what restraints should be in place, and a wider margin accordingly applied.

In *Jersild v. Denmark* (1994) Series A, No. 298; 19 E.H.R.R. 1, para. 31, the Court expressed its approach to an interference under Article 10 in this way:

> "The Court will look at the interference complained of in the light of the case as a whole and determine whether the reasons adduced by the national authorities to justify it are relevant and sufficient and whether the means employed were proportionate to the legitimate aim pursued . . . In doing so the Court has to satisfy itself that the national authorities did apply standards which were in conformity with the principles embodied in Article 10 and, moreover, that they based themselves on an acceptable assessment of the relevant facts . . ."

The state must be able to show a "pressing social need" for the interference (*Handyside v. U.K.* (1976) Series A, No. 24; 1 E.H.R.R. 737, para. 48), in addition to the proportionality of the means employed (*ibid.* at paragraph 49).

2–108   In this assessment, the nature of the interest in free expression being asserted under Article 10 in the particular case is a key factor. In broad terms, the case law has identified, non-exhaustively, three categories of interest: political expression (*e.g. Lingens v. Austria* (1986) Series A, No. 103; 8 E.H.R.R. 407), artistic expression (*Müller v. Switzerland* (1988) Series A, No. 130; 13 E.H.R.R. 212), and commercial expression (*markt Intern Verlag and Beermann v. FRG* (1989) Series A, No. 165; 12 E.H.R.R. 161).

Political expression has been given a wide meaning, comprising not only matters related to politics and politicians, but also discussion of other matters of general public concern (*Thorgierson v. Iceland* (1992) Series A, No. 239; 14 E.H.R.R. 843, para. 64 — a case relating to allegations of police brutality). The principal distinction is between matters belonging to the public arena (as in *Lingens*, above, and *Oberschlick v. Austria (No. 2)* R.J.D. 1997–IV 1266; (1998) 25 E.H.R.R. 357 — defamation cases concerning politicians' public conduct), and essentially personal matters (as in *Barfod v. Denmark* (1989) Series A, No. 149; 13 E.H.R.R. 493 — defamatory accusations against lay judges). Political expression has received very substantial protection under Article 10, linked as it often is to questions of press freedom (see, *e.g. Goodwin v. U.K.* R.J.D. 1996–II 483; (1996) 22 E.H.R.R. 123, where the commercial interests of a company, in obtaining disclosure of the identity of the source who had supplied confidential information to a journalist, were held to be outweighed by the public interest in protecting the source. But contrast *Brind v. U.K.* (1994) 77–A D.R. 42; 18 E.H.R.R. C.D. 76, where the Commission rejected as inadmissible the complaint following *R. v. Secretary of State for the Home Department ex p. Brind* [1991] 2 A.C. 696). In *Castells v. Spain* (1992) Series A, No. 236; 14 E.H.R.R. 445, para. 46, the Court held:

> "The limits of permissible criticism are wider with regard to the Government than in relation to a private citizen, or even a politician. In a democratic system the actions or omissions of the Government must be subject to the close scrutiny not only of the legislature and judicial authorities but also of the press and public opinion. Furthermore, the dominant position which the Government occupies makes it necessary for it to display restraint in resorting to criminal proceedings, particularly where other means are available for replying to the unjustified attacks and criticisms of its adversaries or the media."

In that case, the applicant was not permitted under domestic law to adduce evidence of the truth of his allegations against the government, and the Court held that this interference was not justified. In a case where the media assisted in the dissemination of objectionable and racist statements, without being the author of them, the Court took into account the important rôle of the press as "public watchdog", and considered whether the programme in question had been put together in a responsible fashion (*Jersild v. Denmark* (1994) Series A, No. 298; 19 E.H.R.R. 1). Bearing in mind the legal and moral abhorrence of racist views, it is striking — and a reminder of the importance attached to the right to freedom of expression — that the Court found that the journalist's conviction for aiding and abetting the dissemination of racist remarks was a violation of Article 10.

2–109 In comparison to political expression, artistic and commercial expression have received a lesser level of protection. In both *Müller v. Switzerland* (1988) Series A, No. 133; 13 E.H.R.R. 212 and *Otto-Preminger-Institut* (1994) Series A, No. 295–A; 19 E.H.R.R. 34, finding that no violation had occurred in either case, the Court seemed to give less priority to the interest in artistic expression (concerning respectively paintings containing sexual material, and a blasphemous film). In both cases, the Court stressed the obligations resting on the applicants under Article 10(2). In the latter case, the Court also emphasised that the national authorities had considered the artistic merit of the film, and that they were better placed than the Court to determine the need to prevent offence to Roman Catholics. As regards commercial expression, the decision in *markt intern Verlag and Beermann v. FRG* (1989) Series A, No. 165; 12 E.H.R.R. 161 establishes (not without criticism) a particularly broad margin of appreciation for states, especially in relation to unfair competition (paragraph 33), an approach followed in *Casado Coca v.*

Spain (1994) Series A, No. 285–A; 18 E.H.R.R. 1 and *Jacubowski v. Germany* (1994) Series A, No. 291–A; 19 E.H.R.R. 64. However, the Court has not always accepted the categorisation of expression as commercial: in *Barthold v. FRG* (1985) Series A, No. 90; 7 E.H.R.R. 383 the Court considered that the issue was about public discussion on a matter of general interest (the provision of vetinary services) rather than commerical advertising (concerning an interview given by the applicant for publication, about the fact that he was the only local provider of certain services).

2–110 Questions of proportionality (see generally at paragraphs 2–44—2–46) have arisen in many of the cases decided by the Court, but each case turns on its facts. Essentially, this test involves a practical judgment, relating the purpose of the measures to the means employed and the practical consequences. In *Observer and Guardian v. U.K.* (1991) Series A, No. 216; 14 E.H.R.R. 153 the Court held that the interlocutory injunctions against publication of the "Spycatcher" book were initially proportionate and justified, being temporary and limited. However, once the book had been published in the United States, and the information had effectively lost its character of confidentiality, the Court was firm in its conclusion that the restrictions could no longer be justified on the remaining grounds of deterring other security officers from publishing such material, and maintaining the reputation of the Security Service. In *Open Door Counselling Ltd and Dublin Well Woman Centre Ltd v. Ireland* (1992) Series A, No. 246–A; 15 E.H.R.R. 244 the Court was struck by the absolute and sweeping nature of the injunction granted to restrain the applicants from assisting women to obtain abortions abroad, and on this ground alone found the restriction to be disproportionate. This judgment was supported by the fact that all that the applicants were doing was to provide counselling (giving information as to the options available), the absence of which had created health risks in terms of late abortions and non-take-up of medical supervision. As in the "Spycatcher" case, the Court was also influenced by the fact that the information was anyway available through other sources.

M. ARTICLE 11 — FREEDOM OF ASSEMBLY AND ASSOCIATION

2–111 Most of the cases which have involved Article 11 have arisen in the context of trade union and labour law, and these aspects are dealt with in Chapter 13. This section is accordingly confined to some general observations.

1. State obligations and responsibility

2–112 There is a close and clear relationship between Article 11 and with the rights protected under Articles 9 and 10 (*e.g. Young, James and Webster v. U.K.* (1981) Series A, No. 44; 4 E.H.R.R. 38, para. 57); and as with the latter Articles positive obligations (see generally paragraphs 2–35—2–37) may also be imposed on states pursuant to Article 11 (see *Plattform "Ärzte für das leben" v. Austria* (1988) Series A, No. 139; 13 E.H.R.R. 204, where however the Court declined to develop a general theory of such obligations — paragraph 31). While it is the duty of states to take reasonable and appropriate measures to enable lawful demonstrations to proceed peacefully, they cannot guarantee this absolutely and they have a wide discretion in the choice of the means to be used (*ibid.* paragraph 34).

Linked with the question of positive obligations are the circumstances which may trigger state responsibility under Article 11. In *Young, James and Webster* (above), the applicants were dismissed from their employment with British Rail on account of their refusal to join a trade union, following the making of a "closed shop" agreement by the employer. The Court considered that state responsibility was engaged because it was the domestic law in force at the relevant time (*i.e.* the Trade Union and Labour Relations Act 1974) which made lawful the treatment of which the applicant's complained (paragraph 49). While this ruling seems to give very extensive horizontal effect (see paragraph 2–36) to Article 11 (by suggesting that any behaviour of private individuals, contrary to the Convention, will engage state responsibility unless proscribed under domestic law), it is more likely that it is to be seen as confined by the context — namely a very political and highly legislated area of law. The Court did not go on to examine whether the state may also have been responsible for being the effective employer, or controller of a nationalised industry.

2. Peaceful assembly

2–113   The right to hold public meetings, marches, and demonstrations is an important facet of a free society, and Article 11 protects these methods of expression so long as they are peaceful. A non-violent sit-in, which obstructed access to military premises, has been held nonetheless to be peaceful (*G v. FRG* (1989) 60 D.R. 256). Purposeful — but not incidental — disruption will prevent an assembly from being peaceful (*Christians against Racism and Fascism v. U.K.* (1980) 21 D.R. 138). The Commission has held that the right of assembly did not extend to a right of access to a shopping centre (*Anderson v. U.K.* (1997) 25 E.H.R.R. C.D. 172).

In *Ezelin v. France* (1991) Series A, No. 202; 14 E.H.R.R. 362 the Court made a rare finding of a violation in an Article 11 case, and affirmed the importance of the right of peaceful assembly. The applicant attended a demonstration, in his capacity as a lawyer and trade union official. Violence occurred, though no allegations of unlawful conduct were made against the applicant. The applicant was professionally disciplined and reprimanded by a court, because he had not dissociated himself from the demonstration when the violence occurred, and had refused to co-operate with police enquiries. The Court held that the sanction applied to the applicant had been disproportionate to the need to prevent disorder.

3. Association

2–114   Association has an autonomous meaning in the Convention, so that the definition in domestic law is not conclusive. Although the term is capable of encompassing a wide range of types and purposes, the Strasbourg authorities have excluded public law organisations from the scope of associations, which has particular relevance for professional bodies. In *Le Compte, Van Leuven and De*

Meyere v. Belgium (1981) Series A, No. 43; 4 E.H.R.R. 1 the Court held that the Belgian *Ordre des médecins* was a public law institution. In *Casado Coca v. Spain* (1994) Series A, No. 285; 18 E.H.R.R. 1 the same conclusion was reached in respect of the Spanish Bar. On the other hand, in *Sigurjónsson v. Iceland* (1993) Series A, No. 264; 16 E.H.R.R. 462 an association of taxi drivers, membership of which was compulsory, but which was established under private law, and which predominantly existed to protect the interests of its members, was held to be within Article 11.

The right to freedom of association includes not only the positive right to join, but also the negative right not to join (*Sigurjónsson*, above). However, Article 11 does not guarantee membership of any particular association (*Cheall v. U.K.* (1985) 42 D.R. 178; 8 E.H.R.R. 74).

4. Interference and justification

2–115   The general principles and observations made above in relation to Articles 8–10 apply equally to Article 11, although there are differences in detail as to the wording of paragraph (2) of each Article.

In *Sibson v. U.K.* (1993) Series A, No. 258–A; 17 E.H.R.R. 193, the applicant was dismissed from his union, and his colleagues threatened to strike if he continued to work with them. When faced with the option from his employers to rejoin the union, move to another depot, or be sent home, the applicant alleged constructive dismissal. The Court held that the compulsion to join a union in this case was sufficiently circumscribed by a number of circumstances so as not to have infringed Article 11. Contrastingly, in *Vogt v. Germany* (1995) Series A, No. 323; 21 E.H.R.R. 205, the dismissal of a teacher for membership of the Communist party was not justified.

The second sentence of Article 11(2) specifically permits the imposition of restrictions on the exercise of rights under Article 11(1) by members of the armed forces, the police, and the state administration. In the GCHQ case, *Council of Civil Service Unions v. U.K.* (1987) 50 D.R. 228; 10 E.H.R.R. 269, the Commission upheld the government's ban on trade union membership at the communications centre, holding not only that the staff there were "members of the administration of the state", but also it was within the power of the state to impose restrictions in the form of a total ban.

N. ARTICLE 12 — RIGHT TO MARRY

2–116   This Article is considered in Chapter 6.

O. ARTICLE 13 — RIGHT TO AN EFFECTIVE REMEDY

2–117   Article 13 is not included among the Convention rights which are given effect in domestic law under the Act (see Schedule 1). Instead, the Act expressly provides for remedies (sections 4 and 8), the government's view being that the passage of the Act itself meets the requirement for a right to an effective remedy (see paragraph 1–22). The relevance, under the Act, of Convention law on Article 13 is accordingly limited, and unclear (*ibid.*). An understanding of

Article 13, however, may be relevant to the development of judicial remedies under the Act, and will inform the extent to which the Act complies with the state's obligation under the Convention itself.

1. Relationship of Article 13 to other Convention rights

2–118   The right to an effective remedy is defined in terms of the substantive rights and freedoms under the Convention, and to which it is thus subsidiary. It is accordingly not a freestanding right, though an applicant does not need to establish an actual violation of another Convention right as a necessary condition for being able to establish a breach of Article 13 (*Klass v. FRG* (1978) Series A, No. 28; 2 E.H.R.R. 214, paras 64 and 69; *Silver v. U.K.* (1983) Series A, No. 61; 5 E.H.R.R. 347, para. 113). The requirement for an effective remedy overlaps with other Articles, particularly Article 6 (right to a fair trial), although the latter is not co-extensive with it (*Golder v. U.K.* (1975) Series A, No. 18; 1 E.H.R.R. 524, para. 33). The Strasbourg authorities have taken the view that a breach of Article 6 also absorbs a claim under Article 13, making it unnecessary to determine the latter claim, and that the requirements of Article 13 are less strict (*e.g. Airey v. Ireland* (1979) Series A, No. 32; 2 E.H.R.R. 305, paras 34–35 — though in *British-American Tobacco Company v. Netherlands* (1995) Series A, No. 331; 21 E.H.R.R. 409, para. 89, the Court left open the possibility that the position could be different in a given case).

The scope of Article 13 in any particular case is affected by the context, in particular the position in relation to the applicant's complaint under the Convention (*Chalal v. U.K.* R.J.D. 1996–V 1831; (1997) 23 E.H.R.R. 413, paras 150–151; *Aksoy v. Turkey* R.J.D. 1996–VI 2260; (1997) 23 E.H.R.R. 553, para. 95). Thus in *Klass*, above, the Court held that an effective remedy, in the context of the secret surveillance in that case, meant "a remedy that is as effective as can be having regard to the restricted scope for recourse inherent in any system of secret surveillance" (paragraph 69 — and see also in a similar context *Leander v. Sweden* (1987) Series A, No. 116; 9 E.H.R.R. 433). In *Chalal*, however, the Court rejected the government's argument that this limitation could be used in a case under Article 3, where issues concerning national security were immaterial, and given the seriousness of the applicant's complaints. In *Aksoy*, moreover, the Court held that Article 13 positively required the state to carry out a thorough and effective investigation into incidents of torture alleged under Article 3 (paragraph 98 — see also *Aydin v. Turkey* R.J.D. 1997–VI 1866; (1998) 25 E.H.R.R. 251).

2. Arguability

2–119   The Court has firmly rejected the contention that a claim under Article 13 depends upon establishing an actual violation of another Convention right, and instead has held that it applies to everyone who claims that a Convention right has been violated (*Klass*, above, paragraph 64). Subsequently, however, the Court introduced the limitation that the applicant must be able to show that a violation is "arguable" (see, *e.g. Silver*, above, paragraph 113; and particularly *Boyle and Rice v. U.K.* (1988) Series A, No. 131; 10 E.H.R.R. 425, para. 52). The Court has equated the test of arguability with the test for inadmissibility of an application on grounds of being manifestly ill-founded under *Article 27(2) (*Powell and Rayner v. U.K.* (1990) Series A, No. 172; 12 E.H.R.R. 355, para. 33, and see also *Boyle and Rice*, above, paragraph 54; but see a contrary approach from the Commission in *Plattform "Ärzte für das leben" v. Austria* (1985) 44 D.R. 65, and see criticism of the Court's approach in Harris, O'Boyle and Warbrick, *Law of the European Convention on Human Rights*, 1995, at 448–449).

3. Limitations Of Article 13

2–120 Article 13 does not require a remedy in every respect. Neither Article 13 nor the Convention generally obliges states to implement the Convention in domestic law in any particular manner (*Swedish Engine Drivers' Union v. Sweden* (1976) Series A, No. 20; 1 E.H.R.R. 617, para. 50). Article 13 thus guarantees only the availability within the national legal order of an effective remedy to enforce Convention rights in the form in which they have been secured in domestic law (*James v. U.K.* (1986) Series A, No. 98; 8 E.H.R.R. 132, para. 84). Article 13 does "not go so far as to guarantee a remedy allowing a Contracting State's laws as such to be challenged before a national authority on the ground of being contrary to the Convention or to equivalent domesic legal norms" (*James*, paragraph 85). Primary legislation thus cannot be challenged by this means (*ibid*.) In *Soering v. U.K.* (1989) 161, 11 E.H.R.R. 439, para. 117, the Court declined to rule on the government's submission that the same limiting principle applied in respect of an international treaty. In *Abdulaziz, Cabales and Balkandali v. U.K.* (1985) Series A, No. 94; 7 E.H.R.R. 471, paras 92–93, the Court declined to apply the principle in respect of the Immigration Rules.

4. Source of the required remedy

2–121 Article 13 does not necessarily require a judicial remedy (*Golder v. U.K.* (1975) Series A, No. 18; 1 E.H.R.R. 524, para. 33; *Klass v. FRG* (1978) Series A, No. 28; 2 E.H.R.R. 214, para. 67). The Court has considered that the Home Secretary's executive powers can satisfy the requirement (*Silver v. U.K.* (1983) Series A, No. 61; 5 E.H.R.R. 347, paras 116–119), although such powers will need to be looked at with care to see if they really do ensure an *effective* remedy, particularly in terms of the independence and authority of the decision-maker (see further below).

5. Effectiveness

2–122 The effectiveness of available remedies is considered from a practical as well as a legal point of view (*Aksoy v. Turkey* R.J.D. 1996–VI 2260; (1997) 23 E.H.R.R. 553, para. 95) — *i.e.* including whether legal remedies can practically be utilised. The Court will look at the aggregate of all the available forms of relief (*Klass*, above, paragraph 72), and may conclude that the sum total is sufficient even if the individual components would not be. The effectiveness of a remedy, however, does not depend on the certainty of a favourable outcome, and the Court will not speculate on what that outcome may have been (*Costello-Roberts* (1993) Series A, No. 247–C; 19 E.H.R.R. 112, para. 40). Thus, an argument that a civil claim was bound to fail in domestic law was not successful (*ibid.*). The remedy of judicial review, though limited in its scope, has been held to be sufficient for these purposes (*Soering v. U.K.* (1989) Series A, No. 161; 11 E.H.R.R. 439, paras 121–124; *Vilvarajah v. U.K.* (1991) Series A, No. 215; 14 E.H.R.R. 248, paras 124–126), a conclusion which ought generally to be fortified now that express provision is made under the Act with regard to the effect of Convention rights in domestic law. Where the remedy is not a judicial remedy (such as a complaint to an Ombudsman), the independence of the decision-maker will be relevant (*Silver*, above, paragraph 116), as will the degree to which the remedy is discretionary or not legally binding (*ibid.* paragraph 115). However, these questions depend on the scope of the obligation under Article 13 in the circumstances of the particular case, and weaknesses in the available remedies may be permissible if the circumstances permit a remedy of only limited effectiveness (*Leander v. Sweden* (1987) Series A, No. 116; 9 E.H.R.R. 433, para. 82 — see paragraph 2–118 above).

P. ARTICLE 14 — PROHIBITION OF DISCRIMINATION

2–123   The prohibition of discrimination contained in Article 14 is discussed in a number of the chapters below, particularly Chapters 5, 13 and 14. However, this issue is sufficiently important, broad, and frequently raised, to merit further outline here.

1. Relationship of Article 14 to other Convention rights

2–124   Like Article 13, the prohibition of discrimination has an autonomous role while having no independent existence, being defined in terms of — and thus complementing — the enjoyment of the other rights contained in the Convention (the *Belgian Linguistic* case (1968) Series A, No. 6; 1 E.H.R.R. 252; *Rasmussen v. Denmark* (1984) Series A, No. 87; 7 E.H.R.R. 371, para. 29). As with Article 13, a finding of a violation under Article 14 is not dependent upon having established a violation of another right (*e.g. Inze v. Austria* (1987) Series A, No. 126; 10 E.H.R.R. 394). The trigger for the application of Article 14 is whether the facts at issue "fall within the ambit" of one or more of the other Convention provisions (*Rasmussen*, paragraph 29). Where the facts fall outside the scope of the rights guaranteed under the Convention, no question arises under Article 14 (as in *Marckx v. Belgium* (1979) Series A, No. 31; 2 E.H.R.R. 330, para. 50, where the Court held that Article 1 of the First Protocol did not guarantee a right to acquire possessions on intestacy). Where the Court finds a violation of another Convention provision, it does not generally proceed to consider Article 14 unless there is a clear inequality of treatment in the enjoyment of the particular right which is "a fundamental aspect of the case" (*Airey v. Ireland* (1980) Series A, No. 32; 2 E.H.R.R. 305, para. 30).

It is possible that discriminatory treatment may also amount to a violation of Article 3, although the threshold for such a finding is a high one, involving contempt or lack of respect for the individual and an intention to humiliate or debase (*Abdulaziz, Cabales & Balkandali v. U.K.* (1985) Series A, No. 94; 7 E.H.R.R. 471, para. 91). Such claims in immigration cases have failed (*ibid.*, *Berrehab v. Netherlands* (1988) Series A, No. 138; 11 E.H.R.R. 322; *Moustaquim v. Belgium* (1991) Series A, No. 193; 13 E.H.R.R. 802).

Although Article 14 may impose positive obligations (see generally paragraphs 2–35—2–37) on states (the *Belgian Linguistic* case, above, paragraph I B 9), it is unclear what the scope of these may be. In part, this is because the arguments under Article 14 tend to be subsumed within those relating to other Articles (see *Airey*, above).

2. Analogous situations

2–125 Article 14 safeguards individuals, placed in analogous situations, from discrimination (*Van Der Mussele v. Belgium* (1983) Series A, No. 70; 6 E.H.R.R. 163, para. 46). In *Fresdin v. Sweden* (1991) Series A, No. 192; 13 E.H.R.R. 784 the Court summarised the test in terms of the need to consider "persons in 'relevantly' similar situations" (paragraph 60). It is effectively for the applicant to demonstrate the similarity, and cases often flounder on account of the problems or failure in adducing adequate evidence.

Cases where the applicant has failed to demonstrate an analogous situation include: *Johnston v. Ireland* (1986) Series A, No. 112; 9 E.H.R.R. 203 (persons entitled to recognition in Ireland of foreign divorces could not be compared with the applicants, who wanted a divorce in Ireland); *Moustaquim v. Belgium* (1991) Series A, No. 193; 13 E.H.R.R 802 (a juvenile delinquent subject to deportation could not be compared to juvenile delinquents with a right of abode), *Van der Mussele*, above (no similarity between the positions of lawyers and other professionals); *Lithgow v. U.K.* (1986) Series A, No. 102; 8 E.H.R.R. 329 (cases of nationalisation and compulsory purchase not comparable); and *Stubbings v. U.K.* R.J.D. 1996–IV 1487; (1997) 23 E.H.R.R. 213 (actions for trespass to the person and in negligence not analogous).

2–126 Examples of analogous situations include: *Schmidt v. Germany* (1994) Series A, No. 291–B; 18 E.H.R.R. 513 (men and women, obligation to do fire service); *Abdulaziz*, above (husband and wife, immigration); *Pine Valley Developments Ltd v. Ireland* (1991) Series A, No. 222; 14 E.H.R.R. 319 (different holders of planning permissions, rectification of planning law — but contrast *Fresdin v. France* (1991) Series A, No. 192; 13 E.H.R.R. 784); *Sutherland v. U.K.* (1997) 24 E.H.R.R. C.D. 22 (differential age of consent for heterosexual and homosexual relations); *Gudmunsson v. Iceland* (1996) 21 E.H.R.R. C.D. 89 (age limit for taxi licence, applicable only in certain geographical areas); and *Bullock v. U.K.* (1996) 21 E.H.R.R. C.D. 85 (defined types of dangerous dog).

The degree of similarity between analogous situations may also be relevant to other questions, such as considering the justification for any difference of treatment (*e.g. Gaygusuz v. Austria* R.J.D. 1996–IV 1129; (1996) 23 E.H.R.R. 364, para. 46).

3. Difference in treatment

2–127 Discrimination involves an unjustified difference of treatment between the applicant and other comparable persons (see, *e.g. Abdulaziz, Cabales and Balkandali v. U.K.* (1985) Series A, No. 94; 7 E.H.R.R. 471). The existence of a difference of treatment is clearly linked with the identification of the situation with which that of the applicant is to be contrasted, and again the effective onus is on the applicant (*e.g. Gay News Ltd and Lemon v. U.K.* (1982) 28 D.R. 77; 5 E.H.R.R. 123, where the Commission held that the applicants had failed to adduce evidence that they had been singled out on account of their ·homosexual views). The Strasbourg authorities will consider for themselves what the true ground is for the difference of treatment (*e.g. Hoffmann v. Austria* (1993) Series A, No. 255–C; 17 E.H.R.R. 293, where the Court rejected the state's reasoning). Proving racism, though, in cases of indirect discrimination has been problematic (*Abdulaziz*, above, para. 85).

Article 14 does not define exhaustively the grounds upon which any such difference of treatment will be caught (*Rasmussen v. Denmark* (1984) Series A, No. 87; 7 E.H.R.R. 371, para. 34). The categories are wide and open-ended (though some grounds are treated more rigorously than others, see below paragraph 2–129). Examples of differences in treatment include: gender (*Abdulaziz*); race (*East African Asians* cases (1976) 3 E.H.R.R. 76; language (the *Belgian Linguistic* case (1968) Series A, No. 6; 1 E.H.R.R. 252); religion (*Hoffmann v. Austria*, above); nationality (*Gaygusuz v. Austria*, above); and illegitimate status of a child (*Marckx v. Belgium*, above). In general, the notion of discrimination in Article 14 includes cases where a person or group is treated, without proper justification, less favourably than another, even where the state affords the applicant more favourable treatment in some respects than is called for by the Convention (*Abdulaziz*, paragraph 82).

4. Reasonable and objective justification

2–128   Not every difference in treatment is discriminatory. Although the principles used by the Strasbourg authorities in seeking justification for a difference in treatment are clear, their application is not always easy to follow, with various elements of the test both overlapping and being confused. The essential benchmark is whether the state has shown a "reasonable and objective justification" for the difference in treatment (the *Belgian Linguistic* case, above, paragraph 10). The Court explained this as follows (*ibid.*):

> "The existence of such a justification must be assessed in relation to the aim and effects of the measure under consideration, regard being had to the principles which normally prevail in democratic societies. A difference of treatment in the exercise of a right laid down in the Convention must not only pursue a legitimate aim: Article 14 is likewise violated when it is clearly established that there is no reasonable relationship of proportionality between the means employed and the aim sought to be realised."

It is not only the principle of the differentiation, but also its scope, which requires to be justified (*National Union of Belgian Police v. Belgium* (1975) Series A, No. 19; 1 E.H.R.R. 578, para. 49). States have sometimes offered no justification for certain measures, with the result that findings have been made against them (*e.g. Marckx v. Belgium* (1979) Series A, No. 31; 2 E.H.R.R. 330, para. 62). There is scope for changing conditions to result in the Strasbourg authorities evolving and altering their position, with the result that a previous finding of justification may no longer be decisive or persuasive (*e.g. Sutherland v.*

U.K. (1997) 24 E.H.R.R. C.D. 22, where the Commission decided to reconsider and depart from its earlier case law on a differential age of consent for homosexuals; see also *Marckx*, above, paragraph 41).

2–129 Under Article 14, the Court carries out a supervisory review, the scope and intensity of which depend on the circumstances, allowing contracting states to make appropriate judgments within their margin of appreciation (see generally at paragraphs 2–41—2–43). As the Court held in the *Belgian Linguistic* case, above, paras I B 10:

> "In attempting to find out, in a given case, whether or not there has been an arbitrary distinction, the Court cannot disregard those legal and factual features which characterise the life of the society in the State which, as a Contracting Party, has to answer for the measure in dispute. In so doing, it cannot assume the role of the competent national authorities, for it would thereby lose sight of the subsidiary nature of the international machinery of collective enforcement established by the Convention. The national authorities remain free to choose the measures which they consider appropriate in those matters which are governed by the Convention. Review by the Court concerns only the conformity of those measures with the requirements of the Convention."

The scope of the margin of appreciation varies according to the circumstances, the subject-matter and the background; and one of the relevant factors is the existence or lack of common ground between the laws of the contracting states (*Rasmussen v. Denmark* (1984) Series A, No. 87; 7 E.H.R.R. 371, para. 40). In some contexts, the margin is narrow. Thus, in a number of cases to do with sexual equality, the Court has adopted the approach that "very weighty reasons" have to be put forward to justify a difference in treatment based exclusively on sex (*Abdulaziz*, above, paragraph 78; *Van Raalte v. Netherlands* R.J.D. 1997–I 173; (1997) 24 E.H.R.R. 503, para. 39). The same is true of differentiation based on nationality (*Gaygusuz v. Austria* R.J.D. 1996–IV 1129; (1996) 23 E.H.R.R. 364, para. 42), illegitimacy (*Inze v. Austria* (1987) Series A, No. 126; 10 E.H.R.R. 394, para. 41), and (it would seem) race (*Abdulaziz*, above, paragraphs 84–85) and religion (*Hoffmann v. Austria* (1993) Series A, No. 255–C; 17 E.H.R.R. 293, para. 36). It is not always clear why the Court arrives at a conclusion of this nature, though it tends to be on the basis of a perception of common approach among states. Contrastingly, in matters such as military discipline, the Court has afforded a wide margin of appreciation (*Engel v. Netherlands* (1976) Series A, No. 22; 1 E.H.R.R. 706 para. 72).

2–130 The Strasbourg authorities have identified a number of aims which they consider to be legitimate in this context. These include: the avoidance of trade union anarchy, and ensuring a coherent and balanced staff policy (*National Union of Belgian Police v. Belgium* (1975) Series A, No. 19; 1 E.H.R.R. 578, para. 48); the convenience for the employer of collective bargaining (*Swedish Engine Drivers' Union v. Sweden* (1976) Series A, No. 20; 1 E.H.R.R. 617, para. 46); leaseholder enfranchisement (*James v. U.K.* (1986) Series A, No. 98; 8

E.H.R.R. 123, para. 76); protection of the family (*S v. U.K.* (1986) 47 D.R. 274); preferential treatment in relation to housing for those with strong attachments to an island (*Gillow v. U.K.* (1986) Series A, No. 109; 11 E.H.R.R. 335, para. 65); protection of the health and rights of children (*Hoffmann v. Austria*, above paragraph 34); and the protection of morals and rights of others (*Sutherland v. U.K.* (1997) 24 E.H.R.R. C.D. 22, para. 54). The Strasbourg authorities will, however, consider whether the aim is served by the difference in treatment (*Abdulaziz, Cabales & Balkandali v. U.K.* (1985) Series A, No. 94; 7 E.H.R.R. 471, para. 81), and whether that difference is itself legitimate (*ibid.,* para. 78).

In the *Belgian Linguistic* case, above, the Court held that Article 14 does not prohibit different treatment where this is "founded on an objective assessment of essentially different factual circumstances and which, being based on the public interest, strike a fair balance between the protection of the interests of the community and respect for the rights and freedoms safeguarded by the Convention" (paragraph II 7). This striking of a "fair balance" entails identifying the interests which are actually in play, and as is apparent from the *Belgian Linguistic* case, above, the Court will consider for itself what (and whose) interests are behind measures which have been imposed (paragraph II 32). Thus, in *Spadea v. Italy* (1995) Series A, No. 315–B; 21 E.H.R.R. 482, para. 46, the Court held that the suspension by legislative decree of eviction orders obtained by the applicant landlords against their tenants was justified in circumstances of a serious housing shortage. If the disadvantage suffered by the applicant is excessive, however, in relation to the legitimate aim being pursued, the requirement of proportionality will have been violated (*National Union of Belgian Police v. Belgium* (1975) Series A, No. 19; 1 E.H.R.R. 578, para. 49). In considering this, the uniformity of application of the measure in question may be important (*ibid.*, where no violation was found; *cf.* the *Belgian Linguistic* case (1968) Series A, No. 6; 1 E.H.R.R. 252, para. II 32, where the measure was not uniformly applied, and there was a violation). On the other hand, the use of discretion to give flexibility to statutory powers may assist in the establishment of proportionality (*Gillow v. U.K.* (1987) Series A, No. 109; 11 E.H.R.R. 335, para. 65).

2–131 States have adduced a wide range of matters to provide support for defences of justification, but the Strasbourg authorities will appraise them critically. Thus in *Abdulaziz*, above, the government adduced statistics on immigration and employment, but the Court found these to be unconvincing (paragraph 79). In *Sutherland v. U.K.* (1997) 24 E.H.R.R. C.D. 22, the Commission was prepared to give only limited weight to the fact that the different age of consent for homosexuals had recently been fully debated by a democratically elected Parliament (paragraph 62). A state will need to ensure that the elements making up the justification are current. In *Schmidt v. Germany* (1994) Series A, No. 291–B; 18 E.H.R.R. 513 the compulsory obligation on men to perform fire service, which was the source of a consequential obligation to pay a levy in lieu of doing the service, had become a dead letter in practice, because there was no longer any shortage of volunteers requiring men to be called up. The state's justification for maintaining the levy on men accordingly fell away.

Q. Article 1, First Protocol — Protection of Property

2–132 This provision is considered in detail in Chapters 7, 8 and 14.

R. Article 2, First Protocol — Right to Education

2–133 This provision is considered in detail in Chapter 11, and this section is confined to some general observations.

The origins of Article 2 were surrounded by particularly lengthy and impassioned discussion, and the Court has had particular recourse to the *travaux préparatoires* in respect of this provision (see *Kjeldsen, Busk, Madsen and Pedersen v. Denmark* (1976) Series A, No. 23; 1 E.H.R.R. 711, para. 50 — a case on compulsory sex education). A substantial number of states, including the United Kingdom, have subsequently entered reservations to Article 2.

The Court gave considerable guidance as to the interpretation and scope of Article 2 in the *Belgian Linguistic* case (1968) Series A, No. 6; 1 E.H.R.R. 252. As the Court held, although the first sentence of the Article is couched in negative terms, it nonetheless does constitute a right. The scope of this right, however, is limited. The wording and the *travaux préparatoires* indicate that the Convention does not recognise such a right to education as would require states to establish at their own expense, or to subsidise, education of any particular type or at any particular level. Rather, the limited aim of this provision is to guarantee the right, in principle, of persons to avail themselves of the means of instruction existing at a given time, and this may entail some positive obligation. The right impliedly carries with it the right to be educated in the national language, or in one of the national languages, but not in a language of choice. In summary, the first sentence of Article 2 guarantees a right of access to such educational establishments as exist at any given time, and to have official recognition of the studies completed in order to ensure an "effective" education (*ibid.*, paras I B 3 and 4).

2–134 The second sentence of Article 2 does not guarantee a right to education, nor is its purpose to secure respect for a right to an education in a language of choice, even in combination with Article 14 (*ibid.*, paras I B 6 and 11). The second sentence is to be read with the first, and the former is an adjunct of the latter and thus of similar scope (*Kjeldsen* above, paragraphs 50 and 52). This means that the Article is binding upon all the functions of the state in the sphere of education and teaching, and not just some of them (*ibid.*, para. 50; and see *Campbell and Cosans v. U.K.* (1982) Series A, No. 48; 4 E.H.R.R. 293, para. 33 — the case which led to the abolition of corporal punishment in state schools). The second sentence aims at safeguarding the possibility of pluralism in education, and is to be read not only with the other Convention provisions as a whole, but more particularly with Articles 8, 9 and 10 (*Kjeldsen*, above paragraphs 50 and 52). Thus, the setting of the curriculum falls within the competence of the state subject only to the requirement that the state is forbidden to pursue an aim of indoctrination that might be considered not to respect parents' religious and philosophical convictions (*ibid.*, para. 53). Having regard to Article 17, philosophical convictions denote those which are worthy of respect in a democratic society (*Campbell and Cosans*, above, paragraph 36). The balance of interests to be achieved under the second sentence, and the relatively limited scope of Article 2, are demonstrated in *Valsamis v. Greece* R.J.D. 1996–VI 2312; (1996) 24 E.H.R.R. 294 (as to which see further Chapter 11).

In respect of higher education, the Commission has also held that, where limited facilities are provided by the state, Article 2 in principle permits the restriction of access through requirements for academic qualifications (*Patel v. U.K.* (1980) 23 D.R. 228; 4 E.H.R.R. 256). The limited scope of this provision has also resulted in the Commission rejecting applications complaining about the refusal to provide grants (*App. No. 9461/81 v. U.K.* (1983) 31 D.R. 210; 5 E.H.R.R. 480), to pay the cost of travel to the school of choice (*Cohen v. U.K.* (1996) 21 E.H.R.R. C.D. 104), and to secure admission to single sex, selective grammar schools (*App. Nos 10228–9/82 v. U.K.* (1984) 37 D.R. 96; 7 E.H.R.R. 135).

S. ARTICLE 3, FIRST PROTOCOL — RIGHT TO FREE ELECTIONS

2–135 The right to free elections has been the subject of complaint before the Court only rarely, and in *Mathieu-Mohin and Clerfayt v. Belgium* (1987) Series A, No. 113; 10 E.H.R.R. 1, the Court took the opportunity to express general principles in relation to Article 3 of the First Protocol. The right is considered to be of "prime importance" in the Convention system (*ibid.*, para. 47), its position re-inforced by the wording of the Article which expressly imposes positive obligations (*ibid.*, para. 50). The unusual wording of this provision in this respect, however, does not mean that the right of individual petition has been excluded (*ibid.*, para. 49). The rights protected are the right to vote and the right to stand for election (*ibid.*, para. 51). These rights are not absolute, and are subject to implied limitations (*ibid.*, para. 52). States may make these rights subject to conditions, and enjoy a wide margin of appreciation, subject to review by the Court. Thus the Court will ensure that states do not curtail the rights so as to "impair their very essence and deprive them of effectiveness"; that any conditions are imposed in pursuit of a legitimate aim; and that the means employed are proportionate (*ibid.*, para. 52).

Article 3 applies only to the election of the "legislature", or at least one of its chambers if it has two or more (*ibid.*, para. 53). The term has to be interpreted in the light of the constitutional structure of the state in question, and does not necessarily only refer to the national parliament (*ibid.*). It is unclear whether the European Parliament will be held to be a legislature, the Commission not having originally been convinced of this in *Lindsay v. U.K.* (1979) 15 D.R. 247 and *Tete v. France* (1987) 54 D.R. 52; 11 E.H.R.R. 91, but having more recently admitted the complaint in *Matthews v. United Kingdom* (1996) 22 E.H.R.R. C.D. 175 following the evolution of the Parliament's functions. In *Edwards v.*

U.K. (1985) 8 E.H.R.R. 96, the Commission concluded that, while it had functions of considerable scope, the GLC was not part of the legislature (see also *Booth-Clibborn v. U.K.* (1985) 43 D.R. 236). The Commission has also held that the right does not apply to referenda (*X v. U.K.* (1975) 3 D.R. 165).

Article 3 does not impose an obligation on states to introduce any specific electoral system, there being a wide margin of appreciation (*Mathieu-Mohin*, above, paragraph 54). This is perhaps inevitable in view of the significant differences between the systems of contracting states. In *Liberal Party v. U.K.* (1980) 21 D.R. 211; 4 E.H.R.R. 107, the Commission held that the "first past the post" system did not violate the right by reason of the results obtained under it.

2-136 Article 3 has a clear relationship with Article 10 (freedom of expression), and also with Article 11. All three Articles were relied on by local government officers in *Ahmed v. U.K., The Times,* October 2, 1998, where they complained about the interference to their political activities caused by the Local Government Officers (Political Restrictions) Regulations 1990 (S.I. 1990 No. 851). The Court held that the restrictions were justified under Articles 10 and 11. As for Article 3, given that this right is not absolute and that the state is entitled to impose conditions upon it, the Court held that the restrictions did not limit the very essence of the right and were thus permissible. In *Bowman v. U.K.* (1998) 26 E.H.R.R. 1, the Court observed that while Article 3 and Article 10 often reinforced one another, they could come into conflict with the result that it might be necessary to restrict the freedom of expression. The applicant distributed a large quantity of leaflets in the run-up to the 1992 general election, setting out the position of candidates on abortion, and was guilty of an offence under the Representation of the People Act 1983 for exceeding the £5 limit on election expenses as an "unauthorised" person. The Court held, in relation to Article 10, that the restrictions amounted to an absolute bar, and were not proportionate to the aim of ensuring equality between candidates.

Access to the broadcast media has been considered by the Commission on a number of occasions, both in connection with Article 3 and Article 10, but a substantial margin of appreciation exists in terms (for example) of setting thresholds for the selection of those entitled to issue broadcasts (*Tete v. France,* above; *Huggett v. U.K.* (1995) 20 E.H.R.R. C.D. 104).

2-137 Various forms of restriction on political activity have been considered by the Commission under Article 3. In *Matthews v. U.K.* (above), the Commission admitted a complaint that the restriction of the franchise to the European Parliament in the United Kingdom excluded Gibraltarians. In *App. No. 9588/81 v. U.K.* (1984) 6 E.H.R.R. 545, the Commission upheld the exclusion of a British Protected Person from the franchise. In *App. No. 9914/82 v. Netherlands* (1984) 33 D.R. 242; 6 E.H.R.R. 139, the Commission upheld restrictions on the voting rights of a serving prisoner. In *Glimmerveen and Hegenbeek v. Netherlands* (1979) 18 D.R. 187; 4 E.H.R.R. 260, the Commission held that the rights under Article 3 were restricted by reason of Article 17 in a case concerning racist candidates.

T. SIXTH PROTOCOL

2–138 The Sixth Protocol qualifies the right of states under Article 2 to maintain the death penalty (see further *Soering v. U.K.* (1989) Series A, No. 161; 11 E.H.R.R. 439 for the relationship between these provisions, and with Article 3). Article 1 of the Sixth Protocol requires the state both to abolish the death penalty, and to refrain from imposing or carrying out such a penalty. This prohibition cannot be the subject of reservation or derogation by the state (Articles 3 and 4 of the Sixth Protocol), but a state may make provision in its law for the death penalty in time of war, including the imminent threat of war (Article 2).

CHAPTER 3

Public Law

Jonathan Manning and Alyson Kilpatrick (Barristers, Arden Chambers)

A. INTRODUCTION

3–01   The effect of the Act in terms of administrative and civil remedies is not entirely easy to predict. While the Government could have incorporated the Convention into domestic law, it has chosen not to do so. Nor (though rules of court may change this) does the Act create any specific means for litigating an asserted breach of — or, more accurately, a failure to act in a way which is compatible with — an individual's Convention rights. Instead, it seems that the pre-existing mechanisms for enforcing rights and challenging decisions in a public law context, pre-eminently that of judicial review, will be of central importance in this emerging field of activity.

The provisions of the Act, and the new statutory obligation to comply with Convention rights, will however, undoubtedly modify the judicial review process. In the words of the Lord Chancellor ([1998] P.L. 229):

> "The courts' decisions will be based on a more overtly principled, and perhaps moral, basis. The court will look at the positive right. It will only accept an interference with that right where a justification, allowed under the Convention, is made out. The scrutiny will not be limited to seeing if the words of an exception can be satisfied. The court will need to be satisfied that the spirit of this exception is made out. It will need to be satisfied that the interference with the protected right is justified in the public interests in a free democratic society. Moreover, the courts will in this area have to apply the Convention principle of proportionality. This means the court will be looking substantively at that question. It will not be limited to a secondary review of the decision making process but at the primary question of the merits of the decision itself."

3–02   This reliance upon judicial review is not surprising, nor necessarily inconvenient. Convention law by its very nature is within the realm of public law; concerned primarily with the relationship between individual and State. The Convention regulates the actions of public authorities and impinges on their exercise of discretion. Judicial review, as it has developed in the English courts, similarly regulates public bodies in the exercise of their public functions, and is the central feature of domestic public law — the judicial control of public wrongs.

The aim of this chapter is, first, to explore the way in which public authorities will be obliged to act in order to comply with their duty under section 6 of the Act and, secondly, to describe how rights under the Convention may be protected by the courts, and the manner in which the legal concepts and principles of judicial review proceedings will fall to be operated in cases brought under the Act.

B. PUBLIC AUTHORITIES

1. Definition

3–03   By section 6(1), "It is unlawful for a public authority to act in a way which is incompatible with a Convention right." Section 6(3) defines the term "public authority" so as to include: (a) a court or tribunal, and (b) any person with functions of a public nature. Expressly excluded are both Houses of Parliament and any person exercising functions in connection with proceedings in Parliament, although not the House of Lords acting in its judicial capacity (section 6(3) and (4)). In relation to a particular act, a person is not a public authority by virtue only of (b) above if the nature of the act is private (section 6(5)).

2. Courts

3–04   Courts are comparatively simple to define, ranging from the Magistrates' Court to the House of Lords, but excluding any court when it is exercising a jurisdiction, recognised but not created by Parliament, in spiritual matters (section 6(5)). The obligation imposed by section 6 thus applies both to superior courts (the Judicial Committee of the House of Lords, the Court of Appeal, the High Court and the Crown Court) and to inferior courts (the county court, Coroner's Court and Magistrates' Court).

There is no express limitation upon those functions of a court on which the Act will bite. Nothing in section 6, for instance, indicates that only judicial acts of a court must be compatible with Convention rights. There is a number of functions carried out by a court which are administrative in nature, but which nevertheless would seem to be properly described as "acts", for instance the issue of a warrant for possession, the attachment of a penal notice to an injunction (see *e.g. R. v. Wandsworth County Court, ex p. Munn*) (1994) 26 H.L.R. 697 and decisions relating to the listing of cases.

3–05   Quite how far this may be taken is unclear. It is unlikely that most administrative decisions/acts undertaken by court staff will involve the operation of Convention rights at all. Where an act may involve such rights, but is ancillary to a judicial decision (as where a penal notice is attached or a warrant is issued), the performance of the act would probably not be incompatible with any Convention right, in that the court has already determined the rights of the "victim" of the act. Moreover, where primary legislation obliged the officer so to act (but not secondary legislation, such as rules of court) section 6(2) would operate to disapply the section 6(1) obligation.

However, listing decisions do call for the exercise of discretion by listing officers, and could potentially involve Convention rights, such as the right, in both civil and criminal cases, to a hearing within a reasonable time (under Article 6). Decisions whether to list cases in chambers or in open court (which, at least in the county court, tend currently to depend largely upon the practice of individual courts, or even the convenience of the judge) may also be affected (see also Article 6).

3–06 The important point, in this context, is not whether any individual act is or is not compatible with any particular Convention rights, but that it cannot be assumed that there is no requirement upon court staff to comply with the section 6(1) obligation, and that such staff must therefore be aware of this duty.

As to judicial acts, it is important to bear in mind that in addition to acting in a way which is compatible with Convention rights, any court determining a question which arises under the Act in connection with a Convention right must (by section 2(1)) take account of any relevant Strasbourg jurisprudence. The effect of this and, in particular its impact on the doctrine of *stare decisis*, is considered at paragraphs 1–64—1–65, above.

Another, though unrelated, question arising from the inclusion of all courts within the definition of public authority, is whether this will have any effect upon the current unavailability of judicial review in relation to the superior courts and certain functions of the Crown Court. The immediate answer would appear to be that it will not, since the prohibition upon judicial review in this respect is statutory (Supreme Court Act 1981, section 29(3)) and thus cannot be abrogated by rules of court or by judicial intervention. Even under the Act, the Courts have no power to depart from incompatible primary legislation.

3. Tribunals

3–07 A "tribunal", for the purposes of the Act, is defined in section 21(1) to mean any tribunal in which legal proceedings may be brought. The term "legal proceedings" is not defined. However, in this context, an internal appeals tribunal, such as that provided for under Part VII of the Housing Act (statutory review of homelessness decisions), or a Housing Benefit Review Board (created by Housing Benefit (General) Regulations 1987, S.I. 1987 No. 1971 as amended, reg. 81), or internal disciplinary tribunals, are probably excluded.

This is of more limited significance than may at first appear to be the case, as many of these tribunals will probably fall within the definition of "public authority" by virtue of section 6(3)(b), to the extent that they exercise public law functions. Purely domestic tribunals whose jurisdiction is founded on contract, such as disciplinary tribunals exercising functions under an individual's contract of employment, will be unlikely to be subject to the Act at all (see below, paragraph 3–12).

The comments, above, concerning courts are otherwise equally applicable to tribunals.

4. Bodies performing public law functions: generally

3–08 The definition contained in section 6(3)(b) is very broad, and deliberately so (*Hansard*, H.L. January 19, 1998, col. 1262) (although in relation to private law acts, bodies which might otherwise be public authorities are not necessarily counted as such: see section 6(5) and (6), and see paragraphs 3–03 and 3–15—3–21). The Home Secretary has referred (*Hansard*, H.L., June 17, 1998, col. 409–410) to the increasing number of private bodies now exercising public functions which previously were exercised solely by public authorities, and the extension of judicial review over such bodies.

A substantial body of modern case-law has invented and then developed the common law boundaries between public and private law.The courts have found it necessary to keep expanding these boundaries, particularly with the increase in contracting out, privatisation and self-regulation. In order to ascertain the types of person within the Act's definition, it is therefore useful to examine the position under the current law (see below).

5. The Crown

3–09 Some decision-makers plainly and uncontroversially fall within the definition of public authority. Traditionally, although the Crown itself was not amenable to the prerogative orders, its servants were. However, the courts in *R. v. Secretary of State for Transport, ex p. Factortame (No. 2)* [1991] 1 A.C. 603 (ECJ and House of Lords) spelt out that even the operation of a statute may be suspended pending the resolution of a European challenge. This Act binds the Crown (section 22(5)).

A declaration has always been available against the Crown. In terms of interim relief, a stay may be granted pending the outcome of the application for review and also an injunction: *Re M* [1994] A.C. 377. The Court of Appeal has also held that a stay may be ordered not only of judicial proceedings, but also of decisions of the Secretary of State and the process by which such decisions had been reached (*R. v. Secretary of State for Education, ex p. Avon C.C.* [1991] 1 Q.B. 558, CA).

3–10 Historically, the Courts would not review the exercise of prerogative powers. However, in *Council of Civil Service Unions v. Minister of State for the Civil Service* [1985] A.C. 374, the House of Lords held that the exercise of such powers was reviewable, so long as the subject-matter of the power was justiciable; *e.g.* the courts would not review the exercise of treaty making powers, honours, mercy, etc. It seems that the number of such powers which the courts will regard as justiciable at common law may be increasing. For instance, in *R. v. Secretary of State for the Home Department, ex p. Bentley* [1994] Q.B. 349, DC, where the Secretary of State had refused to grant a pardon, the court held that the prerogative power of mercy was amenable to review in an appropriate case, and requested the Minister to reconsider the matter.

6. Delegated powers

3–11 A person or body exercising powers delegated by statutory or prerogative power may also be susceptible to review. Moreover, it seems that an administrative recommendation to a minister may be susceptible to review (*R. v. Secretary of State for Transport, ex p. APH Road Safety Limited* [1993] C.O.D. 240, although in *R. v. Secretary of State for the Home Department, ex p.*

Westminster Press Limited [1992] C.O.D. 303 it was held that a government circular to police chiefs concerning information to be given to the media was not reviewable.) In *London Borough of Tower Hamlets v. Secretary of State for the Environment* (1994) 25 H.L.R. 534, a declaration was granted to the effect that two paragraphs of the Secretary of State's Homelessness Code of Guidance were wrong in law.

7. Other bodies

3–12 In relation to other bodies, the position is less clear. The test for reviewability now applied by the courts is based on the nature of the functions performed or powers exercised by the body (see, *e.g. Council of Civil Service Unions v. Minister for the Civil Service*, above), *i.e.* whether those functions are essentially public law functions, or exist instead in private law. A non-statutory body whose authority derives solely from contract, such as an employer's disciplinary tribunal, falls outside the scope of review (see *e.g. R. v. British Broadcasting Corporation, ex p. Lavelle* [1983] 1 W.L.R. 23; *R. v. East Berkshire Health Authority, ex p. Walsh* [1985] Q.B. 152; *cf. R. v. Secretary of State for the Home Department, ex p. Benwell* [1985] Q.B. 554). Conversely, non-statutory bodies set up to undertake public functions have been held to fall within the scope of review.

3–13 In *R. v. Panel on Take-Overs and Mergers, ex p. Datafin* [1987] Q.B. 815, CA, the Court of Appeal held that, in seeking to ascertain the nature of a body's functions, the source of power and the functions performed were both relevant factors to be given different weight in different circumstances.

> "In all the reports it is possible to find enumerations of factors giving rise to the [supervisory] jurisdiction, but it is a fatal error to regard the presence of all those factors as essential or as being exclusive of other factors. Possibly the only essential elements are what can be described as a public element, which can take many different forms, and the exclusion from the jurisdiction of bodies whose sole source of power is a consensual submission to its jurisdiction" (*per* Sir John Donaldson MR at 838E.)

It seems, then, in broad terms, that whether a body has a public law element to its functions, so as to render it susceptible to judicial review (and now also to section 6), will depend upon consideration of the source and nature of its powers. Without falling into the fatal error referred to in *Datafin* above, a body may have such an element where (for example):

- it performs or operates in the public domain as an integral part of a regulatory system which performs public law duties;

- is non-statutory by government decision but is established "under the authority of government" (*ibid. per* Lloyd L.J. at 849D);

- is supported by a periphery of statutory powers and penalties;

- is embraced by government and performs functions that government would otherwise perform;

- and/or is under a duty in exercising what amount to public powers to act judicially.

In addition, it seems clear that the source of its power must not derive exclusively from contract, or otherwise from the consent of those over whom it exercises those powers (*ibid.*).

C. ACTS OF PUBLIC AUTHORITIES

1. Definition

3–14 For the purposes of section 6, an "act" includes a failure to act (section 6(6)). Some conduct is excluded from the scope of section 6 (see paragraphs 1–50—1–51, above), in order to preserve the supremacy of Parliament. Acts will include executive and operational matters, decision-making which has resulted in a course of conduct being adopted, and decision-making which is not succeeded by any activity. Accordingly, a written policy adopted by a public authority is, in itself, reviewable, under section 6.

2. Public and private acts: generally

3–15 If the definition of a "public authority" contained in section 6(3)(b) is dependant on the source of its powers and the nature of its functions, this still does not necessarily entail that every decision taken, or act undertaken, by such an authority is subject to section 6(1). In the law of non-Convention judicial review, a private law act by a public body is not justiciable in the Crown Office unless there is an underlying public law element to the dispute. This is exemplified by the cases of *ex. p. Walsh* and *ex. p. Benwell* (above, paragraph 3–12). In *Walsh*, although, the applicant was employed by a Health Authority (a body plainly susceptible to judicial review), the dispute arose from her contract of employment, which was not a public law matter.

The Act maintains a distinction between public and private law activity. By section 6(5), a person is not a public authority in relation to a particular act by virtue only of section 6(3)(b), if the nature of the act is private. It is therefore necessary to understand the distinction between a public law and private law act, as explained by the courts.

3–16 It can be seen from the quantity of litigation that this question has generated, that the distinctions are by no means always hard and fast or easy to draw. Moreover, difficult questions will arise in relation to disputes which involve a mixture of private and public law elements, such as the case where a local authority seeks to evict a tenant for non-payment of rent, following a rent increase which the tenant argues was *ultra vires* (*Wandsworth LBC v. Winder* [1985] A.C. 465, HL). The question in that case was whether the tenant could raise the issue that the rent increase was unlawful in his counterclaim, as this was a public law issue. The court held that he could.

This, and other similar issues raised in the reported cases can (almost) be reduced to a question of venue: Divisional Court or county court? The question under the Act is a matter of law, and more difficult to circumvent. If in future a tenant were to argue, on facts identical to *Winder*, that the act of seeking possession against him was in breach of section 6 because it was founded upon an illegal rent increase and was incompatible with his rights under Article 8 (right to respect for private and family life), the question would become not whether a public law matter could be raised in private law proceedings, but whether the local authority was a public authority at all for the purposes of the eviction, even though it clearly had been for the purposes of increasing the rent.

Such guidance as current case law may be able to provide arises mainly from the extensive litigation on this subject in the field of housing law (see below), but begins with the landmark decision in *O'Reilly v. Mackman* [1983] 2 A.C. 237.

3. *O'Reilly v. Mackman*

3–17 Before *O'Reilly v. Mackman*, the English courts had not developed formal distinctions of this kind. In *O'Reilly* the House of Lords held that it was contrary to public policy and an abuse of the process of the Court to permit a dissatisfied applicant to proceed by way of an ordinary action, when the substance of the complaint was founded in public law, as this would enable the applicant to evade the provisions of RSC, Ord. 53. These are designed to afford safeguards for public authorities against groundless and unmeritorious applications, in the interests of good administration. However, the House of Lords did not proceed to analyse the distinction it had thereby created (at 280G–281D; 284B; see also *Cocks v. Thanet District Council* [1983] 2 A.C. 286, *per* Lord Bridge of Harwich at 294E-H).

It was left to subsequent cases to begin to consider the problem of disputes involving both public and private law elements. In *Davy v. Spelthorne BC* [1984] A.C. 262, it was said that if the public law element of the claim was merely peripheral, then it may not be sufficient to justify proceeding by way of judicial review.

4. *Cocks v. Thanet DC*

3–18 The distinction between public and private law rights was considered again by the House of Lords, in a housing law context, in *Cocks v. Thanet DC* (above), decided on the same day as *O'Reilly*. Lord Bridge held that the general rule enunciated in *O'Reilly* applied where it was necessary, as a condition precedent to the enforcement of a statutory private law right, to impugn an authority's public law decision. In *Cocks*, a homeless plaintiff, who was in local authority temporary accommodation, sought a declaration to the effect that the authority was in breach of its duty under the Housing (Homeless Persons) Act 1977 to provide permanent accommodation, together with a mandatory injunction and damages.

Lord Bridge, giving the only speech, stated there to be a dichotomy between a housing authority's public law "decision-making" functions and private law "executive" functions (at 292D–293B): the decision whether an applicant fulfilled the statutory conditions to entitle him to housing was a matter of public law, whereas the actual obligation to house a qualifying applicant was a matter of private law, enforceable by an action for injunction and damages. The challenged decision fell within the decision-making category, and a declaration was granted that the plaintiff was not entitled to proceed otherwise than by way of judicial review.

5. Hybrid cases

3–19   If the public and private law elements are inextricably linked, then it appears that matters can proceed either way. In *An Bord Bainne Co-operative Ltd (Irish Dairy Board) v. Milk Marketing Board* [1984] 2 C.M.L.R. 584; (1984) Sol. Jo. 417, Sir John Donaldson, M.R. allowed a private action to continue on the basis that although the matter could be said to be one of public law, private rights were involved and it could cause injustice to require the use of the public law procedure. Moreover, more recently, the Courts have appeared to move away from the position that *O'Reilly* had laid down a general rule (applicable to all cases involving challenge to a public law act or decision) that judicial review must be used, subject to the exceptions Lord Diplock set out, where private law rights were also at stake.

3–20   In *Roy v. Kensington and Chelsea Family Practitioner Committee* [1992] 1 A.C. 625, Lord Lowry declined to decide between that approach and the broader approach that *O'Reilly* only applied to cases where no private law right at all was at stake. He said, however, (at 653) that he much preferred the broader approach,

> "which is both traditionally orthodox and consistent with the *Pyx Granite* principle [1960] A.C. 260, 286, as applied in *Davy v. Spelthorne Borough Council* [1984] A.C. 262, 274 and in *Wandsworth London Borough Council v. Winder* [1985] A.C. 461, 510. It would also, if adopted, have the practical merit of getting rid of a procedural minefield."

However, even adopting the narrow approach for the purposes of the appeal, he found that there were many indications in favour of a liberal attitude towards the exceptions to the rule contemplated but not spelt out by Lord Diplock, and concluded (at 651):

> "unless the procedure adopted by the moving party is ill suited to dispose of the question at issue, there is much to be said in favour of the proposition that a court having jurisdiction ought to let a case be heard rather than entertain a debate concerning the form of the proceedings."

6. *Ali v. Tower Hamlets LBC*

3–21   In *Ali v. Tower Hamlets LBC*, above, the Court of Appeal (after *Roy*) held that a homeless person was not entitled to challenge the suitability of the Council's offer of permanent accommodation under the Housing Act 1985, s.65(2) by way of a civil action in the county court, but only by judicial review.

The approach of the Court in *Ali* is instructive of the factors which the Court may consider in concluding whether a duty owed is in the sphere of public or private law, and therefore whether an act or decision may be challenged by ordinary action. Nolan L.J. said (at 413G–414B):

> "The closing words of [section 69(1)] seem to me to call unmistakably for the exercise by the local authority of a subjective judgment as to what constitutes suitable accommodation. This judgment has to be made before the executive act of securing the suitable accommodation for the applicant can be performed. I take this view of the matter the more readily because of the subject-matter of the judgment which is required. In many, if not most cases, the suitability of particular accommodation for a particular applicant is a matter upon which differing views may honestly and reasonably be held. The particular accommodation offered will inevitably depend upon what is available to the local authority from its own resources, or from the accessible resources of others. The amount of available accommodation will constantly vary. It is of the greatest importance that the suitable accommodation required by the homeless applicant should be provided with the least possible delay. All of these factors seem to me to point to the desirability of the judgment being exercised by the local authority with its unique knowledge of the facts, rather than by the courts."

7. Defending proceedings against a public body

3–22   Where a person is defending a private action against a public body, it is permissible to litigate a public law defence and/or counterclaim in those proceedings without seeking an adjournment to apply for judicial review, provided such public law defence/counterclaim is linked to a private law defence: *Wandsworth LBC v. Winder* [1985] A.C. 461. If a defendant, however, seeks to raise by way of a defence only matters which sound in public law alone (*e.g.* a challenge to the decision to institute the proceedings based upon an alleged breach of a public law duty) the proper procedure is to apply for an adjournment of the private action to enable an application for judicial review to be made or (if made already) to be resolved: *Avon CC v. Buscott and Others* [1988] 1 All E.R. 841. An adjournment will generally not be granted unless there is a real possibility that leave will be granted. The leave application must, in any event, be made promptly — *i.e.* in relation to the public law decision challenged, not in relation to the conduct of the private law proceedings.

This issue has received a good deal of judicial consideration in the context of challenging the suitability of accommodation offered to the homeless under section 65(2) Housing Act 1985, in *Ali* (above), *Tower Hamlets LBC v. Abdi* (1992) 91 L.G.R. 300, and *Hackney LBC v. Lambourne* (1993) 25 H.L.R. 172. Each of these cases has held that an offer of accommodation to the homeless is made solely pursuant to public law duties, and an applicant has no private law right to suitable accommodation, save a right to the particular accommodation which is offered. Accordingly, the suitability of accommodation is a matter for the local authority and not for the courts; any challenge to suitability may only be brought by way of judicial review.

3–23   In *Abdi* and *Lambourne*, the court held, following *Ali*, that a challenge to the suitability of accommodation could not be raised as a defence in proceedings brought by the local authority for possession of temporary accommodation following a refusal by the defendant of the permanent accommodation the suitability of which was under challenge. Indeed, in *Lambourne*, the Court of Appeal rejected the submission that a challenge, on public law grounds, to the decision to serve a notice to quit could be raised by way of defence. Although, if successful in quashing the notice to quit, the defendant would have a private law right to remain in the temporary accommodation, to allow the validity of the notice to quit to be questioned in this way would be to circumvent the reasoning and policy of the decisions in *Ali* and *Abdi*. The defence was therefore struck out.

8. Conclusion

3–24   It may be that the answer to the problem posed in paragraph 3–16 above is answered by *Lambourne*. Even if the act of taking possession proceedings is a private law act, the decision to institute those proceedings is itself likely to be a public law act, placing a body within the ambit of section 6.

This analysis is strengthened, it is suggested, by the recent House of Lords decision in the case of *O'Rourke v. Camden LBC* [1998] A.C. 188 for the following reason. In that case, Lord Hoffman, giving the only speech, disapproved the dichotomy posed by Lord Bridge in *Cocks*: namely, that all decision-making functions were public law functions, but that once the decision had been made the executive act of carrying it out was a private law function. Lord Hoffmann described as "anomalous" the concept of a private law duty arising only when it had been acknowledged to exist (at 196G). He concluded that the existence of a private law duty depended upon the normal principles to be applied in deciding whether a statutory duty was owed (see *X (minors) v. Bedfordshire CC* [1995] 2 A.C. 633), and that there was no need to interpose a private law statutory duty actionable in tort "merely to bridge the gap between the acknowledgement of the duty and its implementation" (at 192H–194E; 196H).

3–25   Accordingly, the position would appear to be that, in the case of bodies such as local authorities, which in judicial review terms are clearly public authorities, there will usually be a public law decision prior to any private law act which can itself be attacked under section 6(1).

The position is not so clear in the case of essentially private law bodies some of whose functions are in the sphere of public law. It is possible to devise complex scenarios in relation to such bodies in order to demonstrate the difficulty of the issue. However, in reality, it is impossible to know at this stage in the development of human rights law in the United Kingdom, whether or not such difficulties will, in fact, materialise, and how the courts will resolve such problems as do arise. It may well be that the situation will not become entirely clear for some time to come.

The words "a person is not a public authority by virtue only of subsection (3)(b)" in section 6(5) seem to invite the courts not only to restrict the operation of section 6 in relation to some bodies, but also to maintain a broader application of the section (even in respect of what might be described as private acts) where factors militate in favour of liability. This approach is reinforced by the inclusive definition of public authority in section 6(3).

D. PROTECTION OF RIGHTS

1. The status of Convention rights in national law

3–26 As discussed above, public authorities are required to act in conformity with the Convention when performing their public law functions. If they do not do so, they act unlawfully (section 6(1)). A person who claims that a public authority has acted or proposes to act unlawfully in this way may either bring proceedings or rely on the relevant Convention right in any legal proceedings, so long as he is the victim of the allegedly unlawful act (section 7).

The Act neither incorporates the Convention into domestic law, nor expressly confers Convention rights in domestic law (but instead — putting aside questions of statutory interpretation — merely renders it unlawful for some bodies in some circumstances to act in such a way as is incompatible with those rights). The Act also provides no new regime for the resolution of issues arising from it, but merely imposes this new course of litigation upon the existing court system. In these circumstances, the question clearly arises: what is the status of a Convention right in domestic law? What sort of right is it? In the language of judicial review, is it a public law right or a private law right? Does it, in fact, have any substantive legal status at all, over and above the duty of public authorities to act in accordance with it?

3–27 It seems that, given the decision not to legislate for the incorporation of Convention rights into domestic law, the only right an individual actually enjoys in relation to public authorities by virtue of the Act is the right not to have decisions or actions taken, in relation to which he is a victim, in a way which is not compatible with Convention rights. Such rights appear to exist only in public law, and can give rise to no private law cause of action, save to the extent permitted by section 7 and 8.

Such questions may appear to be of purely academic interest, but, as is discussed below, the answers to them are likely to determine the type of legal proceedings which may be brought to challenge the legality of a public authority's decisions, and the type of remedy to which an individual who is the victim of such illegality may be entitled (though to some extent this is regulated by section 8, and will be further regulated by rules of court which will determine which is the "appropriate court or tribunal" before which proceedings are to be brought).

3–28 If the rights under discussion are correctly categorised as existing only in public law, then it would seem to follow that the only available remedy would be that of judicial review. It may be arguable, however, that a neat equation between public law rights, procedures and remedies is not possible, not least because in creating a right to damages the Act may have created a private law cause of action (see section 31 of the Supreme Court Act 1981 and RSC, Ord,

53, r.7). Accordingly, it may be that the unlawfulness resulting under section
6(1) has to be regarded as having a hybrid nature, carrying potential effects in
both private and public law and being capable (subject to rules of court) of being
litigated in any way appropriate to the remedy being sought.

There are, however, difficulties with this approach, permitting damages claims
to be brought by way of private law action. The primary remedies for controlling
the unlawful acts of public authorities are those available only by way of public
law challenge: *certiorari, mandamus*, prohibition, etc., which the private law
courts have no jurisdiction to grant. Moreover, the Act provides that no award
of damages is to be made unless it is necessary to afford just satisfaction to the
person in whose favour it is made taking account, specifically, any other relief or
remedy granted or order made by that or another court. If a private action for
damages could be commenced without any recourse to the judicial review court,
there could have been no other relief or remedy granted (save, in some
circumstances possibly a declaration or injunction) and so an award of damages
may become the only remedy available, rendering the just satisfaction test more
easily satisfied. This does not appear to have been the intention of section 8.

Accordingly, it may be that the better construction of the Act is that it simply
provides a right to damages for acting incompatibly with a Convention right,
(*i.e.* exceptionally, a statutory right to damages, where appropriate, for breach of
a public law right). If so, a judicial review application will still be necessary to
determine the lawfulness of the act under challenge and afford any appropriate
primary relief, prior to any consideration of damages claimed in the judicial
review proceedings itself, or to any subsequent civil claim for damages.

Accordingly, it is the effect of the Act upon this remedy that is considered in
the following sections of this Chapter.

2. Incompatible action under the Act

3–29   The Act creates no concept of a breach of a Convention right. To have
done so would have been to employ the language of private law, both in terms of
the existence of the right, and the legal consequences of not giving effect to that
right. The Act has not incorporated Convention rights into domestic law, and so,
in this sense such rights have in themselves no more existence in law than they
did prior to the Act. Instead, the Act addresses the issue from the other
direction. A public authority acts unlawfully if it acts incompatibly with any
Convention right. No criminal offence is committed (section 7(8)), but
proceedings may be brought by, or the relevant Convention right relied on in
any proceedings brought against, the individual concerned.

The meaning, as a matter of language and statutory construction, of
"incompatible" is discussed elsewhere (see paragraphs 1–35 and 1–52).
However, it is important to seek to define the way in which incompatibility with
a Convention right should be approached.

Incompatibility is not a question which is likely (at least in many situations) to
admit of a straightforward answer, and so it is unlikely that the officers of public
authorities will themselves, prior to undertaking any act, be able to consider the
Convention in detail, together with the reported decisions of the Strasbourg
authorities, and modify their proposed action accordingly. For the foreseeable
future, at any rate, these issues will require detailed consideration by the courts.

3. Domestic case law in the 1970s

3–30   In a series of cases in the 1970s, the Court of Appeal came close to imposing similar obligations upon public bodies to those now provided in the Act, even though (subsequently) this approach was renounced. (For a very full discussion of the history of the courts' attitude to the Convention, see Murray Hunt, *Using Human Rights Law in English Courts* (1997) Hart Publishing.) In *R. v. Secretary of State for the Home Department, ex p. Phansopkar* [1976] Q.B. 606, Lord Scarman held that it was the duty of public authorities administering the law, as well as the courts, to have regard to the Convention. He said (at 626F–G):

> "It may, of course, happen under our law that the basic rights to justice undeferred and to respect for family and private life have to yield to the express requirements of a statute. But in my judgment it is the duty of the courts, so long as they do not defy or disregard clear unequivocal provision, to construe statutes in a manner which promotes, not endangers, those rights. Problems of ambiguity or omission, if they arise under the language of an Act, should be resolved so as to give effect to, or at the very least so as not to derogate from the rights recognised by Magna Carta and the European Convention."

Similarly, in *R. v. Secretary of State for the Home Department, ex p. Bhajan Singh* [1976] Q.B. 198, Lord Denning stated (at 207F) that both immigration officers and the Secretary of State should take account of the principles set out in the Convention when carrying out their duties, since they were under a public law duty to act fairly and the Convention was a statement of the principles of fair dealing.

4. The Strasbourg approach

3–31   The Act plainly takes matters further than a mere requirement to have regard to Convention rights as an aspect of natural justice. It is now unlawful not merely to fail to have regard to the Convention, but to act incompatibly with the rights it protects. The approach of the Strasbourg authorities must be considered.

The Court distinguishes between two distinct types of complaint. The first relates to "interference" with a right (*i.e.* a positive, detrimental act of interference); the second relates to a claim that positive action is required in order to guarantee the right (see generally paragraphs 2–35—2–37). In either case, the first step must be to establish whether, on the true construction of the Convention, the right relied on is even capable of protecting the applicant from the conduct complained of. The difficulty here is that the rights protected by the Convention are drafted in general terms. Accordingly, the Court has utilised a number of different methods of construction (see generally paragraph 2–28 and following).

Most important amongst these methods, from the perspective of the approach which the national courts may now be obliged to adopt in order to apply the Act in a meaningful way, is the purposive approach, *i.e.* considering the aim of the Convention — the protection of individual rights:

> "In interpreting the Convention, regard must be had to its special character as a treaty for the collective enforcement of human rights and fundamental freedoms . . . Thus the object and purpose of the Convention as an instrument for the protection of individual human beings require that its provisions be interpreted and applied so as to make its safeguards practical and effective . . . In addition, any interpretation of the rights and freedoms guaranteed has to be consistent with 'the general spirit of the Convention, an instrument designed to maintain and promote the ideals and values of a democratic society' " (*Kjeldsen, Busk Madsen and Petersen v. Denmark* (1976) Series A, No. 23; 1 E.H.R.R. 711, paragraph 53).

3–32   The Court has emphasised in a number of decisions (*e.g. Marckx v. Belgium* (1979) Series A, No. 31; 2 E.H.R.R. 330; *Johnston v. Ireland* (1986) Series A, No. 112; 9 E.H.R.R. 203) that the Convention is a living document, and that interpretation of its meaning must be considered in the light of prevailing conditions at the time of the alleged violation, rather that at the date of drafting of the Convention itself. The court cannot, however by means of such an evolutive approach, derive from the Convention and the protocols a right which was not present at the outset. Accordingly, in *Johnston*, the applicant could not make out a right to a divorce under Article 12, as that article made no reference to divorce, and it appeared from the *travaux préparatoires* that this omission was deliberate (*Johnston*, paragraph 53).

If the Convention right relied on, on its true construction, is not capable of protecting the applicant from the conduct complained of, that is plainly an end of the matter. If it is so capable, the Court then looks to see whether that conduct did, in fact, violate the right relied on.

3–33   Some of the approaches of the Court deserve particular mention in the context of the responsibilities of public authorities. The Court accords the national authorities a "margin of appreciation" in the manner in which it guarantees the Convention rights of its citizens. The less consistent the practice of the signatory states, the wider this margin of appreciation is likely to be. Thus, in *Johnston v. Ireland* (above) the Court held, in respect of the applicant's assertion of a right (under Article 8) to be able to obtain a divorce, that:

> "the notion of 'respect' is not clear-cut: having regard to the diversity of the practices followed and the situations obtaining in the Contracting States, the notion's requirements will vary considerably from case to case. Accordingly, this is an area in which the contracting parties enjoy a wide margin of appreciation in determining the steps to be taken to ensure compliance with the Convention with due regard to the needs and resources of the community and of individuals . . ." (at paragraph 55(c)).

The language of the Court's reference to the "needs and resources of the community and of individuals' is in terms of a balance (see generally paragraph

2–38 above). In a case where an obligation to take positive action was asserted, the Court explicitly emphasised the balancing exercise to be undertaken:

"regard must be had to the fair balance that has to be struck between the general interest of the community and the interests of the individual, the search for which balance is inherent in the whole of the Convention (see, *mutatis mutandis*, amongst others, *James v. U.K.* (1986) Series A, No. 98; 8 E.H.R.R. 123, paragraph 50, and *Sporrong and Lönnroth v. Sweden* (1982) Series A, No. 52; 5 E.H.R.R. 35, paragraph 69)." (*Rees v. U.K.* (1986) Series A, No. 106; 9 E.H.R.R. 56, paragraph 37).

3–34   The balancing exercise may sometimes be relevant even in cases where the Convention does not itself allow for limitations or restrictions on rights. In *Soering v. U.K.* (1989) Series A, No. 161; 11 E.H.R.R. 439, it was alleged that the United Kingdom was in breach of Article 3 (which — as the Court emphasised — made provision for no exceptions or derogations), by deciding to extradite the applicant to the United States where he was to be tried for capital murder in Virginia. The applicant thus ran the risk of exposure to the "death row phenomenon", which was alleged to be inhuman or degrading treatment or punishment. It was held (at paragraph 89) that, in interpreting and applying the notions of inhuman or degrading treatment or punishment, one of the factors to be taken into account — indeed inherent in the whole of the Convention — was a.

"search for a fair balance between the demands of the general interest of the community and the requirements of the protection of the individual's fundamental rights. As movement about the world becomes easier and crime takes on a larger international dimension, it is increasingly in the interest of all nations that suspected offenders who flee abroad should be brought to justice. Conversely, the establishment of safe havens for fugitives would not only result in danger for the State obliged to harbour the protected person but also tend to undermine the foundations of extradition."

3–35   Where a balancing exercise is to be carried out, the proportionality of the alleged interference will be likely to be considered (see generally paras 2–44 and following). This may take a number of forms, in relation to the interference itself, or in relation to any number of subsidiary questions which the Court is required to answer in order to arrive at a conclusion. For example, in *Soering*, the Court considered this doctrine to be relevant in the following respects. First, as to whether exposure to the death row phenomenon would make extradition a breach of Article 3, the manner of the imposition or execution of the death sentence was held to be relevant, including any disproportionality between the sentence and the gravity of the offence (paragraph 104). Furthermore, in considering the argument that the United Kingdom could have extradited the Applicant to the Federal Republic of Germany, which had abolished the death penalty, it was held that this possibility was a relevant consideration to the overall assessment under Article 3, in that it "goes to the search for the requisite fair balance of interests and to the proportionality of the contested extradition decision in the particular case" (paragraph 110).

3-36 Similarly, where a lawyer challenged the Belgian legal professional requirement to undertake pro bono work for clients who could not afford to pay, on the basis that this amounted to forced or compulsory labour in contravention of Article 4, part of the Court's judgment was based on its finding that the burden imposed by this requirement was not disproportionate. The amount of time the applicant was required to spend on pro bono work allowed sufficient time for the performance of his paid work (*Van der Mussele v. Belgium* (1983) Series A, No. 70; 6 E.H.R.R. 163, paragraph 39).

In *Gaskin v. U.K.* (1989) Series A, No. 160; 12 E.H.R.R. 36, where it was alleged that the United Kingdom was under a positive obligation under Article 8, to allow the applicant access to personal records concerning his having been taken into care, the Court held that the U.K. system of allowing access to such records with the consent of the contributor was in principle "compatible with the obligation under Article 8, taking into account the State's margin of appreciation." However, such a system had also to secure the right of access where a contributor was not available to consent or withheld that consent improperly. "Such a system is only in conformity with the principle of proportionality if it provides that an independent authority finally decides whether access has to be granted in cases where a contributor fails to answer or withholds consent." Accordingly, a violation of the Convention was established.

5. The courts' response to the Act?

3-37 It remains to be seen whether the English courts will be prepared to adopt, and how they may adapt, the expansive approach of the Strasbourg authorities. While a purposive approach to construction is more common, at least in cases of ambiguity, and recourse to Hansard is also now permissible, within strict limits (see *Pepper v. Hart* [1993] A.C. 593), there nevertheless remains a considerable jurisprudential gap between the English courts and the Strasbourg authorities. It must also be borne in mind that our courts are not familiar with statutory provisions worded as generally as the Convention. It will, therefore, probably be some time before any consistent approach to the Convention emerges. Moreover, while instructive, the Strasbourg jurisprudence is not binding on national courts and tribunals (see section 2(1)), and the concepts and approaches are not necessarily applicable, or applicable in the same way, under the Act. Even so, balancing exercises, margins of appreciation and proportionality are not entirely alien concepts to the courts, bearing in mind the similarities they enjoy with the doctrine of *Wednesbury* unreasonableness.

E. JUDICIAL REVIEW

1. Sufficient interest and the "victim" test

3-38 By virtue of the Supreme Court Act 1981 (SCA 1981), s.31(3) and RSC, Ord 53, r.3(7), an applicant seeking judicial review of a public body must be someone with "sufficient interest" in the matter to which the application relates. What constitutes a sufficient interest is a matter of mixed fact and law. The Act imposes the additional requirement that an applicant relying on section 6 must be a "victim" (section 7(1) and (3)). In reality, however, with one significant exception (below), this adds nothing to the concept of sufficient interest, as it is plain that — on any test — a person who is (or would be) a victim of the act, would also have sufficient interest in the subject-matter of the application to bring judicial review proceedings in any event.

The one exception is the situation in relation to pressure groups and other "public interest" applicants. Here, the courts now adopt a more liberal approach to the question of standing. In suitable cases, pressure groups will have the requisite interest to bring proceedings: *R. v. Secretary of State for Social Services, ex p. CPAG, The Times*, August 16, 1984. More recently, in *R. v. H.M. Inspectorate of Pollution and the Ministry of Agriculture Fisheries and Food, ex p. Greenpeace Ltd* [1994] C.O.D. 116, it was held that the question of standing was primarily one of discretion and that it was appropriate to take into account the nature of the applicant, the extent of their interest in the issues raised in the application, the remedy they sought to achieve and the nature of the relief they sought, the level of support and status of the body, and the fact that — if Greenpeace were denied standing — those it represented would probably not have an effective way of bringing the issues before the court.

3–39 Although the jurisprudence of the Strasbourg authorities has been relatively elastic as to who may properly be considered a "victim" (see paragraph 2–15 and following), it is clear that there must be some connection between the applicant and the injury or violation complained of. In other words, the applicant must show he or she has been, or that there is a reasonable likelihood that he or she will be, directly affected in some way. The Convention does not provide for applications in the form of an *actio popularis*. Thus, although in other respects the Strasbourg jurisprudence is merely something to which due regard must be paid, in relation to the definition of "victim" Convention law appears to be decisive (section 7(7)). Absent a considerable amount of judicial creativity, pressure groups will have no standing to bring matters before the Courts under the Act, even though this is divergent from the courts' current thinking in non-Convention cases.

In so far as it may be possible to rely on the Convention beyond the limits of section 6 (see paragraphs 3–40—3–45 below), the common law principles of standing ought to apply.

2. Grounds for review: introduction

3–40 The classic statement of the grounds for judicial review is that of Lord Greene, M.R. in *Associated Provincial Picture Houses Ltd v. Wednesbury Corporation* [1948] 1 K.B. 223 at 233–234:

> "The court is entitled to investigate the action of the local authority with a view to seeing whether they have taken into account matters which they ought not to take into account, or, conversely, have refused to take into account or neglected to take into account matters which they ought to take into account. Once that question is answered in favour of the local authority, it may still be possible to say that although the local authority have kept within the four corners of the matters which they ought to

consider, they have nevertheless come to a conclusion so unreasonable that no reasonable authority could ever have come to it."

In *Council of Civil Service Unions v. Minister of State for the Civil Service* [1985] A.C. 374, Lord Diplock reformulated the grounds for seeking review under three heads: illegality, irrationality and procedural impropriety.

The Lord Chancellor's words, cited at the beginning of this chapter (at paragraph 3–01), presume that the effect of the Act will be to oblige the courts to adopt a more substantive approach to the issues before it, rather than simply approaching matters in terms of the propriety and legality of the decision-making process, subject only to the question of whether a decision was so unreasonable that no reasonable decision-maker could have reached it. Whether or not this is actually the case, or whether the Act simply creates an additional ground for review, is open to debate. Nevertheless, it seems more likely than not that the court will have to modify its approach, both in cases brought under the Act and in general. Moreover, the traditional grounds of review raised in challenges brought under the Act will have to be approached differently by the courts in the light of Convention law.

What may also become clearer with time is that Convention rights possibly have a number of different applications. Not only are they relevant under section 6, and also under section 3 (statutory interpretation), but they may also come to be relevant — by extension — as considerations in "ordinary" judicial review (see further paragraphs 3–41—3–45 below).

3. Illegality

(a) Misdirection of law

3–41   A decision-maker must understand the law governing his decision making power and must apply it correctly. Any decision will be unlawful if the decision maker has misunderstood or misapplied the law: see *Wednesbury* (above); *Re Islam* [1983] 1 A.C. 688.

The emergence of a general common law presumption of statutory interpretation in favour of international human rights, and of the use of the Convention as an aid to construction of ambiguous statutory provisions, has already affected the courts' approach to illegality as a ground of judicial review: see, *e.g. R. v. Secretary of State for the Home Department, ex p. Anderson* [1984] Q.B. 778. However, there has never been a uniform approach to consideration of the Convention. In a number of cases public bodies successfully resisted review by arguing that as the Convention was not part of English law, no regard need — or could — be paid to it: see, *e.g. R. v. Secretary of State for the Environment, ex p. NALGO* (1993) 5 Admin. L.R. 785; *R. v. Ministry of Defence, ex p. Smith* [1996] Q.B. 517; *R. v. Secretary of State for the Home Department ex p. Brind* [1991] 1 A.C. 696; see generally at paragraphs 1–09—1–14.

3–42   The Act provides an additional element to the body of law which will fall to be applied in all cases by all public law decision-makers. As section 6(1) provides, an act which is incompatible with any Convention right will be unlawful. Moreover, section 3(1) imposes an obligation to interpret legislation (both primary and subordinate), whenever enacted, so far as is possible to do so, in a way which is compatible with Convention rights. In other words, whenever legislation is under consideration it must be given a meaning which is compatible with the Convention unless the wording of the legislation is so plainly incompatible that it is not possible to do so. It would seem (see paragraph 1–33) that this obligation applies not only to courts and tribunals, but also to public authorities (*e.g.* when they are construing their own statutory powers). There seems to be no reason why one could not have a legal challenge to administrative decision-making based on a failure properly to apply section 3, and which did not go so far as to allege unlawfulness under section 6.

3–43 Courts and tribunals will no longer be bound by previous decisions of higher courts where those previous decisions were based on an interpretation of legislation which was incompatible with the Convention. Instead, it will be necessary to reconsider the position, to examine whether the provision in question can be given an interpretation which is compatible with the Convention. Moreover, the answer to the question whether an act, or a piece of legislation, is compatible with Convention rights may change over time, given that the Convention is a living instrument which must be interpreted in the light of changing social attitudes (see generally paragraph 2–33)

Where it is either not possible to interpret legislation in such a way as would be compatible with the Convention, or where the public authority's act was incompatible with Convention rights because of the existence of primary legislation, the Act will not provide the applicant with any effective remedy. The court remains unable to strike down the legislation (see section 4(6)), and the act under challenge is simply not unlawful (section 6(2)). While by section 4 a superior court may grant a "declaration of incompatibility", such a declaration does not affect the validity, continuing operation or enforcement of the legislation (section 4(6)(a)), and is not binding on the parties to the proceedings in which it is made (section 4(6)(b)); *i.e.* it is not a declaration of rights, but merely informs the legislature that legislation requires changing.

(b) Relevant considerations

3–44 A decision-maker must take into account all relevant considerations before making its decision and must ignore the irrelevant: *Wednesbury* (above). What is relevant generally depends on the facts of the individual case. Historically, the English courts refused to hold that international human rights treaties (even those to which the United Kingdom was a signatory) constituted a relevant consideration to which the Secretary of State of administrative officials had to have regard: see *e.g. R. v. Secretary of State for the Home Department, ex p. Kirkwood* [1984] 1 W.L.R. 913; *Chundawadra v. Immigration Appeal Tribunal* [1988] Imm. A.R. 161.

The Act may affect decision-making in a number of ways in this respect, and separately from the obligation to act compatibly with Convention rights under section 6. As a matter of general administrative law, it could become the case that public authorities will be required to show that they have paid proper regard to any relevant Convention rights for their conduct to be confirmed as *intra vires*, even if the applicant does not go so far as to allege or prove that the conduct is unlawful under section 6. The application of Convention rights to general decision-making is likely to broaden the range of potentially relevant facts, and may also affect the weight to be given to them. Rights which are to be treated as fundamental ought in general to be given greater weight than other interests. Moreover, these issues are capable of arising not only in relation to negative obligations, but also positive ones (see paragraphs 3–31—3–36 above).

(c) Promotion of the objects of legislation

3–45   The decision-maker must act so as to promote, rather than to defeat, the objects or policy of the Act, or other instrument, which created the power in question: *Padfield v. Minister of Agriculture, Fisheries and Food* [1968] A.C. 998. This ground, available in all judicial review cases, is a useful reinforcement of the argument that the Court's approach of construing the Convention purposively should be adopted (see above, paragraph 3–29).

4. Irrationality (or "unreasonableness")

3–46   A decision must not be so unreasonable that no reasonable decision-maker could have come to it: if it is, it cannot have been taken properly. This ground is also sometimes referred to as "perversity", or *Wednesbury* unreasonableness.

In cases brought under the Act, this ground will now probably be supplemented by the Strasbourg concept of "proportionality" (see generally at paragraph 2–44). This principle is that a measure must not be disproportionate to the mischief it is intended to address, *i.e.* not taking a sledgehammer to crack a nut. The courts have traditionally been ambivalent as to the use of proportionality as a concept of national law and whether, if it has any existence, it amounts to any more than *Wednesbury* unreasonableness by another name. In *R. v. Brent LBC, ex p. Assegai* (unreported) June 11, 1987, Woolf L.J. said: "Where the response is out of proportion with the cause to this extent, this provides a very clear indication of unreasonableness in a *Wednesbury* sense." (See also the judgment of Lord Donaldson M.R. in the Court of Appeal in *ex. p. Brind* (above), at 721–722).

3–47   While proportionality has not yet found acceptance in English administrative law, the courts have already indicated that it is likely to do so in the future. In particular, Lord Diplock, in *CCSU* (above), having referred to his threefold classification of the grounds for review (*i.e.* illegality, irrationality and procedural impropriety), went on to say, at 410:

> "That is not to say that further development on a case by case basis may not in course of time add further grounds. I have in mind the possible adoption in the future of the principle of 'proportionality' which is recognised in the administrative law of several of our fellow members in the EEC."

In *R. v. Secretary of State for the Home Department, ex p. Brind* [1991] 1 A.C. 696, the House of Lords gave further consideration to the application of this principle. Lord Templeman said, at 751:

"It seems to me that the courts cannot escape from asking themselves whether a reasonable Secretary of State, on the material before him, could reasonably conclude that the interference with freedom of expression which he determined to impose was justifiable. In terms of the Convention, as construed by the European Court, the interference with freedom of expression must be necessary and proportionate to the damage which the restriction is designed to prevent."

Lord Roskill added some "observations" on the subject, at 750:

"I am clearly of the view that the present is not a case in which the first step can be taken for the reason that to apply that principle in the present case would be for the court to substitute its own judgment of what was needed to achieve a particular object for the judgment of the Secretary of State on whom that duty has been laid by Parliament. But to so hold in the present case is not to exclude the possible future development of the law in this respect."

It has been argued that proportionality is no more than *Wednesbury* unreasonableness in a different guise. It remains to be seen if this is how the matter will in fact be. However, as applied by the Strasbourg court, it is a rather different, and potentially more interventionist, principle than is *Wednesbury*. Moreover, while a disproportionate remedy may inevitably be regarded as perverse, it does not follow that a perverse decision must always also be disproportionate. There is therefore potential for these two principles to be developed by the courts into related, but legally distinct, grounds of challenge.

5. Procedural impropriety: introduction

3–48   A decision-maker must act fairly, and in accordance with the principles of natural justice. The nature, content and extent of this duty will depend upon the circumstances and nature of the decision-maker and decision in question. The two fundamental concepts of natural justice are the rule against bias and the right to be heard. Aspects of these concepts are that no-one may be a judge in his own cause, and judges must be (and be seen to be) impartial.

Article 6 offers the Convention model of the principles of natural justice. Perhaps surprisingly, there is a difficulty as to its application in relation to the protection of Convention rights, given the way in which the Government has chosen to legislate. This difficulty arises from the interpretation of Article 6 given by the Court. In non-criminal matters, Article 6 applies in the determination to a person's "civil rights and obligations": Article 6(1). The Strasbourg authorities have construed the word "civil" to mean, in effect, "private law". Accordingly, in relation to a public law right or obligation, the Article does not apply.

Different states have set different boundaries between their concepts of private law and public law, and the Court has, over time, developed its own concepts of those rights which exist in private law and those which do not, and this has been said to depend only on the "character of the right" (*König v. Federal Republic of Germany* (1978) Series A, No. 27; 2 E.H.R.R. 170, paragraph 90).

Case law has determined that cases concerning rights existing in contract and tort, commercial and insurance law, family law and the law of succession, employment law (but not most public sector employment) and the law of real property have been treated as private law rights and hence within the scope of Article 6. Recently, the Court has held that social security and welfare assistance are both private law rights to which Article 6 applies, at least to the extent that the benefit in question is a statutory right rather than a discretionary payment (see *Schuler-Zgraggen v. Switzerland* (1993) Series A, No. 263; 16 E.H.R.R. 405, paragraph 46). Conversely, matters concerning immigration and nationality, tax, legal aid in civil proceedings, state education, prisoners' and tenants assocations' rights, state medical treatment, elections, etc, are outside the scope of Article 6.

6. Public/private law rights

3–49 The Act applies to all acts of courts and tribunals, however they be categorised, and there should therefore be little or no difficulty applying Article 6 in relation to litigation before these bodies. However, as to the acts of those public authorities falling within section 6(3)(b), there is potential for conflict.

The Act only applies to such bodies where there is a public law element to their functions and where the act under challenge was not a private law act. On this basis, it is possible that Article 6 would never apply: if the act existed in private law, it could relate to a civil right or obligation under Article 6(1), but would not give rise to any duty under section 6(1) of the Act; thus it could not be challenged under the Act and so Article 6 would be irrelevant.

Furthermore, the position is unclear where English law classifies an act as existing in public law but Strasbourg classifies it as a private law right. In determining whether the act is public or private, a court is obliged to have regard to the Strasbourg jurisprudence, including, if it considers it to be relevant, that which has emerged as to the public/private law distinctions under Article 6. If the national court accepts the Strasbourg formulation, the act will exist in private law, but the section 6(1) duty will therefore no longer apply: section 6(5). If the court prefers the English law classification, the Act will apply, but, having regard to the Strasbourg approach in defining "civil rights and obligations", it may hold that Article 6 does not apply to the act challenged and that the act was therefore not incompatible with any Convention right under Article 6.

3–50 The English law classification is therefore not conclusive, but if (as appears to be the case, according to the jurisprudence of both the U.K. courts and the Strasbourg authorities) the status of a right can only be ascertained having regard to the character of the right, it is hard to see how the English courts can continue to find that, for example, the housing benefit scheme creates no private law rights in cases where no Convention point is raised (see *e.g.* *Haringey LBC v. Cotter* (1996) 29 H.L.R. 682, CA), when the same issue is, as the Court has held, a matter of private law for the purposes of Article 6.

Moreover, it is difficult to see the English courts wholly adopting the approach of the Strasbourg authorities, given the extensive consideration the former have given to the issue, and the relatively well developed and coherent body of law they have thereby created, and given also that the intention of section 6 of the Act appears to be to preserve the current distinctions applicable in national law. The effects of adopting the Strasbourg approach would be extremely far reaching, creating a right to proceed by writ (and to claim damages) in relation to a potentially vast number of issues which can currently be litigated only using the RSC, Ord. 53 procedure, thus substantially undermining the decision in *O'Reilly v. Mackman* (above) which has been the foundation of English law in relation to this issue.

3–51   The answer may be that, if the Act has the effect that Article 6 applies to the acts referred to in section 6 (*i.e.* public law acts) then the line of Strasbourg decisions establishing that Article 6 only applies to private law rights and obligations will simply be irrelevant, as not representing the law of the United Kingdom under the Act. However, the potential scope of Article 6, under the Act, is a little difficult to predict.

7. The substance of Article 6

3–52   The Court has emphasised that Article 6 does not control or affect the content of, or rights granted, under national law, but provides purely procedural guarantees in relation to how such rights as are accorded to an individual, under his own national law, may be determined. Moreover, in order for Article 6 to apply at all, there must be a "contestation" (*i.e.* a dispute between the individual and a public authority as defined under the Act) as to civil rights and obligations which are (at least arguably) recognised in national law, and a decision which will be determinative of such civil rights and/or obligations. However, in cases where it is held to apply, the scope of Article 6 seems to be broader in some respects than under the common law, in terms of the rights conferred.

8. Right of access to a court

3–53   This raises the question as to what types of decision-making will amount to a determination of civil rights and obligations. Can Article 6 apply to administrative decision-making as well as court or tribunal proceedings? The position appears to be that the Court considers Article 6 to apply, not so as to require a fair hearing, etc., before the administrative decision-maker, but to require that there must be a right of access to a court to challenge administrative decisions, and that the court before whom a challenge may be brought must have power to consider the merits of the applicant's case; a right to seek judicial review may not be sufficient (see, *e.g. Le Compte, Van Leuven and De Meyere v. Belgium* (1981) Series A, No. 43; 4 E.H.R.R. 1, paragraph 51; *W v. U.K.* (1987) Series A, No. 121; 13 E.H.R.R. 453, paragraph 82). This could be of importance under the Act, if it is correct, as this chapter has stated, that judicial review is likely to remain the main (if not the only) forum for the challenge to the administrative decisions of public authorities under the Act; and given that other remedies currently in existence (such as the right of appeal to the county court in relation to certain homelessness decisions — see Housing Act 1996, s.204) generally provide only specific rights to appeal on a point of law.

The ability to raise issues of fact in judicial review proceedings is limited (*i.e.* where it is alleged that the decision-maker simply misunderstood the facts or did not base his decision upon them; where, on the facts, the decision was *Wednesbury* unreasonable; and where, with leave, the calling of oral evidence is permissible in the case of a conflict of affidavit evidence as to what actually occurred below). It remains to be seen whether, in view of this, it will be held by the courts that the right to seek judicial review affords sufficient access to the courts under Article 6. The national courts are, of course, not bound by the Strasbourg case law: section 2(1). If judicial review is not sufficient, the creation of some new right of challenge would seem to be required.

9. Reasons

3–54   English law recognises no general right to reasons from a public law decision maker, though in some cases fairness will demand that reasons be given (see *R. v. Higher Education Funding Council, ex p. Institute of Dental Surgery* [1994] 1 W.L.R. 242, QBD). The right to a fair hearing guaranteed by Article 6 does require that the decision maker "indicate with sufficient clarity the grounds on which they base their decision" in order that the individual may be in a position usefully to exercise any right of appeal (see *Hadjianastassiou v. Greece* (1992) Series A, No. 252; 16 E.H.R.R. 219, paragraph 33; also *X v. Federal Republic of Germany* (1981) 25 D.R. 240).

If, however, in relation to the acts of administrative decision-makers, Article 6 only applies to as to require access to the courts and a fair hearing before the appellate court, it would seem that the right to a fair hearing, and so the right to reasons, would only apply at this appellate stage. Accordingly, Article 6 will probably not alter the current position so as to impose a general duty to give reasons for all administrative decisions.

10. Article 6 v. natural justice

3–55   The bulk of the Article 6 protections exist as requirements of natural justice in any event. Moreover, while the concepts of procedural fairness provided by Article 6 are drafted in absolute terms, the Court has construed them flexibly. For example, on its face, Article 6 requires that judgment always be pronounced in public, not a right which has any real content in the principles of natural justice. However, the Court has interpreted this right with flexibility, having regard to the differing practices of the different Contracting States. In *Axen v. FRG* (1983) Series A, No. 72; 6 E.H.R.R. 195, and *Sutter v. Switzerland* (1984) Series A, No. 74; 6 E.H.R.R. 272, it was held in relation to the requirement for the public pronouncement of judgments that:

> "many member States of the Council of Europe have a long-standing tradition of recourse to other means, besides reading out aloud, for making public the decisions of some or all of their courts . . . The authors of the Convention cannot have overlooked that fact, even if concern to take it into account is not easily identifiable in their working documents." (*Axen,* paragraph 33.)

Accordingly, it would seem that the inclusion of Article 6 as one of the Convention rights with which public authorities must act compatibly is unlikely to create any substantial extension of the procedural protections available to individuals whose rights are routinely determined by administrative decision-makers.

11. Convention grounds

3–56 The Convention's former lack of status in English law meant that it was not, in itself, a ground for seeking judicial review: *R. v. Secretary of State for the Home Department, ex p. Brind* [1991] 1 A.C. 696. The courts have, however, employed the Convention in a number of ways, for example as a guide to the construction of statutory powers. In *R. v. Radio Authority, ex p. Bull* [1997] 2 All E.R. 561, a challenge to the authority's ban on advertising by "Amnesty" was based on illegality. It was argued successfully that the authority had misinterpreted its statutory provisions, which should have been interpreted in such a way as to minimise the impact on freedom of speech. Brooke L.J. held, given that Article 10 and the English common law were identical, that when construing statutory powers the courts must presume that Parliament intends neither to take away common law rights nor breach international obligations.

As a result of the Act, Convention grounds will add considerably to the armoury of arguments which can be employed to challenge the lawfulness of public authority decision-making

F. REMEDIES

3–57 Section 8 gives a court or tribunal power to grant such relief or remedy within its jurisdiction as it considers just and appropriate, if it finds a public authority to have acted unlawfully under Article 6. No new remedies are created, however, other than the right to damages (in appropriate cases) and the power of the courts to grant a declaration of legislative incompatibility (which is not a remedy in the true sense, in that it has no effect on the validity or continued operation of the incompatible legislation, and is not binding on the parties, thus leaving their rights unaffected). Remedies can only be awarded where the court or tribunal already has jurisdiction to award such relief or remedy.

In judicial review the prerogative orders of *certiorari, mandamus* and prohibition will remain the relevant remedies, although their application will probably be broadened. Relief in judicial review proceedings is discretionary, and it remains to be seen whether the courts will consider it permissible to refuse relief, in a case brought under the Act, for reasons similar to those which may lead to the refusal of relief in other cases (*e.g.* delay, the availability of alternative remedies, the conduct of the applicant, or the academic nature of the dispute).

1. Damages

3–58 As a matter of general law, the court may only award damages in judicial review proceedings if it is satisfied that, if the claim had been brought in a private law action, the applicant could or would have been awarded damages. Thus a claim for damages may only be pleaded in order to bring a valid private law claim for damages in the same proceedings as the public law challenge. The court has no wider jurisdiction to award damages to an applicant than it would enjoy if a damages claim came before it in the normal way, nor is an applicant afforded any additional cause of action for damages in respect of a breach of a public law duty: Order 53, r.7 and SCA 1981, s.31(4); *Calveley v. Chief Constable of the Merseyside Police* [1989] Q.B. 136, CA.

By section 8(3), the jurisdiction to award damages is confined by the requirement for the court to satisfy itself that "the award is necessary to afford just satisfaction to the person in whose favour it is made". In particular, the court must consider any other remedy or order which has been granted or made, and the consequences of any court decision. The court, therefore, must consider the extent of the relief granted in so far as it relates to the particular unlawful act.

The exercise of the jurisdiction to award damages is also subject to a general requirement to have regard to the principles of the Court under Article 41. The Court has approached the issue of damages both in terms of the fact of making an award and the amount with some caution. The number of cases in which damages have been awarded and the levels of those awards are fairly limited (see generally at paragraph 2–25 and following). Financial compensation tends only to be awarded where it is impossible to reverse all the consequences of the breach of the Convention right in question, *i.e.* where the applicant cannot be put back in the position in which he ought to have been had the breach not occurred. Where sums are awarded, they are usually of only small amounts (*e.g.* *X & Y v. Netherlands* (1985) Series A, No. 91; 8 E.H.R.R. 235). No damages at all are awarded where the applicant has failed to make out a causal link between the breach of the Convention right and some pecuniary or non-pecuniary loss (*e.g. Moustaquim v. Belgium* (1991) Series A, No. 193; 13 E.H.R.R. 802). The Court has never yet awarded punitive or exemplary damages.

As to whether the Act has created new private law rights in this field of activity, enabling an applicant to bring a private law damages claim for a failure by a public authority to act compatibly with a Convention right, or whether it has simply created (exceptionally) a right to damages in relation to breach of a public law right is not clear, but is discussed in more detail at paragraphs 3–26—3–28 above.

2. Declaration of incompatability

3–59   If a provision of primary or secondary legislation is found to be incompatible, certain specified courts have a discretion to make a declaration of incompatibility. It should be noted that courts with this jurisdiction to make such a declaration have no obligation to make such a declaration.

By section 4(5) only the House of Lords, the Privy Council, the Courts-Martial Appeal Court, the Court of Appeal and the High Court may make such declarations. This power is exercisable in respect of primary legislation in any proceedings where the question of compatibility arises, and the court is satisfied of incompatibility. In relation to subordinate legislation, the courts' power arises where the provision was made in the exercise of a power conferred by primary legislation, and only where the court is satisfied that the primary legislation prevents removal of the incompatibility.

CHAPTER 4

Criminal Justice

PART I: CRIMINAL LAW AND PRACTICE

Nigel Richardson (Solicitor, Hodge Jones & Allen)

A. INTRODUCTION

4–01 Of all areas of domestic law, the impact of the Act is likely to be greatest in relation to criminal proceedings. At any time during the currency of a criminal case issues may arise that require an application of the Act or the Convention. In the prevention and during the investigation of crime, at any stage in the criminal proceedings from police detention to appeal, Convention law will make itself felt.

Consideration of Convention law will not be confined to the higher courts. In numerous police stations, Magistrates' and Crown Courts, decisions are made on a daily basis concerning the detention of defendants and the conduct of their trials. These considerations are the essence of Articles 5 and 6, which most fully deal with the criminal law process. These are dealt with in some detail below.

4–02 The field of application, however, is broad: the right to silence, disclosure by the prosecution, and other important and controversial issues of current criminal jurisprudence are the subject of consideration by Strasbourg; but the Convention rights can also apply to routine and relatively mundane matters, the grant of legal aid, for instance, or the conduct of a police interview. Defence practitioners are likely to be quoting the Convention to judges, magistrates, Crown prosecutors and custody officers. The impact is likely to be greatest in the early years, while the courts become accustomed to dealing with Convention points and precedents have yet to be set.

It is proposed to consider the issues which are liable to face practitioners in the context and order in which they occur in the criminal justice process itself (arrest, detention and bail, trials and sentencing); and then to look briefly at some effects of the Act in relation to substantive offences.

1. General approach of the Act

4–03 The Act lays down a methodology which governs the approach of any court or public authority to Convention rights. Convention rights are relevant in two main ways.

First, section 3(1) requires that: "So far as it is possible to do so, primary legislation and subordinate legislation must be read and given effect in a way which is compatible with the Convention rights." (See generally paragraphs

1–31 and following, above.) If the language of the statute allows no such interpretive licence, and there appears to be a discrepancy between legislation and the Convention, the court is bound by the statute. This approach looks not simply at the literal meaning of statutory words, but interprets the statute by reference to the presumed underlying purpose of the legislation. This is the basic principal of statutory interpretation employed by the Strasbourg authorities, the so-called "teleological approach". The effect of section 3(1) is that a presumed underlying purpose of all domestic legislation is to give effect to Convention rights.

All relevant domestic legislation is subject to section 3. The Police and Criminal Evidence Act, the Magistrates Courts' Act, all criminal justice acts, and all statutes that create offences must be interpreted as though Parliament intended to give effect to Convention rights.

Secondly, section 6(1) makes it unlawful for a public authority to act in a way which is incompatible with Convention rights (see generally paragraphs 1–46 and following, above). A "public authority" includes a court (section 6(3)(a)), but its ambit is far wider than that. In the context of criminal justice it would include all manner of prosecuting authorities, the Crown Prosecution Service, Customs and Excise, local authorities and the Serious Fraud Office; those who investigate offences, the police, trading standards officers, and DTI inspectors; those who carry out the orders of the courts, such as the probation service, the prison service, and perhaps private prison or custodial contractors; the Director of Public Prosecutions, the Home Secretary and the Criminal Review Commission. Any person "certain of whose functions are . . . . of a public nature" will be constrained to act in a way compatible with Convention rights, unless the nature of the act in question is private (section 6(5)).

4–04 Thus, a Crown prosecutor taking a decision on disclosure of unused material in a summary trial must consider not only the Criminal Procedure and Investigations Act, but also Article 6 (right to a fair trial). The prosecutor must ensure that the decision is compatible with Convention rights. If conditions of detention in the cells at court are squalid and unhygenic there may be a breach of Article 3 which prohibits "inhuman or degrading treatment"; Securicor, or indeed the court itself, in keeping prisoners in such conditions, may be acting in a way which is incompatible with rights under the Convention, and which is therefore unlawful under section 6.

In principle, public bodies should regularly scrutinise their actions and review their decisions to ensure that they are in accord with Convention rights.

2. Interpreting and using Convention rights in court

4–05 Section 2 compels a court to take into account decisions of the Strasbourg authorities when determining a question which has arisen under the Act in connection with a Convention right (see generally paragraph 1–18, above). The court must first identify that a relevant Convention right has come into play. In this it is crucial that practitioners are alert to the existence of such rights in specific cases, and that they adduce evidence of possible breaches in the court which establishes the facts at issue, in practice the magistrates' and crown courts.

A crucial feature of the Act is to enable Convention points to be raised and dealt with as they occur in the course of ordinary proceedings (see sections 3(1) and 7(1)(b)). There is no reason to believe that the existing structure and procedures of trials will be affected, though Convention points will form the basis of preliminary applications, *voire dires*, submissions and speeches. Convention points are also likely to arise as grounds of appeal.

It should be noted that Convention rights are not merely defensive, although most often this is likely to be the manner in which they are raised. A person who complains as the victim of unlawful conduct by a public authority under section 6 may also bring their own proceedings in an appropriate court or tribunal (section 7(1)(a) (see generally at paragraph 1–55, above). This is likely to be relevant to the criminal practitioner where complaint is made of unlawful conduct by the courts themselves (in respect of "judicial acts"). Such cases may include cases of allegedly unlawful detention by the courts (as to which see particularly section 9(3)). In such a case, the proceedings must be brought by exercising a right of appeal, or by judicial review, or (if any rules of court so permit) in another forum (section 9(1)). In respect of complaints about unlawful conduct under section 6, other than those relating to judicial acts, proceedings can be brought in any court or tribunal in accordance with rules of court (see section 7(2)). This is likely to be relevant particularly to practitioners concerned with civil actions against the police.

3. General effects of the Act

4–06 The Act is likely to affect the conduct of a criminal case in a number of ways.

First, the Act may provide a defence to a criminal charge on the basis that the definition of certain behaviour as an offence is in breach of a right guaranteed by the Convention. Thus, the prohibition on certain sorts of trespass by the Public Order Act 1986, section 14B, would appear to affect the guarantee to a right of assembly under Article 11 of the Convention (*cf.* paragraph 4–117, below). In such a case, the defence would be arguing that, so far as it is possible to do so, the Public Order Act must be interpeted in a way which is compatible with the Convention, and that Parliament cannot have intended to prohibit certain types of activity since they are guaranteed under the Convention. This can only be an argument about interpretation — if it is not possible to interpret the legislation in accordance with section 3, then the court is obliged to implement the law even if it does not comply with the Convention (*cf.* paragraph 4–08, below).

Secondly, a defence may arise from the manner in which an offence comes to be prosecuted, for instance, because the prosecution infringes the prohibition on retroactive offences (Article 7(1) *cf.* 4–112, below). In such a case the defence would be by way of an abuse of process argument early in the proceedings (or, perhaps, by way of representations to the police or prosecution). Alternatively, the way in which evidence has been obtained may be in breach of a Convention right, for instance because of the manner in which a suspect was detained or interrogated, or because certain forms of questioning infringe, say, the privilege against self-incrimination. The defence would be arguing that the admission of such evidence would breach Article 6 and thereby prevent a fair trial.

4–07 Thirdly, the court will have a positive obligation to ensure compliance with the Convention within the forensic process. In considering whether to grant a defendant bail or legal aid, the manner in which witnesses are treated, or the speed with which cases are listed, the court must take Convention law into account and has an obligation to act in a way which is compatible with Convention rights. The court has such an obligation whether it arises under sections 6(1), 3(1) or 2(1).

The obligations under section 6(1) apply to all public authorities. Defence practitioners may wish to make representations to those authorities that their actions in investigating or prosecuting offences are in breach of one or more articles of the Convention and are therefore unlawful under section 6(1). A victim of such an unlawful act may *inter alia* apply for judicial review of the relevant decision, and may in certain cases be entitled to damages (see section 8, but note the limitation on damages against a court under section 9(3)).

4. Entirely incompatable legislation

4–08 If a court has been through the process envisaged by section 3, and has been unable to interpret the legislation in favour of Convention rights, it must resolve the conflict by implementing domestic law (*cf. R. v. Morrissy and Staines*, below). The courts are obliged to implement the law even if it does not comply with the Convention, and they would not be in breach of section 6 (because of the effect of section 6(2)).

Once a court has reached this conclusion, however, it may make a "declaration of incompatibility" (section 4). This power is provided only to the High Court and higher appellate courts, and neither effects the relevant legislative provision, nor is it binding on the parties to the proceedings. In a criminal case, therefore, a declaration of incompatibility could never be made by a court of first instance, the Magistrates' or Crown Courts. A first instance court might recognise an incompatibility, be unable to resolve it, and be forced to proceed to convict the defendant despite a breach of his Convention rights. The court would have to proceed to sentence the defendant.

Should the matter go to appeal (other than to the crown court), and the higher court upheld the finding of incompatibility, then a declaration of incompatibility could be made. The result would not directly assist the convicted defendant since, by virtue of section 4(6), the declaration would not effect the conviction. The applicant could, however, make an application to the Strasbourg authorities alleging a violation of the Convention, and a conviction under these circumstances might influence the Crown to grant a pardon.

5. Summary

4–09 The Act requires that cognisance be taken by national courts and public authorities of the overall objectives of particular provisions of the Convention. No Article of the Convention deals exclusively with criminal law. However, those provisions of the Convention that impact most heavily on criminal litigation are Article 5 (right to liberty and security), and Article 6 (right to a fair trial). These are addressed in detail below.

B. ARREST, DETENTION AND BAIL: GENERALLY

4–10   Article 5 is a fundamentally important provision which establishes the physical liberty of the individual, and the security of his or her person. In practice, in the area of criminal procedure, it will deal with issues surrounding arrest and detention, bail and remands in custody, and with imprisonment following conviction.

1. The scope of Article 5

4–11   The Article starts by setting out the right to physical liberty. However, this is not an absolute right and can be curtailed when the interests of society outweigh those of the individual. For this reason the Article:

(a) provides an exhaustive list of circumstances in which the individual may be deprived of that right (Article 5(1)a-f), for instance following conviction or upon arrest on reasonable suspicion of having committed an offence;

(b) sets out certain procedures which must be complied with when the state exercises its right to deprive a citizen of his or her liberty, including a duty to notify the detained person of the reason for his detention (Article 5(2)), and an obligation to review that detention promptly (Article 5(3));

(c) creates a duty to compensate those detained in contravention of the Article (Article 5(5)).

2. Meaning of detention

4–12   In the context of English criminal law, the definition of detention is well established. The question of whether an individual has been deprived of his or her liberty will rarely arise. An arrested suspect, held in accordance with the Police and Criminal Evidence Act 1984 or a prisoner held in custody on remand or following conviction will always be deprived of their liberty.

Deprivation of liberty may, however, take less obvious forms. In *Guzzardi v. Italy* (1980) Series A, No. 39; (1981) 3 E.H.R.R. 333, the Court held that the applicant had been deprived of his liberty when he had in effect been exiled to a small island for a period of 16 months, there complying with a number of regulations imposed by the authorities and subject to restrictions on his movements. The court held that "deprivation of liberty" was not always capable of precise definition and that there was a "grey zone" in which mere restrictions shade into full deprivation.

It is unlikely that curfew orders, or proposed electronic monitering of such orders (Criminal Justice Act 1991, ss.12, 13, as amended), would fall within the definition of "detention". The circumstances of the deprivation of liberty — less than 12 hours per day, at the offender's home, and organised to avoid interference with work, schooling or religion — are insufficiently harsh, more resembling restrictions on movement than full detention. In any event, the order is likely to have been imposed in accordance with Article 5(1)a, and therefore be a lawful deprivation of liberty (*cf.* paragraph 4–13, below).

3. Lawfulness

4–13 Of more significance, perhaps, is the requirement that the deprivation shall be "in accordance with a procedure prescribed by law" and that the detention, in each case that detention is allowable, shall be "lawful". In *Sunday Times v. U.K.* (1979) Series A, No. 30; 2 E.H.R.R. 245, the court held that the expression "prescribed by law" meant that the law was both adequately accessible to the ordinary citizen, and sufficiently precise to enable the citizen to regulate his or her conduct. The term has also been held to mean in accordance with applicable national law and consistent with the purpose of Article 5, namely to protect individuals from arbitrariness (*Scott v. Spain* R.J.D. 1996–VI 2382; 24 E.H.R.R. 391).

A period of detention will in principle be lawful if carried out pursuant to a court order. A subsequent successful appeal against conviction, sentence or order will not retrospectively render the detention unlawful (*Benham v. U.K.* R.J.D. 1996–III 738; 22 E.H.R.R. 293).

C. GROUNDS FOR ARREST OR DETENTION

4–14 Paragraphs (a) to (f) of Article 5(1) set out the circumstances in which the state can deprive an individual of his liberty. This list is exhaustive. Any detention, whether governed by criminal procedure or otherwise, which does not fulfil the criteria set out here is likely to be a breach of the Convention. A detention must not be arbitrary, and will be so if it is not in conformity with the purpose of the particular sub-paragraph by which the detention is purportedly authorised. It is necessary to look carefully at the precise circumstances in which the individual came to be detained in order to ascertain whether they fulfil the criteria of paragraphs (a) to (f).

1. Detention after conviction — Article 5(1)a

4–15 This provision allows the state the power to imprison an individual after they have been convicted by a court. It covers detention post-conviction and prior to sentence, as well as sentences of imprisonment and detention. An appeal against the length of a sentence would not, however, succeed under this provision, although a particularly lengthy sentence might be considered inhuman punishment and thereby breach Article 3 (*Weeks v. U.K.* (1987) Series A, No. 114; 10 E.H.R.R. 293).

A detention will be lawful where there is a "causal connection" between the conviction and the detention (*Van Droogenbroeck v. Belgium* (1982) Series A, No. 50; 4 E.H.R.R. 443). In most cases such a connection will be obvious: the defendant is convicted and is sentenced immediately or shortly after for the specific offences which have been proved.

2. Detention for non-compliance with an order, etc. — Article 5(1)b

4–16 Article 5(1)b provides for the detention of persons for "non-compliance with the lawful order of a court or in order to secure the fulfilment of any obligation prescribed by law". Orders of a court might include cases of civil contempt (for instance, non-compliance with injunctions or maintenance orders) or failure to pay fines. In the latter case, the detention must be in order to "secure the fulfilment of the obligation" and may not simply be imposed as a punishment.

3. Arrest on suspicion of committing an offence — Article 5(1)c

4–17 Alongside detention after conviction, the other exception to the right to liberty likely to concern criminal practioners is Article 5(1)c, and in particular the first limb of that provision. Here, we may directly compare the Convention rights with those granted by the Police and Criminal Evidence Act 1994 (referred to below as "PACE"), the statute governing, *inter alia,* the arrest and detention of suspects by police officers and others charged with the investigation of offences. In most circumstances, the national legislation provides a tighter system of control over police actions than does the Convention.

(a) "An offence"

4–18 The first limb of the Convention provision provides for an arrest and detention based on "reasonable suspicion of [the suspect] having committed an offence." An "offence" for the purposes of Article 5(1)c is one created by the criminal law of the relevant state. The most trivial of offences are not excluded from this definition. In *Steel and others v. U.K., The Times,* October 1, 1998, the Court found that proceedings for breach of the peace are proceedings which determine a "criminal offence" within the meaning of Article 5.

By contrast, police powers to arrest in PACE are limited to: (a) arrest with a warrant (in which case there will have been some exercise of judicial discretion prior to the arrest taking place); (b) arrest without a warrant but for an "arrestable offence" (in essence, a more serious offence carrying a potential maximum penalty of five years' imprisonment or more), or for certain other designated offences; or (c) arrest without a warrant for a non-arrestable offence, but where the circumstances of the situation in which the police find themselves necessitate an arrest (the "general arrest conditions"). These circumstances are exhaustively defined by PACE s.25.

The occasions upon which an arrest can be effected thus appear to be more tightly controlled by existing legislation than is envisaged by the Convention.

(b) "Reasonable suspicion"

4–19 Similarly, the requirement in Article 5(1)c that the arrest must be on "reasonable suspicion" mirrors the further provisions of PACE in relation to arrest. In *Fox, Campbell and Hartley v. U.K.* (1990) Series A, No. 182; 13 E.H.R.R. 157, the Court held that reasonable suspicion presupposes the existence of facts or information which would satisfy an objective observer that the person concerned may have committed an offence. The test is thus an objective one although what is reasonable will depend upon all of the circumstances. Article 5(1)c does not presuppose that the authorities already have sufficient evidence to charge, however. It is legitimate to detain persons for the purposes of questioning in order to confirm or dispel the suspicion upon which their arrests were based, subject of course to proper time limits being complied with (*Murray v. U.K.* (1994) Series A, No. 300-A; 19 E.H.R.R. 193).

Again PACE provides an equally rigorous framework: the officer must have reasonable grounds for suspecting that the arrested person is committing or is guilty of having committed the offence. The test as to whether such grounds exist is partly subjective, in that the officer's suspicions must be genuinely held, and partly objective, in that there must be reasonable grounds for forming such a suspicion and an objective observer would regard them as such (*O'Hara v. Chief Constable of the Royal Ulster Constabulary* [1997] A.C. 286). The Codes of Practice to PACE provide examples of factors which, alone, could never give rise to reasonable suspicion, including "colour, age, hairstyle and manner of dress" (Code A:1.7).

(c) Arrest to prevent the commission of an offence

4–20   The second limb of Article 5(1)c allows for arrest and detention for the prevention of the commission of an offence, and again is mirrored in the domestic legislation by PACE, s.24(7) allowing the arrest of anyone an officer believes to be about to commit an arrestable offence, and section 25(3) allowing an arrest for a non-arrestable offence if the officer believes it necessary in order to prevent physical injury, loss or damage to property or certain other consequences.

At first sight the Convention would appear to provide fewer safeguards in this respect than the domestic legislation. Under Article 5(1)c it would not be a breach to arrest and detain in order to prevent the commission of the most minor offence irrespective of the lack of consequences or the fact that the public interest does not require an arrest. Also the wording of the second limb appears not to require an arrest "for the purpose of bringing [the detainee] before the competent legal authority", thus potentially allowing a general power of preventative detention or internment. In *Lawless v. Ireland* (1961) Series A, No. 1; 1 E.H.R.R. 1, however, it was held that the words "for the purpose of . . ." applied to all three limbs of Article 5(1)c implying that the purpose of an arrest and a continued detention must be the initiation of criminal proceedings. The "competent legal authority" in England and Wales will be the Magistrates' Court.

(d) Arrest to prevent flight

4–21   The third limb of Article 5(1)c adds little to the total — any person who is fleeing after having committed an offence may be arrested on suspicion of having committed the offence in the first place.

(e) Conditions of detention — relation to other Convention Articles

4–22   Article 5(1)c does not merely cover arrest, but deals with detention prior to being brought before a judge or other officer authorised by law to exercise judicial power, as stipulated by Article 5(3). The timescale in which this is to be done is governed by the latter provision (*i.e.* promptly). However it should be noted that the detention itself is only lawful so long as the reasonable suspicion subsists. This provision is similar to the requirement under section 39 of PACE, compelling the custody officer to release a suspect in respect of whom the grounds of detention have ceased to apply.

Article 5(1)c does not concern itself with issues such as degree of force which may be applied to effect an arrest, although in extreme cases this may be considered under Article 2(2)b. Nor does Article 5 seek to define the conditions of detention felt to be appropriate or circumscribe what may be done with a detained person (for instance, the taking of bodily samples or forceable fingerprinting). Particularly inappropriate conditions or treatment may fall within the ambit of "inhuman or degrading treatment" under Article 3, which goes further in imposing a positive obligation to protect the physical well-being of persons in custody. In *Hurtado v. Switzerland* (1994) Series A, No. 280–A, a breach of Article 3 occurred when a prisoner, injured during his arrest, was denied immediate access to medical treatment. While poor conditions of detention may breach Article 3, self-imposed poor conditions will not (*McFeeley v. U.K.* (1981) 3 E.H.R.R. 161 — a "dirty protest" case).

The provisions of Article 6(3)c, the right to legal representation (*cf.* paragraph 4–99), apply not merely to trial but also to the preliminary stages of an investigation. A suspect held at a police station thus has a right under the Convention to see a solicitor privately. This right may be subject to certain restrictions for good cause, but such restrictions may deprive the accused of a fair procedure and thereby breach Article 6(1) in conjunction with 6(3)c (*Murray v. U.K.* (1996) 22 E.H.R.R. 29). The effect of this provision on domestic law is to render section 58 of PACE, allowing for denial of access to a solicitor, more circumscribed than ever.

4. Other reasons for detention — Article 5(1)d–f

4–23   These exceptions have little bearing on the criminal law, dealing essentially with the deprivation of liberty of the individual under civil procedures, or indeed in circumstances not considered lawful under domestic law (alcoholics, drug addicts or vagrants). However, the detention of persons of unsound mind might include detention following conviction, a situation that appears to fit within both subsections of Article 5.

D. PROVIDING REASONS FOR THE ARREST — ARTICLE 5(2)

4–24   In order for a detention under one of the above criteria to be lawful, the authorities must comply with certain procedures. Article 5(2) requires that "everyone who is arrested shall be informed promptly, in a language which he understands, of the reasons for his arrest and of any charge against him."

1. The nature of the information

4–25   The purpose of this provision is to ensure that the arrested person may make effective use of the judicial review procedure envisaged by Article 5(3) and (4), and so that he or she may refute or admit the allegation. This is complimented by the matching provision of Article 6(3)a, which provides for information to be given to the accused person for the purposes of ensuring a fair trial (the latter provision requiring a fuller and more substantial disclosure to fulfill its purpose). Article 5(2) requires "the essential legal and factual grounds for [the detained person's] arrest" (*Fox, Campbell & Hartley v. U.K., above*). In that case the applicants had merely been informed on arrest that they were being taken into custody under section 11 of the Prevention of Terrorism Act 1978 on suspicion of being terrorists. This was held not to be a sufficient indication of the reasons for their arrest.

It is necessary that the information be given in a language which the detained person understands. The purpose of the Article is to ensure that the detained person is not addressed in a foreign and unintelligable tongue. However, it is also necessary that the arresting authorities provide the legal and factual reasons for arrest "in simple non-technical language that [the arrested person] can understand". "Legalese" may not suffice.

2. When must the suspect be informed?

4–26   The requirement under Article 5(2) is for the information to be given "promptly", not necessarily immediately upon arrest, a sensible provision bearing in mind the difficult circumstances in which persons are sometimes placed under arrest. Thus, in *Fox, Campbell and Hartley* the full reasons for the applicants' detention were subsequently brought to their attention during their interrogation; although this was several hours after their initial detention the Court held this sufficient to rectify the original deficiency — the purpose of the provision, to allow the detained person to make adequate representations, had been fulfilled. Neither is it necessary that the information be given in any specific form, for instance in writing, or that it be stated expressly. In *Fox, Campbell and Hartley* the full reasons for the detainees' arrests were only brought to their attention during their interrogation. The Court found no fault with this approach.

3. PACE, s.28

4–27   Again, it is the case that the relevant domestic legislation on this point, the Police and Criminal Evidence Act, creates a more stringent set of rules under which the authorities are obliged to act. Section 28 of PACE allows that an arrest is not lawful unless the arrested person is informed that they are under arrest and the ground for the arrest at the time it occurs or as soon as practicable after. Unless very unusual circumstances prevailed it would be hard to argue that a person could be detained for a period of hours without some moment arising when he or she could be informed of the reasons for their arrest. It is submitted that the wording "as soon as practicable" is of rather greater clarity than the term "promptly", allowing as it does for necessary delay if that can be sucessfully argued, but for no more than that.

As with Article 5(2) no specific form of words is needed; it is necessary, however, that the detained person "knows in substance the reason why it is claimed that this [detention] should be imposed" (*Christie v. Leachinsky* [1947] A.C. 573).

PACE also provides that the detained person is informed of various other rights once he or she arrives at the police station (to which he or she must be taken as soon as practicable after arrest). These include the right not to be kept incommunicado, the right of access to a solicitor, and the right to consult the

Codes of Practice governing the detention and treatment of prisoners. The exercise of these rights may only be delayed under certain specific, and exceptional, circumstances.

E. DETENTION AT A POLICE STATION AND BAIL FROM COURT — ARTICLE 5(3)

4–28   Article 5(3) effectively follows the progress of an investigation likely to have been carried out under the provisions of section 5(1)c. The suspect has been properly arrested and detained: Article 5(3) answers the questions concerning how long he may now be detained and what should then happen to him at the conclusion of the police investigation.

1. Period in police detention

4–29   Initially, Article 5(3) provides that a person detained under section 5(1)c shall be brought promptly before a judge or other officer authorised by law to exercise judicial power. In England and Wales, in the first instance, this will be a magistrate who, by virtue of the Bail Act 1976, has the power to review "the circumstances militating for and against detention [and deciding] whether there are reasons to justify detention and of ordering release if there are no such reasons" (*Schiesser v. Switzerland* (1979) Series A, No. 34; 2 E.H.R.R. 417).

The main safeguard for the individual against lengthy periods of police detention subsists, under the Convention, in the word "promptly". The Court explored this concept in the case of *Brogan and others v. U.K.* (1988) Series A, No. 145–B; 11 E.H.R.R. 117, without arriving at a fixed term of hours or days which would place a limit on police detention. In that case the applicants were detained for lengthy periods under the Prevention of Terrorism Act, the shortest period being four days and six hours, before being released without charge. The Court held that there had been violations of Article 5(3) in all cases, despite the fact that there is a limited degree of flexibility attached to the notion of "promptness" and that each case must be assessed according to its own special features and attendant circumstances. Even within the context of terrorism within Northern Ireland, however, detention for over four days without an appearance before a court constituted an unacceptably wide interpretation of the word "promptly". In consequence of this decision, the U.K. government entered a derogation in respect of Article 5(3) (see below).

(a) Length of police detention

4–30   How, then, does Article 5(3) effect detention prior to charge in criminal investigations? The first point to note is that detention for over four days in an ordinary criminal case must almost always breach the concept of "promptness" in the light of *Brogan*, above. Secondly, detention prior to charge is governed by PACE, ss.41–45. This provides a series of time limits governing a suspect's detention, all running from the "relevant time", which will normally be the moment the suspect arrives at the police station. The maximum period during which a suspect may be held without either being charged or brought before a court for further detention to be authorised is 36 hours. This period is, however, limited to more serious matters, those defined as "serious arrestable offences": persons arrested for more trivial offences may not be detained for more than 24 hours — the statute thereby itself reflecting the concepts of promptness yet flexibility in all the circumstances which was defined by the Court in *Brogan*. Detention in police custody for more than 36 hours may be authorised, but only by a magistrates' court upon an application for a warrant of further detention. In this circumstance the police have complied with their duty under Article 5(3) to bring the detained person promptly before a court which may then exercise its judicial power in considering the propriety of the suspect's further detention.

4–31 Overarching these time limits are further procedural requirements on the police to review detention at certain set times, and to charge a suspect when there is sufficient evidence to do so or release the suspect without charge. These are provisions which are not envisaged or required by Article 5.

Following *Brogan*, above, the government of the day entered a derogation under the Convention to preserve the power of the Secretary of State to extend the period of detention of persons suspected of terrorism connected with Northern Ireland. The effect of this is that persons arrested and detained under the Prevention of Terrorism (Temporary Provisions) Act 1984 may be held in custody without charge for periods of up to seven days, without a breach of Article 5(3) occuring. This derogation is retained under Schedule 2, Pt 1 of the Act, although it expires after five years of the Act coming into force unless renewed by both Houses of Parliament (*cf.* White Paper, *Rights Brought Home: the Human Rights Bill*, paragraph 4.4).

2. "Brought before a judge"

4–32 Detention in police custody carried out in accordance with the provisions of PACE is highly unlikely to occasion a breach of Article 5(3). However, one should perhaps note the difference in emphasis between Article 5 and PACE. The former creates an obligation that the detained person be brought before a court promptly. The latter creates strict time limits for the moment of charging ("a person shall not be detained for more than 24 hours without charge"), and thereafter only allows that he be brought before a magistrates' court no later than the first sitting after he is charged, with provision being made in section 46 of PACE that this be no longer than the second day after he is charged. It is possible to envisage situations in which persons are held for quite a number of days before being brought to court, without any infringement of the provisions of PACE.

3. Bail from court

4–33 Having been brought before a court the detainee is entitled to "trial within a reasonable time or to release pending trial". This does not entitle the authorities to detain a suspect for a "reasonable time" and then release them pending trial when it appears that an imminent trial is not likely (*Wemhoff v. FRG* (1968) Series A, No. 7; (1979-80) 1 E.H.R.R. 55). This is not a matter of choice for the authorities, but a dual obligation.

The suspect is entitled to have his detention reviewed and release pending trial ordered unless there are "relevant and sufficient" reasons to justify the detention "having regard to the circumstances and facts advanced by both the authorities and the suspect". In *Wemhoff*, the circumstances held to have been properly taken into account by the national court considering bail included the defendant's connections abroad, his foreign assets and his likely future bankruptcy, all indicating the possibility that he might abscond.

4. Reasons for refusing bail

4-34   Strasbourg case law has identified four broad categories of reasons justifying the refusal of bail.

(a) Risk that the accused may abscond

4-35   To justify detention under this ground the prosecution must show "a whole set of circumstances, particularly, the heavy sentence to be expected or the accused's particular distaste of custody, or the lack of well established ties in the country" all of which make flight a more attractivve option than continued detention (*Stogmuller v. Austria* (1969) Series A, No. 9; 1 E.H.R.R. 155). In that case the fact that the defendant could leave the country was, of itself, insufficient to provide a reason for a fixing bail without further supporting circumstances. Other considerations include the character of the accused (presumably also including any previous record of compliance with bail), his morals, home, occupation, assets, family ties and links with the country in which he was being prosecuted (*Neumeister v. Austria* (1968) Series A, No. 8; 1 E.H.R.R. 91).

In *Wemhoff*, above, it was held that the mere possibility of a severe sentence was not sufficient to justify a refusal of bail, although it might be a factor which would encourage a defendant to abscond. Further, the court is under an obligation to consider the issue of bail throughout a person's detention and to take into account that "the danger of flight necessarily decreases as the time spent in detention passes by", assuming that such time is deducted from any eventual sentence (*Neumeister*, above; *Matznetter v. Austria* (1969) Series A, No. 10; 1 E.H.R.R. 198)

(b) Committing further offences

4-36   The danger of repetition of offences may justify the refusal of bail. It is necessary, however, "that the danger be a plausible one and [detention] appropriate, in the light of the circumstances of the case and in particular the past history and personality of the person concerned" (*Clooth v. Belgium* (1991) Series A, No. 225; 14 E.H.R.R. 717). In both *Matznetter* and *Clooth* the Court has stressed that the judge or magistrate should consider the seriousness of the consequences of further criminal offending when deciding on bail; even a very real danger of the commission of further minor offences might not justify a remand in custody under this criterion.

(c) Interference with the course of justice

4-37   Again, bail may be refused when there is a real risk that the release of the accused might result in an inteference with the course of justice. Examples of this could include intimidating or interfering with witnesses, warning other possible suspects and the supression of evidence. As with the danger of absconding, it may be that the risks diminish with the passage of time, as inquiries are effected, statements taken and verifications carried out (*Clooth*, above). It follows that this objection to bail may not be sustainable through a long period of detention.

(d) Preservation of public order

4–38　In *Letellier v. France* (1991) Series A, No. 207; 14 E.H.R.R. 83 the Court accepted that an appropriate ground for the refusal of bail could arise when there was a significant risk of public disorder should the defendant be released. In that case, the French courts concluded that there was such a risk based only on the seriousness of the offence with which Mme Letellier was charged. This was insufficient. This ground can only be substantiated when it is "based on facts capable of showing that the accused's release would actually disturb public order". The court also suggested that the offence giving rise to such a fear would have to be of a "particular gravity". In order for an objection to bail to be substantiated under this ground, therefore, a court will have to be dealing with a serious offence in relation to which there are manifest indications of some form of public disorder if the detainee were released.

5. Conditions of bail

4–39　Article 5(3) specifically reserves the option for the authorities to grant bail with one condition, "guarantees to appear for trial". In a number of the cases cited above the court has re-iterated that, when the only remaining objection to bail is based on the fear that the defendant would abscond, the domestic court must order release if guarantees would remove that danger (*Wemhoff*, above). "Guarantee" in this context means either surety or security.

While not specifically mentioned in the Article itself, additional conditions may be imposed to alleviate the risks which might otherwise prevent bail being granted. Were this not the case a defendant might well be prejudiced, having to remain in custody when an appropriate condition would remove the risk that causes him to be detained. A requirement as to residence, and the surrender of passport and driving licence have been approved as conditions (*Schmid v. Austria* (1985) 44 D.R. 195).

6. Convention rights and the Bail Act 1976

(a) Common exceptions to the right to bail

4–40　In the English jurisdiction, the refusal of bail is largely governed by the Bail Act 1976, and in particular Schedule 1, Pt. 1. Section 4 of the Bail Act grants a general right to bail to most categories of accused person brought before a court; Schedule 1, Pt. 1 provides for exceptions to that right where there are "substantial grounds for believing" that, if the defendant were granted bail, he would:

(a) fail to surrender; or

(b) commit an offence while on bail, or

(c) interfere with witnesses or otherwise obstruct the course of justice.

Thus far, the Convention rights and the domestic legislation are broadly coincidental, the three grounds for refusing bail mirroring the first three reasons to justify continued detention. Indeed the similarity goes further: under the Bail Act the court is compelled to have regard to other relevant considerations when reaching its decision. These include the nature and seriousness of the offence, although this, of itself, is not a ground for refusing bail. Convention caselaw requires "relevant and sufficient grounds" to justify detention; the Bail Act requires that the court be satisfied that there are "substantial grounds" for belief. There seems little or no difference in meaning between the two tests.

(b) Further exceptions to the right to bail

4–41 However, the Bail Act provides further exceptions to the right to bail. These include a remand in custody for a defendant's own protection, or when a defendant was already on bail in criminal proceedings at the time of the commission of the current offence, or when a defendant has been arrested after absconding. While each of these circumstances hint at the grounds for detention defined by the Convention (public order, commission of further offences and absconding, respectively), under the Bail Act it is not necessary that the court goes on to find those grounds substantiated. The mere finding that a defendant was already on bail at the time of the commission of a further offence is sufficient to justify the refusal of bail under the domestic jurisdiction. There is no requirement that the court find substantial grounds for believing that any further consequences will flow.

These further grounds for refusal of bail do not fall within the categories defined by Convention caselaw. However, those categories are not closed. It is therefore possible that further grounds could be established in which the public interest in keeping a defendant detained would outweigh that individual's right to liberty.

(c) Criminal Justice and Public Order Act 1994, s.25

4–42 In one circumstance all discretion is removed from the judiciary in granting bail. Under the Criminal Justice and Public Order Act 1994, s.25 a defendant may not under any circumstance be granted bail where he is charged with murder, manslaughter or rape, when he has been previously convicted of such an offence. This provision, although rare in its application, would certainly appear to undermine the purpose of Article 5(3): there is little point in bringing a suspect promptly before a judge or other officer if that officer has no discretion to review the appropriateness of the detention; nor can the judge consider "relevant and sufficient" reasons to justify further detention, when his only function is to determine whether the defendant falls within section 25, and if so, to refuse bail; further the Convention case law emphasises review of detention as circumstances change — in a situation such as section 25 envisages there can be no development. In late 1997 the Commission declared admissible two cases challenging the legality of section 25 (*BH v. U.K.* 30307/96; *CC v. U.K.* 32819/96). These currently await consideration by the Court.

7. Trial within a reasonable time

4–43 There must be "relevant and sufficient" grounds to justify detention and, as we have seen, those grounds must subsist throughout the period in which the defendant is in custody pending trial. In addition to this, the trial must take place "within a reasonable time". There is considerable overlap between this provision and Article 6(1) which also grants the right to a hearing "within a reasonable time", but does so whether or not the defendant is in custody. In practice, applications under this provision are normally also made under Article 6(1) and will be considered at paragraphs 4–73—4–76.

F. REMEDIES

4–44 Article 5(4) guarantees the right to *habeas corpus* for all persons detained, whether in criminal or other procedings. Article 5(5) provides for an enforceable right to compensation for anyone detained in contravention of the provisions of Article 5 (*cf.* section 9(3) of the Act). Such a situation will only arise when the basis for a decision to detain an individual was in breach of Article 5; it will not arise when, for instance, a bail decision is overturned by a higher court or a convicted person is freed on appeal, so long as the detention was lawful in the first instance.

G. THE RIGHT TO A FAIR TRIAL: GENERALLY

1. The rights guaranteed

4–45 The provision of the Convention likely to have most far reaching effect on English criminal procedure is Article 6, guaranteeing the right to a fair trial.

The Article begins by defining the general right, "to a fair and public hearing within a reasonable time by an independent and impartial tribunal established by law". It proceeds to set out circumstances in which the press or public may be excluded from the hearing, while establishing the general requirement that "judgment shall be pronounced publicly".

Article 6(2) states the general principal that "everyone charged with a criminal offence shall be presumed innocent until proved guilty" and Article 6(3) sets out five specific minimum rights for the accused person:

    (a) to be informed of the nature and cause of the allegation against him;

    (b) to have adequate time and facilities for the preparation of his defence;

    (c) to defend himself in person or through legal assistance of his own choosing, and to be given free legal assistance if he has insufficient means to pay for it and the interests of justice so require it;

(d) to examine witnesses against him and call his own witnesses under equal conditions;

(e) to have a free interpreter where necessary.

The minimum rights are a non-exclusive list, and the fact that they are respected does not, by itself, guarantee a fair trial. The rights set out in Article 6(3) are specific aspects of the right to a fair trial guaranteed by Article 6(1) which is the overriding purpose of the provision and must be the main consideration (*Edwards v. U.K.* (1992) Series A, No. 247–B; 15 E.H.R.R. 417).

2. Criminal charges

4–46   Although Article 6 governs many civil and all criminal proceedings, the fuller guarantees set out in subsections (2) and (3) apply only to criminal matters; the definition of "criminal charges" is therefore of importance.

The term has an autonomous character, meaning that it cannot merely be interpreted by reference to the domestic law of the individual states. In *Engel v. The Netherlands* (1976) Series A, No. 22; 1 E.H.R.R. 647 the Court considered whether various "charges" — in this instance breaches of military discipline by conscripts — counted as criminal within the meaning of Article 6. The first test to be applied was to ask whether the offence was classified as criminal by the domestic law of the relevant state: if so, then it was automatically a criminal offence for the purposes of Article 6. Next, the nature of the offence and the severity of potential penalty fall to be considered. The general application of the law to all citizens, rather than just a selected group (such as conscripts), is an indicator that the offence is criminal in nature. When considering severity of penalty, the Court held that if "deprivations of liberty [were] liable to be imposed as a punishment" then the offence was criminal in character, unless such deprivations could not be "appreciably detrimental".

How does this affect the domestic jurisdictions? Clearly, the main body of substantive offences will fall within the definition of "criminal" for the purposes of Article 6, since classification as an offence under national law is sufficient to settle the issue. However, the reverse is not true, and some behaviour which is not classified as criminal in the domestic jurisdiction may nevertheless be an offence for the purposes of Article 6. Thus traffic misdemeanours, although decriminalised in the relevant domestic jurisdicton, may be criminal in nature, particularly when the penalty of a fine was accompanied by an order for committal to prison in default (*Pfarrmeier v. Austria* (1995) Series A, No. 329–C; 22 E.H.R.R. 175, *Schmautzer v. Austria* (1995) Series A, No. 328-A; 21 E.H.R.R. 511, and *Umlauft v. Austria* (1995) Series A, No. 328–B; 22 E.H.R.R. 76); and when the offence was of general application, governing the behaviour of large numbers of people (*Ozturk v. FRG* (1984) Series A, No. 73; 6 E.H.R.R. 409).

(a) Examples of "criminal charges"

4–47   Proceedings under the Dangerous Dogs Act 1991 have recently been held by the Commission to be criminal in nature, involving distressing if not severe penalties (*Henry Bates v. U.K.*, App. No. 26280/95; *Bullock v. U.K.*, App.

No. 29102/95). Binding-over proceedings (*Steel v. U.K., The Times,* October 1, 1998) have also been held by the Court to be criminal in nature. Proceedings involving the non-payment of fines or of the community charge may be criminal for the purposes of Article 6; in the latter case, the possibility of a relatively severe sentence of three months' imprisonment, and the general application of the law to all citizens, persuaded the Court that the applicant was "charged with a criminal offence" (*Benham v. U.K.,* R.J.D. 1998–III 738; 22 E.H.R.R. 293). Confiscation proceedings held under the Drug Trafficking Offenders Act 1994 or the Criminal Justice Act 1988, carrying substantial powers of imprisonment in default of payment, will be criminal proceedings for the purposes of Article 6. In *Welsh v. U.K.* (1995) Series A, No. 307–A; 20 E.H.R.R. 247 the Court considered the penalty of confiscation under Article 7, deeming it to be, in that case, a retroactive punishment, closely linked to the conviction for a criminal offence. The same is likely to be true of contempt of court in civil proceedings, where the penalty may be imprisonment (*cf. Harman v. U.K.* (1984) 38 D.R. 53, where admissibility was decided in relation to Article 7(1) — the contempt was a retroactive criminal offence).

Certain proceedings, which are currently of a hybrid nature, are likely to be defined as criminal. Thus, under the Crime and Disorder Bill, a person who breaches an anti-social behaviour order or a sex offender order, made on the civil standard of proof, becomes liable to criminal sanctions including custody. It is arguable that the first stage of those proceedings, the making of the order, should be classed as criminal and thereby benefit from the guarantees of Article 6(2) and 6(3). The order itself should be made after a proper and fair determination of the facts at issue, since the creation of the order is a clear and obvious precursor to possible criminal sanctions which will occur if the order is breached. It is submitted that the initial proceedings are as relevant to the imposition of a criminal penalty as the breach proceedings, and should be subject to the same fair trial safeguards (*cf.* also the similar provisions of the Protection from Harrassment Act 1997).

3. General rights

4–48 Of more fundamental importance are the particular rights which have been established by the Strasbourg courts in determining the meaning of "a fair hearing". These rights are additional to the specific guarantees afforded by Article 6(3), but even the categories listed below are far from exhaustive — the definition of "fair hearing" being wide enough to allow for consideration of all types of procedural variety and irregularity. The Court has, however, been reluctant to examine and assess evidence itself, the consideration of facts being the proper duty of the domestic courts. The Court's own role is to assess the fairness of procedures by which national courts reach their verdicts.

H. EQUALITY OF ARMS

4–49 The principal of "equality of arms" requires that each party to proceedings is treated on an equal basis and has:

> "a reasonable opportunity of presenting his case to the court under conditions which do not place him at substantial disadvantage *vis-à-vis* his opponent" (*Kaufman v. Belgium* (1986) 50 D.R. 98).

This right is an inherent element of a fair trial. Specific guarantees designed to ensure equality for defendants in criminal trials are set out in Article 6(3), in particular the right to call and cross-examine witnesses. Article 6(1) however ensures this principle in a variety of other situations.

Failure to treat equally a witness called by the defendant and a court appointed expert has been held to be a breach of the principle of equality of arms and therefore of Article 6(1) (*Bonisch v. Austria* (1985) Series A, No. 92; 9 E.H.R.R. 191). The principle is also breached if the prosecuting authority is heard in the absence of the defendant or his legal represetative (*Neumeister v. Austria* (1968) Series A, No. 8; 1 E.H.R.R. 91 — although in that case the principle did not apply to proceedings relating to detention on remand, these falling outside the scope of Article 6).

1. Disclosure

4–50   The principle of equality of arms unquestionably overlaps with the specific guarantees of Article 6(3) in the area of disclosure of information by the prosecution to the defence. In *Edwards v. United Kingdom* (1992) Series A, No. 247–B; 15 E.H.R.R. 417 the Court held that the minimum rights in Article 6(3) are specific aspects of the right to a fair trial and, since the applicant was in essence complaining that his trial was unfair, the matter would be considered under Article 6(1)

The Court considered the application of Article 6(1) to disclosure by the prosecution in *Bendenoun v. France* (1994) Series A, No. 284; 18 E.H.R.R. 54. The case dealt with disclosure of documents in administrative proceedings for tax offences. The applicant claimed that he did not have access to the full customs file against him and therefore not to the full facts of the case. The Court found that there had been no breach — the authorities relied only on documents they had disclosed and the applicant had been aware of contents of most of the undisclosed documents which he had seen in linked proceedings. The Court could envisage circumstances in which the concept of a fair trial may entail an obligation to supply the defendant with all available material, but even then it would be necessary for the defendant to provide brief reasons for his request.

4–51   In *Jespers v. Belgium* (1981) 27 D.R. 61, the Commission held that the obligation on the prosecution was to disclose material which might assist the defendant in mounting a defence or in raising mitigatory factors. Assistance to the defendant might be found in material which undermined the credibility of a prosecution witness. The duty of the prosecution included disclosure of materials in its possession but also extended to cover items to which the authorities could gain access. These could include social service files, hospital notes or other similar documentation.

The basic principle that the prosecuting authorities should disclose all material evidence for or against the defendant was reaffirmed in *Edwards v. U.K.* (1992) above. Despite finding a defect in the trial procedure because of a failure to disclose relevant material to the defence, the Court finally held that there had been no violation of Article 6. The defects of the original trial had been remedied by the subsequent procedure of the Court of Appeal, which considered the impact of the newly disclosed material on the conviction and concluded that the conviction was safe.

2. Criminal Procedure and Investigations Act 1996

4–52 Disclosure of unused material in the domestic jurisdiction is governed by the Criminal Procedure and Investigations Act 1996 ("CPIA"). The prosecution is under a duty to disclose to the defence material which "might undermine the case for the prosecution against the accused." Such material must have come into the prosecutor's possession "in connection with the case for the prosecution against the accused" or, if not actually in his possession, must be material which "he has inspected in connection with the case for the prosecution against the accused" (CPIA, s.3).

The defendant may be entitled to further material, "secondary disclosure" which "might be reasonably expected to assist the accused's defence", but only if he has served on the prosecution a defence statement, which gives details of his case to the prosecutor (CPIA, ss.5–7).

The restrictive nature of this legislation may be interpreted as breaching Article 6(1). Strasbourg case law has not to date dealt with a situation where the right of access to prosecution materials was contingent upon some action by the defence (save for making a request for disclosure — *Bendenoun v. France,* above). Although there is a clear link between the defence statement and the secondary disclosure (the prosecution provide further material in support of the defence case as disclosed by the defence statement), there is a sense in which the legislation creates a bargaining system, where full access to the prosecution materials is dependent on full disclosure of the defence case. It may be argued under Article 6(1) that access to relevant prosecution materials should be unconditional.

Further, the wording of section 3 in relation to the manner in which materials have come into the prosecutor's possession, or in which he has inspected them, may be unduly restrictive. Materials that come to the notice of the prosecutor in relation to a different investigation, even if relevant to the present matter, somewhat arbitarily fall outside the ambit of section 3. The prosecution are not obliged to disclose the existence of items which they do not hold, but to which they could gain access (*cf. Jespers v. Belgium* (1981) above).

3. Disclosure of evidence in summary matters

4–53 The CPIA 1996 applies in similar terms to matters heard in the magistrates' court or Crown Court, with one important difference — namely that in the Crown Court the defendant can be compelled to produce a defence statement on pain of the jury being invited to draw an inference from its absence. However, the disclosure provisions relate only to material that is not being directly used by the prosecution in the presentation of their case. This leaves an odd anomaly in English law in respect of cases heard in the magistrates' court: while there is a right to unused material by virtue of the CPIA 1996, there is no obligation on the prosecution to disclose to the defence in advance of the trial the statements of witnesses upon whom they intend to rely. In relation to either-way offences the Magistrates' Court (Advance Information) Rules 1985 require the prosecution to furnish a summary of their case or copies of witness statements to the defence in order to determine the mode of trial. After that stage, or in summary only offences, no such obligation arises. While voluntary disclosure is often provided by the prosecution, a refusal to do so is likely to be a violation of the Article 6 principles of equality of arms and the specific provision of Article 6(3)b that the accused be provided with adequate facilities for the preparation of his defence.

4. Sensitive material

4–54 English law allows the prosecution, in the public interest, not to disclose to the defence all of the evidence or material in its possession. The principle of public interest immunity is retained in the CPIA. Examples are given of the sort of material which might fall into that category, and complex provisions are created for the judicial determination of such an issue. At its most extreme level, the defence may not even be aware that an application to withhold material in the public interest has been made.

To date, no decision has been reached by the Court on the fairness of such procedures. Three applications were declared admissible by the Commission in September 1997 and await consideration by the Court (*Jasper v. U.K.*, 27052/95; *Rowe and Davis v. U.K.*, 28901/95; *Fitt v. U.K.*, 29777/96). However, in *Edwards v. U.K.* (1992) Series A, No. 247–B; 15 E.H.R.R. 433, where the Court did not address the issue of public interest immunity, a dissenting judgment from Judge Pettiti held that once criminal proceedings were underway the whole of the evidence should be communicated to the defendant "in order to be the subject of adversarial argument".

4–55 Complete access to prosecution materials, irrespective of their sensitivity, is highly unlikely. However, it is worth noting the robust decision of the Court in the case of *Chahal v. U.K.*, R.J.D. 1996–V 1831; 23 E.H.R.R. 413. That case involved the withholding of sensitive material in proceedings for judicial review of an order for deportation. The issue was somewhat starker than in criminal proceedings, in that the Divisional Court itself was not given access to the sensitive material, still less was the applicant allowed to review it. The Court found a violation of Article 5(4) and stated that, when the use of confidential material was unavoidable, "this does not mean that the national authorities can be free from effective control by the domestic courts whenever they choose to assert that national security and terrorism are involved." The Court also referred, apparently favourably, to the Canadian system of resolving such issues in deportation proceedings in which sensitive evidence is considered in the absence of the applicant and his or her representative, but with a security-cleared counsel acting on their behalf. It may be the case that the Court is less ready to accept untested claims of sensitivity of material than the U.K. executive or courts, and that further development of the procedure governing disclosure of such material will follow from the Act.

I. EVIDENTIAL RULES

4–56 Article 6 does not seek to establish any uniform set of evidential rules to be followed in national courts. This would be impossible in view of the differing legal systems of the signatories to the Convention. However, the Court has considered particular rules of evidence within certain systems and whether the exercise of those rules in any given case has caused the trial to be unfair.

1. Assessment of the evidence

4–57 The Court will rarely examine the evidence which was put before the national court and substitute its own assessment of the facts. The Court's task is to ascertain whether the proceedings, including the way in which the evidence was taken, were fair (*Edwards v. U.K.* (1992), above).

2. Illegally-obtained evidence

4–58 Because Article 6 does not lay down any rules governing the admissability of evidence, which is a matter for regulation by the domestic courts, the admission of evidence which has been obtained unlawfully under national law will not necessarily breach the right to a fair hearing. The Court will consider whether the admission of the evidence caused the trial as a whole to be unfair. Thus in *Schenk v. Switzerland* (1988) Series A, No. 140; 13 E.H.R.R. 242, which involved the use in evidence of an unlawfully obtained recording of a telephone conversation, the Court held that the admission of the recording was not unfair: the defendant had been able to challenge the use of the tape and there was other evidence upon which the conviction was based. (It should be said, however, that intrusive surveillance techniques may breach Article 8 — the right to respect for private and family life.)

Evidence obtained as a result of "maltreatment with a view to extracting a confession" will almost certainly breach Article 6(1), and may also comprise inhuman or degrading treatment contrary to Article 3 (*Austria v. Italy* (1963) 6 Y.B. 740).

4–59 Currently, under English law the admission of disputed evidence is governed by the provisions of PACE 1984, ss.76 and 78. Section 76 deals with confessions obtained by oppression or in consequence of anything said or done likely to render the confession unreliable; section 78 is used to challenge the admission of any evidence likely to have such an adverse effect on the fairness of the proceedings that the court ought not to admit it. Under the latter provision the court must look at the circumstances in which the evidence was obtained. Section 78 has been invoked to challenge the admission of evidence of identification procedures, of confessions, and that obtained from illegal searches. The basis of the challenge is frequently, but not exclusively, that the evidence has been obtained in breach of PACE Codes of Practice. As under Article 6, the court is not considering whether the evidence was obtained unlawfully or irregularly, but whether its admission will have a detrimental effect on the fairness of the proceedings (*R. v. Khan (Sultan)* [1996] 3 W.L.R. 162).

Section 2(1) of the Act requires that a court, when determining a question which has arisen under the Act in connection with a Convention right, must take into account Strasbourg jurisprudence. In addition, section 7(1) of the Act will allow a victim of an unlawful act by a public authority to rely on Convention rights in any legal proceedings. Taken together, these provisions will allow a defendant to argue that disputed evidence has been obtained not only in circumstances where sections 76 or 78 apply, but also in breach of one or more Articles of the Convention, such as Article 3 (prohibition against inhuman or degrading treatment) or Article 8 (respect for private life). Furthermore, the national court will have to consider the Strasbourg case law in deciding whether to admit the disputed evidence.

3. Other forms of evidence

4–60 The Court has considered the admissibility of hearsay evidence and of anonymous informants under Article 6(1). Applications of this nature tend also to be made under the specific guarantee of Article 6(3)d, the right to examine witnesses, and are dealt with at paragraphs 4–105—4–108.

It is not a breach of Article 6(1) for a defendant's previous convictions to be disclosed during the trial (*X v. Austria* (1967) 23 C.D. 31). Neither is it a violation of the right to a fair hearing for the evidence of an accomplice who has been provided with immunity from prosecution to be admitted, provided a suitable warning is given to the jury (*X v. U.K.* (1976) 7 D.R. 115).

J. SELF-INCRIMINATION

1 61 The right to a fair hearing invoked by Article 6(1) includes a privilege against self incrimination which "lies at the heart of the notion of a fair procedure under Article 6" (*Murray (John) v. U.K.* (1996) 22 E.H.R.R. 29). The rationale for this principle lies in protecting the accused from improper compulsion by the authorities and thereby preventing potential miscarriages of justice. The prosecution must prove its case without relying on evidence obtained by coercion or oppression of the accused.

The principle is usually considered under Article 6(1). However, it is closely linked with the presumption of innocence guaranteed by Article 6(2) and applications are commonly made under both provisions.

In the case of *Funke v. France* (1993) Series A, No. 256–A; 16 E.H.R.R. 297 the applicant was under investigation for customs offences which he was alleged to have committed. In the course of those investigations he was ordered to disclose documentation, and failed to do so. Although no substantive proceedings were brought, he was convicted and fined for failing to disclose materials during the investigation. The Court concluded that there had been a breach of the applicant's right not to incriminate himself: his conviction had been an attempt by the authorities to compel him to produce the evidence of other offences he had allegedly committed, which the customs officers had been unable to obtain themselves.

4–62 Similar issues arose in *Saunders v. U.K.*, R.J.D. 1996–VI 2044; 23 E.H.R.R. 313. In that case the applicant was obliged to answer questions put to him by Department of Trade and Industry officials investigating unlawful share dealing. By virtue of the Companies Act 1985, s.434 a failure to co-operate with the inspectors could lead to criminal sanctions the equivalent of a conviction for contempt of court. The answers given were subsequently relied on by the prosecution at the applicant's criminal trial. The Court criticised the use of powers of compulsory questioning and found that there had been a violation of the applicant's right to a fair hearing. This was such a marked departure from the basic principles of a fair procedure that it could not be justified by considerations of the complexity of corporate fraud or the public interest in thorough investigation of such offences.

In *Saunders v. U.K.* (1997) above, the Court was unwilling to decide whether the privilege against self-incrimination is an absolute right or whether infringements of it may be justified in some circumstances (*cf. Murray (John) v. U.K.*, above). The Court reached its decision on consideration of all the facts of the case, in particular the use made of the material obtained by self-incrimination and its importance to the prosecution case. This reluctance to state the absolute principle is a theme of the decisions of the Court in many cases concerning the general fair trial provisions, and it is coupled with a wish to consider the full circumstances of each case individually in order to determine whether the applicant received a fair trial.

1. The right to silence

4–63   Article 6(1) has specific application to the provisions governing the right of an accused to remain silent under police questioning or at trial. Sections 34–37 of the Criminal Justice and Public Order Act 1994 ("CJPOA") create a sanction on defendants who fail to mention facts when questioned by police that they later rely on at in their defence (section 34); who fail to answer questions about objects, substances or marks on themselves, or their presence at a certain place, at the time of their arrest (sections 36–37); or who fail to give evidence at trial (section 35). In each case, the court or jury can draw such inferences from the failure as appear proper.

This issue was considered by the Court in *Murray (John) v. U.K.*, above, in that case in the context of the anti-terrorist provisions of the Criminal Evidence (Northern Ireland) Order 1988, the precursor of sections 34, 36 and 37 of the CJPOA 1994. The applicant was arrested and interviewed, having been cautioned that adverse inferences could be drawn from his failure to account for his presence at the scene of the offence. He was denied access to a solicitor for 48 hours and refused to answer questions. At his trial the judge, sitting without a jury, drew adverse inferences from his silence.

4–64   The Court held that the denial of access to a solicitor had led to a violation of Article 6(1) and 6(3)c, but, by a majority, it held that the drawing of adverse inferences did not breach the right to a fair trial. The Court stated that it would be incompatible with Article 6 for a conviction to be based solely or mainly on an accused person's silence (a protection also contained in CJPOA, s.38(3)) or for the failure to answer questions to be an offence or a contempt of court by itself. However, the failure to answer questions may be taken into account in assessing the persuasiveness of the prosecution case. The Court again considered the full circumstances of the case and the fairness of the trial as a whole. It was at pains to point to a number of safeguards within the interrogation and trial procedures: that the accused was warned of the consequences of refusing to answer questions; that silence alone could not establish guilt; and that the question of whether to draw inferences was decided by a judge, who gave reasons for his decisions which could be subject to scrutiny by the appellate courts.

The conclusions to be drawn from *Murray* are not entirely obvious. It would seem that evidence gathered from a suspect while he is being denied access to legal advice, will be a breach of Article 6. The right to silence is not absolute, however, and the drawing of inferences will not necessarily be unfair if other safeguards are in place to ensure a fair trial. In *Murray* the Court drew considerable reassurance from the fact that the whole question of inferences was considered by a judge sitting alone. In the crown court, in England and Wales, a jury decides whether to draw inferences, what to infer, and the weight they will attach to those inferences. One of the Court's safeguards in *Murray* is therefore absent, and the Court may reach a conclusion on the right to silence more favourable to the defendant in a criminal trial. In late 1997 a number of cases on the right to silence, both from Northern Ireland and from the mainland, were declared admissible on their merits by the Commission (*Hamill v. U.K.* 22656/93; *Murray [Kevin] v. U.K.* 22384/93; *Quinn v. U.K.* (1997) 23 E.H.R.R. C.D. 41).

2. Scope of the privilege

4–65 The privilege against self-incrimination is essentially concerned with the wishes of an individual to remain silent. It does not extend to the use of powers to obtain evidence independant of the will of the suspect (for instance, breath, blood, fingerprints or other bodily samples, or material acquired following the execution of a search warrant) (*Saunders v. U.K.*, above). Provisions such as sections 61–63 of PACE, allowing for the forceable taking of fingerprints and samples, do not breach the privilege against self-incrimination.

3. Compulsory admissions

4–66 In *Saunders* the Court did not hold that the practice of compulsory questioning (section 434 of the Companies Act 1985), under sanction of criminal penalties for failure to co-operate, was in itself unfair. The use made of the answers so obtained, however, breached the defendant's right to a fair criminal trial. Certain other statutes provide criminal penalties for a failure to answer an investigator's questions: section 178 of the Financial Services Act 1986, for instance, mirrors the provisions of the Companies Act in relation to insider dealing; section 366 of the Insolvency Act 1986 provides for the compulsory examination of a bankrupt by the receiver. The admission in a criminal trial of answers obtained in such compulsory examinations is likely to be a breach of Article 6(1). In *R. v. Morrisey; R. v. Staines* (1997) 2 Cr.App.R. 426, the Court of Appeal accepted that sections 177 and 178 of the FSA, which specifically allow for evidence so obtained to be used in criminal proceedings, were incompatible with the Court's ruling in *Saunders*. However, it could not enforce a judgment of the Court which would render a U.K. statute ineffective. After the Act is in force, it is submitted that a declaration of incompatibility should be made.

K. INDEPENDENT AND IMPARTIAL TRIBUNAL ESTABLISHED BY LAW

4–67 The fair trial guaranteed by Article 6(1) must be heard before an "independent and impartial tribunal established by law." A considerable amount of Strasbourg case law deals with tribunals other than ordinary courts of law (for instance, prison boards of visitors — see *Campbell and Fell v. U.K.* (1984) Series A, No. 80; 7 E.H.R.R. 165). There are several recent decisions concerning the independence and impartiality of courts martial (*Findlay v. U.K.* 22107/93, 24 E.H.R.R. 221 — court martial not independent owing to central position of convening officer, to whom all other members of the court were subordinate; *Coyne v. U.K.*, R.J.D. 1997–V 1842 — confirmed *Findlay*, and the defects in the original proceedings could not be rectified on appeal).

The test for impartiality of a tribunal is twofold:

> "The existence of impartiality for the purpose of Article 6(1) must be determined according to a subjective test, that is on the basis of the personal conviction of a particular judge in a given case, and also according to an objective test, that is ascertaining whether the judge offered guarantees sufficient to exclude any legitimate doudt in this respect." (*Hauschildt v. Denmark* (1989) Series A, No. 154; 12 E.H.R.R. 266).

4–68 So far as the subjective test is concerned, the Court will operate under the presumption that a court is impartial unless there is proof of actual bias. Even strong statements of opinion by judges as to the accused's guilt have failed to satisfy the test of actual bias (*X v. U.K.* (1975) 3 D.R. 10).

The objective test will not be satisfied if the court fails to ensure that justice is seen to be done. Thus, financial or other interests in the outcome of a case should disqualify a tribunal member, unless the interest is disclosed and any objections are considered. Considerable Strasbourg case law deals with the position of judges who are involved in more than one function within a criminal prosecution. Much of this is irrelevant to the domestic criminal justice process. A judge hearing preliminary applications in a case, including making bail decisions, is unlikely to have his or her impartiality compromised, unless such decisions effectively amount to a preliminary finding of guilt (*Hauschildt v. Denmark*, above). Above all, it is the appearance of impartiality that is paramount.

1. Juries

4–69 The requirement for independence and impartiality applies equally to judges and juries, although the secrecy which surrounds juries" deliberations means that evidence of impropriety is rare.

In both *Gregory v. U.K.* (1998) 25 E.H.R.R. 577 and *Remli v. France* (1996) 22 E.H.R.R. 253, there was some evidence of racial bias on the part of a juror. *Remli* involved an overheard racist comment by a juror. The national court effectively took no action, stating that it was "not able to take note of events alleged to have occurred outside of its presence". The Court found that there had been a breach of Article 6(1) in that there was "an obligation on every national court to check whether, as constituted, it is 'an impartial tribunal' . . . where this is disputed".

In *Gregory*, the jury passed a somewhat gnomic note to the judge reading "jury showing racial overtones. 1 member to be excused". The trial judge invited submissions from counsel, and then gave a firm redirection to the jury reminding them to try the case according to the evidence and directing them that "any thoughts or prejudice of one form or another, for or against anybody, must be put out of [your] minds." The Court concluded that there had been no violation of Article 6(1) the trial judge having created sufficient safeguards to exclude any objectively justified doubts as to the impartiality of the jury.

In *Pullar v. U.K.* (1996) 22 E.H.R.R. 391, the applicant sought to challenge the impartiality of a jury on the basis that one member had worked for a firm from whom the applicant was alleged to have solicited money. The Court considered the circumstances of the jury member's employment (a junior employee who had now left the firm) and the safeguard of the judge's directions on assessment of evidence, and concluded that the court's impartiality could not be impugned.

The *Remli*, *Gregory* and *Pullar* cases indicate the extent to which the Court will consider all the circumstances of a trial when assessing the alleged impartiality of a court, and in particular the extent to which the judge can rectify possible defects by appropriate directions.

L. REASONED JUDGMENT

4–70   A further general requirement of a fair hearing is that the court gives reasons for its judgment. This is in order that the defendant may properly exercise his or her right of appeal (*Hadjianastassiou v. Greece* (1992) Series A, No. 252; 16 E.H.R.R. 219), and because both the defendant and the public as a whole have a legitimate interest in knowing the basis for any judgment.

Not all applications to the court require a full response. However, an application which, if successful, would decide the case will require a "specific and express" judgment (*Hiro Balani v. Spain* (1994) Series A, No. 303–B; 19 E.H.R.R. 565). Because of their nature, this requirement does not apply to jury trials. However, it would apply to summary trials, and the failure of many magistrates to give reasons for verdicts or submissions of no case to answer is questionable.

M. RIGHT TO A FAIR AND PUBLIC HEARING BEFORE A COURT

4–71   Article 6 guarantees the right of access to a court — "everyone is entitled to a fair and public hearing". Dispute about the scope of such access is likely to be rare within the criminal jurisdiction, since a criminal prosecution proceeds to a court hearing without requiring the co-operation of the defendant.

The Article also requires that judgment shall be pronounced publically, but allows that the press and public may be excluded from all or part of the trial if one of a number of risks attaches to a public hearing. These risks include a threat to national security, the interests of juveniles and where publicity would prejudice the interests of justice. Although the list is not open-ended, the categories are wide and allow for a variety of circumstances in which hearings in camera could be justified. The Commission has allowed that the screening of witnesses from the accused and the public, in circumstances where their voices could still be heard, did not interfere with the defendant's rights under Article 6(1) or 6(3)d (*X v. U.K.* (1993) 15 E.H.R.R. C.D. 113).

4–72 In this country, the principle of open justice is the basic rule, with hearings in camera, reporting restrictions and limited public access to the courts permissible if statute allows for this in particular circumstances. These include the trial or testimony of children (Children and Young Persons Act 1933, s.39), the reporting of committal proceedings or pre-trial hearings (Magistrates' Courts Act 1980, s.8; CPIA 1996, ss.37–41), and proceedings for offences under the Official Secrets Act (1920 and 1989). The court may also sit in camera if the administration of justice so requires (*Scott v. Scott* [1913] A.C. 417). Criminal courts in this country currently circumscribe the principle of open justice in a number of instances which would need to be justified in order not to breach Article 6(1). These include applications for bail in the Crown Court, which are routinely heard in chambers.

In order for the national court to justify exclusion of press and public where publicity would prejudice the interests of justice, the court must both find "special circumstances" and only exercise its powers to the extent that it is strictly necessary. It is questionable that the automatic reporting restriction on legal argument in jury trials will always fulfill this criterion. In *Hodgson and others v. Imperial Tobacco Ltd and others* [1998] 1 W.L.R. 1056, the Court of Appeal summarised the position regarding hearings in chambers in the High Court, emphasising the possibility of access to the public and press where practical.

N. "REASONABLE TIME"

4–73 A basic element in the right to a fair trial is the presumption that the proceedings should be concluded within a reasonable time. This provision is closely connected to the right to be tried within a reasonable time guaranteed by Article 5(3). However, a different objective lies behind the two provisions: Article 5 ensures that accused persons are not remanded in custody for lengthy periods awaiting trial; Article 6 applies to civil and criminal proceedings and applies whether an accused person is in custody or at liberty. The purpose of Article 6 is to ensure that the administration of justice is carried out expeditiously, since delay "might jeopardise its effectiveness and credibility" (*H. v. France* (1989) Series A, No. 162–A; 12 E.H.R.R. 74).

In criminal cases the relevant time at which the procedings begin will usually be the moment that a suspect is charged. However, the Court has been prepared to accept that proceedings may start before the moment of formal charge, when the suspect is "substantially affected as a result of the suspicion against him" (*Deweer v. Belgium* (1980) Series A, No. 35; 2 E.H.R.R. 439). It is arguable that time may begin to run from the moment of first arrest where the a suspect has then been remanded on police bail for a lengthy period prior to charge (*X v. U.K.* (1979) 17 D.R. 122). When further counts are added against a defendant the relevant time will be when the first charge was laid.

4–74   The relevant time ceases to run at the conclusion of a criminal case, including the determination of any appeal or discontinuance by the prosecution (*Eckle v. FRG* (1982) Series A, No. 51; 5 E.H.R.R. 1; *Orchin v. U.K.* (1984) 6 E.H.R.R. 391).

Three general factors to be taken into account in determining whether proceedings have exceeded a reasonable period will be the complexity of the case, the conduct of the applicant and the conduct of the relevant authorities. There are no strict or absolute time limits, each case must be assessed in the light of its particular circumstances.

The approach to be adopted in considering those circumstances was set out in a number of early cases:

Complexity: factors which may add complexity to a case could include legal issues, the volume of evidence or number of defendants and difficulties in securing evidence (*Neumeister v. Austria* (1968) Series A, No. 8; 1 E.H.R.R. 91; *Eckle v. FRG* (1982) Series A, No. 51; 5 E.H.R.R. 1). Substantial delays caused by an attempt to have two defendants tried together will not be justified (*Hentrich v. France* (1994) Series A, No. 296–A; 18 E.H.R.R. 440).

Conduct of the defendant: no breach of Article 6 will arise if the defendant himself has been responsible for the delay, for instance by absconding (*Girolami v. Italy* (1991) Series A, No. 196 E) or even by exercising his proper procedural rights, should those slow proceedings (*Konig v. FRG* (1978) Series A, No. 27; 2 E.H.R.R. 170).

Conduct of the authorities: the state is responsible for unjustifiable delays in the conduct of proceedings, whether these arise as a result of action or inaction on the part of the police, prosecuting authorities or the courts. It is the duty of the state "to organise [its] legal systems so as to allow the courts to comply with the requirements of Article 6(1)" (*Zimmermann and Steiner v. Switzerland* (1983) Series A, No. 66; 6 E.H.R.R. 17). Complaints of insufficient resources, excessive workloads or backlog of cases will not absolve the authorities from responsibility to process all cases expeditiously.

Finally, what amounts to unreasonableness will also depend on the number of stages the case has had to go through and the nature of the case: criminal cases should, in general, progress faster than civil ones, and cases where the defendant is in custody require special attention.

1. Speed of trial

4–75   Under domestic law, no defined time limits exist within which a criminal case must be heard.

The Prosecution of Offenders Act 1985, s.22 allows the Secretary of State to set time limits for the completion of preliminary stages of the proceedings in cases in which the defendant is in custody on remand. These time limits do not strictly affect the hearing of the case, but merely the length of time during which the defendant may be kept in custody. The effect of non-compliance by the prosecution is that the defendant will be granted bail. A court may extend the time limits if it is satisfied that there is good and sufficient cause for so doing and that the prosecution has acted with all due expedition. In opposing such an application by the prosecution, the defence may now also rely on the guarantee under Article 5(3) preventing detention on remand beyond a reasonable time (*cf.* *Stogmuller* (1969) Series A, No. 9; 1 E.H.R.R. 155; *Neumeister*, above; *Wemhoff* (1968) Series A, No. 7; 1 E.H.R.R. 55).

Under the Act, Article 6(1) may be cited by the defence upon a prosecution application for an adjournment, for instance when not ready to commit to the Crown Court or when not ready for trial. It should be noted that the operation of Article 6(1) will only assist the defence. It does not provide a corresponding obligation on the defendant to prepare his case promptly.

4–76   In accordance with Strasbourg case law, in certain cases an application for an extension of time limits could take into account periods before the defendant was charged, where he was substantially affected by the suspicion against him. Such a situation might occur where a suspect had lost his job as a result of police investigation.

It is submitted that the prosecution should not be entitled to rely on explanations involving staff shortages or administrative problems in the face of defence arguments under Article 6(1). If the delay is unjustifiable in that it has not arisen as a result of the complexity of the case or the actions of the defendant, then the administrative difficulties of the prosecuting authorities ought to be irrelevant.

The application of the reasonable time guarantee to all stages of a criminal case means that it may be relevant in circumstances where the jury are unable to reach a decision. Prolonging the case by requesting a retrial might lead to a violation of Article 6(1). Such an argument could support an abuse of process application and would certainly support any representations made to the prosecution not to proceed.

When looking at individual cases decided by the Court, it is possible to conclude that justice in our national criminal courts is relatively swift (see, for instance, *Ferrantelli and Santangelo v. Italy* (1997) 23 E.H.R.R. 288 — 16 years' delay in a murder trial held to breach Article 6(1); or *Ringeisen v. Austria* (1971) Series A, No. 13; 1 E.H.R.R. 455 — over five years to conclude a complicated fraud trial and appeal, not considered to be an undue delay). By domestic standards the Court has not been generous to applicants in its decisions on judgment within a reasonable time, and the majority of its decisions have involved complicated or unusual cases that have taken a number of years to conclude. Following the Act, however, it must follow that the principles of Strasbourg case law apply to all manner of domestic cases, large or small. The fact that the Court has rarely considered modest cases, or the fact that some European jurisdictions are more tardy than our own in processing criminal cases, should not affect the operation of the principles in national courts.

O. PRESUMPTION OF INNOCENCE — ARTICLE 6(2)

4–77   Article 6(2) enshrines the basic right that "everyone charged with a criminal offence shall be presumed innocent until proved guilty by law". The general principle is set out in the case of *Barberà, Messegué and Jabardo v. Spain* (1988) Series A, No. 146; 11 E.H.R.R. 360:

"When carrying out their duties, the members of the court should not start with the preconceived idea that the accused has committed the offence charged; the burden of proof is on the prosecution, and any doubt should benefit the accused".

This presumption is an overriding obligation on the court, standing independent of the other, often more specific, obligations imposed by Article 6. Thus, proceedings in which all the other rights of the accused are observed may be unfair if the presumption of innocence is not maintained.

The rights conferred by Article 6(2) have close links with the privilege against self-incrimination, since the presumption of innocence presents the prosecution with the burden of proving the case, without assistance from the defendant (*cf. Saunders v. U.K.*, above).

1. Scope of the presumption

4–78   For obvious reasons, the presumption of innocence applies only to those charged with a criminal offence (*cf.* paragraphs 4–46 and 4–47). It does not apply to those being *investigated* for criminal offences, and thus provides no specific rights to those under police interrogation or subjected to identification procedures (*X v. FRG* (1971) 38 C.D. 77).

The presumption applies until the final determination of guilt or innocence, including proceedings on appeal against conviction. However, it does not apply to the sentencing stage of proceedings. In sentencing a convicted defendant, a judge or magistrate may take into account matters which were not put before the court in evidence, for instance his previous convictions or personal history (*Engel v. Netherlands* (1976) Series A, No. 22; 1 E.H.R.R. 647).   While Strasbourg case law has applied Article 6(2) to a number of different areas of criminal procedure, its main field of application is at the trial stage and, more particularly, the basis upon which a conviction is founded. The conviction must be based on the evidence, which itself must be sufficiently strong to rebut the presumption of innocence. The defendant must then be given the opportunity to challenge the evidence against him (*Austria v. Italy* (1963) 6 Y.B. 740). What evidence is required, then, to establish guilt?

2. The evidential requirement

(a) Reverse onus cases

4–79   Although the general burden of proof lies first and foremost with the prosecution, there will not necessarily be a breach of Article 6(2) if the burden is transferred to the defendant when he is seeking to establish a defence. In *Lingens and Leitgens v. Austria* (1981) 26 D.R. 171 the Commission considered the position in a case of criminal defamation, where the burden of showing that the statements at issue were true, and therefore establishing a defence, lay with the defendants. It found that the general burden of proof had not been shifted in that all the elements of the offence, except for the truth of the statements at issue, had to be proved in the normal way by the prosecutor. It would be unfair to impose upon the prosecution the burden of proving a negative; and part of the purpose of the Austrian legislation was to impose a standard of care on those making potentially defamatory statements not only to ensure such statements were true, but to make sure that what was being said could also be proven as true. Reversing the onus in one particular did not necessarily breach Article 6(2).

There has been relatively little Strasbourg case law on the burden of proof. The Court has made general statements of principle, but has considered few specific examples.

4–80   In domestic legislation a number of offences contain "reverse onus" clauses. Under the Prevention of Crime Act 1953, s.1, it is an offence for a person to have in a public place an offensive weapon, unless he has "lawful authority or reasonable excuse, the proof whereof shall lie with him". Similarly it is a defence to a number of offences under the Misuse of Drugs Act 1971 if the defendant can prove that he "neither believed nor suspected nor had reason to suspect that the substance in question was a controlled drug" (MDA 1971, s.28(3)b). In each instance the prosecution still bears the burden of establishing all elements of the offence. The "reverse onus" clause provides a defence which the prosecution may rebut if they have sufficient evidence.

The most common "reverse onus" clause encountered in national courts is contained in the Magistrates' Courts Act 1980, s.101, which provides that where a person relies in his defence on any exception, exemption, proviso, excuse or qualification the burden of proving its existance shall lie with the defendant. This section relieves the prosecution of the impossible burden of proving a negative in many common situations, for instance, proving that a driver did not hold a certificate of insurance. In this case it would seem that the general burden of proof has shifted. In an allegation of driving without insurance the prosecution merely have to prove that the defendant was driving in circumstances where insurance was required; thereafter it is for the defendant to prove that he was insured. In such a situation, the court will not find for the defendant in a case of any doubt. But for the *Lingens* approach, section 101 might breach Article 6(2), albeit with absurd consequences should the full burden of proof fall on the prosecution in such cases.

The standard of proof upon the defendant in reverse onus cases in domestic law will always be the civil standard, on the balance of probabilities (*R. v. Carr-Briant* [1943] K.B. 607). To an extent, this protects the defendant from a complete reversal of the presumption of innocence and makes it less likely that a reverse onus clause will breach Article 6(2).

(b) Rebuttable presumptions

4–81   Article 6(2) does not prevent the operation of rebuttable presumptions of law or fact that may operate against the defendant. However, it may limit such presumptions. The Court stated in *Salabiaku v. France* (1988) Series A, No. 141–A; 13 E.H.R.R. 379:

> "Article 6(2) does not regard presumptions of fact or law provided for in the criminal law with indifference. It requires States to confine them within reasonable limits which take into account the importance of what is at stake and maintain the rights of the defence."

That case dealt with the presumption under French law that a person bringing prohibited goods through customs was guilty of smuggling them, rebuttable by the defence that it was impossible for him to have known the nature of the goods. The Court held that the existence of the possible defence meant that the presumption did not breach Article 6(2). Other presumptions held not to have infringed Article 6 include the Sexual Offences Act 1956, s.30(2) (the presumption that a man living with a prostitute was knowingly living off her earnings (*X v. U.K.* (1972) 42 C.D. 135); and the presumption that liability for a car-parking fine should be based on the ownership of the vehicle (*Duhs v. Sweden* (1990) 67 D.R. 204).

It would seem from the judgment in *Salabiaku* that the Court was taking into account the principle of proportionality (see generally paragraph 2–44 and following, above) in considering infringements on the presumption of innocence. A breach of Article 6(2) may occur more readily in the case of a grave offence where the potential penalty is more severe than in a trivial matter.

A rebuttable presumption operating in favour of a defendant (for instance, the presumption of *doli incapax*) is unaffected by Article 6(2), protecting, as it does, the defendant's innocent status.

(c) Strict liability

4–82 Article 6(2) does not prohibit offences of strict liability, the state being free to define what form of *mens rea* is appropriate to any particular offence. The prosecution, however, must retain the obligation to prove other elements of the offence (*Henry Bates v. U.K.* (1996) App. No. 26280/95).

(d) Standard of proof

4–83 The presumption of innocence does not require that the defendant be proved guilty beyond reasonable doubt. The court must, however, base its judgment on "direct or indirect evidence sufficiently strong in the eyes of the law to establish [the defendant's] guilt" (*Austria v. Italy* (1963) 6 Y.B. 740).

3. Criminal record

4–84 The presumption of innocence will not be violated when the previous criminal convictions of an accused person are brought to the attention of the judge or court prior to conviction (*X v. Austria* (1966) 9 Y.B. 550). In many European jurisdictions disclosure of the defendant's criminal record before conviction is entirely commonplace. Thus, the operation of section 1(f) of the Criminal Evidence Act 1898, and the loss of a defendant's "shield", will not breach Article 6(2).

4. Pretrial publicity

4–85 A fair trial will be impeded, and the presumption of innocence thwarted, by public statements made prior to the defendant's trial which assert his guilt. The danger of such statements is that they "encourage the public to believe [the defendant] guilty and, secondly, prejudge the assessment of the facts by the competent judicial authority" (*Allenet de Ribemont v. France* (1995)

Series A, No. 308; 20 E.H.R.R. 557). This is clearly the case when statements are made by public officials, and it may also impose an obligation upon the state to regulate assertions of guilt in the private press (*X v. U.K.* (1969) 30 C.D. 70).

While pre-trial allegations that a defendant is guilty of a criminal offence will breach Article 6(2), it is proper for the authorities to assert a suspicion or report that a suspect has been arrested or charged (*Krause v. Switzerland,* (1978) 13 D.R. 73).

5. Judicial bias and comment

4–86   While the adverse comments of officials may prejudice a fair trial, bias against the defendant by the judge or jury will by its nature breach the presumption of innocence.

> "The presumption of innocence will be violated if, without the accused's having previously been proved guilty according to law, a judicial decision concerning him reflects an opinion that he is guilty" (*Barberà, Messegué and Jabardo v. Spain* (1988) Series A, No. 146; 11 E.H.R.R. 360 at 392).

There is a clear overlap here with the requirement under Article 6(1) for "an independant and impartial tribunal" (*cf.* paragraph 4–67, above).

A breach of Article 6(2) may occur, however, in circumstances where there is no risk that the outcome of the trial will be prejudiced. If a suggestion is made that a successful defendant was in fact guilty of the offence there will be a violation of the presumption of innocence.

6. Costs

4–87   The right to a fair trial will be breached if courts make pronouncements hinting at a defendant's guilt after he has been acquitted. This has obvious implications for the matter of costs. Although nothing in Article 6 grants a successful defendant a right to his legal or other costs, the proceedings in which the question of costs fall to be determined form part of the trial and the presumption of innocence continues to apply. If an accused person has been acquitted, a refusal to award costs based on suspicions regarding his innocence is not admissible. In *Sekanina v. Austria* (1993) Series A, No. 266–A; 17 E.H.R.R. 221 the court considering costs improperly took into account a range of suspicions against the successful defendant which had not been dispelled during the trial and the jury's majority verdict. This was held to offend his presumption of innocence and was a breach of Article 6(2).

In domestic law, an order for the defendant's costs will normally be made in the case of an acquittal (*cf.* Prosecution of Offences Act 1985, s.16). However, there is a discretion for the magistrates or judge not to award costs if there are "positive reasons for not doing so". Such reasons may be found if "there is ample evidence to support a conviction but the defendant is acquitted on a technicality which has no merit" (Practice Direction (Costs in Criminal Proceedings) 93 Cr.App.R. 89). A court would need to be careful in such a case not to breach Article 6.

Article 6(2) does not prevent a court from voicing suspicions about a defendant's guilt where the proceedings have concluded without a final decision on the merits of the accusation, for instance, where the charge was withdrawn. Such a situation does not confer on the defendant a right to re-imbursement of his legal costs. However, if he has not been given any opportunity to exercise the rights of the defence, Article 6(2) may be breached where the reasons given for the refusal of costs amount to a determination of guilt (*Leutscher v. Netherlands* (1997) 24 E.H.R.R. 181).

P. SPECIFIC RIGHTS — ARTICLE 6(3)

4–88 Article 6(3) provides a number of specific rights which allow the defendant to prepare and conduct his trial on equal terms with the prosecuting authorities. These particular rights are components of the more general guarantees to a fair trial afforded by Article 6(1), in particular the equality of arms principle. Treatment of a defendant which does not breach one of the specific rights of Article 6(3), may nevertheless offend against the principle of a fair trial, and be held to breach the overall guarantee of Article 6(1).

The rights set out in Article 6(3) apply only to persons charged with criminal offences (*cf.* paragraphs 4–46—4–47, above). A criminal charge will continue throughout any appeal process and some aspects of Article 6(3) are therefore applicable to the appellate courts.

1. Right to be informed of the accusation

4–89 The first guarantee for the accused established by Article 6(3) is the right "to be informed promptly, in a language he understands and in detail, of the nature and cause of the accusation against him."

This guarantee is similar in form to Article 5(2), under which a person must be informed of the reasons for their arrest. However, the purpose of the guarantee is different: information must be provided under Article 5(2) in order that the arrested person may challenge their detention; under Article 6(3) it allows the defendant to start preparing his or her defence.

(a) "In detail"

4–90 The requirement that the accused be informed in detail of the nature and cause of the accusation would suggest some form of discloure of evidence by the prosecution. The Strasbourg authorities have not, however, interpreted this phrase broadly. The accused must be informed of the offence with which he is being charged and also the facts which support the allegation, but it is not necessary that he be furnished with the evidence against him. In the case of *Brozicek v. Italy* (1989) Series A, No. 167; 12 E.H.R.R. 371, the Court held that the required information should:

> "list the offences of which [the defendant] was accused, state the place and date thereof, refer to the relevant Articles of the Criminal Code and mention the name of the victim".

The level of detail required by the Indictments Act 1915, s.3 (or the Magistrates' Courts Act 1980, and Rules, in relation to the laying of an information) would appear to fulfil the requirements of Article 6(3)a.

4–91 The prosecution may alter the charges at any stage of the proceedings so long as the defendant is properly notified of the changes (*Ofner v. Austria* (1960) 3 Y.B. 322). This might suggest that the return by a jury of an alternative verdict (as allowed by section 6(3) of the Criminal Law Act 1967) might breach Article 6(3)a, since the defendant is unlikely to have been formally notified of the changes. However the Court has taken a broad approach to the situation in *De Salvador Torres v. Spain* (1997) 23 E.H.R.R. 601, where the applicant had been convicted of an aggravated form of the offence with which he was charged. The Court held that the aggravating element was an intrinsic part of the original accusation and was known to the applicant from the outset of the proceedings; his rights under Article 6(3)a had not been breached. This Article may, however, assist the defence in opposing a prosecution application for a late amendment to an indictment where the substance of the case against the defendant has changed (Indictments Act 1915, s.5, and see *R. v. Johal and Ram* (1972) 56 Cr.App.R. 348).

The duty to inform the defendant of the nature of the allegation applies also to hearings on the facts ("Newton hearings") In *De Salvador Torres v. Spain*, above, the Court found that the applicant must have been aware of the underlying factual element that eventually constituted a aggravating feature in his case. Nevertheless, the Court was willing to entertain an application of this nature under Article 6(3)a. All of the specific guarantees of Article 6(3) would appear to apply to hearings on the facts.

(b) "Promptly"

4–92 The requirement under Article 6(3)a that information be given promptly has not been fully considered by the Strasbourg authorities. The overall purpose of the provision is to enable the defendant to prepare his defence, and if information is provided in time for this to be achieved the requirement will be fulfilled. A charge or summons served on the defendant once a decision has been made to commence proceedings (assuming that it properly identifies the nature and cause of the allegation) would appear to suffice.

(c) "In a language he understands"

4–93 The information must be provided to the defendant in a language that he understands. Thus in *Brozicek v. Italy*, above, the applicant had notified the authorities that he did not understand Italian and had requested a translation of the "judicial notification" which commenced proceedings against him. No such translation was forthcoming and he was convicted in his absence. This was held to be a breach of Article 6(3)a, the authorities being under a duty to provide an appropriate translation unless they could establish that the defendant had sufficient command of the language to understand the information provided.

There is no requirement that the information be in writing (*Kamasinski v. Austria* (1989) Series A, No. 168; 13 E.H.R.R. 36), and the presence of an interpreter at a police station providing an oral translation of the charge will satisfy Article 6(3)a.

If a defendant has legal representation, it is sufficient that the information is provided in a language that the lawyer understands (*X v. Austria* (1975) 2 D.R. 68).

2. Right to prepare a defence

4–94   Article 6(3)b grants to every defendant the right "to have adequate time and facilities for the preparation of his defence".

(a) Adequate time

4–95   On the one hand, the Convention grants a right to a defendant to a hearing within a reasonable time (Article 6(1)); on the other, it guarantees him adequate time to prepare a defence. Between these must lie an appropriate period from the commencement of a case to its final disposal. In a number of cases, the Strasbourg authorities have considered what constitutes an adequate amount of time for the preparation of a defence. Several factors may be taken into account including the complexity of the case (or lack of it), and the fact that the defendant is representing himself. If a lawyer is appointed it has been held to be proper to consider his or her workload, and to allow time for the appointment to be made. If a new lawyer is substituted, time should be allowed for further preparation of the case.

In practice, the decisions of the Court have not been generous in the grant of time to prepare cases. The unhappily regular occurrence of an advocate meeting their client just hours before the trial has not been found to breach Article 6(3)b (*X v. U.K.* (1971) 13 Y.D. 114). Nonetheless, reference to Article 6(3)b may assist defence lawyers in resisting the tendency of some magistrates' courts to list simple cases for almost immediate summary trial; and it may assist in obtaining adjournments of appropriate length for the preparation of more complicated cases in all criminal courts. Finally, the power of both the magistrates' and Crown Court to deal summarily with contempts of court, without allowing the alleged offender time to prepare a defence, would appear to offend against Article 6(3)b (Contempt of Court Act 1981, s.12; Magistrates' Courts Act 1980, s.97(4)).

(b) "Adequate facilities"

4–96   The guarantee that the defendant be given adequate facilities for the preparation of his trial means that:

> "The accused must have the opportunity to organise his defence in an appropriate way without restriction as to the possibility to put all relevant defence arguments before the trial court, and thus to influence the outcome of the proceedings" (*Can v. Austria* (1985) Series A, No. 96; 8 E.H.R.R. 121).

The right to facilities is not limitless. Avenues that are unlikely to prove relevant to the accused's defence will be beyond the ambit of this guarantee.

However, the provision does place upon the authorities an obligation to assist the defendant in the preparation of his case. The defendant must, for example, be afforded access to the results of the authorities' investigations. The prosecution must "disclose to the accused all material evidence for or against the accused" (*Edwards v. U.K.* (1992) Series A, No. 247–B; 15 E.H.R.R. 417) (*cf.* paragraphs 4–50 to 4–55).

4-97 An inability to make sensible use of prosecution material that has been disclosed is likely to be a violation of Article 6(3)b. The Sexual Offences (Protected Material) Act 1997 limits the physical access of the defence, and particularly unrepresented defendants, to certain types of material in sexual offence cases. If this inhibits the defendant in the preparation of his case, it may be incompatable with the Convention.

"Adequate facilities" also include the ability to contact and communicate freely with a lawyer. This right is not absolute and the court has confirmed that restrictions on the right may be appropriate in certain circumstances (*Can v. Austria*, above). Access to a lawyer must include unsupervised consultation, so that confidential information may be passed between lawyer and client. The requirement of some high security prisons that visits by lawyers take place within the sight but not hearing of prison officers, and sometimes that such visits are recorded on video, may be a breach of Article 6(3)b.

It should be noted that this provision may have a bearing on the provision of legal aid (independently of Article 6(3)c), and in particular on payment for specific items of expenditure necessary to the preparation of a defence (for instance, experts' reports, investigations by agents or the cost of travel to interview witnesses). Legal aid practitioners may wish to cite this Article when applying for the costs of such items.

3. Right to representation and legal aid

4-98 Article 6(3)c guarantees an accused person two separate rights:

(i) to defend himself in person or through legal assistance of his own choosing, or

(ii) to be given free legal assistance when he has insufficient means to pay and the interests of justice so require.

These rights have been held to apply to pre-trial proceedings (particularly in appearances before examining judges in civil law jurisdictions) and to appeal proceedings, but not to applications for bail pending trial, the latter falling within Article 5.

(a) The right to defend oneself or have legal assistance

4-99 An accused person has the right to represent himself or to choose a lawyer to represent him. The court cannot prevent a person from being legally represented in criminal proceedings, assuming that he is willing to pay for the representation (*Pakelli v. FRG* (1983) Series A, No. 64; 6 E.H.R.R. 1). The choice is not unfettered: it may be proper to make regulations governing the qualifications necessary to practice in particular courts, and ethical considerations may properly bar individuals from acting in certain cases (*X v. U.K.* (1978) 15 D.R. 242). In general, however, the defendant's wishes should be respected. The right to defend oneself does not prevent the state from imposing a lawyer to assist the defendant if this is a stipulation of national law (*Croissant v. Germany* (1992) Series A, No. 237–B; 16 E.H.R.R. 135).

In the United Kingdom a failure to allow legal representation may result in a successful appeal against conviction, if the lack of representation may have prejudiced the defendant (*R. v. Harris* [1985] Crim.L.R. 244, where an adjournment to seek fresh representation was refused). Article 6(3) adds weight to this as a ground of appeal.

(b) The right to legal aid

4–100 Free legal assistance must be provided if the means of the defendant and the interests of justice so require it. Legal advice is not limited to cases where the defendant is not allowed to represent himself (*Pakelli v. FRG*, above)

Further, the assistance must be effective. The case of *Artico v. Italy* (1980) Series A, No. 37; 3 E.H.R.R. 1 illustrates an extreme example of ineffective legal assistance. In that case the lawyer appointed to represent the defendant under the national legal aid system declined to act, and the Italian court refused to appoint a replacement. The Italian government argued that it had fulfilled its obligations under Article 6(3)c once a lawyer had been appointed. The Court rejected this argument:

> "the Convention is intended to guarantee not rights that are theoretical or illusory but rights that are practical and effective; this is particularly so of the rights of the defence in view of the prominent place held in a democratic society by the right to a fair trial, from which they derive".

Legal assistance must be something worth having rather than a service that "might prove worthless". The Court of Appeal has held that a conviction may be quashed where an appellant may have suffered injustice because of "flagrantly incompetent advocacy" (*R. v. Ensor* (1989) 89 Cr.App.R. 139), a somewhat lower standard than the Strasbourg criteria, and more limited in that it applies to advocacy only.

4–101 Under Article 6(3)c a defendant who is granted free legal assistance does not have an unfettered choice of lawyer. The lawyer may be appointed or employed by the state, so long as he or she is an effective lawyer (*X v. U.K.* (1984) 6 E.H.R.R. 345). The Legal Aid Board is currently considering proposals to limit the numbers of solicitors paid under the legal aid scheme to represent criminal clients. Such a restriction on choice by the defendant would not appear to breach the rights set out in Article 6(3)c. Nor is there any breach by the decision of a Crown Court not to assign a Queen's Counsel in circumstances where effective representation can be provided by junior counsel alone.

Legal assistance must be given if the defendant's means are insufficient and the interests of justice so require. There is no definition within the Convention of "sufficient means" and there has been no case law that assists in determining a specific level of impoverishment which would always justify the grant of legal aid. In *Pakelli v. FRG*, above, the Court considered the fact that the applicant had been in custody for two years and that he had been "engaged in business on a small scale and his financial situation was modest". This offers little enlightenment.

In considering whether the interests of justice require the grant of legal aid, a number of factors must be considered. Foremost among these are the seriousness of the charge and the range of possible sentences open to the court. In *Quaranta v. Switzerland* (1991) Series A, No. 205, the mere fact that the offence carried a substantial prison sentence was enough in itself to warrant the provision of legal aid, without consideration of other criteria. Complexity of the case and the accused's personal inability to mount an effective defence are both important considerations. In the case of *Granger v. U.K.* (1990) Series A, No. 174; 12 E.H.R.R. 469 the Court found that the applicant:

> "Was not in a position fully to comprehend the pre-prepared speeches he read out or the opposing arguments submitted to the court. It is also clear that, had the occasion arisen, he would not have been able to make an effective reply to those arguments or to questions from the bench."

4–102 In considering the grounds for granting legal aid, the Court has held that it is not necessary for the applicant to show that he was actually prejudiced by the lack of representation. It would be impossible to prove that the result of the case would have been substantially different if presented by a lawyer. Instead, the court must consider whether it appears plausible in the particular circumstances that a lawyer would have assisted the defendant (*Artico v. Italy*, above).

It is a duty of the authorities to review any refusal of legal aid in the light of the defendant's case as it develops; unexpected complexities or increased gravity may merit the grant of legal assistance, notwithstanding that it has initially been refused (*Granger v. U.K.*, above).

In *Benham v. U.K.*, R.J.D. 1996–III 738; 22 E.H.R.R. 293, the Court held that the availability of legal advice under the Green Form scheme and the possibility of the appointment of a solicitor at court (the duty solicitor scheme) was insufficient to meet the requirements of Article 6(3)c. The case concerned committal to prison for non-payment of the community charge, involving a potential term of imprisonment of three months and demanded an understanding of the difficult concept of "culpable neglect". The Court considered that the interests of justice demanded that the applicant ought to have benefitted from free legal representation before the magistrates. This decision may prove relevant to current proposals to extend the scope of the Court Duty Solicitor Scheme, with the aim of reducing the numbers of defendants who are granted full legal aid. It is arguable that Article 6(3)c grants a right that is greater than mere extempory advocacy at court.

4. Right to cross-examine and call witnesses

4–103 Article 6(3)d concerns the right of an accused person to call and examine his own witnesses "under the same conditions as witnesses against him" and to cross-examine witnesses called by the prosecution. This right applies to the stage in proceedings in which guilt is being determined, which may include preliminary and investigative procedures in some European jurisdictions; it would not appear to apply to apply to bail applications (*Can v. Austria*, above).

(a) Defence witnesses

4–104 The right to call witnesses is not absolute, and the Strasbourg authorities have generally respected decisions of national courts as to the appropriateness of calling particular witnesses. The refusal of a court to hear a witness whose evidence was irrelevant, for instance, is unlikely to breach Article 6(3)b. In *Bricmont v. Belgium* (1989) Series A, No. 158; 12 E.H.R.R. 217 the Court held that a national court, when deciding not to call a witness who the defendant had requested, must give reasons for its decision. Failure to do so would be a violation of Article 6(3)d. Further, when a witness is called by the defence the court must take suitable steps to ensure attendance.

Protection of a witness, the fact that they may be mentally ill or that they may not have admissible evidence to give, are all good reasons for a court refusing to call witnesses. The interests of victims and witnesses as well as defendants, are protected by the Convention (*MK v. Austria* (1997) 24 E.H.R.R. C.D. 59).

It is vital, however, that witnesses who are called on behalf of the defendant receive similar treatment to that afforded to the prosecution (*Bonish v. Austria*, above). In this aspect Article 6(3)d is a specific instance of the equality of arms principle contained within Article 6(1). Many of the cases cited under Article 6(3)d arise from applications under both limbs of Article 6.

(b) Hearsay

4–105   The right of a defendant to examine or have examined witnesses against him effectively creates a general restriction on hearsay evidence. A considerable body of Strasbourg caselaw has developed which considers the position under Articles 6(1) and 6(3)d where a national court allows untested statements to be given in evidence. Such siuations have arisen where witnesses do not attend court, where the identities of undercover agents are protected, or where certain classes of person are excused from attesting. Consideration of the specific facts of these cases is of limited assistance to the practitioner in this country, owing to the different weight placed on pre-trial hearings and judicial investigation in civil jurisdictions. However, it is possible to extract a number of general principles often repeated throughout the judgments.

- The admissibility of evidence is primarily governed by the rules of domestic law. It is for the national courts to assess the evidence before them (*Barbera et al v. Spain*, above; *Asch v. Austria* (1991) Series A, No. 203–A; 15 E.H.R.R. 597).

- For the purposes of Article 6(3)d, the term "witness" has an autonomous meaning and includes persons who might have, but did not give, evidence in the national proceedings (*Ludi v. Switzerland* (1992) Series A, No. 238; 15 E.H.R.R. 173).

- "In principle, all the evidence must be produced in the presence of the accused at a public hearing with a view to adversarial argument" (*Kostovski v. Netherlands* (1989) Series A, No. 166; 12 E.H.R.R. 434). The court has stressed on many occasions that the hearing of witnesses should, in general, be adversarial in nature (*Barbera et al v. Spain*, above). However, it is not inconsistent with Article 6(1) or 6(3)d for statements to be read at trial provided that there is compliance with the rights of the defence, in particular giving the opportunity to examine and confront witnesses at an earlier stage in the proceedings

(*Unterppertinger v. Austria* (1986) Series A, No. 110; 13 E.H.R.R. 175). Such a provision is not particularly relevant to criminal procedure in this country, especially since the Criminal Procedure and Investigations Act 1996, Sched. 1, para. 4 has all but abolished live evidence and cross-examination in committal proceedings.

4–106 The Commission has held that Article 6(3)d is not violated by the admission of statements taken from a witness in Turkey who could not attend a trial in Germany, where the statements were taken and the witness examined in a Turkish court (*X v. FRG* (1988) 10 E.H.R.R. 521).

- The Court will look at the overall effect of the admission of the "hearsay" evidence on the fairness of the proceedings. If the lack of an opportunity to question witnesses has seriously prejudiced the defendant's position, there is likely to be a violation of Article 6(1) and 6(3)d. In a number of judgments emphasis has been placed on the importance of the evidence in question to the prosecution case. In *Kostovski* and *Unterpertinger*, above, the applicants convictions were based mainly on the disputed evidence, and in those circumstances the Court found that there had been violations of the right to a fair trial. In some more recent cases the Court has made mention of the disputed evidence being the only evidence against the accused, and it is now unclear which test the Court is applying (*Asch v. Austria*, above; *Saidi v. France* (1993) Series A, No. 261–C; 17 E.H.R.R. 251).

In considering the overall effect of the disputed prosecution evidence, it is clear that the Court has applied the principle of proportionality (see generally paragraphs 2–44 to 2–46) to the admission of the evidence. The Court has recognised that it is important to protect certain classes of witness and that it may be impossible to obtain "live" evidence in some circumstances. These difficulties should not always frustrate the prosecution of offenders. However, in *Saidi*, the Court stated that it was "aware of the undeniable difficulties of the fight against drug trafficing — in particular with regard to obtaining and producing evidence — . . . but such restrictions cannot justify restricting to this extent the rights of the defence".

(c) National law

4–107 The main provisions allowing the admission of disputed documentary hearsay into criminal proceedings are sections 23 and 24 of the Criminal Justice Act 1988. In short, these allow for:

(a) the admission of statements of persons who have died, are outside the United Kingdom, who cannot be found or who do not give evidence through fear or because they are being kept out of the way (section 23);

(b) the admission of statements made in the course of a business or profession (section 24).

In each case an application must be made by the party seeking to adduce the evidence without calling the witness. The judge or magistrate has a discretion not to admit the statement if to do so would be contrary to the interests of justice (sections 25 and 26). In deciding this the court must have regard to a number of issues, including the nature and authenticity of the document, whether the evidence is available elsewhere, its relevance, and the risk of unfairness to the accused in view of the impossibility of cross-examination.

Following the Act, national courts will have to consider the Strasbourg jurisprudence in addition to sections 23–26 when ruling on the admissibility of prosecution documentary hearsay. This is likely to reduce the frequency with which such statements are admitted. The legislation sets out specific circumstances in which documentary hearsay may be admitted; the Strasbourg caselaw provides an overall presumption against the admission of evidence in this form. Albeit somewhat inconclusive, the more detailed jurisprudence suggests that the greater the importance of the disputed evidence to the prosecution case, the stronger are the arguments that it should be excluded under Article 6.

It should be noted that nothing in Article 6 prevents the admission of undisputed hearsay evidence, for instance, statements served under section 9 of the Criminal Justice Act 1967.

(d) Anonymous witnesses

4–108 The use of anonymous witnesses by the prosecution is, prima facie, a breach of Article 6(3)d. The defendant should have the opportunity to challenge and question a prosecution witness and, if unaware of the identity of the witness, he would be unable to test their reliability or credibility (*Kostovski v. Netherlands* (1989) Series A, No. 166; 12 E.H.R.R. 434). However, the Court has recognised the necessity of protecting certain witnesses and the legitimacy of the police authorities' wishes to preserve the anonymity of undercover agents, so long as the rights of the defence are respected. Where anonymous police officers gave evidence from a separate room via a sound link without the defendant or his counsel being given the opportunity to observe the witnesses, the Court found a violation (*Van Mechelen v. Netherlands* (1998) 25 E.H.R.R. 647). However, where there were good reasons for maintaining the anonymity of witnesses and the defendant's counsel was able to question the witnesses, albeit not in the presence of the defendant himself, then the procedures were sufficient to establish a fair trial (*Doorson v. Netherlands* (1996) 22 E.H.R.R. 330).

5. Right to an interpreter

4–109 The right to the assistance of an interpreter for those who cannot understand or speak the language of the court is granted to the defendant from the time he is charged with an offence until the conclusion of the case, including any appeal.

The obligation upon the authorities is to provide a free interpreter; the right is not dependant on the means of the defendant, and nor can an unsuccessful defendant be ordered to pay towards the costs of the service, as this prospect might deter the defendant who needs assistance from requesting an interpreter (*Luedicke, Belkacem and Koc v. FRG* (1978) Series A, No. 29; 2 E.H.R.R. 149).

The Practice Direction (Costs in Criminal Proceedings) (1991) 93 Cr.App.R. 89 allows the court a discretion not to order the costs of an interpreter to be paid from central funds, the cost thereby falling on the defendant. This would appear to breach the principle set out in *Luedicke, Belkacem and Koc*, that the costs of an interpreter should always be paid by the court.

Although Article 6(3)e refers to the "language used in court", the right to the free assistance of an interpreter applies not merely to the trial itself, but extends to documentary materials and pre-trial hearings. However not all items of written evidence have to be translated for the defendant, only such as allow him to have knowledge of the case against him and to conduct his defence (*Kamasinski v. Austria* (1989) Series A, No. 168; 13 E.H.R.R. 36). This latter requirement probably encompasses the provision of an interpreter for communications between lawyer and client, since a proper defence requires that instructions be passed between the parties.

Q. SENTENCE AND AFTER

4–110   In principle the procedural rights guaranteed by Article 6 continue to apply at the sentencing stage of the case. Some will, of course, have no practical relevance to proceedings. The presumption of innocence is clearly not applicable to sentencing hearings, save perhaps hearings which establish the facts upon which a defendant is to be sentenced.

Issues relating to retroactive penalties are considered below at paragraph 4–114.

A particular form of punishment may breach Article 3 if it can be classed as "inhuman or degrading". The test here is relatively high, and includes treatment deliberately causing mental or physical suffering, which in the particular situation is unjustifiable. Treatment or punishment of an individual may be said to be degrading if it grossly humiliates him before others. While the conditions under which an individual has to serve their sentence might breach Article 3, it is unlikely that any sentence in itself which can be imposed by a court in this country would violate the right. When considering whether a punishment is inhuman or degrading regard must be had to the suffering which a person of the applicant's sex, age and health would be likely to endure (*cf. Tyrer v. U.K.* (1978) Series A, No. 26; 2 E.H.R.R. 1). Severe punishments imposed on young and susceptable people are therefore more likely to be inhuman or degrading. Use of the death penalty, except in wartime, is prohibited, because the Act gives effect to the Sixth Protocol.

Prisoners' rights are considered further in Part II below.

R. SUBSTANTIVE OFFENCES

4–111   In general, Convention rights and guarantees rarely affect the substance of national criminal law, though they are certainly generally applicable to the definition of crime. Individual states are at liberty to determine what constitutes criminal activity and to legislate accordingly, in so far as the definition or application of those offences does not breach a right granted under the Convention. Such breaches have not often been found. The Strasbourg authorities have considered certain specific U.K. offences and their relationship with human rights, and other, more recently created offences may come under examination in the near future. This section considers a few of the issues which could arise.

1. Retroactive offences

4–112   Article 7(1) states that:

> "No one shall be held guilty of any criminal offence on account of any act or omission which did not constitute a criminal offence . . . at the time when it was committed".

This principle prevents the retrospective creation of criminal offences, and ensures that an act can only be punished by law if it was declared to be an offence before the act was committed.

Article 7 will be breached when a person is found guilty for an act or omission which was not an offence at the time the act or omission occurred. This is so whether the offence was created by statute or by judicial interpretation of the existing law. In the latter situation, a grey area exists between what is merely clarification and adaptation of the law to new circumstances, and the extension of existing offences "to cover facts which previously clearly did not constitute a criminal offence" (*X Ltd and Y v. U.K.* (1982) 28 D.R. 77). The former is an allowable development of the common law; the latter a breach of Article 7.

4–113   In *SW and CR v. U.K.* (1995) Series A, No. 355–B and C; 21 E.H.R.R. 363 the Court considered the English law on marital rape, under which a husband had previously been granted immunity from prosecution for the rape of his wife on account of the consent thought to be inherent in the marriage contract. This common law immunity was confined by a number of judicial decisions, until finally it disappeared altogether (*R. v. R.* [1992] 1 A.C. 599) . The applicants argued that these offences had been committed prior to the changes in the law and that the prohibition against retrospective punishment applied. The Court found there to be no breach, in that the English courts were merely continuing a consistent line of caselaw, and:

> "Article 7 of the Convention cannot be read as outlawing the gradual clarification of the rules of criminal liability through judicial interpretation from case to case, provided that the resultant development is consistent with the essence of the offence and could reasonably be foreseen".

The Court also looked at the "fundamental objectives of the Convention", namely respect for human dignity and freedom, and set these against this particular arbitrary and anachronistic immunity from prosecution.

Changes in the law relating to ancillary matters, such as court procedure, the rules relating to detention on remand or the admissibility of evidence, are unlikely to be regarded as breaching Article 7 (*cf.* Commission's decision in *Quinn v. U.K.* (1997) 23 E.H.R.R. C.D. 41), to the effect that Article 7 was not concerned with retrospective application of rules of evidence).

2. Retroactive penalties

4–114   Article 7 also provides that no-one shall receive a heavier penalty than that which was applicable at the time the offence was committed. The Court considered the concept of a "penalty" in *Welsh v. U.K.* (1995) Series A, No. 307–A; 20 E.H.R.R. 247, which concerned the imposition of a confiscation order under the Drug Trafficking Offences Act 1986, a provision which came into force after these offences had been committed. The Court held that the order was a penalty, in that it had been imposed as a direct result of a conviction; it had a punative purpose; in fixing the amount to be forfeit, the judge could take into account the culpability of the accused; and imprisonment in default of payment was possible.

3. Offences of violence

(a) Consent

4–115   The extent to which the state should involve itself in the private lives of its citizens and impose criminal sanctions on personal, and particularly sexual, behaviour has been a continuing theme in Strasbourg caselaw (*cf. Dudgeon v. U.K.* Series A, No. 45; 4 E.H.R.R. 149; *Norris v. Ireland* Series A, No. 142; 13 E.H.R.R. 186) — criminalisation of homosexuality contrary to Article 8). As a rule, the Court has been prepared to give individual states a wide margin of appreciation (see generally paragraphs 2–41—2–43) to consider all public policy factors when deciding the role of consent in criminal law.

The question of consent arose as a defence to charges of assault contrary to sections 47 and 20 of the Offences Against the Person Act 1861 in *Lasky, Jaggard and Brown v. U.K.* (1997) 24 E.H.R.R. 39. The applicants had been involved in consensual acts of sado-masochistic sex causing actual physical injury. Their unsuccessful defence had been to try to extend the concept of consent to physical harm to include sexual acts. They complained to the Court that their convictions amounted to an unlawful and unjustifiable interference with their right to respect for their private lives, in breach of Article 8. The Court did not uphold their complaint, but found that the Contracting States enjoyed a wide margin of appreciation in considering the public policy factors which are ranged against the freedom of the individual, such as public safety, health and morality, and the rights of others. In this instance the Court held that it was proper for the State to regulate activities which involve the infliction of physical harm, and that the prosecution had not, therefore, breached Article 8(2).

(b) Self-defence

4–116   Article 2 guarantees that everyone's right to life shall be protected by law, and provides for certain circumstances where deprivation of life is not be regarded as breaching the Convention. Use of lethal force in self-defence, to effect arrest or to quell a riot, is allowed so long as the force is "no more than absolutely necessary." Article 2 allows less licence to use force than the relevant domestic provisions: the Criminal Law Act 1967, s.3, and the common law rules that it replicates. The former provides that "a person may use such force as is reasonable in the prevention of crime, or in effecting or assisting the lawful arrest of offenders . . ." (note that the statute does not refer to "self-defence", but cases of this sort will nearly always be covered by the "prevention of crime" provision). Given that Article 2 is non-derogable, except in relation to war (Article 15(2)), the disparity between existing national law and the Convention seems likely to give rise to argument about the compatibility of these provisions. The higher standard of Article 2 would work to the detriment of a defendant, but reliance upon this by the prosecution seems offensive.

4. Public order offences

4–117 Article 11 guarantees the right to peaceful assembly, subject to restrictions which are necessary in a democratic society in the interests of, *inter alia,* public safety or the prevention of disorder or crime. The objective of Article 11 is to allow individuals to come together for the furtherance of their common interests, especially political interests. It covers "meetings in public thoroughfares" (*Rassemblement Jurassien, Unité Jurassienne v. Switzerland* (1979) 17 D.R. 93).

Section 14A–C of the Public Order Act 1986 would seem capable of violating Article 11, in that it allows for the creation of "trespassory assembly orders" where it appears that an assembly may be held on land "to which the public has no right of access or only a limited right of access". Any person taking part in an assembly of more than 20 persons in contravention of the order commits an offence. There is no necessity for the prosecution to show that the group had been disruptive, or had threatened public safety or the rights of others. Further, assembly on the highway may fall within a trespassory assembly order, since the public's right of access to the highway is limited to passing and repassing and does not extend to assembling, protesting and the like (*DPP v. James* [1997] 2 All E.R. 119). The possibility of a blanket ban on demonstrations, without any necessity for the authorities to show that the assembly will not be peaceful, or will infringe one of the restrictions of Article 11(2), runs counter to the right of assembly.

Total bans on demonstrations have been held to be justified in the interests of public safety where the risk of disruption or violence (not necessarily on the part of the applicants) outweighed a limited restriction of freedom of expression (*Rassemblement, etc. v. Switzerland,* above; *Christians Against Racism and Facism v. U.K.* (1980) 21 D.R. 138).

PART II: PRISONERS' RIGHTS

Leon Daniel (Barrister, Doughty St Chambers)

S. INTRODUCTION

4–118 The establishment and development of prisoners' rights in domestic law has already taken place, as a result of a significant body of decisions in national courts and in Strasbourg, particularly in the last decade. These have established certain rights and procedural safeguards for prisoners. Historically, the legislature has subsequently made provision and/or formulated policy in reaction to such decisions. The Act may accordingly be seen to have a lesser impact in relation to prisoners than on some other areas of domestic law. Some aspects of prison law are, however, arguably inconsistent with the Convention, and in this writer's view will require testing in the courts. It is in any event self-evident that the deprivation of individual liberty inherent in a system of punishment by imprisonment is likely to give rise to further issues under the Act and the Convention.

1. Legislative framework

4–119 The Prison Act 1952 confers on the Home Secretary responsibility for the management of prisons in the United Kingdom. Section 4(2) empowers him to ". . . make contracts and do . . . acts necessary for the maintenance of prisons and the maintenance of prisons." The statute also provides for the creation of prison rules:

> ". . . for the regulation and management of prisons, remand centres, young offender institutions or secure training centres respectively, and for the classification, treatment, employment, discipline and control of persons required to be detained therein" (section 47(1)).

The rules are the Prison Rules 1964 (S.I. 1964 No. 388 (as amended)) and the Young Offenders Institution Rules 1988 (S.I. 1988 No. 1422), which cover all matters relating to management. A particular prison rule may be supplemented by detailed standing orders, advice and/or instructions to prison governors. These are the chief mechanisms by which statements about prison policy and the practical workings of prison management are made and amended. The combination of the 1952 Act and the Prison Rules effectively gives the Home Secretary a wide degree of discretion in the operation and the management of prisons. This discretion is not however balanced by reciprocal provisions bestowing any positive rights upon prisoners, save in limited respects. Although some rules (*e.g.* rule 37A — the right to confidential correspondence with legal advisers) do mention certain rights, these are far from comprehensive.

2. Fundamental rights before the Act

4–120 A common law doctrine which has originated in the field of prisoners' rights is the *Leech* principle. Although the 1952 Act does not contain any "built-in" safeguards to protect the rights of prisoners, it was held in *R. v. Secretary of State for the Home Department ex p. Leech (No. 2)* [1994] Q.B. 198 that executive interference with a fundamental right can only be achieved by express statutory provision, or by necessary implication, to the minimum required to secure the statutory objectives. *Leech* concerned a prisoner's right to unimpeded access to the courts, which it was argued was breached as a result of the correspondence with his lawyer being read by prison officers (see below *Silver v. U.K.* and *Golder v. U.K.*). Such practice was held to be unlawful, and was the precursor to the present rule 37A, which prevents legal correspondence with the court and/or a legal advisor being read except where there is reason to suspect that it contains illicit material, or threatens prison security or the safety of others.

Although the fundamental rights doctrine is likely to take a "back-seat" after incorporation, particularly in the light of the present uncertainty as to its applicability in challenging prison policy (*per* Kennedy L.J. in *R. v. Secretary of State for the Home Department, ex p. O'Dhuibhir*, 1997, unreported, CA); it is instructive to consider the domestic cases alongside Convention law, to see how the Act may now affect the position in domestic law.

T. PREVENTATIVE DETENTION

4–121 A series of Strasbourg cases against the U.K. government has been the catalyst for establishing important procedural safeguards for certain life prisoners who have served the part of their sentence recommended for deterrence and retribution, which is known as the tariff period. After the expiry of the tariff period, life prisoners may remain detained on the basis that they would provide an unacceptable risk to the public if released. There are two kinds of life sentence prisoners, mandatory and discretionary lifers. A discretionary life sentence may be imposed for certain grave offences including manslaughter, rape and arson, and where the person's character indicates a propensity to commit offences in the future which pose a serious risk to the public. In contrast, a mandatory life sentence is imposed where a person has been convicted of murder.

Until the landmark decisions of the Court in *Weeks v. U.K.* [1987] Series A, No. 114; 10 E.H.R.R. 293 and *Thynne, Wilson and Gunnell v. U.K.* [1990] Series A, No. 1990; 13 E.H.R.R. 666, the procedure which facilitated a discretionary lifer's eventual release into the community mirrored that of a mandatory lifer. In *Weeks* the Court found a violation of Article 5(4) on the grounds that the applicant was unable to institute proceedings in a court following a decision to recall him to prison in 1977. The Court held that the Parole Board could not be regarded for the purposes of Article 5(4) as a court, because it did not have the power to determine the applicant's release.

4–122 The three applicants in *Thynne* complained of a violation of Article 5(4) on the ground that they were not able to have the continued lawfulness of their detention decided by a court at reasonable intervals throughout their imprisonment, having particular regard to the part of their sentence or tariff which did not relate to punishment and deterrence but was merely protective in nature. The Government argued that, as no clear distinction could be made by reference to the tariff period between the deterrence and retribution and the protective element of the sentence, the applicants could not succeed. In a landmark judgment, the Court concluded:

> "Although the dividing line may be difficult to draw in particular cases, it seems clear that the principles underlying such sentences, unlike mandatory life sentences, have developed in the sense that they are composed of a punitive element and subsequently of a security element designed to confer on the Secretary of State the responsibility for determining when the public

interest permits the prisoners release. This view is confirmed by the judicial description of the 'tariff' as denoting the period of detention considered necessary to meet the requirements of retribution and deterrence."

The Court found in favour of the applicants, holding that after expiry of the punitive term fixed in his case a discretionary life sentence prisoner was entitled to have the lawfulness of his continued detention decided by a judicial process. This decision was given statutory effect by the enactment of the Criminal Justice Act 1991. Section 34 of that Act governs the procedure for discretionary lifers. In short, a judge has to declare in open court the length of the punitive part of the sentence, so that the deterrent and retribution elements may be easily identified. After the expiry of the punitive period of the sentence a prisoner has a right to have his case referred to a panel of the Parole Board which then has the power to order his release. It is significant that the burden is on the prisoner to satisfy the panel that he poses an acceptable risk to the public to be released (see *R. v. Parole Board, ex p. Lodomez, The Times,* August 3, 1994). Having regard to Article 5(4), it may be arguable that the burden should rest with the state to show that a prisoner poses an unacceptable risk and not vice versa.

4-123   The principle in *Thynne* was recently extended by the Court to juvenile murderers detained "during Her Majesty's Pleasure" pursuant to section 53(1) of the Children and Young Persons Act 1933. In *Hussain and Singh v. U.K.* (1996) 22 E.H.R.R. 1, the Court concluded that because considerations as to the danger posed by the applicants were based on an assessment of their character and mental state, the applicants' sentence after expiration of the tariff was more comparable to a discretionary life sentence, and thus the same procedural safeguards should be in place. Following interim measures being put in place to give effect to the Court's judgment, the government made provision in the Crime (Sentences) Act 1997 for a formal process — akin to that for discretionary lifers — to be in place for juvenile mandatory lifers.

4-124   The distinction between discretionary and mandatory lifers was subsequently affirmed by the Court in *Wynne v. U.K.* (1994) Series A, No. 294-A; 19 E.H.R.R. 333. The Court concluded that:

"Although the mandatory life sentence also contains a punitive and a preventive element, it belongs to a different category from the discretionary sentence since it is imposed automatically as the punishment for the offence of murder irrespective of considerations of dangerousness. While the two types of life sentence may now be converging there is still a substantial gap between them. Thus in mandatory life sentences the release of the prisoner is entirely a matter within the discretion of the Secretary of State who is not bound by the judicial recommendation as to the length of the tariff and who can have regard to other criteria than dangerousness in deciding on release."

Thus, the statutory procedure under section 35 of the Criminal Justice Act 1991 (now replaced by section 29 of the Crime (Sentences) Act 1997) whereby the Secretary of State has the final say on whether a mandatory lifer should be released, even after the punitive element of his sentence is served, was expressly approved by the Court. By section 2(2)(b) of the Criminal Justice Act 1991, a court may impose a sentence longer than the normal period for an offence where it is "necessary to protect the public from serious harm." The offences where a person's sentence may be increased as a result of preventative considerations under this provision include indecent assault and actual bodily harm. Although obvious similarities can be drawn between this provision and the system for discretionary lifers, there is no provision for a prisoner sentenced under section 2(2)(b) to have the preventative element of his sentence reviewed by a judicial body. In this writer's view, a strong argument may be made that this breaches Article 5(4) of the Convention, having regard to the decision of *Thynne*. Although this argument was considered by the Divisional Court in *R. v. The Parole Board, ex p. Mansell*, March 7, 1996, unreported, the application for judicial review was rejected solely on the basis of common law principles of fairness (*per* Otton L.J.).

U. PRISONERS' CORRESPONDENCE

4–125   The Court has given extensive consideration to cases relating to interference with prisoners correspondence. In *Silver v. U.K.* (1983) Series A, No. 61; 5 E.H.R.R. 347, the Court considered whether interference with a prisoner's mail by the prison authorities constituted a breach of the right to respect for correspondence and freedom of expression contrary (respectively) to Articles 8 and 10. The Court concluded that, as the correspondence was being censored on a number of grounds unknown to the prisoner, Article 8 had been violated. The Court did, however, indicate that certain restrictions on correspondence imposed by the prison authorities could be justifiable for the prevention of crime and disorder, and would therefore be justified under Article 8(2). It was decided that it was not necessary to consider separately whether there was also a breach of Article 10. *Boyle and Rice v. U.K.* (1988) Series A, No. 131; 10 E.H.R.R. 425 is another example where the Court found a violation of Article 8, arising from interference with four prisoners" correspondence. A similar judgment was given by the Court in *McCallum v. U.K.* (1990) Series A, No. 183; 13 E.H.R.R. 597.

In *R. v. Governor of H.M.P. Whitemoor, ex p. Main* [1997] C.O.D 400, a long term prisoner applied for judicial review to quash the Governor's order which authorised prison staff to search confidential correspondence in the prisoner's cell in his absence. It was argued that any searching of correspondence could only be done in accordance with rule 37A, and that the order was *ultra vires*; or alternatively that it could only be permitted in the prisoner's presence, as the documents were subject to legal professional privilege, and such searches would infringe the fundamental right to communicate freely with a legal adviser. In dismissing the application at first instance, Pill L.J. (sitting with Astill J.) held that rule 37A did not extend to cell searches and was limited to communications in transit between a prisoner and his legal adviser. Additionally, he concluded that, as an attempt was made in the Governor's order to provide a safeguard for the prisoner, and there had to be a margin appreciation in the Governor when considering how searches are conducted, the order was neither *ultra vires* or irrational. The applicant's appeal to the Court of Appeal was subsequently dismissed (see *R. v. Secretary of State for the Home Department, ex p. Simms and another* and *R. v. Governor of Whitemoor Prison, ex p. Main* [1998] 2 All E.R. 491). The Court of Appeal concluded by applying the *Leech* test that there is a "self evident and pressing need" for the prison authorities to examine a prisoner's correspondence so far as it is necessary to ensure that it is bona fide. It was expressly argued on the appellant's behalf that the prison service's actions contravened Article 8(1) of the Convention. In support of this submission reference was made to *Campbell v. U.K.* (1992) Series A, No. 233–A; 15 E.H.R.R. 137 where the Court had held that interference with a prisoner's correspondence by the prison authorities in Scotland amounted to a violation of Article 8. The Court of Appeal distinguished this case on the ground that there was no pressing need that was addressed to justify the interference in *Campbell*.

In considering whether the interference with a prisoner's correspondence in the course of cell searches is in "accordance with the law" for the purposes of Article 8(2), national courts may well reach a similar conclusion to that in *ex p. Main*: namely that the restrictions under rule 37A do not extend to cell searches, with the effect that the interference is in "accordance with the law", and that they are "necessary" on security grounds. In contrast, however, the interference is with legal correspondence, the court may be less disposed to find such actions acceptable, having regard in particular to Article 6(1). In *Golder v. U.K.* (1975) Series A, No. 18; 1 E.H.R.R. 524, it was held that Article 6 implied a right of access to a court, and that this not only related to matters arising from the conduct of proceedings once they had been instituted, but included matters ancillary to such a right (such as the right to institute legal proceedings in the first place). Thus, the act of searching legal correspondence in a prisoner's cell, although not breaching rule 37A, may nonetheless amount to a breach of Article 6(1).

V. FAMILY LIFE

4–126 There have been two attempts by U.K. prisoners to establish a right to conjugal visits, in *R. S. v. U.K.* 17142/90 and *E.L.H. v. U.K.* (1997) 25 E.H.R.R. C.D. 158. Both applications failed at the Commission stage. The Commission acknowledged in *E.L.H.* that several European countries facilitate conjugal visits, but concluded that,

> ". . . although the refusal of such visits constitutes an interference with the right to respect for ones family life under Article 8 of the Convention, for the present time it must be regarded as justified for the prevention of disorder or crime under the second paragraph of that provision".

In *R. v. Secretary of State for the Home Department ex p. ODhuibhir*, 1997, unreported, CA, two exceptional risk category A prisoners at Whitemoor sought to challenge the prison's policy which required all visitors (including legal advisers and family members) to be separated from a prisoner and partitioned by glass and wall, with no opportunity of physical contact. It was argued that the policy infringed the prisoners' right to the free flow of information between them and their legal advisers, which was part of the right to unimpeded access to the courts. A similar submission was made regarding the effect of the policy on family visits which, it was argued, infringed the prisoners' residual right to physical contact with family members, and increased the potential for the break up of the family and the risk of mental illness in prisoners. This was rejected by the Court of Appeal. It is probably unlikely that the outcome of this case would be any different under the Convention, as the policy of strictly limited contact with visitors was based purely on security considerations.

W. FREEDOM OF EXPRESSION

4-127   In *R. v. Secretary of State for the Home Department ex p. Simms and O'Brien* [1998] 2 All E.R. 491, two prisoners, both mandatory lifers, claimed that they were wrongly convicted and were receiving visits from investigative journalists. The judicial review challenge related to the legality of prison policy which prevents journalists visiting prisoners unless they give undertakings that no material information obtained during such a visit would be used for professional purposes. Latham J. concluded, at first instance, that the policy amounted to a restriction on the right of free speech, which was in excess of the minimum necessary in order to achieve the statutory objectives under section 47(1) of the 1952 Act. The fact that prisoners could enter into written correspondence with journalists, provided *inter alia* the matters raised amounted to serious representations about their convictions or sentence, was relied upon by Latham J. as indicative that the policy in question was excessive, as a similar undertaking could adequately meet any concerns regarding visits from journalists. The Court of Appeal, however, overturned this, holding that the policy was lawful having regard to the 1952 Act. In the Court's view, prisoners lost their "right" to communicate orally with the media through a journalist and that this is reflected in Article 10(2) of the Convention. An appeal to the House of Lords is pending. It is anticipated in view of the impending implementation of the Act, that the Law Lords will consider the Convention jurisprudence more strictly in reaching their decisions and will be less disposed to make a finding which may be inconsistent with the Convention.

CHAPTER 5

Immigration and Asylum

Judith Carter (Solicitor, North Islington Law Centre)

5–01 This chapter compares the main principles guiding the developing case law of the Strasbourg authorities with the current position in English immigration law, and suggests areas which may need reviewing as the Act comes into force. "Immigration" is used to mean immigration controls, whether on entry, removal or deportation.

Paragraphs 5–02—5–18 provide a general introduction to the areas where the Convention has already had an impact, and where the Act is going to have an effect in immigration law, pointing to the Convention Articles most used in immigration cases. Paragraphs 5–19—5–25 are an examination of likely procedure in immigration cases under the Act. Paragraphs 5–26—5–36 deal with the general principles relevant to the Articles most used in immigration law.

The structure then considers various aspects where Convention rights may be encountered by the practitioner: deportation/removal (paragraphs 5–37—5–73); extradition (paragraphs 5–74—5–78); entry (paragraphs 5–79—5–82); detention (paragraphs 5–83—5–92); benefits (paragraph 5–93); and nationality (paragraph 5–94).

A. GENERAL INTRODUCTION

5–02 This section covers the underlying principles for review of immigration control by the Strasbourg authorities, and how that impacts on U.K. immigration controls; and interpretation of the relevant provisions under the Act.

1. Legal framework on freedom of movement

5–03 The Convention gives no right to entry or residence, and does not challenge the legal framework whereby states have jurisdiction to decide on entry and residence of aliens. However, it does restrict state jurisdiction where one of the rights in the Convention may be breached (*e.g.* Articles 8 and 3 on deportation, Article 5 on detention).

The Convention is far more limited in its scope than the International Covenant on Civil and Political Rights (Articles 12 and 13 of which give a right to enter the country of nationality and freedom to move within it, and a right of appeal against expulsion). These rights are in optional Protocols to the Convention (the Fourth and Seventh), which the United Kingdom has not ratified and which are not given effect in the Act.

In domestic law, freedom of movement within the United Kingdom is a common law right, but permission for entry to and residence in the territory is the prerogative of the sovereign. That situation has been encroached upon by U.K. legislation setting out a framework for control of entry, residence and deportation (Immigration Act 1971 (IA 1971)), conditions for entry and residence (Immigration Rules) and right of abode (*e.g.* Commonwealth Immigrants Act 1962). However, the Secretary of State retains residuary discretion to allow entry or to desist from expulsion (Immigration Act 1971, s.33(5)), and he has made policies setting out the way in which this discretion may be exercised. The Secretary of State must have regard to those published policies, or he will be acting unlawfully (*Secretary of State for the Home Department v. DS Abdi* [1996] Imm. A.R. 148 at 157).

Nationality law is not the subject of the Convention, apart from the extent to which nationality gives a person right of entry or abode (see paragraph 5–94).

2. Impact of the Act on immigration law

5–04   The main impact of the Act will be on the powers of review in the English courts, including the matters on which adjudicators can make decisions which will be binding on the Secretary of State. If Article 6 (fair hearing) is applicable to immigration proceedings, there will be an effect on appeals procedure. There is also the procedure for obtaining a declaration of incompatibility with Convention rights (see paragraph 5–25).

Convention cases which have already affected immigration controls in the United Kingdom are:

5–05   *East African Asians Case* (1981) 3 E.H.R.R. 76, which found that U.K. entry controls were racist towards that group (Articles 3 and 14);

Abdulaziz, Cabales and Balkandali v. U.K. (1985) Series A, No. 94; 7 E.H.R.R. 471, in which the Court found that U.K. entry controls were sexist (Articles 8 and 14);

Lamguindaz v. U.K. (1993) Series A, No. 258–C; 17 E.H.R.R. 213, where expulsion of a long resident alien would have been in breach of Article 8;

Soering v. U.K. (1989) Series A, No. 161; 11 E.H.R.R. 439, where extradition of a German national to Virginia to face the death penalty would have been in breach of Article 3;

Chahal v. U.K. (1997) R.J.D. 1996–V 1831; 23 E.H.R.R. 413, where deportation of an Indian national on national security grounds would have breached Article 3; and the review of detention was inadequate to comply with Article 5;

D v. U.K. (1997) 24 E.H.R.R. 423, where removal of a person with AIDS would have breached Article 3;

Yousuf v. U.K. (unreported) App. No. 14830/89, June 30, 1992) where the Immigration Rules were held to be insufficient to allow a parent contact with a child.

In addition, the important case of *Berrehab v. Netherlands* (1988) Series A, No. 138; 11 E.H.R.R. 322) has given rise to published policies regarding the factors to be considered on deportation of family members.

3. Which articles may be relevant in immigration cases?

5–06   The Articles which assist migrants are Article 8 (respect for family and private life); Article 6 (fair hearing); Article 5 (liberty and security); and Article 14 (prohibition of discrimination). Articles which may be relied upon indirectly are Article 2 (right to life); Article 3 (prohibition of torture); Article 4 (prohibition of slavery and forced labour); and Articles 9–11 (freedom of religion, expression and association). Article 2 of the First Protocol (right to education) may be put forward in cases involving the removal of children. Article 12 (right to marry) has been of no assistance in immigration cases, as it may be exercised anywhere (*Beldjoudi v. France* (1992) Series A, No. 234; 14 E.H.R.R. 801), and is not discussed further here (see Chapter 6 for the family law context).

Article 16 (restrictions on political activity of aliens) may be raised by the state in respect of Articles 10, 11 and 14. A state may also refer to Article 17 (prohibition of abuse of rights) in Article 3 "asylum" cases. Some issues concerning Article 13 (which is not given effect under the Act) are considered below (paragraph 5–15).

4. Who is a "public authority" for the purposes of section 6?

5–07   In immigration law, "public authority" for the purposes of section 6 will include all persons making decisions relating to entry and exit from the United Kingdom: Entry Clearance Officers; immigration officers; the Home Office; those in charge of detention centres, including Group 4 (as delegated authorities); and police carrying out immigration functions. The reviewing bodies (being the adjudicators, tribunals and the Special Immigration Appeals Commission, and the courts of review and appeal above them) are all public authorities under section 6(3)(a).

Authorities which make decisions which depend on a person's immigration status will be responsible if the consequence of their decision results in a person suffering treatment incompatible with Convention rights (*e.g.* councils, benefits officers and other public officials in relation to claims for benefits or housing (*cf. R. v. SS for the Environment, ex p. Tower Hamlets London Borough Council* [1993] Imm. A.R. 495, [1993] 3 All E.R. 439, CA, and see paragraph 5–09 on jurisdiction).

5. Which matters fall within the scope of functions of public authorities?

5–08   Both positive and negative "acts" which might be incompatible with Convention rights are covered by section 6(6). For the purposes of immigration, both a positive act of expulsion and, in very limited circumstances, a refusal to allow entry, may be actionable. If the state fails to act, it will only be possible to challenge that failure if the state has a positive obligation to act in those circumstances. The capacity to make a challenge is linked with whether the applicant is a victim (paragraph 5–10), and thus with the moment at which Convention issues arise (paragraph 5–22).

Where an issue arises which has an E.C. law nexus, Convention law is relevant through that route (see paragraph 5–18).

6. Jurisdiction and responsibility of the United Kingdom

5–09   States must secure the rights and freedoms guaranteed to everyone physically present within their jurisdiction (Article 1), and section 6 reflects this. The lawfulness of the applicant's residence is not a factor which can be used to exclude their enjoying the rights (*D v. U.K.*, above and see paragraph 5–43). Jurisdiction includes exercising official functions at Embassies abroad (*e.g. X. v. FRG* (1966) 17 C.D.). A state may also be responsible where it has "effective control" outside its national territory (*Loizidou v. Turkey* (1995) Series A, No. 310, paragraphs 62 and 63; 20 E.H.R.R. 99 at 130).

7. Is the applicant a "victim"?

5–10   In order to complain of conduct made unlawful by section 6, a person must be a victim (see paragraph 2–15 and following). The Court has refused to consider a person a "victim" until an expulsion order has actually been served (*Vijayanathan and Pusparajah v. France* (1992) Series A, No. 241–B, para. 46; 15 E.H.R.R. 62 at 75–6); or until an appeal against expulsion has been formally rejected, even though the expulsion has only been stayed (*Paez v. Sweden*, case struck off the list by the Court November 7, 1997, 653/1995). However, in *Nsona v. Netherlands* (R.J.D. 1996–V 1979) a complaint of a breach of Article 8 in respect of past events relating to entry, was dealt with in spite of the fact that the applicant had been granted a residence permit. Although the Act's definition of victim is equated to that under Article 34 (section 7(7)), the wording of section 7(1) (referring as it does to past and proposed conduct) may allow Convention issues to be raised much earlier in domestic proceedings, for example in an appeal against refusal of variation of leave (see paragraphs 5–19— 5–25 on procedural issues). Government proposals to allow only one appeal against refusal of further leave and notice of intention to deport will result in all issues being heard together in any case (1998 White Paper: "Fairer, Faster and Firmer").

Under the Convention, non-governmental organisations have been able to bring proceedings on behalf of a group of people affected by a particular issue (*Open Door and Dublin Well Woman Clinic v. Ireland* (1992) Series A, No. 246, para. 41). This may allow a group such as JCWI or ILPA to take an action under section 7, provided the group can demonstrate that it is itself directly affected.

8. Procedural guarantees in immigration law

5–11   Articles 6 and 13 are related, in that Article 13 requires a remedy to be "effective", which may involve examining the procedures followed. However, Article 13 is not given effect under the Act (see paragraph 5–15). It is also not clear that Article 6 will apply to immigration proceedings.

(a) Immigration status as "civil rights and obligations"

5–12   Article 6 does not, according to the Commission, include rights relating to immigration (*X,Y,Z,V and W v. U.K.* (1967) 10 Y.B. 528, 538; 25

C.D. 117 at 122–3); asylum (*P v. U.K.* (1987) 54 D.R. 211 at 211–212); deportation, even following a criminal conviction (*Agee v. U.K.* (1976) 7 D.R. 164, paras 27–30); nationality (*S v. Switzerland* (1988) 59 D.R. 256); or extradition (*Farmakopolous v. Greece* (1990) 64 D.R. 52). The Commission has in the past found that where a right to family life is in issue, Article 6(1) may apply (*Khan and Singh v. U.K.* (1967) 24 C.D. 116 at 130; 10 Y.B. 478 at 500; *X,Y,Z,V,W v. U.K.*, above) but has not followed this approach in later cases. Proceedings concerning a request for entry to take up a private employment contract do not concern a "civil right" (*X v. U.K.* (1977) 9 D.R. 224 at 226). The Court can however consider whether treatment falling short of the standards in Article 6 in a receiving country may prevent removal (*Soering v. U.K.* (1989) above).

This situation is not necessarily set in stone: the Court has an expansive approach, and the inclusion of social security rights, which were initially considered not to fall under the definition in Article 6, is evidence of this (*Schouten and Meldrum v. Netherlands* (1994) Series A, No. 304; (1995) 19 E.H.R.R. 432. See Chapter 12). Harris, O'Boyle and Warbrick, *Law of the European Convention on Human Rights* (Butterworths, 1995), speak of "the Court's increasingly dynamic understanding of what amounts to a private law right for the purposes of Article 6" and advocate a reformulation of the definition, even to the point of including all proceedings where there are national courts or administrative tribunals in place to consider rights and obligations, including immigration and nationality law (pp. 184–5).

(b) Immigration cases as "criminal proceedings"

5–13   The Strasbourg authorities have not defined any purely immigration proceedings as "criminal". For example, a deportation order is not a penal sanction, but rather a security measure, for the purposes of Article 7 (*Moustaquim v. Belgium* (1991) 13 E.H.R.R. 802 (Com. Rep.). The Commission has distinguished administrative detention pending deportation from detention for the criminal offence of illegal entry or overstaying (*X v. Netherlands* (1965) C.D. 18 at 19; 8 Y.B. 228 at 264). As extradition proceedings are "criminal" in the United Kingdom, the English courts will have to apply Article 6 standards to them (see paragraph 5–78).

(c) U.K. approach to date

5–14   In civil proceedings, Article 6 may, in any case, simply state the fundamental rules of natural justice, which are part of the law for the purposes of the IA 1971, s.19 (*Mustafa v. Secretary of State for the Home Department* [1979/80] Imm. A.R. 32 at 37–38). As regards the relevance of Article 6 in mixed family/immigration cases, the Court of Appeal, in a wardship case, completely discounted the possibility that it might apply (*Re A (A minor) (Wardship: immigration)* [1992] F.L.R. 427 at 430). However, the Court of Appeal in *R. v. Secretary of State for the Home Department, ex p. Canbolat* [1998] 1 All E.R. 161 and the High Court in *R. v. Secretary of State for the Home Department, ex p. A. Uzun* [1998] 1 All E.R. 314 have accepted arguments based on Article 6.

9. Effective remedy

5–15   Article 13 (which, though not given effect under the Act, may nonetheless be of relevance — see paragraphs 1–21—1–22) requires an *effective* remedy. The protection under Article 13 is lower than under Article 6(1) (*Golder v. U.K.* (1975) Series A, No. 18; 1 E.H.R.R. 524, para. 33).

Cases often merit skilled representation. Legal aid may be needed to pay for that representation to ensure full enjoyment of the associated right, and a decision on eligibility should be made speedily (following *Zamir v. U.K.* (1983) 5 E.H.R.R. 242). The restricted availability of legal aid may mean that the United Kingdom does not comply with Article 13 (Harris, O'Boyle and Warbrick, *op. cit*, argue that the principles under Article 6(1) in *Airey v. Ireland* (1979) Series A, No. 32, paras 24–26; 2 E.H.R.R. 305 at 315 should apply here).

The Green Form legal aid system in the United Kingdom provides funding for legal representatives for advice and assistance, but not representation (see *Zamir v. U.K.* above). The government may comply with its obligations:

(1) by providing free legal representation through the Immigration Advisory Service and the Refugee Legal Centre (funded under IA 1971, s.23, as extended by paragraph 4(2)(f) of Schedule 2 of the Asylum and Immigration Appeals Act 1993 and section 3 of the Asylum and Immigration Act 1996);

(2) if a request is made under the Green Form legal aid scheme for funding to appear as "Mackenzie friend" in cases involving complexity etc., it may be granted.

5–16   There are problems with both approaches:

(1) The representation agencies may be unable to cope with demand (the RLC has twice placed a short "moratorium" on new cases).

(2) Anecdotal evidence reveals the inconsistent standards which are applied as the role of a Mackenzie friend: from fully representing in the appeal, to just giving advice to the appellant. Full representation would obviously satisfy Article 13, whereas giving advice, particularly where there are language difficulties or where the case involves complex points of law, would not satisfy the "*Airey*" requirements. Statistics also show that appellants who are represented have a higher chance of winning their appeals.

The Act's failure to give effect to Article 13 means that these issues would have to be argued in Strasbourg.

5–17   To date the Court has found the remedy of judicial review to be adequate to remedy non compliance with the Convention (*Vilvarajah v. U.K.* (1991) Series A, No. 215, paras 122–6; 14 E.H.R.R. 248 at 291–292), on the basis that Article 13 will be satisfied as long as the totality of the procedures are adequate (*e.g. Leander v. Sweden* (1987) Series A, No. 116, para. 77; 9 E.H.R.R. 433). As legal aid is available for judicial review proceedings, the Court has not considered the question of compliance in proceedings before the tribunals.

10. Effect of E.C. law

5–18   European law is interpreted with due regard for fundamental rights, in respect of which the convention has a special position (see generally paragraphs 2–05—2–06). Thus, the ECJ has been willing to link freedom of movement with Convention rights, such as the freedom to join a trade union (*e.g. Rutili v. Minister for the Interior* [1975] E.C.R. 1219; [1976] 1 C.M.L.R. 140), and the right to respect for family life (*Commission v. Germany* [1989] E.C.R. 1263, [1990] 3 C.M.L.R. 540). The U.K. Courts have already considered arguments where the Convention has been relevant to the interpretation of E.U. Law (see paragraph 5–82). The Act imposes a more direct obligation on the courts.

B. PROCEDURE UNDER THE ACT

5–19   In advance of any rules of court, this section addresses general points of procedure: when it will be possible to argue Convention issues; in what form; the suspensive effect of the Act; and remedies under the Act.

1. Use of the Act and Convention as shield and sword

5–20   The Convention can be used both to assert rights and to protect them (see generally paragraph 1–55). Where the state is threatening a positive act, *e.g.* removal, Convention rights are available as a defence. They may also be raised at the stage of requesting leave to enter or remain, and the standard application form may have to be amended to ensure that it obtains the full information necessary to enable the Secretary of State to consider those issues. Representations may be made to the Secretary of State at any time and, according to the rules of natural justice, he will have to consider them before making any decision.

2. Procedure before the Immigration Appeals Authority

5–21   The Secretary of State is required to give a notice stating reasons for the decision taken (Reg 4 of Immigration Appeals (Notices) Regulations 1984, S.I. 1984 No. 2040). This Notice will now have to include reasons where Convention rights have been raised in any way. A letter refusing representations based on the Convention rights will also have to give full reasons. It will then be possible to submit grounds of appeal which relate to any refusal under the immigration rules and under the Convention.

3. When will appeals authorities consider Convention issues?

5–22   It has been made clear that the immigration appellate authorities will have jurisdiction to hear claims under section 6 of the Act (Lord Williams of Mostyn, Second Reading, January 19, 1998, *Hansard*, col. 1361). The result of this is a widening of the ambit of appeals, which are presently limited to examining only whether the Secretary of State has "power in law" to deport/ remove (see paragraph 5–38). It remains to be seen at what stage they will accept jurisdiction in view of the requirement that the applicant be a "victim" of the impugned measure (see paragraph 5–10).

4. Access to the appeals or review procedure

5–23   The right to bring a case under the Act before the courts may be exercised through a statutory right of appeal or, where there is none, by way of judicial review, although the scope of that review should be broader than is now the case (see below). The rules of procedure to be drafted under section 7(11) (see paragraph 5–40) of the Act should allow direct access to the courts to argue Convention points in cases where a positive obligation may arise, *e.g.* to take a decision without undue delay.

It remains to be seen whether such an appeal could be argued on the basis that the impugned decision is "not in accordance with the law" (IA 1971, s.19), or whether it will have to be argued on a separate basis under section 7 of the Act, as a "mixed appeal".

5. Suspension of removal

5–24   The Court (previously the Commission) has a procedure for requesting states to refrain from removal while the Court is considering a case (formerly Rule 36 of the Commission's Rules of Procedure; now Rule 39 of the Court's Rules of Procedure). In order to persuade the Court to make such a request, the applicant has to show that "serious and irreparable harm" is likely to occur if the impugned measure is carried out (*Cruz Varas v. Sweden* (1991) Series A, No. 201; 14 E.H.R.R. 1, para. 93).

In the United Kingdom all statutory appeals have suspensive effect except "safe third country" appeals and appeals against refusal of entry where the appellant does not already have a visa. In the latter cases judicial review and a request for an injunction would provide the remedy (*M v. Home Office* [1994] A.C. 377). The decision as to whether or not the injunction should be made depends on the arguability of the main proceedings.

It is not clear whether the rules of procedure under the Act will specifically provide for a suspensive effect in proceedings where a Convention right is raised. If they do so provide, then a threshold will have to be applied. It is suggested that the test of whether the point is "arguable" would be sufficient as it is the same test used to establish whether there is an effective remedy under Article 13 of the Convention.

6. Relief under the Act

5–25   The question of remedy in immigration and asylum cases is usually straightforward: it will be a grant of entry or leave to remain. The rights or obligations attached to that leave may vary, but they will not be governed by the Convention, as no positive obligation is imposed on states to grant particular forms of leave. Persons who are not removable because of the United Kingdom's obligations under section 6 will be granted exceptional leave to remain (E.L.R.) (Lord Williams of Mostyn, Second Reading, January 19, 1998, *Hansard*, col. 1361). That is already a well-established kind of leave, albeit a discretionary one which can be withdrawn (*Written Answers*, H.C. Vol. 138, ser. 6, col. 425 (July 28, 1988)). The current practice of allowing those with E.L.R. to have recourse to public funds must continue, in view of the acceptance that, whatever the financial circumstances, the person may not be removed. This will have to apply to both Article 3 and Article 8 cases.

The Act provides for the higher courts to make a declaration of incompatibility (section 4) as regards primary and (in some cases) secondary legislation. Primary legislation, such as IA 1988, s.5(1) (limited right of appeal in deportation cases and non-suspensive appeals), could be affected. Even if the Court does make a declaration, *e.g.* in respect of an immigration rule, the procedure does not in fact grant "relief" to the applicant, as it has no suspensive effect and is not binding on the parties to the proceedings (section 4(6)). If such a case were to involve removal of some kind, it would be necessary to obtain some other suspensive remedy (see above).

Financial compensation has not generally been considered an appropriate remedy by the Court in immigration cases.

C. GENERAL PRINCIPLES OF SUBSTANTIVE RIGHTS RELATING TO IMMIGRATION

5–26   This section gives a brief overview of the approach of the Strasbourg authorities to immigration cases under the main, relevant Articles.

1. Article 3

5–27   This Article has been successfully used to prevent the removal of applicants to a country where there are substantial grounds for believing that there is a real risk they would suffer ill treatment contrary to the standards of the Article (*Soering v. U.K.* (1989) above). In summary: there is no right to asylum under the Convention; any person who is being expelled from the territory may raise Article 3 issues; the prohibition on treatment contrary to Article 3 is absolute; and the Court demands a high level of scrutiny of the decision where Article 3 issues are raised. Protection under Article 3 is wider than under the Geneva Convention (*Chahal v. U.K.* (1996) above), but may lead to a less secure status in the host country.

2. Article 8

5–28   Article 8 has been argued successfully in numerous deportation/removal cases. The Court is less willing to find an interference in family life where a refusal of entry is being challenged (so that a state is being asked to carry out a positive act). The Court is more likely to find that there is an interference where applicants can show they enjoy a family life in the host state. Those who can only show they enjoy a private life benefit from a lower level of protection under the Convention. The Court has sometimes confused factors defining private and family life, and the factors which should be weighed in the balance when looking at the proportionality of the measure. The method of the Court's review is dealt with below (paragraph 5–38).

Applicants alleging breaches have been both the person who is the subject of the order and resident family members of applicants for entry.

3. Relationship between Articles 2, 3, and 8

5–29   Article 2 has a very limited effect in removal cases (see paragraph 5–72). Concerns that the health and well-being of the applicant might deteriorate on removal or deportation may raise issues under Article 3 or Article 8. An interference with private life under Article 8 may be alleged where a person's "physical integrity" is threatened (*X and Y v. Netherlands* (1985) Series A, No. 91, para. 22; 8 E.H.R.R. 235). There may be an area where the "minimum level of severity" under Article 3 is not attained, but Article 8 may provide protection, with the possibility that the lesser level of harm is justified under Article 8(2). Many of the cases involving deportation have alleged breaches of Article 3 and failed to show that the harm done was sufficient to engage responsibility under that Article (*e.g. Abdulaziz and Ors v. U.K.* (1985) Series A, No. 94, para. 91; *Djeroud v. France* (1991) Series A, No. 191–B, para. 70; Commission decision (1991) 14 E.H.R.R. 68), and the Strasbourg authorities have gone on to examine a possible breach of Article 8 looking at the more abstract notions of family and private life (see paragraphs 5–37—5–38).

4. Article 5

5–30   Article 5(1)(f) permits deprivation of liberty to prevent illegal entry, for deportation or extradition so long as that detention is not arbitrary or disproportionate (*De Wilde, Ooms and Versyp v. Netherlands* (1971) Series A, No. 12; 1 E.H.R.R. 373). There must be an opportunity for a speedy review of detention to ensure that it is for the purpose stated and lawful (Article 5(4)).

5. Articles 9–11

5–31   These Articles (respectively the rights to freedom of thought, expression, and assembly) do not in themselves give any rights to entry or residence, as there is no obligation on a state to allow a person to exercise them in any particular place. The Commission has not given any weight to these rights when balanced against a state's right to deport. Recently, however, the Court has linked Article 10 to a case of exclusion from a territory (see paragraph 5–82).

6. Article 14

5–32   There is no "free standing" protection against discrimination: Article 14 must be linked to one of the rights in the Convention. Conversely, simply because one of the substantive rights has not been breached, does not mean that a breach of Article 14 cannot be found (*e.g. Inze v. Austria* (1987) Series A, No. 126, paras 43–45). If a particular measure is found to be discriminatory, the state concerned may claim that there is an "objective and reasonable justification" on the grounds that there is a "reasonable relationship of proportionality between the means employed and the aim sought to be realised" (see, *inter alia, Rasmussen v. Denmark* (1984) Series A, No. 87, para. 14; 6 E.H.R.R. 94). The Court will allow the state a certain "margin of appreciation" in assessing whether and to what extent differences in otherwise similar situations justify a different treatment in law, and the scope of the margin will vary according to the circumstances, but the Court will give the final ruling (*Abdulaziz and Ors v. U.K.* (1985) above, paragraphs 71 and 78).

The Immigration Rules say that officers will carry out their duties without regard to the race, colour or religion of persons seeking to enter or remain in the United Kingdom (H.C. 395, para. 2). This protects fewer categories of people than does Article 14, which is non-exhaustive. There is no existing U.K. forum for challenging alleged discriminatory treatment in immigration matters by a public authority. The adjudicators and courts will have to be prepared to hear complaints under Article 14 alongside the existing statutory appeals.

(a) Discrimination on grounds of nationality

5–33 The Commission has stated that discrimination on grounds of nationality is an objective and reasonable justification when dealing with immigration matters. Differential treatment between E.U. and non-E.U. nationals is objectively and reasonably justifiable, since the E.U. states belong to a "special legal order" (*Moustaquim v. Belgium* (1991) Series A, No. 193, para. 49; 13 E.H.R.R. 802 at 816). The same is true as between Commonwealth and non-Commonwealth citizens, since there is a "special relationship which exists between citizens of the Commonwealth and the United Kingdom" (*X and Ors v. U.K.*, App. No. 9504/81, unreported; *Agee v. U.K.* (1997) 7 D.R. 164 at 176). There is no right to obtain nationality (*Beldjoudi and Teychene v. France* (1992) 14 E.H.R.R. 801, para. 79, Commission Opinion), and therefore no breach of Article 14 where there is a discrimination on grounds of sex between those who may acquire a certain nationality (*Family K and W v. Netherlands* (1985) 43 D.R. 216 at 219 220).

U.K. immigration law inevitably discriminates on the ground of nationality, and this distinction is of special significance where the persons hold British passports of some kind, and yet do not have right of abode (see the *East African Asians Case* below).

Professor Schermers of the Commission has argued that expulsion following a prison sentence is a "double punishment" for the offender, and therefore discriminates on grounds of nationality in the context of punishment for a specific crime rather than in the context of immigration controls (Opinion in *Lamguindaz v. U.K.* (above). The effect of double punishment is an important aspect of deportation and removal, and should be argued along with Article 8 where the person is a long resident or has family ties (see paragraphs 5–39—5–58).

(b) Discrimination on grounds of sex

5–34 In *Abdulaziz and Others v. U.K.* (above) the Court found a breach of Article 14 on grounds of sex, together with Article 8, where the Immigration Rules made it easier for men settled in the United Kingdom to bring their wives to join them than it was for settled women to bring their husbands. There are now no differences based on sex on the face of the Immigration Rules.

(c) Discrimination on grounds of sexual orientation

5–35 The Strasbourg authorities have been reluctant to deal with complaints on these grounds. They have:

(1) avoided dealing with complaints under Article 14 (*e.g. Dudgeon v. U.K.* (1981) Series A, No. 45; 4 E.H.R.R. 149); or

(2) chosen a comparator by dubious logic: where a gay couple claimed they were discriminated against on the grounds of sex, the Commission

said: "the only comparable group [was] that of lesbians [who] would, in principle, have been treated in the same way as the applicants" (*X. and Y. v. U.K.* (1983) 32 D.R. 220; 5 E.H.R.R. 601 at 602); or

(3) justified the discrimination on the basis that the heterosexual family deserves greater protection than a homosexual (private life) relationship (*S v. U.K.* (1986) 47 D.R. 274).

This jurisprudence is challengeable on the basis that the Convention is a "living instrument" (*Tyrer v. U.K.* (1978) Series A, No. 26, para. 31). There are signs of change in:

(a) the Court very gradually widening the definition of "family" (*X, Y and Z v. U.K.*, R.J.D. 1997–II 619; 24 E.H.R.R. 143, paras 36–37);

(b) the increasing protection offered to those with private life ties (*C. v. Belgium*, judgment of August 7, 1996); and

(c) the United Kingdom's recent recognition of same sex relationships in a published immigration concession (October 13, 1997 "Concession on Unmarried Partners", reported in *Butterworth's Immigration Law Service*).

(d) Discrimination on grounds of race/ethnicity

5–36 The difficulty with the Convention jurisprudence in this area is its refusal to address indirect discrimination. In the *East African Asians Case* (above) the Commission refused to look behind the face of the law, in spite of its avowed purpose of excluding British protected persons (overwhelmingly non-white people). As the law did not distinguish on the basis of race or colour between "different groups of British protected persons", the Commission concluded that the law could not be discriminatory. The Court failed actively to consider the groups which were suffering discrimination. The same approach was taken in *Abdulaziz* (above), where neither the Court nor the Commission was willing to accept that a breach of Article 14 could be made out by establishing indirect discrimination under the 1980 Immigration Rules (paragraph 85). It might have been better for the Court to admit the discrimination in these circumstances, and justify it on the grounds of the state's right to grant nationality to whom it pleases.

Articles 3 and 14 were linked in a case where an ethnic minority group's difficulty in obtaining identity papers or aliens' passports amounted to degrading treatment under Article 3, even though there was no Convention right to be issued with identity papers (*Kalderas Gypsies v. Federal Republic of Germany and Netherlands* (1977) 11 D.R. 221 at 231 (paragraph 57)).

D. REMOVAL AND DEPORTATION: GENERALLY

5–37 The Strasbourg authorities have consistently stated that, according to international law and the limits of their treaty obligations, Contracting States have the right to control the entry, residence and expulsion of aliens. However, where an *expulsion* (including removal, deportation and extradition) may raise issues under one of the rights in the Convention, there may be a breach of that right (*e.g. Ahmed v. Austria*, R.J.D. 1996–VI 2195; 24 E.H.R.R. 278). Paragraphs 5–39—5–78 below consider issues in respect of the main Convention rights.

5–38   Removal and deportation cases are treated very differently in domestic law. Removal is a purely administrative measure, used to remove a person from the territory who has no legal status there, either because they have not been given leave to enter or because they have entered illegally. No appeal rights are attached (except where a person with a visa is refused entry or the appeal right is exercisable from abroad (IA 1971, s.13(3)), and the only remedy against immediate removal will be judicial review. Deportation describes the process of expulsion of a person who is, or has been, legally present in the jurisdiction (1971, s.3) and a statutory right of appeal attaches (IA 1971, s.5).

The Convention does not distinguish between those who are present in the territory with temporary admission, illegally, or legally (see Article 1, and *e.g. D v. U.K.*, above (1997) 24 E.H.R.R. 23). However, the Court gives more weight to the circumstances of those who are present legally (*Dalia v. France*, judgment of February 19, 1998, unreported, App. No. 154/1996/773/974, unless the right at stake is an absolute one (*e.g. Article 1, D v. U.K.* as above).

Successive U.K. governments have issued policy guidelines to enforcement officers purporting to take into account the United Kingdom's obligations under Article 8 in particular (the "DPs": DP2/93, the first and only document which made specific reference to the Court's jurisprudence under Article 8, replaced by DP 4/95, 3/96, 4/96 and 5/96). These guidelines apply to illegal entrants and potential deportees, but not to those refused entry or on temporary admission (*R. v. Secretary of State for the Home Department, ex p. Comfort Henry* [1995] Imm. A.R. 42). This goes against the Convention jurisprudence and results in the situation where an asylum seeker can live in the United Kingdom on temporary admission, work, receive benefits and marry, for any period (often between five to 10 years) while awaiting a decision on a claim for asylum. If finally refused entry as an asylum seeker, such a person has, under the Immigration Rules, to return to their country of "residence" in order to make an application for entry, *e.g.* on the basis of marriage. This is one of the anomalies of Home Office policy, which should be opened up when Article 8 becomes effective through the Act

The Secretary of State is required to take into account any matters put before him before making a notice of intention to deport (H.C. 395, para. 364), and in particular the factors set out in the policy guidelines (the "DPs"). The problem is not, therefore, with what he may consider, but with the way those factors are weighed in the balance.

All potential deportees have a right of appeal. However, where it is presently limited (*e.g.* Immigration Act 1988, s.5(1)) the Act will require a broadening of jurisdiction to take into account Convention issues. In such a case the adjudicator or tribunal will have to be given full power to hear and assess evidence pertinent to those rights, and to be given reasons for the Secretary of State's decision, since without full reasons the adjudicator will be unable to assess whether the proportionality test has been properly applied. It will also have to have the power to make binding decisions, rather than the present recommendations.

E. Deportation/removal and Article 8

5–39   There are several problems with the Court's interpretation of Article 8 and the United Kingdom's interpretation of the Court's case law in this area. First, the Court's approach is unclear and sometimes leads to unexpected or unpredictable results. Secondly, it has been reluctant to recognise private life as worthy of protection in deportation cases, although that is now changing. Thirdly, although the United Kingdom has issued policy guidelines to comply with the Court's case law, the stringent threshold criteria, the failure to recognise the need for contact with young children, and the limitation on those to whom they apply, all give rise to potential problems under Article 8. Domestic case law shows that there is room to develop a more sophisticated test as to compliance with the Article.

This section suggests a method of approach for cases under Article 8, followed by general comments on the current legal situation. It then applies the suggested approach to the different situations which most commonly arise, with an analysis of the problems of both the Convention case law and U.K. deportation/removal policy.

1. Proposed approach to Article 8

5–40   The following questions should be asked by a public authority which is deciding, or reviewing, expulsion from the United Kingdom:

(a) Is there a family or private life to be protected?

(b) Is there an interference? (*i.e.* is there a deportation measure or restriction on entry which will separate a person from his or her family, or affect his or her private life?)

(c) Is the interference a lawful measure?

(d) What is the legitimate aim pursued?

(e) Is the measure necessary in a democratic society?

   (i) Does it correspond to a pressing social need (*Handyside v. U.K.* (1979) 1 E.H.R.R. 737, para. 48); and
   (ii) is it proportionate?

   • Is the measure relevant? *e.g.*, does it achieve the aim of either preventing further offences being committed in the host country or actually protecting the labour market?
   • Is the measure the minimum necessary to achieve the aim? (*Handyside v U.K.* (1979) 1 E.H.R.R. 737 paras 50 and 55; and see Conclusions of M. Abraham in *Beldjoudi v. France* 14 E.H.R.R. 801 at 811, and Separate Opinion of Judge de Meyer at 839.)

(f) If the measure passes the above tests of necessity, its "proportionality" will be measured by balancing the legitimate public order aim (considering the seriousness of the offences committed) against the strength of the family or private life ties.

This process demands that the public authority state reasons for domestic policy regarding the removal of second generation and long resident immigrants, all cohabiting couples and British children of foreign parents.

2. General comments on the current legal situation

5–41   The Court has carried out all the investigations above, but never in a structured way in any one case. The U.K. policy guidelines (DPs) take a wide variety of factors into account, but it is unclear how they are balanced against each other. National courts have not yet openly acknowledged the role of the proportionality test in Convention case law, in the limited circumstances in which they have examined it. The extent of the existing review, within judicial review of a decision taken under the policy guidelines, was described in *R. v. Secretary of State for the Home Department, ex p. Gangadeen* [1998] Imm. A.R. 106, CA, in terms that it was right for the court to confer a broad measure of discretion on the Home Secretary in relation to the application of the policy, so long as he had regard to it and made a decision which was not inherently irrational. The greater the interference with human rights the more the court would require by way of justification. With explicit reference to Convention case law, the court then noted the great importance which the interests of the child should be given when carrying out the balancing exercise, but did not carry out such an exercise itself, concluding that the Secretary of State had already done so satisfactorily. This process is inadequate to deal with the complex issues which arise in Article 8 cases.

It is important to bear in mind that the U.K. policy guidelines do not apply to all who are physically present in the jurisdiction, but only to those who are illegal entrants or overstayers (see above).

3. General principles

(a) Is there a private or family life to be protected?

5–42   There is a substantial body of case law on the definition of family and private life (see below for particular cases, and Chapter 6). The Court has given a very wide definition of private life:

> "The Court does not consider it possible or necessary to attempt an exhaustive definition of the notion of 'private life'. However, it would be too restrictive to limit the notion of an 'inner circle' in which the individual may live his own personal life as he chooses . . . Respect for private life must also comprise to a certain degree the right to establish and develop relationships with other human beings." (*Niemitz v. Germany* (1992) Series A, No. 251–B, para. 29).

Private life includes physical integrity as well as abstract ties (*X and Y v. Netherlands* (1985) Series A, No. 91, para. 22; 8 E.H.R.R. 235).

There has been confusion over the definition of family as opposed to private life. In *Moustaquim v. Belgium* ((1991) Series A, No. 193, para. 62; 13 E.H.R.R. 802) the Court took into account what were undoubtedly personal matters to conclude that family life exists (*e.g.* nationality, language used, length of residence). More recently the Court has made explicit findings that "private life" exists and may be protected in immigration cases (*C v. Belgium*, above, judgment of August 7, 1996, unreported).

It is important to maintain the distinction between the existence of private or family life and whether there is an interference in it: otherwise there is a risk that the very separation complained of is listed as a reason why there is no interference in family life (*Askar v. U.K.*, App. No. 26373/95, Dec. October 16, 1995, unreported).

(b) Is there an interference?

5–43   According to the Court, there will only be an interference with family or private life if the persons to be removed are unable to live together elsewhere (rights under Article 8 do not allow a family to choose their place of residence: *Abdulaziz and Ors v. U.K.* (1985) Series A, No. 94, 7 E.H.R.R. 471). The Court is more likely to find an interference in a deportation case than a "leave to enter" case, as it will give weight to the legal status of the person at the time the family ties were formed (*Dalia v. France*, above, judgment of February 19, 1998, unreported, paras 41–45). The Court will not find an interference if the relationship was formed after the applicant knew of the enforcement action against her (*El Boujaidi v. France*, R.J.D. 1997–VI 1980). (See further paragraphs 5–79—5–82 on leave to enter.)

5–44   Private life did not initially enjoy protection in immigration cases. The Commission maintained that a "disruption" of private life caused by removal "cannot, in principle, be regarded as an interference with the right to respect for private life . . . unless the person concerned can demonstrate that there are exceptional circumstances . . . justifying a departure from that principle" (*X and Y v. U.K.* (1987) 11 E.H.R.R. 49). This "principle" had, however, been formulated in a case of extradition, and the lesser standard of protection was linked directly to the fact of the extradition request (*Chandra v. U.K.* (1986) 47 D.R. 85; 9 E.H.R.R. 373).

The Court has recently recognised that an immigration measure can indeed interfere with private life (*e.g. Boughanemi v. France*, R.J.D. 1996–II 593; 22 E.H.R.R. 228, at para. 42; *C v. Belgium*, above, judgment of August 7, 1996, unreported). This means that it will be possible to use Article 8 to gain greater protection for gay couples, children and long residents who are deemed to enjoy private not family life under the Convention (see below).

(c) Is the measure "in accordance with the law" and in pursuance of one of the legitimate aims in Article 8(2)?

5–45   The question whether or not a measure is "in accordance with the law" will be considered by establishing whether or not there is a rule of domestic or international law which authorises the act (*Silver v. U.K.* (1983) Series A, No.

61, para. 86; 5 E.H.R.R. 347 and *Groppera Radio AG v. Switzerland* (1990) Series A, No. 173, para. 68; 12 E.H.R.R. 321). See paragraphs 2–88—2–89 for extended discussion. The U.K. government has usually stated that the "legitimate aim" of the measure is for the prevention of disorder or crime, and this has been accepted. In *Berrehab v. Netherlands*, Series A, No. 138; 11 E.H.R.R. 322, the assertion that the immigration measure was for the economic well-being of the country was rejected after the Court examined the claim on its facts, as Mr Berrehab had been legally working in the Netherlands for several years (paragraph 29).

(d) Is the measure necessary in a democratic society?

5–46   The aim of the measure should respond to a "pressing social need", and be proportionate to the legitimate aim pursued, which will be "weighed against the seriousness of the interference with the applicants' right to respect for their family life" (*Berrehab v. Netherlands*, above). In examining the necessity of the interference the Court allows the contracting state a "margin of appreciation" to determine whether the measure is "necessary in a democratic society" (*e.g. Olsson v. Sweden (No. 1)* (1988) Series A, No. 130, at 31–32, para. 67; 11 E.H.R.R. 259). This margin is to allow for different local conditions as between states and is not, therefore, available to the domestic courts to allow a general discretion to the U.K. authorities.

(e) Proportionality

5–47   The factors to be weighed in each case are discussed below.

4. Analysis of the approach of the Court and the United Kingdom in particular cases

(a) Married couples

5–48   Convention case law has established that married couples enjoy "family life", which always exists where people are bound by blood or legal ties and may also exist in a *de facto* family situation (*Abdulaziz, Cabales and Balkandali v. U.K.* (1985) Series A, No. 94; 7 E.H.R.R. 471; *Marckx v. Belgium* (1979) Series A, No. 31, para. 31; 2 E.H.R.R. 330, and *Kroon and Ors v. Netherlands* (1994) Series A, No. 297–C, para. 30; 18 E.H.R.R. 188). The latest version of the U.K. policy guidelines on enforcement action (DP 3/96) only applies to a married couple, who have been married for two years prior to enforcement action commencing (paragraph 5), and does not examine any *de facto* relationship between unmarried couples (see below for this category).

The Court may find an interference in family life if "real and effective family ties" exist (*Beldjoudi v. France* (1992) Series A, No. 234–A, paras 55–6; 14 E.H.R.R. 801). The family life must be "firmly established in the country concerned" to avoid the Court finding that they could live together elsewhere (*X and Y v. Switzerland* (1977) 9 D.R. 57). In the United Kingdom only those who can pass the two year "threshold" may be protected from an interference, but there is no such rigid rule in the Convention case law. The U.K. guidelines which list the factors going to whether the couple could live together elsewhere do not conflict with Convention case law.

5–49 A typical case might concern a spouse who is to be deported following conviction for a serious offence, or for overstaying, or the removal of a spouse who married while on temporary admission, or after entering illegally. In these cases the government will say the legitimate aim which the removal measure pursues is the *prevention* of disorder or crime. The authorities should therefore show a strong likelihood of reoffending (compare *R. v. Nazari* [1980] 3 All E.R. 880). It is not possible to give a concise analysis of the weight which the Court gives to the "legitimate aim" pursued, particularly in the case of people who are deported because of their criminal record: as Judge Martens complained in *Boughanemi v. France*, R.J.D. 1996–II 593; 22 E.H.R.R. 228, the decision is a "lottery for the national authorities and a source of embarrassment to the Court" (Dissenting Opinion).

In general, the removal of one member of the family will not be disproportionate unless "practical and legal obstacles" exist which might "imperil the unity or even the very existence of the marriage" (*Beldjoudi v. France* (1992) 14 E.H.R.R. 801 at 820, Commission Report, para. 55). The U.K. guidelines (DP 3/96 Notes) list a number of factors and suggest in general terms the weight to be given to them.

(b) Unmarried couples

5–50 There are no decisions of the Court on immigration relying purely on a relationship of cohabitation, only a Commission case from 1975, where no interference was found (*X and Y v. Switzerland* (1977) 9 D.R. 57). The Commission may be more willing to find an interference in the lives of unmarried couples now that cohabiting couples may come under the definition of "family" (*X, Y and Z v. U.K.* (1997) above), and the Court has recognised that an immigration measure may be an interference in respect for private life, albeit that of a long resident, not a same sex couple (*C v. Belgium* (1996) above, judgment of August 7, 1996, unreported).

The United Kingdom now has a policy concession (October 13, 1997) "Concession on Unmarried Partners", reproduced in *Butterworth's Immigration Law Service* which applies for unmarried couples on entry. There is now no U.K. policy on deportation/removal applying to unmarried couples, although the fact that one exists for entry cases suggests such relationships may be given more recognition in the future.

A same sex couple, however long they may have been cohabiting, or bringing up children together, enjoy "private life" rather than "family life" (following *Dudgeon v. U.K.* (1981) Series A, No. 45, para. 41; 4 E.H.R.R. 149). According to the Court, this classification is not discriminatory (*S v. U.K.* above, paragraph 5–35). The Court has never found an interference in cases concerning expulsion which affected the private life of gay or lesbian couples (*X and Y v. U.K.* (1983) 32 D.R. 220; 5 E.H.R.R. 601; *X and Y v. U.K.* (1987) 11 E.H.R.R. 49, see paragraph 5–44, above).

5–51 An applicant should put forward evidence that the partner who is settled in the United Kingdom is not able to live elsewhere with the applicant, just as is done in marriage cases.

The Court has now laid aside the "principle" that an immigration measure cannot amount to an interference in private life. This will require the respondent state to address the "legitimate aim" which the measure was intended to pursue, and the necessity for the measure. As there is a concession for in-time applications for leave to remain or enter for cohabiting couples, the government will have to state why it is necessary to have a measure which discriminates against cohabiting couples who enjoy "private life" together for enforcement purposes, but not on entry.

It is with regard to proportionality that the Secretary of State should determine the weight to be given to factors such as the length of the relationship. The Commission has assessed the weight to be given to private life of a gay couple as against the need to enforce immigration controls, and found that subjection of the applicant to hostility and social ostracism because of his homosexuality was of lesser importance than the enforcement of those controls (*B v. U.K.* (1990) 64 D.R. 278 at 283). This example shows how important it is to continue arguing for the importance of private life rights in all categories.

(c) Contact between parents and children

5–52 Family life has been held to include a blood relationship between parent and child, whether or not it is legitimate (*Donehub v. Netherlands* above, paragraph 21). Subsequent events may break the tie, but only in "exceptional circumstances" (*Gul v. Switzerland*, R.J.D. 1996–I 159; 22 E.H.R.R. 93, para. 32). "The mutual enjoyment by parent and child of each other's company constitutes a fundamental element of family life" (*McMichael v. U.K.* (1995) Series A, No. 307–B, at 55; 20 E.H.R.R. 205).

In *Berrehab v. Netherlands* the government wished to deport a Moroccan national who had been married to a Dutch national, and there was a child of that marriage. The marriage had broken down after conception of the child and before her birth, but there was contact between the father and his daughter for several hours four times a week, and he supported her financially. There would have been an interference in family life had the father been deported, because the possibility of his regularly visiting the Netherlands to maintain contact with his daughter was "a somewhat theoretical one", and such contacts were essential as the child was very young.

5–53 In U.K. cases involving contact, the U.K. guidelines (DP4/96) say that there is no interference on expulsion because a parent may exercise access to child by making an application from abroad under the appropriate Immigration Rules (DP 4/96, para. 6; H.C. 395, paras 246–248), and that therefore this is not a factor which should be considered on deportation. Paragraphs 246–248 set out the requirements for leave to *enter* (note, not to remain) to exercise rights of access to a child resident in the United Kingdom. The rules fail those who have never been married, or who are widowed, or who do not have a contact order because they have come to an amicable arrangement (Children Act 1989, s.8, under which contact orders are made, is subject to the stipulation that the family court will not make an order unless it considers that doing so would be better for the child than making no order at all (Children Act 1989, s.1(5)). The visiting parent will need considerable independent financial means to stay without working or claiming benefits. The rules do not permit the level of contact which was protected in the case of *Berrehab v. Netherlands*, or was approved in *McMichael v. U.K.*.

Exceptions may be allowed under the guidelines where the parent to be expelled has a deportation order signed, as this prevents return for three years, and where parents are not married (DP 4/96, para. 8). The United Kingdom's submissions to the U.N. Committee on the Rights of the Child claimed that deportation proceedings will "not normally be initiated" where there is frequent and regular contact with a child (paragraph 5.47 of the initial report submitted to the Committee under Article 44 of the Convention on the Rights of the Child).

The stringent immigration rules and the test in the guidelines are too high, and should be challenged using Article 8, *Yousuf v. U.K.* (unreported), App. No. 14830/89, Dec. of June 30, 1992, above, the model of *Berrehab v. Netherlands* (1988) Series A, No. 138; 11 E.H.R.R. 322, above, and the strong statements about a state's positive obligations towards the family in *McMichael v. U.K.* (1995) Series A, No. 307–B; 20 E.H.R.R. 205, above.

(d) Children

5–54 "Child" has an autonomous meaning under the Convention and includes anyone under 18 years (*X v. Switzerland* (1979) 18 D.R. 238), and U.K. law is in accordance with this (see further Chapter 6). A woman who was married and lived away from home was not considered to have a family life connection with her parents (*X v. U.K.* (1972) 15 Y.B. 564). The U.K. guidelines assume the existence of family ties between the child and the parent following (*e.g. Marckx v. Belgium* (1979) Series A, No. 31, para. 31; 2 E.H.R.R. 330). Children who may be deported with their parents may enjoy a "private life", distinct from their family life, in the United Kingdom (*Fadele v. U.K.* (unreported) App. 13078/87), but it carries almost no weight with the Court.

The Court is unwilling to find an interference on expulsion of an entire family where the private or family life of young children is concerned, even if that child has the nationality of the host state and close relationships with extended family (*e.g. O and OL v. U.K.* (1987) 11 E.H.R.R. 48 and *Sorabjee v. U.K.*, App. No. 23938/94, Dec. of October 23, 1995, unreported). The Court will consider who is available to care for the child, and where, in coming to its decision (*Nsona v. Netherlands*, R.J.D. 1996–V 1979).

5–55 Before making a decision to deport the Secretary of State will have to consider the factors in H.C. 395, para. 364. Internal guidelines have been issued which list the relevant factors a) where children are present in the United Kingdom on their own; and b) where their parents are to be removed or deported (DP 4/95 and 4/96). They accord with Article 8 except in the interpretation of the importance to be attached to contact between the parent and child (at paragraph 6, see above). If a child would face serious risk of harm if returned on his or her own, then deportation action may not be taken, and evidence will be required of this (paragraph 3). If no evidence of any care arrangements abroad is forthcoming then the Secretary of State is likely to concede.

If a school age child is to be removed in his/her own right (H.C. 395, para. 367), or because he/she will have to accompany a parent on removal, the effect of removal on education (*cf.* Article 2 of the First Protocol) and plans for the child's care and maintenance here or abroad are factors to take into account (*i.e.* to weigh in the balance when looking at the proportionality of the deportation) (see, for example, *Ho v. Secretary of State for the Home Department*, IAT 14727).

The nationality of the child has not, so far, been considered a deciding factor where a family is to be deported, and the standard of practical arrangements for a child's care have weighed more heavily (*Sorabjee v. U.K.*, above; *Kamara v. U.K.*, App. No. 24381/94 (1995) unreported; *Jaramillo v. U.K.*, App. No. 24865/94 (1995) unreported and *R. v. Secretary of State for the Home Department, ex p. Lawerteh* (unreported) April 29, 1996, CA).

The United Kingdom has ratified the *U.N. Convention on the Rights of the Child* (November 20, 1989, U.N. Doc. A/44/25) but has entered reservations regarding immigration and nationality law. However, the Committee on the Rights of the Child found that the reservations do not appear to be compatible with the principles and provisions of that Convention imposing an obligation on states to make the best interests of the child a primary consideration (Eighth session of the Committee, U.N. Doc. CRC/C/15Add.34 (1995)). In *R. v. Secretary of State for the Home Department, ex p. Gangadeen*, above, the Court of Appeal stated that Article 8 did not require such emphasis to be placed on the rights of the children, although criticism could be made of the "balancing test" employed by the court, and of its failure to question the status of the U.K. reservation to the Child Convention.

(e) Long residents

5–56   The problem in cases of "long residents" or "integrated aliens" is that of defining who they are and what protection they may benefit from under the Convention. Second generation immigrants who arrived in the host country with their parents when they were very young will not be protected from deportation without the additional proof of links with the country of residence (*e.g. Moustaquim v. Belgium*, above). In the most recent cases concerning long term residents, the Court has found an interference in the applicant's "private and family life", and gone on to consider all the factors as before (*Boujlifa v. France*, R.J.D. 1997–VI 2250).

The United Kingdom government operates 10 and 14 year long residence concessions (121 H.C.O. Official Report (6th Series) written answers, cols 833–834, November 5, 1987 (10 Year Rule); 14 Year Rule announced by Douglas Hurd, Secretary of State for the Home Department, November 30, 1988, both reproduced in *Butterworth's Immigration Law Service*), combined with the factors to be considered under H.C. 395, para. 364. Under U.K. law, children who have been born here and are over 10 years old, and children who have come to the United Kingdom at an early age and accumulated 10 years' residence, benefit from particular guidelines (DP 5/96). In addition, only a person over 17 years old may be the subject of recommendation for deportation by a criminal court, following conviction (H.C. 395, para. 364). The U.K. guidelines for children resident for 10 or more years requires no other threshold to be met before the individual factors going to "proportionality" are considered (DP 5/96). It seems therefore that such children are assumed to enjoy a "private life" in the United Kingdom, independently of family ties, which would suffer an interference on removal. Under the long residence concessions the Secretary of State will consider all factors establishing the applicant's connections with the United Kingdom (see above).

5–57   The proportionality test in these cases has had unpredictable results (see under "married couples" above). Two alternative approaches have been suggested by Judges of the Court:

(1) The Court should fully recognise the private life rights of "integrated aliens" and prevent them from being expelled: the removal of an integrated alien "may *exceptionally* be justified where the alien is convicted of *very serious* crimes, such as serious crimes against the State, political or religious terrorism or holding a leading position in a drug trafficking organisation." (Dissenting Opinion of Judge Martens in *Boughanemi v. France*, R.J.D. 1996–II 593, paragraph 9)

(2) The integrated alien who has lived all, or practically all, his or her life within a State should no more be expelled than nationals, and to do so would be a breach of Article 3 (*e.g.* Concurring Opinion of Mr Schermers and Mrs Thune in the case of *Beldjoudi v. France* (1992) Series A, No. 234–A; 14 E.H.R.R. 801). This approach has the disadvantage of not allowing for exceptions.

Under both these approaches the test for integration depends entirely upon age of arrival and length of residence, which removes the need to examine other areas of private/family life for indications that removal would be disproportionate.

5. Scope of review in Article 8 cases

5–58   The Strasbourg authorities have accepted that judicial review is a sufficient remedy as long as the substantial argument about the breach may be put before the domestic court (*Vilvarajah v. U.K.* (1991) Series A, No. 215, paras 124–126; 14 E.H.R.R. 248). Obviously a statutory appeal before the adjudicator will also satisfy that requirement. The existing case law under the guidelines (DP 3/96, etc.) has concentrated on whether the Secretary of State actually applied them (*R. v. Secretary of State for the Home Department ex. p. Amankwah* [1994] Imm. A.R. 240, QBD), rather than how he weighed the various factors in the balance (*Gangadeen and Khan v. Secretary of State for the Home Department* [1998] Imm. A.R. 106, CA). He must generally accept the adjudicator's findings of fact (*Secretary of State for the Home Department v. Danaie* [1998] Imm.A.R. 84, CA). The Secretary of State, the adjudicator and the courts may examine whether or not deportation is the correct course of action. The proportionality test is not presently used in any of these *fora*. It is not clear whether the English courts will carry out the proportionality test themselves, or whether they will use the tools of judicial review in order to decide whether or not the Secretary of State has carried out that test.

It is impossible for the adjudicator or judge to assess whether or not the above examination has been carried out without having full reasons for the decision (*R. v. Secretary of State for the Home Department, ex p. M. Zighem* [1996] Imm. A.R. 194 at 199). The English courts are increasingly requiring full reasons to be given in cases involving fundamental rights (see, *e.g. Albert Tong v. Secretary of State for the Home Department* [1996] Imm. A.R. 551 at 557; *Launder v. Home Office* [1997] 3 All E.R. 961, HL, and this should be the case now in national security appeals too (under SIACA (Special Immigration Appeals Commission Act) 1997).

F. DEPORTATION/REMOVAL AND ARTICLE 3

1. Introduction

5–59　This section compares protection under the English interpretation of the Geneva Convention 1951 and Protocol relating to the Status of Refugees ((1954) Cmnd 9171 and (1969) Cmnd 3906) with the wider protection offered under Article 3, with brief reference to the protection offered under the U.N. Convention Against Torture ("CAT" U.N. Doc. A/RES/39/46, December 10, 1984) and the scope of review under the different regimes. The Article applies to all cases of extradition (*Soering v. U.K.* (1989) Series A, No. 161; 11 E.H.R.R 439), removal (*D v. U.K.* (1997) R.J.D. 1997–III 37; 24 E.H.R.R. 423) or deportation (*Ahmed v Austria*, R.J.D. 1996–VI 2195; 24 E.H.R.R. 278), regardless of the conduct of the applicant (*Ahmed v. Austria*, above; *D v. U.K.*, above) or national security reasons (*Chahal v. U.K.*, R.J.D. 1996–V 1831; 23 E.H.R.R. 413, para. 80–2).

Article 3 protects (by way of non-removability) but gives no positive rights to residence. The government stated that a person in this position would be granted exceptional leave to remain (Lord Williams of Mostyn, January 19, 1998, col. 1361 (Second Reading), *Hansard*, HL). It will be important to ensure, when a definition of Article 3 in national law is being developed, that this does not become a minimum threshold for obtaining exceptional leave to remain, which presently may have a wider ambit than Article 3.

2. Definition

5–60　Under the Convention, ill-treatment must reach a minimum level of severity to constitute degrading treatment, according to the test in *Ireland v. U.K.* ((1978) Series A, No. 25, para. 162; 2 E.H.R.R. 25 at 79). The assessment of the minimum is relative; it depends on all the circumstances of the case, such as the nature and context of the treatment or punishment, the manner and method of its execution, its duration, its physical or mental effects and, in some instances, the sex, age and state of health of the victim (*ibid.*, para. 162).

Neither the sex discrimination in *Abdulaziz v. U.K.* ((1985) Series A, No. 94; 7 E.H.R.R. 471 nor the refusal to grant a new residence permit in *Berrehab v. Netherlands* (1988) Series A, No. 138; 11 E.H.R.R. 322) reached that minimum level. In the *East African Asians Case* ((1981) 3 E.H.R.R. 76, Com. Rep.) racially discriminatory legislation imposed on the applicants constituted degrading treatment. In regard to the death penalty, the manner in which it is imposed, personal circumstances (including the youth and mental health of the condemned person and any disproportionality to the crime committed), the conditions of detention while awaiting execution, any delay and mental anguish will all be taken into account (*Soering v. U.K.* (1989) Series A, No. 161, paras 100 and 108). The special stigma of "torture" attaches only to deliberate inhuman treatment causing very serious and cruel suffering, which includes rape in custody (*Aydin v. Turkey* (1997) 25 E.H.R.R. 251, para. 82).

5–61   The Commission has maintained a distinction between "prosecution" and "persecution" (*X v. FRG* (1969) 32 C.D. 87 at 95; *X v. FRG* (1976) 5 D.R. 154 at 155); but where there is a risk of prosecution for political reasons which could lead to an unjustified or disproportionate sentence being passed, this might amount to inhuman treatment (*Altun v. FRG* (1983) 36 D.R. 209, and see paragraphs 5–74—5–78 on extradition). In relation to issues which may arise under "safe third country" cases, the Commission has stated that the repeated expulsion of an individual to a country where his admission is not guaranteed may raise an issue under Article 3 (*Giama v. Belgium* (1980) Commission Report, 21 D.R. 73). Article 3 may be violated where a state fails to carry out an investigation into a potential serious breach of the Convention (see paragraph 5–65).

In domestic law, the Bill of Rights 1688 contains the right not to be inflicted with "cruell and unusual punishments" (*R. v. Secretary of State for the Home Department, ex p. Herbage* (No. 2) [1987] Q.B. 1077). There has been no opportunity to obtain a definition of torture in exceptional leave cases, although there is a considerable body of case law on the definition of "persecution" under the Geneva Convention. The United Kingdom is a signatory to the Convention Against Torture (see above), and is subject to its review mechanisms, but has not signed up to the optional protocol allowing the individual right of petition. The definition of "torture" under CAT is that of "severe pain or suffering, whether physical or mental" inflicted for a specific purpose. It is thus narrower than the Article 3 definition (see below).

3. Comparison of Article 3, and Articles 1 and 33(1) of the Geneva Convention

5–62   This section sets out the points which may be argued where a case cannot be made out under the Geneva Convention. The arguments can best be seen by making comparisons between definitions under Articles 1 and 33 of the Geneva Convention, and the Court's Article 3 jurisprudence.

(a) Standard of proof

5–63   The responsibility of the host state will only be engaged where there are substantial grounds which have been shown for believing that an individual would face a real risk of being subjected to treatment contrary to Article 3 if removed to another State (*Vilvarajah v. U.K.* (1991) Series A, No. 215; 14 E.H.R.R. 248, para. 103). A mere possibility of ill-treatment is not enough (*ibid*). In *Chahal v. U.K.* (R.J.D. 1996–V 1831; 23 E.H.R.R. 413) and *Altun v. Switzerland* ((1983) 36 D.R. 209 at 233–234) a violation was found where the risk of ill-treatment was an exceptional but serious breach of the usual standards.

Domestic interpretation of the Geneva Convention requires the applicant to show a "well-founded fear of persecution, the test being whether there is a reasonable degree of likelihood of persecution for a Convention reason if returned" (*R. v. Secretary of State for the Home Department, ex p. Sivakumaran (U.N. High Commissioner for Refugees intervening)* [1988] A.C. 958 at 994). The test has a subjective and objective element, and the lower standard of proof applies to assessment of past events and likelihood of future persecution (*Kaja v. Secretary of State for the Home Department* [1995] Imm. A.R. 1). This test is certainly no more difficult to satisfy than that under Article 3.

(b) Reason for ill-treatment

5–64   Whereas the definition of a refugee in the Geneva Convention requires "persecution" which is for one of a limited number of reasons, Article 3 prohibits any ill-treatment, and no investigation is made of the motive of the agents causing it (*e.g. Chahal v. U.K.*, above).

(c) Source of ill-treatment

5–65   The source of ill-treatment is irrelevant under Article 3 as long as the authorities are unable to afford appropriate protection (*e.g. Ahmed v. Austria,* R.J.D. 1996–VI 2195; 24 E.H.R.R. 278, para. 44). The extent of protection afforded by the "absolute character" of Article 3 includes a situation where "the source of the risk of proscribed treatment in the receiving country stems from facts which cannot engage either directly or indirectly the responsibility of the public authorities of that country, or which, taken alone, do not in themselves infringe the standards of that Article" (*D v. U.K.* above, para. 49). The Court has recently found breaches of Articles 2 and 3 where the state has failed to investigate adequately the killing or abduction of a close relative (*Yasa v. Turkey*, judgment of September 2, 1998, unreported; and *Kurt v. Turkey*, judgment of May 25, 1998, unreported).

The United Kingdom's definition of a refugee already takes into account actions by non-state agents where the government is unable to offer effective protection (following paragraph 65 of the *Handbook on Procedures and Criteria for Determining Refugee Status*, UNHCR (Geneva, 1988); *Secretary of State for the Home Department v. Savchenkov* [1996] Imm. A.R. 28, CA; *Yousfi v. Secretary of State for the Home Department* [1998] I.N.L.R. 136 (IAT). See also European Union developments in this area: Joint Position on recognition of refugees of March 4, 1996, Ref. 96/196/JHA: Justice and Home Affairs Group).

(d) Internal flight

5–66   Where it may be possible to live in another, safe, part of the receiving country, the Court will evaluate the risk of ill-treatment throughout the whole territory (*Chahal v. U.K.*, above, para. 98). This is the equivalent of the "internal flight alternative", which is part of the definition of "refugee" in U.K. law (*Secretary of State for the Home Department v. Ikhlaq and Ikhlaq* [1997] Imm. A.R. 404, and see *Robinson v. Secretary of State for the Home Department* [1997] 4 All E.R. 210; [1997] Imm. A.R. 568).

(e) Exclusion from protection

5–67 Article 3 demands absolute protection. In appropriate cases it will protect those who would otherwise be disqualified, either under the Geneva Convention exclusion clauses (Articles 1(E) and 1(F)), or under the Secretary of State's statutory power to deport, *e.g.* on grounds of being conducive to the public good for reasons of national security (*Chahal v. U.K.*, above). Article 16 (allowing states to restrict the political activities of aliens) will not apply as it is linked specifically to Articles 10, 11 and 14 (but see Harris, Warbrick and O'Boyle at 508 for the argument that Article 14 could indirectly extend its ambit). Article 17 is wider, in that it forbids use of any of the Convention rights to destroy or limit any other rights therein. A state party may not use this Article to avoid ensuring the enjoyment of rights under Article 5 and 6 by a person accused of being a member of a terrorist organisation (*Lawless v. Ireland* (1961) Series A, No. 3, para. 7; 1 E.H.R.R. 15). That argument was not used by the U.K. government in *Chahal v. U.K.* (above), and it seems, were the matter to go to Strasbourg, that it would not be available as a defence to an allegation of breach of Article 3 by removal.

(f) Cessation of protection

5–68 There are no positive obligations on the host state to grant anything more than temporary protection when a person is not removable by reason of a possible breach of section 6. In debate in the House of Lords, January 19, 1998, col. 1361 (Second Reading), *Hansard*, HL, Lord Williams of Mostyn for the government said that such a person would be "eligible for exceptional leave to remain". The Convention is clear that offences committed in the host state cannot negate the duty to provide protection under Article 3 (*Ahmed v. Austria*, above). A person who is refused further exceptional leave to remain will have a full right of appeal before an adjudicator, (under Immigration Act 1971, s.19 or section 7 of the Act) who will be able to decide on the facts whether or not ELR is to be granted.

(g) The point of time for assessment of risk

5–69 The Court considers conditions in the receiving country at the date of judgment (*Ahmed v. Austria*, above, para. 43). In domestic asylum cases under the Geneva Convention the date of the decision on the application, or the date of appeal is the crucial date (*Ravichandran v. Secretary of State for the Home Department* [1996] Imm. A.R. 97, CA and *Adan v. Secretary of State for the Home Department* [1998] 2 W.L.R. 702, HL).

4. Procedural points

5–70 It is intended that rules to be made under section 7(11) will enable special adjudicators to have jurisdiction to hear appeals relating to rights under the Convention, which will considerably broaden their jurisdiction as at present they may only make a recommendation, there is no obligation on them to hear any evidence, and the Secretary of State has no duty to follow the recommendation.

It is clear from the Court's examination of the facts in *Chahal v. U.K.* (above) that full reasons will need to be given by the Secretary of State in order for the adjudicator to properly assess the decision taken under Article 3. These can be given in the explanatory statement.

The Court will assess the issue in the light of all the material placed before it or, if necessary, obtained *proprio motu* (*Cruz Varas v. Sweden* (1991) Series A, No. 201; 14 E.H.R.R. 1, para. 75), and "the existence of the risk must be assessed primarily with reference to those facts which were known or ought to have been known to the Contracting State at the time of the expulsion", although the Court may also have regard to material which comes to light after an expulsion (*ibid.*, para. 76, and *D v. U.K.* (above), para. 50). Domestically, both the immigration adjudicators (under IA 1971, s.19) and the special adjudicators (under the wider, amended jurisdiction of AIAA 1993, s.8) will be able to hear argument going to the facts and merits of human rights cases.

In *Chahal v. U.K.*, above, the U.K. procedure for assessing a possible breach of Article 3 was found to be inadequate in view of the severely restricted powers of review of the national security panel. Shortcomings identified in the procedure have been remedied by the Special Immigration Appeals Commission Act 1997 and Procedure Rules (S.I. 1998 No. 1881) which provide for reasons to be given for decisions to detain and deport on national security grounds; representation before this Commission; and a special advocate who will have access to sensitive material but not show it to the appellant. It is not yet known whether rules to be made under section 7(11) will apply to this Commission. The 1997 Act came fully into force on August 5, 1998 (S.I. 1998 No. 1892).

5. Whether Article 3 protects removal to "safe third country"

5–71   Removal to a third country where there is no risk of ill-treatment contrary to Article 3 is not prohibited by the Convention. However, if the third country were to remove the applicant to a fourth country where there was a risk of torture (the so-called "chain removal"), there may be a breach (see *Giama v. Belgium* above). In domestic law the United Kingdom has a limited right to return an asylum seeker to, for example, France, if that person has travelled through France in order to arrive here (Asylum and Immigration Act 1996, s.2; Dublin Convention; H.C. 395. para. 345). There is a right of appeal on the ground that one of the conditions allowing removal to a third country is/has not been fulfilled (section 3(1)), but that appeal may only be exercised from abroad (section 3(2)).

The result is that the only suspensive remedy against removal is judicial review. It is not yet clear whether, when a breach of the Convention is claimed under section 6(1), the applicant will be able to come immediately before the adjudicator, or whether judicial review will continue to be the remedy available (rules have yet to be made under subsection 7(9) and (11)).

G. DEPORTATION/REMOVAL AND ARTICLE 2

5–72   Article 2 (right to life) may be raised as an indirect issue in asylum and immigration cases, in a similar way to Article 3. Its application is confined to those cases where the evidence of danger to life is certain, and it will not apply where there is only a possibility of ill-treatment (see paragraph 5–63, above). Article 2 is one of the Articles from which there can be no derogation under Article 15 (save in relation to wartime). This section briefly examines the arguments relevant to removal.

In *D v. U.K.*, (above) the applicant argued that there would be a direct causal link between his expulsion and his accelerated death; and that Article 2 denoted a positive obligation to safeguard life which required the government not to take a measure which would further reduce his limited life expectancy (paragraph 56). The government contended that it was not responsible for his having become HIV positive and developed AIDS, nor for the inadequate medical facilities in the receiving country (paragraph 57). The issue was decided by the Commission and the Court under Article 3.

5–73 The extent to which Article 2 carries positive obligations was decided by the Court in a case alleging police negligence in failing to protect the life of someone who claims to be under attack (*Osman and Osman v. U.K.*, App. No. 23452/94, *The Times*, November 1998).

In the extradition case of *Soering v. U.K.* (above) the Court made findings under Article 3, but made no findings under Article 2. Judge De Meyers argued in favour of finding a breach of Article 2 on the basis that, when considering whether or not to grant an extradition request, and the right to life is involved, a state should not be entitled to allow a requesting state to do what the requested state itself is not allowed to do (*i.e.* subject someone to the death penalty when there is no provision for that punishment in English law).

The scope of review in Article 2 cases is the same as in Article 3 in the United Kingdom.

H. EXTRADITION

5–74 This section examines the protection offered by the Convention against extradition including the procedural guarantees under Article 6.

1. General principles

5–75 Neither extradition itself, nor detention pending extradition, are in any way precluded by the Convention (Article 5(1)(f)), but, where the consequences of extradition prevent the applicant from enjoying one of the Convention rights, and the consequences are not too remote, it may attract the obligations of the requested state (*Soering v. U.K.*, above, para. 85).

The Extradition Act 1989 governs English law on extradition. There are two stages, first the decision of the magistrate to commit and detain (section 6), and secondly the decision of the Secretary of State to return the person (sections 11 and 12). In addition, there are either old and new style proceedings, depending on the date of the treaty under which the extradition request is made. For full discussion of the law on extradition, see *The Law of Extradition in the U.K.*, Michael Forde (Round Hall Press, 1995); *Aspects of Extradition Law*, Chapter 4 (G Gilbert, Martinus Nijhoff Pubs, 1991).

2. Comparison of Convention and U.K. extradition law

5–76   Extradition may, exceptionally, give rise to issues under Article 3, where extradition is contemplated to a country in which "due to the very nature of the regime of that country or to a particular situation in that country, basic human rights, such as are guaranteed by the Convention, might be either grossly violated or entirely suppressed" (*Nazih-Al-Kuzbari* (1963) 10 C.D. 26 at 36; 6 Y.B. 462 at 480). These considerations are wider than those which the magistrate may take into account under section 6 of the Extradition Act. Extradition is not allowed where a person may be prejudiced at his trial or punished, detained or restricted in his personal liberty by reason of his race, religion, nationality or political opinions (section 6(1),(9)). The Secretary of State, under section 12 (for new style proceedings), must decide whether it would be unjust or oppressive to return the accused person a) due to the trivial nature of the offence; b) because of passage of time since commission of offence or escape; c) because the accusation is not made in good faith in the interests of justice. Under old style proceedings the Secretary of State must decide whether it would be unjust to return the accused person (*R. v. Secretary of State for the Home Department, ex p. Sinclair* [1992] Imm. A.R. 293). There is no requirement in the Extradition Act that the human rights situation in the requesting country be taken into account.

The Court has not excluded the possibility that an issue might exceptionally be raised under Article 6 by an extradition decision in circumstances "where the fugitive has suffered or risks suffering a flagrant denial of a fair trial in the requesting country" (*Soering v. U.K.*, above, paras 112–13). The High Court has left open the question of whether a breach of Article 6 alone could render an extradition unlawful (*Re Osman, The Times*, December 17, 1990). It is not clear whether the Court will look at the fair trial point divorced from "discrimination". If Article 3 is raised the fairness of a trial will go to the question of whether "prosecution" is in fact "persecution" (see paragraph 5–61).

5–77   The Convention does not prevent extradition to face the death penalty (see *Soering v. U.K.*, above, but compare *Kareem v. Sweden* (1996) 87 D.R. 173), and neither does section 6 of the Extradition Act. However, if the offence is not punishable by death in Great Britain, the Secretary of State may decide not to order the return of the accused person (section 12(2)(b)). The death row phenomenon may raise issues under Article 3 (*Soering v. U.K.*, above. See paragraph 5–60 on Article 3).

An interference with family and private life alone will not prevent extradition, which could in any event be justified under Article 8(2) (*Raidl v. Austria* (1995) 20 E.H.R.R.; C.D. 114 at 120; *Chandra v. U.K.*, above).

3. Using Convention rights in extradition proceedings

5–78   A Convention point could be raised in representations to the Secretary of State (made under section 12, or following *ex. p. Sinclair*). It could be dealt with either as an asylum claim in its own right, or in the context of any judicial review or habeas corpus proceedings relating directly to the extradition proceedings. The forum may be decided by the procedural rules to be made under section 7(2) of the Act. The forum will affect the extent of reasons to be given for the Secretary of State's decision.

Extradition proceedings have been held not to be criminal for the purposes of the due process guarantees in Article 6 (*Agee v. U.K.* (1977) 7 D.R. 164). However, the U.K. courts have decided that extradition proceedings are "criminal" since they have their origin in acts or conduct punishable under the criminal law, and the standards of criminal committal proceedings must apply (*Amand v. Secretary of State for Home Affairs* [1943] A.C. 147). Article 6 therefore does apply to the committal proceedings before the magistrate (following *Engel v. Netherlands* (1976) Series A, No. 22; 1 E.H.R.R. 647; *Funke v. France* (1993) Series A, No. 256–A; 16 E.H.R.R. 297), but not to the discretionary decision of the Secretary of State as to whether to return the accused person (since the committal proceedings are by then terminated — X v. *Austria* (1961) 8 C.D. 9).

I. Leave To Enter

1. Introduction

5–79   This section considers the situation where a person is physically outside the United Kingdom and applying for entry clearance. In such cases, the Convention offers a lower level of protection than for those already present in the jurisdiction. The reason for this is that the grant of entry is a positive act, and the state is allowed a margin of appreciation in its consideration of "the fair balance that has to be struck between the competing interests of the individual and of the community as a whole" (*Gul v. Switzerland*, R.J.D. 1996–I 159; 22 E.H.R.R. 93, para. 38).

2. Article 8 cases where leave to enter is requested

5–80   In *Abdulaziz and others v. U.K.* (1985) Series A, No. 94; 7 E.H.R.R. 471, the Court considered a case brought by the British and settled wives of men abroad, alleging that to refuse their husbands entry interfered unjustifiably with their family life constituted degrading treatment and was discriminatory. The Court repeated the principle that although there was no right to enter as such, immigration controls did have to operate in accordance with the Convention (paragraphs 59–60). This was in spite of the fact that there were specific provisions regarding immigration in the Fourth Protocol.

In the United Kingdom, the Immigration Rules provide the framework for entry. Policy for categories "outside the rules" may supplement the rules. Such policies may not always comply with the requirement that the law be clear and accessible (*Silver v. U.K.* (1983) Series A, No. 61; 5 E.H.R.R. 347).

Applications made under Article 8 have foundered where the Commission considered that applicants could establish family life together elsewhere, as there would be no interference (*Abdulaziz and others v. U.K.*, para. 88). In order to engage Article 8, it is therefore crucial to show that the family member in the United Kingdom could not join the person applying for entry abroad. Therefore, cases of family reunion for refugees, or those with ELR, are more likely to succeed than ordinary immigration cases (*cf. Fadele v. U.K.* (1991) 7 D.R. 159).

5–81 In the case of refugee family reunion, the obligation under Article 8 should be conclusive: the family member in the United Kingdom is unable to return home, and therefore any requirement to set up family life in a third country will almost certainly constitute an interference. Where the family member is a national of, or resident in, the refugee's country of origin, there is no question of return. The Court decision in *Gul v. Switzerland* (above) concerned an application by a Turkish couple, who had humanitarian leave to remain in Switzerland, for a family reunion with their young son. The Court found that there was no interference in their family life, and therefore no violation, in view of the change in circumstances which had occurred since the original grant of residence permit, the fact that the parents had been to visit their son, the temporary nature of their residence permit, and the fact that their son was accustomed to living in Turkey. This case may be interpreted as being confined to its facts, and there was a strong dissenting opinion, together with later criticism of the reasoning. However, in another case, the Court took a similar decision, though by a bare majority (*Ahmut v. Netherlands*, R.J.D. 1996–VI 2017; 24 E.H.R.R. 62).

3. Exclusion

5–82 A person is most likely to be excluded from a country for political reasons. The Commission has stated that expulsion cannot be seen as an interference with Articles 9, 10 and 11 (*Agee v. U.K.* (1977) 7 D.R. 164 at 174–5; and *Omkarananda and the Divine Light Zentrum v. Switzerland* (1981) 25 D.R. 105 and 118). The Court modified that view in *Piermont v. France* (1995) Series A, No. 314, para. 50; 20 E.H.R.R. 301, where it found that France had breached the Convention by refusing to allow entry to French Polynesia to an MEP who was going to engage in political activity. The case of Gerry Adams, the Sinn Fein leader, and Tony Benn, M.P. (*Adams and Benn v. U.K.* (1997) 23 E.H.R.R. C.D. 160), claiming a violation of Articles 6(1), 10 and 13 for preventing Gerry Adams travelling to the United Kingdom to speak to a group of M.P.s, was declared inadmissible. The Commission allowed the U.K. government a margin of appreciation in their assessment of the "pressing social need" justifying the exclusion.

In the United Kingdom exclusion orders only need to be made against those who would otherwise have an automatic right of entry, *i.e.* E.U. and in particular Irish nationals (since Ireland forms part of the Common Travel Area). As exclusion of a person who has a right of entry is such a serious matter, an order will usually only be made when national security is at stake. The primary legislation is the Prevention of Terrorism Act, which sets out the powers which the Secretary of State has to make such an order. There is a very limited right of review in such cases. Criticisms of the appellate procedure in exclusion order cases have been raised before both the Commission and the ECJ (*McCullough v. U.K.*, App. No. 24889/94, Dec. September 12, 1997; *R. v. Secretary of State for the Home Department, ex p. Gallagher* [1995] E.C.R. I–4253; [1996] 1 C.M.L.R. 543).

The review process was addressed in the English courts in *R. v. Secretary of State for the Home Department, ex p. Adams* [1995] All E.R. (E.C.) 177 where breach of Article 10 was argued, and *R. v. Secretary of State for the Home*

Department, ex p. McQuillan [1995] 4 All E.R. 400 where breach of Article 8 was argued, but there is no definitive ruling on exactly what the review process entails. (For a full discussion of these cases see Murray Hunt, *Using Human Rights Law in the English Courts* (Oxford, Hart 1997).)

J. DETENTION

5–83   Immigration and asylum detainees are in particular need of the right of review, as the detention is most likely to be under administrative powers. The focus of attention in immigration cases is on the standard of proof used to determine the immigration status of the detainee, or to assess the proportionality of the length of detention.

1. Main principles under the Convention

5–84   As an exception to the right to liberty of the person, the Convention permits detention in order to prevent illegal entry, and in order to deport or extradite (Article 5(1)(f)). The detainee has a right to a review of the legality of that detention (Article 5(4)) to ensure it is not arbitrary, *i.e.* in conformity with its stated purpose (*Bozano v. France* (1986) Series A, No. 111, paras 54 and 60; (1987) 9 E.H.R.R. 297 at 313), nor disproportionate (*Caprino v. U.K.* (1980) 22 D.R. 5), which would be contrary to Article 5(1). If the substantive proceedings take an unreasonably long time, through failure by the State to pursue them with due diligence, or because a remedy is not effective, the detention could become disproportionate (*Kolompar v. Belgium* (1992) Series A, No. 235–C, 16 E.H.R.R. 197, para. 68) and therefore unlawful (*Quinn v. France*, Series A, No. 311, para. 48; 21 E.H.R.R. 529, and see also *Chahal v. U.K.*, above).

2. Scope of review

5–85   The right to review under Article 5(1)(f) is of the legality of the detention, and there is no requirement to look behind the legality to examine the facts of the case. The protection is accordingly of a lower standard than that in Article 5(1)(c) (*Chahal v. U.K.* above), and Article 6(2) may not be relevant (*X v. Netherlands* (1965) 18 C.D. 19; Y.B. 228 at 264). The burden of proof is on the government to justify continued detention. If identity documents and sureties have been offered and bail is refused, continuing detention may be unlawful (*R. v. Special Adjudicator, ex p. B*, QBD, April 1998, C.L. 382).

In English law, review is carried out through a right to request bail (IA 1971, Schedules 2 and 3), through habeas corpus and the inherent jurisdiction of the court in judicial review proceedings.

(a) Bail

5–86   The statutory right to request bail is restricted, in that for a person who is detained on arrival for questioning it is only available seven days after arrival (IA 1971, Sched. 2, para. 22(1B)). In order to comply with Article 5(1)(f), the detention must be to prevent absconding, rather than to gain further information from someone who has requested entry and is not therefore an illegal entrant. It may be that the fact that the remedy of bail is restricted for a period of seven days could breach the Convention. There are no proposals to change this period in the White Paper "Fairer, Faster and Firmer 1998". Detention for up to 4 days without being brought before a magistrate was not considered lawful in *Brogan v. U.K.* (1989) Series A, No. 145–B, para. 59; 13 E.H.R.R. 439. In *De Jong, Baljet and Van den Brink v. Netherlands* (1984) Series A, No. 77; 8 E.H.R.R. 20, a period of six days before a release could even be requested was a violation (paragraph 58). This was in spite of the fact that habeas corpus is available (as it would have been in *Brogan v. U.K.*). The fact that a decision is about to be made on the substantive claim cannot be used to postpone taking a decision on the application for release (*Sanchez-Reisse v. Austria* (1986) Series A, No. 107; para 56–57; 9 E.H.R.R. 71).

(b) Habeas corpus

5–87   There are gaps in the statutory rights for certain detainees, and in these circumstances the only remedy is habeas corpus, unless the detention is at the discretion of the minister, when only judicial review will lie (*R. v. Secretary of State for the Home Department, ex p. Muboyayi* [1994] 4 All E.R. 72). The court has full power of review over the legality of detention, and may look into precedent facts (*R. v. Secretary of State for the Home Department ex p. Rahman* [1997] 1 All E.R. 196 at 299). For further discussion see R. J. Sharpe, *The law of habeas corpus* (2nd. ed., 1989, Clarendon).

(c) Inherent jurisdiction of the court

5–88   The test for granting bail is whether the applicant can make out one of the grounds for judicial review (*Vilvarajah v. Secretary of State for the Home Department* [1990] Imm. A.R. 457), and the applicant must at the very least "show some credible ground for believing that the [substantive] appeal might succeed" (*Charles v. Secretary of State for the Home Department* [1992] Imm. A.R. 416 at 417).

The Commission considered that habeas corpus and the review under the inherent jurisdiction of the court did not provide sufficient remedies for the purposes of Article 5(1)(5), because it appears that courts cannot go into matters of necessity and proportionality (*Caprino v. U.K.*, above, para. 67), even though they do allow a limited investigation into precedent fact. There is therefore room to argue that the courts should weigh the necessity and proportionality of the detention, after they have made conclusions on the facts. (For persuasive international law on this point, see also paragraph 9 of *A v. Australia* Communication of the U.N. Human Rights Committee, No. 560/1993, *Butterworths Immigration Law Service.*)

3. Remedy where national security issues are concerned

5–89   The U.K. procedure before the national security panel for challenging detention was found to be inadequate in *Chahal v. U.K.*, above. In response, the Special Immigration Appeals Commission Act 1997 was passed, setting up a Commission which has power to hear cases involving national security issues (see paragraph 5–70).

4. Conditions of detention

5–90   Conditions of detention are addressed under Article 3 (*Ashingdane v. U.K.* (1985) Series A, No. 93, para. 44; 7 E.H.R.R. 528 at 543). The English courts will now have to have regard to the standards set by Article 3 when considering the definition of the minimum standard (in contrast to *R. v. Metropolitan Police Commissioner, ex p. Nahar and Anr, The Times*, May 28, 1983).

5. Procedural guarantees

5–91   To satisfy Article 5(4), the "court" must provide guarantees of judicial procedure, not "markedly inferior" to those provided by the criminal courts; and the lengthier the detention, the higher the standards of procedure (*De Wilde, Ooms and Versyp v. Belgium* (1971) Series A, No. 12, paras 78–79; 1 E.H.R.R. 373). Thus hearings which would satisfy the requirements of Article 5(4) should be adversarial (*Sanchez-Reisse v. Switzerland*, above), preferably with an oral hearing (*ibid.*), and with the physical participation of the detained person or the representative (*Farmakopolous v. Belgium* (1992) Series A, No. 235–A); and reasons must be given for the detention (*ibid.*).

The Commission considered that an immigration detainee was entitled to free legal aid for legal representation to make the guarantee under Article 5(4) effective: it would have been "unreasonable to expect the applicant to present his own case in the light of the complexity of the procedures involved and his limited command of English" (*Zamir v. U.K.* (1983) 40 D.R. 42, para. 113). In this case the Commission imported the Article 6(1) test of effectiveness for the provision of legal aid. A decision on legal aid must be taken speedily.

5–92   In the United Kingdom, legal aid is not available for representation at statutory bail applications under the IA 1971. The government funds the Immigration Advisory Service and the Refugee Legal Centre to provide free representation, but these agencies do not have sufficient capacity to do this for all detainees. Following *Vilvarajah v. Secretary of State for the Home Department* [1990] Imm. A.R. 457, a person who has the remedy of going before an adjudicator should take that remedy and not use habeas corpus (for which legal aid is available). A person may be prevented from properly presenting his case at this level. Where the government agencies cannot provide representation, an application for legal aid should be made, citing the obligations of the state under Article 5(4).

Article 5 does not explicitly require an interpreter to be provided for detention proceedings under the Convention jurisprudence. However, if it is possible to import criminal procedural standards, following *De Wilde, Ooms and Versyp v. Belgium* (1971, above), then an interpreter should be available. At the moment there is an administrative presumption against an interpreter being present for bail applications. Where this prejudices the applicant, Article 5(4) should be argued in favour of a further hearing.

K. BENEFITS AND EMPLOYMENT

5–93   There is no right to work or to benefits *per se* under the Convention. This section addresses the question whether denial of all benefits to certain residents is a breach of other Convention rights, in the absence of any positive "economic and social right" to have a minimum income level. Chapter 10 deals with the Court's developing approach to social security rights.

Where English law has excluded entitlement to benefits, the Court has found that local councils have a duty to those in need of care and attention, to provide them with food, warmth and shelter under the National Assistance Act 1948, s.21 (*R. v. Hammersmith and Fulham LBC, ex p. M and others, The Times,* February 19, 1997). This entitlement was linked to the fact that people excluded from benefits had a statutory appeal right, legitimising their presence in the United Kingdom. Those appeal rights are rendered nugatory if the appellant does not have the means to survive pending the appeal, which could be listed for as long as 18 months in the future.

If anyone has an application or appeal pending based on Convention rights, which may render them irremovable, then they should equally be provided with the minimum to survive while awaiting the final decision: this ensures that the remedy under Article 13 is "effective" (*R. v. Brent LBC, ex p. D* (1998) I.C.C.L.R. 234, QBD).

L. NATIONALITY LAW

5–94   The Convention does not interfere in any way with the state's right to grant or refuse nationality. However, if the decision to refuse nationality is linked to a decision to expel, it may come within the Commission's competence (*X v. FRG* (1969) 30 C.D. 107 at 110). Until the United Kingdom ratifies the Fourth Protocol, its own nationals have no protection against expulsion nor right to enter the United Kingdom, without a link to another right. The refusal to allow the applicants to enter the country of their nationality and to require them to wait in India for permission to enter was a breach of Article 3 (*X and Y v. U.K.* (1974) 44 C.D. 29). (See paragraph 5–33 as to discrimination on grounds of nationality.)

M. CONCLUSIONS

5–95   The major impact of the Act in immigration law will be the widening of jurisdiction in asylum cases (assuming appropriate rules are made), to enable the adjudicator to give a binding determination in relation to matters which are not covered by the Geneva Convention. The wider jurisdiction of presently restricted deportation appeals will greatly assist those who previously were able to obtain a recommendation from the adjudicator, but found that increasingly the Secretary of State was not following it.

The United Kingdom's approach to contact between children and their parents will have to be more generous than at present, and, along with other "guidelines", the policies should be spelt out on the face of the rules to ensure that they are clear and accessible.

In all areas the scope of review will have to be broad enough to ensure that Convention rights are fully taken into account. Under Article 8, this means carrying out the proportionality test adequately. Under Article 5, the court will have to weigh the necessity and proportionality of the detention. Under Article 3, there must be adequate procedural and practical guarantees to make the right effective. And under Article 14 it will mean developing the U.K. discrimination law in new areas.

CHAPTER 6

Family and Child Law

Josephine Henderson (Barrister, Arden Chambers)

A. INTRODUCTION

6–01 This chapter explores the relevance and significance of the Act and the Convention in some areas of English family and child law. It does not seek to provide an exhaustive review of the case law, but rather to highlight issues of interest to practitioners.

1. Principal Convention rights

6–02 The main Convention Articles of interest to the practitioner are: Article 8 (right to respect for private and family life); Article 9 (freedom of thought, conscience and religion); Article 12 (right to marry); Article 14 (prohibition of discrimination); and Article 6 (right to a fair trial). The application of these is considered in the various sections below.

The U.N. Convention on the Rights of the Child, while not part of U.K. law (see Geraldine Van Bueren, "The United Nations Convention on the Rights of the Child — The Necessity of Incorporation into United Kingdom Law", [1992] Fam. Law 373), has been referred to by national courts as well as by the Strasbourg authorities. Under Article 3 of the U.N. Convention, to which the United Kingdom is a signatory, it is provided that: "In all actions concerning children, whether undertaken by public or private social welfare institutions, courts of law, administrative authorities or legislative bodies, the best interests of the child shall be a primary consideration." The international standards set by the U.N. Convention were considered relevant by the Commission in *A v. U.K.* [1998] E.H.R.L.R. 82 and by the Court in *Olsson v. Sweden (No. 2)* (1992) Series A, No. 250; 17 E.H.R.R. 134 (but *cf.* Judge Pettiti's judgment in *Olsson v. Sweden (No. 1)* (1988) Series A, No. 13; 11 E.H.R.R. 259, and Van Bueren, "Protecting Children's Rights in Europe — A Test Case Strategy" [1996] E.H.R.L.R. 171). The application of the Hague Child Protection Convention 1996, and issues surrounding the recovery of children, are outside the scope of this Chapter.

2. How and when to raise Convention rights

6–03 While Convention rights have already received some consideration by English courts in family and children cases prior to the Act (see below), practitioners will wish to familiarise themselves with the practical ways in which Convention issues can be expected to arise under the Act. First and foremost, through its application to "public authorities" (see paragraph 1–47 and following), the Act makes Convention rights relevant to the way in which bodies such as social services authorities conduct themselves, by requiring such bodies to act in a manner which is compatible with those rights (section 6). Thus the intervention by such bodies in the lives of individuals and families (which at one extreme can entail the removal of children from the family) must be done in a manner which complies with Convention standards, unless primary legislation clearly requires or authorises a different course (section 6(1) and (2)). For public authorities to act otherwise is unlawful, providing the basis for legal action in certain cases (see further below). Outside the context of litigation, in dealings between social services departments and families, the Convention is relevant to the way in which statutory functions are performed, and may be used in order to persuade a public authority against potentially unlawful action. The same can also be said of other public agencies involved in family and children cases, particularly the police.

Secondly, in the context of litigation, section 7 provides for allegations of conduct made unlawful under section 6 to be capable of being raised in legal proceedings, whether proactively or defensively (see generally paragraph 1–55). Convention issues may thus not merely form the basis of a legal claim, but can also be used, for example, in resisting applications by local authorities for care orders and the like. The defensive uses of the Convention in public law proceedings in respect of children seems likely to be one of the most important aspects of the Act to practitioners in this area. It is important to recognise, however, that only certain classes of person can thus rely on the unlawful conduct of public authorities (see paragraph 6–05, below), and that proceedings to be brought against public authorities for unlawful conduct may be required by rules of court to be brought in a particular court or tribunal (section 7(1)(a) and (2)). It is important too that the courts are themselves public authorities for these purposes, so that the conduct of litigation is itself subject to Convention standards (particularly Article 6, the right to a fair trial, but also other relevant Articles).

Thirdly, Convention law will be of general relevance to the interpretation of all domestic legislation, by reason of section 3 and the requirement that legislation should be read and given effect (so far as possible) in a way compatible with Convention rights (see generally paragraph 1–31 and following). This is likely to be of particular importance, given especially the extensive statutory functions of local authorities in child care. By section 2, whenever a court is faced with a question which has arisen in connection with a Convention right, relevant Strasbourg case law must be taken into account.

6–04   It will immediately be observed that the Convention cannot be used to complain about the actions of an individual, only those of a public authority. There is no duty upon individuals such as parents to act in accordance with Convention rights. So, for example, a parent cannot complain that a grandparent has failed to respect the parent's right to family life under Article 8. This is not to say that the Convention will be irrelevant to the private law sphere: there still exist in particular the obligations on national courts to determine all disputes, and to interpret any applicable legislation, in accordance with Convention rights.

Whether a person or organisation (such as the NSPCC) will be treated as a public authority for the purposes of the Act will doubtless become a much-litigated question, given the broad definition in section 6.

3. Victims

6–05   There is a significant limitation in the class of person who may rely on the unlawful conduct of public authorities under section 6. By section 7(1), only actual or potential "victims" can make use of their Convention rights in legal proceedings. This limitation extends to proceedings for judicial review (section 7(3)). Victim status is to be determined in accordance with Convention law on this question (see generally paragraphs 1–56, 2–15 and following). In practical terms, this means that persons who do not fall within the definition of "family" cannot complain of a violation of their family life.

Furthermore, there is likely to be a requirement that the person should be directly affected by the act of the public authority. In many cases, actions are brought by parents or other relatives on behalf of a child. Unless such a person is directly affected, the complaint is likely to fail. In *A and B v. U.K.* [1998] E.H.R.L.R. 82, for example, a complaint by the father of a boy beaten by his stepfather was considered inadmissible by the Commission, although the boy's own complaint was admissible. This also means that special interest bodies, such as the NSPCC or Homeless Persons' Alliance, will not themselves be able generally to make a complaint, though they may be allowed to be heard as an interested party in the course of existing proceedings.

4. Rights v. the welfare approach

6–06   The use of the word "right" can create difficulties in the application of the Convention in family cases. In many areas, the English courts tend to adopt an investigative rather than adversarial approach. In most children's cases, the focus is on the welfare, or best interests of the child. For example, contact is seen as furthering the welfare of the child, rather than as the right of the parent or child. The courts may, and often do, act against the wishes of the child, or the wishes of the person seeking or resisting contact.

The approach of the Court, in dealing with applications under Article 8, has been to balance the interests of the individual and the interests of others or of the community as a whole. Comparisons can be made with aspects of domestic law. The margin of appreciation (see generally paragraph 2–41 and following) given to states under the Convention can be seen to correspond to the discretion given to local authorities in domestic law. Considerations relating to the protection of health or morals, and the protection of rights and freedoms, of a child under Convention law, are broadly equivalent to the welfare considerations in domestic law. English law, however, goes one stage further than the Convention in stating that the welfare of the child is "paramount". It remains to be tested whether, under the Convention, it is necessary in a democratic society for a child's welfare to be *always* paramount. It may be that in future cases, in interpreting s.1 of the Children Act 1989, the courts will need to examine more closely whether the child's welfare demands a particular course of action. Furthermore it may be necessary to make specific reference to the "rights" of parents and their children when conducting the balancing exercise. Courts will have to ensure that "paramount" does not mean "first".

Parental discretion over the upbringing of their children is given legal recognition under the Convention. It is a part of family life, to be respected under Article 8. The boundaries of this right, and the extent to which interference is justified, are not clear. Some of the difficulties which arise in dealing with issues of parental discipline are considered at paragraph 6–58 and following, below.

5. Effective remedies

6–07   Article 13 (right to an effective remedy) has not itself been given effect under the Act, but the right to an effective remedy is one of the highly contentious issues in family law. Family cases are very different from ordinary civil actions in which the court's task is to provide legal remedies to enforce recognisable legal rights (see Andrew Bainham "Interfering with parental responsibility — a new challenge for the law of torts?", *Journal of Child Law* Oct./Dec. 1990; and *Patel v. Patel* (1988) 18 Fam. Law 213). Furthermore the remedy of damages is not available for most cases where children have suffered as a result of the acts or failure to act of local social services authorities. In future, the boundaries of the relationship between parents and third parties will have to be defined by the courts. It is likely that an adequate remedy will have to be found by the courts (see further paragraph 6–99 and following, below).

6. Discrimination and justification

6–08   Whilst Article 14 is not a free-standing prohibition on discrimination it may be relevant in the context of family law when considering the treatment of the families of married and unmarried persons, legitimate and illegitimate children. Family life protected under Article 8 does not depend on the legal status of marriage or legitimacy. Where rights are denied to persons without such status, or on account of race, colour, sex language, religion, etc., there may be a violation of Article 14 (see, *e.g. Abdulaziz, Cabales and Balkandali v. U.K.* (1984) Series A, No. 94; 7 E.H.R.R. 471, in which there was discrimination in immigration laws which denied women the right to bring a new family into the country, but Article 8 was not breached because families did not have the right to live in the place of their choice). However, States have a wide margin of appreciation in these matters, and it is not always clear whether the denial of some rights (such as the right to adopt, denied to homosexual couples) will be said to pass the requirements of a legitimate aim and proportionality (see generally paragraph 2–44 and following). In this context, it can be particularly important to consider the dynamic quality of Convention law (see generally paragraph 2–33).

B. WHAT IS FAMILY LIFE?

6–09   Respect for private and family life is protected under Article 8. Most of the areas of dispute with which family practitioners are familiar concern "family life", but mention should also be made of the concept of a private life. This is wider than the notion of privacy in English law. It encompasses the development of relationships outside the "inner circle" (see paragraph 2–82). Sexual relations, for example, are an intimate aspect of private life. Relationships between homosexual couples are often considered under private rather than family life, although the boundaries are neither well defined nor fixed. The Strasbourg authorities take into account the current attitudes in the contracting states when approaching such questions (see "The Concept of Family Life under the E.C.H.R." by Jane Liddy [1998] E.H.R.L.R. 15).

Family life does not depend upon marriage alone. It is a matter of fact whether a relationship between partners is sufficiently established to constitue family life. The different types of relationships which constitue family life are considered in paragraphs 6–27—6–30 below, and the changing nature of relationships and family structures is considered in paragraphs 6–31—6–35.

Under the Convention, the identification of a family life is essentially a question of fact, depending on the real existence of family ties. This approach is not adopted universally in English family law. For example, under some parts of the Children Act 1989, the categories of persons who must be made respondents to an application by a local authority, or who are entitled to notification of proceedings or who may make representations, are fixed and limited (see, e.g. Family Proceedings Rules 1991, App. 1). The court has discretion in some areas to consider applications from relevant persons. But in some cases, a person whose relationship with a child is not that of parent, or person with parental responsibility, may find his or her family life or bond with the child is not respected, and may need to invoke Article 8.

For consideration of "family" in other non-family law contexts such as housing law, see paragraphs 7–26—7–27 (and *e.g. Fitzpatrick v. Sterling Housing Association* [1997] Fam. Law 784).

C. MARRIAGE AND DIVORCE

6–10   Although family life does not depend on marriage alone, the institution of marriage is still considered important in domestic law, and is protected under the Convention. Marriage is recognised as a part of family life protected by Article 8, and Article 12 specifically protects the right to marry.

"Sham" marriages may fall outside the scope of Article 8 (see *e.g. Moustaquim v. Belgium* (1991) Series A, No. 193, para. 51; (1991) 13 E.H.R.R. 802). Polygamous unions may establish a family life (*A and A v. Netherlands* (1992) 72 D.R. 118), but in *Alam and Khan v. U.K.* (1967) 10 Y.B. 478, the Court considered that there was no obligation on the state to give legal status to polygamous unions.

1. The right to marry

6–11   There are various restrictions in domestic law on who may marry, which will fall to be tested against the rights under Articles 8 and 12.

(a) Transsexuals and homosexuals

6–12 The right to respect for private and family life connotes a level of positive obligations upon the contracting states (see generally paragraph 2–35 and following), including recognition of legal rights. In the United Kingdom, there is still limited legal recognition of partnerships between persons of the same sex. Interference with relationships between persons born of the same sex has been said to be justified under Article 8 if, for example, it is for the protection of morals.

Since the decision in *Corbett v. Corbett (Otherwise Ashley)* [1971] P. 83, domestic courts have held that a marriage depends on sex (*i.e.* chromosomal, gonadal, and genital factors) rather than gender (which may be determined by psychological factors and operative interventions). In *Rees v. U.K.* [1987] 2 F.L.R. 11; Series A, No. 106; 9 E.H.R.R. 56, a transsexual argued that the refusal to allow him to marry was a breach of Article 12. The Court held unanimously that Article 12 referred to the "traditional marriage between persons of opposite biological sex." The Court pointed out that Article 12 is mainly concerned to protect marriage as the basis of family life, and did not regard homosexual couples, with or without children, as forming a family. The Court found that, in the United Kingdom, the legal impediment to the marriage of persons who are not of the opposite biological sex did not impair the "essence" of the right to marry.

In *Cossey v. U.K.* [1991] 2 F.L.R. 492; Series A, No. 184; 13 E.H.R.R. 622, the Court found that there continued to be little common ground between contracting states, and "no evidence of any general abandonment of the traditional concept of marriage". In considering U.K. legislation, the Court took a different approach from that taken in *Rees*, and held that the impediment to marriage was biological not legal.

6–13 Six years after *Cossey*, counsel for a transsexual argued, in the Court of Appeal, that public attitudes had changed (*J v. S-T (formerly J) (Transsexual: Ancillary Relief)* [1997] 1 F.L.R. 402). The court was aware that *Rees* and *Cossey* had been distinguished in a decision that France was in violation of Article 8, on the ground that science had progressed and attitudes had changed (*B v. France* [1992] 2 F.L.R. 249; Series A, No. 232–C; (1992) 16 E.H.R.R. 1); and also of the "very considerable advances since 1970 when *Corbett* was decided". It was nonetheless held that in English law the "fundamental essence" of matrimony, as a union between persons of the opposite sex, had not changed: on the contrary, that it "must be made inviolable, and must be buttressed". Ward L.J. suggested that it might have been different if the defendant had completed the full gender reassignment programe, including a phalloplasty, but only in respect of the claim for ancillary relief after the declaration of nullity.

More recently, in *Sheffield and Horsham v. U.K.*, *The Times*, September 4, 1998 (see Commission decision in [1997] E.H.R.L.R. 443) , the Court held by a majority that the U.K. government was entitled to a margin of appreciation in refusing to give legal recognition to post-operative transsexuals. The detriment to the applicants was not considered sufficiently serious to override that margin. The Court found that medical science had not advanced significantly since *Rees* and *Cosens*, and that there was still no common legal approach among contracting states, although the matter should be kept under review. Accordingly, by a narrow majority, the Court held there was no violation of Article 8. Nor was there a breach of Articles 12 or 14. In *I v. U.K.* (App. No. 25680/94, Dec. of May 27, 1997), the Commission unanimously declared admissible complaints by a transsexual nurse, under Articles 8, 12, and 14 (see also *X, Y and Z v. U.K.* (1997) 24 E.H.R.R. 143).

(b) Persons under the age of 16

6–14 By Article 12, only men and women "of marriageable age" have the right to marry. English law requires the parties to be 16 (or 18, without parental consent). The justification for establishing a minimum age is that early marriage and childbirth would interfere with a child's education and be "socially and morally wrong" (see, *e.g. Pugh v. Pugh* [1951] 2 All E.R. 680), and that it prevents trafficking in children. This is in accordance with Article 6(3) of the Declaration on the Elimination of Discrimination against Women, but is contrary to the practices of some religious and ethnic groups.

The courts will not recognise certain religious ceremonies conducted abroad, if one or both parties are domiciled in England *e.g.* where one of the parties is under 16 (*Pugh v. Pugh* [1951] P.482; [1951] 2 All E.R. 680). Where neither party is domiciled in England, the marriage may be recognised if it is valid under the *lex loci domicilii* of each party. The Court of Appeal recognised that Moslem culture allows girls to marry at a young age (*Alhaji Mohamed v. Knott* [1969] 1 Q.B. 1). This tolerance of religious practices abroad may not comply with obligations to protect children (see U.N. Convention on the Rights of the Child).

(c) Prohibition on grounds of consanguinity and affinity

6–15 The degree of restriction on these grounds varies between religious groups, and does not always coincide with the prohibitions set out in the Marriage Act 1949. In *Cheni v. Cheni* [1963] 2 W.L.R. 17; [1962] 3 All E.R. 873, the courts recognised a Jewish marriage valid in Egypt between uncle and niece. The test of recognition was said to be "whether the marriage is so offensive to the conscience of the English court that it should refuse to recognise and give effect to the proper foreign law".

Polygamous marriages may not be contracted in England, but may be recognised if contracted by non-domiciliaries abroad (see *Dicey and Morris on the Conflict of Laws*, r.71). In the United States, the Mormons challenged such restrictions as being in breach of their right to free exercise of religion. The courts drew a distinction between the freedom to profess a belief and the freedom to practice it (*Reynolds v. U.S.* 98 U.S. (8 Otto.) 145 (1878)).

Article 9 allows persons to manifest religious beliefs subject to the limitations "necessary in a democratic society in the interests of public safety, for the protection of public order, health or morals, or for the protection of the rights and freedoms of others". It is not clear whether restrictions on the practice of polygamy can be justified under these limitations. It has been suggested that the refusal to recognise polygamy is based on racial discrimination and contrary to Article 14, although the refusal does protect the interests of women in so far as they do not have the same right to enter into marriage under Islamic law (Caroline Hamilton on *Family, Law and Religion* (1995), Sweet & Maxwell).

2. Marriage ceremonies

6–16   It is not a violation of Article 9 that a marriage by a ceremony of a person's own choosing is not legally binding. The marriage ceremony has not been considered as "a form or manifestation of thought, conscience or religion" (*X v. FRG* (1974) 1 D.R. 64). It might, however, be argued that the failure to recognise certain types of marriage discriminates against persons on the ground of religion (Article 9 and 14).

3. The validity of a religious marriage

6–17   English law does not recognise a marriage conducted in the absence of any civil formalities (Marriage Act 1949, *R. v. Bham* [1965] 3 All E.R. 124, *R. v. Ali Mohammed* [1964] 1 All E.R. 653). Whilst it is not an offence to conduct a purely religious ceremony, the parties cannot seek relief from the courts on the dissolution of such a marriage. On the other hand, where the person conducting the solemnisation purports to marry the couple under English law, he may be guilty of a criminal offence. Greater lenience is shown to the parties because the presumption of marriage is strong. If they believed that they were entering into a marriage which was valid under English law, their children will be legitimate (s.1(1) of the Legitimacy Act 1976), although it is not clear whether the marriage would be upheld for other purposes.

The legal requirements for solemnising and registering a marriage means that many people practicing minority religions have two ceremonies of marriage, one civil and one religious. It is arguable that there is no basis for allowing Anglicans to be exempted from the civil preliminaries.

The requirement that a building be certified as a place for religious worship before it is eligible for registration may discriminate against Scientologists, and other religions (see, *e.g. R. v. Register General, ex p. Segerdal* [1970] 2 Q.B. 697). The Marriage Act 1994 allows civil marriages to be solemnised on any premises approved by local authorities, but failure to give approval may still give rise to complaints about discrimination.

4. Failure to conduct a religious ceremony

6–18   Where one party refuses to take part in a religious wedding after a civil marriage takes place, the parties will be married in the eyes of the state, but not within the religious community (the state is upholding a "limping" marriage). The basis on which English courts grant a nullity is failure to consummate, but this ground may not always be available, and it ignores the reality of the problem in these cases. The courts fail to recognise the religious beliefs of the parties, that a marriage is not a marriage until there has been a religious ceremony, and this could be considered a breach of Article 9. Hamilton (*op. cit.*) suggests that recognition of religious beliefs could be achieved by allowing nullity on the ground of consent.

5. Divorce

6–19 There is no absolute right to a divorce under Article 8 (*Johnson v. Ireland* (1986) Series A, No. 112; 9 E.H.R.R. 203). But where families separate, and new families are formed, the state may need to offer some remedy to protect the newly formed family from the other family (*Airey v. Ireland* (1979) Series A, No. 32; 2 E.H.R.R. 305) and relieve the parties of marriage "duties" (such as the duty to live together).

Failure of the State to recognise religious divorces may be breach of the right to practice religion under Article 9. On the other hand, any intervention of the state in religious practices would have to be justified (*e.g.* on the ground of morality). A person may be divorced in civil law, but not under his or her religion. Where the religious laws prohibit remarriage, the state may have a duty to assist parties to remove such barriers to remarriage, if it is to uphold the right to marry under Article 12 (*i.e.* to remarry), and the right to respect for family life under Article 8 (*i.e.* with regard to the new family). In some cases (for example in Judaic and Islamic law), the religious barriers to remarriage discriminate against women: divorce is not offered on an equal basis to men and women (contrary to Article 16(1) Universal Declaration of Human Rights, Article 23(4) of the International Covenant on Civil and Political Rights, and the Convention on the Elimination of All Forms of Discrimination Against Women).

6–20 Divorces which are valid according to foreign laws may be recognised in English law if both parties are non-domiciles, provided it is not contrary to public policy. It is now possible to apply for ancillary relief in England in respect of some overseas divorces (section 12 of the Matrimonial and Family Proceedings Act 1984). The Family Law Act 1986 makes a distinction between divorces obtained overseas by proceedings (section 46(1)) and those obtained otherwise than by means of proceedings (section 46(2)). Arguably, this distinction in civil rights discriminates against certain religions contrary to Article 9. For example, the state will more readily recognise a Jewish divorce (*get*) than certain Hindu divorces.

It has been suggested that the state ought to uphold an agreement between the parties to obtain a religious divorce (such as the pre-nuptial contract mandatory in orthodox Jewish marriages), but this raises the issue as to how far the courts ought to enforce this or any religious obligation, such as attending services. Courts may be prepared to impose sanctions where one party prevents another remarrying according to the religion he or she practices. In *Brett v. Brett* [1969] 1 All E.R. 1007, the Court of Appeal, in assessing maintenance, decided that a lump sum was payable immediately and a further sum payable at a later date if the husband failed to grant his wife a *get*. There are no statutory sanctions at present in this regard. A remarriage (religious barriers) clause, to aid Muslims and Jews in obtaining a religious divorce, was withdrawn from the Matrimonial and Family Proceedings Bill in 1984. Under the Family Law Act 1996, the failure of a party to obtain a religious divorce may delay the divorce.

It should also be emphasised that undue delay in being granted a divorce could give rise to complaint under Article 6(1).

D. FAMILY LIFE OUTSIDE MARRIAGE

6–21 The notion of "family" is not confined solely to marriage-based relationships, as explained below.

1. Partners of the opposite sex and their children

6–22 In Convention law, the "family" may encompass *de facto* family ties, where the parties are living together outside marriage, or the relationship is sufficiently stable (*Johnston v. Ireland* (1986) Series A, No. 112; 9 E.H.R.R. 203; *Keegan v. Ireland* (1994) Series A, No. 290; 18 E.H.R.R. 342, *Wakefield v. U.K.* (1990) 66 D.R. 251, *K v. U.K.* (1986) 50 D.R. 199, *Marckx v. Belgium* (1979) Series A, No. 31; 2 E.H.R.R. 330). It is not essential that the relationship include an element of co-habitation (*Kroon v. Netherlands* (1994) Series A, No. 297–C; 19 E.H.R.R. 263). In *Keegan v. Ireland*, parents who were separated had enjoyed a relationship for two years and cohabited for one year. They made a deliberate decision to have a child and they planned to get married. Their relationship was said to have the "hallmark of family life" for the purpose of Article 8.

In order to invoke Article 8, the applicant must establish a relationship with his or her partner which is sufficiently stable to amount to a "family" tie. In some areas of English family law, a strict delineation (such as a two year co-habitation rule) may result in some persons who would be regarded as having established a "family tie" under the Convention being unable to benefit from family provision or other benefits (see, *e.g.* the definition of cohabitant in section 1(3)(b) of the Fatal Accidents Act 1976). For discussions about definitions used in different jurisdictions, see Hoggett, Pearl, Cooke and Bates, *The Family, Law and Society Cases and Materials* (Butterworths, (1996)).

6–23 In domestic law, if a child is born of a stable relationship, the child is automatically deemed part of the family, and no established bond need be proved with that child. Children born of a casual relationship will automatically have a bond with their mother sufficient to amount to "family life", but not their father unless there is some substantive family life. The investigation by the Strasbourg authorities as to whether there is a bond sufficient to amount to "family life" (see, *e.g. Singh v. U.K.* (1967) 10 Y.B. 478) may be similar to the test for granting parental responsibility developed by the English courts, *e.g.* in *Re H (Illegitimate Children: Father: Parental Rights) (No. 2)* [1991] 1 F.L.R. 214 (but without the welfare element). For discussion of these principles, see *McMichael v. U.K.* (1995) Series A, No. 308; 20 E.H.R.R. 205; [1995] Fam. Law 478; see also, Barton and Bissett-Johnson [1995] Fam. Law 507, and *Dawson v. Wearmouth* [1997] 2 F.L.R. 629. The extent of the protection under Article 8 in respect of unmarried partners was also considered in *U v W* [1997] 2 F.L.R. 282, in relation to *in vitro* fertilisation.

2. Homosexual relationships and children

6–24 The bond between homosexual couples in a stable relationship is still not considered by the Strasbourg authorities to come within the ambit of family life under Article 8 (although certain aspects of private life are protected). This refusal to consider the "real existence in practice of close personal ties" (*K v. U.K.* (1986) 50 D.R. 199 at 207) may be considered to be something of an anomaly. In *Kerkhoven v. Netherlands* (App. No. 15666/89, Dec. of May 19, 1992) the Commission held that the relationship of a woman with the child of her long-term lesbian partner did not fall within the scope of family life, despite the fact that she had taken on a parenting role. The Commission found that homosexual relationships did not fall within the scope of the term family life.

Likewise, in most areas of English law, the definition of co-habitants does not include homosexual couples (see, *e.g. Fitzpatrick v. Sterling Housing Association* (1998) 30 H.L.R. 576). In other areas, such as domestic violence, homosexual couples are not excluded from protection (*e.g.* Family Law Act 1996, Pt. IV; but *cf.* provision for transfer under *ibid.* Schedule 7). Any person, including the homosexual partner of a parent, may apply to be joined in care proceedings.

3. Transsexual relationships

6–25 In *R. v. Registrar of Births, ex p. P & G* [1996] 2 F.L.R. 90, the Divisional Court did not consider Article 8 to be applicable in a challenge made by a transsexual under the Births and Deaths Registration Act 1953 (*cf. R. v. Registrar of Births, ex p. R* (unreported), January 29, 1996, Brooke J.)

There have, since then, been developments in the attitude of the Strasbourg authorities. The situation of a transsexual is now considered to be different from that of a homosexual. In *X, Y and Z v. U.K.*, R.J.D. 1997–II 619; 24 E.H.R.R. 143, family life was held to exist even where there was no blood link or legal nexus of marriage or adoption. In this case, X, a female-to-male transsexual lived in a permanent relationship with Y, a female. After AID treatment, Y gave birth to Z. X was not permitted to be registered as Z's father. The Commission recalled the cases of *Keegan v. Ireland* (1994) Series A, No. 290; 18 E.H.R.R. 342, and *Family X v. U.K.* (1982) 30 D.R. 232, and that "family life" was not restricted only to marriage-based relationships. In the Commission's view, whether other family ties fall within the scope of Article 8 depends on the particular circumstances of the case. Relevant factors will include the existence of blood ties, co-habitation, and the nature of the relationships between the persons concerned, including the demonstrable interest, commitment and dependency existing between them.

6–26 The Court was more cautious, but accepted that the case concerned family life within the meaning of Article 8. The Court did not accept that a change in the U.K. law to allow a transsexual to register as father of a child was to the advantage of the child. In refusing to find a violation of Article 8 (by a majority of 14 to 6), the Court looked at the implications of such a change, which would "be open to criticism on the ground of inconsistency" if the female to male transsexual was not also allowed to marry a female. The Court took into account social research on the welfare of children in such relationships, but decided that a failure to change the law would not cause undue hardship to the applicants.

The English courts, with their emphasis on the interests of the child, may be more willing to find violations of Article 8 in such a situation. In *X, Y and Z v. U.K.*, Judge Gotchev, in his dissenting opinion, considered that in striking a balance between the right to family life and any countervailing general interest, "the welfare of the child should be the prevailing consideration, irrespective of the manner of his or her conception or the transsexuality of the 'social father' ".

E. FAMILY LIFE: THE PARENT/CHILD RELATIONSHIP

6–27   A child born of a marital union is *ipso iure* part of that relationship from the moment of the child's birth, and by the very fact of it there exists between child and parents a bond amounting to "family life" which subsequent events cannot break save in exceptional circumstances (*Keegan v. Ireland* (1994) Series A, No. 290; 18 E.H.R.R. 342, and *Gul v. Switzerland* (1996) 22 E.H.R.R. 93, and see below). Exactly what events constitute "exceptional" circumstances are not clear. In *Berrehab v. Netherlands* (1989) Series A, No. 138; 11 E.H.R.R. 322, it was held that it was not necessary for parents to co-habit with their children for the bond to remain part of their family life.

1. Presumption of paternity

6–28   In *Kroon v. The Netherlands* (1994) Series A, No. 297–C; 19 E.H.R.R. 263, the Court said that legal assumption of a child's legitimacy should not prevail over biological and social reality. The presumption of paternity must be capable of being rebutted. This is one of the few areas in which the rights of parents are said to prevail over the interests of the child in English law (*cf. S v. McC* [1972] A.C. 24).

Questions of human rights also arise in a consideration of whether blood tests should be ordered against a party's wishes. In *Tomlinson v. Ridout* (unreported, July 22, 1993, CA) a man appealed against a paternity order which required him to submit to a blood test. The Court of Appeal considered that any interference with Article 8 would be justified under Article 8(2) because his right interfered with the rights of others.

2. Embryology and surrogacy

6–29   Artificial methods of insemination give rise to complex medical, legal and ethical issues. In such circumstances, states are given a wide margin of appreciation in defining and protecting family life under Article 8 (see *U v. W* [1997] 2 F.L.R. 282). The Commission has upheld the refusal by a state to recognise the biological father of a child born by *in vitro* fertilisation in (*G v. Netherlands* (1993) 16 E.H.R.R. C.D. 38). The biological father complained when he was refused access rights to the child. His complaint was held inadmissible. Also, a father has no relationship with a foetus, whether or not he is married to the woman who is carrying the foetus (*X v. U.K.* (1980) 19 D.R. 244).

F. FAMILY LIFE: OTHER RELATIONSHIPS

6–30   Relationships between siblings (*Moustaquim v. Belgium* (1993) Series A, No. 193; 13 E.H.R.R. 802, para. 56), between grandparents and grandchildren (*Marckx v. Belgium* (1979) Series A, No. 31; 2 E.H.R.R. 330;

Price v. U.K (1988) 55 D.R. 224), and between uncle and nephew (*Boyle v. U.K.* (1994) Series A, No. 282–B; 19 E.H.R.R. 179), fall within the ambit of Article 8. The composition of a family may vary between cultures. Whether Article 8 protects a relationship between members of an extended family will depend on a consideration of the nature of the bond within the real context of everyday life. The existence of family life between adoptive parents and their adopted child is well established (*X v. France* (1982) 31 D.R. 241). The position in relation to a foster parent and a foster child has been raised but not pursued by the Commission (*X v. Switzerland* (1978) D.R. 13; see also *Gaskin v. U.K.* (1989) Series A, No. 160; 12 E.H.R.R. 36).

The width of meaning given to family life may be particularly important when considering the different treatment under domestic law of persons applying for orders in relation to children. Restrictions exist, for example, in relation to those persons entitled to seek orders under the Children Act 1989, s.8. The operation of such provisions, and their justification, will fall to be tested against the requirements of the Convention.

G. ALTERATION OF FAMILY STRUCTURES

6–31 This section considers the ending of family relationships, and how different families close down.

1. Parent/child relationships

6–32 Despite changes in family structures, a parent's established bond with his or her child still constitutes a family within the meaning of Article 8, except when the child is adopted, or in other exceptional circumstances. Where a child is taken into care, a mother and any other person who has or had a family life with the child continues to enjoy the protection of Article 8 (see *O and H v. U.K.* (1988) Series A, No. 120; 10 E.H.R.R. 95), *W, B and R. v. U.K.* (1988) Series A, No. 121; (1988) 10 E.H.R.R. 74). This approach has not been universally adopted by the English courts. In *Re KD (a minor) (ward: termination of access)* [1988] A.C. 806, Lord Templeman held that the English courts could, in accordance with the Convention, consider the extent to which the family life of the parent and child has been supplanted by some other relationship which has become the essential family life for the child, *e.g.* when a child is taken into the care of the local authority.

A relationship between adult partners ceases to be family life within the meaning of Article 8 where parties divorce or separate, but the relationship between each separated or divorced partner and a child of that union may survive as family life (*Berrehab v. Netherlands* (1988) Series A, No. 138; 11 E.H.R.R. 322).

2. Relationships between spouses or partners

6–33 There is a presumption that Article 8 applies after a legal marriage, even though the parties are not co-habiting (*Abdulaziz, Cabales and Balkandali v. U.K* (1985) Series A, No. 94; 7 E.H.R.R. 471). Divorce or separation usually brings family life to an end. But it is not just a matter of looking at formalities. Marriage does not in itself maintain the family.

In most cases, the English courts regard the termination of legal relations upon divorce as termination of family life, but the approach of the Court in considering the real existence of close personal ties is reflected in the English courts in some contexts. In *M v. M* [1981] 2 F.L.R. 39, the Court of Appeal held that a child was not "a child of the family" of the husband of a woman who had become pregnant by another man. Even though they were not divorced, the parties were held together only by the "empty shell" of the marriage. It is not clear whether in applying the Convention, such a couple would have a "family life" within the meaning of Article 8 (see also *W v. W* [1984] F.L.R. 796, *Teeling v. Teeling* [1984] F.L.R. 808).

3. Step-parents

6–34   For the purposes of Article 8, most step-parents will be regarded as having a bond with their step-children sufficient to amount to family life. However in England they are not given the same status as natural parents, which could give rise to complaint under the Convention. Whilst status can be acquired by step-parents (*e.g.* by applying for a section 8 order), a number of commentators have already argued for greater legal recognition of the step-parent relationship (*e.g.* J. Masson, "Old Families into New: A Status for Step-Parents" in M.D.A. Feeman (ed.) *State, Law and Family* (Tavistock, 1984); see also Ines Weyland, "The blood tie: raised to the status of a presumption", [1997] J.Soc.Wel. & Fam.L. 19(2), 173–188).

4. Competing family claims

6–35   Different families may have competing claims. For example, the responsibility of a former partner or spouse to make periodical payments, or to pay child support, does not cease on remarriage. The state's obligations to protect one newly-formed family from another family were considered in *Airey v. Ireland No. 1* (1979) Series A, No. 32; 2 E.H.R.R. 305. The Court held there was violation of Article 6(1) where the applicant wife was unable to afford a legal separation from her husband, a violent alcoholic, in the Irish courts. The Court also held that the obligation on the State to comply with Article 8 might require allowing parties to be relieved of "the duty to live together" (but see dissenting decision of Judge Vilhjamsson).

The effect of a change in residence of one family member was considered in *Ahmut v. Netherlands*, R.J.D. 1996–IV 2017; 24 E.H.R.R. 62. Mr Ahmut moved to the Netherlands from Morocco, leaving behind his former wife and children. He re-married in the Netherlands. The Dutch court later refused an application for a residence permit by Mr Ahmut's son. The Court accepted that the case fell within the ambit of Article 8, following the approach that the bond with a child which amounts to family life cannot be broken save in exceptional circumstances.

H. RESPECT FOR FAMILY LIFE

6–36   Article 8 affords not the right to family life, but rather the right to respect for it. The word "respect" in Article 8 connotes both positive and negative obligations. The negative obligations include the obligation not to interfere with family life. Broadly, any restraint on the activities of the family group or failure to recognise the importance of close and intimate relationships may be regarded as a violation of Article 8.

The positive obligations implied in the meaning of "respect" include a requirement for the state to take positive steps to allow members to maintain their existing family life (see, *e.g. X and Y v. Netherlands* (1985) Series A, No. 91; 8 E.H.R.R. 235, and dissenting judgment of Judge Martens in *Gul v. Switzerland* (1996) 22 E.H.R.R. 93). Respect may include taking measures with a view to reuniting children with their natural parents (*Olsson v. Sweden* (1988) Series A, No. 13; 11 E.H.R.R. 259; *Eriksson v. Sweden* (1989) Series A, No. 156; 12 E.H.R.R. 183; *Margareta and Roger Andersson v. Sweden* (1992) Series A, No. 226; 14 E.H.R.R. 615. Respect may also include providing adequate remedies for individuals in the courts (*e.g. A v. U.K* [1998] E.H.R.L.R. 82; *The Times*, September 24, 1998). Such remedies could include the enforcement of a contact order (*Hokkanen v. Finland* (1994) Series A, No. 299–A; 19 E.H.R.R. 139). In determining whether a positive obligation exists, a fair balance has to be struck between the general interest of the community and the interests of the individual (*Rees v. U.K.* (1986) Series A, No. 106; 9 E.H.R.R. 203).

1. The creation or extention of a family

6–37 The obligation under Article 8 is to respect family life: it does not allow persons to claim a right to establish family life (contrast Article 12, the right to marry and to found a family). Article 8 involves recognition of a family which exists. It is not clear to what extent there will be interference with family life if a family is prevented, by inadequate accommodation or otherwise, from growing.

2. Identity of the individual or family: change of name

6–38 An individual's name is a concern of private or family life. It is a means of personal identification and a link to a family, and falls within the ambit of Article 8 (*Stjerna v. Finland* (1994) Series A, No. 280–B; 24 E.H.R.R. 195, *Burghartz v. Switzerland*, Series A, No. 299–B; 18 E.H.R.R. 101). A balance must be struck between the competing interests of the individual and those of the community as a whole (*Keegan v. Ireland* (1994) Series A, No. 290; 18 E.H.R.R. 342) There appears to be little common ground between Convention countries as to the conditions on which a change of name may legally be effected and there is a wide margin of appreciation.

Parental rights to choose the name of a child were considered to fall within the ambit of Article 8 in *Guillot v. France* [1997] E.H.R.L.R. 196. But the failure by the state to allow a particular name to be registered did not cause sufficient inconvenience to the parents to establish a violation of Article 8.

3. Violence and harassment within the family

6–39 The protection of one family member from the threats of violence of another have been considered to be part of the state's obligations under Article 8 (*Airey v. Ireland* (1979) Series A, No. 32, para. 32; 2 E.H.R.R. 305). This case could be considered as the protection of the private or family life of one person against interference by a third party, or it can be seen as a protection of the family as a unit. Discrimination in the level of protection afforded to people on account of their marital status may give rise to complaints of violation of Article 14.

It is likely that English law provides an adequate remedy in most cases for domestic violence and harassment. The increased level of legal protection has been marked not only by greater statutory intervention in this area, but also by common law developments such as the removal of the concept of "marital immunity" as regards rape (see *R. v. R* [1992] 1 A.C. 599, Criminal Justice and Public Order Act 1994, s.142 and *SW v. U.K.; CR. v. U.K.* [1996] 1 F.L.R. 434, [1996] Fam. Law 275). Claims of discrimination may still arise in respect of treatment under English law, however. The Family Law Act 1996, for example, still offers greater protection to married couples, and to property owners.

Further claims of shortcomings may arise in respect of the protection of private life. In domestic law, the courts have held that non-molestation orders cannot be used to protect privacy. An applicant was refused an order under section 42 of the Family Law Act 1996 forbidding his former wife from harassing him by procuring or seeking to procure the publication of information relating to events occurring during the marriage. The court held that such conduct did not fall within the ambit of the part of the Act concerned with domestic violence (*C v. C, The Independent*, November 27, 1997).

4. Sexual relations

6–40   For some time now, homosexual practices between consenting adults in private have been protected under Article 8, but restrictions are still upheld in some areas (*e.g. Flemming v. U.K.* (1997) 23 C.D. 207, homosexuals in the armed forces; *Marangos v. Cyprus* (1997) 23 C.D. 192, treatment of homosexual men in Cyprus). Private practices between consenting adults may justifiably result in state intervention. In *Laskey, Jaggard and Brown v. U.K.*, R.J.D. 1997–I 120; 24 E.H.R.R. 39, after the House of Lords had held that consent was no defence to offences of assualt, the defendants (who had been carrying out sado-masochistic practices) complained of unlawful and unjustifiable interference with their right to respect for their private life contrary to Article 8. The Court held unanimously that there was no violation of Article 8.

In *Sutherland v. U.K.* [1996] E.H.R.L.R. 554, the Commission concluded that there was a violation of Articles 8 and 14 in the fixing of the minimum age of consent for homosexual relations at 18 rather than 16. The matter has been referred to the Court.

5. Abortion and sterilisation

6–41   This subject is considered in detail in Chapter 9, below.

6. Enjoyment of company

6–42   Article 8 not only covers the right to co-habitation (*Abdulaziz, Cabales and Balkandali v. U.K.* (1984) Series A, No. 94; 7 E.H.R.R. 471), but also protects the right to "the mutual enjoyment by parent and child of each others' company" (*Andersson v. Sweden* (1992) Series A, No. 226; 14 E.H.R.R. 615; see also *W v. U.K* (1987) Series A, No. 121, para. 59; 10 E.H.R.R. 29, and *Olsson* (1988) Series A, No. 13; 11 E.H.R.R. 259). Violation of this aspect of the right to family life has been the subject of a number of applications which concerned contact with children in care (see paragraphs 6–73—6–74). There would seem to be no reason why a right to mutual enjoyment of company should not be extended to other relationships (*Moustaquim v. Belgium* (1991) Series A, No. 193; 13 E.H.R.R. 802).

7. Residence

6–43   The right to live together is said to be an essential ingredient of family life so that relationships may "develop normally" (*Marckx v. Belgium*, see above) and parties may "enjoy each other's company" (*Olsson v. Sweden* (1988), see above). Thus where a family is prevented from living together, there may be a violation of Article 8. But there is no right to choose the most suitable place to develop family life (*Ahmut v. Netherlands*, R.J.D. 1996–VI 2017; 24 E.H.R.R. 62, *Gul v. Switzerland* (1996) 22 E.H.R.R. 93). In *Re A (A Minor) (Wardship: Immigration)* [1992] 1 F.L.R. 427 parents, who were Bangladesh citizens, commenced wardship proceedings seeking an order that their child be not removed from the jurisdiction. The father had been refused leave to remain in the United Kingdom, but did not challenge the Secretary of State's decision. The Court of Appeal decided that no issue arose in wardship, and that the Convention could not have any relevance. Parker L.J. said that the consequences of applying the Convention in such a case would be "alarming in the extreme".

In *Ahmut v. Netherlands*, see above, a father opted to move away from Morocco where his son from a previous marriage resided, and live and re-marry in the Netherlands. When his son was later refused a resident's permit, the Court refused (by a narrow majority) to intervene and decided that the father was not prevented from maintaining the degree of family life which he had opted for when moving to the Netherlands, nor was he prevented from returning to Morocco.

There is no right to a home under Article 8 (see further, paragraph 7–03 below), but a right of access to and occupation of a home may be protected by Article 8 (*Wiggins v. U.K.* (1978) 13 D.R. 40, *Cyprus v. Turkey* (1976) 4 E.H.R.R. 482, *Howard v. U.K.* (1987) 52 D.R. 198). Article 1 of the First Protocol, may also protect the property right in a home (see below). In offering accommodation to a family, a local authority may need to consider Article 8 in considering whether it is suitable for all members of the family, and whether applicants should be offered accommodation away from the support of friends. The enjoyment of a social life was considered an aspect of family life in *Beldjoudi v. France* (1992) Series A, No. 234–A.

8. Property and inheritance rights

6–44   In *Z and E v. Austria* (1986) 49 D.R. 67, the Commission considered that the positive obligations on a state under Article 8 included the implementation of "legislation regulating the use of property insofar as it interferes with the possibility to use this property for family purposes". Although Article 1 of the First Protocol also protects the peaceful enjoyment of possessions, this is not the same as the right to acquire property. In *Marckx v. Belgium* (1979) Series A, No. 31; 2 E.H.R.R. 330, a mother and daughter challeged the impediments placed in the way of an illegitimate child's right to inherit property under Belgian law. The Court held that although the mother had been wrongly denied the right to dispose of her property by will, her daughter had no right to acquire such property.

Discrimination in respect of inheritance rights is likely to give rise to claims under the Convention (see, *e.g. E.C.H. Camp and A. Bourmimi v. Netherlands* [1997] H.R.C.D. Vol. VIII No. 111 p. 731, App. No. 28369/95). Domestic laws on inheritance and financial provision contain examples of a difference of treatment between various classes of person, married and unmarried, and between spouses and children. Married and non-married partners are treated differently on a consideration of property division on separation. The use of the constructive or resulting trust will assist unmarried couples in many cases, but the court cannot take into account all the circumstances of the case as it can in dividing property on divorce under s.25 of the Matrimonial Causes Act 1973. Law Commission proposals on reforming property rights in relation to cohabitees are likely to go some way towards remedying the discrimination which exists at present. In some cases, differential treatment of married and unmarried persons has been justified by the European Court (*e.g. McMichael* (1998) Series A, No. 308; 20 E.H.R.R. 205), but such discrimination is increasingly difficult to justify and in some cases may violate Article 8, Article 14, and Article 1 of the First Protocol. An application has been made against Spain concerning the refusal, following the applicant's separation from her cohabitee to transfer the home which they had shared, to her, on the ground that such a claim could only arise out of a marriage (App. No. 37784/97 noted in [1998] H.R.C.D., Vol. IX, No. 5, p. 390).

9. The right to information

6–45 The right to information was considered to be an aspect of family life protected by Article 8 in *Gaskin v. U.K.* (1989) Series A, No. 160; 12 E.H.R.R. 36, in relation to access to records kept by a local authority in respect of a child in their care. The Court said that "persons in the position of the applicant have a vital interest, protected by the Convention, in receiving the information necessary to know and understand their childhood and early development".

10. Recognition of gender

6–46 At present, neither domestic law nor the Strasbourg authorities recognise any right to legal recognition of gender reassignment, although they are in some cases prepared to admit the possibility of recognition of ancillary rights.

At present, English law does not allow the amendment of birth certificates after a "sex-change" or "gender reassignment" operation (*R. v. Registrar of Births, ex p. P & G* [1996] 2 F.L.R. 90). In *Rees v. U.K.* (1986) Series A. No. 106; 9 E.H.R.R. 203; [1987] 2 F.L.R. 111, the Court found that refusal to amend was not contrary to Article 8, because there was a wide margin of appreciation and it could not be said that the United Kingdom had not struck the requisite balance. However, at that time the court held, by majority, that there was little common ground between the Contracting States and that, generally speaking, the law appeared to be changing. The Court of Appeal in *J v. S-T (Formerly J) (Transsexual: Ancillary Relief)* [1997] 1 F.L.R. 402 did not consider there had been any change in the approach of the English courts or the Strasbourg authorities to legal recognition of a change of gender.

More liberal approaches are seen where issues of legal consequences of gender, rather than legal status, are being considered. In *X, Y and Z v. U.K.*, R.J.D. 1997–II 619; 24 E.H.R.R. 143, the Commission was of the opinion that "there is a clear trend in Contracting States towards the legal acknowledgement of gender re-assignment" and that "in the case of a transsexual who has undergone irreversible gender re-assignment in a Contracting State and lives there with a partner of his former sex and child in a family relationship, there must be a presumption in favour of legal recognition of that relationship". The Court distinguished the case from *Rees v. U.K.* (1986) Series A, No. 106; 9 E.H.R.R. 203, and *Cossey v. U.K.* (1990) Series A, No. 184; 13 E.H.R.R. 622; [1991] 2 F.L.R. 492, only on the basis that it was not possible for a transsexual to be registered as the father of a child, not on the basis that the domestic law did not recognise the transsexual's change of identity.

6–47   In *X, Y and Z v. U.K.*, R.J.D. 1997–II 619; (1997) 24 E.H.R.R. 143, X (a female-to-male transsexual) lived in a permanent relationship with Y (a female). After AID treatment, Y gave birth to Z. In accepting Y for AID treatment, the hospital asked X to acknowledge himself to be the father of the child within the meaning of the Human Fertility and Embryology Act 1990. The Registrar General refused to allow X to be registered as the father under the Births and Deaths Registration Act 1953. In other areas too, X was not treated as a father. Whilst he could apply for parental responsibility, this does not confer the right to inherit or to financial support, nor to succeed to tenancies. Furthermore, X could only apply for parental responsibility if he had a joint residence order with Y. The Court held that, while Article 8 applied to the case, by a majority there had been no violation having regard to the lack of agreement between states, the apparent state of transition in the law, and the wide margin of appreciation afforded to national authorities.

The matter came before the Court again in *Sheffield and Horsham v. U.K.*, *The Times*, September 4, 1998 (see paragraph 6–13).

I. PARENTS' RIGHTS

6–48   The Convention rights which have particular relevance for parents can be grouped and summarised as follows.

1. Article 8 — respect for family life

6–49   While the only right enshrined in Article 8 is the right to respect for *inter alia* one's family life, the Strasbourg authorities have explored this in various contexts, including the upbringing of children by their parents. The right has thus been translated into specific rights which arise according to the circumstances of the case.

The rights of parents are likely to be thrown into particular relief in the face of conduct by local authorities in relation to children in care. In *W, B and R. v. U.K.* (1987) Series A, No. 121; 10 E.H.R.R. 29 and *O & H v. U.K* (1988) Series A, No. 136; 13 E.H.R.R. 449, for example, the rights of parents to maintain relationships with their children was held to have been violated through the action of local authorities in taking decisions to terminate parental access and (in some cases) to place for adoption. Access to children was considered a civil right (*cf.* the emphasis in domestic law on access being the right of the child not that of the parent), with the effect that Article 6 (right to a fair trial) was also held to have been violated by the lack of access to a court and delay.

The right of a parent to place restrictions on a child's freedom of movement was upheld by a majority of the Court in *Nielsen v. Denmark* (1989) Series A, No. 144; 11 E.H.R.R. 175, but this case may have been decided differently if the detention of the child had been for the purpose of punishment rather than treatment (see *A v. U.K* [1998] E.H.R.L.R. 82).

2. Article 9 — freedom of thought, conscience and religion

6–50   The right to bring children up in the religion of parental choice is usually accepted as a parental right (*e.g.* the United Nations Convention on the Rights of the Child, Art. 14). In *Re S (Minor) (Access: Religious Upbringing)* [1992] 2 F.L.R. 313, the Court of Appeal decided that the Convention did not assist a father seeking access to his children and orders concerning their religious upbringing. There could be a different result in cases of this type when the Act comes into force. Albeit not decided under Article 9, in *Hoffman v. Austria* (1993) Series A, No. 255–C, the Court considered that there had been violation of Article 14 and Article 8 in respect of a mother, when the Austrian court awarded custody to the father after their divorce on the grounds that she was a Jehovah's Witness.

3. Article 14 — prohibition of discrimination

6–51   Persons with parental responsibility, and those without, are treated differently under the Children Act 1989. For example, in respect of persons who must be made respondents in care proceedings. Discimination against unmarried fathers was considered justified by the Court in *McMichael v. U.K.* (1995) Series A, No. 307–B; [1995] 2 F.C.R. 718. The difference in treatment the applicant received when he was not married, in comparison with the treatment of married fathers, was said to have an objective and reasonable justication, namely the protection of the interests of the child and mother.

4. The application of Convention rights in English law

6–52   Convention law should not be interpreted as giving rise to rights which may be demanded by all parents at all times. In particular, how "respect" is afforded to a particular applicant, depends on the circumstances of the case, but the Strasbourg decisions are useful indicators as to what is considered to be worthy of protection.

What is particularly noticeable in domestic law is the change in terminology in recent years from "parental rights" to "parental responsibility", reflecting a reluctance to accept that parents have rights (see, *e.g.* J. Eekelaar "The Eclipse of Parental Rights" (1986) 102 L.Q.R. 4, and "The Emergence of Children's Rights" (1986) 6 *Oxford Journal of Legal Studies* 161). In *F v. Wirral Metropolitan Council* [1991] Fam. 69, the Court of Appeal examined the common law relating to parental rights. Common law recognised the right of a father to control the religious upbringing, apprenticing and training of his children and enjoy their services. There has never been a right to enjoy consortium, nor any right vested in the mother. Purchas L.J. considered that the parental right recognised in cases such as *Re KD (A Minor) (Ward: Termination of Access)* [1988] A.C. 806 "stems from the parental duty towards the child to care for and protect the child and is subservient to the welfare of the child" (p. 93). The court accordingly decided that there was no tort of interference with parental rights. In *A. v. C.* [1985] F.L.R. 445 at 455 Ormrod L.J. said : "So far as access to a child is concerned, there are no rights in the sense in which lawyers understand the word" (see also, *e.g. A v. Liverpool CC* [1982] A.C. 363). Parental rights to refuse medical treatment for their child were respected in *Re T (A Minor) (Wardship: Medical Treatment)* [1997] 1 W.L.R. 242; [1997] 1 All E.R. 906, and specific reference to rights (rather than responsibilities) has been made in some cases, *e.g. Re K (A Minor) (Custody)* [1990] 2 F.L.R. 64, *Re K (A Minor) (Wardship; Adoption)* [1991] 1 F.L.R. 57.

The Act seems likely to influence, at the very least, the terminology used by the courts in considering the interests of parents.

J. CHILDREN'S RIGHTS

6-53 The Convention does not specifically mention children's rights, but in many cases the Strasbourg authorities have upheld the rights of children as well as adults under the Convention, see, *e.g. Marckx v. Belgium* (1979) Series A, No. 31; 2 E.H.R.R. 330; *Costello-Roberts v. U.K.* (1993) Series A, No. 247–C; 19 E.H.R.R. 112; *Gaskin v. U.K* (1989) Series A, No. 160; 12 E.H.R.R. 36 — the right under Article 8 to information; *Costello-Roberts v. U.K, A v. U.K.* (see above) — the right under Article 3 not to be beaten; *Johnston v. Ireland* (1986) Series A, No. 112; (1987) 9 E.H.R.R. 203 — the right under Article 14 not to be discriminated against on the ground of legitimacy; *Berrehab v. The Netherlands* (1989) Series A, No. 138; 11 E.H.R.R. 322 — the right under Article 8 to maintain family ties; *X, Y and Z v. U.K.*, R.J.D. 1997–II 619; 24 E.H.R.R. 143 — the right under Article 8 of a child in relation to a transsexual carer.

In all these cases, the right of the child to respect for family life was translated into a specific right in the circumstances of the individual case, *e.g.* to information, to contact with a parent, or to a remedy. These cases should not be interpreted as giving rise to rights which may be demanded by all children at all times. Ultimately, Article 8 requires that family life be respected. How this respect is afforded, depends on the circumstances of the case.

In theory a child has right not to suffer discrimination on account of age or status in the exercise of Convention rights (Article 14). There will usually be an objective and reasonable justification for interfering with the rights of the child, for example in connection with property rights. The right of a child to freedom of expression under Article 10 and to have a say in matters such as choice of religion and education was considered in *Khan v. U.K* (1986) 48 D.R. 253.

The rights of a child under the Convention may need to be considered as part of the "welfare" of a child. In some cases, the exercise of the rights of a child, *e.g.* to respect for private life and for belief, may conflict with the court's view of what is in the child's best interest. It is not clear to what extent interference with a child's rights under Article 8, can be justified by the protection of the child's own interests. In order for the private and family life of a child and his or her beliefs to be respected, it will normally be necessary for the child's wishes and opinons to be considered.

K. INTERFERENCE WITH RIGHTS IN CHILDREN'S CASES

6–54   This section considers how the interests of the State, the child and its parents are to balanced under the Convention. Article 8(2) requires that any interference by a public authority with the exercise of the right under Article 8(1) must meet certain criteria. In addition to being in accordance with the law, any interference must also be necessary in a democratic society. Necessity is to be judged in terms of the interests set out in Article 8(2), the most relevant of which here are the protection of health or morals, and the protection of the rights and freedoms of others.

Differences in approach between English law and the Convention are particularly noticeable here. The former emphasises the welfare of a child rather than the rights of a child, and the obligations of parents rather than parental rights. These differences may amount to more than merely a matter of form. However, the justification for interference is still a matter to be determined primarily by national authorities, particularly given the margin of appreciation which the Convention affords them.

1. Convention rights in English law before the Act

6–55   Examples are given below of the contrasting approaches in the English courts before the Act in handling Convention rights against the background of the welfare approach. Hardly suprisingly, Convention rights have been considered irrelevant in a number of cases. In other cases, the courts have sought to justify their approach as being in harmony with the principles of the Convention, but a closer analysis shows that the balancing act required by Article 8, where there are competing interests, has rarely been applied.

The effect of decisions of the courts prior to the Act will have to be considered in each case. Certainly, cases which are found to be in conflict with the requirements of the Act will have to be re-considered; and decisions in which the courts have decided not to apply the Convention may need to be confined.

In *Re A (a Minor) (Wardship: Immigration)* [1992] 1 F.L.R. 427, Parker L.J. said that the consequences of applying the Convention in the circumstances of that case would be "alarming in the extreme". In *Re M (A Minor)* (unreported) May 3, 1996, the Court of Appeal refused to accede to a request from the Commission, and said that it had its own responsibilities to fulfil, its principle concern being the welfare of the child. In *Rowan v. Canon* (unreported) July 20, 1995, the Court of Appeal did not consider Convention rights to be relevant on an application for the transfer of possessions. In *Re S (Minor) (Access: Religious Upbringing)* [1992] 2 F.L.R. 313, the court decided that the Convention did not assist a father seeking access to his children and orders concerning their religious upbringing. In *Re M and H (Minors) (Local Authority: Parental Rights)* [1990] 1 A.C. 686, *Newton v. Newton* [1990] 1 F.L.R. 33, *Re D (A Minor)* July 20, 1989, CA, and *Re W (A Minor)*, September 28, 1989, CA, questions of breach of Convention rights were held to be irrelevant to the English proceedings. In *F v. S (Wardship: Jurisdiction)* [1991] 2 F.L.R. 349, the court considered that an application of the Convention would put too great a strain on the language of sectin 41 of the Family Law Act 1986, so it was not applied.

6–56 Some decisions which pre-date the Act have taken into account Convention rights. In *Re P-B (A Minor) (Child Cases: Hearings in Open Court)* [1997] 1 All E.R. 58, the Court of Appeal considered that in exercising its discretion to conduct a hearing in open court, the court can take account of Article 6, but recognised that Article 6 is a qualified right. In *Re W (Wardship: Discharge: Publicity)* [1995] 2 F.L.R. 466, the Court of Appeal decided that Articles 8 and 10 must be taken into account when deciding whether restraint of publicity was justified (see also *Re W (A Minor) (Wardship: Restriction on Publication)* [1992] 1 W.L.R. 100). In *Re KD (A Minor) (Ward: Termination of Access)* [1988] A.C. 806, the House of Lords considered whether English law, putting the interests of the child first, was in conflict with Convention rights, in particular Article 8. The qualified nature of the right to private and family life was recognised. Lord Templeman held that there was no inconsistency of principle or application; and that children ought to be brought up by their natural parents, with state intervention being justified only to protect the child from harm.

Where the welfare principle does not apply, the courts have more easily been able to have regard to Convention rights. In *Re M (A Minor)* (unreported) August 22, 1996, Johnson J. considered that in wardship proceedings the court should seek to exercise its discretion in a way which does not violate the Convention. The court decided that the right to petition should outweigh any other matter. In *Re H-S (Minors) (Protection for Identity)* [1994] 1 W.L.R. 1141, the Court of Appeal considered whether to discharge an injunction banning publication of the identity of parties. The Court held that where Convention rights under Articles 8 and 10 were in issue, they must be taken into account by the court in its balancing exercise, and the welfare of the child was not then the court's paramount consideration. Such a balancing exercise could be carried out under the inherent jurisdiction of the court.

2. Conflicts between individuals and the State

6–57 The interests of parents and/or their children may come into conflict with those of the state in a wide variety of situations. Commonly this may be because a local authority exercises powers, or seeks the approval of the courts, in making decisions about the upbringing of children. The interests of the state may not be easy to define; nor are they necessarily compelling. In *Berrehab v. The*

Netherlands (1989) Series A, No. 138; 11 E.H.R.R. 322, the Court held that the State's duty to preserve a dependant child's ties outweighed any perceived need of the State to protect its economic well-being. And in *Johnston v. Ireland* (1987) Series A, No. 112; 9 E.H.R.R. 203, it was held that the failure of the State to give equal status to illegitimate children was not justified. Broadly, the Convention requires a fair balance to be struck between the various interests involved.

In *Olsson v. Sweden (No. 1)* (1988) Series A, No. 13; 11 E.H.R.R. 259, the restrictions on parental access to a child in care were held not to be justified on the grounds of "administrative difficulties" and "the parents' unco-operative attitude". On the other hand, in *Rieme v. Sweden* (1992) Series A, No. 226–B; 16 E.H.R.R. 155, the interference was justified in view of the unco-operative attitude of the parents and the efforts made by the authority. The interests of the child are often justification for interference (the risk to the child was one of the factors which led to a finding of justification in *Rieme*), but not always. In *Eriksson v. Sweden* (1989) Series A, No. 156; 12 E.H.R.R. 183, the authority's contentions that an abrupt transfer of custody would be harmful to a child were not considered sufficient justification.

The Court has found that there was no interference by the state with the family life of a Turkish national who was refused permission to bring his sons to Switzerland (*Gul v. Switzerland* [1996] 22 E.H.R.R. 93). It was not necessary to consider Article 8(2), because there was no interference. The applicant was not prevented from visiting his son in Turkey. In contrast, in *Berrehab v. The Netherlands* (1988) Series A, No. 138; 11 E.H.R.R. 321, the separation of a Moroccan applicant from his daughter by a Dutch citizen was held to be unjustified interference.

(a) State intervention in relation to parenting functions

6–58   English courts and local authorities rarely intervene merely because they disapprove of the manner of parenting, as opposed to cases where practices cause or threaten to cause serious physical harm to a child or are considered by the court to be detrimental to the child's welfare. Where a parent wished a child to be sterilised, the English courts were prepared to intervene (*Re D* [1976] 2 W.L.R. 279) on the ground that it was against the child's best interests.

Interference with parental rights may be justified by English courts under Article 8(2) either because it is necessary for the protection of the child (*e.g. Re KD (A Minor) (Ward: Termination of Access)* [1988] A.C. 806, or for some other reason. For example, the separation of woman prisoners from their babies is justified on the grounds of national security, public safety and the like (*e.g. R. v. Secretary of State, ex p. Togher*, unreported, February 1, 1995, CA (also, *Togher v. U.K.* (1988) C.D. 99).

The chastisement of a child by a parent or person *in loco parentis* has been considered in *A v. U.K.* [1996] 3 F.C.R. 569; [1998] E.H.R.L.R. 82 (see also Commission decision at *The Times*, September 24, 1998). The applicant complained in relation to beatings by his stepfather, alleging violation of Articles 3, 8, 13 and 14. The boy and his brother had been placed on the local Child Protection Register because of known physical abuse. Their stepfather admitted hitting them with a cane, and was given a police caution. Subsequently, the boys were removed from the register. Later, when the applicant was nine years old, his headteacher reported to the local Social Services Department that the boy was being hit with a stick. His stepfather was arrested and charged with causing actual bodily harm. At the trial, the judge directed the jury that it was a defence that the alleged assault was merely the correcting of a child by its parent, provided the correction was "moderate in the manner, the instrument and the quantity of it, or put another way, reasonable."

6–59   The Court referred to changes in English law on corporal punishment in schools since *Costello-Roberts v. U.K.* (1993) Series A, No. 247–C; 19 E.H.R.R. 112. The Education (No. 2) Act 1996 was at that time amended so that corporal punishment in schools could not be justified if "inhuman or degrading". But the Court noted that the law relating to the use of corporal punishment on a child by a parent or other persons *in loco parentis* remained unchanged.

The Court decided that the injuries, though without severe or long lasting effects, and lacking the aggravating factor of being institutionalised, were considerably more serious than those in *Costello-Roberts*. The state was not directly responsible for the acts of the stepfather, but the Court nonetheless found that the state was responsible for failing, through its domestic legal system, adequately to protect the boy.

6–60   In *Costello-Roberts*, the Court reviewed previous decisions and considered the factors which are relevant to a determination of whether punishment reaches a minimum level of severity to be "degrading" in breach of Article 3. The factors include "the nature and context of the punishment, the manner and method of its execution, its duration, its physical and mental effects and in some instances, the sex, age and state of health of the victim". It is the physical and emotional integrity of the child which must be protected.

A majority of the Commission in *A v. U.K* did not consider that every physical rebuke, however mild, by a parent would be in breach of Article 3, though this was the subject of disagreement. The question whether some disciplinary measures which do not amount to breach of Article 3 may amount to breach of Article 8, was left open in *Costello*. In his concurring opinion in *A v. U.K*, Mr E. A. Alkema said that he would have prefered to consider that application under Article 8, so that the rights of others (such as other children) could be taken into account.

Where the punishment does not involve an assault on the child, the Court has been less willing to attach state responsibility. In *Nielsen v. Denmark* (1988) Series A, No. 144; 11 E.H.R.R. 175, the Court considered by a majority that the state was not responsible under Article 5 for the detention of a child in a closed psychiatric ward at the request of his mother. The detention was considered to be the lawful exercise of a parental right, within the boundaries of Article 8.

6–61   In English law, parents may be restrained from exercising what local authorities consider to be excessive punishment by the latter's powers under Parts IV and V of the Children Act 1989. A care or supervision order may be made if the section 31 "threshold" criteria are satisfied. It is not clear, though, how far the state can endorse the use of violence in carrying out parental duties.

It can be noted here that English law does not recognise wrongful interference with parental rights, and offers no remedy in tort. There is no tort of interference with parental responsibility (*F v. Wirral Metropolitan Borough Council* [1991] Fam. 69, *Re S (A Minor) (Parental Rights)* [1993] Fam. Law 572, *M v. Newham London Borough Council* [1993] 2 F.L.R. 575. All rights to damages for loss of a child's services have been abolished by the Law Reform (Miscellaneous Provisions) Act 1970, s.5 and the Administration of Justice Act 1982). This approach has been said to be in direct conflict with that of the Court (see *Butterworths Family Law Service* at A [102], and see *Hokkanen v. Finland* (1994) Series A, No. 299–A; 19 E.H.R.R. 139; [1996] 1 F.L.R. 289).

(b) State intervention in cases of parental inaction

6–62 Where a parent refuses medical treatment for a child in a life-threatening situation, on the grounds of religious belief, the courts will intervene. (As to treatment issues in the context of healthcare, see generally Chapter 9.) A doctor has the right to proceed in administering treatment despite parental opposition. A local authority may be granted a care order, on the basis that the child is likely otherwise to suffer significant harm. Alternatively the child could be made a ward of court. In deciding whether to intervene and what steps to take, the court and/or local authority must give respect and weight to the right to respect for private and family life under Article 8, and a parent's religious beliefs under Article 9 (see *Re O* [1993] 2 F.L.R. 149, *Jane v. Jane* (1983) 4 F.L.R. 712, *Re S* [1993] 1 F.L.R. 376), as well as considering the child's right to life under Article 2. Intervention in ordering medical treatment may be justified under Article 9(2) where there is an obvious risk of harm. Where treatment will merely prolong life (*Re J* [1992] 2 F.L.R. 165), where the illness is less serious, or where the risks of treatment are very high (*R. v. Cambridge Health Authority ex p. B* [1995] 2 All E.R. 129), parental rights may carry greater weight.

Parental opposition to a course of action, such as the stubborn and extreme opposition of a mother to contact with a father, is sometimes held to justify refusal by the courts to intervene, on the basis that it is not in the child's best interests. Sometimes it is difficult to rationalise this approach of the English courts, particularly where the child or child's representative agrees that the course of action should take place. An extreme example of the court's decision that it was not in the child's best interests for the court to oppose parental wishes is *Re T (Wardship: Medical Treatment)* [1997] 1 F.L.R. 502. The parents (who were both health care professionals) of a sick baby refused to allow the child to have a liver transplant. The Court of Appeal supported the parents' decision on the ground that it was in the interest of the child; but in doing so stretched the meaning of "in the interest of the child" to its limits, and made it clear that it considered the facts of the case to be unusual. There was no consideration of the Convention, so the court was not concerned with Article 2 (right to life), nor Article 8.

It can be noted that in English law, it is a criminal offence to neglect wilfully a child, under the Children and Young Persons Act 1933, s.1(1), and it is no defence to this charge, or to manslaughter, that the parent was manifesting a religious belief (*R. v. Senior* [1899] 1 Q.B. 283).

(c) The use of force in removing or detaining a child

6–63 The use of force in removing a child from its family was justified under Article 8(2) in *Dunkel v. FRG* (1985) App. No. 10812/84, but it was held that subsequent measures, such as a refusal to indicate the child's whereabouts, might constitute unjustified violation. Interference by the state, against the wishes of both child and parent, may be justified under Article 8(2) where the life or health of a child is at risk (*e.g. Re W (A Minor) (Consent to Medical Treatment)* [1993] 1 F.L.R. 1), but not for administrative convenience or to punish parents or children, where no criminal offence is suspected.

The absence of effective control and supervision by the courts may raise questions of violations of Articles 6 and 8 (right to a fair trial). Substantial powers for local authorities and the police exist under the Children Act 1989, which can be exercised without recourse to the courts. Not only may the unjustified exercise of such powers give rise to complaints under Article 8, but practical problems in obtaining effective access to a court are capable of engaging Article 6 as well.

3. Conflicts between individuals

6–64 The conflicting interests of individuals, particularly as between parents and children, can be a matter of concern under the Convention. Where such conflicts are being litigated, state responsibility is engaged particularly through the courts' duty under Article 6 to ensure a fair trial. Additionally, although the primary purpose of the Convention has been to provide some regulation of the legal relations between individuals and the state, the obligations of the state go further than this (see generally paragraph 2–35 and following). Thus, in *X and Y v. The Netherlands* (1986) 8 E.H.R.R. 235, the Court found that Article 8 could involve positive obligations on the State including "the adoption of measures designed to secure respect for private life even in the sphere of relations of individuals between themselves". In *Airey v. Ireland* (1979) Series A, No. 32, such positive obligations included the right (under Articles 6 and 8) to have effective access to legal protection in recognition of a *de facto* separation between husband and wife. Under the Act, the extension of the Convention is relevant in terms of possible positive obligations on public authorities to secure the observance of Convention rights in the sphere of private law.

Broadly, the Strasbourg authorities tend to conduct a balancing act between the rights of parents and the rights of children. The English approach is less adversarial, and focuses on the paramouncy of the welfare of a child. Some parental rights seem always to override children's rights in both European and English law. For example, the right to bring children up in the religion of parental choice is usually accepted as a parental right which will not be overruled by the courts (*e.g.* the United Nations Convention on the Rights of the Child, Art. 14). Whether this approach is justified or not remains to be tested.

(a) Strasbourg decisions

6–65 The right of parents to control their children and make decisions about their upbringing is an aspect of family life which is protected by Article 8 (*R. v. U.K.* (1987) Series A, No. 121–C, para. 64, *Neilsen v. Denmark* (1988) Series A,

No. 144; 11 E.H.R.R. 175, *X v. Netherlands*, 10 E.H.R.R. 74, and *Hoffman v. Austria* (1993) Series A, No. 255–C. On the other hand, the importance of children's wishes and rights were emphasised in *X v. Denmark* (1976) 7 D.R. 81, *Rieme v. Sweden* (1992) Series A, No. 226–B; 19 E.H.R.R. 155, and *Hokkanen v. Finland* (1994) Series A, No. 299–A; 19 E.H.R.R. 139. The balancing of competing rights may mean that less weight is given to certain rights of the child. However the right to freedom from degrading treatment under Article 3, is an unqualified one.

In *Nielsen v. Denmark* (1988) Series A, No. 144; 11 E.H.R.R. 175, the Court accepted that parents have the right to impose restrictions on their child's freedom of movement. The wishes of the child were subjugated to those of the parents. The Court may have been influenced by the fact that the detention was said to be in the interests of the boy's health, and not a form of punishment. Traditionally the Court has not adopted a child centred approach (see Geraldine Van Bueren, "Protecting Children's Rights in Europe — A test Case Strategy" [1996] 2 E.H.R.L.R. 171). But increasingly reference is made to the interests of the child, and to the U.N. Convention on the Rights of the Child.

If childhood is considered to be a status, there ought to be no discrimination based on childhood or minority (Article 14), but in some situations, where there are competing interests, those of the adult will prevail. The emphasis on the welfare of the child, rather than the wishes of the child, may make it difficult to determine whether the child's rights under the Convention are properly respected by local authorities and courts. It is likely, however, that both the Strasbourg authorities and the English courts will justify the differential treatment of children and adults on the ground that young children are vulnerable (*cf. Ginsberg v. New York* 390 U.S. 629 (1968)).

(b) English decisions

6–66   The approach of the English courts, which requires a balancing act to be carried out, has been said to be in harmony with the principles of the Convention, *e.g. Re S (A Minor) (Paternal Rights)* [1993] Fam. Law 572 in which English law was said to be consistent with the Convention. But in practice a balancing exercise is only carried out when there is no risk to a child's welfare. Where the wishes of a mature child conflict with his or her parents" views, or of a person *in loco parentis*, the English courts will take into account the wishes of the child. There is no rule of absolute parental authority, and no absolute right of a child to make decisions. In English law, the rights of parents, such as they are, tend to yield to the mature child's right to make his or her own decisions.

After *Gillick* (see below), the weight given to the child's views will depend on his or her age, maturity, understanding, and intelligence. In *Re P* [1986] 1 F.L.R. 272, a 15-year-old girl, who was in care, wanted to have an abortion against the wishes of her parents who were practising Seventh Day Adventists. The court decided, in wardship proceedings, that the interests of the parents should not prevent the abortion (see also *Re B* [1991] F.C.R. 889). In most English cases, older children's wishes are respected (see *Gillick v. West Norfolk and Wisbech Area Health Authority and Another* [1986] 1 F.L.R. 224, *M v. M (Minors: Removal from the Jurisdication)* [1993] 1 F.C.R. 5, *Re P (A Minor) (Education: Child's Views* [1992] 1 F.L.R. 316, *Re F (Minors) (Denial of Contact)* [1993] 2 F.L.R. 677, and *Re M (Contact: Welfare Test)* [1995] 1 F.L.R. 274).

6–67   The refusal of local authorities and courts to accede to a child's wishes gives rise to concern about the effectiveness of a child's Convention rights. For example, the wishes of older children were overridden in *Re R (Minor) (Residence: Religion)* [1993] 2 F.L.R. 163, and *Re C (Minor) (Care: Child's Wishes)* [1993] Fam. Law 400. The court can also decide issues against the wishes of a ward of court (see *e.g.* Re W [1992] 4 All E.R. 627). And a child's right of veto may be overriden by the English court in urgent cases under their inherent jurisdiction (*South Glamorgan County Council v. W and B* [1993] 1 F.L.R. 575). This potential interference with Article 8 is likely to be justified by the courts under Article 8(2) either on the ground that the child is not "*Gillick*-competent" or, even if "*Gillick*-competent", on the ground that parental rights are being exercised by a person with parental responsibility (*e.g. Re R (Minor) (Wardship: Medical Treatment)* [1991] 4 All E.R. 177, and *Re K, W and H (Minors: Medical Treatment)* [1993] 1 F.L.R. 854) or by the court *in loco parentis (Re W (A Minor) (Medical Treatment)* [1993] Fam 64, *Re S (Minor) (Medical Treatment)* [1994] 2 F.L.R. 1065, and *Re E (Minor) (Wardship: Medical Treatment)* [1993] 1 F.L.R. 386).

L. LOCAL AUTHORITIES AND CHILDREN

6–68   This section considers the application of Convention rights against the practical framework of local authority involvement in cases involving children, this context being not only one of the most significant in terms of individual rights in family cases, but also in terms of administrative and legal practice.

1. Children in care

(a) The child protection conference

6–69   Authorities need to be aware of both the substantive and procedural applications of Article 8. Failure to consult parents or other relevant persons may be a violation of Article 8 which needs to be justified, whether or not the authority has a statutory obligation to consult. The English courts have found no breach of natural justice in some cases where parents did not attend case conferences (see, *e.g. R. v. Harrow LBC, ex p. D* [1990] Fam. 133, *R. v. East Sussex County Council, ex p. R* [1991] 2 F.L.R. 358, and *R. v. Devon County Council, ex p. L* [1991] 2 F.L.R. 541), but it is open to parents, and other relevant persons, to claim that there is an unjustified violation of their rights. In addition to Article 8, it is possible that the administrative decision-making process may also be subject to the due process requirements of Article 6 (*W v. U.K.* [1987] Series A, No. 121; 10 E.H.R.R. 29).

(b) Making a care order

6–70   Removing a child from his or her family is perhaps the most serious interference with family life. On the other hand, there is little doubt that the protection of a vulnerable child is of paramount importance and is justification for that interference. In *Johansen v. Norway* (1996) 23 E.H.R.R. 33, the Court held that the taking and keeping of the child in care did not breach Article 8; but the deprivation of access and other parental rights while the child was in care was a violation.

The rights of a child to private and family life under Article 8 may be in issue. For example, it is not clear whether the preservation of cultural identity would justify interference under Article 8(2) (see, e.g. H v. Trafford Metropolitan Borough Council [1997] 3 F.C.R. 113). Religious and cultural issues may also be relevant to the issue whether the threshold criteria for making a care order are satisfied. Some commentators have argued that allowance for religious and cultural background ought to made (e.g. M.D.A. Freeman, Children, Their Families and the Law, (MacMillan, 1992)). If allowance is not made for the differences in attitudes to child-rearing, there is a danger of discrimination in the exercise of parental rights under Article 14.

(c) Decisions about children in care

6–71 Where family relationships are affected, the failure of the state to provide access to the courts may be regarded as a breach of Articles 8 or 6. These Articles may be invoked in cases where procedural unfairness exists. In W, B and R. v. U.K (1988) 10 E.H.R.R. 29, the procedural rather than substantive aspects of Article 8 were held to be violated. The views and interests of parents were not taken into account in the local authority's decision making process. Similar failings were considered under Article 6 in O v. U.K. (1988) Series A, No. 136; 13 E.H.R.R. 449. On the other hand, the requirement to conduct regular reviews (under the Review of Children's Cases Regulations 1991, S.I. 1991 No. 895 etc.), the remedy of judicial review, the Secretary of State's default powers (under the Children Act 1989, s.84), and the complaints procedure may, in any case, sufficiently protect the interests of an affected person.

Challenges are likely under Articles 6 and 8. The monitoring by the courts of a child in care has been specifically excluded by the Children Act 1989 (Re B (Minors) (Care: Contact: Local Authority's Plans) [1993] 1 F.L.R. 543, CA, and see A v. Liverpool City Council [1982] A.C. 363). At present, the court cannot interfere with the plans made for children in care, such as plans for adoption, even if those plans change after a care order is made (see also Re T (A Minor) (Care Order: Conditions) [1994] 2 F.L.R. 423). Save for religious issues (section 33(6)(a) of the 1989 Act), the retention of parental responsibility by parents (and parents alone) is largely illusory because its exercise is controlled by the local authority.

6–72 Attempts have been made to continue to involve the courts, for example by the use of interim care orders, but these have been largely unsuccessful (see, e.g. Berkshire County Council v. C and others [1993] 1 F.L.R. 569, Re C (Interim Care Order: Residential Assessment) [1997] 1 F.L.R. 1, Re J (Minors) (Care: Care Plan) [1994] 1 F.L.R. 253, and Re L (Sexual Abuse: Standard of Proof) [1996] 1 F.L.R. 116). For a consideration of whether parents can invoke the inherent jurisdication of the court, see Re L (Sexual Abuse: Standard of Proof) [1996] 1 F.L.R. 116.

(d) Contact with children in care

6–73 Any curtailment of family relations is likely now to receive greater scrutiny by the courts. In practice, in recent years at least, the paramountcy principle has meant that the concept of parental rights has been given little weight, although the principle of working together with parents is emphasised in Departmental Guidance. The domestic courts are likely increasingly to give weight to parental rights, including rights of access.

6–74 (i) Strasbourg cases In a number of cases before the Court, it has been held that the absence of a proper procedure for challenging refusal to allow access to children in care was a breach of Article 6 and a denial of "due process", and in some cases breach of Article 8 (see, *e.g. O and H v. U.K.* (1988) Series A, No. 136; 13 E.H.R.R. 449, and *W, B and R. v. U.K.* (1987) Series A, No. 121; 10 E.H.R.R. 29). Consideration as to whether a decision made by an authority fails to respect family life, and therefore is in breach of Article 8, cannot be divorced from the decision-making process. In *W, B and R*, authorities terminated parental access to children taken into care. The Court found violations of both Article 6(1) and 8, because the authorities did not consider the views and interests of the applicants. Where delays in the proceedings lengthened the period of no contact, and prejudiced future relations with the child, the Court has found a violation of Article 8 (see *H v. U.K.* (1987) Series A, No. 120 at paras 89–90; 10 E.H.R.R. 95).

In *Johansen v. Norway* (1996) 23 E.H.R.R. 33, the applicant's child was taken into care on the basis that she was incapable of taking care of her daughter, because of her physical and mental state of health. She was later refused access and the child was placed in a foster home with a view to adoption. She complained that the State had violated Articles 6, 8 and 13. The Court held that taking and keeping the child in care did not breach Article 8, but that the depravation of access and other parental rights, when the child was in care, was a violation. The authorities had overstepped their margin of appreciation under Article 8(2) in wholly depriving the applicant of her family life with the child. The steps taken were inconsistent with the aim of reuniting mother and daughter and did not correspond to any overriding requiement in the child's best interests (see also *Andersson v. Sweden* (1991) Series A, No. 212–B; 14 E.H.R.R. 615, *Hokkanen v. Finland* (1995) Series A, No. 299–A; 19 E.H.R.R. 139, *Olsson v. Sweden (No. 1)* (1988) Series A, No. 13; 11 E.H.R.R. 259, *Olsson v. Sweden (No. 2)* (1992) Series A, No. 250; 17 E.H.R.R. 134, and *W v. U.K.* (1987) Series A, No. 121; 10 E.H.R.R. 29.)

An applicant father's lack of a court remedy to have a determination of access rights to his son, who was in care, was held not to give rise to a violation of Article 6(1) in *Paulsen-Medalen and Svensson v. Sweden* (1998) App. No. 16817/90; 26 E.H.R.R. 259. The Court found that he could have made use of domestic remedies.

6–75 (ii) English law Under the Children Act 1989 there is a duty to allow reasonable contact (although the duty in respect of relatives other than parents is less onerous), and termination of contact with a child in care may now be challenged in court proceedings (s.34), but in some cases the court's hands are tied. Contact will usually be terminated if it conflicts with the authority's plans, which cannot be challenged. During the passage of the Children Act, the Lord Chancellor stated that "partnership with parents based on agreement so far as possible will be the guiding principle" for the provision of services (*Hansard,* H.L. Vol. 502, col. 491). But duties to consult parents are often qualified by the test of reasonable practicability. The termination of parental contact with children may be justified on the ground that it is contrary to the interests of the child, but this may beg the question whether the child's interests should remain paramount once Convention rights become part of domestic law under the Act. Access to the courts may itself also be restricted by order of the court (*Re Y (Child Orders: Restricting Applications)* [1994] 2 F.L.R. 699), which may give to rise to complaint under Articles 6(1) and 8.

2. Adoption

6–76 The reform of adoption law was considered by the government in 1996. Proposals included obligations to consult children, parents and others, and which may doubtless come to be the subject of scrutiny in connection with Convention rights.

(a) Rights of natural parents

6–77 In *Keegan v. Ireland* (1994) 18 E.H.R.R. 342, a child, born outside marriage, was placed for adoption without the knowledge or consent of the father. The father applied to be appointed as guardian which would allow him to challenge the proposed adoption. The national court ruled that his wishes should not be considered if, in the opinion of the court, the prospective adopters would provide the child with a better quality of welfare. The national court then heard evidence of a psychiatrist that the child would be likely to suffer trauma if it was separated from its prospective adopters, and an adoption order was made. The Court held that the secret placement amounted to a breach of Article 6(1) and 8. In *Sőderbǎck v. Sweden* (App. No. 24484/94 noted in [1998] H.R.C.D., Vol. IX, No. 3, p. 209, also noted in [1998] E.H.R.L.R. 343) the Commission referred a case to the Court in which the applicant complained that the adoption of his daughter by his mother's partner, without his consent, violated Article 8.

Various issues may arise with regard to the Convention rights of natural parents in connection with the making and consequences of an adoption order. These may include questions of contact, religious upbringing, and access to information.

(b) Rights of adoptive parents

6–78 In *Re S (A Minor) (Adoption Order: Conditions)* [1994] 2 F.L.R. 416, the Court of Appeal held that a judge erred in imposing conditions in an adoption order, restricting the religious practices of prospective adopters. The county court judge had required the prospective adopters, who were Jehovah's Witnesses, to undertake not to withold consent to blood transfusions being given to the child without applying to a court. The court held that the imposition of conditions in an adoption order ought to be very rare indeed. The court was able to base its decision, not out of respect for family and private life under Article 8, but on a consideration of the child's welfare as it was required to do under the Children Act 1989, holding that it was far better that the child be adopted by the family she had been with for two years, than there be no adoption order, and on a consideration of the practicalities of imposing such a condition. The addition of Convention rights to these considerations may at least provide an alternative approach.

(c) Rights of children

6–79   In some respects, Convention rights of children may be seen to add little to existing practice. The English courts, for example, have upheld the right of a child to make his or her views known, with the effect that a failure of the authority to ascertain the child's wishes contributed to vitiate the decision to remove the child from prospective adopters (*R. v. Devon CC, ex p. B* [1997] 3 F.C.R. 411, *sub nom R. v. Devon CC, ex p. O* [1977] 2 F.L.R. 388). In other respects, there may at least be a change in emphasis. The right to respect for private life under Article 8 may include, for example, the right to confidentiality. It was said by Waite J. in *Re X, Y and Z (Wardship: Disclosure of Material)* [1992] 1 F.L.R. 84 that "The privilege of confidentiality is that of the court, not of the child . . ." (see also *Re D (Minors) (Adoption Reports: Confidentiality)* [1996] A.C. 593). There is no doubt that the rights of the individual in respects such as these will require greater attention.

(d) The right to adopt

6–80   Adoption does fall within the scope of Article 12 (right to marry and found a family), and the Strasbourg authorities have considered the imposition of conditions on adoption imposed under national law (see *X and Y v. U.K.* (1977) 12 D.R. 32). However, this falls short of any right to adopt, which is important when considering the scope of responsibilities on publc authorities in this context.

3. Children in need but not in care

6–81   The various aspects of local authority functions with regard to children in need, who are not taken into care, will also fall to be scrutinised against the requirements of the Convention. As in other respects, the paramountcy of the welfare principle may not always fit easily with the various rights of those involved. While the emphasis of the Children Act 1989 is on working together, and towards the upbringing of children by their own families, this by no means can be said to guarantee observance of the wishes and interests of those concerned. In discharging their responsibilities, authorities will have to be aware particularly of the possible requirements of Articles 8 and 12, and also to pay due regard to the need to avoid discrimination under Article 14.

Given the extension of state responsibilities under Article 8 to cover certain positive obligations, the provision of services (such as accommodation) by local authorities in respect of children in need seems likely to engage discussion of Convention rights. Authorities will probably need to be particularly astute in dealing with demands on their resources coupled with possibly erroneous or unjustified assertions of entitlement under Article 8. Questions of available resources are likely to be of prime concern to authorities in the manner in which they discharge their duties, but these will need to be balanced appropriately against other considerations having regard to Convention rights.

4. Emergency protection

6–82   The decision whether to seek a child assessment order (CAO) or emergency protection order (EPO), or to offer voluntary assistance is left to local authorities. An EPO is usually made *ex parte*. The absence of the parent may be justified if the threshold criteria of risk of harm to the child is satisfied.

The fact that children, rather than their abusers, are usually removed from the home, even where a parent or other person would be able to care for them at home, may be thought to suggest that inadequate emphasis is placed on the rights of the child in some situations. A local authority has the power to assist the perpetrator to find accommodation under Schedule 2, paragraph 5, of the Children Act 1989, but this power is seldom used. Possible reliance on Article 8 in such situations can certainly be envisaged.

The exercise of police powers to remove children under the Children Act 1989, s.46, and their detention in police protection for up to 72 hours without legal challenge, will engage responsibility under Article 5, as well as under Articles 6 and 8.

5. Secure accommodation

6–83   Section 25 of the Children Act 1989 provides for the use of secure accommodation for restricting the liberty of children being looked after by a wide category of bodies, including a social services authority, certain health authorities or trusts, local education authorities, and children in residential care, in nursing or mental homes. Even children who are not in care may be incarcerated, if they are being looked after by a local authority. The detention of a young person in a hospital maternity ward, to which entry was restricted to those with a pass or a key, was regarded as secure accommodation within the meaning of section 25 of the Children Act 1989 (*Re B (A Minor) (Treatment and Secure Accommodation)* [1997] 1 F.C.R. 618), but a hospital or clinic for treating eating disorders was not (*Re C (A Minor) (Medical Treatment)* [1997] 2 F.C.R. 180, [1997] Fam. Law 474).

In some (and not unknown) circumstances, the detention of children may amount to degrading treatment within the meaning of Article 3. In general, however, concern will focus upon the requirements of Article 5 (right to liberty and security). The justification for the detention of children, other than in criminal cases or under the Mental Health Act 1983, will need to be considered carefully given the circumstances prescribed by Article 5(1). Department of Health Guidance states that secure accommodation should not be used simply for the convenience of the authority or as a form of punishment. The Convention may be expected to provide some clear protection against inappropriate use of secure accommodation.

6–84   In *Neilsen v. Denmark* (1988) Series A, No. 144; 11 E.H.R.R. 175 Judge Carillo Salcedo considered that that absence of adequate procedures for reviewing the committal of a child to a psychiatric hospital by the parent with custody was of major concern. Similar observations might be made in respect of secure accommodation orders. Under the Children Act 1989, the authority must apply for a court order before placing a child in secure accommodation, but the court's powers on considering the application are limited, which means many applications are rubber stamped. The court must make the order if it finds that either of the two section 25 criteria are (or do not need to be) satisfied. The court cannot enquire into whether the authority have considered the factors they are required to consider, so far as practicable, under section 22 of the Children Act 1989, such as the wishes of the parents (*Re M (A Minor) (Secure Accommodation Order)* [1995] 3 All E.R. 407). The limited jurisdiction of the court may give rise to complaints of a violation of Articles 6 and/or 8. Furthermore, the right to be notified of proceedings docs not extend to any "family" members or other persons who do not have parental responsibilty. It has also been suggested that the court has the power to hear the case without letting the child himself know that the application has been made, which would breach Article 5 (Baum and Walker, *Legal Action*, April 1996).

If a parent or other interested party believes that the court has not considered any of the relevant factors, or that the order is not in the best interests of the child, and objects to the making of the order, the remedy is to make a complaint under the Children Act 1989, s.27, or an application for judicial review. It remains to be seen whether this would satisfy the requirements of Article 6. Representations may not be made at the hearing of the application for the order unless they are directed to the section 25 criteria, or to any issue as to whether section 25 applies to the child. The Court of Appeal has indicated that the welfare of the child may be relevant (it cannot be paramount), but the statutory contraints remain (*Re M* [1995] 1 F.L.R. 418).

M. CHILDREN AND PRIVATE LAW PROCEEDINGS

6–85   The courts are themselves public authorities for the purposes of the Act (section 6), and must not act in a way which is incompatible with Convention rights. Article 6 provides specifically for the right to a fair trial. Furthermore, all legislation (primary and secondary) must be read and given effect, so far as possible, in a way which is compatible with Convention rights. In these respects, the Convention is relevant to private law proceedings, as well as cases where the state (commonly in the form of a local authority) is directly involved. The Court, for example, has held that a judicial order with respect to the relative rights of contending parents in a custody dispute may represent an interference with the right to respect for family life, and the fact that it arose out of a dispute between private individuals made no difference (*Hoffman v. Austria* (1993) Series A, No. 255–C).

1. Disputes about contact or residence

6–86   The interests of the child may justify failure of the courts to grant orders under section 8 of the Children Act 1989. In *Peter Whitear v. U.K* [1997] E.H.R.L.R. 291, an access order was made in favour of the father of a child. After many applications to the court, face-to-face and telephone contact with the father was refused. Further applications were made, but the father did not succeed in getting a contact or residence order. Specialist opinion considered the stability of the child to be significantly threatened. The father complained to the

Commission that the refusal to grant him access was *inter alia* a violation of Article 8. The Commission unanimously declared the application inadmissible. The Commission decided that the interests of the child made the refusal justifiable and necessary under Article 8(2).

The courts do need to be careful not to make decisions on unacceptable grounds. In *Hoffman v. Austria* (1993) Series A, No. 255–C, the Court found that the decision of the national authorities on custody of the children violated Articles 8 and 14, because it was based essentially on the ground of religion (the mother was a Jehovah's Witness). It may be said, on the facts of that case, that the courts in this country are rarely prepared to find that certain religions and religious practices have a deleterious effect on children, such as alienating them from a parent (*e.g. Re B and G* [1985] F.L.R. 493, but see *T v. T* [1974] Fam. Law 191 and *Re R* [1993] 2 F.L.R. 163). Decisions based largely on gender, or sexual orientation, are likely to be difficult to justify. In a case against France an application by a foreign national who had been required to surrender his passport to a court when exercising his right of access to his children was declared inadmissible (App. No. 33562/96 noted in [1998] H.R.C.D., Vol. IX, No. 7, p. 593).

2. Enforcement of orders

6–87　　The positive obligations on the State to respect family life include the implementation of legislation regulating family relationships. Finland was criticised for its failure to enforce a father's right of access to his daughter against the wishes of the maternal grandparents in *Hokkanen v. Finland* (1994) Series A, No. 299–A; 19 E.H.R.R. 139. It is not clear, though, to what extent there would be justification under Article 8 for refusing to enforce a contact order on the ground that it would not be in the interests of the child. The inability of a non-custodial parent to enforce rights of access and the length of the enforcement proceedings will be considered in *Nuutinen v. Finland*, App. No. 32842/96.

3. Removal from the jurisdiction

6–88　　While the international aspects of family practice are outside the scope of this Chapter, there is no reason why Convention rights should not be applied here. Until now, the courts have been unwilling to consider their relevance. For example, in *Re M (A Minor)* [1996] 3 F.C.R. 185, and [1996] 3 F.C.R. 377, on an application for a stay of an order granting leave to take a child out of the jurisdiction, the Court of Appeal declined to accede to a request from the Commission that interim relief be granted (*Salome Stopford v. U.K.*, App. No. 31316/96 [1998] E.H.R.L.R. 207). (The Court of Appeal considered that its principle concern was the welfare of the child, which was best served by being reunited with his natural parents.

N. Procedural Aspects

6–89　　The procedural guarantees to a fair trial under Article 6, relevant to all family proceedings, are likely to have somewhat different application where children are involved, by reason of the non-adversarial approach in such cases. Furthermore, the involvement and decision-making of local authorities, while not generally subject to Article 6 considerations, may nonetheless have aspects which do attract the procedural guarantees. The importance of implementing fair procedures for the determination of matters affecting the family unit has also been considered under Article 8 (see, *e.g. Olsson v. Sweden (No. 1)* Series A, No. 13; (1988) 11 E.H.R.R. 259, and *W, B and R. v. U.K.* (1987) Series A, No. 121; 10 E.H.R.R. 29). The Strasbourg authorities have also emphasised the procedural aspect of the right to family life protected by Article 8. In *Boyle v. U.K.* (1994) Series A, No. 282–B; 19 E.H.R.R. 179 an uncle was denied a fair consideration of his views regarding contact with a child in care, in violation of Article 8.

The English courts have previously considered the relevance of the Convention in a number of cases concerning procedural issues. In *Re L (A Minor)* [1996] 2 W.L.R. 395, the House of Lords thought that it was doubtful that a parent who had been denied the opportunity to obtain legal advice in confidence had been accorded a fair hearing, and Articles 6 and 8 were considered.

1. Access to records

6–90   In *Gaskin v. U.K.* (1989) Series A, No. 160; 12 E.H.R.R. 36, the Court held that a person who has been in the care of the local authority has the right, inherent in Article 8, to obtain information about his or her treatment while in care. Other cases which have been considered by the Strasbourg authorities in this context include *Willsher v. U.K.* (1997) 23 C.D. 188 (request for access to personal social services records, including records of investigation into alleged abuse of mental patients); *Leander v. Sweden* (1987) Series A, No. 116; 9 E.H.R.R. 433 (the use of and access to information); and *McMichael v. U.K.* (1995) Series A, No. 308; 20 E.H.R.R. 205 (denial of a parent's access to reports concerning her son during care proceedings). At present access to records is still limited. The Children's Hearings (Scotland) Rules 1996 came into force as a result of the *McMichael* case. The restriction of access to personal files prior to April 1, 1989, and the requirement that consent is given by a third party, means that human rights issues are still likely to arise. Another example is the restriction on the rights afforded to a guardian *ad litem*. He or she can have access to the records of social services departments, but not to the records of heath authorities (except where they are part of the local authority's own records).

2. Is there a right to apply to a court?

6–91   The right of access to the courts in the determination of civil rights is an important (but not absolute) aspect of Article 6 and Article 8 (see generally paragraphs 2–52 and 2–72). Article 6 only comes into play when the determination of civil rights and obligations is in issue. What rights can be said to exist, and whether or not they can be said to be in dispute so as to trigger the application of Article 6, are moot questions in the context of some of the public law aspects of the Children Act 1989. The Court has upheld restrictions on the right of access to courts, provided these have a legitimate aim and comply with the concept of proportionality (see, *e.g. Ashingdane v. U.K.* (1985) 7 E.H.H.R. 528). Restrictions were considered justified in the case of a prisoner in *Golder v. U.K* (1975) 1 E.H.R.R. 54.

It may be necessary to examine the requirements and justification for leave to be obtained before certain applications to the courts may be made. Children have the right to apply for leave to issue proceedings under section 8 of the Children Act 1989 (see, *e.g. Re AD (A Minor) (Child's Wishes)* [1993] Fam. Law 405), but even if the child has sufficient understanding, leave may not be given (*e.g. Re SC (A Minor) (Leave to Seek Residence Order)* [1994] 1 F.L.R. 96, and *Re C (Residence: Child's Application for Leave)* [1995] 1 F.L.R. 927). In respect of other parties, a natural parent can be prevented from being a party to proceedings (*Re W (Discharge of Party to Proceedings)* [1997] 1 F.L.R. 128, *Re X (Care: Notice of Proceedings)* [1996] Fam. Law 139). In some cases, local authority foster parents are automatically prevented from applying for section 8 orders.

6–92 In *Crabtree v. U.K.* (1997) 23 C.D. 202, the applicant complained about the decision of a fostering panel to deregister him as a foster carer. He alleged that the tribunal was not impartial, that he was not given any/or any proper notice of meetings, was excluded from parts of a meeting, and was not given the opportunity to examine witnesses. The Commission did not decide whether the right to work as a home foster carer was a "civil right" within the meaning of Article 6(1), because the application was held to be manifestly ill-founded. The Commission was satisfied that, in judicial review proceedings, the court had found that the panel had not acted unfairly, so there was no violation of Article 6, even though the court, by way of judicial review, could not substitute its own decision on the merits (see also *Bryan v. U.K* (1995) Series A, No. 335–A; 21 E.H.R.R. 342).

At present, there is a reluctance on the part of the judiciary to interve in the local authority's exercise of powers under the Children Act 1989, and this might be thought to increase the potential for the Convention to make a real difference. In *R. v. London Borough of Brent ex p. Sawyers* [1994] 1 F.L.R. 203 an application for judicial review was made by an autistic child whose grandparents wished to foster him and asked to be rehoused. The Court of Appeal considered that the complaints procedure under section 26 of the Children Act 1989 was a suitable alternative remedy (see also *R. v. Birmingham City Council, ex p. A* [1997] 2 F.L.R. 841).

3. Delay

6–93 Many of the Strasbourg cases under Article 6 have concerned unacceptable delays in the course of legal proceedings. While the need for expedition has often been emphasised particularly in cases involving children, practitioners are all too familiar with examples of delay at different stages of procedures and proceedings. Even in case of urgency, the courts have however been unwilling to review the conduct of the local authority. In *R. v. Birmingham City Council, ex p. A, The Times,* February 19, 1997, a child urgently needed to be provided with accommodation in a special foster placement. There was considerable delay and her condition deteriorated. Her mother applied on her behalf for judicial review. The court declined to hear the matter, and said that the appropriate course was to seek relief under the complaints procedure because the court could not consider the precise circumstances of the delay (see also *R. v. Royal Borough of Kingston upon Thames, ex p. T* [1994] 1 F.L.R. 798).

Article 6(1) requires particular diligence in dealing with children's cases (*Hokkanen v. Finland* (1994) Series A, No. 299–A; 19 E.H.R.R. 139), and diligence also in dealing with marital status (*Bock v. FRG* (1989) Series A, No. 150; 12 E.H.R.R. 247). A violation of Article 8 was found in *H v. U.K.* (1988) Series A, No. 136; 13 E.H.R.R. 449, because the delays in proceedings challenging restrictions on access to a child in care would have the effect of a *de facto* determination of the matter. The longer the parent was unable to see the child, the more the future relations would be prejudiced. In *P, P & T v. U.K.* [1996] E.H.R.L.R. 526, the court listing system was criticised in a case where wardship/care proceedings were protracted, so that boys bonded to their temporary foster parent, jeopardising the local authority's plans. The Commission accepted that the lawyers had the right to make a complaint to the Commission about the delay (see also *GF v. Austria* (1996) 22 E.H.R.R. C.D. 145, and *SP, DP & T v. U.K.* (1996) 22 E.H.R.R. C.D. 148). In *Paulsen-Medalen and Svensson v. Sweden* (1988) App. No. 16817/90; 26 E.H.R.R. 259 the Court held unanimously that there was a violation of Article 6(1) where there was undue delay in proceedings relating to access by a mother with a child in care.

4. Impartiality

6–94   The Children Act makes provision for an independent person to take part in the process, but there are concerns about whether the local authority's complaints procedure is sufficiently neutral. Whilst an independent person is required to sit on the complaints panel, the majority on the panel will be members or officers of the authority. It is not clear whether, if Article 6 were applicable to this process (see *W v. U.K.* [1987] Series A, No. 121; 10 E.H.R.R. 29, but note *Bryan v. U.K.*, above), this arrangement would satisfy the requirement for a tribunal to be independent and impartial under Article 6(1) (see, *e.g. Stramek v. Austria* (1984) Series A, No. 84; 7 E.H.R.R. 351, and *Langborger v. Sweden* (1989) Series A, No. 155; 12 E.H.R.R. 416).

5. Notification of proceedings

6–95   Notification of proceedings must be one of the most fundamental aspects of the right to a fair trial, yet in many cases applications are heard *ex parte*. In such cases, the right to apply to set aside or appeal the order, may adequately protect the rights of the party against whom the order was made. In other cases, the courts may interfere with family life in a more permanent way, without a party being notified of proceedings. A party may prevented from being served with notice of confidential serial number adoption proceedings applications (*Re K (adoption: disclosure of information)* [1997] 2 F.L.R. 74).

There are limited categories of persons who have right to be informed of, or to challenge, applications under the Children Act 1989, *e.g.* an application for an emergency protection order. In most cases, parents or persons with parental responsibility must be notified, but other persons may be part of the family for the purposes of Article 8 and may be deprived of the right to a fair hearing. Any person may be excluded by a local authority from their home under directions made in interim care orders and emergency protection orders (Schedule 6 to the Family Law Act 1996). Those persons may not even be aware of proceedings.

6. Conduct of hearings

6–96 Family proceedings are not usually heard in public. In the case of Children Act proceedings, hearings and directions appointments take place in chambers unless the court otherwise directs. Judgment may be given in open court if to do so is in the public interest. In *Re P-B (A Minor) (Child Cases: Hearings in Open Court)* [1997] 1 All E.R. 58, the Court of Appeal considered that Articles 6 and 10 (freedom of expression) were not violated by conducting hearings in chambers. The present procedures were considered to be within the spirit of the Convention, which recognises the right to a public trial is qualified in the interests of minors or the protection of the private life of the parties. In exercising its discretion, the court can take account of Article 6. In *Re R (A Minor)*, (unreported), July 22, 1996, CA, the Court of Appeal considered that the Convention was not in conflict with the rule that proceedings under the Children Act 1989 are to be held in chambers unless otherwise directed. The Court of Appeal considered that the Convention provided for the exclusion of the press and public from all or part of a trial on grounds including the protection of juveniles. An approach which balances the need to protect the ward from harm, and the freedom of the press, is unlikely to violate Convention rights (*Re W (A Minor) (Wardship: Restriction on Publication)* [1992] 1 W.L.R. 100, *Re W (Wardship: Discharge: Publicity)* [1995] 2 F.L.R. 466, *M v. BBC* [1997] 1 F.L.R. 51, *Re P-B (Children Act: Open Court)* [1996] Fam. Law 606, and "The Review of Access to and Reporting of Family Proceedings" (Lord Chancellor's Department, 1993)).

In civil cases, there is no general right under the Convention to be present at a hearing. However, where the issue affects a fundamental right, such as the right to liberty (in applications for secure accommodation orders) or family life (*e.g.* decisions about taking a child into care, or adoption), the right to attend court may be protected. Under domestic law, a child may be prevented from attending court in Children Act 1989 proceedings if the court considers this to be in the child's interests, having regard to matters to be discussed or the evidence likely to be given, and if the child is represented by a guardian or solicitor.

6–97 Under the Convention, there is no absolute right to be heard, but violation of Article 6 or Article 8 may be argued in any case in which the failure to allow representations to be made is unfair to the applicant. In *X, Y and Z v. U.K.*, R.J.D. 1997–II 619; 24 E.H.R.R. 143, the Commission felt that the children ought to have had separate representation. Parties to proceedings should have a reasonable opportunity of presenting their case under conditions which do not place them at a substantial disadvantage (*e.g. Dombo Beheer BV v. Netherlands*, Series A, No. 274–A; (1993) 18 E.H.R.R. 213). In domestic law, the right of a child to take part in proceedings is not absolute. A guardian *ad litem* must be appointed in care and supervision proceedings unless the court is satisfied that that it is not necessary to safeguard the child's interests. The question of whether a child can instruct a solicitor is also determined by the court. Questions can certainly arise as to whether the views of a child have been adequately represented.

There are no absolute rights under the Convention of access to documents held by another party or disclosed to the court. But failure to provide discovery may result in unfairness. In *McMichael v. U.K.* (1995) 20 E.H.R.R. 205, the Scottish courts had sight of documents which were withheld from the parents. The child was adopted after the court had dispensed with the necessity for parental consent. The Court decided that the parents' rights under Article 6 (in respect of the mother only) and Article 8 (in respect of both parents) had been violated.

Refusal to provide discovery may be justified in some situations. In *Re K (Adoption: Disclosure of Information)* [1997] 2 F.L.R. 74 it was held that the previous convictions of a prospective adopter need not be disclosed to the mother. The court applied the three-stage test laid down in *Re D (Minors) (Adoption Reports: Confidentiality)* [1996] A.C. 593, namely (a) whether the disclosure involved a real possibility of significant harm to the child; (b) the overall benefit to the child of non-disclosure, having regard to the magnitude of risk and gravity of harm that disclosure would cause; and (c) if the child's interests are first served by non-disclosure, then the parents' interests in disclosure must be weighed against this. The House of Lords considered the cases of *Hendriks v. Netherlands* (1982) 5 E.H.R.R. 223 and *McMichael v. U.K.* (1995) Series A, No. 308; 20 E.H.R.R. 205, and decided that there was no conflict between English law and Convention rights (see also Lindsey Mendoza, "Confidentiality in Child Proceedings", [1998] Fam. Law 30, and Kevin Barnett, "Adoption and confidential information", [1997] Fam. Law 489).

O. REMEDIES

1. Remedies under the Act

6–98   While in many cases the use of Convention rights under the Act will be confined to the way in which statutory provisions are to be interpreted, and to defensive measures by individuals against the actions of public authorities, the courts have a wide discretion as to the remedies available for unlawful conduct by public authorities (*i.e.* for conduct which is incompatible with Convention rights within the meaning of section 6). Section 8(1) enables the court to make any order within its jurisdiction as it considers just and appropriate, including the power to award damages (but subject in the latter case to the restrictions in sections 8 and 9). It is therefore possible that the courts will fashion new forms of remedy for use in these cases, and no less so in family and children's cases than in other types of litigation. Given that Convention issues may be raised in the course of any legal proceedings, an essential matter for the practitioner will be to ensure that the proceedings are before an appropriate tribunal with jursidiction to grant any relief which may be sought. This is likely to be particularly relevant if damages are to be claimed, bearing in mind the absence of such jurisdiction in some courts. It will be important also to consider any rules of court which may be made under section 7(2) for the purpose of defining which courts may entertain claims against public authorities under section 7(1)(a).

It is also relevant to bear in mind the limited extent of the jurisdiction to make declarations of incompatibility in the exceptional cases where legislation cannot be read and given effect consistently with Convention rights (see sections 3 and 4). Among the courts of first instance, only the High Court has this power (section 4(5)).

2. Adequacy of existing remedies

6–99 In view of the exclusion of Article 13 (right to an effective remedy) from those Convention rights which are given effect under the Act (see generally paragraphs 1–21—1–22), it seems likely that there will remain an unresolved tension in domestic law between the remedies which the courts may be prepared to grant in particular cases (whether or not under section 8), and claims that the failure or refusal of the courts to grant relief amounts to a violation of Article 13. This tension can be demonstrated by comparison with cases prior to the Act, and in relation to which it may remain necessary to exhaust attempts to obtain a remedy before national courts as a prelude to taking proceedings in Strasbourg.

A decision on the recovery of damages from the police is due be given shortly by the Court. In *Osman v. U.K*, App. No. 23452/94, Commission decision of July 1, 1997, H.R.C.D. Vol. VIII, No. 11, the applicants complained about the State's failure to protect the lives of a father and son. The father was murdered and his son was injured by the boy's teacher. The son and his mother commenced a civil action in negligence against the police, who were aware of the dangerous behaviour of the teacher, but it was struck out, on the ground that no cause of action could lie against the police for negligence in the investigation of crime [1998] E.H.R.L.R. 101 and 269. The Commission decided there was no violation of Article 8, but that there had been a violation of Article 6. The immunity of the police from suit could be equated to a bar to the applicant's civil action, and was held to be a disproportionate restriction on their access to a court.

6–100 The decision in *Osman* may prove to be relevant to the refusal to provide a remedy in damages on public policy grounds in other areas such as local government. The landmark decision in *X (Minors) v. Bedfordshire CC* [1995] 2 A.C. 633 is the subject of an application to the Commission in *K.L. and others v. U.K.*, App. No. 29392/95 and *T.P. and K.M. v. U.K.*, App. No. 28945/95 (see [1998] H.R.C.D., Vol. IX, No. 7, p. 604). The refusal of the House of Lords in *X (Minors)* to allow claims for damages to be brought against child care professionals and local authorities is clearly significant against the background of the responsibility of public authorities (including the courts) under the Act to honour Convention rights. The application before the Commission alleges a failure by the United Kingdom to protect children from degrading treatment (Article 3), and violation of Articles 6, 8 and 13.

CHAPTER 7

Housing Law

Caroline Hunter (Lecturer, Nottingham University; Barrister, Arden Chambers) and Andrew Dymond (Barrister, Arden Chambers)

A. INTRODUCTION

7–01 Housing law has no easily defined provenance, but has always roamed far and wide in seeking to protect what may be called "the home". As Arden and Partington put it in the preface to the first edition of *Housing Law* (Sweet & Maxwell, 1982), housing law concerns all areas of law "in so far as they touch upon the ways in which people's occupation of their homes is regulated by law". In England and Wales the law, and the state in its broadest context, touches on occupation of the home in a number of different ways. For owner-occupiers this may be through constraints on the way they can use the home, laws controlling possession for mortgage arrears, income support when they are unemployed, or the destination of the home on matrimonial breakdown. For tenants there is, in particular, control of the landlord/tenant relationship, giving rights to tenants and duties to landlords (*e.g.* to repair). Where the state provides housing there are questions of access to it, and the rights of the homeless.

From a human rights point of view, it has been suggested by Scott Leckie ("The Justiciability of Housing Rights" (1995), *The Right to Complain about Economic, Social and Cultural Rights, SIM Special* No. 18, Netherlands Institute of Human Rights) that the areas of legislation (and common law rights) which will have a bearing on the satisfaction of housing rights in any given country include: (a) landlord and tenant laws; (b) security of tenure laws; (c) protection from eviction laws; (d) laws on maintenance and repairs; (e) rental laws; (f) property laws; (g) laws on housing subsidies and benefits; (h) homelessness legislation; (i) land use and distribution laws; (j) housing finance laws; (k) building codes and standards legislation; (l) laws regulating property speculation; (m) environmental health and planning laws; (n) laws relating to the privatisation of public housing; (o) non-discrimination laws; (p) compensation laws; and (q) laws availing legal aid and judicial remedies.

7–02 Leckie considers human rights in their broadest context, encompassing not only civil and political rights, but also social and economic rights. The Convention is, however, concerned mainly with civil and political rights. The Convention does not provide a right to housing, whether this be done directly by the state, or by the state providing other mechanisms (such as income support) which will give access to housing. Nor does it require directly that housing should be of a certain standard. The significance and application of the Act for housing law in this country accordingly needs to be viewed against this limited background.

The main provision of relevance in the Convention is Article 8, which requires "respect" *inter alia* for the "home" and also "family life". Also of direct relevance is Article 1 of the First Protocol, which protects the "peaceful enjoyment of possessions". It is also necessary to consider the rights under Article 6(1) to a fair and public hearing.

B. A RIGHT TO HOUSING?

7–03   The principal Article of relevance when considering the application of the Convention to housing issues is Article 8(1): "Everyone has the right to respect for his private and family life, his home and his correspondence". The most important aspect of this, here, is the respect for "home". What is clear from the jurisprudence, however, is that Article 8 does not establish the right to a home. Thus in *X v. FRG* (1956) 1 Y.B. 202 an East German refugee sought to establish that there was a breach of Article 8 through the failure by the then West German government to provide him with a decent home. The application was ruled inadmissible.

In any event, in this country, we probably have a greater protection for those who find themselves homeless than in most other signatory states, through the provisions of the Housing Act 1996, Pt VII. It should be remembered, however, that Convention jurisprudence is dynamic rather than static, and it is possible that the view taken in *X v. FRG* may change if the consensus amongst the signatory states moved. Respect for the home, and also family life, could be interpreted as requiring positive steps by the state to ensure that there is an adequate home.

7–04   In relation to some of the rights under Article 8, the Court has been willing to identify positive acts which were required on the part of the State (see, *e.g. Marckx v. Belgium* (1979) Series A, No. 31; 2 E.H.R.R. 330, in relation to positive obligations as regard respect for family life, including for illegitimate children). In *Powell and Rayner v. U.K.* (1990) Series A, No. 172; 12 E.H.R.R. 355 where the Court was considering respect for the home, the Court was willing to accept that there might be a positive obligation on the government in relation to regulating a non-state interference (by aircraft noise). (See also *López Ostra v. Spain* (1995) Series A, No. 303–C; 20 E.H.R.R. 277.) In *Whiteside v. U.K.* (1994) 76A D.R. 80, the Commission held that there was a positive duty on the Government to provide remedies against harassment by the individual in and around her home by her former cohabitee.

The current interpretation of the meaning of "respect for home", however, makes it unlikely at the moment that the Strasbourg authorities will impose any positive obligations in respect of housing directly upon the state. If this were to change in the future, it may be possible to question, for example, whether the exclusion of large numbers of immigrants and many single people from the protection afforded by Part VII of the Housing Act 1996 is justifiable.

1. Other human rights approaches to the right to housing

7–05   The narrow interpretation given to housing rights under the Convention is in part explained because the latter's primary concern is with civil and political rights. Other human rights charters have, however, taken a broader view. Thus the Covenant on Economic, Social and Cultural ᵣᵢᵍₕₜs, Art. 11(1) provides a positive obligation to provide adequate housing. The Committee on the Covenant have asserted that in defining adequacy the following must be considered: legal security of tenure; availability of services, materials and infrastructure; affordability; fitness for habitation; accessibility; location and cultural adequacy (see General Comment No. 4, para. 8; see further Leckie, *op. cit.*)

The European Social Charter, does not, as yet, go as far as the Covenant, and does not contain an express right to adequate housing. Housing issues have, however, been considered under the Charter in the context of Article 16 (the right of the family to social and legal protection). The Committee of Independent Experts has suggested that this Article requires the provision of an adequate housing policy for families. Article 19 on migrant workers, may also be considered, particularly in the context of housing policies which discriminate against such workers.

C. Who is Governed by the Act?

7–06   In addition to questions as to the general interpretation and effect of primary and subordinate legislation under section 3, the legality of the conduct of "public authorities" in the housing context arises under section 6. It is necessary to consider what persons and bodies are covered by this phrase.

Housing in this country is provided through both the public and private sectors. The vast majority of those in England and Wales (around 70 per cent) are owner-occupiers, their purchases on the whole being financed through mortgages provided by private finance. About 17 per cent of dwellings are let by local authority landlords, with just over 4 per cent let by registered social landlords. The remaining 10 per cent or so are let by private landlords.

For those who are tenants of local authorities it is clear that they will be able, if the circumstances arise, to avail themselves of section 6 to challenge the actions of their landlord. Similarly those who approach local authorities for housing, either through the homelessness route in Part VII of the Housing Act 1996 or through the waiting list under Part VI of the Housing Act 1996, would also be able to bring proceedings in an appropriate case.

7–07   Private sector tenants and owner-occupiers will only come into contact with local authorities in more indirect ways. Local housing authorities have extensive powers in relation to compulsory purchase (Housing Act 1985, s. 17), unfit housing (Housing Act 1985, Pts VI and IX), houses in multiple occupation (Housing Act 1985, Pt XI) and statutory nuisances (Environmental Protection Act 1990, Pt III). There are also other areas of local authority decision making which may clearly include housing issues, such as planning (see Chapter 8) and duties under the Children Act 1989 (see Chapter 6). Where decisions are being made in relation to action by the local authority under these powers, those affected (owner-occupiers, tenants and landlords) would be able to take direct action under sections 6 and 7.

The definition of "public authority" in section 6(3) is a broad one, encompassing courts, tribunals and any person whose functions are of a "public nature". In the context of housing, there are numerous bodies which potentially are public authorities. The Housing Corporation, which regulates, and makes grants of public money to, registered social landlords would seem to fall within the definition, as exercising a pre-eminently public role (see generally the Housing Act 1996, Pt I, as to its powers). In addition, other bodies which provide avenues of redress on housing matters are potentially covered. In particular, ombudsmen (both the Commissioners for Local Government in the context of local authority housing, and the Housing Ombudsman in relation to registered social landlords) and certain internal local authority tribunals, such as Housing Benefit Review Boards.

1. Registered Social Landlords

7–08   Until the Housing Act 1996, registered social landlords were known as housing associations. Such organisations cannot easily be described, ranging as they do from very small local specialist organisations, to national landlords with many thousands of properties, to associations which have taken over the complete stock of particular local authorities. Could the actions of such a landlord be challenged? Section 6(3) defines a "public authority" as including "(b) any person certain of whose functions are functions of a public nature."

This broad, and indeed rather opaque, definition does not provide an easy answer as to whether it encompasses registered social landlords. What is meant by "public" in these circumstances? A number of factors could be said to illustrate the public nature of registered social landlords:

- registration under a statutory scheme with a public regulator;

- receipt of public funds through both the Housing Corporation and local authorities;

- the close relationship that many registered social landlords have with local authorities, particularly regarding nomination rights;

- controls on allocation to registered social landlords by local authorities to be found in the Housing Act 1996, Pts VI and VII.

Other factors, however, would suggest that they are not public:

- the fact that a large part of their funding is raised from private institutions and that some operate with no public funding at all;

- the regulation of their landlord and tenant relationships through the same regime as other private sector tenants.

7–09   In the context of judicial review, the Court of Appeal has held that a housing association is not subject to the supervisory jurisdiction of the High Court (*Peabody Housing Association v. Greene* (1978) 38 P. & C.R. 644). This case was, however, decided in relation to a landlord and tenant dispute. In a different context, in Scotland, where the housing association was exercising statutory powers, judicial review of their decision was permitted: see *Hoyle v. Castlemilk East Housing Co-operative Ltd, The Times*, May 16, 1997. In *R. v. West Dorset D.C. and West Dorset Housing Association, ex p. Gerrard* (1994) 27 H.L.R. 150 the applicant sought to challenge a decision made under the Housing Act 1985, Pt III. The authority had delegated the inquiry function to the housing association to which they had transferred all their stock. The association was joined as one of the respondents to the application, and no objection was taken to this. Thus Handy has suggested ("Housing Associations: Public or Private Law" (1997) J.H.L. 14) that:

> "Whether an issue in the context of [registered social landlords] is private or public law will depend upon the particular context and particular nature of the power in question."

It seems an unattractive proposition that certain bodies could be public authorities under the Act for some purposes but not for others, but this result seems to be implicit from the wording of section 6. When considering any particular act by a person which might be a public authority because its functions are of a public nature, the person is not for that reason alone to be considered a public authority if the nature of the act is private (section 6(7)). It may be arguable that, in their individual relationships with tenants, the acts of registered social landlords may be considered private. At this stage, it seems very difficult to predict which side of the line the courts are likely to find that registered social landlords fall.

D. Rights Under Article 8

7–10   The most important Article in relation to housing is Article 8, which requires respect for the home.

1. What is a "home"?

7–11   "In general 'home' is where one lives on a settled basis" (Harris, O'Boyle & Warbrick, *Law of the European Convention on Human Rights* (Butterworths, 1995), p. 317). Accordingly, it would seem that "holiday homes" and possibly work hostels would fall outside this (see *ibid.* at 318). This is consistent with the English law on security of tenure under the Rent Acts and Housing Acts, which exempts certain categories of occupation, including holiday homes, from protection.

In the same context, the English courts have reached a similar definition of a home, which has been held to connote "a substantial degree of regular personal occupation by the tenant of an essentially personal nature" (*Herbert v. Byrne* [1964] 1 All E.R. 882, CA). A home is where someone carries out the everyday activities of sleeping, eating and cooking (*Curl v. Angelo* [1948] 2 All E.R. 189, CA). It is, of course, not essential that someone should be in the dwelling all the time. Someone may be away from the property for an extended period of time owing to the nature of their work, illness or imprisonment. A substantial body of case law developed concerning a tenant's absence from the property and the point at which it ceases to be a home. Once there is a prolonged absence from the property, the tenant needs to establish both the subjective intention to return there, and outward and visible signs of that intention, such as a person living in the property as a caretaker or the presence of the tenant's personal belongings (*Brown v. Brash and Ambrose* [1948] 2 K.B. 247, CA). Under the Rent Acts it was even accepted that, in limited circumstances, someone could have more than one home, as long as these requirements were fulfilled. The contrast is between a house which can truly be said to be someone's home with one kept as a "mere convenience", such as a postal address.

7–12 The Commission adopted a very similar approach in *Gillow v. U.K.* (1986) Series A, No. 109; 11 E.H.R.R. 335. The case concerned the housing licensing system in Guernsey, which made it unlawful to occupy housing in Guernsey without the necessary licence. The Gillows had lawfully occupied the house they owned on the island for five years. They then lived in different parts of the world for 18 years because of Mr Gillow's work. The Gillows also maintained a home in England. Before the Commission, it was argued that the Gillows' had a home in England. The argument that they no longer had a home in Guernsey was rejected, on the basis that they had always had an intention to return to their house there. When the case came before the Court, it was accepted that the applicants did not have a home in England. The Court concluded that the Gillows' home was in Guernsey.

The Court's decision is largely based on a factual approach (paragraph 46):

> "Although they [the Gillows] had subsequently left Guernsey, they had retained ownership of the house, to which they always intended to return, and had kept furniture in it. On their return in 1979, they had lived in the property with a view to taking up permanent residence once the negotiations with the Housing Authority . . . had been concluded . . ."

A similar approach can be seen in *Buckley v. U.K.* R.J.D. 1996–IV 1271; 23 E.H.R.R. 101. The Government sought to argue that, as the Buckley's "home" was an illegally stationed caravan, it did not fall within the meaning of "home" for the purposes of Article 8. This approach was rejected by the Court, which considered purely whether the applicant had an established residence and did live there. Although the case was held to fall within Article 8, the applicant's claim was not in fact upheld (see Chapter 8, below).

7–13 This may, however, be contrasted with the decision in *Loizidou v. Turkey* (1995) Series A, No. 310; 20 E.H.R.R. 99, where a factual test led to the opposite conclusion. The applicant owned land in Northern Cyprus on which she had intended to build a block of flats, one of which was going to be for the use of her own family. Because of the military occupation of Cyprus she was unable to build the flats. The Court rejected the alleged breach of Article 8, because the applicant did not have any "home" on the land: "it would strain the meaning of the notion "home" in Article 8 to extend it to comprise property on which it is planned to build a house for residential purposes".

7–14 Although there is a distinction between domestic and business use of premises, this is hard to draw in practice where premises are being used for both domestic and business use. In the context of mixed use of property, the English courts have held that business activities which are merely incidental to residential occupation do not prevent a property being occupied as a home. Thus, it was held that a doctor who installed a consulting room in residential premises, at which he occasionally saw patients in residential premises, while he kept his main practice elsewhere, did not occupy the property for business purposes (*Cheryl Investments Ltd v. Saldanha* [1979] 1 All E.R. 5, CA). Similarly, the fact that an art historian did much of his work at his home did not prevent him from enjoying residential security of tenure (*Wright v. Mortimer* (1996) 28 H.L.R. 719, CA).

The Court, too, has found it difficult to draw a line between where the home ends and the business begins, and indeed has taken quite a broad view. In *Niemitz v. Germany* (1992) Series A, No. 251 B; 16 E.H.R.R. 97, it was held that a lawyer's home extended to his office.

2. "Respect" for the home

> "Article 8(1) protects the right to *respect* for the various interests it lists. This makes it clear that not every act of a public authority which has an impact on the exercise of the interest will constitute an interference with the Article 8(1) right" (Harris, O'Boyle & Warbrick, at 320).

In some contexts the narrow interpretation of the meaning of "respect" has been used to justify a finding that the Article does not give rise to any positive obligations, although in other circumstances the Court has taken a different approach, and found a requirement, *e.g.* for the law to regulate the relationships between private individuals, so as to provide effective remedies (see *X and Y v. Netherlands* (1985) Series A, No. 91; 8 E.H.R.R. 235). The court has taken a narrow view of the meaning of the right to respect for the home (see paragraph 7–03 above), and accordingly positive obligations in this field have been limited. (See further the discussion under paragraph 7–25, below.)

3. The rights which are protected

7–15 Given the limited interpretation that has been put on Article 8 in relation to housing rights, there has only been a limited number of cases where it has successfully founded a claim.

(a) Deprivation of the home

7–16 Most obviously there is a right to access and occupation, which the state must not unjustifiably interfere with. Where the state excludes an applicant from his or her home, there may be a breach of Article 8. The most extreme example of this can be seen in the case of *Cyprus v. Turkey* (1976) 4 E.H.R.R. 482 where, following the invasion of Cyprus by the Turkish army, Greek Cypriots were forced from their homes and refugees were refused permission to return to their homes. This was held, unsurprisingly, to be a breach of Article 8(1).

Such precipitate action is likely to be rare in this country, although the interrelation between the procedures for eviction of trespassers and the rights of gypsies show how problems could arise. The Criminal Justice and Public Order Act 1994 was passed to enable local authorities to take swifter action to remove people living in vehicles on unoccupied land or trespassing on occupied land. Under section 77 of that Act, the authority may make a direction for such persons to leave the land. If they fail to leave, a criminal offence is committed. The direction may be enforced in the magistrates' court, and it has been held that once the direction is issued there should be as little delay as possible between the giving and enforcing of it (*R. v. Wolverhampton M.B.C., ex p. Dunne & Rafferty* (1996) 29 H.L.R. 745, DC).

In *Dunne,* however, it was accepted that the remedy under the 1994 Act was draconian and that authorities must give careful consideration to the exercise of their powers. In particular, the Gypsy Site Policy and Unauthorised Camping Circular 18/94, issued by the Department of the Environment, gives guidance to local authorities as to preliminary steps to be taken before using these powers. Paragraph 9 reminds them that they ". . . should not use their powers to evict gypsies needlessly. They should use the powers in a humane and compassionate fashion and primarily to reduce nuisance and to afford a higher level of protection to private owners of land." In particular, where the occupiers may include children or vulnerable persons, the effect of the use of the procedure on such persons should be considered.

By contrast, in *R. v. Brighton & Hove Council, ex p. Marmont, The Times,* January 15, 1998, QBD, instead of using their powers under the 1994 Act, the authority used the summary possession procedure available under RSC, Ord. 113. Using this procedure, an owner of land may obtain possession against trespassers within days. On the facts of the case, the court found that the authority had paid sufficient attention to the guidance before exercising their powers, but it was also held that the guidance in the Circular was irrelevant where the authority were using the summary possession procedure. This presents a possible area of challenge using Article 8.

7–17 A home may be taken away through the compulsory purchase procedure, whether to be replaced by other homes, or road building or the like. It is also possible for authorities to take action to close or demolish properties which are unfit for human habitation: Housing Act 1985, Pt IX. To the extent that this deprives owners of their property rights, the matter is more properly considered an infringement of Article 1 of the First Protocol (see paragraph 7–28, below). However, where the applicant lives in the home (either as an owner-occupier, or as a tenant or other occupier) the matter could be considered as an infringement of Article 8. In *Howard v. U.K.* (1985) 52 D.R. 198, the local authority had exercised their powers to purchase compulsorily the house and land of two elderly brothers under the Town and Country Planning Act 1971. The land was in an area zoned primarily for housing redevelopment. It was accepted by the Government that this was an interference with rights in breach of Article 8(1), but a justification was pleaded and accepted under Article 8(2) (see below paragraph 7–24).

7–18   In *Gillow* (above), where the law in Guernsey prevented occupation of the home without a licence, which the Gillows were refused, occupation without a licence led to a criminal prosecution. In these circumstances the Court found that there was an interference with the applicants' right to respect for their home.

In other circumstances, public landlords routinely evict tenants and other occupiers from their homes, *e.g.* because they are in arrears of rent, or because they are unlawful occupiers. The response under the Convention to such cases is likely to be unsupportive, provided proper legal processes have been observed. Thus in *S. v. U.K.* (1986) 47 D.R. 274, the applicant claimed that respect for her home had been violated, when under the Housing Act 1980 she was not entitled to succeed to her lesbian partner's secure tenancy, and was evicted from her home. The Commission found the application inadmissible. Taking a narrow view of "home", the Commission noted that the applicant had no legal title to the property, the contractual relationship having been between her former partner and the landlord. The Commission also noted, at 278, that:

". . . on the death of the partner, under the ordinary law, the applicant was no longer entitled to remain in the house, and the local authority was entitled to possession so that the house could no longer be regarded as "home" for the applicant within the meaning of Article 8."

If they were wrong on this view of home, the Commission considered, in any event, that the interference was in accordance with the law, and necessary for the protection of the contractual rights of the landlord to have the property back at the end of the tenancy.

(b) Peaceful enjoyment

7–19   The right to respect for home life has been held to extend to peaceful enjoyment of the home. This has primarily been established through cases relating to aircraft noise. Thus in *Arrondelle v. U.K.* (1982) 26 D.R. 5, the applicant owned a cottage, which was just over a mile away from the east end of the runway at Gatwick airport. The runway was extended in 1973, and in 1975 the M23 was completed about 500 feet from the home. The applicant was denied planning permission for a change of use on the property and was unable to sell it. The government settled the case by making an *"ex gratia"* payment. (See also *Powell and Rayner v. U.K.* (1990) Series A, No. 172; 12 E.H.R.R. 355, discussed more fully below at paragraph 7–25.)

The law in this country does provide protection in a variety of ways against interference with peaceful enjoyment of a home. Such protection exists in common law, as a matter of contract and tort. This is complemented by, for example, statutory control of environmental nuisances, such as under the Environmental Protection Act 1990; by protection from eviction, such as under the Protection from Eviction Act 1977; and by a recent widening of sanctions against anti-social behaviour (see the Housing Act 1996, Pt V, and the Crime and Disorder Act 1998, s.1). In so far as these protect occupiers from interference with their peaceful enjoyment of the home, it can be said that there is compliance with such positive duties as there may be under Article 8. Where a public authority, however, fails to use powers available to it, it may be arguable that there has been a failure to protect occupiers.

At the moment, for example, it is generally thought that there is no obligation on landlords to take action to protect tenants against the effects of anti-social behaviour by other tenants of the landlord. In *O'Leary v. Islington L.B.C.* (1983) 9 H.L.R. 81, the Court of Appeal held that there was no implied covenant in a tenancy agreement on the landlord's part to enforce a covenant not to commit a nuisance against other tenants. In *Smith v. Scott* [1973] Ch. 314, ChD, a tenant of a local authority brought proceedings for an injunction against them on the basis that the authority had let the neighbouring property to a family whom they knew regularly engaged in anti-social conduct. It was held that the authority could not be liable in nuisance for the acts of the neighbouring family. *Scott*, however, has been the subject of some academic criticism but has recently been followed in *Hussain v. Lancaster City Council* [1998] E.G.C.S. 86. Where tenants receive no protection from their public landlord, it may be that they could make a claim under the Act for violation of Convention rights.

As to the scope of the law itself, it is notable that the aircraft cases (above) were cited in the dissenting speech of Lord Cooke in *Hunter v. Canary Wharf Ltd* [1997] A.C. 655, at 714B, when he sought to justify the extension of rights to sue in nuisance, to occupiers of land beyond those who had a legal interest in the land. In so far as the law does not protect all occupiers of the home equally, there may yet be more to be said on this.

(c) Housing conditions

7-20 Closely linked to peaceful enjoyment of the home, is the maintenance of it in a fit condition. Indeed, in English law a failure to repair by a landlord may amount to a breach of the covenant for quiet enjoyment. Thus, a landlord was held to be in breach of the covenant for quiet enjoyment because of a failure to keep a building watertight (*Gordon v. Selico Co.* [1985] 2 E.G.L.R. 79, ChD).

While existing law itself provides a number of safeguards as to housing conditions for tenants (Landlord and Tenant Act 1985, s. 11; Environmental Protection Act 1990, Pt III; Housing Act 1985, Pts VI and IX), it is also undoubtedly the case that much housing is in very poor condition (see the English National House Condition Survey, 1996). It is possible to envisage that, in cases where local authorities fail to respond to poor conditions, they might be in breach of their obligations under Article 8.

This might arise because the authority refuse (or more likely fail) to take any action in relation to a property in the private rented sector which they know to be in very poor condition. More commonly, this may also arise where public sector landlords fail to respond to the problems of their own tenants, and leave them in appalling condition for many years. While many cases demonstrate that substantial damages (together with injunctive relief) for poor housing conditions may be available to a tenant, in some cases redress is not possible under breach of repairing covenant. The most notorious example arises where there is severe condensation damp, caused not by a breach of repairing covenant, but rather by the inherent design of the building (see *Quick v. Taff Ely B.C.* [1986] Q.B. 809, CA).

7–21   The presence of such damp may well render the dwelling unfit for human habitation within the definition of Housing Act 1985, s.604. Local authorities are under a duty to take action against unfit housing, and Parts VI and IX of the 1985 Act give them extensive powers in this regard. But an authority cannot use these enforcement provisions against themselves (*R. v. Cardiff CC, ex p. Cross* (1981) 6 H.L.R. 6, CA), so the duty to act does not arise where an authority are themselves the landlord. This gap could be redressed if parliament enacted the Law Commission's recommendation — made in 1996 — that there should be an implied covenant in every short letting that the dwelling is fit for human habitation. (Such a covenant is already implied by Landlord and Tenant Act 1985, s.8, into certain tenancies let at a low rent, but the definition of low rent is such that the section is currently redundant.) Certainly, many tenants have used Environmental Protection Act 1990, s.82, to force landlords, including local authorities, to take action to remedy condensation damp (*Dover D.C. v. Farrar* (1982) 2 H.L.R. 32, DC), but such proceedings do not always provide a satisfactory remedy. In particular, there are considerable limitations on the compensation available, even if the premises are found to be "prejudicial to health" (see Hunter, "Costs and Compensation in Statutory Nuisance Claims" [1997] J.H.L. 27). In such circumstances, there will doubtless be occasions when reliance will be placed on Article 8.

(d) Facilitating rights to live in the home

7–22   Many states offer forms of protection for occupiers of rented homes, which limit the rights of landlords to evict them at will. Given that there is no positive duty under the Convention on states to provide a home, it is hard to argue that states have a duty to provide such a system of security of tenure. The last 20 years or so have, however, seen a gradual withdrawal of rights for tenants in the private sector in this country. Although it is very unlikely that this trend (if challenged) would be found to violate Convention rights, the exclusion and operation of statutory protections could possibly engage responsibility under Article 8 in some respects (for example if existing protections were removed).

(e) Affordability

7–23   The lack of any positive duty makes it impossible to argue that there is a duty on the government to provide affordable housing, either by ensuring rents are low (through rent control or subsidy), or by providing some form of housing income, such as housing benefit or income support for owner-occupiers. What we have seen, however, has been a series of cuts in all forms of assistance towards affordability. Rent control in the private sector has all but been abolished (by the Housing Act 1988), and subsidy of public sector housing has been withdrawn. For occupiers of housing there have been extensive cuts in housing benefit and income support for mortgage costs. Some of these cuts, given that they hit existing occupiers, have led to the loss of the home. In these circumstances it is possible to envisage issues arising under Article 8.

4. Justification for interference

7–24   Even if the applicant can show that there has been an interference with his or her rights under Article 8, it is a defence (under Article 8(2)) to show that this is:

> "in accordance with law and is necessary in a democratic society in the interest of national security, public safety or the economic well-being of the country, for the prevention of disorder or crime, for the protection of health or morals, or for the protection of the rights and freedoms of others."

The defence was successfully used in *Howard* (above). The question to be addressed is whether "the competent authorities have struck a balance between the applicants' interests and the interests of the community as a whole." The factors which weighed in favour of the Government were that:

- The interference was in accordance with law under a clear statutory enactment.

- The inspector's report had expressly addressed whether or not the applicants' particular property should be included within the order.

- The inspector balanced the advantage of the exclusion of the property against the disadvantage to the community as a whole, namely that certain sheltered housing would not be built or would be rendered substantially more expensive.

- The applicants were offered alternative suitable residential accommodation in the immediate vicinity.

- The applicants were entitled to full compensation.

7–25   In *Gillow* (above), the Government also sought to argue that the requirement of a licence and the refusal of it, were justified. The Court found that the requirements were made in accordance with law, under a valid statute, which was sufficiently certain in its terms and operation. Furthermore the legislation had a legitimate aim of promoting the economic well-being of the island, which was not disproportionate in a democratic society. However, the way that the law had been applied to the Gillows, taking into account their individual circumstances, had been disproportionate to the legitimate aim being pursued. (As to the principle of proportionality, see generally paragraph 2.44 and following.)

Housing policies which deprive people of their homes, or the right to occupy them, will generally be upheld if there is a proper basis for them, particularly where alternative provision is made. In each case, however, public authorities must consider the individual application of the policy.

A number of claims relating to interference with the peaceful enjoyment of the home by environmental pollution have also been considered by the Court. In *Powell and Rayner v. U.K.* (1990) Series A, No. 172; 12 E.H.R.R. 355, the interference stemmed from aircraft noise at Heathrow airport. While the Court found that increasing noise from the airport did interfere with applicants' "scope for enjoying amenities" of their homes, the legitimate economic benefits flowing from the airport had to be weighed against the interference to the applicants' enjoyment of their homes. Furthermore, the government had introduced a number of measures to assist those living around the airport, including restrictions on night flying, noise insulation grant schemes and purchase of noise-blighted properties. Accordingly the Court concluded, at paragraph 45:

"In forming a judgment as to the proper scope of the noise abatement measures for aircraft arriving at and departing from Heathrow Airport, the United Kingdom Government cannot arguably be said to have exceeded the margin of appreciation afforded to them or upset the fair balance required to be struck under Article 8."

In framing claims under Article 8 it will always be necessary to consider questions of justification. Where a policy has been framed which is part of a larger economic policy (*e.g.* cuts in benefit or investment in public housing), a wide margin of appreciation is often likely to be allowed. (As to the margin of appreciation, see generally paragraph 2–41 and following.)

5. Protection of family and private life

7–26 In addition to respect for the home, Article 8(1) provides for respect for family and private life. This subject is covered in detail in Chapter 6, but some points in relation to housing law are made here.

The Strasbourg authorities have taken a broad view of the duties of states in respecting family life. In *Marckx v. Belgium* (1979) Series A, No. 31; 2 E.H.R.R. 330, for example, the Court found that states had a positive duty to provide a system of domestic law which safeguarded the illegitimate child's integration into his family. Many family law matters will relate to the family home. The maintenance of the family may require effective laws as to the destination of the family home on relationship breakdown. In relation to married couples and owner-occupied homes, this protection is provided through the Matrimonial Causes Act 1973. For tenants, whether married or unmarried, provision is made in the Family Law Act 1996.

This leaves a gap, in which unmarried owner-occupiers are still subject to arcane property laws in order to establish their rights. Where the property is in the sole name of (usually) the man, a woman on the ending of the relationship may find herself homeless, and without rights. While some provision may be made (where there are children) under the Children Act 1989, this does not usually provide a cohabitant with any long term rights to the property. It has accordingly been suggested that unless the law in this area is reformed, the government may be susceptible to challenge.

7-27   The Court of Appeal has already cited Article 8 in the case of *Albany Home Loans Ltd. v. Massey* (1997) 29 H.L.R. 902, when seeking to solve the issue of whether a court should exercise its powers to order possession of the family home against a husband (who admitted he had no defence to the claim made by a mortgagee) when the wife had raised a claim which was yet to be tried. The husband's appeal against the possession order made against him was allowed, so that the husband and wife could remain together in the home, at least until her defence was finally adjudicated upon.

Respect for family life, private life and home may overlap. Thus in *S. v. U.K.* (1986) 47 D.R. 274, in addition to a claim based on respect for the home, a claim for breach of respect for family life was also made. The application was, however, declared inadmissible by the Commission. Homosexual relationships were held not to fall within the scope of the right to respect for family life. Although the relationship fell to be protected by the right to private life, the partner had died, and accordingly there was nothing to protect, save S's individual occupation of the home (as to which see paragraph 7-18, above).

E. PROPERTY RIGHTS

1. Interference with and deprivation of possessions

7-28   Article 1 of the First Protocol provides for the "peaceful enjoyment of possessions". No one is to be deprived of his possessions "except in the public interest and subject to the conditions provided for by law and by general principles of international law." The second paragraph of the Article provides, however, that: "the proceeding provisions shall not . . . in any way impair the right of a State to enforce such laws as it deems necessary to control the use of property in accordance with the general interest. . . ."

"Possessions" for these purposes clearly encompass all forms of interest in land, including leases (*Mellacher v. Austria* (1989) 12 E.H.R.R. 391). As it also encompasses contractual rights (*A, B and Company AS v. FRG* (1978) 14 D.R. 146 at 168), it will also encompass occupiers who merely have a contractual licence to occupy. Where an occupier has no legal rights, there can be no claim under this provision (*S v. U.K.* (1986) 47 D.R. 274).

7-29   It has been held that Article 1 of the First Protocol comprises three distinct rules. The first is expressed in the first sentence of the first paragraph and lays down the principle of peaceful enjoyment of property. The second expressed in the second sentence of the first paragraph, covers deprivation of possessions and subjects it to certain conditions. The third, contained in the second paragraph, recognises that states are entitled, amongst other things to control the use of property in accordance with the general interest, by enforcing such laws as they deem necessary for the purpose (see *Mellacher v. Austria* (1989) Series A, No. 169; 12 E.H.R.R. 391, and *Sporrong and Lönnroth v. Sweden* (1983) Series A, No. 52; 5 E.H.R.R. 35).

From a housing point of view, deprivation of property rights can be seen from two different angles (as further explained below). First, the state may deprive an occupier of his or her rights of occupation. This is illustrated by *Howard*, above.

Secondly, the state may reduce the rights of an owner of land as against other occupiers. This is illustrated by *James v. United Kingdom* (1986) Series A, No. 98; 8 E.H.R.R. 123.

2. Deprivation of rights of occupation

7–30   In *Howard* (above), in addition to the claim under Article 8 (see above), a claim was also made under Article 1 of the First Protocol. The Commission recognised that the two provisions of the Convention overlapped, and held that it was required to reconcile them. In answering the question as to whether the deprivation was in the "public interest" under Article 1 of the First Protocol, the same approach was to be taken as to whether the interference was justified under Article 8(2). Thus it must be shown that (at 206):

"the competent authorities struck a fair balance between the rights of the individual property owner and the rights of the community, in any expropriation of the property. A significant factor in any such balance will be the availability of compensation, reflecting the value of the property expropriated".

Given the conclusion reached under Article 8(2) (see paragraph 7–24 above), the Commission concluded that the applicants had no claim.

It is unusual for public bodies to deprive occupiers of land of their rights without justification, and without recourse to legal procedures. It is not unknown, however, as is illustrated by *Akinbolu v. Hackney LBC* (1996) 29 H.L.R. 259, where a secure tenant, who had been arrested as an illegal immigrant was released on bail, only to find that the locks to his flat had been changed. The Court of Appeal held that this was an illegal eviction, and it could also, arguably, be said to have been a breach of Article 1 of the First Protocol.

3. Reduction of rights as against other occupiers

7–31   In *James* (above), the trustees of the Duke of Westminster complained as to the effect of the Leasehold Reform Act 1967, which entitled long leaseholders of houses to purchase the freehold, at an advantageous price. The Court found that the trustees had been deprived of their possessions, accordingly the question was whether this was justified within the terms of Article 1 of the First Protocol. It was argued that there could be no public interest where the benefit of the legislation went to individuals (*i.e.* those leaseholders who sought to enfranchise). The Court rejected this argument holding, at paragraph 41, that: "The taking of property in pursuance of a policy calculated to enhance social justice can properly be described as being 'in the public interest'."

Was the deprivation in the public interest in this case? The Court emphasised (at paragraph 46) that this was an area where national governments should be given a "wide margin of appreciation", as "the decision to enact laws expropriating property will commonly involve considerations of political, economic and social issues on which opinions within a democratic society may reasonably differ widely". Furthermore the aim pursued by the legislation was a legitimate one: "modern societies consider housing of the population to be a prime social need, the regulation of which cannot entirely be left to the play of market forces". The means for achieving the aim was appropriate and not disproportionate, and the compensation was adequate.

7–32   A similar argument was raised in *Mellacher* (above), in relation to rent controls imposed on landlords. The Court found that the legislation did not amount to expropriation of the landlord's property, nor were they deprived of their right to use it, though there was a control of the use of the property. The Court therefore considered whether under the second paragraph of the Article the interference with the property rights was justified in the general interest. It held (at paragraph 45) that laws controlling the use of property "are especially called for and usual in the field of housing, which in our modern societies is a central concern of social and economic policies". Again the Court emphasised the wide margin of appreciation that states have in this area, and found that the interference was in the general interest. Furthermore the detailed means by which this was achieved in the legislation were not "so inappropriate or disproportionate to take them outside the State's margin of appreciation" (paragraph 55).

The approach in *Mellacher* was followed in two Italian cases concerning the suspension of possession orders: *Spadea v. Italy* (1995) Series A, No. 315–B; 21 E.H.R.R. 482 and *Scollo v. Italy* (1996) Series A, No. 315–C; 22 E.H.R.R. 514. In considering the balance between the general interest and the private interest in matters of rent control, security of tenure and suspension of eviction, the Court emphasised that each case must be examined individually to assess whether the preference given to the tenant was justified with respect to the aim of the law. The legislation relating to the suspension of suspending or staggering eviction orders was subject to certain exceptions which balanced the housing needs of the landlord and the tenant. (Compare, in the domestic context, the balancing exercise in determining whether it is "reasonable" to make a possession order.) Both cases turned on how this balancing exercise had been carried out. In *Spadea* the landlord had no urgent need for the accommodation, but the tenants were elderly and on low incomes and it was held that there had been no breach. By contrast, in *Scollo* the landlord established a breach because he was disabled, unemployed and in need of the flat, and although he fell within the exceptions the eviction had been repeatedly suspended.

F. RIGHTS TO A FAIR HEARING

7–33   The due process requirements of Article 6(1), relating to the determination of a person's civil rights and obligations, have led the Strasbourg authorities to make and apply a distinction between matters of public and private law, the latter not falling within the Article. (For a detailed discussion see paragraphs 2–67—2–68; see also Harris, O'Boyle & Warbrick, at 174–186). This distinction is likely to be of particular significance where rights may be seen to straddle the public/private divide, as is particularly the case in housing law (see also paragraphs 7–06 and 7–09). Where the rights involved concern property rights, Article 6(1) will be applicable. Thus it will encompass decisions as to the purchase and retention of land, compulsory purchase and the like. In *Gillow* (above), it was held that the Gillows had a right to a fair hearing under Article 6(1), a right which had been fulfilled in the particular circumstances.

Other aspects of housing practice can be contrasted with this, such as internal review procedures in relation to decisions on the allocation of housing under Part VI of the Housing Act 1986, and homelessness under Part VII. Given the attitude of the English courts, which have consistently held that matters of this type are public (see, *e.g. Camden LBC v. O'Rourke* [1998] A.C. 188, HL), it seems likely that Article 6(1) will not apply to these procedures.

From the perspective of domestic law, the provision of social welfare benefits by the state would also generally seem to fall within the scope of public law matters. The Strasbourg authorities, however, after a number of cases which turned on the particular nature of the benefits and their contributory nature and link to employment contracts, now seem to have established that Article 6(1) applies to all social security rights (see paragraph 12–13). This would accordingly seem to include housing benefit. Although the initial determination of entitlement to benefit will not engage Article 6(1) (by reason of the requirement for a dispute — see paragraph 7–34 below), the review of housing benefit determinations by officers and by housing benefit review boards, following representations that there had been an error, might at first sight seem to need to comply with the due process requirements (see generally paragraphs 2–72—2–79). Apart from other issues, this could be said to raise the question of whether housing benefit review procedures comply with the requirement for an independent and impartial tribunal, given that the reviews are carried out (in the first instance) often by the same officers who made the initial determination, and (upon further review) by members (councillors) of the local housing authority itself.

The Court's jurisprudence, however, is that the procedural guarantees in Article 6 do not have to be satisfied at every stage in the process: it is sufficient if there is access to a court with full jurisdiction over the subject-matter and which does provide the guarantees (see *Bryan v. U.K.* (1995) Series A, No. 335–A; 21 E.H.R.R. 342, paragraph 40). Since the internal housing benefit review procedures are themselves subject to judicial review, it would seem that that the former would not, on account of their structure alone, violate the requirements of Article 6.

1. Disputes

7–34 In order to have a claim under Article 6(1), there must be a dispute concerning civil rights and obligations (see generally paragraphs 2–70—2–71). The Article is, moreover, a procedural guarantee of a right to a fair hearing only in the determination of whatever legal rights and obligations a state in its discretion provides. In *James* (above), it was held that Article 6(1) "does not in itself guarantee any particular content for (civil) "rights and obligations' in the substantive law . . .". It also does not require that there be a national court with competence to invalidate or override national law. Although the freeholders could not challenge the tenant's entitlement to a transfer of title once the conditions of the Leasehold Reform Act 1967 were satisfied, there was access to a tribunal to determine whether the legislation had been complied with. In this latter respect the Court distinguished *Sporrong and Lönnroth v. Sweden* (1983) Series A, No. 52; 5 E.H.R.R. 35, and held there had been no breach of Article 6(1).

2. Adequacy of rights of challenge

7–35   In many instances, statutory rights to a hearing exist in housing matters, and these can be quite extensive (such as in relation to compulsory purchase, and closing or demolition orders). Where such rights do not exist (as in the case of short-term tenants, including periodic tenants, occupying premises subject to a closing or demolition order — see Housing Act 1985, s.269(2)), judicial review may yet be possible, though the availability of this is limited (*R. v. Woking B.C., ex p. Adam* (1996) 28 H.L.R. 513, CA). Similarly, although repossession generally has to be sought through legal process, the courts' powers and responsibilities may be limited. For example, in the case of introductory tenants (under the Housing Act 1996), before seeking possession a local authority must (if asked) go through a review procedure, which is entirely internal. In relation to such reviews, considerations arise similar to those regarding housing benefit review boards (see above). Once the procedural requirements are complied with, however, the court must grant possession (Housing Act 1996, s.127(2)). The possibility remains, however, of challenge by way of judicial review to the authority's original decision to evict.

Where determinations of civil rights and obligations are made administratively, the adequacy of any right of challenge before a tribunal must satisfy the right of access to a court inherent in Article 6 (see generally *Golder v. U.K.* (1975) Series A, No. 18; 1 E.H.R.R. 524). Where the jurisdiction of the court (and thus the right and scope of challenge) is limited (as in judicial review), the due process requirements may not be met (see *W, B and R v. U.K.* (1987) Series A, No. 121; 10 E.H.R.R. 82). The decisions of the Court in this area are not entirely consistent, with the outcome dependant on the nature of the complaints made by the applicant (see *Zumbotel v. Austria* (1993) Series A, No. 268–A; 17 E.H.R.R. 116). In general, however, where administrative decisions are at issue, it seems likely that judicial review would be an adequate protection (see *IKSCON v. U.K.* (1994) 76A D.R. 90; 18 E.H.R.R. C.D. 133).

G. DISCRIMINATION

7–36   Article 14 provides for the protection of the rights in the Convention without discrimination "on any ground, such as sex, race, colour, language, religion, political or other opinion, national or social origin, association with a national minority, property, birth or other status" (see generally paragraph 2–123 and following). It is only the rights protected by the Convention that fall within this provision, so it is important first to identify the housing right which it is alleged is being breached prior to adding a claim under Article 14.

Several of the cases discussed above have included a claim under Article 14. In *James* (above), the Court accepted that the 1967 Act rendered Article 14 applicable, since it did entail "differences of treatment in regard to different categories of property owners". There was, however, no discrimination, since treatment is discriminatory only "if it has no objective and reasonable justification, if it does not pursue a legitimate aim or if there is not a reasonable relationship of proportionality between the means employed and the aim sought to be realised".

In *S. v. U.K.* (1986) 47 D.R. 274, the Commission considered whether the differential treatment between homosexual and heterosexual partners under the Housing Act 1980 was justified. It considered that the aim of the legislation (in giving succession rights to families) was to protect the family. The family (including unmarried heterosexual partners) was considered by the Commission as meriting special protection in society. Accordingly, families could be afforded particular assistance, and therefore "a difference in treatment between the applicant and somebody in the same position whose partner had been of the opposite sex can be objectively and reasonably justified".

H. PROCEEDINGS AND REMEDIES

7-37 A victim of an unlawful act under section 6 may bring proceedings against a public authority in the appropriate court or tribunal under s.7 (as to victims, see generally paragraphs 2–15 and following). The nature of housing law is such that private law rights and public law rights, as traditionally defined, often overlap in given circumstances. There are numerous cases in a housing law context as to whether the public law duties of local authorities, enforceable by judicial review, also give rise to private law rights which may be enforced by way of action and for which a claim in damages may lie. The choice of court or tribunal has been of great significance. (See *O'Rourke v. Camden LBC* [1998] A.C. 188, in which the House of Lords held that there was no cause of action for alleged failure to provide an applicant with temporary accommodation pending his homelessness application; and *Haringey v. Cotter* (1996) 29 H.L.R. 682, CA, in which it was held that a landlord had no cause of action in relation to an alleged failure to pay housing benefit.) Subject to the rules which may be made under s. 7(2) as to the appropriate tribunal for proceedings, it seems that no such general problems will face those bringing claims for unlawful acts under section 6, although claims for damages will need to surmount the requirement of just satisfaction (see generally paragraph 1–58).

It is notable that Convention issues may be raised by way of claim, counterclaim or similar proceeding (see section 7(1) and (2)). It is also open for a victim to raise an unlawful act as a defence, perhaps most obviously in a claim for possession. Counterclaims are already commonly brought against possession actions for rent arrears on the basis of damages for breach of repairing covenant. Comparison may also be made with the present practice by which a defendant may — albeit in limited circumstances — raise a public law defence in a private law action (see *Wandsworth LBC v. Winder* [1985] A.C. 461, HL, in which the authority brought a claim for possession based on rent arrears, and the tenant counterclaimed on the basis that the authority's rent increases were unlawful).

7-38 The definition of "court" in section 8(5) envisages that unlawful acts may be raised in tribunal proceedings, but the limitation on when damages may be awarded may remain relevant as to the choice of the appropriate forum for proceedings. Only courts which have the power to award damages may do so for an unlawful act (section 8(2)). Thus, rent assessment committees could not award damages. As damages are available in proceedings commenced by way of judicial review, this may remain the most appropriate remedy in such circumstances.

CHAPTER 8

Planning Law

Iain Colville (Barrister, Arden Chambers)

A. INTRODUCTION

8–01 The sophisticated system of planning control which operates throughout England and Wales is central to modern society, and has become increasingly important in an age of heightened awareness about environmental issues. Moreover, in their broadest sense, those issues transcend national boundaries and interests.

The nature and operation of this system of control is deeply political, in a wide sense. Planning law has exclusively statutory origins. Implicit within the concept of control is a considerable degree of intervention by the state, entailing a balance of economic, political, social and environmental factors. Against this background, it is not difficult to see how human rights law could have a good deal of relevance. The Convention, however, touches on areas relevant to planning control in only a limited and often indirect way, though nonetheless with undeniable significance.

In the context of the areas covered by this chapter, the Act can be expected particularly to affect the way in which public authorities, as defined under section 6, perform their functions; and also to affect the grounds upon which the decisions of public authorities come to be challenged. Thus, for all those involved in planning processes, in whatever capacity, it will be important to have an understanding of the operation and impact of the Act and the Convention.

B. PUBLIC AUTHORITIES

8–02 Apart from courts and tribunals concerned with planning matters (which will come under the forensic obligation — by sections 2 and 3 — to interpret and apply legislation correctly in accordance with Convention law, as well as the general obligation to conduct themselves in accordance with Convention rights), the broad definition in section 6 of "public authority" comprises two main elements: the general nature of the functions of the legal entity; and the particular nature of any specific acts or omissions which are under consideration. In each case, it will be necessary to determine whether, in the particular context, the functions and conduct belong to the public or private sphere.

1. Planning

8–03   Under Part I of the Town & Country Planning Act 1990, the direct responsibility for controlling development has been vested in the various local planning authorities ("LPAs"): county planning authorities; district planning authorities; unitary authorities; mineral planning authorities; Joint Planning Boards; National Parks authorities; the Broads Authority; Enterprise Zone authorities; Urban Development Corporations; Housing Action Trusts; and the Urban Regeneration Agency. The Secretary of State for the Environment, Transport and the Regions is responsible for overseeing and controlling the local planning authorities in the discharge of their duties in England, and in Wales the power is vested in the Secretary of State for Wales. There is no doubt that these will be public authorities for the purposes of section 6 in relation to planning and environmental functions.

The Wildlife and Countryside Act 1981 established the Nature Conservancy Council for England (English Nature), and the Countryside Council for Wales. These bodies are responsible for the designation of two categories of areas, namely the Sites of Special Scientific Interest and National Nature Reserves. Both these designations will have a significant impact on any proposal to develop on or within the vicinity of such an area. In discharging their duties, both these bodies will also be public authorities under the Act.

2. Compulsory Purchase

8–04   Many bodies have statutory powers of compulsory purchase which overlap with the statutory framework of planning functions. The exercise of such powers clearly falls within the public law sphere, although in other respects the particular body may possess characteristics more akin to those of a private law entity. It seems likely that, in connection with compulsory purchase, such bodies would be considered to be public authorities for the purposes of the Act.

C. VICTIMS

8–05   In certain respects, a person will need to possess the characteristics of a "victim" in order to articulate Convention rights for the purposes of legal proceedings. While this will not be necessary in order for a person or group to rely on Convention rights with regard (for instance) to the interpretation and application of planning legislation, victim status is essential in order for a party to be able to bring proceedings or rely on the alleged unlawful conduct of a public authority in any legal proceedings on grounds of incompatibility with Convention rights.

Victim status under the Act seems destined to be more confined than, for example, the approach of the English courts to standing in judicial review proceedings. (As to the definition of victims generally, see paragraph 1–56, and Chapter 3.) The Convention law which is applicable in determining who is a victim for these purposes can be said, in general, to adopt a more rigorous approach.

In *Tauira and Others v. France* [1995] D.R. 83–B112, the applicants were residents of Tahiti, and claimed that they were victims of breaches of the

Convention by France's plan to test nuclear weapons. The residents lived over 1000 km from the test site. The Commission held that the applicants were not "victims". The Strasbourg authorities, though, are prepared to look at substance rather than form. In *Pine Valley Developments Ltd v. Ireland* (1992) Series A, No. 222; 14 E.H.R.R. 319 the Court considered that two companies (the first and second applicants — one of which had been struck off the register, while the other was in hands of a receiver) were no more than vehicles for the third applicant (the sole beneficial shareholder) to obtain planning permission, and that to draw a distinction between the applicants was artificial.

8-06   The limitation of those entitled to rely upon aspects of the Act has a particular relevance to planning issues, where groups rather than individuals have commonly been those in the forefront of protest and challenge. These groups have taken many forms, from local amenity groups to national and international environmental pressure groups. A pressure group objecting to a proposed development is not likely to be regarded as a victim unless it can show that it is directly affected. Many will doubtless consider it to be unsatisfactory that such groups will generally have to rely on the discretion of the court to allow them to take part in proceedings by way of *amicus* briefs, rather than being entitled to participate as of right.

However, there seems no warrant for saying that this restriction of rights and remedies under sections 6 to 9 of the Act should result in any equivalent restriction of other rights of legal action in which the Convention may be relied upon. Thus, to the extent that Convention rights may be relevant other than under section 6 (for example as a matter of general administrative law), access to the courts through judicial review for environmental groups should be unaffected.

D. CONVENTION RIGHTS IN DOMESTIC LAW BEFORE THE ACT

8-07   A number of planning cases prior to the Act has demonstrated what can best be described as ambivalence towards Convention rights. In *R. v. Secretary of State for the Environment, ex p. Davis* (1990) 59 P. & C.R. 306, the duty to respect human rights in administrative decision-making was described as "common ground", but the weight to be attached to Convention rights was said primarily to be for the decision-maker. In contrast, in *R. v. Dacorum Borough Council, ex p. Cannon* (1996) 2 P.L.R. 45 reliance on Convention rights was comprehensively rejected in the absence of any statutory ambiguity. In *Britton v. Secretary of State for the Environment* [1996] J.P.L. 617, the reference in an earlier version of PPG1 to international commitments being a relevant consideration in the planning process was the source of a finding of irrationality, given the failure to address to address the possible violation of Convention rights. Subsequently, PPG1 was altered, by removing the relevant passage.

E. RAISING CONVENTION RIGHTS UNDER THE ACT

8–08 Convention issues may arise in a number of ways. Not only must public authorities act compatibly with Convention rights (except where legislation provides otherwise — see section 6(2)), but their statutory powers fall to be interpreted, where possible, so as to be compatible with those rights. It will accordingly be incumbent on public authorities to be able to demonstrate that they have taken Convention rights into account, where relevant. This applies as much to the initial decision-makers as to public authorities charged with hearing appeals.

However, it should be noted that, if an appellant does not initially raise an alleged violation of Convention rights at the appropriate stage, it may subsequently be too late to do so effectively. Thus, in *Wellhead v. Secretary of State for the Environment and Epping Forest District Council* (1991) 71 P.& C.R. 419, 426, it was observed that the factual basis for arguing a breach of Article 8 would have to be raised before the Inspector.

Given that the Act creates no new procedures for legal challenge, and subject to any rules which may be made under section 7(2), alleged breaches of section 6 are capable of being raised under section 7 both on statutory appeals and judicial review. In this respect, the Act will create new, and "hard" grounds of challenge.

F. CONVENTION RIGHTS RELEVANT TO PLANNING CONTROL AND COMPULSORY PURCHASE

8–09 In terms of substantive rights, the Convention provisions of most general relevance to the operation of the planning system and the compulsory acquisition of land are Article 8 (right to respect for private and family life) and Article 1 of the First Protocol (protection of property). Other Articles may also be relevant, such as Article 14 (prohibition of discrimination). With regard to procedural rights, the guarantees contained in Article 6 (right to fair trial) will be relevant in some (but not all) planning and compulsory purchase contexts.

1. Application of Article 8

8–10 Under this Article there is a general requirement not only to respect the rights contained in the Article, but also (to some extent) to protect them. The main right that is relevant in the planning and compulsory purchase context is the right of respect for one's home.

There is only a right to respect for the home, not a right to a home, and the court therefore has the ability to interpret how far "respect" should go. Moreover, Article 8(2) allows for the justification of interferences with this right, so far as they are in accordance with law, for a proper purpose, and necessary in a democratic society. These elements permit a considerable (but not unfettered) degree of policy.

8–11 In *Gillow v. U.K.* (1989) Series A, No. 109; 11 E.H.R.R. 325 the Court held that the decision of the authorities in Guernsey to refuse to grant the applicants a licence to occupy their own home, on their return to the island, was an interference with their right under this Article which was disproportionate to the legitimate aim of the legislation. The authorities were applying the relevant housing legislation which was aimed at restricting the residential population of the island, and the decision was in accordance with its provisions. However, since the applicants had built the house to live in when they had possessed residence qualifications, the refusal to issue the licence was disproportionate to the legitimate of the legislation.

In *Buckley v. U.K.* R.J.D. 1996–IV 1271; (1997) 23 E.H.R.R. 101, the applicant was a gypsy who had purchased land on which she parked her caravans. The LPA had refused to grant planning permission for the stationing of caravans on the land, and enforcement action was commenced. The appeal against the enforcement notice was dismissed. The applicant alleged that she was prevented from living with her family in caravans on her own land and from following the traditional lifestyle of a gypsy, contrary to Article 8. The Court was satisfied that there was nothing in Article 8, or in the case law, to suggest that the concept of "home" was limited to residences which have been lawfully established, as was the case in *Gillow*. However, the interference was held to be justified.

The latitude of this Convention right is highlighted by *Powell and Rayner v. U.K.* (1990) Series A, No. 172, 12 E.H.R.R. 355. The applicants alleged that excessive noise generated by the air traffic in and out of Heathrow Airport violated Article 8. The Court held that the quality of the applicants' private life and the scope for enjoying the amenities of their home had been adversely affected, and that Article 8 was a material provision. Similar issues arose in *López Ostra v. Spain* Series A, No. 303–C; (1994) 20 E.H.R.R. 277, where the release of gas fumes, pestilential smells and contamination from the operations of a waste management plant, harmful to the health of the applicant, were held to give rise to a violation of Article 8.

2. Application of Article 1 of the First Protocol

8–12   The Commission, in its report in *Powell v. United Kingdom* (1987) 9 E.H.R.R. C.D. 241, expressed the opinion that "this provision is mainly concerned with the arbitrary confiscation of property and does not in principle, guarantee a right to the peaceful enjoyment of possessions in a pleasant environment". This Article is concerned with the protection of property rights, and the Court has principally been involved in the question of compensation awarded for the compulsory acquisition of property. There is some overlap with Article 8 (see below).

The Court has broken down this Article into three rules which relate with each other. In *Sporring and Lönnroth v. Sweden* (1983) Series A, No. 52; 5 E.H.R.R. 35, paragraph 61, the Court stated:

". . . this provision comprises three distinct rules. The first rule, set out in the first sentence of the first paragraph, is of a general nature and enunciates the principle of peaceful enjoyment of property; the second rule, contained in the second sentence of the same paragraph, covers deprivation of possessions and makes it subject to certain conditions; and the third rule, stated in the second paragraph, recognises the contracting states are entitled, amongst other things, to control the use of property in accordance with the general interest. The three rules are not 'distinct' in the sense of not being unconnected: the second and third rules are concerned with particular instances of interference with the right to peaceful enjoyment of property and should therefore be construed in the light of the general principle enunciated in the first rule . . ."

It may be the case that the public authority can satisfy the second and third rule, but the Court may find a violation of the Article on the first rule: *Erkner and Hofauer v. Austria* (1987) Series A, No. 117; 9 E.H.R.R. 464, and *Poiss v. Austria* (1988) Series A, No. 124–E; 10 E.H.R.R. 231.

8–13 The term possessions covers a wide range of proprietorial interests. In *Powell & Rayner v U.K.* (above) the Court held that the nuisance caused by aircraft noise, because it may seriously affect the value of the property or even render it unsaleable, could amount to a partial taking of property. The fact that domestic law does not acknowledge as a legal right a particular interest does not mean that the interest is not a possession. In *Tre Traktorer Aktiebolag v. Sweden* (1991) Series A, No. 159; 13 E.H.R.R. 309 the Court did not accept the argument that because a liquor licence conferred no rights in national law, it could not be a possession. In that case the applicant had a restaurant, and without the licence there would be an adverse effect on his business. Other possessions include economic interests connected with the grant of planning permission (*Pine Valley Developments Ltd. v. Ireland* (1992) Series A, No. 222; 14 E.H.R.R. 319), and rights to extract gravel (*Fredin v. Sweden* (1991) Series A, No. 192; 13 E.H.R.R. 142).

The Article cannot be used to seek compensation for the cessation of an unlawful use: *Charter v. U.K.* (1988) 10 E.H.R.R. C.D. 534. Nor can it be relied upon as a ground for extending the permitted use of the property, without the need for planning permission: *ISKCON v. U.K.* (1991) 76–A D.R. 90.

8–14 In order to fall within the second rule of the Article, there must be actual deprivation (*Sporrong and Lönnroth*, above). The "public interest" justification for a deprivation covers a wide field and affords a wide margin of appreciation, since the decision to enact law expropriating property will commonly involve consideration of political, economic and social issues on which opinions within a democratic society may reasonably differ widely (*James v. U.K.* (1986) Series A, No. 98; 8 E.H.R.R. 123). The public interest may be engaged even where property is to be transferred between private persons (*ibid.*). Expropriation must pursue a legitimate aim, and the means employed must be proportionate (*ibid.*).

Under the third rule, the state may seek to control property by requiring positive action, as well as imposing restrictions on the type of activity undertaken at the property. Restrictions may take the form of planning control: *Allan Jacobsson v. Sweden* (1990) Series A, No. 163; 12 E.H.R.R. 56 and *Pine Valley Developments Ltd v. Ireland* (above). Not only does the State have to show that that the action of restricting the use of the property is lawful, but it must show that the burden on the individual is not disproportionate to the public benefits achieved by the control of use, *i.e.* the "fair balance test".

3. Justification for interference

8-15 It is important to recognise the considerable degree of latitude which exists in complying with Article 8, and Article 1 of the First Protocol. The justifications for interference which are built into these provisions are likely to be of particular relevance in planning matters, where questions of policy, and the balancing of interests, predominate.

In *Sporrong and Lönnroth v. Sweden* (above) the Court stated, at paragraph 69:

> ". . . the Court must determine whether a fair balance was struck between the demands of the general interest of the community and the requirements of the protection of the individuals rights. The search for this balance is inherent in the whole of the Convention and is also reflected in the structure of Article 1."

In that case, the Court was asked to consider whether expropriation permits granted to the City of Stockholm in respect of the applicants' properties, for the purposes of redevelopment of the city centre, was a breach of this Article. The expropriations had not been executed, but in the interim the applicants were prohibited from carrying out construction work on the sites, which were therefore subject to planning blight. The Court, in applying the fair balance principle, found that, despite the complex and difficult matters involved in the planning of the city centre, the arrangements left the applicants in a position where there was no effective remedy for a considerable period of time, and there was a violation of the Convention right.

8-16 The Commission has considered the interaction of Article 8 with Article 1 of the First Protocol, particularly in the case of compulsory purchase of property. It has been recognised that where there is an overlap, the application of the relevant provisions must be reconciled. When Article 1 of the First Protocol applies to the compulsory acquisition of private property, "the measure of necessity referred to in the second sentence of Article 1 of the First Protocol closely resembles that which applies to the justification for an interference with the rights guaranteed by Article 8(1) of the Convention": *Howard v. U.K.* (1987) 9 E.H.R.R. CD 116, see also *App. No. 9261/81 v. U.K.*, 28 D.R. 177, and the Commission's Report in *Gillow v. U.K.* (1985) 7 E.H.R.R. 292; but *cf. James v. U.K.*, above, at paragraph 51.

In *Buckley v. U.K.* R.J.D. 1996–IV 1271; (1997) 23 E.H.R.R. 101, interference with the right under Article 8 was held to be justified. The LPA had served an enforcement notice under the Town & Country Planning Act 1990, requiring the removal of the applicant's caravans. This notice was upheld by the Secretary of State. The LPA prosecuted the applicant for failing to comply with the enforcement notice. The applicant alleged that she was prevented from living with her family in caravans on her own land, and from following the traditional lifestyle of a gypsy, contrary to Article 8. The Court considered that "it was for the national authorities to make the initial assessment of the 'necessity' for an interference, as regards both the legislative framework and the particular measure of implementation"; and that in this case the interference was in accordance with the law, for a proper purpose, and necessary in a democratic society. The Court went on to state that "it is not for the court to impose its own view of what would be the best policy in the planning sphere or the most appropriate individual measure in planning cases". There seems no reason to believe that domestic courts are likely to take a more interventionist approach than the Strasbourg authorities in this respect.

The Commission has recently considered seven applications by applicants (all gypsies) arguing, as in *Buckley* (see above), that the planning laws are in violation of Article 8 and Article 1 of the First Protocol. The Commission in all but one held that the applications were admissible, as they "raised serious issues of fact and law under the Convention": *Coster v. U.K.* (1998) 25 E.H.R.R. C.D. 24, *Beard v. U.K.* (1998) 25 E.H.R.R. C.D. 28, *Smith v. U.K.* (1998) 25 E.H.R.R. C.D. 42, *Lee v. U.K.* (1998) 25 E.H.R.R. C.D. 46, *Varey v. U.K.* (1998) 25 E.H.R.R. C.D. 49, *Smith v. U.K.* (1998) 25 E.H.R.R. C.D. 52, *Chapman v. U.K.* (1998) 25 E.H.R.R. C.D. 64. Each case has the same common thread running through the facts, namely that the applicant purchased land, stationed his caravan on it without planning permission, and was then subjected to action taken by the LPA under the planning legislation to secure its removal. In each case the applicant lost his appeal(s) against the planning decisions, and successful prosecution proceedings had been brought against a number of the applicants. Only in the case of *Smith v. U.K.* (1998) 25 E.H.R.R. C.D. 52 did the applicant refuse to accept an offer of a pitch on an official site, and the Commission held that under Article 8 and Article 1 of the First Protocol the applicant had not established that there was no alternative to him but to resort to the unauthorised stationing of his caravan. The Commission found that in this case, that "having regard to the wide margin of appreciation, the measures taken by the Council may be regarded as necessary in a democratic society for the protection of the rights of others", and that the measures taken by the authority were not incompatible with the fair balance required under Article 1 of the First Protocol. That application was held to be inadmissible.

4. Application of Article 6

8–17   Article 6(1) applies to the determination of both civil rights and obligations and any criminal charges, whereas Article 6(2) and (3) apply only to criminal matters. Both the civil and criminal aspects of Article 6 may be relevant in a planning context, given that criminal proceedings may be involved in the enforcement of planning controls.

The phrase "civil rights and obligations" in Article 6(1) relates to civil rights and obligations in private law, not public law (see generally paragraphs 2–67— 2–68, above). In *Sporrong and Lönnroth v. Sweden* (above), the Court held that the application of planning laws, the refusal to grant permission for the applicant to remain living at her property, and the expropriation of property, were subject to Article 6. The right of property is clearly a "civil right" within the meaning of Article 6(1): *Zander v. Sweden* (1994) Series A, No. 279–B; 12 E.H.R.R. 175. In *Skarby v. Sweden* (1991) Series A, No. 180–B; 13 E.H.R.R. 90, the Court held that the applicant's right under Swedish law to choose the site of a new building, and the decision of the Building Committee to refuse to grant the applicant an exemption from the building plan, was a "civil right" within the meaning of

Article 6(1). In *Bryan v. U.K.* (1996) Series A, No. 335–A; 21 E.H.R.R. 342, the Government did not even contest that the impugned planning proceedings involved a determination of the applicant's "civil rights". Accordingly, the decision of an LPA to grant (conditionally or unconditionally) or refuse planning permission, or commence enforcement action, will be subject to Article 6.

In the seven applications recently before the Commission (see paragraph 8–16) three of the applicants argued that there had been a violation of Article 6. In *Varey v. U.K.* and *Chapman v. U.K.* (see above) the complaint was that the review of planning decisions by the High Court was unduly limited, and prevented any effective challenge or review of the issues of fact. This was considered admissible, but in *Smith v. U.K.* (1998) 25 E.H.R.R. C.D. 52 the Commission, in referring to *Bryan,* found that scope of review of planning decisions available in the High Court was sufficient to comply with this Article.

8–18   For Article 6 to apply there must, at least on arguable grounds, be a genuine and serious dispute over a civil right recognised by national law. In *Powell and Rayner v. U.K.* (above) the Court held that since Civil Aviation Act 1982, s.76(1) excluded liability in nuisance with regard to the flight of aircraft in certain circumstances, the applicants could not claim to have a substantive right under English law to obtain relief, and therefore there was no "civil right" recognised under domestic law to attract the application of Article 6(1). In *Lithgow v. U.K.* (1986) Series A, No. 102; 8 E.H.R.R. 329, at paragraph 192, the Court stated "that Article 6(1) extends only to '*contestations*' (disputes) over (civil) 'rights and obligations' which can be said, at least on arguable grounds, to be recognised under domestic law; it does not in itself guarantee any particular content for (civil) 'rights and obligations' in the substantive law of the 'Contracting States.'" The dispute may relate to both the existence and exercise of the civil right.

Where this Article is found to apply to the particular case, numerous requirements are imposed on public authorities in the exercise of their functions. The rights can be summarised as follows (see generally paragraph 2–72 and following):

    (a) A right of access to a court;

    (b) A fair hearing;

    (c) A right to public hearing and judgment;

    (d) Prompt adjudication; and

    (e) A right to an independent and impartial tribunal, established by law.

One of the most important rights within Article 6 is the right to an independent and impartial tribunal. In *Bryan v. U.K.* (above) an inspector appointed to hold an public inquiry and report to the Secretary of State with his recommendation was held not to be an independent and impartial tribunal, since the Secretary of State could, at any time during the course of the proceedings revoke the power of the Inspector to decide the appeal. However, the subsequent review by the High Court on appeal was held to have complied with the requirements of Article 6, even though the court did not rehear the matter.

5. Article 14

8–19   The essence of Article 14 is a person's right to enjoy Convention rights without there being unjustified difference of treatment (see generally paragraph 2–123 and following). In the planning context, the LPA is bound to have regard to all material planning considerations that are relevant to, for example, a planning application. Each applicant is entitled to have his application determined on the same basis as another in the same position, and failure to do so on the part of the LPA may be a violation of Article 14. In *Pine Valley Developments Ltd v. Ireland* (1992) Series A, No. 222; 14 E.H.R.R. 319, for example, the Court held that this right was violated where the public authority refused to validate void planning permissions, when for different people under the same circumstances it had done so. However, an LPA can take into account the personal circumstances of the applicant as an exceptional or special circumstance.

Circumstances where the applicant is discriminated against should be rare, but this Article has been relied upon in the gypsy cases that have come before the Strasbourg authorities. In *Buckley v. U.K.* (above), it was argued that the applicant was the victim of discrimination on the ground of her gypsy status when the LPA refused to grant planning permission for the stationing of her caravans on her land and subsequently took enforcement action. The Court rejected this argument since there was national policy aimed at enabling gypsies to cater for their own needs, *i.e.* currently Circulars 1/94 and 18/94. This approach has been followed by the Commission in subsequent cases, most recently in *Turner v. U.K.* (1997) 23 E.H.R.R. C.D. 181. The Commission found that, to the extent that gypsies are referred to in the various circulars, gypsies are treated better than other applicants for planning permission, as the LPAs are exhorted to give special consideration to their needs.

In the cases recently before the Commission concerning gypsies (paragraph 8–16, above), each applicant argued that there had been a violation of this Article, and it was only in the case of *Smith v. U.K.* (1998) 25 E.H.R.R. C.D. 52 that the Commission found that there had been no violation. It concluded that Contracting States enjoyed a margin of appreciation when assessing whether and to what extent difference in otherwise similar situations justified a different treatment. In this case all the circumstances had been taken into account and it was not unreasonable for the planning authority, by applying the same criteria as in other case, to treat the applicant's application for planning permission in the same way.

G. CONVENTION RIGHTS IN THE PLANNING PROCESS

8–20   Convention rights could well have an impact on the activities of local planning authorities and the Secretary of State in the following respects.

1. Preparation of the Development Plan

8–21   Each local planning authority is under a duty to prepare a development plan, which is then fundamental to any determination under the Planning Acts (see Town & Country Planning Act 1990, s.54A ("T&CPA 1990"). Part II of the T&CPA 1990 sets out the procedure to be followed, from the preparation of the plan through to its adoption. The procedure includes, where there are objections to policies in the deposit draft, either an examination in public or a public inquiry where the objections are heard by either the panel or the inspector appointed to consider the objections to the draft plan. The panel, or as the case may be the inspector, will produce a report together with recommendations, which the LPA will consider and decide what action to take on each recommendation. The LPA is not required to accept each recommendation, but where a recommendation is not accepted then it must set out its reasons and properly consider the report. An LPA is entitled in setting out its reasons to do so briefly. The final step is the adoption of the development plan for development control purposes, and any person aggrieved by the plan can, within the prescribed period, question the validity of the plan in the High Court.

The effect of a development plan has been considered by the Court in *Katte Klitsche de la Grange v. Italy* (1994) Series A, No. 293–B; 19 E.H.R.R. 368. The applicant owned a large area of land of which the local authority approved a plan in respect of development. It signed an agreement to that effect. At a later date the Council adopted its land-use plan, which excluded part of the applicants land from the area designated for residential development, contrary to the agreement. This plan was adopted. The applicant alleged a violation of Article 1 of the First Protocol, and Article 6. The Court held that the approval of the land-use plan was sufficient to restrict the applicant's exercise of his right to the peaceful enjoyment of his possessions and therefore fell within the first sentence of Article 1 of the First Protocol. However the Court went on to find that in determining whether the fair balance had been struck, the balance between the interests of the community and those of the applicant had not been upset. In line with this decision, Article 1 of the First Protocol may be violated by an LPA adopting restrictive planning policies in its development plan, and it is expected that the courts will have to determine whether a fair balance has been struck, if an aggrieved person questions the validity of the development plan under T&CPA 1990, s.287.

8–22   The adoption of planning policies, which may infringe the enjoyment of property and reduce its market value, may give rise to a "civil right" within Article 6(1): *Ortenberg v. Austria* (1995) Series A, No. 295–B; 19 E.H.R.R. 524. Therefore, each objector to an emerging development plan is entitled to the rights afforded under Article 6(1), though where their objection has not been accepted it is likely that, in line with *Bryan*, above, the court would find that it has sufficient powers under the T&CPA 1990 to review the actions of the LPA/ Secretary of State to comply with Article 6. However, there may be a violation of this Article since, unlike the enforcement appeal process, the reasons given by the LPA need only be brief when deciding not to accept the recommendation of the Panel, or the inspector. This will of course limit the ability of the aggrieved person to challenge the decision (and thus affect the sufficiency of subsequent review).

Section 35B(4) of the T&CPA 1990 provides that "no person shall have the right to be heard at an examination in public". If a person is refused permission to present his case to the panel, is there a violation of Article 6(1)? Under

T&CPA 1990, s.287 the person would be "aggrieved" for the purposes of the Act, and would be able to challenge the validity of the structure plan. This right of appeal should satisfy the requirements of Article 6 in such a case.

2. Determination of a planning application

8–23   The process of determination of any application is set out in Part III of the T&CPA 1990, which includes public consultation. In certain cases an environmental impact assessment will be required, and also an appropriate assessment of the impact of development on designated sites under the Council Directives on Habitats and Wild Birds. Once all the necessary information is before the LPA, a decision will be made to grant consent either conditionally or unconditionally, or refuse the application.

The right to develop property in accordance with the laws and regulations applicable at the time is a "civil right" within the meaning of Article 6(1): *Fredin v. Sweden* (1990) Series A, No. 192; 13 E.H.R.R. 785. In *Skarby v. Sweden* (1990) Series A, No. 180–B; 13 E.H.R.R. 90 the applicant applied for permission to build a house and garages on land that had been designated as a nature park. The application was refused as it did not comply with the development plan. As there was no right of appeal against the decision, there was a violation of Article 6(1). However, following *Bryan*, since the scope of review of the High Court on appeal from the decision of the Secretary of State may be considered sufficient to comply with Article 6(1), it is unlikely that a court will find that an applicant has not received a fair and public hearing by a tribunal in the determination of his application for planning permission.

8–24   In terms of substantive rights, the determination of a planning application is capable of engaging the responsibility of the LPA under the Act to conduct themselves in a manner which is compatible with — for example — Article 8 or Article 1 of the First Protocol. It is not at all difficult to see how the grant or refusal of planning permission will be said to affect the lives, homes, and property of both the applicant and the occupiers and owners of neighbouring property.

Under current planning procedure, LPAs should take into account only material planning considerations, and the personal circumstances of the applicant are to be considered only in exceptional or special circumstances. PPG 1: General Policy and Principles (February 1997) at paragraph 64 states that the planning system is not there to protect the private interests of an individual. However, within a legislative framework which is to be construed generally in accordance with Convention rights, and in view of the general obligation on public authorities to act compatibly with those rights, it would seem that due consideration will have to be given by LPAs to any Convention issues. By reference to the development plan, however, justification for interference with any Convention rights under Article 8 or Article 1 of the First Protocol, is likely to be forthcoming.

3. Determination of an appeal against the decision of the local planning authority

8–25   An applicant for planning permission may appeal against an LPA decision to refuse, or to grant only conditionally, planning permission: T&CPA

1990, s.78. Since the right of appeal is limited to the applicant, a third party has no such right, and will need to rely on judicial review in order to challenge the grant of planning permission. The appeal is to the Secretary of State, and either he will determine it or it will be determined by an appointed inspector.

The planning appeal procedure was the subject of complaint in *Bryan v. U.K.* (above). That decision was followed by the Commission in *ISKCON v. U.K.* (1994) 18 E.H.R.R. C.D. 133, where it was argued by the applicant that, under the enforcement provisions of T&CPA 1990, it did not have the right of access to a court with "full jurisdiction" in determining its appeal against the enforcement notice. The Commission found that the High Court had the right to interfere with the decision of the Inspector and/or Secretary of State where the decision was irrational having regard to the facts, or where he had failed to take into account an actual fact, or that he even took into account an immaterial fact. The complaint of a violation of Article 6 was found to be ill-founded.

8–26   It seems likely that the availability of judicial review will generally satisfy the requirements of Article 6, in terms of affording the right of access to a court for those (other than applicants for planning permission) who seek to challenge the decision of the LPA: *Kaplan v. U.K.* (1980) 4 E.H.R.R. 64; *Ortenberg v. Austria* (above). Where an applicant for planning permission has exercised the right of appeal to the Secretary of State, some third parties have no right to be heard at the inquiry. It is only with the inspectors' leave that such a person falling within this category can appear at the inquiry. If there was ever a case where the Inspector refused to grant such leave, then that third party may be able to argue that Article 6 had been infringed. However, such a decision of the Inspector could be challenged by way of judicial review, and it is likely that the court would find that its powers to review the decision are sufficient to comply with Article 6(1).

Considerations as to the effect of substantive Convention rights should apply in relation to appeal decisions as in relation to planning decisions by LPAs (see above).

4. Enforcement action

8–27   Where there is a breach of planning control, Part VII of the T&CPA 1990 sets out the powers which the LPA have to enforce compliance. The normal course, in the first instance, is for an enforcement notice or breach of condition notice to be served on the owner, the occupier and any other person having an interest in the land. Stop notices may also be served. Injunctive and/or criminal proceedings may follow.

Enforcement action clearly restricts the way in which land may be used, in a material way. Such action was in issue both in *Bryan v. U.K.* and *Buckley v. U.K.* (above), but in neither case was any violation of Convention rights found to have occurred. However, it is possible to envisage situations in which Convention rights may yet be invoked in this context, where for example the interference implicit in the enforcement action cannot properly be justified.

Human rights issues may also arise in relation to the steps taken by LPAs in preparation for enforcement action. The LPA may need to ascertain the ownership of the land and identify those parties who have an interest in the land. Section 171C of the T&CPA 1990 empowers the LPA to serve a planning contravention notice on the owner or the occupier or a person who has an interest in the land, or is carrying out operations on the land or is using it for any purpose. The recipient is required to return the completed form giving relevant information. Failure to return the notice duly completed may result in the recipient being prosecuted. Furthermore, if the notice is returned but contains misleading or false information, an offence may be committed. Assuming that the LPA can prove its case, there is every incentive for the recipient to return the planning contravention notice, even though the information supplied may very likely incriminate that person. The same is applicable to the power that enables a local authority to serve a requisition for information under section 16 of the Local Government (Miscellaneous Provisions) Act 1976, though the information that can be required of the recipient is not as extensive.

Following the recent admissibility decisions of the Commission on the gypsy applications (see paragraph 8–16) the Court will once again have to determine whether the enforcement powers of LPAs are in violation of Convention rights. What can be drawn from the recent decisions is that where the applicant has refused an offer of a pitch on an official site, then this application is likely to falter as was the case in *Smith* (see above).

8–28   Similar issues may therefore arise in this context as arose in *Saunders v. U.K.* R.J.D. 1996–VI 2044; (1997) 23 E.H.R.R. 313. In that case, the applicant complained of a violation of Article 6 in that the information he was required to provide to DTI inspectors in the course of their investigation was subsequently used in criminal proceedings against him. The Court held that there was a violation in respect of the right to silence and privilege against self-incrimination, having regard to the difference between the purpose for which the information was required and that for which it was used. It was not a breach of Article 6 for the information to be used for the purpose for which it was obtained. Accordingly, it would seem that information supplied under a requisition for information should only be used for the purpose for which it was obtained, not for any other purpose.

5. Issue of a revocation/modification or discontinuance order

8–29   Sections 97 to 104 of the T&CPA 1990 set out the powers that enable the LPA or the Secretary of State to order the revocation or modification of any permission, or the discontinuance of the use of any land. Orders made by the LPA are subject to the confirmation of the Secretary of State. Compensation may be payable. Those affected can make representations to the Secretary of State. It seems inevitable that, in future, such representations will include reference to Convention rights.

The situation can arise where the Secretary of State issues, for example, a revocation order, pursuant to T&CPA 1990, ss.100 or 102, only to have to confirm the order he has made. The only right of appeal is to the High Court on the grounds that the order is not within the powers of the T&CPA, or that any of the relevant requirements have not been complied with: T&CPA 1990, s.288. It is hard to see how this procedure complies with the requirements of Article

6(1), though it may be argued that, as in *Bryan*, the power of the High Court to review the decision is sufficient to comply with Article 6.

H. COMPULSORY PURCHASE

8–30   The legal powers under which land is compulsorily acquired are mostly statute-based, and have the effect of taking or affecting private property for a variety of purposes. The statutory powers are needed to authorise what would otherwise be unlawful. Usually, these powers derive from public general Acts, *e.g.* Part IX of the T&CPA 1990. The procedure for the preparation, making and confirmation of the compulsory purchase order is found in the Acquisition of Land Act 1981. The enabling Act will generally set out the right to compensation for an identified group of persons affected by the acquisition. In both the decision to acquired land compulsorily, and in assessing who is entitled to compensation and the basis of any compensation, consideration will need to be given to Convention rights.

1. Compulsory purchase orders

8 31   There Is some overlap in the application of Article 8 and Article 1 of the First Protocol, In the context of compulsory acquisition. In the process of expropriating private property, a proper balance has to be struck between the demands of the community's general interest and the requirements of protecting the fundamental rights of the individual.

In *Lithgow v. U.K.* (1986) Series A, No. 102; 8 E.H.R.R. 329, the Court held that "the taking of property in the public interest without the payment of compensation is treated as justifiable only in exceptional circumstances". Compensation provisions are material to the assessment whether a fair balance has been struck, and in assessing whether or not a disproportionate burden has been imposed on the person who has been deprived of his possessions. A State is vulnerable where there is no right to any compensation in national law: see *Katte Klitsche de la Grange v. Italy* (above).

8–32   It is not correct to say that all persons in the United Kingdom are entitled to receive compensation, let alone receive the value of the land expropriated. The War Damages Act 1965 provides that there shall be no compensation for expropriated properties during a time of war. This Act was introduced following the decision of the House of Lords in *Burmah Oil Co. Ltd v. Lord Advocate* [1964] A.C. 75, where it was held that compensation was payable under such circumstances.

Where statute provides for compensation to be payable, it does not follow that there is no violation of the Convention rights. The assessment of compensation does not always lead to a fair award. The general rule is that in assessing compensation regard shall be had not only to the value of the land to be purchased, but also to the damage sustained by the owner caused by severing land purchased from another owner, or for injuriously affecting that land by the exercise of the powers under which the land is acquired. The rules, both statutory and judicial, have been developed with the aim that any person whose land has been acquired is not left in a worse position as a result of the acquisition.

However, there are occasions where the owner does not receive full compensation. In *James v. U.K.* (1986) Series A, No. 98; 8 E.H.R.R. 123, a violation of Article 1 of the First Protocol, was claimed as a result of rights of enfranchisement in the Leasehold Reform Act 1967. The Court held that the purpose of the Act was to remove social injustices, and if the Act required the payment of the full market value then the purpose of the Act would be thwarted. The acquisitions by the tenants did not result in the placing of an excessive burden on the applicants, over and above the disadvantageous effects generally inherent for landlords in the application of the scheme set up under the leasehold reform legislation. Therefore was thus no violation.

I. REMEDIES

8–33   In general, a local authority is not liable in negligence in carrying out its statutory functions (*Stovin v. Wise* [1996] A.C. 923). This is illustrated by *Strable v. Dartford BC* (1984) J.P.L. 329 where it was held that the LPA was not liable in negligence for the grant of planning permission that adversely affected the interests of a third party: see also *R. v. Lam and Brennan (t/a Namesakes of Torbay) and Torbay District Council* [1998] P.L.C.R. 30. Other causes of action may exist, such as where there has been deceit on the part of the authority (*Slough Estates plc v. Welwyn Hatfield District Council* [1996] 2 P.L.R. 50), or actionable mis-statement (but see *Tidman v. Reading B.C.* [1994] 3 P.L.R. 72).

The introduction of a new statutory remedy in damages under section 8 clearly raises the possibility of an extension of the circumstances in which compensation may be payable by public authorities in respect of planning matters. How far this new remedy develops will very much depend upon the courts' judgment under section 8(3) as to whether the award of damages is necessary to afford just satisfaction. The practice of the Court, however, has tended to be conservative, both as to the fact and amount of awards (see generally paragraph 2–25 and following).

CHAPTER 9

Health

Tim Wright (Solicitor, Wansbroughs Wiley Hargrave)

A. INTRODUCTION

9–01 This chapter considers the position under the Act in relation to the provision and regulation of health care, other than in respect of mental health (for which see Chapter 10).

1. Background: health care law prior to the Act

9–02 Without health, there seems little point in having a concept of human rights. But even without the Convention, the protection of life, the promotion of health, and the prevention of ill-treatment are all recognised and represented as essential components of domestic law.

The provision of health care in the United Kingdom, in the form of the National Health Service, has built into it certain statutory obligations by the state in favour of the individual which are summed up by the National Health Service Act 1977 ("NHSA 1977"), s.(1):

> "It is the Secretary of State's duty to continue the promotion in England and Wales for a comprehensive Health Service designed to secure improvement:
>
> (a) in the physical and mental health of the people of those countries; and
>
> (b) in the prevention, diagnosis and treatment of illness and for the purpose to provide or secure the effective provision of services in accordance with this Act."

By NHSA 1977, s.3(1) those obligations are to be implemented to meet, in the discretion of the Secretary of State, "all reasonable requirements" for "medical, dental, nursing and ambulance services".

9–03 While the courts have acted on frequent occasions to review the quality and provision of such services, the Convention has had very little direct impact on this duty to date. The English courts have tended to review these matters either within the context of administrative law and judicial review, or within a body of case law derived from the courts' inherent jurisdiction, particularly concerning the rights and interests of those under a disability.

As to the former, the decisions made by the Secretary of State for Health or a National Health Service Body, for instance a Health Authority or an NHS Trust, are necessarily administrative decisions and subject to review by the courts on the basis of "reasonableness" (see *Associated Provisional Picture Houses Limited v. Wednesbury Corporation* [1948] 1 K.B. 223) but in the context of this statutory requirement to provide health care.

9–04   As to the latter, the courts have looked to consider and protect the rights and interests of individuals in the context of medical and other treatment, for instance: in withdrawing treatment from a patient who was in a permanent (persistent) vegetative state (see *Airdale NHS Trust v. Bland* [1993] A.C. 789); giving potentially life saving treatment to a child in the face of parental refusal (see *Re C (a Minor) (Wardship: Medical Treatment)* [1989] 2 All E.R. 782); or in the context of a competent adult's right to refuse treatment which appears to be in his best interests (see *Re C (Mental Patient: Medical Treatment)* [1994] 1 All E.R. 819).

A particularly important area has been the failure to provide treatment. This has been looked at in the "rationing" cases (see paragraph 9–21 below), which have generally been decided in favour of the health care provider on the basis of there being only a qualified right to treatment. Where injury is caused, the patient can pursue a claim in negligence alleging breach of a duty of care on the part of the health care body or professional concerned.

2. Scope of Convention case law

9–05   Outside the field of mental health care, there does not seem to be any decided case in English courts in this area where the Convention has had a substantial effect on the ultimate decision. The United Kingdom has, however, been the respondent in the following cases dealing with the more specific context of individual rights within the provision of health care:

- as to the requirements of the state to take adequate measures to protect life in the form of a vaccination programme (see *Association X v. U.K.* (1978) 14 D.R. 31); and

- in the context of whether a prospective father has any rights in connection with the termination of a pregnancy (see *Paton v. U.K.* (1980) 19 D.R. 244; (1980) 3 E.H.R.R. 408).

In addition, applications in respect of other states have considered health care issues, for example:

- the power of the state to impose compulsory health testing for tuberculosis (*Acmanne v Belgium* (1984) 40 D.R. 251);

- the status of a sperm donor in the context of the right to respect for family life and his interest in the resulting child (*M v. Netherlands* (1993) 74 D.R. 120);

- the legitimacy of abortion legislation generally in the context of the right to life set out in Article 2 (*H v. Norway* (1992) 73 D.R. 155);

- the possibility that medical treatment of an experimental nature could be regarded as inhuman or degrading treatment contrary to Article 3 (*X v. Denmark* (1983) 32 D.R. 282).

B. PUBLIC AUTHORITIES IN HEALTH CARE

9–06 The definition of public authority in section 6(3), for health purposes, will include health authorities, special health authorities, National Health Service trusts, and to some extent local authorities in the form of county, unitary and district councils. The definition must also include the statutory persons and bodies set up to administer and regulate various aspects of health care including, for instance the Human Fertilisation Authority, the Health Service Commissioner, the Medical Devices Agency, the Medicines Control Agency, the United Kingdom Transplant Support Services Authority, and the Unrelated Live Transplant Regulatory Authority.

The various regulatory bodies of the health care professions for instance the General Medical Council, the United Kingdom Central Council for Nursing, the Royal Pharmaceutical Society Great Britain, and the Council for Professions Supplementary to Medicine, must also come within the definition. The organisations set up to protect the health care professions, for instance the British Medical Association or the Royal Colleges, will probably not. The Registered Homes Tribunal and the Family Health Service Appeal Authority, which deals with disputes concerning the registration of pharmacists, will clearly come within s.6(3)(a), as presumably will the activities of H.M. Coroner.

C. CONVENTION RIGHTS IN PRACTICE

9–07 While there seem to be a number of possible applications of the Act in the health care field, the reality is that the Convention rights may well have quite restricted application. Convention rights may well be appropriately raised in judicial consideration of a number of contexts involving the provision of health care. In particular, an applicant will necessarily look to the Convention rights as a route to attack those areas where the courts have traditionally protected health care organisations, doctors and other Health Service professionals. In matters where Convention rights are raised, the applicant is likely to be a patient or a patient's relative, and the defendant a public authority. A doctor or a nurse in an NHS treatment environment will usually be an employee of an NHS body, which will be vicariously liable for that employee's acts, omissions and breaches of the Convention's positive and negative obligations performed on behalf of the NHS body. The Convention is unlikely to be relevant in circumstances concerning private medicine, where the relationship between patient and doctor will usually be a contractual relationship between those two individuals.

9–08 A doctor in general practice is in a different position again. Each is an independent practitioner within the NHS, and is therefore not an employee of an NHS body. The decisions of a general practitioner cannot be seen as made on behalf of an NHS body, and the activities of general practitioners as individuals are unlikely to be those of a public authority within the Act. However, ultimate responsibility for handling complaints against general practitioners, and in particular in connection with decisions regarding purchasing future healthcare, presently falls mostly on a Health Authority, which clearly is a public authority within the Act. Furthermore, as general practitioners combine to form Primary Care Trusts, as part of the rearrangement of healthcare purchasing and the strengthening of the role of primary care, these bodies would seem to be public in nature.

As to the decisions of health care organisations, the courts have usually taken the view that those organisations are best placed to exercise their own discretion in exercising their own affairs, and have not sought to enquire too deeply into the processes used to reach decisions. In the same way, the courts have been reticent in interfering with an apparently appropriate clinical decision as to future medical treatment (or care) reached by a doctor or other health care professional.

D. ABORTION

9–09　Questions concerning abortion raise some of the most fundamental issues of all. Abortion has been considered in three ways to date under the Convention, but only by the Commission. It would seem likely that, in at least two of those areas, the legitimacy of the current legislation under the Abortion Act 1967 (as amended) may continue to be reviewed.

1. Article 2

9–10　When life begins is a primary issue under the Convention. Thus, does legal abortion conflict with the right set out in the first sentence of Article 2: "Everyone's right to life shall be protected by law"? The exceptions to that right, set out within the latter part of Article 2, deal only with self-defence and judicial killing. This Article, however, places a positive obligation on the state to preserve life, and to have laws ensuring the right to life.

In approaching this fundamental question, the status of the foetus was considered by the Commission in *Paton* (above). This was a case that had previously come before the English courts (see *Paton v. British Pregnancy Advisory Service* [1979] Q.B. 276) when an injunction had been refused to a husband for restraining termination of pregnancy, on the ground that an injunction could only be granted to restrain an infringement of a legal right. In English law the foetus has no legal rights until it is born and has acquired a separate existence from its mother. In consequence, the father of the foetus, whether or not married to the mother, has no legal right to prevent the mother having an abortion if the provisions of the 1967 Act have been complied with. The status of the foetus has since been confirmed by the English courts on a number of occasions (see for instance *Re F (in Utero)* [1988] 2 All E.R. 193, and *Re MB* (1997) 38 B.M.L.R. 175). In the latter case, the court took the view that it could not take "into account the interests of the unborn child at risk from the refusal of a competent mother to consent to medical intervention". In *C v. S* [1988] Q.B. 135, another case where a father was attempting to prevent a termination, Heilbron J. — citing various Canadian cases — affirmed that an unborn child was *not* a person, and that any rights accorded to it were contingent upon its subsequent birth alive.

9–11 In *Paton* (above), the Commission reviewed the position of the foetus in great detail. It examined the ordinary meaning of the first sentence of Article 2(1), and looked also at the French text: "*Le droit de toute personne à la vie est protégé par la loi*". It noted that the term "everyone's" ("toute personne") is not defined in the Convention, although it also appears in Articles 5, 6 and 8 to 11. In nearly all of those other cases, the instances of the word are such that it can apply only post-natally. The other parts of Article 2 are also phrased in such a way that they can only apply post-natally. The Commission also considered the word "life" as it appears in the first part of Article 2(1), as to whether it could apply to "unborn life". In the German Federal Constitutional Court, "life" has been defined as existing from the 14th day after conception, this being the origin of "individual development". In Germany, Article 2 has thus been applied to "every human individual possessing life"; and unborn human beings have been included in the term "everyone" (see *Brüggeman and Scheuten v. Federal Republic of Germany* (1977) 21 Y.D. 638, 3 E.H.R.R. 244). In the leading American case on abortion, the Supreme Court found that the "compelling" point at which potential life began was "at viability" (see *Roe v. Wade* 401 U.S. 113 (1973)).

The Commission found that the life of the foetus is intimately connected with and cannot be regarded in isolation from the life of a pregnant woman. To view it otherwise would be to prohibit abortion even where there was serious risk to the mother. Thus, the "right to life" of the pregnant woman would be subject to a limitation over and above that set out in the latter part of Article 2. All the original signatories to the Convention in 1950, with one possible exception, had legal abortion when necessary to save the life of the mother; and since then there had been a general liberalisation of laws on abortion.

The Commission went on to consider if Article 2 should be interpreted as recognising a right to life of the foetus with certain limitations, or as not covering the foetus at all. It noted that the termination of pregnancy in this case was carried out at 10 weeks under Abortion Act 1967, s.1(1)(a) in order to avert the risk of injury to the physical and mental health of the mother. The Commission was thus concerned only with the right to life during the initial stages of pregnancy. It took the view that, if it was assumed that Article 2(1) did apply to the foetus at that stage, it was nonetheless covered by an implied limitation of the right of life of the foetus, "protecting the life and health of the woman at that stage".

9–12 This problem was considered again by the Commission in 1992 in *H v. Norway* (1992) 73 D.R. 155 (see above), when it found that the term "everyone" did not seem to be applicable to the unborn child, but it did not exclude the possibility that the life of the foetus could in certain circumstances be protected. The Commission acknowledged in particular that states have a certain discretion in legislation in this area.

Thus, in summary, it is unlikely that the first part of Article 2(1) would be interpreted as giving an absolute right to life to a foetus. It also seems that the mother's right to life would be seen as paramount in circumstances where the foetus is aborted to protect the physical and mental health of the pregnant woman. It is unlikely that the provisions of the Abortion Act 1967 can be challenged to the extent that they provide for abortion on this basis. It is easy to see how the arguments applied in *Paton* could be extended to a situation where termination is carried out to protect from injury existing children of the pregnant woman (see Abortion Act 1967, s.1(1)(a)).

However, any further liberalisation of abortion legislation would have to be carefully considered in the light of the above decisions, which do not rule out the possibility that the foetus has some rights under Article 2(1). For instance, any provision for abortion which was not based on the balance of rights to life may well be incompatible with Article 2. It is difficult to see how termination based on ethnic or eugenic considerations — or even social need — can be reconciled with the Convention.

2. Article 8

9–13 The other respects in which the Commission has considered abortion concern the application of Article 8 (respect for private and family life). Article 8(2) limits the permissible interference by a public authority with the exercise of this right (thus imposing a negative obligation), and requires any interference to be necessary *inter alia* "for the protection of health or morals, or for the protection of the rights and freedoms of others". This has been pleaded in an application challenging national legislation restricting abortion (see *Brüggeman and Scheuten*, above). The Commission took the view that there were limits to the personal nature of this right, stating that "pregnancy cannot be said to pertain uniquely to the sphere of private life". Article 8 allows very considerable scope for the application of the principle of "proportionality" in balancing the right established under Article 8(1) against the interests of others. It seems unlikely that this Article could be used effectively to force a widening of the scope of the Abortion Act 1967.

Abortion has been also challenged under Article 8 by fathers seeking to prevent termination. In this respect it has been alleged not only that abortion interferes with family life, but that the Abortion Act 1967 is defective and that it denies the father a right to be consulted and to make applications about the proposed abortion (see *Paton*, above). The Commission very simply found in that case that Article 8(2) allows interference with any rights that exist under Article 8(1), on the grounds of the necessity for protection of the rights of the mother. In such cases, the courts must first of all take into account the rights of the pregnant woman, being the person primarily concerned with the pregnancy. Having regard to the father's concern at lack of a right of consultation or veto under the Abortion Act 1967, the Commission found that, in considering the rights of the pregnant woman, the father's rights under Article 8 could not be interpreted so widely as to embrace such procedural matters.

9–14 In another case, the Commission affirmed that the woman's rights under Article 8(1) prevailed, and that interference with the family and religious rights of the father was necessary under Article 8(2) to protect others (see *H v. Norway* above). In that case the father had also sought relief under Article 6, in that he claimed that he was entitled to be heard in judicial proceedings "in the determination of his civil rights and obligations". This was also rejected as there was no legal basis for such an assertion of civil rights in that country.

While the decisions on fathers' rights in this context are remarkably consistent, it will always be a matter for review by the courts as to the balance between competing interests of parties under Article 8, and further applications are likely.

3. Risk of serious handicap

9–15   The fourth ground in domestic law upon which a lawful abortion may be carried out is "that there is a substantial risk that if the child were born it would suffer some physical and mental abnormalities so as to be seriously handicapped" (Abortion Act 1967, s.1(1)(d)). This is a ground which has not been considered under the Convention, and it would clearly not be possible to rely on the qualified right to life exception suggested in *Paton*. Protection of the mother's right to life is not relevant. As a ground, this would appear to conflict with Article 2(1), unless the courts find that the foetus in question has no right to life. That may depend upon the gestational age, but it seems unlikely that it will be held that the foetus has no right to life simply because it may have been born disabled. Article 8 might be pleaded, but it seems inconceivable that a court would hold that the right to respect for "private and family life" should allow a mother to reject a child because it was disabled. It is perhaps in any event relatively unlikely that anyone would seek to challenge a termination on this ground.

E. WITHDRAWAL OF TREATMENT

9–16   As with abortion, issues relating to the withdrawal of treatment involve fundamental principles concerned particularly with life and death.

1. Generally

9–17   The inherent jurisdiction of domestic courts is engaged where a patient is either unable to consent or his consent is in doubt. Where a patient is competent to consent, it is accepted beyond doubt that he has the right to refuse medical treatment (see *Re T (Adult: Refusal of Medical Treatment)* [1993] Fam. 95) even if that leads to the patient's death. Similarly, it is accepted that an advance directive (or advance "refusal" or living will) can validly be made by a competent patient to the effect that certain treatment be withheld if certain circumstances occur that render him unable to consent (*per* Lord Goff in *Airdale NHS Trust v. Bland* [1993] A.C. 789 (see above)), again possibly leading to the patient's death. In both cases the patient rejects the benefit of such rights as he might have under Article 2(1). A patient might be well advised to include in a written advance directive a clear statement that such rights are rejected in so far as they apply to the circumstances envisaged.

In the case of an adult patient who has made no such election but has become incompetent or unable to consent, no other individual may exercise a power of consent on his behalf. However, it is settled law that a doctor may act in the best interests of such a patient by administering treatment that is necessary to preserve the patient's life, health or wellbeing (see in *Re F* [1989] 2 W.L.R. 1025). Thus a doctor is allowed *not* to give treatment if he feels that to be in the patient's best interests. Clearly, the failure to give treatment could have the consequence that the patient dies earlier than he might have done if he had been treated. This power does not allow a clinician to withdraw treatment solely to bring about an earlier death. Doctors will often make a decision, if possible in consultation with the patient or the patient's family, that in the event of a particularly serious clinical occurrence the patient will not be actively resuscitated. This decision will be recorded in the clinical records and act as a specific direction to those involved in the patient's care.

9–18   Such steps were undoubtedly legitimate in English law prior to the Act. However, under Article 2(1) the effective shortening of a patient's life must represent a denial of the "right to life". The Commission has in other respects sought to find ways of imposing a limit on that right where conflicting interests lie. In this case however, it cannot be said that any other person's rights under Article 2 are prejudiced, except for the argument that health care resources are limited, and that these might be better diverted to other persons who might benefit more. This argument is dealt with further, below. The doctor will defend his decision not to give treatment perhaps on the basis that such treatment would cause unnecessary further pain and suffering without any corresponding benefit. The doctor might plead that to give such further treatment would amount to "degrading" treatment contrary to Article 3 (considered further, below, in the context of medical treatment generally). It must be the case that, in the absence of any such implied limitation to the rights under Article 2(1), any person, including presumably the patient (or in any case the official solicitor on behalf of the incompetent patient), could seek to challenge the proposal not to give treatment. The court could only reject such an application if it could find a limitation upon the patient's right to life; otherwise a patient has a right to medical treatment to prolong his life. This argument was forcefully approved by Laws J. in *R. v. Cambridge Health Authority ex p. B* [1995] 25 B.M.L.R. 5. In practice, it will be very unattractive to a court to impose treatment upon a patient who is so ill that that treatment will not improve that patient's quality of life. Apart from any limitation available by applying Article 3, the concept of proportionality would surely be employed in an environment of limited resources to balance the individual's rights under Article 2(1) against those of the community in general to share in the state's provision. This is considered further, below, where various specific rights to treatment are noted. In general, however, the right to treatment is an important potential positive obligation upon the state which exists only collaterally to the expressed provisions in the Convention.

2. Permanent (Persistent) Vegetative State

9–19   Permanent (or persistent) vegetative state ("PVS") occurs where a patient, though not in a coma, is insensate but able to breathe spontaneously, with reflex reaction to painful stimuli. Such patients do not improve and receive hydration and nutrition artificially in order to survive. They are extremely rare and have no apparent quality of life, although they are usually extremely well cared for. Their legal position, and a proposal by clinical staff to withdraw the feeding and hydration, were considered at length in *Airdale NHS Trust v. Bland* (above). Lord Mustill raised the possibility that it was in the "best interests of the community at large" that the patient's life should end, particularly in view of the large resources of skill, labour and money then employed in keeping the patient alive. Although he considered that the argument had great force "in social terms", he did not think that the adoption of it was a task that the courts could possibly undertake. The Convention was not relied on at all, but it can easily be seen that Article 2(1) could be pleaded by any party, including the official solicitor on behalf of the patient, seeking to oppose withdrawal of treatment. The courts would need to seek to imply a limitation to Article 2(1), possibly in terms of the interests of the community at large.

In one PVS case (see *Re G* [1995] 2 F.C.R. 46) the court made the order for withdrawal of treatment even though the patient's mother objected. In that case the judge took the view that the family's views should be noted but that the treatment decision was ultimately one for the doctor. In the context of Article 2(1), it might be more difficult for a court to make such an order in the presence of an objecting relative.

F. THE RIGHT TO HEALTH CARE

9–20 The rationing of health care and resources, and rights to demand treatment (such as fertility treatment), give rise to some well-publicised problems. Rights to health care under the National Health Service legislation are contained in NHSA 1977, ss.1 and 3. The statutory rights of the individual patient are tempered substantially by the requirement of the Secretary of State to meet "all reasonable requirements" for the various health care services, as set out in section 3.

In those cases where an individual has sought to compel provision of certain services which have been refused, the courts have almost always construed the word "reasonable" in favour of the Health Service body concerned, taking the broad view that (provided there is no gross evidence of unlawful activity or a defective decision making process) the Health Service body concerned is best placed to make complicated judgments as to how to allocate its resources. The courts have therefore upheld no more than a qualified right to health care under this legislation.

There is no provision in the Convention that gives a direct right to health care. The first sentence in Article 2(1) will be relevant in the case of life-threatening conditions, but not to preventative medicine, or simply care. To what extent, therefore, could there be a right to medical treatment?

This is not an area that has come before the Strasbourg authorities, but in *Association X v. U.K.* (1978) 14 D.R. 31 (concerning a complaint as to the administration of a voluntary vaccination programme) the Commission conceded that Article 2 requires states to take adequate measures to preserve life.

It seems inevitable that the courts must apply Article 2 in this context subject to implied limitations, and the concept of proportionality could be employed in balancing the rights of the individual against those of the community at large in the context of limited resources. It is possible, therefore, that outside cases where the right to life of an individual is immediately threatened, Article 2 is unlikely to have any direct effect.

1. Rationing/resources

9–21 The courts have been called upon to decide a number of relatively high profile cases where individuals have sought to compel the provision of treatment that was being refused. For example in *R. v. Cambridge District Health Authority ex p. B* [1995] 2 All E.R. 129, a specialised form of treatment was refused on grounds of cost and lack of likely effectiveness. The courts have usually upheld such treatment decisions unless it is shown that the decision is manifestly wrong or contrary to specific Department of Health guidance (see *R. v. North Derbyshire Health Authority, ex p. Fisher* (1997) 38 B.M.L.R. 76). In considering such matters, the court will not place itself in a position where it directs a clinician to perform certain treatment contrary to his own clinical judgment or his professional conscience (see *Re J (a Minor) (Wardship: Medical Treatment)* [1992] 3 W.L.R. 758).

It seems unlikely that Article 2 would have any effect, unless refusal of treatment offended the principle of proportionality. Articles 8 and 12 may also be relevant in very specific circumstances, perhaps with regard to fertility treatment (see below).

2. The right to have or refuse treatment

9–22 There can be no doubt that a competent individual can refuse medical treatment. Such decisions can be made by the court in respect of an incompetent patient, and by a parent in respect of a child under the age of 16 (see above at paragraph 9–17). There are certain circumstances where treatment could be compelled, such as the power of the state to take steps in controlling disease. Thus, it has been accepted by the Commission that the state has power to impose a compulsory vaccination programme (see *Acmanne v. Belgium* (1984) 40 D.R. 251 — see below). Further, there are established compulsory powers of treatment of a mental patient (see Chapter 10). The right to refuse treatment is therefore subject to some limitations, which can be expected to be upheld under the Convention.

In this context the positive obligation upon the state to guarantee freedom of thought, conscience and religion under Article 9 might be pleaded in rejecting compulsory treatment. However the limitations upon this right, set out in Article 9(2), "as are prescribed by law and are necessary in a democratic society in the interests of public safety, for the protection of public health, or for the protection of the rights and freedoms of others", would inevitably be relevant and would allow the majority of currently permitted compulsory treatment. Thus an individual who rejected a blood transfusion upon religious grounds might have the protection of Article 9, but that individual's attempt to impose such rejection upon another, for instance his child, might be overturned under the exception in Article 9(2). Before the Act, a child could have relied upon a specific issues order under the Children Act 1989 on the application of a local authority or under the inherent jurisdiction of the court in a health care context, for an order to allow a transfusion. In the latter case, the Act might therefore provide some statutory rights.

9–23 The right to insist on certain treatment is more difficult. Apart from decisions based upon available resources (see above), a court would not compel the provision of treatment which was against the professional judgment of the clinician (see *Re J (a Minor) (Wardship: Medical Treatment)*, above). Article 2, and possibly Article 8, might be pleaded, but even here it would be surprising if a public authority's margin of appreciation did not prevent an individual's attempt to compel treatment. Article 9 might again be pleaded, for instance, in support of a refused request for circumcision for religious reasons. However, the limitation set out in Article 9(2) as to interests of a child ("others") could easily be raised to defeat such a claim.

3. Fertility treatment

9–24 State-funded fertility treatment, in the form of *in vitro* fertilisation, is controversial for being expensive and being able to extend artificially the fertility of a mother beyond the menopause. Some Health Service bodies will provide it and others will not. Access to it has been considered by the Divisional Court (see *R. v. Sheffield Health Authority ex p. Seale* (1994) 25 B.M.L.R. 1) where the court upheld the Health Authority's right to ration this treatment, subject to clearly defined criteria. In addition to general points about rationing (see above), a possible further argument might be considered under Article 12. In *X&Y v. U.K.* (1978) 12 D.R. 32, the Commission found that while the positive obligation imposed on the state under Article 12 (right to marry) extended to the foundation of a family by adoption, there was no implied or expressed right to adopt a child. It is submitted that, similarly, the courts are not likely to extend the right to found a family to include a right to receive fertility treatment.

4. Treatment of aliens

9–25 Medical treatment of non-residents is dealt with under NHSA 1977, s.121. The section provides that regulations can be made for charging those persons who are not ordinarily resident in Great Britain. That is in contrast to the requirements under NHSA 1977, s.1, that treatment for a resident is free. Thus, the treatment of visitors on both an emergency and non-emergency basis is technically chargeable to that individual.

On the basis that the Convention does provide some right to health care, the right as granted by the 1977 Act obviously differentiates as between a resident and a non-resident patient. The same statutory requirement applies to the provision of health care to both, but the non-resident's use of it is subject to the qualification imposed by section 121, above. Allowing for the possible application of Article 14 (prohibition of discrimination — as to which see generally paragraph 2–123 and following), it seems likely that the courts would have no difficulty in approving this differential stance.

G. PUBLIC HEALTH

9–26 Statutory powers in relation to public health (many of which are compulsory in nature) trace their origins from well before the National Health Service, and before the advent of Convention rights. Some of these powers fall more naturally within the scope of areas such as environmental health. The rights of the patient are to be balanced against the interests of the community as a whole, and (in addition to other questions) the procedural guarantees in Article 6 are likely to be relevant where these powers are exercised (see generally paragraph 2–65 and following).

1. Compulsory testing

9–27 Compulsory testing for disease, or perhaps genetic abnormality, has only been a feature of the control of disease or medical treatment in England to the extent that it is allowed under the Public Health (Control of Disease) Act 1984. An order by a Justice of the Peace can only be made in connection with specific diseases, as listed in section 10 of that Act.

The Commission considered compulsory testing in other jurisdictions (see *X v. Austria* (1979) 18 D.R. 154 and *Acmanne v. Belgium* (1984) 40 D.R. 251), particularly in relation to Article 8. In both cases, an interference with the right to respect for private and family life was found, but was held to be justified by Article 8(2) in the interests of the protection of health generally and the rights and freedoms of others. In *X v. Austria*, Article 2 was also considered, but the blood test in question was regarded as being such a minor procedure as not to be a threat to the right to life. It seems likely that the courts would interpret Convention rights in this area in the same way, and uphold the powers given by the 1984 Act. Article 9 (freedom of thought, conscience and religion) might have some relevance here, but the limitations set out in Article 9(2) would inevitably be available to defeat this right in the context of public health.

A voluntary vaccination programme in the United Kingdom was found to be justified under Article 2(1) on the basis that the state has an obligation to protect life. It was further found by the Commission not to be a breach of Article 8, again on the basis of justification under Article 8(2) (see *Association X v. U.K.*, above).

2. Controlling disease

9–28 The Public Health (Control of Disease) Act 1984, s.37 permits the removal of a person suffering from a notifiable disease to a hospital by order of a Justice of the Peace. That order is directed to a local authority, to be implemented by officers of the local authority and the health authority. Section 38 provides for a Justice of the Peace to make an order detaining a patient suffering from a notifiable disease in hospital, if that person has no lodging or accommodation to go to in which proper precautions could be taken to prevent the spread of the disease. It is an offence under section 38 for the patient to leave the hospital during the duration of the order, which may be for such period as the Justice of the Peace directs. That period can be extended from time to time. There is no statutory mechanism in place to allow the period of detention to be reviewed.

There would appear to be no decision under the Convention upon these provisions, but they must be seen in very much the same way as compulsory treatment powers under the mental health legislation (see Chapter 10). The protection of Article 5 is potentially engaged, because the patient is deprived of his right to liberty. However, there can be no doubt that the detention is capable of justification under Article 5(1)(e). The lack of any express review process does not engage Article 5(4), because the initial decision to detain is itself taken by a court (*de Wilde, Ooms and Versyp v. Belgium* (1971) Series A, No. 12; 1 E.H.R.R. 373, para. 76), but general judicial remedies (such as *habeas corpus*) would seem to lie in any event.

Similar propositions apply also to the power under the National Assistance Act 1948 ("NAA 1948") s.47, to make an order in respect of a person suffering grave chronic disease or who is aged, infirm or physically incapacitated, who is living in insanitary conditions and is unable to devote to themselves and is not receiving from other persons proper care and attention. The order requires removal of that person to a hospital or other suitable place for "detention and maintenance" there, and will be limited to detention for a period of three months subject to extension from time to time for further periods of three months. Section 47(6) of the NAA 1947 allows the patient to apply to the court after six weeks for revision of the order, but disobedience of the order is a criminal offence.

H. TREATMENT ISSUES GENERALLY

1. Confidentiality

9–29 It is an established matter of medical practice that a doctor and other health care professionals have a duty to maintain confidentiality of information regarding their patient. That duty is a matter of practicality in preserving a suitable relationship between the doctor and patient, to allow the most efficient possible treatment of the patient. To breach that duty is a disciplinary matter from a professional point of view, and may lead to a claim for damages.

It seems likely that any breach of confidentiality could also be a breach of the positive obligation on the state under Article 8(1) to preserve the right to respect for private life. Article 8(2) provides exceptions to that right, in the interests of national security, prevention of crime and disorder, protection of health and the protection of the rights and freedoms of others.

It was accepted before the Act that the doctor/patient duty of confidentiality can legitimately be breached in certain circumstances, including: compliance with a court order; to prevent or in connection with investigation of a serious crime; the registration of births and deaths; and in connection with communicable diseases, abortion, drug misuse and serious accidents. There are also certain obligations to pass on information under the National Health Service legislation. All of these exceptions would appear to lie within the exceptions set out in Article 8(2). It is important to note that Article 8(1), as applied by the Act, appears to create a statutory right to confidentiality in circumstances which before mostly amounted to a professional duty.

2. Torture, etc.

9–30   Under Article 3 no one shall be subjected to torture or to inhuman or degrading treatment or punishment. In *X v. Denmark* (1983) 32 D.R. 282 (see above), the Commission took the view (in respect of gynaecological treatment of an experimental nature) that treatment could be sufficiently humiliating and debasing as to amount to inhuman or degrading treatment, contrary to Article 3, although the Convention right was not found to have been breached in that case. Article 3 was also considered in an abortion case (see *H v. Norway* above), in the context of pain suffered by the foetus during the procedure. There was no evidence presented to convince the Commission in that case that the foetus did suffer pain, although some still allege this to be the case.

It must be conceivable, however, that a medical procedure could be performed so badly that it could amount to a breach of Article 3. For example, a painful procedure carried out without anaesthetic might be sufficient, but it must be doubtful whether this would make any practical difference to existing law.

A special case exists with regard to individuals in detention, no doubt because the individual's care rests entirely upon the state as administrator of the prison system, but also because the prisoner lives in a closed environment which is less available to public scrutiny. (See in particular *Hurtado v. Switzerland* (1994) Series A, No. 280–A, where it was found that there was a positive obligation on the state to provide medical attention, and review arrangements for an injured prisoner.) The Court has also considered whether a prisoner of full mind can be treated medically without his consent while in prison. In *Herczegfalvy v. Austria* (1992) Series A, No. 244; 15 E.H.R.R. 437, para. 242, it was held not to be a breach of Article 3 to treat a prisoner without his consent where this was necessary to save the prisoner from death or serious injury. Thus force feeding of (or forced administration of medicine to) a hunger striker would be permitted. Such treatment may be degrading in the mind of the prisoner, but the obligation to the prisoner under Article 2(1) to secure the right to life of such a person would surely prevail over any consideration of Article 3. The position is clearly different in relation to forced treatment designed to act as part of the patient's punishment, or to destroy clinically his tendency to commit further offences (for instance, chemical castration).

I. REGULATION OF HEALTHCARE PROFESSIONS

9–31   This section notes the possible effect of the Act on the activities of the professional practice committees of the General Medical Council (GMC) and the other bodies set up to regulate the healthcare professions. These committees are usually convened to consider complaints regarding the professional conduct of that body's members. They consist of senior members of those professions and co-opted lay members. They make decisions which may lead to suspension or removal of the member's right to practice, and which may well, of course, affect an individual's employment prospects.

In the case of the professional conduct committee of the GMC a decision striking off, suspending or imposing conditions of registration upon a doctor can be appealed to the Judicial Committee of the Privy Council. In such cases, the court will look to matters of law but also will review whether the professional conduct committee could reach a decision that there has been serious professional misconduct upon the evidence before it, and thus review the reasonableness of the decision.

In the case of the nursing, midwifery and health visiting professions, regulation and disciplinary matters are governed by the United Kingdom Central Council for Nursing Midwifery and Health Visiting (UKCC). These functions are performed in much the same way as the GMC does with doctors, save that the U.K.C.C. has only to find "professional misconduct" without finding it to be "serious", to take disciplinary steps. Appeal is to the High Court on points of law, procedural irregularities, or on whether there is sufficient evidence to support the decision. The Court will be otherwise hesitant to challenge the findings of that professional misconduct committee.

Similarly some professions outside the mainstream of clinical practice are regulated by legislation (for example, the Chiropractors Act 1994) which provide for disciplinary control of its members.

9–32   Of relevance here will be Article 6 (right to a fair trial), and the procedural rights which are imported through it (see generally 2–65 and following). While that Article's application is clear in the context of courts and tribunals set up by the State, it is less clear as regards administrative decisions that affect civil rights. The tenor of the case law in this area is that where the primary purpose of such decisions is to determine directly a civil right or obligation, there should be in place a mechanism of appeal to a tribunal which has appropriate appellate jurisdiction (see particularly *Le Compte, Van Leuven and Demeyere v. Belgium* (1981) Series A, No. 43; 6 E.H.R.R. 583, para. 47). That appellate jurisdiction should be as to both law and fact, and not merely judicial review.

The subsequent case of *Albert and Le Compte v. Belgium* (1983) Series A, No. 58; 5 E.H.R.R. 533, para. 29 is particularly relevant in this context in that it concerned decisions by a Belgian medical disciplinary body in connection with the practices of doctors in that state. That system allowed a right of appeal to another professional body with subsequent appeal to the Belgian Court of Cassation. Article 6(1) was not complied with in that the professional bodies sat in private and the subsequent appeal was only allowed on points of law. A full appellate jurisdiction is required as this tribunal was directly determinative of the doctors' civil rights. Article 6(1) would however not apply if the disciplinary proceedings had simply lead to a reprimand (see *Le Compte v. Belgium*, above). In *Zumtobel v. Austria* (1993) Series A, No. 268–A; 17 E.H.R.R. 116, para, 32, administrative decisions involving matters of policy were distinguished in that the Court found that Article 6(1) only required that, in effect, judicial review be available by way of appeal.

9–33   In the context of decisions of the professional practice committees of the GMC and other such bodies, it is clear that there are limitations imposed on the extent to which the relevant appellate courts will review these decisions. It seems likely that those limitations may be subject to review in the light of Article 6(1).

While internal disciplinary proceedings against doctors within the NHS are notoriously tortuous, they have now been reformed, clarified and accelerated. Under the former procedures, in *Darnell v. U.K.* (1989) Series A, No. 272 it took nearly nine years to bring proceedings for unfair dismissal to a conclusion, and this was held to be a breach of Article 6 for being an unreasonable delay.

There is no express right to employment in the Convention, although Articles 4 and 11 have been relied on in this respect (see Chapter 13). Subject to this, it is possible that the powers of professional regulatory bodies may be governed to some extent also by Article 8 (respect for private and family life).

CHAPTER 10

Mental Health Law

David Hewitt (Solicitor, Roland Robinsons & Fentons)

A. INTRODUCTION

10–01 The Act is likely to have a significant effect upon domestic mental health law. The fact that it will cover both courts *and* tribunals (section 2(1)) means that it will be applicable wherever psychiatric legal decisions are made — even at first instance, within the Mental Health Review Tribunal ("MHRT"). The fact that it carries, not only the corpus of the Convention itself, but also all judgments, declarations and decisions made under it (section 2(1)(a)–(d)), means that a knowledge of Convention case law will be essential for lawyers in this field.

Neither the Commission nor the Court has faced a large volume of cases concerning U.K. mental health law. Nevertheless, the decisions which they have each been required to make have had a significant influence upon the development of that law. It seems likely, however, that their greatest influence is yet to come.

In order to explain the chief implications of the Act, this chapter will examine each aspect of mental health law which has been affected by decisions from Strasbourg and, in each case, the effect that those decisions have had. Though it cannot hope to do so either comprehensively or infallibly, it will also attempt to foresee some of the developments which will follow once the Convention has been given full effect in English law.

1. The Convention Rights

10–02 The provision under which most of the significant challenges to domestic mental health law have been brought is Article 5 (right to liberty and security) — as it is particularly delineated in sub-articles (1), (2) and (4). Other major cases have been founded upon the prohibition of torture in Article 3, and the right to respect for private and family life in Article 8. Reference will also be made to the right to a fair trial, to freedom of expression and to marry enshrined, respectively, in Articles 6, 10 and 12.

2. Mental Health Act 1983

10–03 The principal source of U.K. mental health law is the Mental Health Act 1983 ("MHA 1983"). At least in its original conception, MHA 1983 owed little to the Convention. The general strategy of the legislators was largely a reactive one, with most apparently content for the law to be shaped by future rulings from Europe. Lord Wallace, an Opposition spokesman, who did not favour this approach, spoke of "the Government, in their role as avid pupil awaiting instruction from the headmaster in Strasbourg" (*Hansard*, H.L., Vol 426, cols. 801–07).

The primary influences of MHA 1983 were the report of the Butler Committee on Mentally Abnormal Offenders (Cmnd 6244) and the MIND study *A Human Condition*, both of which were published in 1975. They were followed by a government Consultative Document in 1976 (*A Review of the Mental Health Act 1959*, DHSS) and a White Paper in 1978 (*Review of the Mental Health Act 1959*, DHSS *et al.*, Cmnd 7320). Though these proposals did not survive the fall of the Labour government in 1979, its Conservative successor subsequently introduced a Mental Health (Amendment) Bill and published a further White Paper (*Reform of Mental Health Legislation*, DHSS *et al.*, Cmnd. 8405).

10–04   The final form of MHA 1983 does, however, show clear signs of influence by the Convention. In 1974–75, MIND had laid a series of cases before the Commission. Probably the most important of these was *X v. U.K.* (1981) Series A, No. 46; 4 E.H.R.R. 181, in which a breach of Article 5(4) was found (see further paragraph 10–19 below). The new administration thought it prudent to acknowledge this decision in its amendment bill. Reflecting upon the case, a government spokesman, Lord Renton, urged a different, more anticipatory, approach:

> "We do not want this kind of proceeding to go on indefinitely — we come out of it badly every time — and it is so obvious on this occasion that we could save ourselves trouble and, indeed, some degree of ignominy" (House of Lords Debates, January 25, 1982, Vol. 426, cols. 801–07).

A subsequent raft of cases, which was initiated by MIND in 1977–78 and came before the Commission as Parliament was debating the Mental Health Bill, is thought to have been highly influential (L. Gostin, *Mental Health Services: Law and Practice* (Shaw & Sons, 1986), 1.10. See: *Ashingdane v. U.K.* (1985) Series A, No. 93; 7 E.H.R.R. 528; *Collins v. U.K.* (1982) App. No. 9729/82, withdrawn; *Barclay-Maguire v. U.K.* (1981) App. No. 9117/80, decision as to admissibility, December 9, 1981 (case withdrawn)). The Royal Assent was granted on May 9, 1983, and MHA 1983 came into force on September 30 that year.

3. Human Rights Act 1998

10–05   The two main approaches of the Act, statutory construction and the obligation of public authorities to act compatibly with Convention rights, are likely to make their presence felt in each area of mental health law.

The relevant judicial bodies will have to interpret MHA 1983 in a way which is consistent with the Convention rights (section 3(1)), and some will be empowered to make a declaration of incompatibility if they cannot (section 4(2)). However, when considering subordinate legislation, such as the Mental Health (Hospital, Guardianship and Consent to Treatment) Regulations 1983

(S.I. 1983 No. 893), the Mental Health Review Tribunal Rules 1983 (S.I. 1983 No. 942), the Court of Protection Rules 1994 (S.I. 1994 No. 3046) or the Mental Health (After care Under Supervision) Regulations 1996 (S.I. 1996 No. 294), those courts have the additional power to declare the incompatibility of such legislation where the primary legislation prevents removal of the incompatibility (section 4(4)).

Among the "public authorities" which will be obliged to act compatibly with the Convention rights, the Act specifies both "a court" and "a tribunal which exercises functions in relation to legal proceedings" (section 6(3)(a) and (b)). The former category will include, for example, the county court when it comes to determine applications for the displacement of a nearest relative under MHA 1983, s.29, while the latter category will clearly contain the MHRT, in both its judicial and its administrative functions (see paragraph 10–36 and following, below). As they probably do not "exercise functions in relation to *legal proceedings*", hospital managers' review hearings probably cannot be so regarded, and therefore will not be so constrained. However, the final category of public authority — "any person certain of whose functions are functions of a public nature" (section 6(3)(c)) — may well embrace hospital managers, at least when they exercise the powers and perform the specific duties described in MHA 1983 (see, for example, section 6(2) and 132(1) of the MHA 1983). It will certainly cover local authorities which, *inter alia*, act as guardians under MHA 1983, s.7 or provide after-care under section 117, and may also extend to the policy and practices of the Legal Aid Board (see paragraph 10–42 and following, below).

B. BASIC PRINCIPLES

10–06 The manner in which the Convention has been applied to domestic mental health law has been shaped by the response in Strasbourg to two cases: *Winterwerp v. Netherlands* (1979) and *X v. U.K.* (1981).

1. Winterwerp v. Netherlands

10–07 This decision, given on October 24, 1979, remains the most significant Convention ruling on psychiatric law ((1979) Series A, No. 33; 2 E.H.R.R. 387). The Court held that, except in an emergency, the detention of a person of unsound mind will be lawful only where each of the following minimum conditions is fulfilled:

(i) The person to be detained must reliably be shown to be of unsound mind. In other words, a true mental disorder must be established on the basis of objective medical expertise; and

(ii) The relevant mental disorder must be of a kind or a degree warranting compulsory confinement; and

(iii) The validity of the continued confinement must depend upon the persistence of such a disorder.

How closely does domestic mental health law comply with these conditions?

2. True mental disorder warranting compulsory confinement

10–08   This section effectively consolidates the first two of the *Winterwerp* criteria.

Most of the routes by which a patient may be detained in hospital (MHA 1983, ss.2, 3, 4, 5(2) and 5(4) for civil admissions; sections 37 and 41 for admissions ordered by a court; and sections 47 and 49 for transfers from prison to hospital) require at least one, and usually two, psychiatric recommendations stating that the patient is suffering from a form of mental disorder which makes it appropriate for him to be so detained. It is likely that these recommendations will satisfy the *Winterwerp* requirement for "objective medical expertise".

There are, however, certain detention provisions — those contained in sections 42(3), 135 and 136 of the MHA 1983 — which require no such recommendation. Can they be rendered compatible with the Convention?

(a) Section 42(3) of the MHA 1983

10–09   This provision enables the Home Secretary to recall to prison a restricted patient who has been conditionally discharged either by himself (under the MHA 1983, s.42(2)) or by the MHRT (under the MHA 1983, s.73). Crucially, there is no requirement that he obtain objective medical evidence before doing so.

In *Kay v. U.K.* (App. No. 17821/91, Committee of Ministers, Decision July 7, 1993) a patient argued that his recall was unlawful because, at the time when he ordered it, the Home Secretary lacked any medical evidence that he was mentally ill. The Court of Appeal had rejected his appeal from an adverse first instance decision, stating:

> "It has been held by this court in *R. v. Secretary of State for the Home Department, ex p. Brind* [[1990] 2 W.L.R. 787] that where the words of an English statute are plain and unambiguous, it is not open to the courts of this country to look to the Convention for assistance in their interpretation. The words of section 42(3) are in our judgment plain and unambiguous. There is no requirement that the Secretary of State cannot by warrant recall a patient who has been conditionally discharged unless he has medical evidence that the patient is then suffering from mental disorder" (*R. v. Home Secretary, ex p. K* [1991] Q.B. 270, *per* McCowan L.J. at 280).

However, the Committee of Ministers held that there had been violations of Articles 5(1) and 5(4). As the offending practice has remained substantially unaltered since 1994, this ruling must still obtain. (The fact that it did not come from either the Commission or the Court is irrelevant as, under section 2(1)(b) of the Act, decisions of the Committee of Ministers will also be binding upon courts and tribunals.) Thus, without a significant change — such as, for example, the introduction of a speedy means by which a patient might challenge his recall — it is hard to see how the current practice can be reconciled with the requirements of the Convention.

(b) Sections 135 and 136 of the MHA 1983

10–10   Section 135 of the MHA 1983 permits a police constable, in possession of a warrant issued by a justice of the peace upon information laid by an approved social worker, to enter the premises of a person,

> ". . . believed to be suffering from mental disorder — [who] has been, or is being, ill-treated, neglected or kept otherwise than under proper control, in any place within the jurisdiction of the justice, or — [who,] being unable to care for himself, is living alone in such a place" (subsection (1)).

That person may then be removed to a "place of safety" with a view to his admission to hospital under MHA 1983 or the making of "other arrangements for his treatment or care". He may, however, only be detained in the place of safety for a maximum of 72 hours (subsection (3)).

10–11   Section 136 of the MHA 1983 permits a police constable to remove to a "place of safety" any person whom he finds "in a place to which the public have access . . . who appears to him to be suffering from mental disorder and to be in immediate need of care and control", though he may only do so if "he thinks it necessary . . . in the interests of that person or for the protection of other persons" (subsection (1)). The purpose of such a detention is to permit arrangements to be made for the detainee to be admitted to hospital, if such is considered necessary. Again, he may only be kept at the place of safety for a maximum of 72 hours (subsection (2)).

Once again, the power to detain is not contingent upon objective medical evidence, but is triggered simply by the belief of an approved social worker or police constable.

Because of the apparent urgency of the circumstances anticipated by sections 135 and 136, and also the relative brevity of the periods of detention permitted thereunder, it is unlikely that these powers would be held to be inconsistent with the *Winterwerp* reading of Article 5.

3. The persistence of mental disorder

10–12   In *Winterwerp*, the Court held that detention would only be valid whilst the patient continued to suffer from mental disorder. However, domestic practice has tended toward a somewhat different view.

(a) The unrestricted patient

10–13   Though an unrestricted patient should be subject to continuous review by his Responsible Medical Officer [RMO], who may discharge him at any time, there is nothing in MHA 1983 to compel discharge immediately the statutory grounds for admission cease to exist. It is therefore arguable that the current position is incompatible with the Convention, and that urgent changes should be made, both in statute and, perhaps more immediately, in clinical practice.

(b) The restricted patient

10–14 The position is even more troublesome in respect of the restricted patient, whom only the Home Secretary or a MHRT may discharge. If the grounds for detention of such a patient should cease to exist while he awaits a decision from either of these bodies, that detention would appear no longer to be supported by "contemporary medical expertise", and might well therefore violate the Convention.

The government might, of course, claim that it is itself permitted, under Article 5(4), to await the judicial decision of the MHRT. Alternatively, it might argue that it is entitled to place perpetual reliance upon the psychiatric opinions which were originally supplied in support of the patient's detention and restricted status. This latter course may be possible where no subsequent report has contained a different conclusion, or even where a different conclusion has been reached on the same clinical facts. If, however, there has been a demonstrable change in the patient's condition, then such a practice surely cannot be consistent with the Convention.

Thus, in order to ensure compliance with the Convention where a restricted patient's application for discharge is supported by his RMO, the Home Secretary should establish whether there are any earlier reports which conflict with this view. If there are none, he should either discharge the patient or seek alternative psychiatric advice. If any such advice should conflict with the opinion of the RMO, the patient would, once again, have to be discharged; if not, continued detention would probably be justified, for the Court has accepted that:

> "In deciding whether an individual should be detained as a 'person of unsound mind', the national authorities are to be recognised as having a certain discretion, since it is in the first place for the national authorities to evaluate the evidence adduced before them in a particular case" (*Winterwerp*, above, at para. 40).

(c) The case of R. v. Merseyside Mental Health Review Tribunal

10–15 The problems inherent in the present practice are illustrated by this domestic case ([1990] 1 All E.R. 694). Though an MHRT had accepted that the applicant was not mentally disordered, it had only granted him a conditional discharge as it believed that he should remain liable to be recalled to hospital for further treatment. The applicant claimed that as he was not now mentally disordered he should not be subject to the MHA 1983. He pointed out that the preamble to the statute speaks of "mentally disordered persons"; that it has effect with respect to the "reception, care and treatment of mentally disordered patients" (section 1); and that "patient" is defined as "a person suffering or appearing to be suffering from mental disorder" (section 145). He added that a conditional discharge under section 73(2) must pre-suppose possible recall to hospital for further treatment, which would be impossible in his case because there was no longer anything to treat.

At first instance, it was held that a restricted patient who was not mentally disordered remained a "patient" under the MHA 1983 for the purposes of section 73(2) and could, therefore, be conditionally discharged so that he remained liable to recall to hospital. Any other conclusion would be untenable because:

"If at the date of the decision the tribunal was wholly satisfied that the person concerned was not suffering from mental disorder but there was substantial expert evidence that he was liable to relapse, nevertheless the tribunal would be obliged to let him loose" (*R. v. Mental Health Review Tribunal, ex p. Kay, The Times*, May 25, 1988, DC).

Section 73 specifically provided for conditional discharge where the tribunal found that he should remain liable to recall: "It was clear that in section 72 and associated sections the context did require another meaning of the word 'patient'" (*ibid.*).

10–16 The Court of Appeal agreed with this decision. Butler-Sloss L.J. conceded that, under section 72, an MHRT must discharge a patient if satisfied that he is not then suffering from mental disorder. She argued, however, that the tribunal's duty under section 73 is somewhat different; that it cannot absolutely discharge a restricted patient unless satisfied that it is not appropriate for him to remain liable to be recalled to hospital for further treatment. Even where he is not mentally disordered, a person will remain a "patient" within the meaning of the MHA 1983.

"At the time the offender is detained under a hospital order he is a patient within the interpretation in section 145. By section 41(3)(a) a restricted patient continues to be detained until discharged under section 73 and in my judgment remains a patient until he is discharged absolutely, if at all, by the tribunal. Any other interpretation of the word 'patient' makes a nonsense of the framework of the Act and the hoped-for progression to discharge of the treatable patient, treatability being a prerequisite of his original admission" (at 699).

10–17 Not surprisingly, this decision has been taken to confirm that section 73 of the MHA 1983 conflicts with the Convention. Larry Gostin's criticism has been particularly trenchant. He has written:

". . . the very purpose of mental health legislation is to have control over, and to treat, mentally disordered persons . . . Once the purposes for detention (treatment of mentally disordered persons) are no longer applicable, a person should no longer be subject to the [Mental Health] Act . . . Arguably, [Article 5(1)] would prohibit the restraint of liberty of persons who are not currently of 'unsound mind' because of the possibility that they may become mentally ill in the future. The 'lawful detention' of persons under Article 5(1)(e) requires a reliable showing that the person is of unsound mind on the basis of objective medical expertise. Further, the European Court of Human Rights recognised [in *Winterwerp*] that mental disorder is subject to amelioration and cure. Once the person is "cured" and is no longer of unsound mind, the logic of the European Court's decision suggests that restraint under mental health legislation is no longer compatible with the Convention" (*Mental Health Services: Law and Practice* (Shaw & Sons, 1986), para. 18.13 1).

It is possible to find support for Gostin's view in the response of the European Commission in the more recent case of *Joseph Roux v. U.K.* (1996) 22 E.H.R.R. C.D. 196, below.

(d) The case of Joseph Roux

10–18   Mr Roux had been convicted in both October 1974 and September 1975 of offences involving, *inter alia*, threats to prostitutes. On the second occasion he was placed under a hospital order without limit of time and admitted to a special hospital. Following an MHRT hearing, he was conditionally discharged on April 11, 1994. On May 24, 1994, one of the psychiatrists responsible for supervising Mr Roux in the community received information that he had brought a prostitute to his accommodation and had been heard to argue with her about money. At the request of that psychiatrist, and with the consent of his other supervisor, a warrant of recall was issued to Mr Roux under section 42(3) of the MHA 1983. A letter giving the reasons for his recall was sent to his hospital psychiatrist, who discussed them with Mr Roux shortly after his return. The matter was referred to the MHRT on June 17, 1994 and, following a hearing in December 1994, Mr Roux was conditionally discharged once again on January 9, 1995.

In his complaint to the Commission, Mr Roux alleged breaches of, *inter alia*, the right to liberty and security contained in Article 5. Referring to the criteria set out in *Winterwerp*, he pointed out that no court had determined the state of his mental health at the time of his recall and argued that as he had not broken the conditions of his discharge he should not have been compelled to return.

The U.K. government pointed to the fact that when the MHRT had ordered Mr Roux's conditional release in February 1994, and again when it reconvened after his recall, it had decided that he was suffering from a psychopathic disorder. Recall had been effected at the request and upon the advice of the two psychiatrists who were responsible for supervising Mr Roux in the community, and their clear view, expressed as late as May 25, 1994, was that he was suffering from a form of mental disorder which required him to be recalled to hospital for treatment in the interests both of his own health and safety and also of the safety of the general public. Finally, the government argued that the power to recall is not linked to the conditions attached to release. It suggested that there may be occasions when recall is appropriate even though those conditions have not been breached, just as there may be breaches of the conditions which do not, in fact, warrant recall.

On September 4, 1996, the Commission unanimously ruled Mr Roux's application admissible, holding that it "raises complex and serious issues under the Convention".

4. X v. U.K.

10–19   This was the earliest domestic mental health case to reach Strasbourg ((1981) Series A, No. 46; 4 E.H.R.R. 188), and was at the forefront of the series presented by MIND in 1974–5 (see paragraph 10–04, above). Like a number of those which were to follow it, including that of Mr Roux, it concerned the conditional discharge of a restricted patient.

The applicant had been convicted of a serious assault upon a workmate and made the subject of a restriction order imposed under sections 60 and 65 of the Mental Health Act 1959. Though he received a conditional discharge in May 1971, he remained liable to recall at any time during the life of the restriction order. In April 1974, in consequence of allegations made by his wife, he was duly recalled to Broadmoor Hospital. Though the allegations had been uncorroborated, and though he had always complied with the conditions of his discharge, an application for a writ of habeas corpus was dismissed. He would be unable to apply to the MHRT for his release until at least six months after his recall.

(a) The first ground of complaint

10–20   The applicant claimed that there had been a violation of Article 5(1), which is subject only to a very few specific exceptions. He argued that the *Winterwerp* interpretation of those exceptions had not been fulfilled. In response, the U.K. government suggested that there would be at least one species of case which would remain untouched by the decision in that case. It pointed out that the applicant's detention was the result of conviction by a competent court (the first exception to the prohibition in Article 5(1)) and argued that in those circumstances the fact that the applicant may have been a person of unsound mind (the other material exception) was irrelevant and the *Winterwerp* protection, which related solely to such persons, could not apply. For its part, the Commission decided that as the state had purported to select a "therapeutic disposal", the conditions would indeed have to be fulfilled. The Court steered a slightly more complex course. Before the applicant's conditional discharge, it ruled, his detention was due both to his conviction and to his mental illness. Afterwards, however, the position would be less clear. Nevertheless, the Court held that it was unnecessary to decide the point because, on the evidence of the special hospital's own psychiatrist, the *Winterwerp* conditions had been fulfilled at the time of the applicant's recall.

(b) The second ground of complaint

10–21   Secondly, the applicant pointed to the absence of any means by which the merits of his recall and detention could be judicially reviewed. He argued that it constituted a violation of Article 5(4), which entitles a detained or arrested person to take proceedings by which the lawfulness of his detention shall be decided speedily by a court. The Commission accepted this argument, and its decision was upheld by the Court. The restriction order imposed upon the applicant under section 65 of the 1959 Act breached the Convention for two reasons. First, because mental illness is subject to amelioration and cure, a person who is detained because of unsound mind must have the right to a periodic judicial review. That review must consider, not merely whether the detention conforms to domestic law, but also whether it remains justified on its merits. In this case, habeas corpus proceedings had been the only immediate way in which the applicant could challenge his detention. However, the 1959 Act permitted the Home Secretary an almost unfettered discretion, and it would therefore be virtually impossible to show that he had acted unlawfully, in bad faith or arbitrarily. This particular form of judicial review could not, therefore, fulfil Article 5(4). Secondly, it was noted that under Article 5(4) a detained person should be able to have the lawfulness of his detention decided by a "court" possessing certain judicial characteristics, such as "independence of the executive and of the parties to the case". The Court held that the Home Secretary could not be a "court" within Article 5(4), nor could any body — such as the MHRT — which merely advised him as to the execution of his powers. (A similar approach was adopted in the subsequent case of *Keus v. Netherlands* ([1990] Series A, No. 185–C; (1990) 13 E.H.R.R. 700), in which *X v. U.K.* was specifically approved.)

(c) The third ground of complaint

10–22 Finally, the applicant complained that he had been given no explanation of the reasons for his recall to Broadmoor, and argued that this constituted a violation of Article 5(2), the right of an arrested person to be informed promptly of the reasons for his arrest. The Court decided that this deficiency was subsumed into the much greater failure to provide a swift means of review. Had such a review taken place, it decided, the applicant would inevitably have received the explanation he desired. The dissenting view, however, was that the right to an explanation:

". . . constitutes a safeguard of personal liberty whose importance in any democratic system founded on the rule of law cannot be underestimated . . . it is the embodiment of a kind of legitimate confidence or expectation . . . in the relations between the individual and the public powers" (*per* Judge Evrigenis).

(d) The consequences of X v. U.K.

10–23 This is one of the cases which can be shown to have had a very direct effect upon the form of the MHA 1983.

Section 42 of the MHA 1983 perpetuates the Home Secretary's power to order the recall to hospital of a conditionally discharged restricted patient. That power can be exercised at the Home Secretary's discretion and without any need for a prior breach of the discharge conditions. However, there is now a two-stage procedure for informing restricted patients of the reasons for their recall (Home Office Circular No. 117/1980; Department of Health & Social Security Circular LA SSL (80) 7), under which the person responsible for bringing the patient back into custody will inform him that he is being recalled to hospital by the Home Secretary under the MHA 1983 and that a further explanation will be given later. As soon as possible after admission, but in any case within 72 hours, the RMO or his deputy should explain to the patient the reasons for his recall. Those reasons should also be relayed by the RMO to the patient's supervisor in the community and to a responsible member of his family or, if appropriate, to his legal representative. Further guidance upon this procedure is contained in the Code of Practice to MHA 1983 (para. 28).

10–24 Both the information which must be given to patients and the occasions upon which they must receive it are now more clearly defined. The Code of Practice provides that "All patients should be given, throughout their stay in hospital, as much information as possible about their care and treatment" (para. 14.1). It stresses that informal patients should be in no doubt that they are permitted to leave at any time, that periodic checks be made to ensure that patients still understand their rights, and that patient information be displayed on ward notice boards and in other appropriate places. Section 132 of the MHA 1983 imposes a positive duty to inform in respect of detained patients. It states:

"(1) The managers of a hospital or mental nursing home in which a patient is detained under this Act shall take such steps as are practicable to ensure that the patient understands —

(a) under which provisions of this Act he is for the time being detained and the effect of that provision; and
(b) what rights of applying to a Mental Health Review Tribunal are available to him in respect of his detention under that provision;

and those steps shall be taken as soon as practicable after the commencement of the patient's detention under the provision in question".

A corresponding duty is owed in respect of certain other provisions in the MHA 1983, such as the power to impose medical treatment without consent and the limitations upon that power (*ibid.*, subsection (2)). The duty to provide information is owed, not only to the patient, but also to his "nearest relative", as that term is defined elsewhere in the MHA 1983 (*ibid.*, subsection (4)).

10–25 Following his recall to hospital, a conditionally discharged restricted patient now has the right to apply to the MHRT for the restriction order to be removed (MHA 1983, s.75(2)). Should he fail to do so within one month of his recall, the Home Secretary must himself submit an appeal on the patient's behalf (MHA 1983, s.75(1)(a)). However, in view of the delays which are currently being encountered in arranging tribunal hearings, especially those requested by restricted patients, it may be that the United Kingdom still stands in breach of Article 5(4) in this regard (see paragraph 10–39, below).

The rest of this chapter will consider the impact of the Strasbourg authorities upon various aspects of mental health law and practice. It will also attempt to assess the extent to which the latter are compatible with the Convention.

C. ADMISSION

10–26 Under the MHA 1983 a significant role is played by a patient's "nearest relative", as that term is there defined (section 145). In particular, should he raise any objection, a patient's proposed admission for treatment under section 3 of the MHA 1983 cannot take place without an order of the county court (section 11(4)). The precise identity of the nearest relative, and the nature of his relationship with the patient, is therefore of great importance, as the Mental Health Act Commission has acknowledged:

> "The Commission continues to receive reports of instances where it is inappropriate for a person to remain as the nearest relative for the purposes of the [Mental Health] Act: for instance where the patient has been abused, physically, emotionally or sexually by that person in the past. At present, there are no provisions in the [Mental Health] Act for that person to be removed from exercising the functions of the nearest relative on these grounds" (*Seventh Biennial Report, 1995–1997* (The Stationery Office), paragraph 10.10.3).

It would seem that this deficiency constitutes a further breach of the Convention. In *J. T. v. U.K.* (Commission decision as to admissibility; Legal Action, July 1997, p. 16), the applicant had been detained under section 3 of the MHA 1983 in 1984 and finally discharged only in January 1996. She was concerned that if she was compulsorily detained again personal information would be released to her mother, her statutory nearest relative, with whom she had had a very difficult relationship, or to her stepfather, against whom she had made allegations of sexual abuse. She wished to appoint a new nearest relative and claimed that the fact that domestic law did not permit her to do so amounted to a violation of Article 8 (right to respect for private and family life). The Commission unanimously declared her complaint admissible.

    10–27 In fact, the Convention would seem to confer considerable freedom upon the relative of a mentally disordered person. In *Nielsen v. Denmark* ((1988) Series A, No. 144; 11 E.H.R.R. 175), the 12-year-old applicant had been admitted to a Danish psychiatric hospital at the request of his mother. As she possessed sole parental rights over him, he had no redress under Danish law and therefore claimed a breach of the Convention. He criticised the lack of a means of judicial review and claimed that he had been detained without any evidence that he was of unsound mind. He did not succeed, however, as the Court held he was "still of an age at which it would be normal for a decision to be made by the parent even against the wishes of the child", and that his detention was "a responsible exercise by the mother of her custodial rights in the interests of the child".

    It would seem that English law has reached a similar point. The case of *R. v. Kirklees Metropolitan Council, ex p. C* (1992) 8 B.M.L.R. 110 concerned a 12-year-old girl who was admitted by her local authority to a psychiatric hospital, against her will and without the MHA 1983. It was held at first instance that, just as an adult might enter hospital voluntarily, so might a child. It was necessary only that consent was present, and that could be given on behalf of a child by a parent or local authority. Here, the applicant's age and general behaviour showed that she was not competent according to the test in *Gillick v. West Norfolk & Wisbech Health Authority* [1986] A.C. 112, and the local authority could therefore consent to admission on her behalf. This decision was subsequently upheld in the Court of Appeal [1993] 2 F.L.R. 187, and in the light of the *Nielsen* decision would seem to be unassailable.

D. Rights During Detention

10–28 At least in the early years of Convention litigation, it was common for applicants to complain, not so much of the *fact* of their detention, but of the physical degradations to which it had exposed them.

1. Environment

10–29 The suggestion that the conditions in which a patient was kept violated Article 3 of the Convention was the basis of one of the first decisions to be made against the United Kingdom. In *A v. U.K.* (App. No. 6840/74) a Broadmoor patient alleged that he had been subjected to inhuman and degrading treatment or punishment during a five-week period of seclusion. He complained that he had been allowed limited opportunities for exercise or association; that he had been deprived of adequate clothing; and that the seclusion room had been insanitary and inadequately furnished, lit and ventilated. Having visited Broadmoor, the Commission approved a friendly settlement which included an *ex gratia* payment to the applicant of £500 and the introduction of a new seclusion regime with the following features:

(i) The seclusion room to have natural lighting and a floor area of at least 4.7 square metres;

(ii) All secluded patients to have suitable clothing and footwear, mattresses and bedding, and reading matter;

(iii) Patients secluded for more than three hours to receive an individual programme of care;

(iv) Unless precluded by their condition, all secluded patients to be permitted to leave the seclusion room to visit the toilet, and to have access to visitors and at least 30 minutes' exercise in the morning and afternoon;

(v) All secluded patients to be observed at intervals of no more than 15 minutes, such observations to be recorded in a special book alongside other information such as the reason for seclusion and the time at which it began and ended;

(vi) Hospital management to be made aware of any patient secluded for more than 24 hours.

Subsequently, the Department of Health and Social Security carried out its own review of seclusion procedures in the special hospitals (*Review of Special Hospitals' Seclusion Procedures*, DHSS, April 1985).

10–30 The conditions in Broadmoor hospital were to be the subject of another complaint to the Commission under Article 3. In *B v. U.K.* (1984) 6 E.H.R.R. 204 a patient claimed, not only that his detention in a special hospital was unmerited, but also that the hospital was grossly overcrowded, pervaded by an atmosphere of violence and lacking in adequate sanitary facilities. He alleged that dormitory beds were only six to 12 inches apart, that observation lights were left on all night, and that there was no privacy and little fresh air or exercise. He said that he received no treatment whatsoever and almost never saw his doctor. Nevertheless, his application failed, it being held that there was no single incident which was so grave as to warrant a finding of inhuman or degrading treatment.

Such matters are unlikely to be a fruitful source of further litigation. As Larry Gostin has concluded, the decision in *B* "leaves in doubt whether Article 3 would take cognizance of the totality of conditions in the absence of a single factor which was so gross as to shock the conscience" (*Mental Health Services: Law and Practice* (Shaw & Sons, 1986), paragraph 20.29A).

2. Treatment

10–31   Though never the subject of a complaint against the United Kingdom, the question of whether medical treatment might violate Article 3 has reached Strasbourg on several occasions.

In *Ireland v. U.K.* (1978) Series A, No. 25, para. 162, the Court held: "Treatment will be inhuman only if it reaches a level of gravity involving considerable mental or physical suffering, and degrading if the person has undergone humiliation or debasement involving a minimum level of severity".

The key case on this subject is that of *Herczegfalvy v. Austria* (1992) Series A. No. 242–B; (1993) 15 E.H.R.R. 437, in which the applicant had been admitted to an Austrian psychiatric hospital in September 1979. He was in a weakened condition due to a hunger-strike, and had therefore been force-fed under domestic law and sedated against his will. He was handcuffed, fastened to a security bed by straps and a net, and his ankles were secured by a belt. When he complained of a breach of Article 3, the Court held:

> "The position of inferiority and powerlessness which is typical of patients confined in psychiatric hospitals calls for increased vigilance in reviewing whether the Convention has been complied with. While it was for the medical authorities to decide, on the basis of the recognised rules of medical science, on the therapeutic methods to be used, if necessary by force, to preserve the physical and mental health of patients who are entirely incapable of deciding for themselves, such patients nevertheless remain under the protection of Article 3, whose requirements permitted of no derogation" (at para. 82).

However, the established principles of medicine would generally be decisive, and a measure could not be regarded as inhuman or degrading where it was a therapeutic necessity. The Court would still have to be satisfied that such a necessity did in fact exist, and it expressed concern about the prolonged use of handcuffs and the security bed. Nevertheless, the applicant had failed to disprove the argument advanced by the Austrian government that his treatment was justified by medical necessity according to contemporary psychiatric standards. There had, therefore, been no breach of Article 3.

10–32 This approach applies a similar standard to that imposed by the domestic case of *Bolam v. Friern Hospital Management Committee* [1957] 1 W.L.R. 582 (which, of course, concerned injuries sustained by the plaintiff during a session of electro-convulsive therapy).

Mr Herczegfalvy also argued that, by forcibly feeding and medicating him, the authorities had violated the right to respect for private and family life enshrined in Article 8. In dismissing this contention, the Court noted that it concerned the same facts as those adduced in the complaint under Article 3, and found that they again did not disprove the Austrian government's view that the hospital authorities were entitled to treat the applicant as incapable of taking a decision for himself.

For the moment, the matter would appear to rest with the case of *Grare v. France* (1993) 15 E.H.R.R. C.D. 100), in which it was affirmed that psychiatric treatment which may have unpleasant side effects is not of such a nature or seriousness as to violate Article 3 (or Article 5 or Article 8(1)).

3. A minimum standard of treatment?

10–33 It might be thought that the corollary to the decision in *Herczegfalvy* would be an expectation that psychiatric hospitals will provide a minimum standard of medical treatment. However, those who have sought to propound such a view have invariably been disappointed.

In *Ashingdane v. U.K.* (1985) Series A, No. 93; 7 E.H.R.R. 528, which was among the second wave of cases to influence the MHA 1983, there was evidence that the applicant's continued detention in secure accommodation was proving harmful to his health. His transfer from a special hospital had been prevented by industrial action taken by the CoHSE trade union. Following the *Winterwerp* decision, the Commission found that in principle, Article 5(1), under which the complaint was made, concerned the actual deprivation of a patient's liberty, and not his treatment. Arbitrary detention could not be lawful and, furthermore, there must be some relationship between the ground upon which detention was claimed to be permitted and the place and conditions of detention. In that regard, the detention of a person of unsound mind would comply with the Article only if it took place in a hospital, clinic or other appropriate therapeutic institution. Nevertheless, it was held, Article 5(1)(e) does not make any requirement as to the actual manner in which detention is effected, for example, as to treatment or environment. Gostin regards this approach as "disappointing". He argues that:

". . . if the government is to deprive a person of liberty not on the grounds of dangerous behaviour but because of the person's need for treatment, then it must be incumbent upon [it] to provide a minimally adequate standard of treatment so that a person's mental health does not deteriorate, but can actually improve" (*Mental Health Services: Law and Practice* (Shaw & Sons, 1986), paragraph 20.29).

4. Conjugal rights

10–34   The existing authority on the subject suggests that mental patients do not have a right under the Convention to conjugal relations. In *X and Y v. Switzerland* (1979) D.R. 13, the Commission found against two prisoners who had been denied such facilities, holding that restrictions were necessary "for the prevention of disorder or crime". This was also the decision in the more recent cases of *ELH and PBH v. U.K.* (1997) 25 E.H.R.R. C.D. 158.

It is surely conceivable, however, that if a similar case were brought in respect of a psychiatric institution, it would succeed: the normal punitive considerations, by which a prison might seek to justify its policy, would be absent in such a case; and it could be argued that conjugal relations might help to preserve a patient's marriage and thereby improve his or her prognosis. A general prohibition might easily be held to contravene Article 12, which preserves the right to marry and to found a family. Though different considerations might be supportable in special hospitals, there could be difficulties even there, for not every restricted patient represents a serious and continuous threat.

Though Article 12 is confined to formalised heterosexual relationships, Article 8 will extend to common-law marriages, long-term cohabitations and maybe even homosexual relationships.

5. Mail

10–35   In *Y v. U.K.* (1977) 10 D.R. 37, a Broadmoor patient complained that he had been forbidden to send a telegram to his mother concerning his appeal. The Commission decided that there had been no material interference with Article 8 — which, alongside private and family life, also preserves the right to respect for correspondence — because he had not been prevented from sending a letter and had, in any event, been able to deliver his message to his mother in person when she visited him two days later.

The MHA 1983 contains certain provisions permitting the interception, and in some cases the withholding, of detained patients' mail, both incoming and outgoing (MHA 1983, s.134). The subject is also covered in the Code of Practice (paragraph 24.15) and is the only area in which the Mental Health Act Commission possesses direct, as opposed to delegated, authority (MHA1983, section 121(7)). That authority permits the MHAC to review decisions by the managers of special hospitals to withhold the correspondence of detained patients, and in some cases to order its release. Between July 1, 1995 and March 31, 1997, the MHAC received nine such requests and granted two (*Seventh Biennial Report, 1995–1997*, pp. 91/2).

It is likely that section 134 complies with Article 8. It will probably also be justified under Article 10 which, though it safeguards the right to freedom of expression and to receive and impart information and ideas without interference by public authority, also permits (at para. (2)) such restrictions as are necessary in a democratic society in the interests of, *inter alia*, public safety, for the protection of health or morals or for the protection of the reputation or rights of others.

E. MENTAL HEALTH REVIEW TRIBUNALS

10–36　As MHRTs have the power, *inter alia*, to discharge patients from detention under MHA 1983, it is not surprising that several aspects of their work have been subjected to scrutiny under the Convention. As we shall see, it is unlikely that that scrutiny has come to an end.

1. The regularity of review

10–37　Every patient who is detained under sections 2, 3, 7 and 37 of the MHA 1983, together, in some circumstances, with the "nearest relative" of an unrestricted patient, is entitled to apply to the MHRT for release at least once in every period of detention (MHA 1983, ss.66(1) and (2) and 70). As the maximum period of detention is initially six months, followed by a further period of six months and then 12 months at a time, this right of appeal will accrue at least annually. It is not thought that such a position would infringe the Convention.

However, in a somewhat esoteric exception in MHA 1983, patients who had been continuously detained as "imbeciles" under section 6 of the Mental Deficiency Act 1913 — which operated until 1959 — were permitted to apply to the MHRT only every *two* years. This state of affairs probably *does* breach the Convention. Thankfully, it will not arise very often, though it seems that a patient detained under the 1913 Act finally obtained her discharge as recently as 1993.

10–38　More recently, the Commission was required to adjudicate in the case of *Pauline Lines v. U.K.* [1997] E.H.R.L.R. 297. In 1961, the applicant had been a patient in a psychiatric hospital when she assaulted and seriously injured a fellow patient. She was subsequently detained by warrant under the Mental Health Act 1959, which, following the introduction of MHA 1983, had the effect of a restriction order without limit of time. She was conditionally discharged and then recalled to hospital several times between 1970 and 1992. On July 21, 1992, she was admitted to hospital under section 3 of the MHA 1983. Although there was a dispute as to her right to do so, she applied to an MHRT, which refused to order her discharge. On July 30, 1993, the Home Secretary granted a conditional discharge, but Ms Lines subsequently attempted suicide and was re-admitted to hospital under MHA 1983, s.3. On December 3, 1993, she was recalled under MHA 1983, s.42(3) on the ground that her condition had not sufficiently improved. Her case was again referred to the MHRT, which again declined to order discharge, ruling that she continued to present a danger to herself and to the public. On March 14, 1995, the Home Secretary discharged the applicant into a group home, and she subsequently complained to the Commission of a violation of Article 5(4).

Ms Lines argued, first, that it had taken too long to stage a review of her detention on July 21, 1992 and again on July 27, 1993; and secondly, that she had not been permitted to apply to the MHRT during her detention under MHA 1983, s.3, between July 27 and December 3, 1993. For its part, the U.K. government acknowledged that the applicant had not been permitted to appeal against her section 3 admissions, but argued that this prohibition was in fact intended to facilitate her early release. It suggested that MHA 1983, s.3, had been used to allow health professionals to retain control over her treatment in a way which formal recall would have precluded. The Commission held that the complaint concerning the applicant's detention between July 21, 1992 and July 8, 1993 had been lodged outside the strict six-month time-limit and was therefore inadmissible. In respect of the applicant's detention from July 27, 1993, however, the Commission held that the application raised serious issues under Article 5(4) — the right of a detained person to take proceedings by which the lawfulness of his detention shall be decided speedily by a court — and would therefore be admissible.

2. Delay

10–39 A constant theme of complaints by detained patients, particularly restricted patients, is the length of time taken for their applications to come before an MHRT.

In *Barclay-Maguire v. U.K.* (App. No. 9117/80; decision as to admissibility, December 9, 1981 (case withdrawn)) the Commission held that a delay of 18 weeks in this regard contravened the right to have the lawfulness of detention decided speedily by a court in accordance with Article 5(4). In seeking a friendly settlement, the U.K. government had suggested a period of 13 weeks as a reasonable target. A subsequent amendment to the MHRT Rules (S.I. 1983 No. 942) sought to control excessive delay. It provides that "the [mental health review] tribunal may give such directions as it thinks fit to ensure the speedy and just determination of the application" (Rule 13).

A number of more recent cases concern this or a similar point. In *Van der Leer v. Netherlands* (1990) Series A, No. 170–A; 12 E.H.R.R. 567 the Court held that a delay of five months in arranging a hearing was "excessive", while in *Koendjbihaire v. Netherlands* (1990) Series A, No. 185–B; 13 E.H.R.R. 820 it described a wait of four months as "unreasonable". (In the latter case, however, the Court drew a distinction between the urgency to be expected in the processing of appeals against an *initial* detention and that which will be appropriate for subsequent reviews.)

10–40 An even more rigorous standard was applied in *E v. Norway* (1990) Series A, No. 181–A; 17 E.H.R.R. 30, where a psychiatric patient's application to the Oslo city court had been made on August 3, 1988 and heard on 7 September. Though judgment was given on September 27, one day less than eight weeks after proceedings had begun, the Court held that this was not a "speedy determination" and that there had, therefore, been a breach of Article 5(4).

In the United Kingdom, the Mental Health Act Commission has recently reported that delays of as much as 12 weeks have been encountered in arranging tribunals for unrestricted patients. The delay is often longer for restricted patients, especially those in the special hospitals, and it seems that many patients detained under MHA 1983, s.3, are now discharged well before they have access to a MHRT (*Seventh Biennial Report, 1995–1997*, para. 3.1.4). The perils of this state of affairs for the U.K. government are evident from the following case.

10–41 In *Joseph Roux v. U.K.* (see paragraph 10–18, above) the applicant's third ground of complaint was that the time taken for his case to be put before the MHRT following his recall was greater than that permitted under the Convention. The U.K. government argued as follows:

(i) The case was referred to an MHRT within the one month prescribed by MHA 1983, s.75(1)(a);

(ii) The applicant was told of the reasons for his recall immediately upon his recall to hospital and his solicitors were informed of those reasons immediately they asked for them;

(iii) The MHRT hearing had been set for the first date when both a judge and the RMO were available — November 18, 1994;

(iv) On that date the hearing had been adjourned to December 16, 1994, when the applicant received his conditional discharge;

(v) The lawfulness of the applicant's continued detention was therefore determined "speedily" within Article 5(4).

Notwithstanding these arguments, the Commission unanimously held that the application "raises complex and serious issues under the Convention which require determination on their merits", and would be admissible.

It seems, therefore, that the procedure — rather more than the law — which governs the scheduling of MHRT hearings will be compatible with the Convention only once any delay has been reduced to something consistent with the Strasbourg decisions. In this regard there have recently been introduced the Mental Health Review Tribunal (Amendment) Rules 1998 (S.I. 1998 No. 1189) which require that the recall of a restricted patient be referred to the MHRT within a month and that a hearing take place within a further eight weeks.

3. Legal Aid

10–42 Though once a keenly disputed topic, the funding of adequate legal representation for detained patients would now seem to be an established feature of U.K. law. As we shall see, however, it is debatable whether the cover guaranteed by the legal aid system is as comprehensive as the Convention demands.

When, in November 1981, the Conservative government of the day introduced into the House of Lords the Bill which subsequently became the Mental Health (Amendment) Act 1982, the Opposition twice unsuccessfully sought to insert into it a clause extending legal aid to MHRTs (H.L. Debates, Vol. 427, col. 891). Shortly afterwards, the government had to face a claim brought by Mr Collins, a Broadmoor patient detained under an unrestricted hospital order (*Collins v. U.K.* (App. No. 9729/82 (withdrawn))). Because at that time legal aid would only cover the giving of initial advice and not formal representation, his solicitor had refused to appear for him at a forthcoming MHRT hearing. This situation was made the more acute because Mr Collins had been denied access to a psychiatric report which his RMO had prepared for the tribunal, and could not therefore be aware of the legal case which he would have to meet. Mr Collins alleged a violation of Article 5(4) — in that he had been denied the opportunity to take proceedings by which the lawfulness of his detention might be decided — and the Commission declared his complaint admissible. On December 1, 1992, however, the government announced that the existing Assistance By Way Of Representation ("ABWOR") legal aid scheme would be extended to cover full tribunal representation, and Mr Collins withdrew his complaint. Had he been compelled to continue, it is likely that he would have succeeded.

10–43   In any case, both the Court and the Commission have often stressed that effective legal representation is a key component of the "special procedural guarantees" which will be required in mental health cases (*Winterwerp v. Netherlands*, above, paragraphs 60–61, 101–102; *X v. Belgium* (1984) 3 D.R. 13). Larry Gostin concludes:

> "These cases suggest that where a patient has expressed clearly a desire to be represented, and he is prevented from being represented either because the tribunal does not ensure that someone is appointed and/or he cannot afford representation, a claim under Article 5(4) . . . conceivably could arise" (*Mental Health Services: Law and Practice* (Shaw & Sons, 1986), paragraph 18.21).

10–44   But does the Convention require more even than this? In *Megyeri v. Germany* (1992) Series A, No. 237–A; 15 E.H.R.R. 584 a psychiatric patient complained that he had not been represented by a lawyer at proceedings reviewing his detention. Though he conceded that he had not in fact requested a lawyer, the Court nevertheless found that Article 5(4) had been violated. It said:

> "[W]here a person is confined in a psychiatric institution on the ground of the commission of acts which constituted criminal offences but for which he could not be held responsible on account of mental illness, he should — unless there are special circumstances — receive legal assistance in subsequent proceedings relating to his detention. The importance of what is at stake for him — personal liberty — taken together with the very nature of the affliction — diminished mental capacity — compels this conclusion".

Thus, it may not be sufficient simply to provide legal aid to all MHRT applicants. Very many patients are detained under the MHA 1983 because they have behaved in a way which, in other circumstances, would have been deemed criminal. It may now be necessary to ensure that they are each represented by a lawyer, and any patient who is not, and whose detention is upheld, may — whether or not he actually wanted to be represented — be able to seek redress for a violation of the Convention. Such a state of affairs would have implications, not only for the MHRT, which would have to arrange such representation, but also for the Legal Aid Board which, even in the absence of an application from the patient himself, would have to fund it.

4. The burden of proof

10–45 In order for a patient to be detained under MHA 1983, it is incumbent upon those who wish to detain him to establish that he then fulfils the relevant statutory criteria (sections 2(1), 3(2) *et al.*). However, where a patient seeks his discharge from valid detention, the burden will shift to him. He must show, not that the admission criteria are no longer made out, but that he now satisfies different — *discharge* — criteria. An MHRT need only order discharge if it satisfied, in the case of a patient detained for treatment (under section 3).

"(i) that he is not then suffering from mental illness, psychopathic disorder, severe mental impairment or mental impairment or from any of those forms of disorder of a nature or degree which makes it appropriate for him to be detained in a hospital for medical treatment; or

(ii) that it is not necessary for the health or safety of the patient or for the protection of others that he should receive such treatment" (MHA1983, s.72(1)(b)).

On occasions, therefore an MHRT will refuse to discharge a patient simply because there is doubt as to whether he continues to suffer from a mental disorder. Though the matter has yet to be tested at Strasbourg, it would seem that in order to ensure compliance with the Convention it will be necessary to re-allocate the statutory burden of proof so as to compel those seeking to prevent discharge to demonstrate that the admission criteria still obtain.

5. Deferred discharge

10–46 Even though it may find that he is not then suffering from mental disorder of a nature or degree sufficient to warrant continued detention, an MHRT may defer the discharge of an unrestricted patient until a future date (MHA 1983, s.72(3)). It is likely that, under the conditions expressed in *Winterwerp* (see paragraph 10–07, above), such a practice would constitute deprivation of liberty without objective medical evidence to the effect that the detained person was then a person of unsound mind, and that it would therefore violate Article 5 of the Convention.

With regard to a restricted patient, an MHRT may defer an order for discharge (MHA 1983, s.73(7)), but only where it has first come to the conclusion that his condition is not such as to require that he continue to be liable to be detained in hospital (MHA 1983, s.73(2)). The tribunal has no power to *order* that suitable arrangements be made, though it is permitted to subpoena witnesses to explain why they have not (Mental Health Review Tribunal Rules S.I. 1983 No. 942, Rule 14). It is now clear that this position is not compatible with the Convention.

(a) The case of Stanley Johnson v. U.K.

10–47 This recent case ([1998] H.R.C.D., Vol. IX, No. 1, p. 41; [1997] E.H.R.L.R. 105–108) exhibits many of the features of those which preceded it.

In 1984, Mr Johnson, who was found to be suffering from mental illness, was convicted of assault occasioning actual bodily harm. He was made the subject of a hospital order and a restriction order without limit of time under sections 37 and 41 of the MHA 1983. He was admitted to a special hospital and subsequently made a number of MHRT applications. On June 15, 1989, his RMO informed an MHRT that Mr Johnson was now free of any symptoms of mental illness, but that he was not fit for immediate discharge because he needed rehabilitation. However, reports from two independent psychiatrists recommended that he be released to hostel accommodation immediately. The tribunal accepted that Mr Johnson was no longer suffering from mental illness, but found that if he was released without rehabilitation he might become ill again. It therefore granted him a conditional discharge which it deferred until suitable accomodation could be found. Mr Johnson's next MHRT application was heard on May 9, 1990, when, as no suitable accomodation had yet become available, the result was precisely the same. In September 1990, Mr Johnson commenced trial leave at a less secure hospital, but he was returned to the special hospital in October following an assault on a fellow patient. On April 9, 1991, his discharge was again deferred by the tribunal until accomodation could be found. On January 12, 1993, he came before the MHRT for the final time. In a written report, his RMO conceded that Mr Johnson had not suffered from mental illness since 1987, did not require to be detained in hospital and was unlikely to accept any conditions upon his discharge. He was released several days later.

Mr Johnson argued that his detention between 1989, when his RMO had first confirmed that he no longer suffered from mental illness, and 1993 violated Article 5(1) and Article 5(4) (and also Articles 3 and 8), because:

(i) The factor which determined the imposition of indefinite detention — mental illness — was no longer present during that period;

(ii) The possibility that his illness would recur was not sufficient to justify his continued detention;

(iii) The imposition of conditions for his discharge constituted a deprivation of his liberty.

For its part, the U.K. government argued:

(i) The Convention had not been violated, because successive tribunals were trying to discharge Mr Johnson, not detain him. The fact that he was not released until 1993 was in part due to his own lack of co-operation;

(ii) The conditional discharge procedure had been recommended by experts in order to provide for Mr Johnson's successful rehabilitation into the community;

(iii) That procedure, and the deferral of release until suitable accommodation was available, fell within the state's margin of appreciation;

(iv) To interpret the Convention in any other way would reduce the availability and effectiveness of the "care in the community" principle and would result in unacceptable risks to the public;

(v) The conditions imposed upon Mr Johnson did not amount to a deprivation of liberty sufficient to contravene Article 5(1)(e).

10–48   On June 25, 1996, the Commission expressed the opinion, by 15 votes to one, that there had been a violation of Article 5(1). It stated:

> "[T]he Commission considers that the tribunal in June 1989 was entitled to proceed with caution and with due regard to the interests of the community. It could, in principle, have been justified in deciding that a phased discharge was called for even if this entailed some period of deferment of the applicant's release. However, such a release cannot be indefinitely deferred . . . The margin of appreciation afforded to the national authorities, allowing a deferral of the discharge of a person who has been found to have recovered from mental illness, must be correspondingly limited and must be subject to strict procedural safeguards to ensure the discharge of such a person at the earliest opportunity." ([1996] E.H.R.L.R. 89).

The Commission found that the necessary safeguards were lacking, in that the MHRT had made no detailed examination of the availability of accommodation and there was no certainty as to whether, or when, a suitable hostel place would be found. The tribunal had no power to prevent discharge arrangements from being unduly delayed, and if they were, Mr Johnson would have to wait another 12 months for a further MHRT hearing. Thus, there was a violation of the Convention from the date of the first MHRT decision (June 15, 1989).

The Court concurred with the Commission and awarded Mr Johnson non-pecuniary damages of £10,000 together with costs of £25,000 and expenses. No change has subsequently been made to the powers governing the deferred discharge of restricted — or, for that matter, unrestricted — patients, and the United Kingdom would therefore appear still to be in violation of the Convention in this regard.

F. COMPULSORY COMMUNITY TREATMENT

10–49   The response of the U.K. government to a series of tragedies, such as the killing of Jonathan Zito by a former mental patient, Christopher Clunis (see Ritchie J., Dick D. and Lingham R., *The Report of the Inquiry into the Care and Treatment of Christopher Clunis* (HMSO, 1994)), was to create the statutory power of Supervised Discharge. This was contained in the Mental Health (Patients in the Community) Act 1995, which, with effect from April 1, 1996, inserted new sections into MHA 1983 (sections 25A–J). It was supplemented by a NHS Guidance Note (*Guidance on Supervised Discharge (After-Care Under Supervision) and Related Provisions*, HSG (96)11), which in fact constituted a formal Code of Practice to the new provisions. Though the new power enabled newly-discharged patients to be required to reside at a particular place and to comply with arrangements for their treatment, education and training (MHA 1983, s.25D(4)), it did not permit medical treatment to be imposed upon them against their will (see generally, Hewitt D., *The Supervised Discharge of Former Mental Patients*, [1997] *Litigation* 149 and 197). Despite, or — more likely — because of, that fact, the question of forcing former patients to accept medication in the community has excited considerable comment, much of which has assumed that such a course would violate the Convention. On the basis of established authorities, that would seem not to be so.

In *W v. Sweden* (1988) 59 D.R. 158, the applicant had been required to accept psychiatric medication as an outpatient as a condition of her discharge from hospital. The Commission ruled her complaint inadmissible. Article 5 did not apply:

> "The provisional discharge was accompanied by an order that the applicant should take medicine and present herself for medical control at the hospital once every second week. The Commission considers that these conditions attached to the provisional discharge were not so severe that the applicant's situation after her provisional discharge could be characterised as a deprivation of liberty" (at 160).

10–50 This case had been preceded by a similar one in which a challenge was brought under Article 8. In *L v. Sweden* (1986) 8 E.H.R.R. 269 the Commission, holding a complaint inadmissible, stated:

> "It is clear from the decision of the [Swedish] Discharge Council that the reason for not discharging the applicant permanently was that there were reasons to believe that the applicant would stop taking her medication if permanently discharged and that that would lead to a deterioration of her health. The decision thus pursued the aim of protecting the Applicant's health, which is an aim permissible under Article 8(2) . . . The Commission finds that the decision not to discharge the applicant permanently was 'necessary in a democratic society' for the protection of her health. It follows that this aspect of the application is manifestly ill-founded".

In its submission to a House of Commons committee, the Law Society's Mental Health and Disability Sub-Committee concluded from this decision; "Thus, measures to allow leave from detention on condition that the patient continues to accept medical treatment do not violate Article 8, so long as they comply with Article 8(2)" (*House of Commons Health Committee Report on Community Supervision Orders*, Vol. II, p. 8, Memorandum, para. 8).

10–51 It is difficult to disagree with the finding of one recent enquiry, that "The case-law would . . . appear to demonstrate that provisional discharge (or a community treatment order, in U.K. parlance), with a requirement to take medication to prevent a deterioration of health, is most unlikely to fall foul of Convention obligations" (Blom-Cooper L., Hally H. and Murphy, E., *The*

Falling Shadow: One Patient's Mental Health Care 1978–1993, (Duckworth, 1995)). The same is even more likely to be true of the present arrangements for "after-care under supervision", which, as we have seen, contain no more draconian a sanction in default than the power to "review" those arrangements and "consider" whether it might be appropriate for the patient to be detained in hospital once more (MHA 1983, s.25E(4)(a) and (b)).

G. GENERAL PROCEDURAL GUARANTEES

10–52 In *Winterwerp v. Netherlands* (see paragraph 10–07, above), compulsory detention in hospital had the effect under Dutch law of divesting the applicant of the capacity to administer property. In such circumstances, the Court held, there was a determination of civil rights within the meaning of Article 6(1) — the entitlement to a fair and public hearing within a reasonable time by an independent and impartial tribunal:

> "Whatever the justification for depriving a person of unsound mind of the capacity to administer his property, the guarantees laid down in Article 6(1) must be respected. While mental illness may render legitimate certain limitations upon the exercise of the 'right to a court', it cannot warrant the total absence of that right as embodied in Article 6(1) . . ." (at paragraph 75).

Article 6 will, of course, apply both to the Court of Protection and to MHRTs. However, the Court has held that Article 6 guarantees do not have to be satisfied at every level of the decision-making process, so long as there exists a tribunal of full jurisdiction which *does* satisfy those requirements (*Bryan v. U.K.* (1995) Series A, No. 335–A; 21 E.H.R.R. 342). Therefore, the possibility that certain of its decisions may subsequently be subjected to judicial review will to some degree shield the MHRT from the provisions of Article 6. (As to the procedural requirements of Article 6, see generally paragraph 2–65 and following).

The Article 6 "guarantees", of course, include the right to a "fair and public hearing". This, it has been held, implies a right to an oral hearing at the trial court level (*Fredin v. Sweden (No. 2)*, Series A, No. 283–A, para. 21). However, though the Court of Protection entertains approximately 6,000 receivership applications each year, together with a further 10,000 applications for the registration of enduring powers of attorney, those cases in which oral representations are heard number no more than one in a 100 (Public Trust Office, private correspondence with author, March 10, 1998). It is perhaps of some significance that the relevant rules (Court of Protection Rules, S.I. 1994 No. 346) contain no provision which expressly entitles applicants to a hearing, much less one which is conducted in public: rule 7 expressly states: "Except where these rules otherwise provide, any function may be exercised — (a) without fixing an appointment for a hearing"; while rule 10(1) allows the hearing of a receivership application to be dispensed with where the Court "considers that the application can properly be dealt with without a hearing".

Rule 56 contains at least one form of remedy in so far as it provides that: "(1) Any person who is aggrieved by a decision of the court not made on a hearing . . . may apply to the court . . . to have the decision reviewed by the court." However, there is nothing to *require* the court to carry out such a review, and even if it does decide to do so, there is nothing to require any review to take the form of an oral hearing. Furthermore, the Government's recent Green Paper on changes to the Court of Protection contained nothing which would entitle incapacitated adults to the sort of hearing envisaged by Article 6(1) (*Who Decides? Making decisions on Behalf of Mentally Incapacitated Adults*, Cmnd 3803, December 1997). It is at least conceivable, therefore, that the United Kingdom is in breach of the Convention in this regard, and that it is likely to remain so for some considerable time.

The Court of Protection Rules require not a public hearing, but one in chambers (rule 39(1)). Our understanding of the phrase "in chambers" may, of course, alter in the light of the sentiments recently expressed by Lord Woolf M.R. (*Hodgson v. Imperial Tobacco Limited* [1995] 1 W.L.R. 1056). In any case, the exclusion of the public from court hearings has been justified under the Convention where it is necessary for the "protection of the private life of the parties" (*X v. U.K.* (1980) 2 Digest 456 and *X v. Norway* (1970) 35 C.D. 37; *Genoum v. France* (1990) 66 D.R. 181 and *Imberechts v. Belgium* (1991) 69 D.R. 312). As the Court of Protection regularly dabbles its fingers in the stuff, not only of individuals' psychological lives, but also of their fiscal affairs, it is likely that it will be permitted to continue to do so in private, notwithstanding the other requirements of Article 6.

H. REMEDIES UNDER THE ACT

10–53 For mental patients, the most significant features of the limited right to redress under the Act are likely to be the following:

(i) the power of certain courts to make a declaration of incompatibility with Convention rights (section 4(2) and (4));

(ii) the continuing validity even of incompatible provisions (sections 3(2) and 6);

(iii) the protection for public authorities whose acts contravene Convention rights merely because they were performed in accordance with incompatible primary legislation (section 6(2));

(iv) the restriction upon available remedies, especially damages (sections 8 and 9(3)).

It is not possible to anticipate each and every conflict between MHA 1983 and the Convention. However, two brief examples may help to illustrate the possibilities for judicial challenge and the limits which have been placed thereupon.

Example 1

10–54   Ms Z, who is detained under section 3 of MHA 1983, applies to the MHRT for her discharge. Her RMO believes that she still suffers from mental illness; the independent psychiatrist whom Ms Z has commissioned says that she does not.

In weighing the two conflicting opinions, the MHRT will have a second difficult choice to make (see paragraph 10–45, above): whether to ignore the onus imposed by section 72 and discharge Ms Z or dismiss her application and violate the Convention. Faced with unambiguous primary legislation, the MHRT is likely to eschew the former course and find, instead, that the applicant has failed to discharge her statutory burden of proof.

Such a decision is permissible within the discretion afforded to the MHRT, which will therefore enjoy the protection of section 6(2) and, under section 9(3), immunity from liability for damages in any case. Though it finds itself unable to reconcile section 72 with the Convention, the tribunal will lack the status to strike it down or even make a declaration of incompatibility (section 4(2) and (4)). It may, of course, choose to "state a case" for further determination (MHA 1983, s.78(8)), and Ms Z may seek to compel it to do so by way of an appeal (RSC, Ord. 56). Alternatively, Ms Z might make application for a judicial review of the tribunal's decision (RSC 1965, Ord. 53). These are the only courses by which proceedings for a violation of the Convention may be brought against a court (section 9(1)), though either will propel the matter into the High Court, where the question of incompatibility may be formally addressed.

Despite its relative seniority, however, and also despite the fact that section 8 permits any "court" to "grant such relief or remedy, or make such order, within its jurisdiction as it considers just and appropriate", the High Court may not order Ms Z's discharge from detention simply for a breach of the Convention. This is because the section 8 power applies only where the court finds that the relevant act — in this case, the failure to grant discharge — is "unlawful", as that term is defined in section 6(1). However, the act of a public authority — here, the MHRT — cannot be "unlawful" if "as the result of . . . primary legislation, the authority could not have acted differently" (section 6(2)(a)). The High Court, like the MHRT, is bound by section 72 of the MHA 1983 — and by the onus of proof which it imposes — even though it may demonstrably violate the Convention.

10–55   In a case where a violation of Convention rights did make the action of the MHRT or other public authority unlawful under section 6, a right to damages may exist under section 8. However, there are two important qualifications which may yet further affect a claimant's prospects for recovering compensation under the Act. First, section 9(3) prevents any such award of damages being made in respect of a "judicial act done in good faith", except to the extent required by Article 5(5) (*i.e.* the right to compensation for detention in violation of Article 5). If detention is affected by unlawful conduct of a tribunal or court in other ways (*e.g.* breach of Article 6 guarantees), damages will not be recoverable unless (in very rare cases) the applicant could prove bad faith. Secondly, it is not every court or tribunal which will have the power to award damages. Unless special provision is made by rules under section 7(11), courts and tribunals (such as MHRTs) which do not have general jurisdiction to award damages will not be able to do so under the Act. The High Court, of course, can award damages in judicial review proceedings (RSC 1965, Ord. 53, r.14).

Thus, even if the MHRT is found to have acted in breach of the Convention, Ms Z will be unable either to secure her liberty or recover damages. She may, of course, console herself in the knowledge that her efforts may have lightened the burden of succeeding generations of detained patients.

Of course, the absolute prohibition on damages will not apply to other, non-"court", public authorities, such as social services departments and hospital trusts. If such authorities act, or propose to act, in a manner which is incompatible with the Convention, then they may be subjected to the usual armoury of remedies, such as judicial review or habeas corpus (section 8(1)). In addition, those authorities may be compelled to make financial compensation to those who have been, or are likely to be, aggrieved.

Of course, the Act is intended to provide, not merely a sword, but also a shield. As is evident from the following example.

Example 2

10–56 Frank is a restricted patient who has been granted a conditional discharge. He refuses to comply with an order for his recall to hospital made under section 42(3) of the MHA 1983. He alleges that the Home Secretary has no evidence that he continues to suffer from mental illness. He is given shelter and material assistance by Mr Q, who is aware both of the recall order and of Frank's allegation. After Frank has been successfully retaken, Mr Q is charged with an offence under MHA 1983, s.128.

Because Frank refused to return to hospital, he may be treated as if he had absented himself from hospital without leave (MHA 1983, s.42(4)(b)). It is in such circumstances that he can be retaken (MHA 1983, s.18(1)) and that any attempts to give him succour will constitute a criminal offence (MHA 1983, s.128(3)). Mr Q might, of course, hope to plead that the circumstances of Frank's recall — in particular, the fact that it was apparently effected without evidence of his current mental state — place it in breach of Article 5 (*per Joseph Roux v. U.K.* — see paragraph 10–18, above), and that, under section 7(1)(b) of the Act, he therefore has a complete defence to the charge. Sadly, Mr Q is likely to be confounded, for such a defence is available only to a person who "is (or would be) a victim of the unlawful act" — *i.e.* recall by the Home Secretary. Given that the Act expressly adopts the definition of "victim" contained in Article 34 (see paragraph 2–15 and following, above), it is hard to see how Mr Q can be held so to have been aggrieved. However, it is likely that Mr Q will be able to rely on section 3, and require the (criminal) court to construe the MHA 1983 in a manner which is compatible with the Convention. If so, it is likely that the apparent incompatibility between the MHA 1983 and the Convention will afford him a defence to a charge under the MHA 1983, s.128(3) (see, for example: *R. v. Wicks* [1998] A.C. 92; *Boddington v. BTP* [1998] 2 All E.R. 203). Thus, the mere fact that he is not a "victim" of the apparently unlawful recall order will not prevent Mr Q raising the Convention issue in his defence.

I. CONCLUSION

10–57 Some comfort may be derived from the fact that certain aspects of mental health legislation — the power to detain in a place of safety, for example, and to impose "supervised discharge" in the community — do not appear to infringe the Convention. It is clear, however, that other practices are somewhat less compatible.

The Home Secretary's power to recall a conditionally-discharged restricted patient must now be fettered: with a requirement that he obtain objective medical evidence of persisting mental illness and with a speedy means of judicial challenge to recall. In the absence of such fetters, section 42(3) of the MHA 1983 will continue to violate Articles 5(1) and 5(4).

The discharge powers of the MHRT will also require amendment to ensure compatibility with the Convention. The burden of proof which MHA 1983, s.72(1), imposes upon a patient seeking his discharge should be reversed; and the power to defer discharge under section 72(3) confined to those unrestricted patients who can reliably be shown still to suffer from a mental disorder. With regard to restricted patients, the tribunal should be permitted absolutely to discharge a patient without the need for evidence that is not appropriate for him to remain liable to be recalled to hospital for further treatment; and some means should be introduced by which it might compel the performance of conditions imposed upon a discharge deferred under section 73(7).

10–58 There is also a number of omissions which will require a statutory remedy. Provisions should be introduced to compel the discharge of unrestricted patients where the statutory grounds for their admission no longer obtain, and of restricted patients whose psychiatric condition has demonstrably improved and whose application for discharge is supported by their RMO. Furthermore, any person should be given the statutory right to appoint a new nearest relative where physical, sexual or financial abuse have rendered the statutory holder of that post inappropriate.

With regard to the relevant subordinate legislation, it is to be hoped that the recent amendments to the rules governing MHRT procedure — at least in so far as they concern recalled restricted patients — will finally reduce the delay in fixing hearings for discharge applications. Similar measures in respect of unrestricted patients — and especially those detained under section 3 — would be welcomed even beyond Strasbourg. Furthermore, and in so far as the common law does not resolve the problem, the practice in the Court of Protection ought more fully to reflect the Convention right, not only to a hearing, but also to one which is both fair and public.

10–59 It is not only the courts, but also certain public authorities, which will be affected by the Convention: hospital trusts (or the respective special hospital authorities) may be susceptible to challenge if they attempt to restrict the conjugal rights of those whom they detain; while the Legal Aid Board may be obliged to extend assistance even to those who do not want, and who have not requested it.

These, at least, are the more likely consequences of giving effect to the Convention. What is certain is that other consequences will flow, in ways which cannot yet be foreseen and with a significance which it is impossible yet to conceive.

CHAPTER 11

Education

John Friel and Deborah Hay (Barristers, Goldsmith Building)

A. THE DEVELOPMENT OF EDUCATION RIGHTS

11–01 The development of education as a specialist area of practice is relatively recent. Until the early 1980s, although there were a few well-known cases, the extent of this body of law was extremely restricted. Educationalists largely applied their own interpretation without a view from the courts. Despite the late start, this is now an important area of law, in which essential human rights are considered.

In *Gateshead Union v. Durham County Council* [1918] 1 Ch. 146, the Court of Appeal held that a child's right to free education was enforceable. *Meade v. Haringey LBC* [1979] 1 W.L.R. 637 is a good example of the type of case that subsequently arose. That case concerned schools in Haringey closed by an industrial dispute. The parents sought an injunction to keep the schools open. The Court of Appeal held that there was a right for the individual to apply directly to enforce a duty to provide education.

11–02 Despite the dearth of litigation, the statutory provisions — particularly the Education Act 1944 — did give effect to individual rights in education. The right to free education for all children was established (section 8) with the standard of education being that suitable to age, aptitude and ability (section 8(2)). Local Education Authorities ("LEAs") were also required to have regard to children with special educational needs, and the 1944 Act (like its earlier predecessors) included specific provisions for children with special educational needs (at that time termed special educational treatment). Section 76 of the 1944 Act (which predates the Convention) itself provided for children to be educated in accordance with the wishes of parents, subject to the avoidance of any unreasonable public expenditure. The 1944 Act thus created rights in a manner which largely predicted the later Convention.

A major and continuing principle of the 1944 and subsequent Acts, however, was that the LEA had to make "efficient use of resources". Despite parents being given, on the face of it, an important right to have children educated in accordance with their wishes, this right was overridden by the claim that to do so would not be an efficient use of resources or would involve unreasonable public expenditure.

11–03 Parliament has continued to enact education legislation which has given increased rights to parents. The Education Act 1980 introduced the right of choice of school for parents (section 6), so that they were no longer at the mercy of the LEA allocation system. Children faced with expulsion were also given an appeal via their parent to a neutral body. The Education Act 1981 created a separate detailed body of legislation to protect children with special educational needs. The Education Reform Act 1988 improved the opportunities for parental involvement in schools, the independence of schools, and affirmed parental rights. The Education Acts 1993 and 1996 (largely a consolidatory Act) have both extended the concept of parental rights, which is matched with increasing parental involvement.

Nonetheless, the proviso of efficient use of resources and avoidance of unreasonable expenditure, which acts as a counterbalance to parental rights, continues to defeat parental choice. Indeed, in relation to choice of schools, it can properly be argued that the choice is illusionary. Good schools can only take a limited number of pupils, and parents will in any event be dependent on geographical area, religious practice and other entry criteria.

11–04 The courts in this country have accepted significant claims for individual rights. The attitude of the courts has, in general, been to apply the legislation in a way which develops positively the rights of the individual child. Parents were able to establish, through the Education Act 1981, the right to a detailed Statement of Special Educational Needs which accurately reflected the diagnosis of the child's needs and the provision to meet their needs (*R. v. Secretary of State for Education, ex p. E* [1992] F.L.R. 377). The right to sue negligent educationalists, education officers and psychologists was established by the House of Lords in *X (Minors) v. Bedfordshire County Council* [1995] 2 A.C. 633 (this is considered in the decision in *Phelps v. London Borough of Hillingdon*, November 4, 1998, CA). In *R. v. East Sussex County Council, ex p. Tandy* [1998] 2 W.L.R. 884, the House of Lords held that the duty to make arrangements for suitable education was a directly enforceable statutory duty owed to the individual, and which could not be fulfilled "unless the arrangements do in fact provide suitable education for each child". The development of domestic legislation and its interpretation by national courts has resulted in those education cases which have gone to Strasbourg involving very specific rather than wider issues.

11–05 The Education Act 1944 recognised the right of individuals to be educated at schools of their own religious background. Such schools were termed "voluntary maintained schools", and there continue to be a large number of such schools throughout the country. There are in addition a number of other schools maintained by individual charities. This diversity has been preserved throughout the education legislation, and is an accepted part of our society. This diversity appears to conform to the interpretation of Article 2 of the First Protocol, whose aims have been defined as:

"Safeguarding the possibility of pluralism in education, which possibility is essential to the preservation of the 'democratic society' as conceived by the Convention . . . The second sentence of Article 2 implies on the other hand that the state, in fulfilling the functions assumed by it in regard to education and teaching, must take care that information or knowledge included in the curriculum is conveyed in an objective, clinical and pluralistic manner. The State is forbidden to pursue an aim of indoctrination that might be considered as not respecting parent's religious and philosophical convictions. That is the limit that must not be exceeded" (*Kjeldsen, Busk Madsen and Pedersen v. Denmark* (1976) Series A, No. 23; 1 E.H.R.R. 711, a case concerning compulsory sex education).

The present legislation accordingly makes allowances for the maintenance of such schools, the employment of staff, and admission of children, who come from the appropriate religious background. The legislature has been careful to preserve minority rights, to foster development of the concept of parental rights, and parental involvement.

B. THE PARTICULAR RELEVANCE OF THE ACT TO EDUCATION

11–06   Article 2 of the First Protocol, provides:

"No person shall be denied the right to education. In the exercise of any functions which it assumes in relation to education and to teaching, the State shall respect the right of parents to ensure such education and teaching in conformity with their own religious and philosophical convictions."

This is to be contrasted with Education Act 1996, s.9, which re-enacts Education Act 1944, s.76, namely:

"In exercising or performing all their respective powers and duties under the Education Acts, the Secretary of State, Local Education Authorities and the funding authorities shall have regard to the general principle that pupils are educated in accordance with the wishes of their parents, so far as is compatible with the provision of efficient instruction and training and the avoidance of unreasonable public expenditure".

In addition, Education Act 1996, s.14, imposes upon the LEA a duty to secure efficient primary education, secondary education and further education. For those children who are out of school, through illness or otherwise, the duty is again to provide suitable education, which means efficient education suitable to his age, ability and aptitude and any special educational needs he may have.

11–07   The U.K. government entered a reservation to Article 2 of the First Protocol, stating that the second sentence of the Article is accepted only insofar as it is compatible with the provision of efficient instruction and training, and with the avoidance of unreasonable public expenditure. It is therefore highly unlikely that the introduction of the Convention right into English law will extend the present statutory provisions.

The House of Lords has made it clear that while effective and adequate provision for each child's education must be made irrespective of the LEA's resources, if there are two possibilities and one is cheaper, the LEA is entitled to chose the cheaper of the two options. In *R. v. East Sussex County Council, ex p. Tandy* (above) Lord Browne-Wilkinson stated, at 890:

> ". . . I should make it clear, as did Keene J. (first instance) and Staughton L.J. (in the Court of Appeal) in their judgments, that if there is more than one way of providing suitable education, the LEA would be entitled to have regard to its resources in choosing between different ways of providing suitable education".

Although this decision has given firm guidance on the rights of the child, and ensured that the duty to provide education cannot be watered down by reliance on resources, it falls far short of the provisions of Article 2 of the First Protocol, and of the jurisprudence of the Strasbourg authorities.

1. Respect for personal beliefs

11–08   It is with regard to parental belief and viewpoint that the Convention is likely to give rise to a number of issues. In *Campbell and Cosans v. U.K.* (1982) Series A, No. 48; 4 E.H.R.R. 293, the Court defined "philosophical conviction" as "those ideas based upon human knowledge and reasoning concerning the world, life, society, etc., which a person adopts and professes according to the dictates of his or her conscience".

Valsamis v. Greece, R.J.D. 1996–VI 2312; 24 E.H.R.R. 294 illustrates both the development of the Strasbourg jurisprudence, and its likely implications for domestic law. The parents and child were all Jehovah's Witnesses, theirs being a religion recognised by the state. A fundamental tenet of their religion was pacifism. As the religion of the state in schools in Greece was the Greek Orthodox Church, the parents applied for exemption from religious lessons, together with other events including national holiday celebrations and public processions, which involved military parades. Despite this request, the child was told to attend a school parade, which included a military parade. After the parents refused to allow their child to participate, the child was suspended from school for one day.

11–09   The Court held by seven votes to two that there had been no breach of Article 2 of the First Protocol by itself. This was largely because the Greek State itself did recognise the particular religious belief, although the Court expressed surprise at the actions taken in this case. The Court unanimously held, however, that there had been a breach of Article 13 taken together with Article 2 of the First Protocol, and with Article 9. This was because it was not possible to apply to the Greek administrative courts for judicial review (as in English law), because the event had taken place and there was no judicial remedy available.

The Court reiterated that Article 2 of the First Protocol, enjoined the State to respect the parent's convictions, be they religious or philosophical, throughout the entire State education programme.

"That duty is broad in extent as it applies not only to the content of education and the manner of its provision but also to the performance of all the 'functions' assumed by the State. The word 'respect' means more than 'acknowledge' or 'take into account'. In addition to primarily negative undertakings applies some positive obligation on the part of the State." (paragraph 27)

In addition, the Court referred to its earlier judgment in *Young, James & Webster v. United Kingdom* (1981) Series A, No. 44; 4 E.H.R.R. 38, para. 64, where it was held that,

"Although individual interests should on occasion be subordinated to those of a group, democracy does not simply mean that the views of the majority must always prevail: a balance must be achieved which ensures the fair and proper treatment of minorities and avoids any abuse of a dominant position."

The Court went on to point out that the setting and planning of the curricula were, in principle within the competence of the contracting states. The state must not pursue a form of indoctrination that might be regarded as not respecting parent's religious and philosophical convictions (*Trimble & Cosans v. U.K.* [1982] 4 E.H.R.R. 293).

2. The tension between education rights and efficient use of resources

11–10 The essential tension between Convention law and its restricted application in the United Kingdom, by reason of the Reservation and the concurrent provisions of national law, means that any extension of rights (particularly parental rights) is likely to be limited. In the present system, parental choice of school may effectively be limited for various reasons. This is illustrated by children with special educational needs being placed in secular, nominally Christian, schools. The curriculum taught, for example, to an orthodox Jewish child is a modern secular non-religious curriculum, admitting of other faiths, and ignoring the particular religious views and practices of the parents. (Problems of this type are explored in relation to children with special needs, concerning tribunal decisions, in "Education Public Law and the Individual" (1998) Vol. 1, p. 13, Rabinowicz and Shaffer, *Religious Education and Special Educational Needs*.) The LEA will normally not maintain voluntary special religious schools and, as it maintains secular special schools, it will seek to place the child in an LEA secular special school, unless it can be established in a child's case that education in a religious and cultural background is a special educational need. The parents will need to establish that the child requires such education for its mental wellbeing and/or adequate educational development to qualify as a special educational need (*R. v. Secretary of State for Education ex p. E* [1996] F.L.R. 312). Unless that can be established, it is clear that the authority, in complying with statute (*i.e.* the efficient use of resources test), must place the child within its LEA maintained school.

As an indication of the considerable effect which the Reservation may have, the Government has only now agreed to fund Muslim schools and Seventh Day Adventist schools, after a lengthy and controversial refusal to do so.

3. Effective remedies

11–11 The Act is likely to give rise to more rather than less domestic litigation; in education, litigation has in any event been growing at a steady rate. In addition, the failure to implement the Convention fully in English law is likely to increase the number of cases in this area going to Strasbourg from this country. Given that Article 2 of the First Protocol deals specifically with and is the key to rights in education, the Reservation may be unwise. (See *Cohen v. U.K.* [1996] 21 E.H.R.R. C.D. 105).

In *Valsamis*, above, the Court observed that the Applicants were entitled to have a remedy to raise their allegations in domestic law (paragraph 48).

> "It must accordingly be asked whether Greece's legal order afforded the Applicants an effective remedy within the meaning of Article 13 of the Convention that enabled them to put forward their arguable complaints and obtain redress. . . . [T]he Applicants could not obtain a judicial decision that the disciplinary measure of suspension from school was unlawful. Such a decision, however is a pre-requisite for submitting a claim for compensation."

11–12 Many remedies in education law involve a reconsideration of a decision by way of judicial review, or by way of a statutory appeal. The reconsideration of a case, or a fresh decision, does not involve compensation. Further, the decision in *X (Minors) v. Bedfordshire CC* [1995] 2 A.C. 633 affects any claim for breach of statutory duty in education law. The House of Lords allowed cases in professional negligence to be brought against negligent educational psychologists, teaching staff and education officers in cases of children with special educational needs; a cause of action was not available for a failure to provide any education in breach of statutory duty (see *Phelps v. London Borough of Hillingdon*, above). Although the Act now enables awards of damages to be made against LEAs for conduct which is incompatible with Convention rights (see sections 6 and 8), this entitlement is dependant upon the content of those rights (*i.e.* as limited by the Reservation), and is subject to the binding effect of domestic primary legislation (see section 6(2)). An LEA that is giving effect to domestic legislation (such as the efficient use of resources test) is unlikely to be caught by section 6(1).

C. PARTICULAR ISSUES

11–13 There have been numerous statutory reforms which have taken place since 1979. There is yet another Education Bill passing through Parliament, and a Green Paper to deal with children with special educational needs has been the subject of recent consultation. Statutory provision has altered considerably in a relatively short space of time, due to pro-active and well-organised lobbying.

Moreover, the courts have only recently started looking at the issues on a frequent basis. Education remains an unpredictable area.

The requirement under section 2(1), for any court or tribunal to take Strasbourg case law into account where relevant, is likely further to complicate matters. The Strasbourg authorities have certainly developed their jurisprudence in this field, but there are often important dissenting judgments. Indeed the dissenting judgment in *Valsamis v. Greece*, R.J.D. 1996–VI 2312; 24 E.H.R.R. 294 by two judges is a good example. There are nonetheless distinct trends that have substantial implications in education law.

Under the Act, Convention rights may be relevant in a number of ways within the existing practical framework. Children and parents enforce their rights by:

- Judicial review against all public bodies;

- Statutory appeals which largely involve parental choice of school or special educational needs;

- Actions in negligence, largely against local authorities, but often against individual schools;

- Actions in relation to independent schools either in negligence, or in breach of contract·

- Complaints to the local Government Commissioner.

Convention rights may arise in each of these contexts.

1. Whose right is it?

11–14 It is important to remember that the actual right is that of the individual child, although the parent exercises it. The Education Acts speak clearly about parental rights, but they are not so clear in relation to duties owed to the child. A parent, of course, gives expression to the child's rights through making choices in respect of and on behalf of the child. The courts have recognised the right of the child to receive education, from *Gateshead Union v. Durham C.C.* [1918] 1 Ch. 146 through to the decision in *R. v. East Sussex County Council, ex p. Tandy* [1998] 2 W.L.R. 884. A duty to provide education is actually owed to the individual child, as is the duty to provide special educational provision to match special educational needs (*R. v. Secretary of State for Education and Science ex p. E* [1992] F.L.R. 377).

The Education Acts do not recognise the best interests and/or welfare of the child as being a paramount test (as enshrined in family law under the Children Act 1989). Efforts to import this test into the statutory framework were defeated in the House of Lords during the passage of the Education Act 1993, and have not been resurrected (although widely promoted). While the Code of Practice on special educational needs, issued under the Education Act 1993, does refer to ascertaining the child's wishes, it is relatively woolly and does not give any clear guidance. Although the Special Educational Needs Tribunal in practice does look at the interests of the child on the date of the hearing, in accordance with current needs and provision, the tribunal is clearly restricted by the statutory framework, and cannot avoid the efficient use of resources test (*Richardson, White, Solihull & Others v. London Borough of Ealing* [1998] E.L.R. 319).

The Strasbourg authorities have taken a different approach. In *Johnston v. Ireland* (1986) Series A, No. 112; 9 E.H.R.R. 203, where the daughter of a couple was illegitimate on account of the father's inability to obtain a divorce in respect of a prior marriage, the daughter's claim of a violation of Article 8 succeeded, but the parents' claim was rejected. Family members may be protected because of the child's rights, although they themselves have no claim, as in *Berrehab v. The Netherlands* (1988) Series A, No. 138; 11 E.H.R.R. 322.

In its developing jurisprudence, the Strasbourg authorities will also use non-binding instruments, such as the U.N. Convention on the Rights of the Child, to look at the child's case applying the best interests of the child approach. Article 3(1) of the UN Convention of the Rights of a Child did not create a new right, but establishes a principle of interpretation that, in all actions concerning children, the best interests of the child shall be considered a primary consideration. In *Nielsen v. Denmark* (1988) Series A, No. 144; 11 E.H.R.R. 174 the Court agreed that the rights of the holder of parental authority cannot be unlimited and do not involve any restricted power of decision over the child and its personal conditions This implies that as a child becomes older and matures the entitlement to participate in the enjoyment of their rights is strengthened.

11–15 The acceptance by the Strasbourg authorities of the test of the best interests of the child, and the recognition of the developing capacity of the child, is in direct conflict with the approach of English education law. In *S v. Special Needs Tribunal* [1995] 1 W.L.R. 1637 Latham J. held that a young person had no right to an individual appeal against his Statement of Special Educational Needs. This was despite the fact that the statute defined a child as a person under the age of 19, and thus included an adult of full capacity. The Court of Appeal ([1996] 1 W.L.R. 382), while appreciating the fact that a person over the age of majority could not appeal, confirmed the decision. It is difficult to see how the decision in these cases can stand if there is a direct conflict between the legislation and the interests of the child. The normal rule is that a child of sufficient age and capacity, although only a minor, is able to bring proceedings. Indeed in *Hendricks v. Netherlands* (1982) 29 D.R. 5, followed in *Hokkanen v. Finland* (1994) Series A, No. 299–A; 19 E.H.R.R. 139, the Commission observed that, where there were conflicts between the interests of the child and one of its parents which "can only be resolved to the disadvantage of one of them, the interests of the child under Article 8(2) prevail" (paragraphs 55–58).

Where parental control and the state restricts the child's right to exercise independence the incorporation of the Convention is likely to produce substantial changes. Van Bueren, in her article "Protecting Children's Rights in Europe — A Test Case Strategy" [1996] E.H.R.L.R. 171, points out that the recent trends of the Strasbourg authorities have been to take greater account of children's rights, and to give considerable prominence to the U.N. Convention.

2. Special educational needs tribunals/school choice appeals

11–16 Apart from actions for negligence concerning personal injuries to children, the most frequent areas in which parents become involved in litigation about their children's education are the exercise of rights in respect of a choice of school, and making sure their children (where they have special educational needs) are given adequate care and appropriate special educational provision. Although the present Education Bill will effect changes to the procedures in respect of the last two areas, there are no real changes of substance, and issues will remain in relation to Article 6.

Special Educational Needs Tribunals consist of two lay persons (with expertise) and a lawyer chairman. The Lord Chancellor's Department appoints the lawyer. The tribunal, in consultation with the DfE, appoints the lay members, with the focus on those with experience of local government or special educational needs, preferably both. However, often those appointed within the education system have worked for LEAs themselves. The criteria may restrict appointments, by eliminating those who have great expertise in the area of special educational needs, but who do not have sufficiently direct experience of local government.

11–17   The method of appointment used for the admissions and exclusions appeal panels examination may be open to criticism under Article 6, in view of the jurisprudence of the Strasbourg authorities. In *Findlay v. United Kingdom*, R.J.D. 1997–I 263; 24 E.H.R.R. 20 the constitution of a court martial was found to be in breach of Article 6 for failing to secure that the court was independent and impartial, due to the fact that a single officer brought the charges, chose the members of the court, selected the prosecuting and defending officers, and was responsible for ensuring that witnesses attended. In *Mantovanelli v. France* (1997) 24 E.H.R.R. 370 the Strasbourg authorities applied the procedural guarantees under Article 6 in relation to the preparation of an expert report for use by an administrative court. Given the central role played by the LEA or Governing Body in the appointment of persons to the appeal committees, the very high likelihood of an association with the LEA, and the reality that continued appointment is dependent on the LEA, the method of appointment and composition of the panel is questionable.

The approach of the Court, in using the test of the best interests of the child, and in developing the concept of the child as having individual rights and the ability to express them, comes into conflict with the statutory provisions governing the rights of appeal. Under the Education Acts, it is the parent who has a right of appeal. The decisions of the High Court and the Court of Appeal in *S (A Minor) v. The Special Educational Needs Tribunal* [1995] 1 W.L.R. 1657; [1996] 1 W.L.R. 382 will need to be reviewed, representing as they do a considerable restriction on the development and exercise of children's rights.

3. Independent schools

11–18   Whilst independent schools are not public authorities for the purposes of the Act, the interpretation of any legislation may have implications for such schools, and state responsibility may be engaged under the Convention in respect of activities within independent schools. In *Costello-Roberts v. U.K.* (1993) Series A, No. 247; 19 E.H.R.R. 192, the Court relied on several factors in finding that the use of corporal punishment in an independent school could engage state responsibility: the extent of the obligation to secure the right to education under Article 2 of the First Protocol, and its application to internal disciplinary systems; the co-existence of state and private schools; and the non-delegable nature of Convention obligations by states. Bullying within the independent school sector may also raise the issue of state responsibilities (see further *A v. U.K.*, T.L.R. September 23, 1998 for a further interpretation of the State's duty to intervene in preventing a child suffering harm which amounted to a breach of Article 3 of the Convention. The Act may also have some indirect impact, by encouraging greater examination under domestic law of aspects of independent education affecting pupils and their parents).

CHAPTER 12

Social Security

Robin C.A. White* (Professor of Law, Leicester University; Deputy Social Security Commissioner)

A. BACKGROUND

12-01 The Convention is largely, though not exclusively, about civil and political rights. It is rooted in the traditions of Western liberal democracies, which have regarded civil and political rights as first order rights from which other human rights protections will flow. There is a separate European Social Charter, to which the United Kingdom is a party. Article 12 of the Charter contains a right to social security, and Article 13 contains a right to social and medical assistance. There is also a series of Council of Europe Conventions as set out at paragraph 12-42 dealing with issues of social security, but all these conventions operate as international agreements and have not been incorporated into U.K. law. There is also a body of E.C. law affecting social security entitlements, which deals both with the co-ordination of national social security systems and with equal treatment between men and women in entitlements to social security benefits.

Furthermore, the administration and adjudication of benefits are frequently seen as administrative acts and so belong more to the realm of public law than private law. The casual observer might therefore assume that the introduction of the Convention into U.K. law would have little potential impact upon the administration and adjudication of social security benefits. That is not so. The interpretation and development of Convention rights over 45 years have resulted in areas of both procedural and substantive protection applicable to social security benefits.

12-02 It is now clear beyond doubt that the judicial determination of claims to benefit in the various tribunals with jurisdiction to determine appeals must comply with the due process requirements of Article 6 (right to a fair trial). The same must also be true of appeals to the Social Security Commissioners. On the substantive level, there are possibilities of using a number of Articles to challenge aspects of the existing social security system. The Convention cannot, however, be used to argue for the creation of new benefits (see, for example, *X v. Germany* (1967) 23 C.D. 10).

* The views expressed are purely personal.

Though the Convention has had effect for the United Kingdom since 1953, the Act will add a further dimension to domestic social security administration and adjudication. It will require both policy-makers and decision-makers to have regard to the impact of Convention rights as a matter of national law, in addition to rights accruing under E.C. law. For legal advisers, there will be additions to the strategies which may be adopted in seeking to advance the position of clients before national tribunals. In some cases, E.C. law will be preferred, but in other circumstances (particularly where nationals of countries other than those in the European Union and the European Economic Area are concerned), Convention rights will be the vehicle for a challenge to established policy and practice.

B. INTERPRETATION AND APPROACH

1. The scheme in the Act

12–03   Section 6 of the Act makes it unlawful for a public authority to act in a way which is incompatible with a Convention right (see generally paragraph 1–46 and following). There can be no doubt that the Department of Social Security, the Benefits Agency, the Central Adjudication Services, and the tribunals which hear appeals by claimants are all public authorities. They will all need to consider whether they are acting in a manner compatible with Convention rights.

Any person who is a victim, as defined by Convention case-law of the Commission and Court, is entitled to bring proceedings (including judicial review proceedings) against the public authority which it is claimed has acted in a manner incompatible with Convention rights, and in such proceedings may rely on Convention rights (section 7(1)). The proceedings are to be brought before the "appropriate court or tribunal" (section 7(1)(a)), which is to be determined by rules (section 7(2)). Where the alleged violation of Convention rights touches on entitlement to a social security benefit, then it is likely that the rules to be made will give jurisdiction to a social security appeal tribunal, a disability appeal tribunal, or a medical appeal tribunal. If the matter is taken on appeal to the Social Security Commissioners, they too will have to deal with Convention rights. That said, certain matters involving the Convention (see below) would seem to lend themselves more appropriately to judicial review.

2. Who is a victim?

12–04   The Strasbourg authorities have taken a broad view of the circumstances in which a person will be a victim of an alleged violation of Convention rights (see generally paragraph 2–15 and following). Because the contracting parties to the Convention undertake under Article 1 "to secure to everyone within their jurisdiction the rights and freedoms" defined in the Convention, there is no requirement of nationality or residence. In addition to those who are victims in fact, the Commission has admitted claims from those who are "indirect" victims. So, for example, claims of violations of the right to life in Article 2 have (understandably and logically) been accepted by relatives of those who have died. The Commission has also admitted claims on behalf of children made by their parents or guardians. Both approaches are of relevance in the social security context, since many claims are made on behalf of children, and the Secretary of State enjoys a wide power to appoint persons to act for those who are unable to handle their own affairs or have died (section 5(1)(g), Social Security Administration Act 1992, and regulation 33 of the Social Security (Claims and Payments) Regulations (S.I. 1987, No 1968), as amended). Potential victims have also been granted standing to complain where a legislative provision was likely to affect them, or where an impending deportation could, if implemented, result in a violation of Convention rights. But the Strasbourg authorities have set their face against a general public interest claim:

". . . the applicant cannot complain as a representative for people in general, because the Convention does not permit such an 'actio popularis'. The Commission is only required to examine the applicant's complaints that he himself was a victim of a violation." (*X Association v. Sweden*, (1982) 28 D.R. 204, 206.)

3. Determining the appropriate forum

12–05   Issues of standing are likely to be significant in determining the appropriate forum for complaint in the national legal order. Suppose, for example, that a recipient of a social security benefit wished to argue that the formal structures of social security appeal tribunals breached the requirements of Article 6. Is such a claim best dealt with by the tribunal itself, or by an application to the High Court for judicial review? It is certainly arguable that the latter venue is more appropriate for this type of claim. But a different type of problematic bias might best be taken on appeal to the Social Security Commissioner, as where, for example, a claimant might complain that a medical member of a tribunal who had seen the claimant as a patient at some time in the past did not recuse themselves at an appeal hearing. This would currently be regarded as a breach of natural justice which would result in any decision of the tribunal being set aside by the Commissioner, but could also amount to a breach of Article 6.

4. The Strasbourg approach to interpretation

12–06   In considering any question arising in connection with a Convention right the decision-maker must, under section 2, have regard to Convention case-law. Furthermore, section 3 of the Act requires both primary and secondary legislation to be read, as far as possible, in a manner which gives effect to Convention rights. A glance at the Convention rights set out in Schedule 1 to the Act is enough to indicate that Convention rights are not drafted in the detailed manner of United Kingdom primary and secondary legislation. The rights have also been considered and interpreted over several decades by the Strasbourg authorities (see generally paragraph 2–28 and following; and see Jacobs, F. and White, R. *The European Convention on Human Rights* (2nd ed., Oxford: Clarendon Press, 1996), Chap. 3; and Harris, D. O'Boyle, M. and Warbrick, C., *Law of the European Convention on Human Rights,* (London: Butterworths, 1995), pp. 5–19.)

The Strasbourg approach to interpretation has particular importance in the field of social security for two main reasons. First, the application of the due process guarantees in Article 6 depends upon a dynamic interpretation of the text of that Article, and the extent to which decision-making involving social security benefits falls within the determination of civil rights and obligations. Secondly, the substantive protections of the Convention in this area depend largely on the development of the protection of family and private life under Article 8 and the protection of property rights in Article 1 of the First Protocol often when read in conjunction with the prohibition on discrimination in Article 14.

C. PROCEDURAL GUARANTEES

1. Does the resolution of social security disputes involve the determination of civil rights and obligations?

12–07 The guarantee of due process in Article 6 is central to the system of protection in the Convention. Article 6 is an omnibus provision which contains a blueprint for what constitutes a fair trial.

The first question which must be addressed is whether decision-making in social security constitutes "the determination of . . . civil rights and obligations" for these purposes. Answering this question requires detailed discussion of a line of Convention cases. The formulation in Article 6 excludes the initial decisions of adjudication officers since the Article contemplates a situation in which there is a dispute. This is clearer from the French text, which refers to "contestations". It cannot be said that there is a dispute when what is at issue is an initial determination of entitlement to benefit (see *Feldbrugge v. The Netherlands* (1986) Series A, No. 99; 8 E.H.R.R. 425, para. 25); the vast majority of such decisions are not the subject of appeal to a tribunal. But what of the tribunals? Are they determining civil rights and obligations? The essential question is whether Article 6 covers only private law rights to the exclusion of public law matters: a distinction which is much more formal in continental systems of law than in the United Kingdom's common law system.

12–08 It was not long before the issue came before the Court in *Ringeisen v. Austria* (1971) Series A, No. 13; 1 E.H.R.R. 455, after the majority of the Commission had concluded that Article 6 should be construed restrictively as including only those proceedings which are typical of relations between private individuals and as excluding those proceedings in which the citizen is confronted by those who exercise public authority. The Court took a different view. Article 6 covers all proceedings the result of which is decisive for the private rights and obligations of individuals, and neither the character of the legislation (whether, for example civil, commercial or administrative) nor that of the authority with jurisdiction over the dispute (whether, for example, court, tribunal or administrative body) are of great consequence. Since the decision in this case, the Court has adopted a liberal interpretation of the concept of civil rights and obligations.

Several cases have considered whether social security disputes involve the determination of civil rights and obligations.

(a) The Feldbrugge case

12–09   *Feldbrugge v. The Netherlands* (1986) Series A, No. 99; 8 E.H.R.R. 425 concerned a dispute over entitlement to a sickness allowance in The Netherlands. Mrs Feldbrugge had been registered as unemployed, but then ceased to register because she had become ill and did not consider herself fit for work. The Occupational Association (the body responsible for administering sickness allowance in The Netherlands) arranged for her to be medically examined by their consulting doctor, who concluded that she was fit for work. The sickness allowance was stopped. The claimant appealed to the Appeals Board and the President of the Appeals Board arranged for her to be seen by a gynaecologist who was one of the permanent medical experts attached to the Appeals Board. That doctor examined her and gave her an opportunity to comment. The doctor consulted another gynaecologist and two general practitioners (one of whom was the claimant's GP). They all agreed with the decision that the claimant was fit for work, but the permanent medical expert considered that an orthopaedic specialist should also be consulted. An orthopaedic surgeon examined the claimant who was again given an opportunity to comment. The three practitioners consulted by the gynaecologist were also consulted following this examination. The orthopaedic surgeon concluded in the light of all the medical findings that the claimant was fit for work in accordance with the initial contested decision. The President of the Appeals Board then ruled against the claimant, who filed an objection which raised the matter before the Appeals Board itself, which found the objection lacking in substance. An appeal to the Central Appeals Board was unsuccessful. Mrs Feldbrugge complained that she had not had a fair trial before the President of the Appeals Board in violation of Article 6(1). The Court had to face squarely the issue of whether the adjudication of the claimant's dispute was a matter concerning her civil rights and obligations. The Court weighed the features of the case which suggested that the matter was one of public law against the features which suggested that it was one of private law. The public law nature of the legislation on sickness allowances, the compulsory nature of insurance against illness, and the assumption by the State of responsibility for social protection had to be weighed against the personal and economic nature of the asserted right, its connection with the contract of employment, and affinities with insurance under the ordinary law. After weighing these interests, the Court ruled by a majority of ten votes to seven, that, taken together, the private law aspects of the sickness allowance scheme were "predominant" and the adjudication of Mrs Feldbrugge's claim was therefore covered by Article 6(1).

(b) The Deumeland case

12–10   *Deumeland v. Germany* (1986) Series A, No. 100; 8 E.H.R.R. 448, decided on the same day as the *Feldbrugge* case, concerned industrial injury pensions in Germany. The proceedings in Germany were extraordinarily protracted, and this was the substance of the applicant's complaint. Gerhard Deumeland had in January 1970 slipped on a snow-covered pavement as he was coming home from an appointment with an ear nose and throat specialist whom he had consulted on leaving his workplace. He died in March 1970, and his widow claimed a widow's supplementary pension on the basis that the death of Gerhard had been the consequence of an industrial accident. The first set of proceedings before the Berlin Social Security Court of Appeal lasted from June 1970 to December 1972. The outcome of these proceedings was a decision that the accident in question was neither an industrial accident nor an accident on the way to or from work. There was accordingly no entitlement to a widow's supplementary pension. Mrs Deumeland appealed to the Berlin Social Security Court of Appeal, where the first set of proceedings lasted from November 1972 to September 1973. These were unsuccessful. An appeal on a point of law was pursued before the Bundessozialgericht (Federal Social Security Court) which lasted from October 1973 to May 1975. In the course of these proceedings, the claimant challenged a judge for bias accusing him of delaying the proceedings. That challenge was not successful and the appeal decision was taken by a panel which included the unsuccessfully challenged judge. The decision of the Bundessozialgericht was to set aside the decision of the Berlin Social Security Court of Appeal and to remit the case for a fresh hearing.

The second set of proceedings before the Berlin Social Security Court of Appeal lasted from May 1975 to March 1979. In December 1976 during the course of these proceedings, Mrs Deumeland died and her son, Klaus, was allowed to continue the proceedings. The outcome was a decision that the claim to the widow's pension was unfounded. Klaus Deumeland sought to appeal to the Bundessozialgericht. Leave to appeal was eventually refused. Leave for a further appeal to the Bundesverfassungsgericht (Federal Constitutional Court) was refused by that Court, and a subsequent application to the Berlin Social Security Court of Appeal by Klaus Deumeland to have the proceedings re-opened was not only unsuccessful but also resulted in his being fined 800 German marks for bringing vexatious proceedings. For reasons which are very similar to those in the *Feldbrugge* case, the Court, by a majority of nine votes to eight, concluded that the proceedings of which the applicant complained had been concerned with the determination of civil rights and obligations.

(c) Limited to insurance based benefits?

12–11 These two cases had involved benefits which flowed from an insurance principle, and this feature might be seen as critical in drawing a distinction between social insurance and social assistance. The latter term refers to those benefits which fall outside the sphere of social insurance and involve the State stepping in to provide benefits for those who have no entitlement to insurance-based benefits, or whose entitlement is such that their income is below subsistence level. The distinction came before the Court in *Salesi v. Italy* (1993) Series A, No. 257–E. Enrica Salesi had claimed a monthly disability allowance in the Lazio social security department, which had been refused. In February 1986, she brought proceedings against the Minister of the Interior before the *pretore del lavoro* (magistrates' court exercising their labour jurisdiction) in Rome seeking payment of the benefit. The Minister appealed against the decision of the pretore awarding the benefit, and the Rome District Court dismissed the appeal in May 1989. A subsequent appeal to the Court of Cassation was also dismissed. Even though the claimant was ultimately the winning party, she complained to the Commission alleging a violation of Article 6(1) by reason of the length of the proceedings.

The Court re-affirmed its decisions in *Feldbrugge* and *Deumeland* noting,

". . . the development in the law that was initiated by those judgments and the principle of equality of treatment warrant taking the view that today the general rule is that Article 6(1) does apply in the field of social insurance."

The Court went on,

"In the present case, however, the question arises in connection with welfare assistance and not . . . social insurance. Certainly there are differences between the two, but they cannot be regarded as fundamental at the present stage of development of social security law. This justifies following, in relation to the entitlement to welfare allowances, the opinion which emerges from [the judgments in *Feldbrugge* and *Deumeland*] as regards the classification of the right to social insurance benefits, namely that State intervention is not sufficient to establish that Article 6(1) is inapplicable" (para. 19).

12–12   The Court concluded that there were no convincing reasons for distinguishing welfare benefits from the rights to social insurance benefits asserted in the earlier cases. The decision of the Court may be criticised for its poverty of reasoning, but nevertheless remains an authority for the extension of Article 6(1) to all disputes concerning social security benefits.

Schuler-Zgraggen v. Switzerland (1993) Series A, No. 263; 16 E.H.R.R. 405 concerned a claim to an invalidity pension. The claimant had been employed and paid contributions into the federal invalidity insurance scheme. She contracted open pulmonary tuberculosis and applied for an invalidity pension. The Compensation Office awarded a half pension, which was subsequently increased to a full pension. In 1984 the applicant gave birth to a son. In 1985 she was required to undergo a medical examination by doctors appointed by the Invalidity Insurance Board. This resulted in a decision to terminate the award of the invalidity pension. The claimant appealed to the relevant Appeals Board. In the course of these proceedings she was refused a sight of her medical file which had been seen by the Appeals Board. The Board subsequently dismissed her appeal. The claimant lodged an appeal against this decision with the Federal Insurance Court, whose decision was to remit the case to the Compensation Office, whose reconsideration did not result in the award of a pension. The Court followed its earlier decisions in concluding that the proceedings in issue were concerned with the determination of civil rights and obligations. The Court also followed the decision in *Salesi* in virtually identical language:

". . . the development in the law that was initiated by those judgments [in *Feldbrugge* and *Deumeland*] and the principle of equality of treatment warrant taking the view that today the general rule is that Article 6(1) does apply in the field of social insurance, including even welfare assistance" (para. 46).

Schouten and Meldrum v. The Netherlands (1994) Series A, No. 304; 19 E.H.R.R. 432 concerned the liability of persons in similar positions to employers to pay contributions to an occupational association in respect of physiotherapists who worked for them. This was the first case in which the Court had been called upon to determine an issue involving the payment of contributions under a social security scheme as distinct from disputes concerning entitlement to benefits. The Court took the view that the approach adopted in *Feldbrugge* and *Deumeland* was appropriate in the case of liability to pay contributions. The public law and private law aspects of the arrangements should be weighed to see whether one or the other were predominant. Using exactly the same factors as had been in issue in *Feldbrugge*, the Court concluded that the private law aspects were predominant and that Article 6(1) applied.

(d) The current position

12–13   These cases establish beyond a peradventure that adjudication of social security disputes involves the determination of civil rights and obligations to which the procedural guarantees of Article 6(1) apply. They have been followed even in cases where the pensions of those employed in the public service were involved (*Lombardo v. Italy* (1992) Series A, No. 249–B; 21 E.H.R.R. 188; and *Massa v. Italy* (1993) Series A, No. 265–B; 18 E.H.R.R. 266). It follows that the rules on what constitutes a fair trial apply to the proceedings of tribunals, the Commissioners and the courts when dealing with social security questions.

2. What is a fair trial under Article 6(1)?

12–14   The Strasbourg authorities have indicated that Article 6(1) demands not only an overall requirement of a fair hearing but also the presence of specific features in order for there to be a fair trial. The overall requirement has been summarised as follows,

> "The effect of Article 6(1) is, *inter alia,* to place the "tribunal" under a duty to conduct a proper examination of the submissions, arguments and evidence adduced by the parties, without prejudice to its assessment of whether they are relevant to its decision." (*Kraska v. Switzerland* [1993] Series A, No. 254–B; 18 E.H.R.R. 188, para. 30.)

It is important that the general requirements for a fair trial are appreciated, since they continue to be developed in specific circumstances by the Strasbourg authorities. Certain of the requirements are of a general nature, whereas others are more specifically stated in Article 6.

(a) General requirements

12–15   Four features inherent in the concept of a fair trial appear to have flowed from this general notion of a fair trial.

The first and perhaps most important is the concept of *égalité des armes*, which translates inelegantly into English as "equality of arms". In English law, it is an aspect of the requirement of natural justice. It requires that each party has a broadly equal opportunity to present a case in circumstances which do not place one of the parties as a substantial disadvantage as regards the opposing party (see *Dombo Beheer BV v. The Netherlands* (1993) Series A, No. 274–A; 18 E.H.R.R. 213, para. 33).

Secondly, there must be a judicial process, which requires each side to have the opportunity to have knowledge of and comment on the observations filed or evidence adduced by the opposing party (*Ruiz-Mateos v. Spain* (1993) Series A, No. 262; 16 E.H.R.R. 505, para. 63). Non-disclosure of material by one side to the other is likely to give rise to violations of this feature of a fair trial, as might issues of the circumstances in which evidence was acquired. In the *Feldbrugge* case, the applicant complained that she had not had a proper opportunity to present her case. The Court found that the proceedings before the President of the Appeals Board "were not attended to a sufficient degree, by one of the principal guarantees of a judicial procedure" (para. 44) in that, although the applicant had been afforded the opportunity to comment on her condition during the medical examinations, she was neither able to present oral argument nor to file written pleadings before the President of the Appeals Board; nor was she able to consult the two reports of the consultants and to formulate objections to them.

12–16 Thirdly, there is a requirement for a reasoned decision, which is regarded as implicit in the notion of a fair trial. The level of reasoning need not be detailed. If a court gives reasons, then the requirement for a reasoned decision is *prima facie* met, but a decision which on its face shows that it was made on a basis not open to the judge cannot be said to be a reasoned decision (see *De Moor v. Belgium* (1994) Series A, No. 292–A; 18 E.H.R.R. 372). The introduction of short-form decisions in tribunals is unlikely to fall foul of this provision, since a party is entitled to a full written decision on application within 21 days of the day on which the decision notice was notified to the parties. Decisions of the Commissioners are always given in full, except a decision made with the consent of the parties to set aside a tribunal decision and remit the case for a rehearing by the tribunal.

The final issue is whether a trial can be fair if there is no right of appearance in person. The law here remains in a state of development and the Court has yet to pronounce in detail on this in civil cases, but the Commission has held that in some cases a fair trial is only possible in the presence of the parties. An example would be a case where the personal character and manner of life of a party are directly relevant to the formation of the court's opinion on the point at issue. Custody disputes over children might be such cases (See *X v. Sweden* (1958–9) 2 Y.B. 354, 370).

12–17 Presence may need to be distinguished from participation. In the *Schuler-Zgraggen* case, the applicant had not availed herself of the opportunity to request a hearing, but nevertheless complained that the proceedings were unfair because the Federal Insurance Court had not ordered a hearing of its own motion. The Court accepted the arguments of the Government that purely written proceedings did not in the circumstances of this case prejudice the interests of the litigant. It was accepted that a written procedure would offer advantages of efficiency and speed which might be jeopardised if oral hearings became the rule. The Court concluded,

"The Court reiterates that the public character of court hearings constitutes a fundamental principle enshrined in Article 6(1). Admittedly, neither the letter nor the spirit of this provision prevents a person from waiving of his own free will, either expressly or tacitly, the entitlement to have his case heard in public, but any such waiver must be made in an unequivocal manner and must not run counter to any important public interest" (para. 58).

These comments have relevance both for paper hearings before tribunals and for procedure before the Commissioners (see below).

(b) Requirements specifically mentioned in Article 6(1)

12–18 There are four specific features of a fair trial to be found on the face of Article 6: trial before "an independent and impartial tribunal established by law"; a qualified requirement for a public hearing; public pronouncement of judgment; and judgment within a reasonable time. These are considered generally at paragraph 2–74 and following.

3. The application of Article 6(1) to appeal proceedings

12–19 Article 6 does not require contracting states to have a system of appeals from decisions at first instance in civil cases (*De Cubber v. Belgium* (1984) Series A, No. 86; 7 E.H.R.R. 236, para. 32), but if the state does provide a system of appeals, it too must comply with the guarantees to be found in Article 6(1) (*Fedje v. Sweden* (1991) Series A, No. 212–C; 17 E.H.R.R. 14, para. 32). It follows that a defect at first instance might be corrected at the appellate stage of the proceedings. Where there is an appeal, the requirement to exhaust domestic remedies before a complaint can be made under the Convention means that it must be used, and it will then be the totality of the domestic proceedings which is considered by the Commission and Court. It will always be necessary to look at the character of the appellate proceedings to determine the extent to which they are able to remedy any deficiency at first instance. For example, the shortcoming identified in the *Feldbrugge* case could not be remedied on appeal, because the nature of the appeal was restricted to four very narrow grounds, none of which offered the opportunity for the applicant to participate to the extent required by Article 6 in the proceedings which determined her dispute.

A fair appeal is unlikely to be able to correct a defect arising from a structural problem in the first instance court or tribunal which results in its not being an independent and impartial tribunal (*De Cubber v. Belgium* (1984) Series A, No. 86; 7 E.H.R.R. 236, para. 33). There is a suggestion that the quashing by an appeal court on the specific ground that the first instance court or tribunal was not independent and impartial might have cured the defect, but this could amount to recognition that there was no right to a court in the particular instance. This is a right which the Court has read in to Article 6.

4. The right to a court

12–20 The Court has recognised that Article 6 must contain a right of access to a court for the determination of a particular issue (see generally paragraphs

2–72—2–73; *Golder v. United Kingdom* (1975) Series A, No. 18; 1 E.H.R.R.
524; also *Keegan v. Ireland* (1994) Series A, No. 290; 18 E.H.R.R. 342). The
right might even include a right to some sort of representation in order to make
the right effective, where "such assistance proves indispensable for an effective
access to court" (*Airey v. Ireland* (1979) Series A, No. 32; 2 E.H.R.R. 305, para.
26).

The introduction of short-form decision notices in tribunals has a
consequential effect on appeals to the Commissioner, which might be argued to
operate as a denial of the opportunity of appeal. Where a short-form decision is
issued by a tribunal, a party has 21 days in which to request a full written
decision, in which case one must be prepared (regulation 23(3C) of the Social
Security (Adjudication) Regulations (S.I. 1995 No. 1801) as amended). There is
no provision in the legislation for extension of that time, though the President of
the Independent Tribunal Service has expressed the hope that the discretion to
write a full decision will be exercised sympathetically (President's Circular No.
2, para. 16). The time limit for appealing to the Commissioner is three months
beginning with the date when a copy of the full statement of the tribunal's
decision was given or sent to the applicant (regulation 3 of the Adjudication
Regulations 1995). But Regulation 24 provides that any application for leave to
appeal to the Commissioner shall . . . have annexed to it a copy of the full
statement of the tribunal's decision." The effect of these provisions taken
together is that parties who have only received a short-form decision may be
precluded from making application for leave to appeal to the Commissioner if
they have not exercised their right to request a full statement of reasons within
the 21-day time limit. The question, accordingly, is whether the need to seek a
full statement of reasons sufficiently close in time to the hearing to ensure that
the chairman is able to write up the decision of the tribunal outweighs the
interests of a party seeking to appeal in enjoying the full period allowed by the
regulations for making that application. In other words, are the circumstances in
which someone might lose any opportunity to appeal justified, or is there a
denial of a right to a court? There appears to be no discretion to allow the
application for leave to appeal where it does not have annexed to it a copy of
the full statement of the tribunal's decision. The relationship between the two
provisions is certain to be the subject of case-law from the Commissioners, but
might also raise issues under Article 6.

5. Application to English social security procedure

12–21 As noted above, initial decision-making by adjudication officers on
claims to benefit does not fall within Article 6, though appeals to tribunals
within the Independent Tribunal Service structure and onward appeals to the
Social Security Commissioners do attract the due process guarantees of the
Article.

Procedure before the tribunals is unlikely to raise any difficulties under Article
6. It is just possible that an issue could arise from the introduction of paper
hearings. However, paper hearings will only arise where the claimant does not
ask for an oral hearing. There might be an arguable violation of Article 6 where
a paper hearing proceeds in a case which is for particular reasons more
appropriate for an oral hearing. A good example might be a case involving a

substantial overpayment of benefit where the claimant maintained that disclosure had taken place. Here issues of credibility are raised which can best be resolved by seeing and hearing the claimant. It will also be important to ensure that the requirements implicit in "*égalité des armes*" are always met; this will mean that the claimant always has the opportunity to respond to the case put forward on behalf of the adjudication officer, and that new evidence is not put before the tribunal at such a late stage that the claimant has no opportunity to comment upon it.

12–22 It is possible that a claimant might take issue with the composition of a tribunal in which there is no guarantee that, for example, a medical member of a disability appeal tribunal is not also a member of the panel of examining medical practitioners used by the Benefits Agency. There would clearly be a breach of natural justice (and a violation of Article 6(1)) if a doctor who had examined a claimant sat on the tribunal which heard the appeal, but it is clear that this would be obvious from the papers and that the normal expectation is that the doctor would not sit. The requirement that an applicant must exhaust all domestic remedies before complaining of a breach of the Convention would mean that an applicant would need to pursue an appeal to the Social Security Commissioner, who would, in the face of the circumstances described, have no hesitation in setting the tribunal decision aside for breach of natural justice and remitting the case for an oral hearing before a properly constituted tribunal. In this way, a remedy would be provided for the breach of Article 6 in the domestic courts. However, where the objection related to the *possibility* of inclusion of a doctor on the tribunal who also conducted examinations for the Benefits Agency, it is difficult to see how a remedy could be provided by the tribunal. A claimant might find little sympathy given to the argument that he or she has no complaint about the impartiality of the specific individuals on the tribunal, but objects that a medical member might also be an examining medical practitioner for the Benefits Agency. There is something slightly odd about a tribunal holding in the abstract that it is not an independent and impartial tribunal. For this reason, it may well be that judicial review would be the proper route to raise such a challenge, although to be a victim for the purposes of the Convention, the claimant would of necessity also have an appeal to the tribunal.

The tribunals are structured in such a way that claimants can appear in person. It is unlikely that the significant evidence that represented claimants do better than unrepresented ones (Genn, H. and Genn, Y., *The Effectiveness of Representation at Tribunals* (London: Lord Chancellor's Department, 1989)) would persuade the Court that proceedings before the tribunals were such that the state was obliged to provide legal assistance.

12–23 Perhaps the tribunals are most at risk of complaints that judgment has not been given in a reasonable time, particularly where an appeal to the Commissioner has resulted in the setting aside of the decision and the remission of the case for a fresh hearing. Current delays both before the tribunals and the Commissioners can result in four or more years passing before a final decision is made. This could in a simple case be regarded as excessive under Article 6, particularly if the case had lain dormant for some time either in the

Commissioner's office after the papers were ready for determination, or within the Independent Tribunal Service awaiting listing for the rehearing. The existence of backlogs and excessive workloads on the judiciary are not accepted as justifications for unreasonable delays. The Court has consistently stated that the contracting states must organise their judicial systems in such a way that their tribunals can meet the requirement to give judgment within a reasonable time (see, for example, *Massa v. Italy* (1993) Series A, No. 265–B; 18 E.H.R.R. 266, para. 28).

Two particular aspects of procedure before the Commissioner might be problematic. The first relates to entitlement to an oral hearing. The Social Security Commissioner Procedure Regulations (S.I. 1987 No. 214, as amended) provide that, where a request is made for an oral hearing, the Commissioner "shall grant the request unless, after considering all the circumstances of the case and the reasons put forward in the request for the hearing, he is satisfied that the application or appeal can properly be determined without a hearing" (regulation 15(2)). Most appeals to the Commissioner are determined without an oral hearing, but many applications for an oral hearing are refused. The standard reasons simply repeat the words of the regulation. Many appeals are pursued before the Commissioner without the benefit of expert advice and assistance. Since the appeal to the Commissioner lies only on a point of law, the underlying argument is that an unrepresented appellant is unlikely to be able in oral argument to advance the position established by the exchange of written arguments between adjudication officer and appellant. There is a provision that a Commissioner can of his or her own motion direct an oral hearing (regulation 15(3)). It would be conceivable that an appellant might try to argue that the presumption in the regulation has effectively been reversed in practice, and that an oral hearing will only be granted if the appellant can show reasons why there should be one.

12–24 A second exposure under Article 6 could result from argument that legal assistance is necessary to enable a person to pursue an appeal effectively before the Commissioner. The arguments that would be advanced by the appellant would be that the jurisdiction of the Social Security Commissioners is described by themselves as broadly equivalent to an appeal to the High Court and is available only on points of law. Furthermore, social security law is of great complexity and specialist assistance is needed to construct and argue legal points involved in appeals. The countervailing arguments would, no doubt, be that the Commissioners adopt an inquisitorial approach to the file, and considerable preparatory work is undertaken by nominated officers (specialist legal staff working under the direction of a Commissioner) to ensure that the file is complete before it is placed before a Commissioner for determination of the appeal. There is force in both arguments. Which would prevail if the matter came before the Court is hard to predict.

D. SUBSTANTIVE ISSUES

1. Key articles

12–25 Three provisions of the Convention have particular relevance in the context of social security. They are Article 8 (respect for private and family life);

Article 1 of the First Protocol (protection of property); and Article 14 (prohibition of discrimination) (see generally paragraphs 2–81 and following, 2–132 and 2–123 and following, respectively).

Article 8 is a broad provision, and is frequently coupled with Article 12 (right to marry), Article 2 of the First Protocol (right to education), and Article 5, Seventh Protocol (equality between spouses). The United Kingdom is not a signatory to the Seventh Protocol (though it has indicated an intention to become a party), but its impact on the interpretation of Article 8 has some adjectival impact on the United Kingdom. The grouping of respect for private life, family life, home and correspondence in Article 8 has led to the protection afforded by it being considered more than the sum of its parts. This is the provision which contains an embryonic right to privacy. Its significance in relation to social security is its recognition of family units, and it is easy to see how it could be argued that certain conditions of entitlement to social security might produce a situation which inhibits keeping the family together. Respect for private life has been interpreted to include respect for same sex relationships, and again it is not difficult to envisage situations in which the social security system does not reflect any recognition of such relationships. The Article also offers some protection against abuse of the use of covert surveillance, which might arise when social security authorities are investigating suspected fraud.

12–26 There have, however, been no examples of successful use of Article 8 before the Court in the context of social security entitlements. It was pleaded in the *Gaygusuz* case discussed below, but neither the Commission nor the Court considered it necessary to examine the case under this head in the light of its conclusions on other aspects of the application.

The Commission has held that there was no hindrance to family life where a wife was obliged to pay insurance contributions for her husband who was a house-husband, even though husbands did not have to pay contributions in respect of housewives. Since the matter could not be brought within Article 8, the question of discrimination under Article 14 could not be considered. The matter could also not be considered as a property question, since Switzerland has not ratified Article 1 of the First Protocol (*Uwe Klöpper v. Switzerland* (1996) 84A D.R. 101).

Article 1 of the First Protocol — as explained in *Sporrong and Lönnroth v. Sweden* (1982) Series A, No. 52; 5 E.H.R.R. 35 — comprises three distinct rules. First, there is a right to peaceful enjoyment of possessions. Secondly, persons can only be deprived of their possessions subject to certain conditions; and, thirdly, states are entitled to control the use of property in accordance with the general interest.

12–27 Article 14 is a provision which prohibits discrimination on the grounds of sex, race, colour, language, religion, political or other opinion, national or social origin, association with a national minority, property, birth or other status. However, the protection is only applicable to the enjoyment of the rights and freedoms set forth in the Convention. It is the linking of Article 14 with another Article of the Convention which gives the former substance. In order to have effect, it does not have to be shown that there is a violation of the substantive article, merely that the alleged discrimination operates in a field which is covered by the protections afforded by those provisions. Indeed the practice of the Court has been to decline to consider Article 14 in conjunction with another Article if they find a violation of the latter on its face.

Where Article 14 is considered, the Court asks itself whether there is a difference of treatment between two groups which may properly be compared on one of the grounds mentioned (and the list is not closed by reason of the last two words referring to "other status"). The question is then asked whether that difference of treatment pursues a legitimate aim. Finally, the Court considers whether the means employed are proportionate to the legitimate aim pursued. In making this judgment, due regard will be had to the state's margin of appreciation, which will vary depending on the circumstances of each case. Where the discrimination is based on sex, there is little room for a margin of appreciation, but where broader policy issues are under consideration (such as housing allocation policies to ensure a supply of housing for poorer people), the margin of appreciation will be wider (see *Gillow v. U.K.* (1986) Series A, No. 109; 11 E.H.R.R. 335, para. 66).

2. Property rights and social security

12–28 In *Müller v. Austria* (1975) 3 D.R. 25, the Commission considered the nature of any property rights in pension entitlements. The applicant had been a member of a compulsory contributory pension scheme in Austria and had become a frontier worker moving into Liechtenstein for work. He was permitted for a while to continue to contribute to the Austrian scheme on a voluntary basis, but this was treated as a supplementary pension arrangement. The result was that, on his retirement, the applicant considered that he received a lesser pension than if he had continued to pay the same contributions into the compulsory scheme. His attempts to seek redress before the Austrian courts left him aggrieved and he complained to the Commission. The Commission was willing to consider that Article 1 of the First Protocol was applicable, but that Article only gave the applicant a right as a beneficiary of a compulsory social insurance scheme to any payments made by the fund; it did not give him any entitlement to a specific sum. The applicant's second line of argument was that his position as a frontier worker was different from that of resident workers, and that, in the enjoyment of his property rights, he was the victim of discrimination in violation of Article 14. The Commission disagreed. There was a difference of treatment (and it was legitimate to compare resident and frontier workers) but this was justified because frontier workers would gain an entitlement to two pensions: one in Austria under the voluntary arrangements, and one under the Liechtenstein scheme. There was furthermore no difference of treatment of Liechtenstein frontier workers and frontier workers working in other neighbouring states. The Commission's opinion that there was no violation of the Convention was confirmed by the Committee of Ministers.

Similar issues came before the Court in *Gaygusuz v. Austria* (1997) 23 E.H.R.R. 364. The key issue in the case proved to be a simple one. Gaygusuz was a Turkish national who had worked in Austria. He had paid contributions under the Austrian social security scheme, but had experienced periods of unemployment and periods when he was unfit for work. He applied for an advance on his retirement pension as a form of emergency assistance, but was refused because he was not an Austrian national. His attempts to redress his grievance using domestic procedures were unsuccessful and he complained to the Commission that there had been a violation of a number of articles of the Convention. Among his complaints was a complaint of a violation of Article 14 taken in conjunction with Article 1 of the First Protocol. The first question was whether the substance of the claim was a matter covered by the protection of property in Article 1 of the First Protocol, since otherwise Article 14 could have no application. Both the Commission and the Court concluded that Article 1 of the First Protocol was relevant, but for somewhat different reasons. The Commission concluded that the Article was brought into play because the obligation to pay "taxes or other contributions" falls within its field of application, and so the ensuing benefits are also within its field of application (paragraph 47 of Commission Opinion). The Court, however, considered that,

> "the right to emergency assistance — in so far as provided for in the applicable legislation — is a pecuniary right for the purposes of Article 1 of Protocol 1. That provision is therefore applicable without it being necessary to rely solely on the link between entitlement to emergency assistance and the obligation to pay 'taxes or other contributions'." (para. 41)

12–29 This was enough to engage Article 14. The discrimination here was blatant. Nationals had an entitlement, and non-nationals did not. It is difficult to see how such discrimination might be justified. The Austrian government argued that there was a special responsibility on a state to care for its own nationals, and there were certain exceptions to the nationality condition (which had not assisted Gaygusuz). Neither the Court nor the Commission was persuaded by these arguments. There had been a violation because there was discrimination within Article 14 which was not capable of objective and reasonable justification.

Attempts have been made to argue that the suspension of a retirement pension for those serving terms of imprisonment breached the property rights in Article 1 of the First Protocol, but the applications were declared inadmissible (*Josef Szrabjer v. U.K.*, App. 27004/95; *Walther Clarke v. U.K.*, App. 27011/95); and also in respect of invalidity benefit (*George Carlin v. U.K.*, App. 27537/95). The public interest was served by avoiding a situation in which prisoners enjoyed the advantage of accumulating a lump sum by receiving a state benefit without any outgoing living expenses. Arguments based on discrimination between prisoners and non-prisoners were dismissed as a comparison of two different factual situations. Other comparisons were also found to be without merit.

A challenge to the system of recovering state benefits from personal injury awards has also failed at the admissibility stage (*Graeme Kightley v. U.K.*, App. 28778/95).

3. Family and private life

12–30 Article 8 guarantees respect, *inter alia,* for family life, subject to the limitation contained in the Article. In the *Gaygusuz* case, the applicant had complained that the refusal to award him the emergency assistance requested violated respect for his family life (presumably on the grounds that refusal of the assistance threatened the break up of, or hardship to, his family); the admissibility decision is not specific on the basis for declaring this part of his complaint admissible (see (1994) 18 E.H.R.R. C.D. 51). Neither the Commission nor the Court found it necessary to consider this aspect of the complaint since they had concluded that there was a violation of Article 14 read in conjunction with Article 1 of the First Protocol. Nevertheless, it remains open for the limits of the protection under Article 8 to be explored in the context of entitlements to social security. But it would be fair to say that there are few indications that the Strasbourg authorities regard the Convention right here as including an obligation on the state to make payments to families for their support.

4. Discrimination

12–31 The importance of the prohibition of discrimination in the enjoyment of the rights protected by the Convention has already been mentioned. Furthermore the *Gaygusuz* case provides a clear example of the application of the provision in a social security context.

The coupling of Article 14 and Article 1 of the First Protocol opens up the possibility for considerable case-law development of the principle of equality in social security entitlement. The adjudicating authorities have already had to wrestle with issues of discrimination flowing from Community law under the equal treatment directives, but that has focused on discrimination between men and women. Community rights are also linked in some cases to worker status under Community law. By contrast, there are no such limitations in relation to equal treatment under Article 14. In *Van Breedam v. Belgium* (1989) 62 D.R. 109) the Commission ruled inadmissible an application concerning liability to pay supplementary social security contributions where the discrimination alleged was between painters and sculptors on the one hand and writers and musicians on the other in relation to the treatment of royalties as a basis for levying contributions. Although the application was ruled inadmissible, the Commission does not appear to question the legitimacy of the comparative groups put forward by the applicant, since the grounds of their decision are that there was a legitimate reason for the difference of treatment.

12–32 In *Krafft and Rougeot v. France* (1990) 65 D.R. 51 the calculation of judicial pensions in France was in issue, and again the Commission did not appear to question the legitimacy of comparing the treatment of those appointed to judicial office from private practice and those appointed from within the court service. Again the difference of treatment was found to have a legitimate basis.

It is not difficult to imagine the sort of comparisons which might be raised challenging aspects of the U.K. social security system. The whole system is replete with differences. Examples are differences between single and married people, between students and non-students, between those who are habitually resident and those who are not. It may even be possible to re-open some of the challenges on grounds of alleged sex discrimination which have been made and lost under Community rules. Such cases are bound to be very complex and time-consuming, involving as they do issues of the legitimacy of the comparators chosen and whether there is objective and reasonable justification of any difference of treatment between those groups.

5. Education rights

12–33   Article 2 of the First Protocol provides that no one is to be denied the right to education. The full scope of this right is yet to be determined. The existing case law is mainly concerned with primary education, but the Commission has not ruled out the application of the provision to higher education (see, for example, *Sulak v. Turkey* (1996) 84 D.R. 101). The confused state of the exclusion of students in full-time higher education from entitlement to most social security benefits might well leave the United Kingdom exposed to challenge under this provision. On the assumption that the provision applies to higher education, it could be argued that students are currently required to abandon their courses completely in order to become eligible for certain social security benefits with the result that they lose entitlement to the balance of a mandatory award to support their studies if they wish to return to their courses later on. This could be argued to operate to deny them the right to an education.

E. FURTHER ISSUES IN ENGLISH SOCIAL SECURITY LAW

1. Declarations of incompatibility

12–34   Neither the tribunals nor the Commissioners are within the group of judicial authorities with power to make declarations of incompatibility. Both can, however, declare secondary legislation incompatible with the Convention. Prior to the Act, both could (and have) declared secondary legislation incompatible with its enabling legislation. While the absence of a power on the part of tribunals to make a declaration of incompatibility can be explained by their dispersed nature and the multiplicity of personnel which sit in them, similar objections cannot be made in respect of the Commissioners, who clearly ought to have this power. They are a small specialist group of judges with acknowledged expertise in the application of social security law. Lord Bridge has described them as having "great expertise in this somewhat esoteric area of the law" (*Chief Adjudication Officer v. Foster* [1993] A.C. 754, 767).

Occasions may well arise where both the first instance tribunals and the Commissioners hear argument that primary legislation cannot be read in a manner compatible with Convention rights. When that occurs, there will inevitably be much argument on the proper interpretation of the relevant primary legislation. Where the arguments as to its incompatibility are not convincing, the decision can be written up without difficulty. But where those arguments are convincing, there will be a difficulty in writing up the decision. Clearly the primary legislation must be followed and applied. But care may need to be taken to avoid "pseudo-declarations" of incompatibility, that is, statements which clearly indicate that if the adjudicating authority had the power to make such a declaration, it would have done so. Nevertheless, the decision-writer may wish to indicate the argument which was put on the issue, since that might assist the Court of Appeal if the case is taken on appeal.

2. The Social Security Administration (Fraud) Act 1997

12–35   Section 14 of the Social Security Administration (Fraud) Act 1997 adds a section 122(1A) to the Social Security Administration Act 1992, making it an offence for a person, without reasonable excuse, to fail to notify a change of circumstances, or, knowingly, to cause or allow another person to fail to notify a change of circumstances which is required to be notified to the Benefits Agency, where the person knows that the other person is required to notify the change. The effect of this provision is that a welfare rights adviser might commit an offence if a client provides information which would have an effect on the award of a benefit and indicates that this information has not been disclosed to the Benefits Agency. If the adviser gave clear advice that there was a duty to disclose the information to the Benefits Agency, that would probably constitute reasonable excuse for not then themselves notifying the information. The provision is designed to catch those likely to benefit from the failure to disclose, such as fraudulent landlords receiving housing benefit.

12–36   The conflict faced by the adviser is clear. It is between confidentiality and the proper administration of the social security benefits schemes. It is not difficult to imagine claimants complaining that disclosure of the confidential information by the adviser was a breach of their private life. They could argue by analogy with the surveillance cases (see Jacobs, F. and White, R., *The European Convention on Human Rights* (2nd ed., Oxford: Clarendon Press, 1996) pp. 206–10) that there was an interference with private life under Article 8 which would then need to be tested against the permitted limitations in paragraph (2) of the Article. It would follow that if the claimant is to be protected, so too should the adviser who is exposed to possible prosecution, though the adviser would probably avoid the commission of the offence by advising that disclosure should be made by the claimant. This would, it is argued, result in the adviser having reasonable excuse for not making the disclosure.

The 1997 Act also contains sweeping provisions on the exchange of information by Government departments which might be open to challenge for similar reasons. But such challenges would be highly speculative and would require development of the law protecting private life beyond that which is currently recognised in the case-law of the Court.

3. Jobseeker's allowance

12–37   Section 7(3) of the Jobseekers Act 1995 permits certain steps a person has taken actively to seek work (a condition of entitlement to a Jobseeker's Allowance) to be disregarded where the person's "appearance" is considered to undermine the prospect of securing the employment he or she is seeking (see also Regulation 18(4) of the Jobseeker's Allowance Regulations (S.I. 1996 No. 207)). The provision has been described as "remarkable" (Wikeley, N., "The Jobseekers Act 1995: What the Unemployed Need is a Good Haircut" (1996) 25 I.L.J. 71).

Article 8 of the Convention protects the right to "private life" which can certainly be read to include a right to determine a personal identity. This could involve matters of dress or appearance. Much will turn on the way in which these rules are applied, but it is not difficult to imagine circumstances in which matters of appearance are argued to be manifestations of the personal identity protected by the demand for respect for private life in Article 8. This is an area where the development of Article 8 rights is not yet complete, and remains to be tested.

4. The Social Security Act 1998

12–38   A number of aspects of the Social Security Act 1998 ("SSA 1998") would appear to leave open the possibility of challenge for compatibility with Convention rights.

One of the great achievements of the Office of the President of Social Security Appeal Tribunals (OPSSAT) and its successor, the Independent Tribunal Service (ITS), has been to emphasise the independence of the tribunals hearing appeals by claimants against decisions of adjudication officers in the Department of Social Security. That success has dramatically increased respect for the tribunals. Certain provisions of the Social Security Act 1998 at best undermine that independence, and at worst may leave the structure exposed to challenges under the Convention as not constituting independent and impartial tribunals. New "unified appeal tribunals" replace the tribunals which formed part of the ITS, which is itself abolished. Appointment to the panels is happily not a matter for the Secretary of State for Social Security, but for the Lord Chancellor (or Lord Advocate in Scotland). But tribunals in the future may consist of one, two or three members and the requirements for a lawyer chairman of the tribunals goes. The authority of the new tribunals is, however, undermined by the provision that the Secretary of State may supersede any decision of a tribunal or of a Social Security Commissioner (section 10(1) of the SSA 1998). That power is subject to regulations, which it is understood will limit the exercise of the power to situations where there is a change of circumstances or new evidence comes to light. At present such limitations appear in the primary legislation (section 35 of the Social Security Administration Act 1992), and it is disturbing to see that this practice has been discontinued.

Section 26 of the SSA 1998 would appear to be objectionable in that it enables the Secretary of State who is one of the parties to the dispute to direct the tribunal on the determination of the appeal. Such a provision must result in the tribunal not being independent and impartial, since it is a characteristic of an independent and impartial tribunal that it is not susceptible to instructions concerning the exercise of its judicial function (*Ettl v. Austria* (1987) Series A, No. 117; 10 E.H.R.R. 255, para. 38).

The Council on Tribunals has suggested that the proposed new structure for the tribunals could resemble the unsatisfactory system which was abandoned many years ago, and has suggested that the new arrangements are a cause for concern (*Annual Report of the Council on Tribunals for 1996/97* (1997–98) H.C. 376).

5. A recent case

12–39   An interesting recent judgment of the Court originated in two applications lodged against the United Kingdom (*McGinley and Egan v. U.K.* judgment of June 9, 1998). Both applicants were men who had served in the armed forces in the 1950s and had taken part in atmospheric nuclear tests in the Pacific Ocean. They both subsequently suffered health problems which they attributed to exposure to ionising radiation caused by the nuclear tests. They pursued claims before the Pensions Appeals Tribunal but were frustrated by their inability to gain access to detailed contemporaneous records on the nature of the tests in which they had played a part. Their claims were unsuccessful. They complained that the denial of access to records effectively denied them access to a hearing, and deprived them of their right to a fair hearing, as well as constituting a failure to respect their private lives. The Commission took the view unanimously that there was a violation of Article 6(1) and by a vote of 23 to three that there was a violation of Article 8. The Court disagreed and found no violation of either Article 6, Article 8 or Article 13 of the Convention, because there was a procedure for seeking disclosure of documents in the rules of procedure of the Pensions Appeal Tribunal which the applicants had not used.

6. Other matters

12–40 The restructuring of social security decision-making in the Social Security Act 1998 will remove the sharp distinction which is made at present between contribution questions and entitlement questions. The former have never been the province of the tribunals, but have been subject to a right of appeal to the High Court (Social Security Administration Act 1992, s.18). Some of those appeals are now brought within the jurisdiction of the tribunals. In other cases, a right of appeal may disappear. The world of contributions is among the most arcane areas of the law, and there may well be numerically and problems which surface as matters come to be explored by the adjudicating authorities. Such questions certainly give rise to dispute in other jurisdictions.

Other areas of social security adjudication which are not considered in this chapter are decisions and reviews under the social fund which are dealt with by the Independent Review Service, and the whole area of housing benefit. It would be surprising if adjudication in these areas did not throw up potential challenges under the Convention.

F. CONCLUDING COMMENT

12–41 Once the Convention is given effect in U.K. law, it is unlikely that the adjudicating authorities will be swamped with Convention points, but this chapter has shown that there is a number of areas where challenges might be made to the practices of tribunals and the Social Security Commissioners, and to the substantive rules of entitlement to benefit.

One feature of the application of Convention law in tribunals, where parties are frequently not represented, will be the unpredictability of the points which are raised. A number of claimants already make generalised references to their human rights in their appeals. To date, these could be safely ignored. But in an inquisitorial jurisdiction and with directly enforceable Convention rights, that will not be an option for the future, just as it is not an option for a tribunal to ignore a generalised reference to the impact of E.C. law. This will require confidence and a robustness of approach in the tribunals, where time does not allow a relaxed consideration of every issue raised by claimants. An example of the sort of argument which can speedily be dismissed by a well-informed tribunal is the claim by a person that he or she was subjected to a humiliating interrogation about their lifestyle by the examining medical practitioner, which they consider to be inhuman and degrading treatment contrary to Article 3. The short answer to such a point in virtually all such claims will be that Article 3 does not bite until the alleged ill-treatment reaches a particular level of severity which does not appear to have been reached here (*Ireland v. United Kingdom* (1978) Series A, No. 25; 2 E.H.R.R. 25, para. 162). A tribunal familiar with this principle could speedily come to this view, particularly where the claimant had not made any complaint under the complaints procedures applicable to medical examinations. But a tribunal not so informed could struggle with a hopeless point. The key to effective decision-making in the tribunals will be the provision of sufficient training to give tribunal adjudicators confidence to dispose speedily of hopeless points and to deal effectively with more meritorious ones. These are likely to be complex and time-consuming, and, unless spotted in advance, might well require an adjournment.

G. SOCIAL SECURITY CONVENTIONS TO WHICH THE UNITED KINGDOM IS A PARTY

12–42   European Interim Agreement on Social Security Schemes Relating to Old Age, Invalidity and Survivors 1953 and Protocol 1953 (ETS 12 and 12A).

European Interim Agreement on Social Security other than Schemes for Old Age, Invalidity and Survivors 1953 and Protocol 1953 (ETS 13 and 13A).

European Convention of Social and Medical Assistance 1953 and Protocol 1953 (ETS 14 and 14A).

European Code of Social Security 1964 and Protocol 1964 (ETS 48 and 48A).

The United Kingdom is also a party to ILO Convention No. 102 concerning Minimum Standards of Social Security.

CHAPTER 13

Employment and Labour Relations Law

David Carter (Barrister, Arden Chambers)

A. INTRODUCTION

13–01 This chapter is concerned with the possible effects of the Act on employment and labour relations law. It is helpful to begin by outlining the sources and context of existing law in these areas.

1 Employment Law

13–02 Employment law is essentially the law of contract as applied to the employment relationship. As such, it draws heavily on common law principles. The contract of employment may be subject to express and implied terms, including several arising out of the nature of the employment relationship; such as the implied term of mutual trust and confidence. In particular areas, the contract is modified by statute, principally the Employment Rights Act 1996 ("ERA 1996"), generally for the benefit of employees. This provides for *e.g.* the right to written terms and conditions of employment (section 1), not to work on Sundays (section 43), time off for public duties (section 50) and for ante-natal care (section 55), maternity rights for female employees (section 81), minimum periods of notice (section 86) and written reasons for dismissal (section 92). Grafted on to the contract are such additional rights as the right not to be unfairly dismissed (section 94), to pay when laid-off (section 28) and to receive compensation when made redundant (section 135).

There are further "stand-alone" statutory rights designed to prevent employees and prospective employees from being discriminated against on the ground of sex or marital status (Sex Discrimination Acts 1975 and 1986 ("SDA 1975 and 1986"), and Equal Pay Act 1970), race or nationality (Race Relations Act 1976 ("RRA 1976")) and disability (Disability Discrimination Act 1995 ("DDA 1995")).

13–03 Of particular importance to the discussion in this chapter is the discretion exercisable by industrial tribunals in deciding unfair dismissal and discrimination cases. In the former, as a general rule, a dismissal is fair if it is for an admissible reason (ERA 1996, s.98(2)) and the tribunal is satisfied that the employer acted reasonably in treating it as sufficient reason for dismissing the employee (ERA 1996, s.98(4)). In discrimination cases, indirect discrimination on the basis of sex or race is capable of justification (RRA 1976, s.1(1)(b), SDA 1975, s.1(1)(b)) as is both direct and indirect disability discrimination (DDA 1995, s.5(1)(2)). The judgment as to whether different treatment is justifiable requires "an objective balance between the discriminatory effect of the condition and the reasonable needs of the party who applied the condition" (*Hampson v. Department of Education and Science* [1989] I.C.R. 179, *per* Balcombe L.J. at 191F). This statement was subsequently approved by the House of Lords in *Webb v. EMO Air Cargo (U.K.) Ltd* [1993] I.C.R. 175, *per* Lord Keith at 182H–183A.

This chapter also considers employment law in a wider context, as the law that touches upon an individual's right to work, for instance, the regulation of a self-employed solicitor by the Law Society.

2. Labour Relations Law

13–04 This area of law governs relations between employers on the one hand and employees collectively on the other. Originally collective action by workers was illegal, viewed as an unlawful interference with trade. Modern labour relations law dates from 1871 when trade unions were legalised. Labour relations law encompasses the rights of employees to join together in trade unions or similar organisations, to be represented, to enter collective agreements and to take industrial action.

3. European Union Law

13–05 When the United Kingdom joined the European Economic Community (the predecessor to the European Union), English law became subject to European law (European Communities Act 1972, s.2(1)). Since then, both European Union legislation and decisions of the Court of Justice of the European Communities ("the ECJ") have played an increasingly important role in the development of domestic employment law. European Union legislation takes effect through treaty rights (*e.g.*, Article 119 of the E.C. Treaty) and Council Directives (*e.g.*, 77/187, given effect by the Transfer of Undertakings (Protection of Employment) Regulations (S.I. 1981 No. 1794). Council directives have been a particularly fertile area in relation to equality between the sexes.

13–06 It is now settled law that domestic legislation must be interpreted so far as possible as is consistent with European law, even to the extent of "rewriting" a statute (*Marshall v. Southampton and South-West Hampshire Area Health Authority (Teaching)* [1986] I.R.L.R. 140). For instance, in *Bossa v. Nordstress Ltd* [1998] I.R.L.R. 284, the applicant complained that he had been refused employment in England for a job in Italy because he was not an Italian citizen. The Employment Appeal Tribunal held that the prohibition in the Race Relations Act 1976 that discrimination on the ground of nationality was only unlawful if in respect of employment within the United Kingdom, must be disapplied. The basis for the decision was that Article 48 of the Treaty on European Union ("the Maastricht Treaty") prohibited discrimination in relation to employment in any Member State of the European Union.

Further, an individual can sue the State for damages for failing to take necessary steps to achieve the results required by a directive (*Francovich v. Italian Republic, Bonifaci v. Italian Republic* [1992] I.R.L.R. 84) or for breaching European law (*Brasserie du Pêcheur SA v. Federal Republic of Germany, R. v. Secretary of State for Transport, ex p. Factortame Ltd (No. 3)* [1996] I.R.L.R. 267).

B. A RIGHT TO WORK?

13–07 The Convention is principally concerned with individual rights and freedoms as opposed to social, political and economic rights (*cf.*, the European Social Charter, Article 1(2), which refers to protecting the right of the worker "to earn his living in an occupation freely entered upon"). In *X v. Denmark* (1976) 3 D.R. 153, the applicant claimed that his dismissal was an infringement of his right to work. Rejecting his claim as inadmissible, the Commission stressed that the right to work was an economic and social right, and that it was not guaranteed by the Convention. This orthodoxy was restated by the minority of the Court in *Young, James and Webster v. U.K.*, Series A, No 44; [1981] I.R.L.R. 408, (see below), yet the majority stressed the individual's right to earn a livelihood. It may appear to be a small step from this to the "right to work", yet it is a step which, to date, the Court has been unwilling to take.

C. ARTICLE 8 — RESPECT FOR PRIVATE AND FAMILY LIFE

1. Nature of the right

13–08 The Strasbourg authorities have decided that the right to a private life includes the right to a personal identity, to intimacy and private space and to personal autonomy. The right to intimacy includes subordinate rights, such as not to have correspondence looked at or interfered with. This has been extended to conversations on an internal office telephone line (*Halford v. U.K.* (1997) 24 E.H.R.R. 523). By the same reasoning, it would extend to other forms of surveillance, for instance by close circuit television and the monitoring of other forms of private communication, such as electronic mail.

The essence of family life is the right of members to live together for the enjoyment of each other's company (*Olsson v. Sweden* (1988) Series A, No. 130; 11 E.H.R.R. 259, at para. 59). Further, the State must act in such a way that individuals can lead a normal family life (*Marckx v. Belgium* (1979) Series A, No. 131; 2 E.H.R.R. 330, at para. 31). Article 8(2) permits lawful interference with the right if "necessary" for particular purposes, including the economic well-being of others and the protection of the rights and freedoms of others. In relation to Article 10(2), which is similarly worded, the Court has decided that "necessary" implies a pressing social need (*Barthold v. Germany* (1985) Series A, No. 90; 7 E.H.R.R. 383).

Article 8 is considered below in relation to employee privacy and its effect on employees wishing to work part-time in order to fulfil family commitments.

2. Privacy at work

13–09   There is no general right to privacy under English law, regardless of the employment relationship. Increasingly, in the context of the modern workplace, employers may be tempted to (and in many cases, do) invade the privacy of their employees, for instance, by obtaining information about previous criminal convictions, conducting psychometric testing and random drug-testing, reading correspondence, monitoring telephone conversations (whether it is eavesdropping or merely compiling a list of telephone numbers), video-surveillance, and carrying out body-searches. All or any of such behaviour comes within the ambit of *Halford* (above).

13–10   In *Halford*, the applicant was a senior serving police officer, who had taken industrial tribunal proceedings alleging that she had been discriminated against on the ground of sex, in that she had not been promoted. During the course of those proceedings, she alleged that her employer had "bugged", *inter alia*, her office telephone in order to obtain evidence for use in the tribunal case. The Court decided that Article 8 had been violated because there had been an interference with her private life and correspondence. Of particular importance was the fact that the calls had been made on her employer's telephone, at her employer's premises and during her working time.

Despite the significance of *Halford*, it should not be overstated. Given that the employer had assured her that she could use the telephone line in question privately for the purposes of her industrial tribunal litigation, the facts of the case were particularly favourable to the applicant. Regrettably, the Court did not lay down any guidelines or indicate in what circumstances interference might be justified. Clearly a number of factors may be relevant to the issue of justification, for instance whether the employer had a legitimate purpose for the interference, on grounds such as security, health and safety, quality control, compliance with statutory obligations, or supervision of performance. In addition, it may be relevant to take into account how necessary the interference was in respect of the employer's business, whether the information was obtained inadvertently, what safeguards were built in to avoid gathering private information, how and in what circumstances such information was used and whether any confidentiality was preserved. It is suggested that a further (and possibly crucial) factor will be whether the employee has consented to the interference.

3. Family commitments

13–11   The issue here is illustrated by *Home Office v. Holmes* [1984] I.R.L.R. 299. Ms Holmes was a full-time employee, who, following the birth of her second child asked her employer to allow her to return to work on a part-time basis so that she could care for her child. Her request was refused as there were no such posts available. The Employment Appeal Tribunal upheld the finding that she had been discriminated against on the ground of sex, rejecting the employer's argument that the condition that she work full-time was justifiable irrespective of her sex. They found that she had been indirectly discriminated against because the proportion of women who could comply with the requirement to work full-time was less than the proportion of men, having regard to the burden placed on women in modern society in the bringing up of children. The approach in *Holmes* was subsequently endorsed by the Northern Ireland Court of Appeal in *Briggs v. North Eastern Education and Library Board* [1990] I.R.L.R. 181. Although (since *Holmes*) there have been cases tending to limit its effect (see, for instance, *Kidd v. DRG (U.K.) Ltd* [1985] I.R.L.R. 190, and *Clymo v. Wandsworth London Borough Council* [1989] I.R.L.R. 241), the general position now is that the burden is squarely on employers to show objective justification for refusing to accommodate returning mothers (see, for instance, *British Telecommunications plc v. Roberts* [1996] I.R.L.R. 601). Most recently, in *London Underground Ltd v. Edwards (No. 2)* [1998] I.R.L.R. 364, the Court of Appeal held that the industrial tribunal was entitled to find that there was a high preponderance of single mothers having care of a child without specific evidence (in the words of Potter L.J. "it was a matter of common knowledge"). The issue has been taken a stage further in *Edwards*, where a change in working arrangements for existing employees (the introduction of flexible working), which was more difficult for working mothers to comply with, was held to be sex discrimination.

13–12 Article 8 clearly reinforces the existing position in domestic law so far as working mothers are concerned, but it raises the possibility of employers being required to accede to requests for other forms of arrangement to facilitate family life, for instance to accede to a request for job-sharing or flexi-time working. The cases in domestic law have all concerned indirect discrimination against women and have been founded on assertions that a proportionately larger number of working women than working men have child-care responsibilities. Article 8 may come to the assistance of employees where such an imbalance cannot be shown (for instance, *Kidd v. DRG Ltd* (above)). It is significant that, in 1999, the United Kingdom is due to implement the European Union directive giving three months' leave to men and women after the birth of a child, which gives recognition to the role of both parents in the upbringing of a child. Nevertheless, it does not meet the issue of the continuing care of a young child which may be the responsibility of a male or female parent by choice or necessity. There seems no reason why Article 8 should not be relied on by a working father to require his employer to adopt working arrangements that facilitate the care of (and enjoyment of time with) his child.

D. ARTICLE 9 — FREEDOM OF THOUGHT, CONSCIENCE AND RELIGION

1. Nature of the right

13–13 There are two distinct parts to Article 9(1), which can be characterised as the freedom to believe and the freedom to manifest that belief. The former is given greater protection as it is not subject to Article 9(2), which enables the State to impose limitations on the manifestation of any belief in the interests of others. Article 9(1) expressly refers to "thought, conscience and religion". The Strasbourg authorities have yet to find it necessary to define a religion, possibly because a set of beliefs falling short of a religion will be encompassed by "thought" and "conscience". In general, it is only "coherent views on fundamental problems" that qualify for protection (*X v. FRG* (1981) 24 D.R. 137, and *Campbell and Cosans v. U.K.* (1982) Series A, No. 48; 4 E.H.R.R. 293, at paragraph 36). Clearly, there is no difficulty with the major world religions. For one of the more obscure faiths, the applicant will need to demonstrate that it exists (see, for instance, *X v. U.K.* (1977) 11 D.R. 55, and *Chappell v. U.K.* (1987) 53 D.R. 241; 10 E.H.R.R. 510, in relation to the Wicca religion and Druidism respectively).

Under Article 9(2), the State may justify interference with the manifestation of belief on certain grounds, *e.g.* in the interests of public safety. The Strasbourg authorities allow States a large margin of appreciation and in only one reported case (*Kokkinakis v. Greece* (1993) Series A, No. 260–A; 17 E.H.R.R. 397) has the Court found that interference was not justified. It is also the case that a common reason for finding against applicants is that they are not satisfied that the particular manifestation was necessarily required as part of their set of beliefs (see *Ahmad v. U.K.* (1981) 4 E.H.R.R. 126). The Court has decided that a provision of the general domestic law which incidentally interferes with a manifestation of a belief is generally not a violation (*Ahmad v. U.K.* (above).

13–14   Absent specific statutes (for instance, the Education Act 1944, s.30), there is no provision in English law against discrimination on the ground of religion (*n.b.* there is in Northern Ireland), although it may arise indirectly as a form of race discrimination. Thus, a Rastafarian man (not a member of a distinct ethnic group under the Race Relations Act 1976 — see *Dawkins v. Department of the Environment* [1993] I.R.L.R. 284), who was dismissed for wearing his hair in a particular way in accordance with his religious beliefs, may refer to Article 9 in support of a claim for unfair dismissal.

In the context of employment, Article 9 impinges upon the conflict between the obligations arising out of the contract of employment and the personal obligation imposed by the employee's faith. It is mostly likely to be relevant in relation to disciplinary action (including dismissal) where instructions from the employer conflict with the employee's beliefs, to requests for time off to observe religious obligations and to appearance codes. (As to the last, see paragraphs 13–22—13–24, below.)

2. Workplace discipline for beliefs

13–15   The essence of the right to believe is that the citizen is permitted to believe what he or she wishes, free of indoctrination by the State (*Angelini v. Sweden* (1986) 51 D.R. 41). In *Knudsen v. Sweden* (1985) 42 D.R. 247, the Commission suggested that Article 9 might apply where an applicant is already employed and faces dismissal unless he changes his beliefs. It is suggested that this is correct, as the Convention affords the right to believe great protection, not allowing any justification for an interference with the freedom.

An employee who manifests his or her beliefs is likely to be in a weaker position. Article 9(2) allows interference to be justified. By way of analogy, an employer was justified (under Article 10(2)) in dismissing a teacher who disobeyed an instruction not to put up posters advocating evangelism (*X v. U.K.*

(1979) 16 D.R. 101). Further, in relation to Article 10, the Court has declined to protect freedom of expression where a political belief is in conflict with a condition of holding public office, characterising such applications as a right to public office which is not protected by the Convention (see *Glasenapp v. Germany* (1986) Series A, No. 104; 9 E.H.R.R. 25, and *Kosiek v. Germany* (1986) Series A, No. 105; 9 E.H.R.R. 328). It is suggested that such reasoning could be applied in relation to Article 9(2) which concerns the manifestation of a belief, but not 9(1).

3. Time off for religious purposes

13–16   An employee who wants to take time off as a requirement of religious observation is clearly manifesting his or her religious beliefs. Accordingly, Article 9(2) can apply to justify interference.

In *Ahmad v. ILEA* [1978] 1 Q.B. 36, the plaintiff was employed full-time as a primary school teacher by the defendant authority. He was a devout Muslim. Before his employment commenced, he told his employer that his religion could require him to attend prayers at a mosque every Friday and then return to work. No difficulty arose for six years, when he was transferred to a school within easy reach of a mosque. He felt obliged to attend the mosque for some 45 minutes each Friday. His employer would only sanction his absence if he did so in his own time and offered to vary his contract so that he worked part-time (four and a half days per week). He declined the offer, as it meant that he would receive reduced pay and other benefits. Instead, he resigned and claimed that he had been constructively dismissed. Section 30 of the Education Act 1944 provided that a teacher should not be disqualified from being a teacher *inter alia* because of the need to attend religious worship. Article 9 was prayed in aid of the employee's case. By a majority, the court decided that he was not entitled to absent himself from work for the purpose of religious worship in breach of his contract of employment. His subsequent application under the Convention was ruled inadmissible (*Ahmad v. U.K.* (1981) 4 E.H.R.R. 126). The Commission decided (at para. 9) that, in denying the applicant time off for worship during working hours, the employer had given due consideration to his Article 9 rights by offering to employ him part-time to enable him to attend the mosque in his own time.

13–17   In *Stedman v. U.K.* (1997) 23 E.H.R.R. C.D. 168, the applicant objected to working on Sundays because, amongst other reasons, it offended her religious convictions. The Commission decided that her application was inadmissible as she had been dismissed for failing to work her contractual hours, not for her religious beliefs and that she always had the option of resigning.

On the face of it, Article 9 appears to give hope to minorities who are discriminated against on the ground of their beliefs, but, to date, the interpretation by the Strasbourg authorities would seem to belie this. In relation to prospective employees, they have adopted a highly pragmatic (and arguably intellectually weak) approach, namely that an employer cannot be forced to offer employment because the Convention does not guarantee a right to work. Existing employees may be in a stronger position. The Court has yet to give any definitive ruling, but the Commission has said that an employee can resign if a contractual term conflicts with his or her religious beliefs (*Stedman v. U.K.* (above)).

4. Article 9 v. Article 10

13–18   Article 9 rights often overlap with those under Article 10 — for instance, a person adopting a particular appearance in deference to his or her religion. In *Otto-Preminger-Institut v. Austria* (1994) Series A, No. 295–A; 19 E.H.R.R. 34, the applicant's freedom of expression (under Article 10) came into conflict with the right to freedom of religion, the right to show a film which offended the Catholic majority. In finding against the applicant, the Court put greater emphasis on the freedom of religion than the freedom of expression. Accordingly, wherever possible, it may be advantageous for applicants to frame their applications under Article 9.

E. ARTICLE 10 — FREEDOM OF EXPRESSION

1. Nature of the right

13–19   Freedom of expression specifically includes the freedom to hold opinions and to receive and impart information and opinions. Information and opinions extend to ideas and speculation (*Handyside v. U.K.* (1976) Series A, No. 24; 1 E.H.R.R. 737). It includes all forms of expression, verbal, written or otherwise. The right to impart opinions is, however, not completely unfettered. Article 10(2) entitles the State to impose restrictions. Thus, the Commission has upheld the right to prevent the dissemination of propaganda and opinions maintaining racial supremacy or the spreading of race hatred (*Glimmerveen and Harderbeek v. Netherlands* (1979) 18 D.R. 187). The Court appears to have accepted that the right extends to the workplace (*Vogt v. Germany* (1995) Series A, No. 323; 21 E.H.R.R. 205).

2. Freedom of expression and the common law

13–20   It should be noted that the concept of freedom of expression is not alien to the common law. In *Attorney-General v Guardian Newspapers Ltd (No. 2)* [1990] 1 A.C. 109, Lord Goff (at 283E–284A) expressed the view that in the field of freedom of speech, there was no difference in principle between English law and Article 10. In *Derbyshire County Council v. The Times* [1993] A.C. 534, while making reference to Article 10, Lord Keith (at 550E–551G) felt able to reach his conclusion without relying on the Convention.

3. Workplace discipline for expressing views

13–21   The freedom of an employee to express his or her views may come into conflict with the employer's right to manage the workplace. In *Glasenapp v. Germany* (1986) Series A, No. 104; 9 E.H.R.R. 25 and *Kosiek v Germany* (1986) Series A, No. 105; 9 E.H.R.R. 328, the applicants were teachers employed on a temporary basis by different *Länder* (*i.e.*, the provincial states) within what was then West Germany. Both were dismissed, in one case for suspected sympathy with the Communist Party and in the other for membership of an extreme right wing party. Holding such political views, the applicants could not swear allegiance to the German constitution, as was required in their employment as civil servants. The Court rejected their applications, because they had a choice as to their employment (*i.e.* they could have taken another job which allowed them to hold their particular views) and the Convention did not give them a right to work. The same issue arose again in *Vogt v. Germany* (1995) Series A, No. 323; 21 E.H.R.R. 205, where the Court upheld the application. It reasoned (first) that the political group in question (the Communist party) was not a proscribed organisation in Germany, (secondly) that there was no consistency of approach between different *Länder*, and (finally) on the basis of proportionality (the applicant was employed as a language teacher and to stop her working was out of proportion to the aim of the ban).

It is perhaps of significance that, in *Vogt*, the applicant was being disciplined for holding her views, whereas in *Glasenapp* and *Kosiek* the applicants were being refused employment. Similarly, in *Rekvenyi v. Hungary* (1997) 89–A D.R. 47; 23 E.H.R.R. C.D. 63, the Commission declared admissible an application arising out of the demand of the employer (a police force) that officers refrain from political activities and that, if they did not do so, they would have to leave their employment. It would appear, therefore, that once admitted to employment an employee is in a stronger position to resist interference with the freedom of speech than when applying for a job.

Ahmed and others v. U.K., The Times, October 2, 1998, concerned a restriction imposed by statute rather than an employer. A number of senior local government officers challenged the legality of statutory regulations which limited their ability to participate in certain types of political activity, such as standing for election as a local councillor. The European Court of Human Rights found that there was no violation of Article 10 on the ground that the restrictions were not disproportionate to the applicants' right to freedom of expression, having regard for the legitimacy of the need addressed by the regulations and the margin of appreciation enjoyed by the State.

4. Appearance codes

13 22 The Commission has decided that freedom of expression extends to expressing an idea or presenting information, including by the way in which a person dresses (*Stevens v. U.K.* (1986) 46 D.R. 245).

In most jobs, as a part of their management prerogative, employers lay down rules as to the appearance of their employees. In some instances these may have little to do with the way the employee performs his or her duties (as in *Burrett v. West Birmingham Health Authority* [1994] I.R.L.R. 7, where a female nurse objected to wearing a cap which served no practical purpose, as a matter of principle, because she regarded that it was "undignified and demeaning"). Put simply, can the bus driver refuse to wear a uniform because it does not affect his or her ability to do the job? Likewise, can the employer make the workforce dress smartly; can the female shop assistant who strictly observes Islam wear a veil against the express instructions of her employer; and does a woman have a right to wear trousers at work rather than a skirt?

13–23 Cases have been brought before industrial tribunals for unfair dismissal (where the termination of employment has resulted from the employee's failure to obey an instruction) and for sex and race discrimination. In domestic law, the leading case is *Smith v. Safeway plc* [1996] I.R.L.R. 456, in which a male employee was dismissed because he refused to cut his long hair, which offended the employer's appearance code. Women were allowed to have hair of any length, provided it was pinned back, if long; men were not. He claimed sex discrimination. The Court of Appeal held that he had not been discriminated against, because the employer was entitled to enforce a common code of smartness and conventionality, and in so doing it was entitled to differentiate between men and women. It was only discriminatory if, looking at the appearance code as a whole rather than garment by garment, one sex was treated less favourably than the other (*per* Phillips L.J. at 459 para. 17). *Smith* followed the principle laid down by the Employment Appeal Tribunal in *M Schmidt v. Austicks Bookshops Ltd* [1977] I.R.L.R. 360, another sex discrimination case, in which the applicant was dismissed for wearing trousers in contravention of a work-place rule that banned such clothing for women employees, such as the applicant, who came into contact with members of the public. The EAT found no discrimination, on the basis that there was a dress code for men, albeit different, as well as for women, and there was no discrimination in the way both codes were applied (see also *Burrett v. West Birmingham Health Authority* (above)).

The issue can be fairly postulated as the employee's freedom of expression versus the employer's right to manage: ". . . an employer is entitled to a large measure of discretion in controlling the image of his establishment . . ." (*Schmidt* at page 361, para. 10). English law acknowledges an employee's right to freedom of expression, but it will always attempt to achieve a balance with competing interests, in this case the need of the employer to determine what is best for the business. This was made clear in *L.M. Boychuk v. H.J. Symons Holdings Ltd* [1977] I.R.L.R. 395, where a lesbian employee was found to be fairly dismissed for refusing an order that she should not wear a badge saying "Lesbians ignite". Whilst acknowledging that there were limits to the employer's control over the employee's appearance, the Employment Appeal Tribunal declined to define where they lay, holding that it was essentially a matter for the industrial tribunal when considering reasonableness.

13–24 The same principles are evident in relation to race discrimination. In *Panesar v. Nestlé* [1980] I.C.R. 144, the applicant (a Sikh) was refused employment because he refused to cut off his beard for religious reasons. He claimed that he had been subject to indirect discrimination. The employer required employees to be clean shaven for reasons of food hygiene. Whilst acknowledging that application of the rule was undoubtedly discriminatory, the Court of Appeal held that it was justifiable (this being a defence to indirect discrimination, under Race Relations Act 1976, s.1(1)(b)). It is interesting to note that the Court dismissed the applicant's reliance (in part) on Article 9, on the basis that Article 9(2) would come to the assistance of the employer. Similarly, in *Singh v. British Rail Engineering Ltd* [1986] I.C.R. 22, and *Kingston and Richmond Area Health Authority v. Kaur* [1981] I.R.L.R. 337, two other Sikh applicants failed to establish indirect race discrimination, when the respondent employers were able to justify the requirements. In the former, the applicant refused to wear protective headgear which was introduced after he had been employed for over 10 years without an accident. In the latter, the applicant refused to wear a nurse's uniform unless her legs were covered.

As with all questions of what is reasonable, it is a matter of taking into account relevant factors and balancing them fairly. In *Schmidt*, the Employment Appeal Tribunal observed that one of these factors would be whether the employee came into contact with the public, but this is only one factor. Other factors justifying an employer's insistence on conformity to a standard would include: the better performance of duties (a railway ticket inspector wearing a uniform to give him or her authority to demand tickets from the public); health and safety (protective clothing for a factory worker); illegality (a helmet for a motor-cycle courier); and food hygiene (a head covering for a baker).

5. Whistle blowing

13–25   If an employee reveals information relating to his or her employment, he or she may be in breach of an express term in the contract of employment not to do so and/or the implied term of mutual trust and confidence between the employer and the employee. Disclosure can lead to disciplinary action, including dismissal, and a court has the power to grant an injunction to prevent disclosure or further disclosure. This behaviour, particularly where it occurs for reasons of conscience, is commonly referred to as "whistle blowing". The issue that arises is whether Article 10 acts to override (or at least mitigate) a contractual restriction on the dissemination of information by an employee.

Article 10(2) provides that lawful interference in the exercise of the freedom of expression may be justified where *inter alia* it is "necessary in a democratic society . . . for the protection of the reputation or the rights of others . . . (or) . . . for preventing the disclosure of information received in confidence". In *Barthold v. Germany* (1985) Series A, No. 90; 7 E.H.R.R. 383, the Court decided that "necessary" implies a pressing social need. In most whistle blowing cases, it will not be difficult for the restriction to be framed in these terms, for instance to protect the employer's business interests, its customers or other employees. Whether the particular interference complained about is justifiable depends on whether it is proportionate to the object of the restriction. In the final analysis, this depends on the circumstances of the case. The Strasbourg authorities have proceeded on a case by case basis, considering whether the proper balance has been achieved between the competing interests of the employer and employee. Because of this, there is no clear jurisprudence but a number of different strands, which have to be balanced against each other.

13–26   From the aspect of restrictions on the disclosure of information, it is recognised that employment carries with it duties which must be set against any right to freedom of speech. In *Morissens v. Belgium* (1988) 56 D.R. 127, a teacher was dismissed after claiming on television that she was not promoted because she was a lesbian. Her application was rejected by the Commission, in part on the basis that, by accepting the post, she had implicitly accepted the responsibilities that went with it, including a restriction on her freedom to speak out about matters of concern. As a general rule, the more responsible the post, the more the employee is expected to accept restrictions on the freedom of expression. The same point emerges from *Tucht v. Federal Republic of Germany* (1982) App. 9336/81, unreported, where the Commission ruled inadmissible the application of a medical consultant who had been dismissed for publicly criticising his employer. Further, the duty on the employee is likely to be greater if a breach of confidentiality would cause damage to the employer's business (*Van Der Heijden v. The Netherlands* (1985) 41 D.R. 264; 8 E.H.R.R. 279). The mode of expression and the way in which the issue is raised are significant. An employee who uses inflammatory language is likely to be treated less sympathetically than one who is temperate in criticising his or her employer (see *Tucht v. Federal Republic of Germany* (above), where the applicant had been abusive in the manner of his criticism). The employee is expected to take up any concern with the employer first before publicising it in the press (*Morissens* (above), *Grigoriades v. Greece* (1995) 20 E.H.R.R. C.D. 92).

Nevertheless, the more well-founded the criticism, the more protection the employee might expect under Article 10 (in *Morissens*, the Commission noted that the applicant had no evidence for her allegations). The same equation exists, depending upon the extent of public concern (*Thorgeir Thorgeirson v. Iceland* (1992) Series A, No. 239; 14 E.H.R.R. 843). The employee is also likely to be given more latitude if the criticism is aimed at an organ of the state (*Thorgeir Thorgeirson*).

F. ARTICLE 11 — FREEDOM OF ASSEMBLY AND ASSOCIATION

1. The right to join a trade union

13–27   Article 11 expressly refers to "the right to form and to join trade unions". The right to belong to a trade union is enshrined in English law by the Trade Union and Labour Relations (Consolidation) Act 1992 ("TULR(C)A 1996"). A trade union may not refuse membership to any person except on specified grounds, for instance where exclusion is caused by the applicant's own conduct (section 174, *ibid.*). Further, it is not a crime to join a union (section 11(1), *ibid.*); an employer must not discriminate against a trade union member in selection for employment (section 137, *ibid.*); an employer must not victimise an employee for belonging to a trade union (section 146, *ibid.*); and a dismissal for membership of a trade union or for trade union activities is automatically unfair (section 152, *ibid.*).

2. The right to be represented by a trade union

13–28   Although Article 11 gives individuals the right to join together in trade unions, it does not deal with any rights enjoyed by the unions themselves. Yet, in practice, the right to join a union only has any real meaning if the union is entitled to act on behalf of its members. In *Swedish Engine Drivers' Union v. Sweden* (1976) Series A, No. 20; 1 E.H.R.R. 617, the Court decided (at para. 39) that Article 11 did not secure any particular treatment of trade unions or their members by the State. In support, the Court pointed to the fact that the right to conclude a collective agreement was not expressed in Article 11. Furthermore, it decided that such a right could not be implied because not all the contracting states incorporated it into their domestic law, nor was it indispensable for the effective enjoyment of trade union freedom. The Court did not doubt, however, that trade unions derive certain rights from Article 11. As the Court noted (at para. 4): "No-one disputes the fact that the applicant union can engage in various kinds of activity *vis-à-vis* the government. It is open to it, for instance, to present claims, to make representations for the protection of the interests of its members . . . and to negotiate." The Court held that the phrase "for the protection of his interests" was not otiose. It followed from the use of these words that it was intended that Article 11 should enable members of a union to be heard through their union, but not necessarily anything more (see also *National Union of Belgian Police v. Belgium* (1975) Series A, No. 9; 1 E.H.R.R. 578).

In *Associated Newspapers Ltd v. Wilson* and *Associated British Ports v. Palmer* [1995] 2 A.C. 151, the employers offered their employees personal contracts in substitution for collective agreements and denied pay rises to those employees who refused to sign them. The House of Lords, in holding that there had been no discrimination against those who refused to do so, made it clear that there was no right of union representation in English law (*per* Lord Lloyd at 486C–D). There is thus a clear conflict between domestic law and Article 11. In both cases, the Commission has declared the employees' applications admissible.

13–29 Whilst the *Swedish Engine Drivers' Union* case clearly resolves the principle of representation, it does not deal with the form of representation. What if an employer recognises one union (or indeed other staff representative organisation), but not another union, possibly because the former is less effective on behalf of its members? It is arguable that the right to representation means the right to effective representation.

3. The right not to join a trade union

13–30 Until relatively recently, trade union membership was not uncommonly a prerequisite to the employment of an individual (notoriously, for instance, in the newspaper industry). This arose out of both the desire of unions to obtain the best possible bargaining position *vis-à-vis* the employers and the view that non-members should not benefit from the improvement of terms and conditions obtained through collective bargaining. This state of affairs is known colloquially as "the closed shop", but is more accurately termed a "union membership agreement". If the individual is refused membership, he or she may be denied the opportunity to earn a living in a chosen occupation.

From time to time, the operation of a closed shop has been permitted under English law, most recently by the Trade Union and Labour Relations Act 1974 ("TULRA"), which provided that it was not unfair to dismiss an employee who refused to join a trade union in circumstances where there was a closed shop (TULRA Sched. 1, para. 6(5)). The only exception was where the individual refused on religious grounds. In 1976, British Rail, which had some 250,000 staff at the time, entered into a union membership agreement, under which all employees were required to be members of one of three unions. The agreement provided that the only permissible reason for not joining was a religious conviction, but in this respect it was narrower than the statutory scheme in that union membership had to be against the tenets of the particular religion (as opposed to the personal beliefs of the individual employees). Fifty-four staff members refused to join and were consequently dismissed. Because of TULRA, they were deprived of the right to claim unfair dismissal. In *Young, James and Webster v. U.K.* (1981) Series A, No. 44; [1981] I.R.L.R. 408, three employees (whose refusals to join were unconnected with matters of religious conviction) complained that TULRA contravened their freedom of association under Article 11. The Court found in favour of the applicants. Paradoxically, by the time the case was heard, the United Kingdom's position was being defended by a Conservative government which was committed to wholesale trade union reform and had already abolished the closed shop (see Employment Act 1980). Indeed some commentators have criticised the case on the basis that the defence was not as fully argued as it might have been, but it is fair to point out that the Court heard from the Trades Union Congress and considered the question of justification of its own motion. The immediate effect of the case was that the U.K. government made provision for compensation to be paid to those employees who had lost their jobs between 1974 and 1980 (Employment Act 1982, Sched. 2).

13–31 In *Young, James and Webster*, the most radical interpretation of Article 11 was given by six of the judges. They held that a freedom to join a trade union implied a concomitant (and opposite) freedom not to join a union. At the other end of the spectrum, three judges (who found in favour of the United Kingdom) pointed out that, on a literal interpretation, Article 11 merely guaranteed the freedom to join a trade union: the contracting parties could have chosen to include a right not to join, but they deliberately chose not to (as is clear from the *travaux préparatoires*). The majority of nine judges considered (at para. 55) that there was a limited right not to join:

". . . a threat of dismissal involving loss of livelihood is a most serious form of compulsion and, in the present instance, it was directed against persons engaged by British Rail before the introduction of any obligation to join a particular trade union.
    In the Court's opinion, such a form of compulsion, in the circumstances of the case, strikes at the very substance of the freedom guaranteed by Article 11. For this reason alone, there has been an interference with that freedom as regards each of the three applicants."

Thus, the result of the case was not that the operation of a closed shop was ruled out completely. It is of course open to speculation but, had the three become employed knowing full well that they had to join a particular union, the result may have been different.

13-32 The principle in *Young, James and Webster* is that the negative aspect of freedom of association is necessarily complimentary to, and inseparable from, its positive aspect. As the Court put it (at page 416), "the notion of freedom implies some freedom of choice as to its exercise". It has since been applied in *Sigurjonsson v. Iceland* (1993) Series A, No. 234; 16 E.H.R.R. 462.

Young, James and Webster is of little direct practical value in the late 1990s, as it continues to be the law that closed shop agreements can only be effective if all employees agree to join the union; and, in the current political climate, a return to the position as it was between 1974 and 1980 seems unlikely. Any dissident is also protected from unfair dismissal (TULR(C)A 1992, s.152). Nevertheless, the decision acts as a constraint on any future government wishing to reintroduce the closed shop.

4. Collective bargaining

13-33 The leading case on collective bargaining is *Swedish Engine Drivers' Union v. Sweden* (1976) Series A, No. 20; 1 E.H.R.R. 617. The Swedish Government refused to enter into a collective agreement with the applicant trade union; it had entered into another such agreement with a larger union. The Court found against the applicant, holding that Article 11 did not guarantee any particular treatment of unions or their members by the State so as to require the State to conclude a collective agreement with them. The union merely had the right to be heard. The State had freedom of choice as to the means to be used to achieve this end.

In *Gustafsson v. Sweden* (1996) 22 E.H.R.R. 409, the issue resurfaced under a different guise. Mr Gustafsson's business comprised a youth hostel and a restaurant. In the particular industry, the employers' organisation and the union had concluded collective agreements in relation to the terms and conditions for the employees. Mr Gustafsson was not a member of the employers' organisation nor were his employees members of the union. As a result, they were not contractually bound by the collective agreements. The union (but not his own staff) took lawful, albeit secondary, industrial action against Mr Gustaffson, leading him to suffer economic loss. He asked the Swedish Government to intervene on his behalf, but they declined on the basis that it was a dispute between private subjects. In his application under the Convention, Mr Gustaffson complained that his freedom not to associate was being violated by him being forced to join the employers' organisation. The court decided that, whereas under Article 11 there is an implied right to refuse to join a trade union, there is no similar implied right to refuse to enter into a collective agreement. The decision was based on the *Swedish Engine Drivers' Union* case: if there was no right under Article 11 to enter into collective bargaining, there could be no negative equivalent.

G. ARTICLE 14 — PROHIBITION OF DISCRIMINATION

1. Nature of the right

13–34   At its simplest, discrimination is a difference in treatment between different people or groups. It may arise directly or indirectly. Direct discrimination is where the difference in treatment arises from a failure to afford equality of treatment; indirect discrimination where there is inequality of outcome.

The Convention does not guarantee freedom from discrimination. Article 14 is not a freestanding right, whatever the reason for the discrimination. It has been described as "parasitic" by some commentators (see Harris, O'Boyle and Warbrick, *Law of the European Convention on Human Rights* (Butterworths, 1995) at page 463). By contrast, in international law, anti-discrimination measures are central to human rights, as in the International Convention on the Elimination of All Forms of Racial Discrimination 1966, the Convention on the Elimination of All Forms of Discrimination against Women 1979 and the U.N. Declaration on the Elimination of All Forms of Intolerance and Discrimination based on Religion and Belief 1981. The most comprehensive provision is found in Article 26 of the International Covenant on Civil and Political Rights, which provides that:

> "All persons are equal before the law and are entitled without any discrimination to the equal protection of the law. In this respect the law shall prohibit any discrimination and guarantee to all persons equal and effective protection against discrimination on any ground such as race, colour, sex, language, religion, political or other opinion, national or social origin, property, birth or other status."

13–35   Article 14 thus merely provides that the other rights and freedoms in the Convention must not be applied in a discriminatory manner. This clearly limits its application. In consequence, claims under Article 14 are usually appended to breaches of other "substantial" rights and freedoms. Despite this, it is possible for there to be a breach of Article 14 alone: see, for instance, *Case Relating to Certain Aspects of the Laws on the Use of Language in Education in Belgium* (1968) Series A, No. 6; 1 E.H.R.R. 252, (the *"Belgian Linguistics Case"*), in which the Court found that there was no breach of Article 6 (the right to a fair trial), as the Convention did not require the State to provide for appeals in criminal trials, but where the State had chosen to have an appeals system, it was obliged not to discriminate by denying access to particular groups.

Article 14 is drawn in wide terms. In contrast to English law, it forbids discrimination "on any ground"; the references in the Article to different ways in which discrimination may arise (for instance, sex, race, etc.) are merely examples. It is thus open-ended and does not include an exhaustive list of possible forms of discrimination (*Cossey v. U.K.* (1990) Series A, No. 184; 13 E.H.R.R. 622, at para. 35; see also Bayefsky, *The Principle of Equality or Non Discrimination in International Law* (1990) 11 H.R.L.J. 1). Accordingly, the Convention envisages prohibiting discriminatory practices that have not been identified in the text of Article 14.

13–36 Nevertheless, the Strasbourg authorities clearly disapprove of certain forms of discrimination more than others. The Court has held that discrimination on the ground of sex needs "weighty reasons" to justify it (*Abdulaziz, Cabales and Balkandali v. U.K.* (1985) Series A, No. 94; 7 E.H.R.R. 471). European Union law has placed (and continues to place) great emphasis on equality of treatment between men and women and it would be surprising if the Court did not reflect this. By contrast, despite ruling in *S v. U.K.* (1986) 47 D.R. 274 that the meaning of "sex" included sexual orientation (see also the similar view taken by the United Nations Human Rights Committee in relation to the International Covenant on Civil and Political Rights), the Commission has persistently declared inadmissible cases where discrimination is alleged on the basis of sexual orientation, so that the Court has not had the opportunity to adjudicate on the question of whether it is discriminatory. There is no clear jurisprudence from the Strasbourg authorities on this issue, the tendency being to look at the merits of each individual case and conflate them with whether a difference in treatment can be justified.

The Court appears to be ready to confront the assumption that men and women behave stereotypically. In *Schuler-Zgraggen v. Switzerland* (1993) Series A, No. 263; 16 E.H.R.R. 405, the Court found a breach of Article 14 (coupled with Article 6) where the applicant (a woman) was denied an appeal against the refusal of a disability pension on the grounds that, having a child, it was unlikely that she would want to work.

13–37 Difference in treatment alone, however, does not constitute discrimination under Article 14. In the *Belgian Linguistics Case* (above, paragraph 13–35), the Court decided that there must also be a lack of a legitimate aim and a lack of proportionality between the end sought and the means to achieve it (para. 10). States rarely experience difficulties in establishing a legitimate aim. If the Court is to intervene, it is more likely to be on the basis of the means being disproportionate to the end. There appears to be no consistency of approach. Where the Court is considering a form of discrimination that it clearly disapproves of, it is likely to apply a far more rigorous test in deciding whether the difference in treatment can be justified. This, in turn, is often determined by the Court's view of the consensus amongst the States, evidenced by treaties, agreements, etc. In *Marckx v. Belgium* (1979) Series A, No. 31; 2 E.H.R.R. 330, at paragraph 31, the Court was able to point to a resolution of the Committee of Ministers of the Council of Europe to demonstrate general European agreement that illegitimate children should not be treated differently to those born to married parents (note, similar reasoning was used by the ECJ in *Grant v. South West Trains Ltd* [1998] I.R.L.R. 206 (see paragraph 13–58, below) to justify, in part, that decision). In relation to proportionality, states are generally allowed a margin of appreciation. How wide that margin is often turns on the consensus amongst the States.

2. Indirect discrimination

13–38 Although the Court has recognised indirect discrimination (*Marckx v. Belgium* (1979) Series A, No. 31; 2 E.H.R.R. 330), there have been few cases and none has been successful to date.

3. Positive discrimination

13–39 There have been few cases before the Strasbourg authorities dealing with positive discrimination (sometimes referred to as affirmative action). This is an issue of great importance in terms of the employment of minorities, particularly where it is considered that they are under-represented in the work force (for instance to increase the number of black officers in the police force). Both the Sex Discrimination Act 1975, s.7 and the Race Relations Act 1976, s.5 permit the recruitment of staff in a discriminatory way, where there is a genuine occupational qualification. Clearly this can, and usually will, amount to a difference in treatment between, say, separate ethnic groups, but it does not follow that there is a breach of Article 14. Applying the test in the *Belgian Linguistics Case* (above), the State is entitled to argue that a legitimate aim and proportionality exist in support of discrimination. For example, in *Lindsay v. U.K.* (1986) 49 D.R. 181; 9 E.H.R.R. 555, the Commission found that a more generous tax regime to encourage married women to take up employment could be justified.

In relation to European Union law the ECJ has considered the issue of positive discrimination. Article 2(1) of Directive 76/207 (Equal Treatment) sets out the general principle that equal treatment means no discrimination, direct or indirect, on the grounds of sex; but sub-para. (4) provides that this is "without prejudice to measures to promote equal opportunity between men and women, in particular by removing existing inequalities which affect women's opportunities". The effect of this provision was considered in *Kalanke v. Freie Hansestadt Bremen* [1996] I.C.R. 314, where a national rule provided that, where equally qualified men and women were candidates for the same promotion in fields and there were fewer women than men at the level of the relevant post, women were automatically to be given priority. This was held to be discriminatory on the ground of sex, contrary to the directive. More recently, however, the ECJ has held that such priority is permissible where there was a saving clause requiring the employer to consider whether reasons specific to the individual male candidate tilted the balance in his favour (*Marschall v. Landl Nordrhein-Westfalen* [1998] I.R.L.R. 39).

3. Summary

13–40 Given the lack of a free-standing right not to be discriminated against, Article 14 is likely to be of use only when appended to a breach of another right or freedom, particularly Articles 8, 9, 10 and 11. When considering claims under these articles, practitioners should always be aware of the possibility of an Article 14 claim.

H. ARTICLE 6 — THE RIGHT TO A FAIR TRIAL

1. Nature of the right

13–41 Article 6 provides procedural protection in relation to the determination of civil rights and obligations and criminal charges. In relation to employment law, it is the former that is significant.

2. Civil rights and obligations

13–42 This phrase broadly means private law as opposed to public law rights (*Ringeisen v. Austria (No. 1)* (1971) Series A, No. 13; 1 E.H.R.R. 455 at para. 94). The distinction between public and private law rights is of course well known in domestic law, but it is an autonomous concept under the Convention which does not sit comfortably with English jurisprudence. In essence, it is "the character of the right" that is important and not the State's categorisation of it as private or public (*Konig v. Federal Republic of Germany* (1978) Series A, No. 27; 2 E.H.R.R. 170 at paras 88–90).

The Commission has decided that rights under a contract of employment are civil rights: see *Darnell v. U.K.* (1991) 69 D.R. 306 (an NHS employee) and *C v. U.K.* (1987) 54 D.R. 162 (a school caretaker). Further, Article 6 extends beyond the contract of employment to include the right to pursue a particular type of work, such as, medicine (*Konig v Federal Republic of Germany* (above)), law, (*H v. Belgium* (1987) Series A, No. 127; 10 E.H.R.R. 339), architecture (*Guchez v. Belgium* (1984) 40 D.R. 100) and acting as a business agent or a property manager (*Jaxel v. France* (1987) 54 D.R. 42; 11 E.H.R.R. 87). Thus, Article 6 is wide enough to encompass proceedings which in English Law might be regarded as issues of public law, for instance, regulation by a public body.

3. Disciplinary proceedings

13–43 Article 6 guarantees the right to a fair and public hearing by an independent and impartial tribunal and thus raises the question whether it applies to proceedings concerned with workplace discipline. An individual may be subject to discipline affecting his or her job in a number of ways: by an employer, by a professional organisation, by a statutory body or by other executive regulation.

Most large and medium-size employers have comprehensive provisions regulating discipline; it is not uncommon for such procedures to be modelled on court proceedings with, for instance, the right to representation, to call and cross-examine witnesses to appeal. There are, however, rarely if ever public hearings, nor are cases likely to be heard by independent tribunals. In general, employees who have been employed for less than two years do not have a right to claim unfair dismissal in industrial tribunal proceedings (ERA 1996, s.108(1)).

13–44 Certain professions are subject to regulation by their own professional bodies, for instance, doctors, dentists, nurses, solicitors and barristers. Their powers extend well beyond the employment relationship. Whereas an employer can decide whether to employ a person, a professional body exercises a far wider and more significant influence, *i.e.*, the power to determine the right to work in a chosen occupation. Other bodies exercise similar control in relation to particular industries, for instance, professional footballers by the Football Association, athletes by the British Athletics Federation. Depending on the offence, disciplinary tribunals established by a professional or trade body can impose penalties of great significance including fines, suspension from practice and indefinite disqualification.In some instances, disciplinary matters are subject to a statutory code: for instance, police officers (Police Act 1996) and employees in the financial services industries (Financial Services Act 1986).

There are other (less obvious) ways in which a person's right to engage in their chosen employment is regulated: for instance, the Department of Education and Science maintains "List 99" which identifies teachers about whom there are particular concerns, for instance because they have been convicted of serious offences. Similarly, the Department of Health keeps "the Consultancy Register" in respect of social workers. In either case, a person is effectively prevented from working in that type of employment whilst on the register.

13–45   In *Le Compte, Van Leuven and De Meyere v. Belgium* (1981) Series A, No. 43; 4 E.H.R.R. 1, the Court decided that Article 6 applied to a disciplinary tribunal established by a medical association (independent of the State, albeit established by statute) with which all doctors other than those employed in the armed services were required to register in order to practice. Article 6 is a procedural right. It does not give a substantive right to take court proceedings where one does not exist in domestic law. It provides for the right to a fair hearing only in the determination of whatever substantive rights there are (see *H v. Belgium* (1987) Series A, No. 127; 10 E.H.R.R. 339 at para. 40). It follows that it does not give employees the right to take court or tribunal proceedings where they are excluded from doing so, say, by virtue of not having worked for two years.

Further, it only apples to disputes at a national level between private persons or between a person and the state. Accordingly, internal disciplinary proceedings held by an employer are outside the ambit of the right. Nevertheless, there is no reason why other forms of discipline should not be caught, for instance, regulation by a professional body or a regulator.

13–46   Article 6 does not impose any obligation on the instigator of the proceedings; it operates as an entitlement of the person against whom proceedings are brought. So, for instance, proceedings held in camera are not in themselves contrary to Article 6, provided both sides are happy to adopt such a procedure. If, however, the defendant (for want of a better term) objected to a private hearing, it would have to be held in public.

Disciplinary proceedings often result in a penalty which falls short of loss of employment, for instance, a warning by an employer or a financial penalty imposed by a professional body. The Commission has decided that disciplinary proceedings resulting in a reprimand do not fall within Article 6 (*App. 10331/93 v. U.K.* (1983) 6 E.H.R.R. 583). This is somewhat anomalous, given that the decision on the appropriate penalty cannot be made until proceedings are completed. One answer to this could be that Article 6 rights apply where the tribunal is minded to impose a penalty that will lead to the loss of the right to work.

I. WAIVER OF CONVENTION RIGHTS

13–47 It is accepted that Convention rights can be waived (*Deweer v. Belgium* (1980) Series A, No. 35; 2 E.H.R.R. 439, para. 49; see also *R. v. Switzerland* (1987) 51 D.R. 83) but only if it is done in an unequivocal manner (*Pfeiffer and Plankl v. Austria* (1992) Series A, No. 227; 14 E.H.R.R. 692, at para. 37).

This issue is of importance, as employees may be required to sign contracts of employment containing terms expressly excluding Convention rights (*e.g.* a confidentiality clause restricting freedom of speech). The Commission has accepted that an individual may contract out of Convention rights (*Vereiging Rechtsinkels Utrecht v. The Netherlands* (1986) 46 D.R. 200), but the mere signing of the contract is not sufficient (see *Rommelfanger v. FRG* (1989) 62 D.R. 151, in relation to Article 10). It is suggested that if an employer wishes to exclude Convention rights, the employee must be made aware of what is being imposed on him or her in clear and unequivocal terms (whether the waiver is contained within a contract of employment, or expressed in some other way).

13–48 There may be a difference in the position of existing and prospective employees, although the Court has not adjudicated upon this question. A common reason relied on by the Court for refusing applications by employees is that they always have the choice of whether or not to take the job: see *Glasenapp v. Germany* (1986) Series A, No. 104; 9 E.H.R.R. 25 and *Kosiek v. Germany* (1986) Series A, No. 105; 9 E.H.R.R. 328. Arguably, the Court cannot avail itself of this line of reasoning where the employee is already in the post. Faced with the consequences of not signing a waiver of rights, the employee may face the loss of his or her job by refusing to comply (see also, *Knudsen v. Sweden* (1985) 42 D.R. 247).

J. REMEDIES

1. Power to grant relief

13–49 In *Secretary of State for Employment v. Mann* [1997] I.C.R. 209, the Court of Appeal held that the jurisdiction of industrial tribunals is solely defined by statute and, accordingly, they had no inherent or general jurisdiction (in that case to hear and determine a claim for damages against the State for failing to implement European Union law). Jurisdiction is conferred by a variety of statutes (see, for instance, paragraph 13–03, above). In addition, it has been extended to encompass breaches of the employment contract or of contracts connected with employment (Industrial Tribunals Act 1996, s.3, Industrial Tribunals Extension of Jurisdiction (England and Wales) Order 1994 (S.I. 1994 No. 1623)). Under the Act, the remedies available to a court or tribunal which finds that a public authority has acted in a way which is incompatible with the Convention are widely drawn (section 8(1)). At first glance, it might be thought that this extends the jurisdiction of industrial tribunals to grant relief for a breach of a Convention right. The Act itself, however, does not confer jurisdiction on tribunals, although provision is made for this to be done by rules made by the Secretary of State or the Lord Chancellor (section 7).

It should be possible to frame the majority of claims for breach of a Convention right in terms that enable them to be brought within the present jurisdiction of industrial tribunals, for instance as unfair dismissal, unlawful discrimination, breach of contract, etc. Absent this, claims may only be brought if the rules made under the Act so provide, failing which, an applicant's recourse is to take action in the High Court or a county court, which can award damages, to grant an injunction or to make a declaration.

2. Monetary compensation

13–50   Most employment disputes are decided by industrial tribunals whose principal remedy is compensation, although in cases of breach of contract there is a parallel jurisdiction in the civil courts.

In proceedings for breach of a Convention right, there is no automatic right to damages even if a breach is proved. There are two limiting factors. First, it is provided that no award shall be made unless it is "necessary in order to afford just satisfaction to the person in whose favour it is made" (section 8(3)). This is a novel formulation by contrast with, for instance, the right to compensation for unfair dismissal where the basic award is calculated according to a mathematical formula and the compensatory award is "such amount as the tribunal considers just and equitable in all the circumstances" (ERA 1996, s.123(1)). Secondly, in deciding whether to make an award, regard must be had for the principles applied by the European Court of Human Rights under Article 41 (section 8(4)).

K. CONCLUSIONS

1. New hierarchy between public and private employees

13–51   Practical use of Convention rights under the Act by employees, otherwise than in relation to the interpretation and effect of legislation, will involve application of the term "public authority" as defined in section 6 (see generally Chapter 3). Thus, in relation to employment by public authorities, employees may enjoy the additional benefits of protection against violations of Convention rights by the employer. Central to this will be the operation of section 6(5), which has the effect of limiting the definition of public authority where acts of a "private" nature are in question.

In English law, matters of contract (including employment) are generally regarded as issues of private law, whether the employer is a public authority or not. This has arisen under the Convention in the context of establishing whether a particular employment is a civil right for the purposes of Article 6 (right to a fair trial). In *Darnell v. U.K.* (1991) 69 D.R. 306 and *C v. U.K.* (1987) 54 D.R. 162, the Commission decided that a National Health Service employee and a school caretaker (both having public sector employers) were entitled to Article 6 protection because employment under an ordinary contract of employment was a civil right. In *Lombardo v. Italy* (1992) Series A, No. 249–B; 21 E.H.R.R. 188

at para. 17, the Court characterised a dispute about a judge's pension as a civil right by equating it to "a contract of employment governed by private law".

13–52 Nevertheless it does not follow from the fact that both English law and the Strasbourg authorities characterise a contract of employment as a private law matter that all employment law issues are axiomatically outside the scope of section 6. The limitation under section 6(5) applies if "the nature of the act is private". It is suggested that this is likely to involve considerations other that just whether the legal relationship is governed by private law (see generally, paragraph 1–48, above). It involves categorising the act itself as private or public as opposed to the nature of the legal relationship. In so doing, regard should be had to a range of characteristics, for instance the nature of the function that is being performed, why the authority is performing it, whether there is a statutory obligation to do so, whether it is in the nature of a business and whether it is touched by issues of public policy. For instance, a contract of employment between a teacher and a local education authority is clearly governed by private law, but arguably the nature of the employment is public because of the statutory obligation on the employer to educate children in its area, the lack of any requirement for parents to pay for the service and because state education is essentially a matter of public policy.

Public authorities (such as central and local government, and the health service) are amongst the biggest employers in Britain. To the extent that such bodies are held to be public authorities for employment purposes under the Act, the most immediate effect will be to lead to differential rights as between the public and private sectors (though see further at paragraph 13–53, below). Private sector employees will not have the same level of protection.

2. Development of the common law

13–53 In terms of the development of employment law, it has been suggested by a leading academic that incorporation of the Convention is not an end in itself, but a means to an end; in broad terms, it represents a change in ideology and will eventually lead to a change in culture (Hepple, *"Human Rights and Employment Law"* — lecture to Society for Advanced Legal Studies, March 18, 1998). Over the medium to long term, the greatest influence that the Act will have on employment law may well be in the development of the common law (see generally paragraph 1–64). If so, it will apply equally to all employees, regardless of whether they are employed by a public authority.

There is ample scope for the interpretation of the implied term of trust and confidence in accordance with Convention rights. This is the experience of other common law jurisdictions. For instance, in *Re Canadian Pacific Ltd v. United Transportation Union* (1987) 31 L.A.C. 179, it was decided that the employer's policy of random drug testing offended the rights of employees to privacy under the Canadian Charter of Rights and Freedoms. Similarly, in the United States, the California Court of Appeal applied a human rights interpretation to the implied term in *Luck v. Southern Pacific Transportation Co.* (1990) 267 Cal. Rptr. 618.

13–54   In unfair dismissal proceedings, when considering reasonableness, the industrial tribunal must carry out a balancing act between the interests of the employer and those of the employee. In discrimination cases (whether on the basis of sex, race or disability), a similar balancing act is required in judging whether the employer's difference in treatment is justifiable. If proportionality is applied to reasonableness in unfair dismissal cases and to justification in discrimination cases, it may lead to a re-evaluation of the employer's prerogative to manage. By way of example, in *L. M. Boychuk v. H. J. Symons Holdings Ltd*, (see paragraph 13–23, above), the industrial tribunal found that dismissal was within the range of reasonable responses of the employer where the employee insisted on wearing a badge displaying her sexuality. By having to acknowledge the employee's freedom of expression and by applying a test of proportionality, the tribunal might have reached the conclusion that dismissal was out of proportion to the disciplinary offence.

3. Influence on new legislation

13–55   The Convention imposes positive obligations upon States to enable their citizens to benefit from Convention freedoms, at least in some respects (see generally at paragraph 2–35 and following). Thus, in *Plattform "Artze Fur Das Leben" v. Austria* (1988) Series A, No. 139; 13 E.H.R.R. 204, which concerned Article 11, the Court (at paragraph 32) held that in some circumstances there may be an obligation on the State to prevent interference where it comes from a private source. In *X and Y v. Netherlands* (1985) Series A, No. 91; 8 E.H.R.R. 235, the Court commented (at paragraph 23), in relation to Article 8, that if there is such a positive obligation, it "may involve the adoption of measures designed to secure respect for private life even in the sphere of the relations of individuals between themselves".

Thus, by reference to *Halford* (above), the State could be obliged to provide a means for the employee to protect his or her privacy right within the working environment, although the choice of the means of compliance is subject to a wide margin of appreciation on the part of the State (see *X and Y v. The Netherlands* (above) at paragraph 24).

4. The European Union and human rights

13–56   The European Communities Treaty does not guarantee human rights, and the European Union itself has yet to accede to the Convention (the ECJ having ruled that this can only take place by treaty rather than through a measure of the Council (see *Opinion 2/94* [1996] E.C.R. I–1759)). The ECJ has, however, long accepted human rights as part of the jurisprudence of European Union law when considering national rules that fall within the scope of community law (see *Internationale Handelsgesellschaft mbH v. Einfuhr-und Vorratsstelle Eür Getreide und Futtermittel* [1970] E.C.R. II–1125, at para. 4; *Johnston v. Chief Constable of the Royal Ulster Constabulary* [1986] I.R.L.R. 263, at para. 18; *Kremzow v. Austria, The Times*, August 11, 1997). In *Elliniki Radiophonia Tileorassi AE v. Pliroforissis and Kouvelas* [1991] E.C.R. I–2925

("*ERT*"), the ECJ observed (at para. 41) that the Community "cannot accept measures which are incompatible with the observance of human rights thus recognised and guaranteed."

Indeed European Union law has progressed further along the human rights path than just looking at the Convention. In the *ERT* decision, it noted that the ECJ drew upon guidelines supplied by international treaties for the protection of human rights on which the Member States had collaborated or of which they were signatories (see also *J. Nold and Others v. Commission of the European Communities* [1974] E.C.R. I–491, at para. 13; and *Hubert Wauchauf v. Federal Republic of Germany* [1989] E.C.R. III–2609, at para. 19). Thus the ECJ permits itself to consider, for instance, the International Covenant on Civil and Political Rights, the treaties of the International Labour Organisation and the European Social Charter, all of which arguably provide greater human rights protection than the Convention.

13–57 European law is of great importance in employment law, particulary in relation to equality, where there is substantial protection from discrimination on the ground of sex: see Article 119 of the European Community Treaty (Equal Pay for Men and Women) and various directives in particular, 75/117 (Equal Pay for Equal Value), 76/207 (Equal Treatment), 86/738 (Equal Treatment in Occupational Pension Schemes), 86/113 (Equal Treatment for the Self-employed). To these may be added further directives relating to parental leave (three months' leave to men and women after the birth of a child) and part-time and atypical work (no need to show disparate impact between men and women to prove discrimination), which are due to be implemented in 1999 and 2000 respectively.

13–58 Discrimination for reasons other than sex has not been afforded equivalent importance under European law. The E.C. Treaty only provides for non-discrimination on the ground of nationality (Article 6). Pressure is mounting for difference in treatment on account of sexual orientation to be recognised as discriminatory. The European Parliament has declared that it deplores such discrimination, but the European Union has not legislated on the issue. It should be noted that, even in the ECJ, such discrimination has been held not to be unlawful: most recently in *Grant v. South West-Trains Ltd* [1998] I.R.L.R. 206, where the employer refused to grant a travel concession to an employee's homosexual partner which would have been allowed had the relationship been heterosexual. The Treaty of Amsterdam inserts a new Article 6a into the European Communities Treaty, which when in force will give the Council power to "take appropriate action to combat discrimination based on sex, racial and ethnic origin, religion or belief, disability, age or sexual orientation". It is suggested that when directives are issued in relation to these forms of discrimination, there is likely to be a change in the attitude of the ECJ.

13–59 Because English law is subservient to European Union law including the judgments of the ECJ, Convention and other human rights law is thus incorporated indirectly into English law and, in some respects, in a more effective and broader way than is envisaged by the Act. If an issue can be framed in terms of a breach of European Union law, this may be a better mechanism for airing a human rights violation concerning employment than applying Convention law under the Act.

CHAPTER 14

Tax Law

Jonathan Peacock and Francis Fitzpatrick* (Barristers of 11 New Square, Lincoln's Inn, London)

A. INTRODUCTION

14–01 Surprising as it may seem at first sight, the Human Rights Act 1998 does have important implications in the fields of direct and indirect taxation on a number of different levels. Whilst the Convention predictably gives a broad measure of discretion to states in the design and implementation of their taxation policies (nothing is quite as fundamental to the "nation state" as the levying of taxes), the jurisprudence of both the Commission and the Court shows that this discretion is by no means untrammelled. Although the number of successful challenges to acts by states in this field is low as yet, commercial and tax lawyers are now looking more closely at rights derived both from the European Union and from the Convention, specifically where large sums of money are at stake or the issues transcend national boundaries.

The implications of the Act for tax advisers can be examined on two levels: substantive and procedural. In outline, issues under the Act and the Convention will arise (and have already arisen) on a substantive level where, notwithstanding the broad measure of discretion conferred on the Inland Revenue and HM Customs and Excise, the U.K. government purports to levy or collect taxes of any sort by measures or decisions which amount to arbitrary confiscation of property or which are discriminatory as between different taxpayers in a relevantly identical position, without objective and reasonable justification. This is examined in detail at paragraphs 14–05 and following, and 14–16 and following, respectively below. On a procedural level, issues will arise (and have arisen) where, in some (but not all) disputes over liability to tax before the special tax tribunals or in the courts, taxpayers are deprived of a fair hearing. Disputes which are covered by this procedural protection are those which determine a taxpayer's "private rights and obligations". This is examined at paragraph 14–20 and following below.

14–02 A number of general features of the Act specifically relevant to tax matters can be noted here.

* We are extremely grateful for the comments of H.H. Stephen Oliver Q.C., President of the VAT and Duties Tribunal and the Presiding Special Commissioner, on an earlier draft of this chapter. All errors and omissions remain however entirely our own work.

First, all U.K. legislation has to be construed, so far as possible, to accord with the Convention rights (see section 3(1)) even if this means overturning previous judicial interpretations of words and phrases. The jurisprudence of the Court and the Commission on tax matters will be persuasive but not binding on U.K. courts (see generally paragraphs 1–18—1–19, above).

Secondly, and where this is not possible, the U.K. courts can declare that a particular provision of primary or secondary legislation is incompatible with the Convention; such a declaration will not itself invalidate the offending law and will have no effect on the parties to the litigation concerned (see section 4, and generally at paragraphs 1–40—1–43, above). This power is only available in the High Court and above; on the face of it, it is not available in the lower courts, the VAT and Duties Tribunal or before the General or Special Commissioners. There remains however the possibility that such tribunals will be able to strike down primary U.K. legislation where the provision in question is contrary to European Community law, underpinned by reference to the Convention — see the landmark case of *Hodgson v. HM Customs and Excise* [1996] V.&D.R. 200 (relying on *Elliniki Radiophonia Tileorassi AE* [1991] E.C.R. I–2925). This is considered further at paragraphs 14–30—14–44 below.

Thirdly, all public authorities — that is, including the Inland Revenue, H.M. Customs and Excise and all tribunals — are obliged to act in accordance with Convention rights (unless barred by legislation) so that an aggrieved party may bring proceedings against the authority concerned or rely on Convention rights in any legal proceedings (see section 6, and generally paragraph 1–46 and following, above). If a breach is found then all remedies will be available, including payment of damages (computed in accordance with Convention jurisprudence) in appropriate cases. This leaves open the possibility that a taxpayer will be able to bring proceedings against, say, the General Commissioners (who are a "public authority") for breach of Convention rights.

1. Summary of Chapter

14–03   This Chapter discusses the Articles of the Convention most directly relevant to tax matters in light of the existing Convention jurisprudence (paragraphs 14–05—14–30 below); examines the impact on U.K. tax matters which Convention law has had to date, via European Community ("E.C.") law (paragraphs 14–31—14–33 below); considers a number of specific areas of U.K. tax law where the Convention may be most relevant in practice (paragraphs 14–34—14–44 below); considers the impact of the Act on the taxation of damages (paragraphs 14–45—14–48 below); and finally discusses the main cases considered by the Commission and the Court on tax matters, including the recent decision of the Court in the *Building Societies Case (National & Provincial, Leeds Permanent and Yorkshire Building Societies v. U.K.* [1997] S.T.C. 1466 at paragraph 14–49 and following below).

2. The relevant articles for tax purposes

14–04   The three Articles most directly relevant are Article 1 of the First Protocol (deprivation of possessions), Article 14 (discrimination — see generally, paragraph 2–123 and following, above) and Article 6 (right to a fair hearing) see generally, paragraph 2–65 and following, above.

B. ARTICLE 1 OF THE FIRST PROTOCOL — PROTECTION OF PROPERTY

1. Construction of Article 1 of the First Protocol

14–05 It will immediately be noted that the tax raising powers of a state are *specifically* referred to in the second paragraph of the Article. However, the true meaning and scope of this part of the second paragraph can only be appreciated from an examination of the Article as a whole, in light of the case law of the Court. The Article can conveniently be broken down into three parts and this is how the Court approaches it (see *Sporrong and Lönnroth v. Sweden* (1982) Series A, No. 52; 5 E.H.R.R. 35 at paragraph 61). The first — the first sentence of the first paragraph — ensures that all "persons" (which includes companies and all other legal entities) are entitled to peaceful enjoyment of their "possessions"; this is the primary right.

The second part — the second sentence of the first paragraph — permits interference with the primary right in the public interest or in accordance with international law; this is the public interest defence. The reference to principles of international law relating to the confiscation of property has no relevance for U.K. resident taxpayers in the normal course of events because, somewhat surprisingly, the Court has held that international law has no application to a dispute between a state and its own nationals — see *X v. Federal Republic of Germany* (1965) 8 Y.B. 218 and *Lithgow v. U.K.* (1986) Series A, No. 102; 8 E.H.R.R. 329, paragraph 119. International law remains, however, relevant to a foreign national or foreign domiciliary who complains of discriminatory taxation in the U.K. in the sense that he is not being treated in the same way as a U.K. national or domiciliary would be in the same position. In effect, therefore, a person who is an alien in a particular country may find that his rights are better protected than those of a national of that country. This is considered further in the context of E.C. law at paragraph 14–31 and following, below.

14–06 The third part — the second paragraph — specifically authorises interference with the primary right where such a course is necessary to "secure" the payment of taxes; this is the tax raising defence. For a while it was thought that the use of the word "secure" in the tax raising defence meant that it only applied to the *collection* of taxes rather that the *levying* of the tax in the first place — see *Gasus Dosier und Fordertechnik GMBH v. Netherlands* (1995) Series A, No. 306–B; 20 E.H.R.R. 403 at paragraph 60 ("*Gasus Dosier*"); this has now been clarified by the Court in *the Building Societies Case,* above.

The Court has held that these three separate rules must be read together and in particular that the public interest defence and the tax raising defence must be construed in the light of the primary right (see *Lithgow v. U.K.* (1986) (above) at paragraph 106 and *Tre Traktörer Aktiebolag v. Sweden* (1990) Series A, No. 159; 13 E.H.R.R. 309, paragraph 54).

2. The primary right and taxation

14–07 The term "possessions" in Article 1 of the First Protocol has been interpreted in the Convention in a broad, non-technical, way as meaning identifiable legal rights. Thus tangible property like chattels and land clearly qualify, as do intangibles like shares, debts, intellectual property rights and goodwill. For example, the jurisprudence of the Commission and the Court recognises that contractual rights and thus quasi-contractual rights (*e.g.* to restitution) can be regarded as "possessions" — see *X v. Federal Republic of Germany* (1980) 18 D.R. 216 in relation to a notary's fees for services rendered and *A, B and Company AS v. Federal Republic of Germany* (1978) 14 D.R. 146 in which a debt was treated as a "possession". Similarly, in *Gasus Dosier* the right of the German company to the concrete mixer under the retention of title clause was capable of being a "possession" whether the right was one merely of possession or some form of security right in or charge over the asset itself (at paragraph 53). More difficult to analyse in view of the jurisprudence of the Court is whether an interest under an English common law trust is capable of being a "possession" within Article 1 of the First Protocol. By analogy with pension and social security rights, a trust interest which is vested and thus capable of being valued will be regarded as falling within Article 1 of the First Protocol — see *Muller v. Austria* (1975) 1 D.R. 46. Conversely where the interest is merely contingent or (more nebulous still) a mere "spes" under a discretionary trust, no such "possession" exists — see *X v. The Netherlands* (1972) 38 C.D. 9.

14–08 More recently in cases such as *Stran Greek Refineries and Stratis Andreatis v. Greece* (1995) Series A, No. 301–B; 19 E.H.R.R. 293 and *Pressos Compania Naviera SA v. Belgium* (1995) Series A, No. 322; 21 E.H.R.R. 301 the Court has held that a legal claim to recover a sum is a "possession" if "sufficiently established". In *Stran Greek Refineries* the refinery company won an arbitration award in its favour, and at the expense of the Greek government. The government responded by overturning the award by legislation. In response to the application, the Court held that the arbitration award amounted to a debt in favour of the refinery company since the proceedings had gone to judgment. In particular, the award was final and binding, enforceable in its own right and not subject to appeal — it was therefore "sufficiently established" (see paragraphs 61–62). In *Pressos Compania*, the company ("PCN") brought a claim in tort against the Belgian Government in relation to a marine collision allegedly caused by the negligence of the state authorised pilotage service. Rather than defend the claim, the Belgian government took away, by retrospective legislation, PCN's right to pursue the matter before the courts. Although the claim had not proceeded to judgment, the Court was prepared to regard it as a "possession" (since the claim in tort accrued at the time the damage occurred) because the applicant had a legitimate expectation that the claim would be determined in accordance with the normal rules of tort (paragraphs 30–32).

14–09 However, if for any reason there is real doubt about the success of the legal claim, it is unlikely to be "sufficiently established" — see *the Building*

Societies case where the Court made clear that proceedings which disclose no clear legal right at the time launched and which will or may be overtaken by further legislation may not give the litigant a "legitimate expectation" such that the claim is "sufficiently established" (see [1997] S.T.C. 1466 at paragraphs 67–70). In practice a legal claim is likely to meet the test only where the complainant has a decision of a court or tribunal in his favour or he can demonstrate that he has an accrued right and is in an identical position to another case which has been decided. Difficult questions arise where an appeal against the precedent authority has been lodged or is open — see *Stran Greek Refineries* (above) at paragraph 60.

There will be "interference" with the possession where any form of "enjoyment" has been affected. Thus, where properties suffer "planning blight" from conditional compulsory purchase orders and prohibition on construction there has been interference with some of the rights of possession and ownership — see *Sporrong and Lönnroth* (above) and *Erkner and Hofauer v. Austria* (1987) Series A, No. 117; 9 E.H.R.R. 464. As for the levying and collecting of taxes, such activities can (and almost certainly will) amount to interference within the scope of Article 1 of the First Protocol; indeed the levying of taxes by the state is perhaps the most visible interference with a person's right to property and this is recognised by the Strasbourg jurisprudence — see the decision of the Commission in *D. G. and D. W. Lindsay v. U.K.* (1986) 49 D.R. 181 at 189. It follows that a state may impose taxation only if the conditions of either the public interest defence or the tax raising defence are satisfied.

3. The public interest defence

14–10   Not surprisingly the Court has held that a state has an extremely wide measure of discretion in deciding what fiscal laws to pass. Indeed the Court has observed that the intention of the framers of the Article was to allow states to pass whatever fiscal laws they considered desirable provided that measures in this field did not amount to arbitrary confiscation (see *Gasus Dosier* (1995) (above) at paragraph 59). This itself throws up considerable difficulties of perception: tax to one person is arbitrary confiscation to another. In practice, the Commission and the Court have interpreted the public interest defence in a practical way — it will be satisfied provided that there is a "fair balance" between the general interests of the community and the rights of the individual. In assessing this balance, it is necessary to have regard to the principles of proportionality, the degree of Parliamentary consideration of the measure in question and any retrospective effect of the measure.

4. Proportionality

14–11   The concept of proportionality (for which see generally paragraph 2–44 and following, above) may be formulated in various ways, but in essence it requires that there be a reasonable relationship between ends and means (see, in the English common law, Lord Diplock in *CCSU v. Minister for the Civil Service* [1985] A.C. 374 at 410C–E). In the context of the Article this means that there should be a fair balance between the protection of the right of property and the public interest in imposing, securing and collecting taxes. (The concept of proportionality has also been developed in an almost identical way as a principle of E.C. law; this is considered at paragraph 14–31 and following, below in so far as it impinges on tax matters in the United Kingdom.)

In deciding whether a measure is proportionate, the Court looks to see whether a measure which infringes the right to property is "manifestly without reasonable foundation" and to whether the measure imposes on a citizen an "individual and excessive burden" (see *Gasus* (above) at paragraph 67).

An act will be held to be disproportionate if the same result could have been achieved without imposing the same deprivation of possessions on the complainant. In this sense, taking property without reasonable compensation will normally be regarded as disproportionate — see *Holy Monasteries* (1994) Series A, No. 301–A; 20 E.H.R.R. 1 and *Pressos Compania* (1995) (above) at paragraph 43. This is because it is not usually necessary to confiscate without compensation to satisfy the public interest in depriving X of his property. In the tax context, levying and collecting taxes will be in the public interest if taxpayers are protected by procedural safeguards (so that all taxpayers can know what their obligations are) and fair compensation is offered by the state in appropriate circumstances — see *Hentrich v. France* (1994) Series A, No. 296–A; 18 E.H.R.R. 440 where a taxpayer successfully challenged the French Revenue's right of pre-emption over land acquired by her.

5. Parliamentary consideration

14–12   It will be easier to demonstrate that the deprivation is arbitrary or disproportionate where there is no evidence that the act complained of was considered, or properly considered, in Parliament. Specifically, a state cannot automatically rely on its "margin of appreciation" (*i.e.* its discretion as a nation to act in the public interest of the nation) if the legislature cannot be seen to have given due consideration to the measure and any alleged public interest. Conversely, if there is evidence of a full debate in Parliament, it is easier for the government to contend that the public interest has been duly considered. This will entail consideration both of the legal form of the legislation in question — primary statute, statutory instrument subject to negative or positive resolution or public notice with legislative effect (a particular favourite of H.M. Customs and Excise) — and of the degree of consideration actually given. Although the Court and the Commission are permitted to examine the record of Parliamentary proceedings without limit, there may well be a reluctance in the U.K. courts to move beyond the principles laid down in *Pepper v. Hart* [1993] A.C. 593, at least until the notion of looking at Hansard as *evidence* of Parliamentary consideration (or the lack of it) rather than merely as an aid to *construction* takes hold.

6. Retrospection

14–13   The mere fact that an applicant has been deprived of his possessions by retrospective legislation is not in itself sufficient for the Court to treat the confiscation as arbitrary or otherwise incapable of being in the public interest. In *A, B, C and D v. U.K.* (1981) 23 D.R. 203 the Commission held that retrospective legislation in the Finance Act 1978 to plug a loophole which was permitting tax avoidance was not a breach of Article 1 of the First Protocol. It accepted a public interest in preventing tax avoidance schemes which involved "artificial losses, incurred in a non-commercial venture". But the Commission also recognised that retrospective legislation was inherently questionable since it undermines the principle of legal certainty. It said that (at 20):

". . . a retrospective provision imposing a tax liability or restricting the availability of tax relief must be regarded as more severe than a similar prospective provision especially by virtue of the uncertainty which it is bound to engender . . ."

14-14   This has been endorsed as a general principle in *the Building Societies* case where the Court indicated that it is "especially mindful" of the dangers inherent in retrospectivity (see [1997] S.T.C. 1466 at paragraphs 107 and 112). Despite this the Court went on to rule (at paragraph 112) that retrospective tax legislation is permissible where it is introduced to restore what it regarded as Parliament's "original intention" (itself a notoriously difficult concept to identify when complex fiscal legislation is passed by a largely uncomprehending Parliament after cursory — or even inaccurate — explanation). Attention should therefore be paid to Hansard (in accordance with *Pepper v. Hart (above)*, White Papers, Ministerial Statements, Government press releases, etc., although again there may well be reluctance to move beyond the principles laid down in *Black-Clawson International Limited v. Papierwerke Waldhof-Aschaffenberg AG* [1975] 1 All E.R. 810 as to the circumstances in which reference can be made to such matters before English courts.

Particularly relevant for the future, the Court went on in *the Building Societies* case to indicate that although retrospective tax legislation undermines legal certainty and defeats "legitimate expectations", such legislation is less objectionable where the taxpayer should have expected that it would be introduced, *e.g.* where a technical defect is being corrected, where there are large sums at stake or (bizarrely) where the government has *secretly* decided to legislate retrospectively before the taxpayer has taken steps to protect his position (see [1997] S.T.C. 1466 at paragraphs 107–112).

7. The tax raising defence

14-15   This defence specifically permits legitimate measures which are necessary to secure the collection of "tax". This often leads to the question of what is a "tax" for these purposes. Neither the Court or the Commission have attempted any definition of the term; what is clear is that a state cannot simply expropriate assets in the guise of "tax". There is obviously considerable uncertainty as to the distinction between a "tax" on one hand and "state appropriation" or "penalty" on the other, *e.g.* a windfall tax directed at a narrow section of society. These issues have yet to be resolved (although the Commission has indicated that there is nothing wrong with a "windfall tax" *per se* — see *Wasa Liv v. Sweden* (1988) 58 D.R. 163 and paragraphs 14–37—14–38 below), as has the extent to which a levy can be challenged on the basis that it amounts to "double taxation". In *the Building Societies* case the Court indicated that "double taxation" is not itself automatically objectionable if it is merely so in a "theoretical sense" ([1997] S.T.C. 1466 at paragraph 60); no indication is given by the Court as to what this means.

Even if "tax" properly so-called is involved, the Court has held that the proviso does not permit measures which are discriminatory, "disproportionate" or (see above) amount to arbitrary confiscation — see *Sporrong and Lönnroth* (above) and *Gasus Dosier* (above). In *Gasus Dosier* the Dutch Revenue seized a concrete mixer, held by a Dutch company but owned — under a retention of title clause — by a German company, in satisfaction of the Dutch company's tax debts. The German company (Gasus) contended that the seizure amounted to confiscation of its "possessions" in satisfaction of the tax liability of another and that such was impermissible interference for the purposes of Article 1 of the First Protocol. The Court rejected this on the basis that the public interest in ensuring payment of taxes outweighed the individual's rights under a retention of title clause. This then led to the question of proportionality (see above). In effect, the state must be able to justify the act concerned in terms of public interest and necessity even in a tax context — at all times the Court is looking for the "fair balance" between the rights of the individual and the "public interest" (see *Hentrich* (above)).

C. ARTICLE 14 — DISCRIMINATION

14–16   Article 14 in effect provides that the enjoyment of the rights and freedoms set out in the Convention shall be secured without discrimination on *any* basis — note the reference to "other status". It stands above other articles in the Convention and can be breached without evidence of a breach of another protected right (see the *Belgian Linguistic* case (1979–1980) Series A, No. 5; 1 E.H.R.R. 241). Thus, a measure which is otherwise in conformity with the Convention, say with Article 1 of the First Protocol, may nonetheless infringe Article 14 if it is of a discriminatory nature. A breach will be found if there is a differential treatment of equal cases without there being *both* an objective and reasonable justification *and* proportionality between the aims sought and the means employed.

There is no doubt that Article 14 applies to the duties imposed on citizens of contracting states to pay tax (see *Darby v. Sweden* (1991) Series A, No. 187; 13 E.H.R.R. 774). In *Darby* an occasional resident of Sweden who was Finnish by nationality objected to paying a Swedish church tax which, had he been a Swedish resident, he could have avoided by registering as a non-member of the Church of Sweden. Although the Court preferred not to reach a view as to whether Article 1 of the First Protocol was breached, it considered that there was a breach of Article 14 because the applicant was in a worse tax position than he would have been had he been a Swedish resident and such discrimination could not be justified.

14–17   In order to found a claim under Article 14 it is necessary in the first place to demonstrate that a particular taxpayer is in a materially identical position to another taxpayer — in other words that they are "equal cases". Although there is no need for complete unity of position the two persons must be directly comparable in all material respects. Having established comparability, taxpayer A must then show that he has not been treated in the same manner as taxpayer B and that the difference in treatment is more than of *de minimis* effect.

Once this is proven it is for the state concerned to justify the difference in treatment between the two on the basis of objective and reasonable criteria and to demonstrate that such differentiation is not "disproportionate", *i.e.* there is no reasonable relationship of proportionality between the means and aim (see for example *A, B, C, D v. U.K.* (above) at 210 and *Darby v. Sweden* (above) at paragraph 31).

14–18 A common ground of alleged discrimination between taxpayers is residence. The U.K. adopts in many areas a radically different treatment of taxpayers depending on whether they are resident or not resident in the U.K. There seems no doubt that a difference in treatment between taxpayers based on residence which has no legitimate aim or reasonable or objective justification or which is disproportionate would fall foul of Article 14 (see *Darby v. Sweden*). It is instructive in this regard to note that similar issues as to whether residents and non-residents are in a similar position and whether discrimination based on residence can be justified in the light of the coherence of the tax system of the state concerned have arisen in E.C. law in actions based on Article 52 of the Treaty of European Union (see for example *Finanzamt v. Schumacker* [1995] S.T.C. 306 and *Wielockx v. Inspecteur der Directe Belastingen* [1995] S.T.C. 876). Aspects of the United Kingdom corporate tax legislation have been found to offend against such principles — see *ICI v. Colmer* [1998] S.T.C. 874 and paragraph 14–31 below.

14–19 Another common ground of alleged discrimination in the tax field concerns retrospective legislation, introduced to overturn a decision of the courts or to close a loophole, which is often targeted at a specific group of taxpayers. Where the retrospective legislation seeks to draw distinctions between such taxpayers (*e.g.* in *the Building Societies* case where the distinction was between those who had launched legal proceedings based on the invalidity of the original legislation by a certain date and those who had not), it is for the state to contend that there is objective justification for such a step.

Such a submission now seems likely to be accepted given that the Court has decided that one taxpayer can be "objectively different" from another if he takes steps to protect his position by litigating (thereby incurring costs and running other risks) and securing a court decision in his favour — see *the Building Societies* case at [1997] S.T.C. 1466 at paragraphs 89–92. Therefore the taxpayer who relies on a "test case" brought by someone else will not necessarily be protected from retrospective legislation by Article 14 even if the test case is otherwise fully applicable to him since he has not taken an "independent and bold" stance (paragraph 89). Protection may only be afforded if the taxpayer launches proceedings of his own, although it remains an open question as to how far he must pursue the litigation to enjoy the full protection of Article 14. Put shortly, a "precautionary writ" is a necessary step but possibly not a sufficient one on its own.

Different treatment on the ground of gender is a particularly obvious form of discrimination and will be difficult to justify on objective grounds. In *McGregor (Helen) v. U.K.* App. No. 30548/96 Commission decision December 3, 1997 (unreported but summarised in [1998] E.H.R.L.R. 354) a woman challenged the compatibility with the E.C.H.R. of section 259 of the Taxes Act 1988. That section until amended by the Finance Act 1998 gave relief in the form of an increased tax allowance to a man married to and living with a totally incapacitated wife with a dependent child but not to a woman. It has now been amended by the Finance Act 1998 to cover both men and women.

In its unamended form, the applicant claimed that it contravened Article 14 read together with Article 1 of the First Protocol, in that if male she would have been entitled to the exemption. The Commission found the complaint admissible and it will go forward to a full hearing at which the government will seek to show it is objectively justifiable and proportionate.

D. ARTICLE 6(1) — RIGHT TO A FAIR HEARING

14–20   Article 6(1) guarantees the right to a fair trial in the determination of "civil rights and obligations". This right is regarded as fundamental and is jealously guarded by the Court — see *Golder* (1975) Series A, No. 18; 1 E.H.R.R. 524. It will not however necessarily apply automatically in the tax field.

1. What rights are protected

14–21   No definitive interpretation has been given to the term "civil rights and obligations"; specifically, the term does not mean (as it might to a common lawyer) a right which relates to matters other than "criminal". Instead, the Court has held first that the phrase is a Convention concept and national courts should follow the guidance given by the Court and, secondly, that it should have a broad interpretation. In arriving at such a broad meaning the Court has sought to distinguish civil rights from public law rights — a distinction better developed in some European countries than it is in U.K. law. In the absence of a clear-cut definition, it is necessary therefore (as the Court has done) to categorise rights on a case by case basis, moving by analogy.

A civil right will normally involve a pecuniary claim so that a claim to damages or restitution will both fall into the protected category. A claim to be entitled to the benefit of, say, an administrative practice will prima facie not be a civil right. However if a claim of this type has direct pecuniary consequences, it may be treated as a claim involving a civil right. Indeed, the Court has stated that Article 6(1) applies irrespective of the status of the parties and of the nature of the legislation which governs the procedure by which the matter is to be resolved. In other words the form of the litigation in question is not determinative of the applicability of Article 6. What matters is the substance — it is enough that the outcome of the proceedings should be decisive for private rights and obligations (*Stran Greek Refineries v. Greece* (above) at paragraph 39).

2. Are tax disputes within Article 6(1)?

14-22   On the face of it Article 6(1) may appear not to apply to disputes about taxation since they are, in form and substance, disputes between the citizen and the state and thus not private law matters — see *X v. France* (1983) 32 D.R. 266 (where it is baldly stated that "Article 6.1 does not apply to proceedings relating to tax assessments") and *Editions Périscope v. France* (1992) Series A, No. 234–B; 14 E.H.R.R. 597 at 606, 612–613. As a statement of general principle this must be correct, whatever the exact distinction between private and public law rights in a U.K. context.

However, the Court has, in two recent cases, explored the extent of the civil/public law distinction in the tax law context. The first of those cases, *Editions Périscope v. France* (1992) Series A, No. 234–B; 14 E.H.R.R. 597 concerned a claim by a taxpayer that a refusal to grant certain tax concessions had led to pecuniary loss. French law required that the taxpayer apply for a certificate entitling him to those concessions. Applications were lodged in 1960, 1961, 1964 and 1970. The first three applications were rejected. However, the last application was simply ignored. In 1974, the taxpayer went into liquidation. In 1976, the taxpayer instituted proceedings in the administrative court alleging that it had suffered loss of 200,000,000FF "through the faults committed by the public authorities". The company alleged that it had been the victim of discrimination in that concessions had been granted to direct competitors. The French authorities adopted a number of delaying tactics with the result that the matter was not first heard until 1981 and the appeal until 1985. The taxpayer lost at trial and on appeal. The grounds appear to have been that the taxpayer's competitors were in a different position from the taxpayer and, accordingly, there was no discrimination. In September 1985, the taxpayer applied to the Commission alleging breaches of Article 6(1) in that its case had not been heard within a reasonable time. On the threshold issue of whether the taxpayer was claiming it had not received a fair trial of a civil right, both the Commission and the Court found in the taxpayer's favour. The Commission held (at paragraph 35):

> "[T]he right claimed by the applicant company was not the right to tax concessions but the right to compensation for an administrative error consisting in alleged discriminatory application of rules governing eligibility for such concessions."

The Court noted (at paragraph 40) that:

> "[T]he subject-matter of the applicant's action was 'pecuniary' in nature and that the action was founded on an alleged infringement of rights which were likewise pecuniary rights. The right in question was therefore a 'civil right', notwithstanding the origin of the dispute and the fact that the administrative courts had jurisdiction."

The Court found that there was excessive delay by the French courts in breach of Article 6(1). However, the applicant was unable to show that the excessive delay had caused it any injury over and above that caused by the substance of the determination.

14–23   The second of the two cases was the *Building Societies* case ([1997] S.T.C. 1466). The facts were complex (see paragraph 14–51 below) but related to a series of claims for restitution of tax alleged to be overpaid. After proceedings had been commenced, the Government persuaded Parliament to pass retrospective legislation to defeat the claim. When the case came to be heard by the Court, the applicants claimed *inter alia* that the retrospective legislation had, in contravention of Article 6(1), been adopted with the intention of thwarting their right to access to a court. On the threshold issue, the Court found in favour of the applicants declaring that the restitution proceedings (paragraph 97):

> "were private law actions and were decisive for the determination of private law rights to quantifiable sums of money. This conclusion is not affected by the fact that the rights asserted in those proceedings had their background in tax legislation and the obligation of the applicant societies to account for tax under that legislation."

14–24   It would, however, be misleading to rely overly much on the precise formulation adopted by the Court in these two cases. The *Building Societies* case refers to "quantifiable sums of money". Yet it is clear from the facts of *Editions Périscope*, upon which reliance was placed by the Court in the *Building Societies* case, that a claim need not be for a liquidated sum in order to comprise a civil right. Nor can real assistance be derived from the reference in *Editions Périscope* to "pecuniary rights". The Court appeared to use the phase in a sense no narrower than the applicant was seeking a money judgment. Yet this can hardly be the criteria given that Article 6 plainly protects an application for an injunction in *locus classicus* private law proceedings.

Moreover, it would seem that the character of the tribunal in which the case is brought is also irrelevant. Such a distinction would subordinate the right to a fair trial to the vagaries of national procedural rules. This analysis is confirmed, at least in part, by the Court which held in the *Building Societies* case that the right to a fair trial applied both to judicial review proceedings and an ordinary writ action. The correct approach is to revert to the text of Article 6 which focuses on the subject-matter (*res*) of the case. Nothing in the *ratio* of the *Building Societies* case or *Editions Périscope* departs from this approach. It follows that, in order to identify whether Article 6 protects an applicant's right to a fair trial, care must be taken in identifying the subject-matter. Where, properly identified, the *res* is the liability of any person to tax, then no protection is afforded by Article 6(1) as regards the manner in which that liability is determined.

14–25   However, where the applicant is asserting a breach of a private right — in *Editions Périscope* the right to be treated in the same manner as his competitors and in the *Building Societies* case, the right to restitution of monies overpaid — Article 6(1) will provide certain procedural safeguards. It is irrelevant in this regard that the private law right has its genesis in a tax claim.

Thus a pure tax claim such as an appeal under the statutory procedure against an assessment or determination of liability will not be within Article 6(1). It does not matter why the taxpayer claims that the assessment is wrong: whether because the officer concerned refused to admit relevant evidence or extend deadlines. Even a claim — based on the strongest evidence — that the bias of the officer led to an inaccurate assessment would fall outside Article 6(1).

However, if, in relation to an underlying tax dispute, a claim is brought against the Inland Revenue or Customs and Excise for damages or for restitution, *e.g.* for misfeasance in a public office or the recovery of sums overpaid — that is a claim of which the subject-matter is pecuniary in nature and founded on an infringement of pecuniary rights (see *Editions Périscope*). It can therefore fall within the protection of Article 6. Likewise, a tax based application for judicial review of the Revenue or Customs and Excise on the basis that the authority in question has acted in *ultra vires* will probably be treated as a civil claim where the judicial review proceedings are "closely interrelated" with, and part of a "calculated strategy" to assert private law claims, *e.g.* to recover money (see [1997] S.T.C. 1466 at paragraph 98). Article 6(1) will also safeguard the determination of a claim that the Revenue breached a (binding) agreement as to a basis of assessment and a claim for restitution of overpaid tax; however, it will not protect a claim which seeks to establish that tax was overpaid.

14–26 In *Hodgson v. H.M. Customs and Excise* [1996] V.&D.R. 200 the VAT and Duties Tribunal decided that the imposition of a particular type of tax penalty involved the determination of the civil rights of a person who had imported hand rolling tobacco for his personal use. In the case law of the Court a liability to make social security contributions was regarded as deriving from tax legislation and thus fell outside Article 6 (see *Schouten and Meldrum v. The Netherlands* (1995) Series A, No. 304; 19 E.H.R.R. 432); conversely, the seizure of an airliner as a result of unlawful importation of drugs and the demand that the owner should pay a penalty before it could be returned was accepted by the Court to involve the owner's civil rights within Article 6 (see *Air Canada v. United Kingdom* (1995) Series A, No. 316; 20 E.H.R.R. 150). In *Hodgson*, the penalty was imposed for more than breach of a procedural requirement of the tax legislation; instead (and close to *Air Canada*) it affected a person's rights to bring his own property into the United Kingdom for his own use and for this reason the Tribunal was satisfied that Article 6 applied. This does not however necessarily mean that the imposition of any tax penalty will be capable of challenge under Article 6; what will matter is the particular conduct which the penalty is seeking to punish. It is interesting to note that the application of Article 6 to a VAT penalty appeal was assumed by the VAT Tribunal, apparently without Customs" objection, in *Ellinas v. H.M. Customs* [1998] S.T. I 705. The case concerned a claim to public interest immunity by Customs, and the conflict with the appellant's rights to a fair hearing.

14–27 Finally in relation to the nature of Article 6 it should be noted that criminal tax matters (*e.g.* prosecutions for fraud) will be governed by the full rights set out in that Article for criminal cases; this falls outside the scope of this chapter (see Chapter 4). What remains relevant however is the extent to which tax penalties can be said to be "criminal" in nature such that the full protection of Article 6 is afforded to, say, a penalty under ss.98 and 100 of the Taxes Management Act 1970 or to a misdeclaration penalty for VAT purposes under sections 63 and 64 of the Value Added Tax Act 1994. In *Hodgson* (above), the tribunal held that tax penalties which are imposed by administrative action, which do not involve a formal "charge", where there is no formal criminal record of offenders and where there is no risk of imprisonment, do not fall within the wider protection of Article 6. Should any tax penalties be very substantial and/or involve a risk of imprisonment, it remains open whether they would be treated as "criminal" matters notwithstanding that they are imposed by an administrative body — see *Ozturk v. Germany* (1984) Series A, No. 73; 6 E.H.R.R. 409, *Bendenoun v. France* (1994) Series A, No. 204; 18 E.H.R.R. 54 and the litigation before the French Conseil d'Etat in the *Meric* case (1995) *Receuil des décisions du Conseil d'État* 154.

3. What is the content of the right?

14–28 The right to a fair hearing involves access to a court, procedural equality, judicial process (impartiality and the absence of bias) and normally a reasoned decision. This may be breached in the tax context where, for example, a right to challenge the actions of the tax raising body is dependent upon paying the sum in dispute prior to the hearing itself (see *Formix* discussed at paragraph 14–32 below).

Similarly, and as frequently occurs in tax cases, where the U.K. Government loses a test case on a particular tax point it frequently persuades Parliament to legislate to reverse the decision of the courts in a manner which preserves the position of the litigant in question but does not necessarily benefit all other taxpayers involved in the dispute. The same course is even adopted where the Government fears that it is about to lose such a test case — see the "pre-emptive strike" legislation in *Willoughby v. IRC* [1997] S.T.C. 995 (Finance Act ("FA") 1997, s.81) and in *Glaxo Group plc v. IRC* [1996] S.T.C. 191 (Finance Bill 1995, cl. 162). In such cases the effect of the legislation is often to prevent some or all of the taxpayers concerned from pursuing their rights in the courts. This is capable of amounting to a breach of Article 6, particularly since the legislation allows the State to determine the outcome of legal proceedings to which it is party (see *Stran Greek Refineries* (above) at paragraph 42). Such interference with the right to a fair hearing may however be justifiable where it has the effect of restoring the intention of the legislature in circumstances where the citizen should have expected such a step (see the discussion of *the Building Societies Case* below).

4. A breach of the right

14–29 An interference in a person's civil rights will be a breach of Article 6(1) unless the state can show that the measure complained of is within its "margin of appreciation", is not disproportionate and is not discriminatory (see above).

Although procedural restrictions on a right of access to a court are permitted — and indeed are a fundamental part of any legal system — the restrictions must not be such as to impair the right protected by Article 6 entirely — see *Stubbings v. U.K.* R.J.D. 1996–IV 1487; 23 E.H.R.R. 213. This can give rise to difficult questions where a right of appeal is limited in scope or where there is no appeal but a taxpayer has the option of bringing judicial review proceedings.

An example in the former category is the present system for challenging a demand for national insurance contributions. Should a person wish to contend that no contribution is due from him, he must make a written application to the Office for the Determination of Contributions Questions which will determine a question to be asked of the Secretary of State for Social Services. This question will then be heard by a senior legal officer of the DSS and advice given to the Secretary of State for him or her to issue a decision (often without reasons). The contributor can then seek a further review by the Secretary of State, appeal to the High Court on a point of law or bring judicial review proceedings (see Social Security Administration Act 1992, ss.17, 18 and 58). Assuming that the payment of contributions involves the determination of civil rights, it seems only a matter of time before this procedure is challenged under Article 6.

14–30 An important example in the second category — where the taxpayer has no right of appeal but can bring judicial review proceedings — is the case of *Hodgson*, above. Here H had no effective right to appeal against the penalty (see *H.M. Customs and Excise v. Carrier* [1995] 4 All E.R. 38); instead H had the right to bring judicial review proceedings in the High Court. However H's right to challenge the penalty in this way was regarded by the tribunal as not being an adequate remedy for the purposes of Article 6. The reasoning of the tribunal was that judicial review could not be a remedy where the Customs and Excise officials concerned had acted "reasonably", but in breach of E.C. law, since such a breach could not undermine the legality of the officials" decision. This had the result that the U.K. legislation had to be construed in a way which protected H's E.C. law rights and provided a remedy before U.K. courts for breach of those rights. *Hodgson* thus opens up recourse to Article 6 in other areas of tax law where there is no right of appeal *per se*; the extent of the "*Hodgson* principle" is likely to be a source of fertile debate as the impact of the Convention is felt in the United Kingdom.

In relation to tax investigations the conduct of those investigations will not necessarily fall within Article 6 such that a taxpayer will be able to refuse to answer questions on the grounds of self-incrimination — see *Abas v. The Netherlands*, Commission (1997) 88–B D.R. 120.

In contemplating proceedings for breach of Article 6(1) itself it should be remembered that the Court will not consider the lawfulness or otherwise of the original action (*e.g.* an assessment to tax), the validity of which the plaintiff was barred or restricted from challenging fairly in court proceedings. In other words, a victory under Article 6(1) alone will not overturn the original complaint and any damages awarded to a plaintiff will only reflect the breach of Article 6(1) itself. This point is amply illustrated by the *Editions Périscope* case (above).

E. E.C. LAW AND THE CONVENTION

1. Introduction

14–31 Although consideration of E.C. law is outside the scope of this book, there is an important overlap between Convention law and E.C. law (see generally paragraphs 1–13 and 2–05—2–06). Principles of human rights have already been developed in E.C. law and been applied in a tax context. They are thus a part of the existing jurisprudence against which the Convention can be applied in the U.K. tax field, and U.K. courts have already taken account of such principles. Originally these E.C. principles of human rights were only binding on Community institutions in making law. In *Wachauf v. The State* [1989] E.C.R. 2609, the ECJ stated, however, that where a Member State is implementing a provision of Community law, it is in the same position as a Community institution and should observe E.C. law concepts of human rights. A failure to observe such principles could therefore mean that the national act is in conflict with E.C. law and thus invalid.

The E.C. human right most frequently cited in the United Kingdom to date is the right to proportionality (derived, in the main, from the Convention jurisprudence) and requires that where a burden is placed on a citizen, the burden should only be such as is strictly necessary to achieve the objective of the legislation under which it is imposed (see paragraph 14–11 above). This has been considered recently in *Garage Molenheide* [1998] S.T.C. 126 where the ECJ stated that measures adopted by national authorities which are within their discretion but which are liable to have an effect on E.C. objectives, must be proportionate and must cause as little detriment to E.C. objectives as is compatible with achieving the domestic aim. The issue arose in this case because Belgian law allowed VAT which a taxpayer claimed as repayable to be retained by the Government where it was alleged that the repayment claim was fraudulent. Whilst the ECJ held that Member States were permitted to take such steps, they had to be such as to cause as little detriment as possible to the E.C. objective of enabling traders to reclaim VAT properly repayable. The Belgian procedure went further than was necessary since it included in the relevant provisions irrebuttable presumptions which had the effect of preventing a taxpayer from adducing evidence on the appeal against the decision to retain VAT.

2. Challenges to U.K. law on the ground of human rights under E.C. law

14–32 The E.C. law concept of proportionality has already been used to challenge aspects of U.K. VAT law. At first instance in *Commissioners of Customs & Excise v. P & O* [1992] S.T.C. 809, the taxpayer relied unsuccessfully on the principle to challenge a substantial VAT penalty which Customs had sought to impose despite no loss of revenue to the Exchequer (the taxpayer later won on appeal on a different point). Likewise, in *Formix (London) Ltd v. C & E Commissioners* [1998] S.T.I. 117 the taxpayer appealed against a notice requiring it to provide security for VAT. Customs objected that the VAT tribunal could not hear the appeal as the legislation required the taxpayer to make tax returns and to pay the tax due. Unlike other types of VAT appeal there was no provision for the tribunal having authority to dispense with the requirement on grounds of hardship (see VATA 1994, s.84(3)). The tribunal was of the view that it might be argued that the requirement to pay the tax before an appeal could be made and the absence of a hardship exception was disproportionately severe and that the right of Member States to impose such obligations for the collection of VAT was under E.C. law restrained by the principles of the Convention. The tribunal adjourned the application in order to approach the Attorney-General to consider appointing a person to assist the Court by presenting argument on the legal issues involved. This will be determined later in 1998.

At least one unsuccessful attempt has also been made on the basis of the E.C. law concept of proportionality to impugn the powers of Customs to seize and destroy goods on which excise duty has not been paid (*Sandhar & Kang v. H.M. Customs and Excise* (1994) (unreported)). For comparison, in *AGOSI v. U.K.* (1986) Series A, No. 108; 9 E.H.R.R. 1, Customs and Excise seized coins smuggled into the United Kingdom from a person innocently in possession of the goods, and a challenge under the Convention failed.

14-33 A striking demonstration of the application of concepts of human rights via E.C. law in U.K. law is the decision of the VAT and Duties Tribunal in *Hodgson* (above) where the taxpayer was successful. The taxpayer entered the United Kingdom with 11.2 kg of hand-rolling tobacco. The U.K. legislation provided that the taxpayer would be liable to a penalty unless the Commissioners were satisfied that it was not imported for a commercial purpose; the Commissioners were not so satisfied. In such circumstances as a matter of domestic U.K. law the VAT tribunal could not review the decision. However, as the taxpayer was exercising a directly effective Community law right to import tobacco for his own use, the compatibility of any domestic law restrictions on that right had to be considered in the light of the principles of human rights recognised by E.C. law, which include Convention rights (see *Elliniki Radiophonia* (above)). The VAT tribunal decided, in effect, that the Convention is a part of E.C. law and thus directly effective in the United Kingdom; it went on to hold therefore that the taxpayer's right to import tobacco for his own use was the exercise of a civil right within Article 6(1) and that he was entitled to a fair trial which included, in the circumstances, a right to appeal on the merits. By exercising this newly created right of appeal, the tribunal considered that the taxpayer had satisfied the "personal use" requirement and that no penalty could be levied.

This case establishes therefore the supremacy of E.C. law including principles of human rights as embodied in the Convention and is a striking example of the effect of the Convention on U.K. tax legislation.

F. POSSIBLE CHALLENGES TO U.K. TAX LAW ON THE GROUND OF INFRINGEMENT OF HUMAN RIGHTS

14-34 A challenge under the Act may lie where there is incompatibility between U.K. legislation and the rights guaranteed by the Convention, where a public authority acts in breach of the Convention, or where the U.K. provision is to be construed in light of the Convention rights. The areas of U.K. tax law where the Act is likely to be relevant are many and difficult to specify at this stage. Cases to watch out for will be those where there is an element of retrospectivity, of discrimination, an unfair procedure, or where there is a particularly harsh regime (*e.g.* large penalties for minor infringements) or a particular taxpayer suffers an individual and excessive burden.

1. Substantive rights

(a) Recovery of overpaid tax

14–35 Where a taxpayer pays a sum by way of income or corporation tax pursuant to a lawful demand which turns out to be excessive, there is a statutory right to recover the sum in question — see, for example, Taxes Management Act 1970, s.33. However, there are considerable limits on a taxpayer's statutory rights to recover tax both in terms of time limits and the "generally prevailing practice" defence (see section 33(2A)). Such barriers to recovery are capable of challenge under Convention rights.

Scrutiny will also fall on other bars or limitations on the recovery of excessive tax paid to the revenue authorities. For example, the introduction of the three year limit on overpaid VAT with effect from July 18, 1996 (see FA 1997, s.47(1)) was clearly retrospective. It reduced with immediate effect the period in respect of which overpaid VAT could be reclaimed from six years to three years. Since the period in which Customs could raise assessments was also limited to three years this is not, on its face, disproportionate (see FA 1997, s.47(10)). However, at the time that the change was first introduced in the autumn of 1996 some taxpayers recovered, by private agreement with Customs, on account of claims going back the full six years whilst other taxpayers in a substantially similar position did not. Whilst the change in the law itself may not have amounted to unlawful deprivation of possessions and/or unlawful discrimination (and this is being challenged by certain taxpayers — see *Marks & Spencer plc v. H.M. Customs and Excise* (1998) unreported) the way in which it was implemented is open to challenge — see *R. v. H.M. Customs and Excise ex p. Kay & Co. Limited* [1996] S.T.C. 1500. Indeed, there seems likely to be further litigation in this area since the Customs' approach to the consequences of capping is still developing (see *Business Brief* 2/98).

14–36 Where a taxpayer has overpaid sums on account of VAT, there is a statutory right to recover the excessive sums (see Value Added Tax Act ("VATA") 1994, s.80) but Customs have a statutory defence if repayment would "unjustly enrich" the taxpayer (see section 80(3)), because (for example) the taxpayer has passed on the burden of the tax to his customers. If Customs are to justify a refusal to repay sums paid as VAT which were not VAT owing to them, they will have to do so by reference to Article 1 of the First Protocol as well as by reference to the E.C. law jurisprudence on unjust enrichment (*e.g. Société Comateb v. Directeur Générale des douanes et droits indirects* [1997] S.T.C. 1006). This will apply equally to the new "reimbursement" regulations — see VATA 1994, s.80A.

Where a sum is paid to the Revenue authorities pursuant to a demand which is *ultra vires* (and thus void rather than *intra vires* but merely excessive), there is a common law right to recover the sum in question — see *Woolwich Building Society v. IRC* [1993] A.C. 70. However, this right is possibly limited by the defences available to the government of payment under a mistake of law (depending upon the facts of the case), change of position and passing on (see Lord Goff in *Woolwich* at 164, 177F–177B).

(b) Windfall/punitive taxes

14–37 Questions arise in relation to windfall taxes. Is it proportionate and non-discriminatory to tax (in effect) the present shareholders in privatised utilities so as to recapture for the public purse benefits allegedly enjoyed by previous shareholders (see FA (No. 2) 1997, ss.1–5 and Schedules 1, 2)? Such taxes are vulnerable to challenge on the basis that they may be said to be discriminatory as between different categories of persons, arbitrary in the manner in which the tax is charged and so disproportionate as to be outside of the state's margin of appreciation, particularly where some element of retrospection is involved. Conversely, it may be easier to justify a windfall tax in Convention terms where there is a "clear" legislative mandate for it, the matter is freely discussed in Parliament and there is some sound policy reason (*e.g.* raising sums to fund employment projects) for the imposition of the tax. Similar considerations apply to the 1981 windfall tax on bank deposits (see FA 1981, s.134 and Schedule 17) and any future windfall taxes on the "excessive" profits of particular taxpayers.

Taxes may be "punitive" whether in terms of the level of taxation borne by all taxpayers or the unfair and disproportionate burden borne by a particular group of taxpayers. In the former category would fall taxes like the investment income surcharge introduced in the Finance Act 1974 which can (and did) approach a marginal rate of 98 per cent and the more narrowly defined surcharge on the gains of non-resident trustees which can, when payment is made to U.K. beneficiaries, amount to 64 per cent under the Taxation of Chargeable Gains Act ("TCGA") 1992, s.91. In each category of case a challenge could be mounted on the basis that the "public interest" defence to deprivation of possessions is not met or on the basis of discrimination or lack of proportionality.

14–38 In the latter category there would perhaps fall the imposition of, or increases in, taxation on particular products or activities, *e.g.* cigarettes, alcohol, company cars, etc. Should there be a specific, "punitive", increase in taxation of such matters, it would be open to challenge on the basis of proportionality (see, by way of example, the challenge on a related basis to the 1997 increase in beer duty in *R. v. H.M. Treasury, ex p. Shepherd Neame*, *The Times*, February 2, 1998).

Closely linked to both categories are cases involving "double taxation" (where either two taxpayers are charged in respect of the same profit or gain or one taxpayer is charged twice in respect of the same profit or gain) and any element of "discretionary taxation" (where the Revenue or Customs exercise a degree of choice in the *levying* of taxes). Courts in the United Kingdom have, understandably, shied away from approving of such taxation (see *Vestey v. IRC* [1980] A.C. 1148 *per* Lord Wilberforce at 1171F–1172F, *R. v. IRC, ex p. Woolwich Equitable Building Society* [1990] 1 W.L.R. 1400 *per* Lord Oliver at 1412H and Lord Lowry at 1433G–1435E). This natural reluctance will be enforced by reference to rights under the Convention.

(c) Discrimination

14–39   There are cases involving discriminatory treatment of taxpayers on a substantive (*i.e.* tax charging) rather than procedural (*i.e.* tax collecting) basis. For example, Customs and Excise have attempted to apply bad debt relief for VAT on the basis that debts not payable in money are excluded from the relief (see *Goldsmiths (Jewellers) Limited v. H.M. Customs and Excise* [1997] S.T.C. 1073) and this has finally been struck down by the ECJ. Similarly, the refusal by the revenue authorities to apply a published practice to particular taxpayers is open to challenge on this basis — see *R. v. IRC, ex p. SG Warburg & Co. Limited* [1994] S.T.C. 518 and *R. v. IRC, ex p. Kaye* [1992] S.T.C. 581. Finally, substantive discrimination in Convention terms would have afforded an additional basis of challenge to the Revenue's policy of selective prosecution (see *R. v. IRC, ex p. Mead and Cook* [1992] S.T.C. 482, which should not now be assumed to be good law, and *R. v. IRC, ex p. Allen* [1997] S.T.C. 1141).

Following from the above, there are also the provisions of U.K. corporation tax which discriminate on the ground of residence. There have been a number of challenges to such aspects of the U.K. corporation tax regime on the basis of Article 52 (freedom of establishment) of the Treaty of European Union (*e.g.* *Commerzbank v. IRC* [1991] S.T.C. 271 and [1993] S.T.C. 605 — repayment supplement; *ICI v. Colmer* [1998] S.T.C. 874 — consortium relief) and there is ongoing litigation over the right to make a group income election and thus to avoid the need to pay advance corporation tax on dividends.

(d) Retrospective legislation

14–40   With the passing of the Act, all retrospective tax legislation will be tested by the courts not just by reference to whether Parliament clearly intended the provision to be retrospective (see paragraph 14–12 above) but also by reference to the principles of proportionality and discrimination (see paragraphs 14–11 and 14–16 and following above). For example, in *R. v. IRC, ex p. Woolwich Equitable Building Society* (above) the question for the House of Lords would have been whether the legislation accorded with Convention rights and not whether the result contended for by one party or another accorded with "the words which Parliament has chosen to use" (see Lord Oliver at [1990] 1 W.L.R. 1412F). Similarly, the decision of the Court of Appeal in *Boote v. Banco do Brasil* [1997] S.T.C. 327, where it was held that a provision of the FA 1976 (limiting the use of losses generated by the exclusion, under the U.S./U.K. Double Tax Treaty, of interest received from the bank from U.S. corporations) had retrospective effect, is open to considerable doubt if viewed through the lens of Article 1 of the First Protocol and Article 14. It is insufficient to conclude that the result "reflects the intention of Parliament ascertained from the words it has used" (*per* Morritt L.J. at 333a). Many other recent cases may have either produced different results had Convention rights been in issue or may have been resolved without the need for litigation at all — see (by way of example) *R. v. H.M. Customs and Excise, ex p. Littlewoods Home Shopping Group Ltd* [1998] S.T.C. 445 (retrospective removal of agreed basis for the calculation of output tax), *Jenks v. Dickinson* [1997] S.T.C. 853 (retrospective effect of FA 1989, s.139) and *B.J. Rice v. H.M. Customs and Excise* [1996] S.T.C. 581 (time of supply for VAT purposes).

(e) Prospective "legislation"

14–41 An increasingly common feature of the day-to-day management of the U.K. tax system is the willingness of the Government to announce by press release that a particular tax scheme or type of transaction is no longer tax effective as from the date of the announcement. Frequently, however, the details of the legislation only appear months later (in a Finance Bill) and, once passed, have retrospective effect. This can, and does, leave taxpayers in a "twilight" zone in the interim unaware of the exact extent of legislative changes. Since this clearly undermines legal certainty it is only a matter of time before a challenge under the Convention is made by a taxpayer who has relied on the terms of the press release only to find himself caught by the terms of the legislation.

(f) Enforcement

14–42 The seizure of goods and/or documents, etc. by the revenue authorities (*e.g.* under TMA 1970, s.20) either as a consequence of alleged illegal importation or in pursuance of a separate tax liability is open to challenge under Article 1 of the First Protocol by reference to proportionality — see *Sandhar & Kang* (above), *Air Canada v. U.K.* (above) (seizure of airliner for unlawful importation of drugs) and *Bell v. H.M Customs and Excise* [1996] V.&D.R. 300 (seizure of car for unlawful use of derv). Challenges will also be possible to any penalty or surcharge which can be said in the circumstances to be disproportionate — see paragraph 14–11, above.

2. Procedural rights

14–43 Tax legislation which does not provide for a right of appeal (see *Hodgson* (above)) or restrict the right to appeal against assessments to tax except on payment of the amount in dispute may infringe the right to possessions or to a fair trial (see *Procola v. Luxembourg* (1996) Series A, No. 326; 22 E.H.R.R. 193). As mentioned above, a challenge has been made to the requirement in VATA 1994, s.84(2) that in order to appeal against the imposition of a requirement to provide security, a taxpayer must complete and pay tax shown as due on any VAT returns outstanding and there is no "hardship" exception. The ground of the challenge (still to be determined) is that the requirement to complete returns and pay the tax was disproportionately severe (see *Formix* (above)).

14–44 Likewise, Customs and Excise have now conceded (in Business Brief 7/98) that written demands and civil recovery proceedings for unpaid excise duty which are not covered by the normal time limits for assessments shall not be pursued if an assessment itself would not have been lawful. In effect, the procedural unfairness and discrimination is removed by concession when, arguably, it reflects the proper legal position in view of the Convention (see [1998] S.T.I. 285). Other recent cases involving procedural unfairness which may have been resolved differently or faster if Convention rights had been in issue include *R. v. IRC, ex p. Allen* [1997] S.T.C. 1141 (decision to prosecute taxpayer after alleged assurance that monetary settlement of liabilities would be accepted), *R. v. IRC, ex p. Kingston Smith* [1996] S.T.C. 1210 (improper execution of Revenue search warrant under TMA 1970, s.20) and *R. v. IRC, ex p. Unilever* [1996] S.T.C. 681 ("unfair" refusal of loss relief claims).

At the tribunal level (*i.e.* before proceedings get to the High Court) it is possible that there will be a distinction between cases involving Convention rights but no E.C. rights (when the tribunal will not be able to strike down primary U.K. legislation) and cases involving Convention rights interpreted through E.C. rights (when such striking down will be permissible) — see *Hodgson* and paragraph 14–02 above. How this will apply in the context of a procedural challenge is difficult to forecast at present; what seems certain is that the distinction itself — whereby taxpayers whose human rights come through E.C. law are in a better position — will cause further discrimination.

Although it is not unique to tax litigation, the availability of a right to costs for the successful litigant is obviously a factor to be considered in determining whether the terms of Article 6(1) are satisfied. At present there is no such right in cases before the General Commissioners and only a very limited right before the Special Commissioners. Thus, for example, it is possible (at the very least) that the decision as to costs in *Homeowners Friendly Society v. Barrett* [1995] S.T.C. (S.C.D.) 90 would have gone the other way had Convention rights been in issue.

G. TAXATION OF DAMAGES

14–45   On a conceptual level, the Act and the Convention could have an impact on the current U.K. position on the taxation of damages in two ways — first, on the taxation of damages payable in satisfaction of a court order (*e.g.* for breach of contract or in tort); secondly, on the proper treatment of damages payable for breach of Convention rights themselves.

As regards the former there is no real risk that the Act and the Convention will have any practical effect on the taxation of damages. Damages are taxable or not according to the principles laid down by the House of Lords in *BTC v. Gourley* [1956] A.C. 185: if the sum for the non-receipt of which compensation is sought (*e.g.* lost wages) would have been taxable had it, in fact, been received (*e.g.* under Schedule E) and the compensation now will, in fact, be taxed on receipt, it can be paid without adjustment on account of tax. The same is true if sums not taxable on receipt are paid in compensation for sums which would not have been taxed had they been received (see, most recently, the discussion of the relevant principles in *Deeny v. Gooda Walker Limited* [1996] S.T.C. 299).

14–46   However, the position in respect of payments made as compensation for breach of Convention rights themselves (see s.8) is more difficult, particularly in the employment field. As the law stands at present, the position is as follows:

(1)   Damages awarded pursuant to a claim for wrongful or unfair dismissal which are referable to earnings — failure to give notice, loss of future earnings, etc. — may be "emoluments" subject to income tax under Schedule E. Where this is not so, the sums will in general be taxable under Schedule E as termination payments within Income and Corporation Taxes Act ("ICTA") 1988, s.148 subject to a number of statutory exceptions (see ICTA 1988, s.188).

(2) Damages for distress, embarrassment, injury to feelings, loss of dignity, discrimination and loss of reputation are, in practice, regarded as being outside the scope of income tax. On analysis such sums are unlikely to be "income" for the purposes of the Taxes Acts and (generally) should not be regarded as derived "from" an employment. Thus where payment for injury to feelings, etc., is made:

(a) In connection with the termination of employment, it is outside the charge to income tax either because the sum is paid on account of "injury" within ICTA 1988, s.188(1)(a) or (in practical terms) because it falls within the £30,000 exemption in s.188(4).

(b) As compensation or aggravated damages for racial, sexual or disability discrimination (see Sex Discrimination Act 1975 s.66(4), Race Relations Act 1976, s.59(4) and Disability Discrimination Act 1995, s.8(4)), it is in respect of a breach of an individual's rights *as a person* and is thus outside the charge to income tax, even if it arises in the employment context. (See the awards of aggravated damages in the recent case of *D'Souza v. London Borough of Lambeth* [1997] I.R.L.R. 677 and the comments of Lord Radcliffe in *Hochstrasser v. Mayes* [1960] A.C. 376 at 392.)

(3) Where such injury to feelings payments are made in the course of an on-going employment relationship it is easier to see how the Revenue may contend that they are emoluments for tax purposes. Indeed, there is a small category of cases involving compensation for injury to feelings, distress, etc., where, notwithstanding the general rule in (2) above, the sum is liable to income tax where payment is made in an employment context. Thus, for example, where compensation is paid in respect of the breach of an employee's right to membership of a trade union (see Trade Union and Labour Relations (Consolidation) Act ("TULR(C)A") 1992, ss.137, 146), or the right to time off for trade union duties, trade union activities or public duties (TULR(C)A 1992, ss.168, 170 and Employment Rights Act ("ERA")1996, s.50) it is taxable as Schedule E income — see the Inland Revenue's "Schedule E Manual" at paragraph 1141. This is so even though such compensation is calculated in part by reference to injury to feelings etc (*i.e.* non-pecuniary loss) — see *Cleveland Ambulance NHS Trust v. Blane* [1997] I.R.L.R 332.

(4) Such payments for injury to feelings, etc., are also outside the scope of capital gains tax since they are damages for a "wrong or injury suffered by an individual in his person" — see TCGA 1992, s.51(2). "In his person" is used in contrast to "in his finances". The relief extends to compensation received by person other than the individual who suffers the injury (*e.g.* relatives of a deceased person) and even to compensation for distress caused by the death of another — see Extra Statutory Concession D33.

14–47 The reason for the Revenue's apparently anomalous approach in this narrow area of income tax is the decision of the Court of Appeal in *Hamblett v.*

Godfrey [1987] S.T.C. 60 where the £1000 paid to each employee at GCHQ as compensation for loss of employment rights under the equivalent provisions to those at (3) above (see *CCSU v. The Minister for the Civil Service* (above)) was held to be taxable — see Knox J. at [1986] S.T.C. 213 at 227h–228j and Purchas L.J. at [1987] S.T.C. 60 at 69c–h. In effect the Court held that the rights were so closely tied to the employment relationship that the payment must be regarded for tax purposes as deriving from the employment, *i.e.* payment for breach of an individual's rights *as an employee*. Contentions on behalf of the taxpayer that the rights in question were "personal" rights unconnected with GCHQ were rejected.

How this relates to the tax treatment of sexual and racial discrimination damages arising out of an employment contract is unclear. It is difficult to identify any basis upon which a payment made in consideration of the relinquishment of a right (*Hamblett*) can be taxed differently from a payment made in accordance with that right (*Cleveland Ambulance*) or one which permits the taxation of a sum paid as compensation for the breach of a trade union right but which bars the taxation of a sum paid as compensation for the breach of a statutory right of non-discrimination.

14–48   There remains a risk therefore that there are two categories of case in which compensation can be paid for injury to feelings — the first (not taxable) where the breach is of an individual's personal, or human, rights unconnected with an employment and the second (taxable) where the breach is of an individual's employment related rights.

For present purposes, and despite the shadow cast by *Hamblett* (above), where damages are awarded as compensation for a breach of Convention rights involving humiliation, loss of dignity and injury to feelings, such sums should not be regarded as taxable income *even if payment arises in an employment context*. It is to be hoped that the Inland Revenue will accept this, by analogy with the present treatment of discrimination payments, whatever the true position in relation to *Hamblett*.

If the Revenue are seeking guidance on the matter, valuable help can be drawn from the position in New Zealand where the equivalent Human Rights Act has been in force since 1993. There the New Zealand Revenue have indicated that they do not regard such damages for injury to feelings, etc., as falling within the equivalent income tax provisions even where the breach arises in an employment context (see the Draft Public Ruling, Ref: PU0020); a similar approach is taken to payments made under employment discrimination legislation — see Public Ruling BR 97/3.

H. The Principal Decisions of the Court on Tax Matters

1. Where the taxpayer lost

14–49   *D. G. and W. D. Lindsay v. U.K.* (1986) 49 D.R. 181 — the complainants, a married couple, contended that the U.K. income tax legislation which denied the single person's tax allowance, discriminated on the grounds of sex, marital status and religion. The Commission dismissed the application on the basis that the U.K. legislation was within the State's margin of appreciation and, in any event, the distinction drawn between married and single people was objectively justifiable.

A, B, C, D, v. U.K. (1981) 23 D.R. 203 — the Commission found that retrospective legislation in FA 1978, s.31 to combat a particular form of tax avoidance (the creation of artificial tax losses on commodity trades) was justified in the circumstances. In particular any discriminatory effect of the legislation was justified given the artificial nature of the tax scheme which had no commercial validity.

14–50 *AGOSI v. U.K.* (1986) Series A, No. 108; 9 E.H.R.R. 1 — this case concerned the seizure of krugerrands by Customs which had been smuggled into the U.K. by X. At the time of the seizure AGOSI retained title to the coins which had been stolen from it; AGOSI thus complained that, in the absence of wrongdoing by it, its right to property had been breached contrary to Article 1 of the First Protocol. The Court examined the remedies open in U.K. law to the party from whom the goods had been seized and reached the conclusion that in the circumstances the right balance had been struck between the protection of the public interest and the rights of the owner of property.

In *Gasus Dosier und Fordertechnik GmbH v. Netherlands* (1995) Series A, No. 306-B; 20 E.H.R.R. 403 — Gasus (a German company) complained of the seizure by the Dutch tax authorities of goods it had sold to another company with a retention of title clause. The tax authorities seized the goods in respect of the purchaser's Dutch tax debt. At the time of seizure the full purchase price had not been paid. The Court found that there was prima facie a breach of the right to property but that the measure was justified in securing the payment of tax, *i.e.* the tax raising defence. In the circumstances the acts complained of passed the proportionality test.

14–51   *National & Provincial, Leeds Permanent and Yorkshire Building Societies v. U.K.* [1997] S.T.C. 1466 — in 1986, the U.K. Government changed the basis upon which the building societies collected, on behalf of the Inland Revenue, income tax on interest payable to account holders. One consequence of the change was that some societies (depending upon the date on which their accounting period ended) were required to collect tax under the old system, under the new system and in a "gap" period between the two. In legal proceedings launched at the time, the Woolwich Building Society contended that this particular consequence was *ultra vires* the primary legislation under which the changes were made. This was accepted by the House of Lords (see [1990] 1 W.L.R. 1400) on the basis that, whether such "double taxation" was intended by Parliament, the regulations were technically *ultra vires*. The Woolwich ultimately recovered around £100 million. In reliance on this outcome, at least three other societies (the Leeds Permanent, the National & Provincial and the Yorkshire) claimed to recover similar amounts from the Inland Revenue. Despite the universal application of the decision of the House of Lords in *Woolwich* the Government persuaded Parliament to legislate retrospectively to take away all such vested rights from all societies save for the Woolwich. After the three societies attempted to recover their money by an indirect route which the Government again thwarted by retrospective legislation, an application was made to the Court in Strasbourg. The Court found no substantive breach of either Article 6(1) or Article 1 of the First Protocol, whether read alone or in tandem with Article 14. In short, the steps taken by the Government were all intended to restore the position to what Parliament had originally intended and thus fell within the state's "margin of appreciation" in tax matters. While the decision itself is open to serious challenge (compare the summary of facts at [1997] S.T.C. 1472–1474 with those relied on by the House of Lords at [1990] 1 W.L.R. 1403–1411 (*per* Lord Oliver)) the effect is to set out valuable principles in the tax field.

14–52 *Wasa Liv Omsesidigt* (1988) 58 D.R. 163 — this concerned a challenge under Article 1 of the First Protocol by a Swedish mutual life insurance company to a one-off windfall tax on life insurance companies and other types of financial institutions, imposed with a view to curbing Sweden's budget deficit. The Commission held that such a tax was within a State's margin of appreciation since it was introduced with a specific public purpose in mind and was considered by the State to be in the public interest.

2. Where the taxpayer won

14–53 In *Darby v. Sweden* (1991) Series A, No. 187; 13 E.H.R.R. 774, the taxpayer was a Finnish citizen who worked in Sweden during the week but returned to Finland on the weekends. He was not registered as a resident of Sweden. He was subjected to the Swedish Church Tax. In his particular circumstances, if he had been a resident of Sweden, he would not have had to pay it. The Court found that the taxpayer had been discriminated against and that there was no objective justification for the difference in treatment.

Editions Périscope (1992) Series A, No. 234–B; 14 E.H.R.R. 597 — the taxpayer sued the French State for damages for discrimination in refusing to grant certain tax concessions to it. The Court dismissed a preliminary objection that, being founded on a tax dispute, the claim was not within Article 6(1), and found there had been a breach because the proceedings had exceeded a reasonable time.

14–54 *Hentrich v. France* (1994) Series A, No. 296–A; 18 E.H.R.R. 440 — the tax authorities exercised a right of pre-emption to purchase a property bought by the taxpayer on the ground that the price paid by the purchaser was too low. The Court found that there had been a violation of the right to property as there was no proper justification for the interference, the exercise of the power was arbitrary and the burden placed on the taxpayer was an individual and excessive burden and disproportionate to the aim which the state wanted to achieve. The Court also found a breach of the right to a fair trial because the procedure did not allow the taxpayer to mount a reasoned challenge to the state's action as there was no obligation on the state to give sufficiently detailed reasons for its action and, further, the length of the proceedings (some seven years) was unacceptable.

14-55 *McGregor (Helen) v. U.K.* (above) the applicant challenged Taxes Act 1988, s.259 (in its pre-Finance Act 1998 form) which gave relief in the form of an increased tax allowance to a man married to and living with a totally incapacitated wife with a dependent child but not to a woman. The principal ground of the challenge was sex discrimination contrary to Article 14. The Commission held the complaint admissible and the matter should proceed to a hearing before the full Court.

APPENDIX 1

Human Rights Act 1998

(C.42)

A–01   ## ARRANGEMENT OF SECTIONS

HUMAN RIGHTS ACT 1998

(C.42)

An Act to give further effect to rights and freedoms guaranteed under the European Convention on Human Rights; to make provision with respect to holders of certain judicial offices who become judges of the European Court of Human Rights; and for connected purposes.

[November 9, 1998]

B E IT ENACTED by the Queen's most Excellent Majesty, by and with the advice and consent of the Lords Spiritual and Temporal, and Commons, in this present Parliament assembled, and by the authority of the same, as follows: —

Introduction

1.—(1) In this Act, "the Convention rights" means the rights and fundamental freedoms set out in —

  (a) Articles 2 to 12 and 14 of the Convention,

  (b) Articles 1 to 3 of the First Protocol, and

  (c) Articles 1 and 2 of the Sixth Protocol.

as read with Articles 16 to 18 of the Convention.

(2) Those Articles are to have effect for the purposes of this Act subject to any designated derogation or reservation (as to which see sections 14 and 15).

(3) The Articles are set out in Schedule 1.

(4) The Secretary of State may by order make such amendments to this Act as he considers appropriate to reflect the effect, in relation to the United Kingdom, of a protocol.

(5) In subsection (4) "protocol" means a protocol to the Convention —

  (a) which the United Kingdom has ratified; or

  (b) which the United Kingdom has signed with a view to ratification.

(6) No amendment may be made by an order under subsection (4) so as to come into force before the protocol concerned is in force in relation to the United Kingdom.

2.—(1) A court or tribunal determining a question which has arisen under this Act in connection with a Convention right must take into acocunt any —

  (a) judgment, decision, declaration or advisory opinion of the European Court of Human Rights,

  (b) opinion of the Commission given in a report adopted under Article 31 of the Convention,

  (c) decision of the Commission in connection with Article 26 or 27(2) of the Convention, or

  (d) decision of the Committee of Ministers taken under Article 46 of the Convention, whenever made or given, so far as, in the opinion of the court or tribunal, it is relevant to the proceedings in which that question has arisen.

(2) Evidence of any judgment, decision, declaration or opinion of which account may have to be taken under this section is to be given in proceedings before any court or tribunal in such manner as may be provided by rules.

(3) In this section "rules" means rules of court or, in the case of proceedings before a tribunal, rules for the purposes of this section —

(a) by the Lord Chancellor or the Secretary of State, in relation to any proceedings outside Scotland;

(b) by the Secretary of State, in relation to proceedings in Scotland; or

(c) by a Northern Ireland department, in relation to proceedings before a tribunal in Northern Ireland —

    (i) which deals with transferred matters; and

    (ii) for which no rules made under paragraph (a) are in force.

Legislation

3.—(1) So far as it is possible to do so, primary legislation and subordinate legislation must be read and given effect in a way which is compatible with the Convention rights.

(2) This section —

(a) applies to primary legislation and subordinate legislation whenever enacted;

(b) does not affect the validity, continuing operation or enforcement of any incompatible primary legislation; and

(c) does not affect the validity, continuing operation or enforcement of any incompatible subordiante legislation if (disregarding any possibility of revocation) primary legislation prevents removal of the incompatibility.

4.—(1) Subsection (2) applies in any proceedings in which a court determines whether a provision of primary legislation is compatible with a Convention right.

(2) If the court is satisfied that the provision is incompatible with a Convention right, it may make a declaration of that incompatibility.

(3) Subsection (4) applies in any proceedings in which a court determines whether a provision of subordinate legislation, made in the exercise of a power conferred by primary legislation, is compatible with a Convention right.

(4) If the court is satisfied —

(a) that the provision is incompatible with a Convention right, and

(b) that (disregarding any possibility of revocation) the primary legislation concerned prevents removal of the incompatibility,

it may make a declaration of that incompatibility.

(5) In this section "court" means —

(a) the House of Lords;

(b) the Judicial Committee of the Privy Council;

(c) The Courts-Martial Appeal Court;

(d) in Scotland, the High Court of Judiciary sitting otherwise than as a trial court or the Court of Session;

(e) in England and Wales or Northern Ireland, the High Court or the Court of Appeal.

(6) A declaration under this section ("a declaration of incompatibility") —

(a) does not affect the validity, continuing operation or enforcement of the provision in respect of which it is given; and

(b) is not binding on the parties to the proceedings in which it is made.

5.—(1) Where a court is considering whether to make a declaration of incompatibility, the Crown is entitled to notice in accordance with rules of court.
(2) In any case to which subsection (1) applies —

(a) a Minister of the Crown (or a person nominated by him);

(b) a member of the Scottish Executive;

(c) a Northern Ireland Minister,

(d) a Northern Ireland department,

is entitled, on giving notice in accordance with rules of court, to be joined as a party to the proceedings.
(3) Notice under subsection (2) may be given at any time during the proceedings.
(4) A person who has been made a party to criminal proceedings (other than in Scotland) as the result of a notice under subsection (2) may, with leave, appeal to the House of Lords against any declaration of incompatibility made in the proceedings.
(5) In subsection (4) —

"criminal proceedings" includes all proceedings before the Courts-Martial Appeal Court; and
"leave" means leave granted by the court making the declaration of incompatibility or by the House of Lords.

Public authorities

6.—(1) It is unlawful for a public authority to act in a way which is incompatible with a Convention right.
(2) Subsection (1) does not apply to an act if —

(a) as the result of one or more provisions of primary legislation, the authority could not have acted differently; or

(b) in the case of one or more provisions of, or made under, primary legislation which cannot be read or given effect in a way which is compatible with the Convention rights, the authority was acting so as to give effect to or enforce those provisions.

(3) In this section, "public authority" includes —

(a) a court or tribunal, and

(b) any person certain of whose functions are functions of a public nature,

but does not include either House or Parliament or a person exercising functions in connection with proceedings in Parliament.
(4) In subsection (3) "Parliament" does not include the House of Lords in its judicial capacity.
(5) In relation to a particular act, a person is not a public authority by virtue only of subsection (3)(b) if the nature of the act is private.
(6) "An act" includes a failure to act but does not include a failure to —

    (a) introduce in, or lay before, Parliament a proposal for legislation; or

    (b) make any primary legislation or remedial order.

7.—(1) A person who claims that a public authority has acted (or proposes to act) in a way which is made unlawful by section 6(1) may —

    (a) bring proceedings against the authority under this Act in the appropriate court or tribunal, or

    (b) rely on the Convention right or rights concerned in any legal proceedings,

but only if he is (or would be) a victim of the unlawful act.

(2) In subsection (1)(a) "appropriate court or tribunal" means such court or tribunal as may be determined in accordance with rules; and proceedings against an authority include a counterclaim or similar proceeding.

(3) If the proceedings are brought on an application for judicial review, the applicant is to be taken to have a sufficient interest in relation to the unlawful act only if he is, or would be, a victim of that act.

(4) If the proceedings are made by way of a petition for judicial review in Scotland, the applicant shall be taken to have title and interest to sue in relation to the unlawful act only if he is, or would be, a victim of that act.

(5) Proceedings under subsection (1)(a) must be brought before the end of —

    (a) the period of one year beginning with the date on which the act conplained of took place; or

    (b) such longer period as the court or tribunal considers equitable having regard to all the circumstances,

but that is subject to any rule imposing a stricter time limit in relation to the procedure in question.

(6) In subsection (1)(b) "legal proceedings" includes —

    (a) proceedings brought by or at the instigation of a public authority; and

    (b) an appeal against the decision of a court or tribunal.

(7) For the purposes of this section, a person is a victim of an unlawful act only if he would be a victim for the purposes of Article 34 of the Convention if proceedings were brought in the European Court of Human Rights in respect of that act.

(8) Nothing in this Act creates a criminal offence.

(9) In this section "rules" means —

    (a) in relation to proceedings before a court or tribunal in Scotland, rules made by the Lord Chancellor or the Secretary of State for the purposes of this section or rules of court,

    (b) in relation to proceedings before any other court or tribunal in Scotland, rules made by the Secretary of State for those purposes,

    (c) in relation to proceedings before a tribunal in Northern Ireland —

        (i) which deals with transferred matters; and
        (ii) for which no rules made under paragraph (a) are in force,

and includes provision made by order under section 1 of the Courts and Legal Services Act 1990.

(10) In making rules regard must be had to section 9.

(11) The Minister who has power to make rules in relation to a particular tribunal may, to the extent he considers it necessary to ensure that the tribunal can provide an appropriate remedy in relation to an act (or proposed act) of a public authority which is (or would be) unlawful as a result of section 6(1), by order add to —

(a) the relief or remedies which the tribunal may grant; or

(b) the grounds on which it may grant any of them.

(12) An order made under subsection (11) may contain such incidental, supplemental, consequential or transitional provision as the Minister making it considers appropriate.

8.—(1) In relation to any act (or proposed act) of a public authority which the court finds is (or would be) unlawful, it may grant such relief or remedy, or make such order, within its powers as it considers just and appropriate.

(2) But damages may be awarded only by a court which has power to award damages, or to order the payment of compensation, in civil proceedings.

(3) No award of damages is to be made unless, taking account of all the circumstances of the case, including —

(a) any other relief or remedy granted, or order made, in relation to the act in question (by that or any other court), and

(b) the consequences of any decision (of that or any other court) in respect of that act,

the court is satisfied that the award is necessary to afford just satisfaction to the person in whose favour it is made.

(4) In determining —

(a) whether to award damages, or

(b) the amount of an award,

the court must take into account the principles applied by the European Court of Human Rights in relation to the award of compensation under Article 41 of the Convention.

(5) A public authority against which damages are awarded is to be treated —

(a) in Scotland, for the purposes of section 3 of the Law Reform (Miscellaneous Provisions) (Scotland) Act 1940 as if the award were made in an action of damages in which the authority has been found liable in respect of loss or damage to the person to whom the award is made;

(b) for the purposes of the Civil Liability (Contribution) Act 1978 as liable in respect of damage suffered by the person to whom the award is made.

(6) In this section —

"court" includes a tribunal;
"damages" means damages for an unlawful act of a public authority; and
"unlawful" means unlawful under section 6(1).

9.—(1) Proceedings under section 7(1)(a) in respect of a judicial act may be brought only —

(a) by exercising a right of appeal;

(b) on any application (in Scotland a petition) for judicial review; or

(c) in such other forum as may be prescribed by rules.

(2) That does not affect any rule of law which prevents a court from being the subject of judicial review.

(3) In proceedings under this Act in respect of a judicial act done in good faith, damages may not be awarded otherwise than to compensate a person to the extent required by Article 5(5) of the Convention.

(4) An award of damages permitted by subsection (3) is to be made against the Crown; but no award may be made unless the appropriate person, if not a party to the proceedings, is joined.

(5) In this section —

"appropriate person" means the Minister responsible for the court concerned, or a person or government department nominated by him;

"court" includes a tribunal;

"judge" incudes a member of a tribunal, a justice of the peace and a clerk or other officer entitled to exercise the jurisdiction of a court;

"judicial act" means a judicial act of a court and includes an act done on the instructions, or on behalf, of a judge; and

"rules" has the same meaning as in section 7(9).

Remedial action

10.—(1) This section applies if —

(a) a provision of legislation has been declared under section 4 to be incompatible with a Convention right and, if an appeal lies —

(i) all persons who may appeal have stated in writing that they do not intended to do so;

(ii) the time for bringing an appeal has expired and no appeal has been brought within that time; or

(iii) an appeal brought within that time has been determined or abandoned; or

(b) it appears to a Minister of the Crown or Her Majesty in Council that, having regard to a finding of the European Court of Human Rights made after the coming into force of this section in proceedings against the Untied Kingdom, a provision of legislation is incompatible with an obligation of the United Kingdom arising from the Convention.

(2) If a Minister of the Crown considers that there are compelling reasons for proceeding under this section, he may by order make such amendments to the legislation as he considers necessary to remove the incompatibility.

(3) If, in the case of subordinate legislation, a Minister of the Crown considers —

(a) that it is necessary to amend the primary legislation under which the subordinate legislation in question was made, in order to enable the incompatibility to be removed; and

(b) that there are compelling reasons for proceeding under this section,

he may by order make such amendments to the primary legislation as he considers necessary.

(4) This section also applies where the provision in question is in subordinate legislation and has been quashed, or declared invalid, by reason of incompatibility with a Convention right and the Minister proposes to proceed under paragraph 2(b) of Schedule 2.

(5) If the legislation is an Order in Council, the power conferred by subsection (2) or (3) is exercisable by Her Majesty in Council.

(6) In this section "legislation" does not include a Measure of the Church Assembly or of the General Synod of the Church of England.

(7) Schedule 2 makes further provision about remedial orders.

Other rights and proceedings

11. A person's reliance on a Convention right does not restrict —

(a) any other right or freedom conferred on him by or under any law having effect in any part of the United Kingdom; or

(b) his right to make any claim or bring any proceedings which he could make or bring apart from sections 7 to 9.

12.—(1) This section applies if a court is considering whether to grant any relief which, if granted might affect the exercise of the Convention right to freedom of expression.

(2) If the person against whom the application for relief is made ("the respondent") is neither present nor represented, no such relief is to be granted unless the court is satisfied —

(a) that the applicant has taken all practicable steps to notify the respondent; or

(b) that there are compelling reasons why the respondent should not be notified.

(3) No such relief is to be granted so as to restrain publication before trial unless the court is satisfied that the applicant is likely to establish that publication should not be allowed.

(4) The court must have particular regard to the importance of the Convention right to freedom of expression and, where the proceedings relate to material which the respondent claims, or which appears to the court, to be journalistic, literary or artistic material (or to conduct connected with such material), to —

(a) the extent to which —

(i) the material has, or is about to, become available to the public; or
(ii) it is, or would be, in the public interest for the material to be published;

(b) any relevant privacy code.

(5) In this section —

"court" includes a tribunal; and
"relief" includes any remedy or order (other than in criminal proceedings).

13.—(1) If a court's determination of any question arising under this Act might affect the exercise by a religious organisation (itself or its members collectively) of the Convention right to freedom of thought, conscience and religion, it must have particular regard to the importance of that right.

(2) In this section, "court" includes a tribunal.

Derogations and reservations

14.—(1) In this Act, "designated derogation" means —

(a) the United Kingdom's derogation from Article 5(3) of the Convention; and

(b) any derogation by the United Kingdom from an Article of the Convention, or of any protocol to the Convention, which is designated for the purposes of this Act in an order made by the Secretary of State.

(2) The derogation referred to in subsection (1)(a) is set out in Part I of Schedule 3.

(3) If a designated derogation is amended or replaced it ceases to be a designated derogation.

(4) But subsection (3) does not prevent the Secretary of State from exercising his power under subsection (1)(b) to make a fresh designation order in respect of the Article concerned.

(5) The Secretary of State must by order make such amendments to Schedule 3 as he considers appropriate to reflect —

(a) any designation order; or

(b) the effect of subsection (3).

(6) A designation order may be made in anticipation of the making by the United Kingdom of a proposed derogation.

15.—(1) In this Act, "designated reservation" means —

(a) the United Kingdom's reservation to Article 2 of the First Protocol to the Convention; and

(b) any other reservation by the United Kingdom to an Article of the Convention, or of any protocol to the Convention, which is designated for the purposes of this Act in an order made by the Secretary of State.

(2) The text of the reservation referred to in subsection (1)(a) is set out in Part II of Schedule 3.

(3) If a designated reservation is withdrawn wholly or in part it ceases to be a designated reservation.

(4) But subsection (3) does not prevent the Secretary of State from exercising his power under subsection (1)(b) to make a fresh designation order in respect of the Article concerned.

(5) The Secretary of State must by order make such amendments to this Act as he considers appropriate to reflect —

(a) any designation order; or

(b) the effect of subsection (3).

16.—(1) If it has not already been withdrawn by the United Kingdom, a designated derogation ceases to have effect for the purposes of this Act —

(a) in the case of the derogation referred to in section 14(1)(a), at the end of the period of five years beginning with the date on which section 1(2) came into force;

(b) in the case of any other derogation, at the end of the period of five years beginning with the date on which the order designating it was made.

(2) At any time before the period —

(a) fixed by subsection (1)(a) or (b), or

(b) extended by an order under this subsection,

comes to an end, the Secretary of State may by order extend it by a further period of five years.

(3) An order under section 14(1)(b) ceases to have effect at the end of the period for consideration, unless a resolution has been passed by each House approving the order.

(4) Subsection (3) does not affect —

(a) anything done in reliance on the order; or

(b) the power to make a fresh order under section 14(1)(b).

(5) In subsection (3) "period for consideration" means the period of forty days beginning with the day on which the order was made.

(6) In calculating the period for consideration, no account is to be taken of any time during which —

(a) Parliament is dissolved or prorogued; or

(b) both Houses are adjourned for more than four days.

(7) If a designated derogation is withdrawn by the United Kingdom, the Secretary of State must by order make such amendments to this Act as he considers are required to reflect that withdrawal.

17.—(1) The appropriate Minister must review the designated reservation referred to in section 15(1)(a) —

(a) before the end of the period of five years beginning with the date on which section 1(2) came into force; and

(b) if that designation is still in force, before the end of the period of five years beginning with the date on which the last report relating to it was laid under subsection (3).

(2) The appropriate Minister must review each of the other designated reservations (if any) —

(a) before the end of the period of five years beginning with the date on which the order designating the reservation first came into force; and

(b) if the designation is still in force, before the end of the period of five years beginning with the date on which the last report relating to it was laid under subsection (3).

(3) The Minister conducting a review under this section must prepare a report on the result of the review and lay a copy of it before each House of Parliament.

Judges of the European Court of Human Rights

18.—(1) In this section "judicial office" means the office of —

(a) Lord Justice of Appeal, Justice of the High Court or Circuit judge, in England and Wales;

(b) judge of the Court of Session or sheriff, in Scotland;

(c) Lord Justice of Appeal, judge of the High Court or county court judge, in Northern Ireland.

(2) The holder of a judicial office may become a judge of the European Court of Human Rights ("the Court") without being required to relinquish his office.

(3) But he is not required to perform the duties of his judicial office while he is a judge of the Court.

(4) In respect of any period during which he is a judge of the Court —

(a) a Lord Justice of Appeal or Justice of the High Court is not to count as a judge of the relevant court for the purposes of section 2(1) or 4(1) of the Supreme Court Act 1981 (maximum number of judges) nor as a judge of the Supreme Court for the purposes of section 12(1) to (6) of that Act (salaries etc.);

(b) a judge of the Court of Session is not to count as a judge of that court for the purposes of section 1(1) of the Court of Session Act 1988 (maximum number of judges) or of section 9(1)(c) of the Administration of Justice Act 1973 ("the 1973 Act") (salaries etc.);

(c) a Lord Justice of Appeal or judge of the High Court in Northern Ireland is not to count as a judge of the relevant court for the purposes of section 2(1) or 3(1) of the Judicature (Northern Ireland) Act 1978 (maximum number of judges) nor as a judge of the Supreme Court of Northern Ireland for the purposes of section 9(1)(d) of the 1973 Act (salaries etc.);

(d) a Circuit judge is not to count as such for the purposes of section 18 of the Courts Act 1971 (salaries etc.);

(e) a sheriff is not to count as such for the purposes of section 14 of the Sheriff Courts (Scotland) Act 1907 (salaries etc.);

(f) a county court judge of Northern Ireland is not to count as such for the purposes of section 106 of the County Courts Act (Northern Ireland) 1959 (salaries etc.).

(5) If a sheriff principal is appointed a judge of the Court, section 11(1) of the Sheriff Courts (Scotland) Act 1971 (temporary appointment of sheriff principal) applies, while he holds that appointment, as if his office is vacant.

(6) Schedule 4 makes provision about judicial pensions in relation to the holder of a judicial office who serves as a judge of the Court.

(7) The Lord Chancellor or the Secretary of State may by order make such transitional provision (including, in particular, provision for a temporary increase in the maximum number of judges) as he considers appropriate in relation to any holder of a judicial office who has completed his service as a judge of the Court.

Parliamentary procedure

19.—(1) A Minister of the Crown in charge of a Bill in either House of Parliament must, before Second Reading of the Bill —

(a) make a statement to the effect that in his view the provisions of the Bill are compatible with the Convention rights ("a statement of compatibility"); or

(b) make a statement to the effect that although he is unable to make a statement of compatibility the government nevertheless wishes the House to proceed with the Bill.

(2) The statement must be in writing and be published in such manner as the Minister making it considers appropriate.

Supplemental

20.—(1) Any power of a Minister of the Crown to make an order under this Act is exercisable by statutory instrument.

(2) The power of the Lord Chancellor or the Secretary of State to make rules (other than rules of court) under section 2(3) or 7(9) is exercisable by statutory instrument.

(3) Any statutory instrument made under section 14, 15 or 16(7) must be laid before Parliament.

(4) No order may be made by the Lord Chancellor or the secretary of State under section 1(4), 7(11) or 16(2) unless a draft of the order has been laid before, and approved by, each House of Parliament.

(5) Any statutory instrument made under section 18(7) or Schedule 4, or to which subsection (2) applies, shall be subject to annulment in pursuance of a resolution of either House of Parliament.

(6) The power of a Northern Ireland department to make —

(a) rules under section 2(3)(c) or 7(9)(c), or

(b) an order under section 7(11),

is exercisable by statutory rule for the purposes of the Statutory Rules (Northern Ireland) Order 1979.

(7) Any rules made under section 2(3)(c) or 7(9)(c) shall be subject to negative resolution; and section 41(6) of the Interpretation Act (Northern Ireland) 1954 (meaning of "subject to negative resolution") shall apply as if the power to make the rules were conferred by an Act of the Northern Ireland Assembly.

(8) No order may be made by a Northern Ireland department under section 7(11) unless a draft of the order has been laid before, and approved by, the Northern Ireland Assembly.

21.—(1) In this Act —

"amend" includes repeal and apply (with or without modification);
"the appropriate Minister" means the Minister of the Crown having charge of the appropriate authorised government department (within the meaning of the Crown Proceedings Act 1947);
"the Commission" means the European Commission of Human Rights;
"the Convention" means the Convention for the Protection of Human Rights and Fundamental Freedoms, agreed by the Council of Europe at Rome on November 4, 1950 as it has effect for the time being in relation to the United Kingdom;
"declaration of incompatibility" means a declaration under section 4;
"Minister of the Crown" has the same meaning as in the Ministers of the Crown Act 1975;
"Northern Ireland Minister" includes the First Minister and the deputy First Minister in Northern Ireland;
"primary legislation" means any —

(a) public general Act;
(b) local and personal Act;
(c) private Act;
(d) Measure of the Church Assembly;
(e) Measure of the General Synod of the Church of England;
(f) Order in Council —

(i) made in exercise of Her Royal Prerogative;
(ii) made under section 38(1)(a) of the Northern Ireland Constitution Act 1973 of the corresponding provision of the Northern Ireland Act 1998; or
(iii) amending an Act of a kind mentioned in paragraph (a), (b) or (c);

and includes an order or other instrument made under primary legislation (otherwise than by the National Assembly for Wales, a member of the Scottish Executive, a Northern Ireland Minister or a Northern Ireland department) to the extent to which it operates to bring one or more provisions of that legislation into force or amends any primary legislation;
"the First Protocol" means the protocol to the Convention agreed at Paris on March 20, 1952;
"the Sixth Protocol" means the protocol to the Convention agreed at Strasbourg on April 28, 1983;
"11th Protocol" means the protocol to the Convention (restructuring the control machinery established by the Convention) agreed at Strasbourg on May 11, 1994;
"remedial order" means an order under section 10;
"subordinate legislation" means any —

   (a) Order in Council other than one —

      (i) made in exercise of Her Majesty's Royal Prerogative;

      (ii) made under section 38(1)(a) of the Northern Ireland Constitution Act 1973 or the corresponding provision of the Northern Ireland Act 1998; or;

      (iii) amending an Act of a kind mentioned in the definition of primary legislation;

   (b) Act of the Scottish Parliament;

   (c) Act of the Parliament of Northern Ireland;

   (d) Measure of the Assembly established under section 1 of the Northern Ireland Assembly Act 1973;

   (e) Act of the Northern Ireland Assembly;

   (f) order, rules, regulations, scheme, warrant, byelaw or other instrument made under primary legislation (except to the extent to which it operates to bring one or more provisions of that legislation into force or amends any primary legislation);

   (g) order, rules, regulations, scheme, warrant, byelaw or other instrument made under legislation mentioned in paragraph (b), (c), (d) or (e) or made under an Order in Council applying only to Northern Ireland;

   (h) order, rules, regulations, scheme, warrant, byelaw or other instrument made by a member of the Scottish Executive, a Northern Ireland Minister or a Northern Ireland department in exercise of prerogative or other executive functions of Her Majesty which are exercisable by such a person on behalf of Her Majesty;

"transferred matters" has the same meaning as in the Northern Ireland Act 1998; and

"tribunal" means any tribunal in which legal proceedings may be brought.

(2) The references in paragraphs (b) and (c) of section 2(1) to Articles are to Articles of the Convention as they had effect immediately before the coming into force of the 11th Protocol.

(3) The reference in paragraph (d) of section 2(1) to Article 46 includes a reference to Articles 32 and 54 of the Convention as they had effect immediately before the coming into force of the 11th Protocol.

(4) The references in section 2(1) to a report or decision of the Commission or a decision of the Committee of Ministers include references to a report or decision made as provided by paragraphs 3, 4 and 6 of Article 5 of the 11th Protocol (transitional provisions).

(5) Any liability under the Army Act 1955, the Air Force Act 1955 or the Naval Discipline Act 1957 to suffer death for an offence is replaced by a liability to imprisonment for life or any less punishment authorised by those Acts; and those Acts shall accordingly have effect with the necessary modifications.

22.—(1) This Act may be cited as the Human Rights Act 1998.

(2) Sections 18, 20 and 21(5) and this section come into force on the passing of this Act.

(3) The other provisions of this Act come into force on such day as the Secretary of State may by order appoint; and different days may be appointed for different purposes.

(4) Paragraph (b) of subsection (1) of section 7 applies to proceedings brought by or at the instigation of a public authority whenever the act in question took place; but otherwise that subsection does not apply to an act taking place before the coming into force of that section.

(5) This Act binds the Crown.

(6) This Act extends to Northern Ireland.

(7) Section 21(5), so far as it relates to any provision contained in the Army Act 1955, the Air Force Act 1955 or the Naval Discipline Act 1957, extends to any place to which that provision extends.

SCHEDULES

SCHEDULE 1

THE ARTICLES

PART I

THE CONVENTION

RIGHTS AND FREEDOMS

Article 2

Right to life

1. Everybody's right to life shall be protected by law. No one shall be deprived of his life intentionally save in the execution of a sentence of a court following his conviction of a crime for which this penalty is provided by law.

2. Deprivation of life shall not be regarded as inflicted in contravention of this Article when it results from the use of force which is no more than absolutely necessary:

(a) in defence of any person from unlawful violence;

(b) in order to effect a lawful arrest or to prevent the escape of a person lawfully detained;

(c) in action lawfully taken for the purpose of quelling a riot or insurrection.

Article 3

Prohibition of torture

No one shall be subjected to torture or to inhuman or degrading treatment or punishment.

Article 4

Prohibition of slavery and forced labour

1. No one shall be held in slavery or servitude.

2. No one shall be required to perform forced or compulsory labour.

3. For the purpose of this Article the term "forced or compulsory labour" shall not include:

(a) any work required to be done in the ordinary course of detention imposed according to the provisions of Article 5 of this Convention or during conditional release from such detention;

(b) any service of a military character or, in case of conscientious objectors in countries where they are recognised, service exacted instead of compulsory military service;

(c) any service exacted in case of an emergency or calamity threatening the life or well-being of the community;

(d) any work or service which forms part of normal civic obligations.

Article 5

Right to liberty and security

1. Everyone has the right to liberty and security of person. No one shall be deprived of his liberty save in the following cases and in accordance with a procedure prescribed by law:

(a) the lawful detention of a person after conviction by a competent court;

(b) the lawful arrest or detention of a person for non-compliance with the lawful order of a court or in order to secure the fulfilment of any obligation prescribed by law;

(c) the lawful arrest or detention of a person effected for the purpose of bringing him before the competent legal authority on reasonable suspicion of having committed an offence or when it is reasonably considered necessary to prevent his committing an offence or fleeing after having done so;

(d) the detention of a minor by lawful order for the purpose of educational supervision or his lawful detention for the purpose of bringing him before the competent legal authority;

(e) the lawful detention of persons for the prevention of the spreading of infectious diseases, of persons of unsound mind, alcoholics or drug addicts or vagrants;

(f) the lawful arrest or detention of a person to prevent his effecting an unauthorised entry into the country or of a person against whom action is being taken with a view to deportation or extradition.

2. Everyone who is arrested shall be informed promptly, in a language which he understands, of the reasons for his arrest and of any charge against him.

3. Everyone arrested or detained in accordance with the provisions of paragraph 1(c) of this Article shall be brought promptly before a judge or other officer authorised by law to exercise judicial power and shall be entitled to trial within a reasonable time or to release pending trial. Release may be conditioned by guarantees to appear for trial.

4. Everyone who is deprived of his liberty by arrest or detention shall be entitled to take proceedings by which the lawfulness of his detention shall be decided speedily by a court and his release ordered if the detention is not lawful.

5. Everyone who has been the victim of arrest or detention in contravention of the provisions of this Article shall have an enforceable right to compensation.

Article 6

Right to a fair trial

1. In the determination of his civil rights and obligations or of any criminal charge against him, everyone is entitled to a fair and public hearing within a reasonable time by an independent and impartial tribunal established by law. Judgment shall be pronounced publicly but the press and public may be excluded from all or part of the trial in the interest of morals, public order or national security in a democratic society, where the interests of juveniles or the protection of the private life of the parties so require, or to the extent strictly necessary in the opinion of the court in special circumstances where publicity would prejudice the interests of justice.

2. Everyone charged with a criminal offence shall be presumed innocent until proved guilty according to law.

3. Everyone charged with a criminal offence has the following minimum rights:

(a) to be informed promptly, in a language which he understands and in detail, of the nature and cause of the accusation against him;

(b) to have adequate time and facilities for the preparation of his defence;

(c) to defend himself in person or through legal assistance of his own choosing or, if he has not sufficient means to pay for legal assistance, to be given it free when the interests of justice so require;

(d) to examine or have examined witnesses against him and to obtain the attendance and examination of witnesses on his behalf under the same conditions as witnesses against him;

(e) to have the free assistance of an interpreter if he cannot understand or speak the language used in court.

Article 7

No punishment without law

1. No one shall be held guilty of any criminal offence on account of any act or omission which did not constitute a criminal offence under national or international law at the time when it was committed. Nor shall a heavier penalty be imposed than the one that was applicable at the time the criminal offence was committed.

2. This Article shall not prejudice the trial and punishment of any person for any act or omission which, at the time when it was committed, was criminal according to the general principles of law recognised by civilised nations.

Article 8

Right to respect for private and family life

1. Everyone has the right to respect for his private and family life, his home and his correspondence.

2. There shall be no interference by a public authority with the exercise of this right except such as is in accordance with the law and is necessary in a democratic society in the interests of national security, public safety or the economic well-being of the country, for the prevention of disorder or crime, for the protection of health or morals, or for the protection of the rights and freedoms of others.

Article 9

Freedom of thought, conscience and religion

1. Everyone has the right to freedom of thought, conscience and religion; this right incudes freedom to change his religion or belief and freedom, either alone or in community with others and in public or private, to manifest his religion or belief, in worship, teaching, practice and observance.

2. Freedom to manifest one's religion or beliefs shall be subject only to such limitations as are prescribed by law and are necessary in a democratic society in the interests of public safety, for the protection of public order, health or morals, or for the protection of the rights and freedoms of others.

Article 10

Freedom of expression

1. Everyone has the right to freedom of expression. This right shall include freedom to hold opinions and to receive and impart information and ideas without interference by public authority and regardless of frontiers. This Article shall not prevent States from requiring the licensing of broadcasting, television or cinema enterprises.

2. The exercise of these freedoms, since it carries with it duties and responsibilities, may be subject to such formalities, conditions, restrictions or penalties as are prescribed by law and are necessary in a democratic society, in the interests of national security, territorial integrity or public safety, for the prevention of disorder or crime, for the protection of health or morals, for the protection of the reputation or rights of others, for preventing the disclosure of information received in confidence, or for maintaining the authority and impartiality of the judiciary.

Article 11

Freedom of assembly and association

1. Everyone has the right to freedom of peaceful assembly and to freedom of association with others, including the right to form and to join trade unions for the protection of his interests.

2. No restrictions shall be placed on the exercise of these rights other than such as are prescribed by law and are necessary in a democratic society in the interests of national security or public safety, for the prevention of disorder or crime, for the protection of health or morals or for the protection of the rights and freedoms of others. This Article shall not prevent the imposition of lawful restrictions on the exercise of these rights by members of the armed forces, of the police or of the administration of the State.

Article 12

Right to marry

Men and women of marriageable age have the right to marry and to found a family, according to the national laws governing the exercise of this right.

Article 14

Prohibition of discrimination

The enjoyment of the rights and freedoms set forth in this Convention shall be secured without discrimination on any ground such as sex, race, colour, languge, religion, political or other opinion, national or social origin, association with a national minority, property, birth or other status.

Article 16

Restrictions on political activity of aliens

Nothing in Articles 10, 11 and 14 shall be regarded as preventing the High Contracting Parties from imposing restrictions on the political activity of aliens.

Article 17

Prohibition of abuse of rights

Nothing in this Convention may be interpreted as implying for any State, group or person any right to engage in any activity or perform any act aimed at the destruction of any of the rights and freedoms set forth herein or at their limitation to a greater extent than is provided for in the Convention.

Article 18

Limitation on use of restrictions on rights

The restrictions permitted under this Convention to the said rights and freedoms shall not be applied for any purpose other than those for which they have been prescribed.

PART II

THE FIRST PROTOCOL

Article 1

Protection of property

Every natural or legal person is entitled to the peaceful enjoyment of his possessions. No one shall be deprived of his possessions except in the public interest and subject to the conditions provided for by law and by the general principles of international law.

The preceding provisions shall not, however, in any way impair the right of a State to enforce such laws as it deems necessary to control the use of property in accordance with the general interest or to secure the payment of taxes or other contributions or penalties.

Article 2

Right to education

No person shall be denied the right to education. In the exercise of any functions which it assumes in relation to education and to teaching, the State shall respect the right of parents to ensure such education and teaching in conformity with their own religious and philosophical convictions.

Article 3

Right to free elections

The High Contracting Parties undertake to hold free elections at reasonable intervals by secret ballot, under conditions which will ensure the free expression of the opinion of the people in the choice of the legislature.

PART III

THE SIXTH PROTOCOL

Article 1

Abolition of the death penalty

The death penalty shall be abolished. No one shall be condemned to such penalty or executed.

Article 2

Death penalty in time of war

A State may make provision in its law for the death penalty in respect of acts committed in time of war or of imminent threat of war; such penalty shall be applied only in the instances laid down in the law and in accordance with its provisions. The State shall communicate to the Secretary General of the Council of Europe the relevant provisions of that law.

SCHEDULE 2

REMEDIAL ORDERS

Orders

1.—(1) A remedial order may —

    (a) contain such incidental, supplemental, consequential or transitional provision as the person making it considers appropriate;

    (b) be made so as to have effect from a date earlier than that on which it is made;

    (c) make provision for the delegation of specific functions;

    (d) make different provision for different cases.

(2) The power conferred by sub-paragraph (1)(a) includes —

    (a) power to amend primary legislation (inlcuding primary legislation other than that which contains the incompatible provision); and

    (b) power to amend or revoke subordinate legislation (including subordinate legislation other than that which contains the incompatible provision).

(3) A remedial order may be made so as to have the same extent as the legislation which it affects.

(4) No person is to be guilty of an offence solely as a result of the retrospective effect of a remedial order.

Procedure

2. No remedial order may be made unless —

    (a) a draft of the order has been approved by a resolution of each House of Parliament made after the end of the period of 60 days beginning with the day on which the draft was laid; or

(b) it is declared in the order that it appears to the person making it that, because of the urgency of the matter, it is necessary to make the order without a draft being so approved.

Orders laid in draft

3.—(1) No draft may be laid under paragraph 2(a) unless —

(a) the person proposing to make the order has laid before Parliament a document which contains a draft of the proposed order and the required information; and

(b) the period of 60 days, beginning with the day on which the document required by this sub-paragraph was laid, has ended.

(2) If representations have been made during that period, the draft laid under paragraph 2(a) must be accompanied by a statement containing —

(a) a summary of the representations; and

(b) if, as a result of the representations, the proposed order has been changed, details of the changes.

Urgent cases

4.—(1) If a remedial order ("the original order") is made without being approved in draft, the person making it must lay it before Parliament, accompanied by the required information, after it is made.

(2) If representations have been made during the period of 60 days beginning with the day on which the original order was made, the person making it must (after the end of that period) lay before Parliament a statement containing —

(a) a summary of the representations; and

(b) if, as a result of the representations, he considers it appropriate to make changes to the original order, details of the changes.

(3) If sub-paragraph (2)(b) applies, the person making the statements must —

(a) make a further remedial order replacing the original order; and

(b) lay the replacement order before Parliament.

(4) If, at the end of the period of 120 days beginning with the day on which the original order was made, a resolution has not been passed by each House approving the original or replacement order, the order ceases to have effect (but without that affecting anything previously done under either order or the power to make a fresh remedial order).

Definitions

5. In this Schedule —

"representations" means representations about a remedial order (or proposed remedial order) made to the person making (or proposing to make) it and includes any relevant Parliamentary report or resolution; and
"required information" means —

(a) an explanation of the incompatibility which the order (or proposed order) seeks to remove, including particulars of the relevant declaration, finding or order; and

(b) a statement of the reasons for proceeding under section 10 and for making an order in those terms.

Calculating periods

6. In calculating any period for the purposes of this Schedule, no account is to be taken of any time during which —

(a) Parliament is dissolved or prorogued; or

(b) both Houses are adjourned for more than four days.

SCHEDULE 3

DEROGATION AND RESERVATION

PART I

DEROGATION

The 1988 notification

The United Kingdom Permanent Representative to the Council of Europe presents his compliments to the Secretary General of the Council, and has the honour to convey the following information in order to ensure compliance with the obligations of Her Majesty's Government in the United Kingdom under Article 15(3) of the Convention for the Protection of Human Rights and Fundamental Freedoms signed at Rome on November 4, 1950.

There have been in the United Kingdom in recent years campaigns of organised terrorism connected with the affairs of Northern Ireland which have manifested themselves in activities which have included repeated murder, attempted murder, maiming, intimidation and violent civil disturbance and in bombing and fire raising which have resulted in death, injury and widespread destruction of property. As a result, a public emergency within the meaning of Article 15(1) of the Convention exists in the United Kingdom.

The Government found it necessary in 1974 to introduce and since then, in cases concerning persons reasonably suspected of involvement in terrorism connected with the affairs of Northern Ireland, or of certain offences under the legislation, who have been detained for 48 hours, to exercise powers enabling further detention without charge, for periods of up to five days, on the authority of the Secretary of State. These powers are at present to be found in section 12 of the Prevention of Terrorism (Temporary Provisions) Act 1984, Article 9 of the Prevention of Terrorism (Supplemental Temporary Provisions) Order 1984 and Article 10 of the Prevention of Terrorism (Supplemental Temporary Provisions) (Northern Ireland) Order 1984.

Section 12 of the Prevention of Terrorism (Temporary Provisions) Act 1984 provides for a person whom a constable has arrested on reasonable grounds of suspecting him to be guilty of an offence under sections 1, 9 or 10 of the Act, or to be or to have been involved in terrorism connected with the affairs of Northern Ireland, to be detained in right of the arrest for up to 48 hours and thereafter, where the Secretary of State extends the detention period, for up to a further five days. Section 12 substantially re-enacted section 12 of the Prevention of Terrorism (Temporary Provisions) Act 1976 which, in turn, substantially re-enacted Section 7 of the Prevention of Terrorism (Temporary Provisions) Act 1974.

Article 10 of the Prevention of Terrorism (Supplemental Temporary Provisions) (Northern Ireland) Order (S.I. 1984 No. 417) and Article 9 of the Prevention of Terrorism (Supplemental Temporary Provisions) Order (S.I. 1984 No. 418) were both made under sections 13 and 14 of and Schedule 3 to the 1984 Act and substantially re-enacted powers of detention in Orders made under the 1974 and 1976 Acts. A person who is being examined under Article 4 of either Order on his arrival in, or on seeking to leave, Northern Ireland or Great Britain for the purpose of determining whether he is or has been involved in terrorism connected with the affairs of Northern Ireland, or whether there are grounds for suspecting that he has committed an offence under Section 9 of the 1984 Act, may be detained under Article 9 or 10, as appropriate, pending the conclusion of his examination. The period of this examination may exceed 12 hours if an examining officer has reasonable grounds for suspecting him to be or to have been involved in acts of terrorism connected with the affairs of Northern Ireland.

Where such a person is detained under the said Article 9 or 10 he may be detained for up to 48 hours on the authority of an examining officer and thereafter, where the Secretary of State extends the detention period, for up to a further five days.

In its judgment of November 29, 1988 in the case of *Brogan and Others*, the European Court of Human Rights held that there had been a violation of Article 5(3) in respect of each of the applicants, all of whom had been detained under section 12 of the 1984 Act. The Court held tht even the shortest of the four periods of detention concerned, namely four days and six hours, fell outside the constraints as to time permitted by the first part of Article 5(3). In addition, the Court held that there had been a violation of Article 5(5) in the case of each applicant.

Following this judgment the Secretary of State for the Home Department informed Parliament on December 6, 1988 that, against the background of the terrorist campaign, and the overriding need to bring terrorists to justice, the Government did not believe that the maximum period of detention should be reduced. He informed Parliament that the Government were examining the matter with a view to responding to the judgment. On December 22, 1988, the Secretary of State further informed Parliament that it remained the Government's wish, if it could be achieved, to find a judicial process under which extended detention might be reviewed and where appropriate authorised by a judge or other judicial officer. But a further period of reflection and consultation was necessary before the Government could bring forward a firm and final view.

Since the judgment of November 29, 1988 as well as previously, the Government have found it necessary to continue to exercise, in relation to terrorism connected with the affairs of Northern Ireland, the powers described above enabling further detention without charge for periods of up to five days, on the authority of the Secretary of State, to the extent strictly required by the exigencies of the situation to enable necessary enquiries and investigations properly to be completed in order to decide whether criminal proceedings should be instituted. To the extent that the exercise of these powers may be inconsistent with the obligations imposed by the Convention the Government has availed itself of the right of derogation conferred by Article 15(1) of the Convention and will continue to do so until further notice.

Dated December 23, 1988.

The 1989 notification

The United Kingdom Permanent Representative to the Council of Europe presents his compliments to the Secretary General of the Council, and has the honour to convey the following information.

In his communication to the Secretary General of December 23, 1988, reference was made to the introduction and exercise of certain powers under section 12 of the Prevention of Terrorism (Temporary Provisions) Act 1984, Article 9 of the Prevention of Terrorism (Supplemental Temporary Provisions) Order 1984 and Article 10 of the Prevention of Terrorism (Supplemental Temporary Provisions) (Northern Ireland) Order 1984.

These provisions have been replaced by section 14 of and paragraph 6 of Schedule 5 to the Prevention of Terrorism (Temporary Provisions) Act 1989, which make comparable provisions. They came into force on March 22, 1989. A copy of these provisions is enclosed.

The United Kingdom Permanent Representative avails himself of this opportunity to renew to the Secretary General the assurance of his highest consideration.

March 23, 1989.

PART II

RESERVATION

At the time of signing the present (First) Protocol, I declare that, in view of certain provisions of the Education Acts in the United Kingdom, the principle affirmed in the second sentence of Article 2 is accepted by the United Kingdom only so far as it is compatible with the provision of efficient instruction and training, and the avoidance of unreasonable public expenditure.

Dated March 20, 1952. Made by the United Kingdom Permanent Representative to the Council of Europe.

SCHEDULE 4

JUDICIAL PENSIONS

Duty to make orders about pensions

1.—(1) The appropriate Minister must by order make provision with respect to pensions payable to or in respect of any holder of a judicial office who serves as an ECHR judge.

(2) A pensions order must include such provision as the Minister making it considers is necessary to secure that —

(a) an ECHR judge who was, immediately before his appointment as an ECHR judge, a member of a judicial pension scheme is entitled to remain as a member of that scheme;

(b) the terms on which he remains a member of the scheme are those which would have been applicable had he not been appointed as an ECHR judge; and

(c) entitlement to benefits payable in accordance with the scheme continues to be determined as if, while serving as an ECHR judge, his salary was that which would (but for section 18(4)) have been payable to him in respect of his continuing service as the holder of his judicial office.

Contributions

2. A pensions order may, in particular, make provision —

(a) for any contributions which are payable by a person who remains a member of a scheme as a result of the order, and which would otherwise be payable by deduction from his salary, to be made otherwise than by deduction from his salary as an ECHR judge; and

(b) for such contributions to be collected in such manner as may be determined by the administrators of the scheme.

Amendments of other enactments

3. A pensions order may amend any provision of, or made under, a pensions Act in such manner and to such extent as the Minister making the order considers necessary or expedient to ensure the proper administration of any scheme to which it relates.

Definitions

4. In this Schedule —
"appropriate Minister" means —

> (a) in relation to any judicial office whose jurisdiction is exercisable exclusively in relation to Scotland, the Secretary of State; and
> (b) otherwise, the Lord Chancellor;

"ECHR judge" means the holder of a judicial office who is serving as a judge of the Court;

"judicial pension scheme" means a scheme established by and in accordance with a pensions Act;

"pensions Act" means —

> (a) the County Courts Act (Northern Ireland) 1959;
> (b) the Sheriffs' Pensions (Scotland) Act 1961;
> (c) the Judicial Pensions Act 1981; or
> (d) the Judicial Pensions and Retirement Act 1993; and

"pensions order" means an order made under paragraph 1.

APPENDIX 2

Other Relevant Convention Provisions

PART I: AFTER THE ELEVENTH PROTOCOL

Article 1

A–02   The High Contracting Parties shall secure to everyone within their jurisdiction the rights and freedoms defined in section I of this Convention.

Article 13

Everyone whose rights and freedoms as set forth in this Convention are violated shall have an effective remedy before a national authority notwithstanding that the violation has been committed by persons acting in an official capacity.

Article 15

1. In time of war or other public emergency threatening the life of the nation any High Contracting Party may take measures derogating from its obligations under this Convention to the extent strictly required by the exigencies of the situation, provided that such measures are not inconsistent with its other obligations under international law.

2. No derogation from Article 2, except in respect of deaths resulting from lawful acts of war, or from Articles 3, 4 (paragraph 1) and 7 shall be made under this provision.

3. Any High Contracting Party availing itself of this right of derogation shall keep the Secretary General of the Council of Europe fully informed of the measures which it has taken and the reasons therefor. It shall also inform the Secretary General of the Council of Europe when such measures have ceased to operate and the provisions of the Convention are again being fully executed.

Article 34

(as substituted by Eleventh Protocol, Art. 1, 1994)

The Court may receive applications from any person, non-governmental organisation or group of individuals claiming to be the victim of a violation by one of the High Contracting Parties of the rights set forth in the Convention or the protocols thereto. The High Contracting Parties undertake not to hinder in any way the effective exercise of this right.

Article 35

(as substituted by Eleventh Protocol, Art. 1, 1994)

1. The Court may only deal with the matter after all domestic remedies have been exhausted, according to the generally recognised rules of international law, and within a period of six months from the date on which the final decision was taken.

2. The Court shall not deal with any individual application submitted under Article 34 that:

(a) is anonymous; or

(b) is substantially the same as a matter which has already been examined by the Court or has already been submitted to another procedure of international investigation or settlement and contains no relevant new information.

3. The Court shall consider inadmissible any petition submitted under Article 34 which it considers incompatible with the provisions of the present Convention or the protocols thereto, manifestly ill-founded, or an abuse of the right of application.

4. The Court shall reject any petition referred to it which it considers inadmissible under this Article. It may do so at any stage of the proceedings.

Article 41

(as substituted by Eleventh Protocol, Art. 1, 1994)

If the Court finds that there has been a violation of the Convention or the protocols thereto, and if the internal law of the High Contracting Party allows only partial reparation to be made, the Court shall, if necessary, afford just satisfaction to the injured party.

Article 46

(as substituted by Eleventh Protocol, Art. 1, 1994)

1. The High Contracting Parties undertake to abide by the final decision of the Court in any case to which they are parties.

2. The final judgment of the Court shall be transmitted to the Committee of Ministers, which shall supervise its execution.

Article 57

(as renumbered by Eleventh Protocol, Art. 2, 1994)

1. Any State may, when signing this Convention or when depositing its instrument of ratification, make a reservation in respect of any particular provision of the Convention to the extent that any law then in force in its territory is not in conformity with the provision. Reservations of a general character shall not be permitted under this article.

2. Any reservation made under this article shall contain a brief statement of the law concerned.

PART II: PREVIOUS PROVISIONS

*Article 25

1. The Commission may receive petitions addressed to the Secretary General of the Council of Europe from any person, non-governmental organisation or group of individuals claiming to be the victim of a violation by one of the High Contracting Parties of the rights set forth in this Convention, provided that the High Contracting Party against which the complaint has been lodged has declared that it recognises the competence of the Commission to receive such petitions.

[2. . . . 4. not reproduced]

*Article 26

The Commission may only deal with the matter after all domestic remedies have been exhausted, according to the generally recognised rules of international law, and within a period of six months from the date on which the final decision was taken.

*Article 27

1. The Commission shall not deal with any petition submitted under Article 25 which:

(a) is anonymous, or

(b) is substantially the same as a matter which has already been examined by the Commission or has already been submitted to another procedure of international investigation or settlement and if it contains no relevant new information.

2. The Commission shall consider inadmissible any petition submitted under Article 25 which it considers incompatible with the provisions of the present Convention, manifestly ill-founded, or an abuse of the right of petition.

3. The Commission shall reject any petition referred to it which it considers inadmissible under Article 26.

*Article 28

(as amended by Third Protocol, Art. 2, 1963 and Eighth Protocol, Art. 4, 1985)

[1. Not reproduced.]

2. If the Commission succeeds in effecting a friendly settlement, it shall draw up a report which shall be sent to the States concerned, to the Committee of Ministers and the Secretary General of the Council of Europe for publication. This report shall be confined to a brief statement of the facts and of the solution reached.

*Article 31

(as amended by Eighth Protocol, Art. 7, 1985)

1. If the examination of a petition has not been completed in accordance with Article 28 (paragraph 2), 29 or 30, the Commission shall draw up a Report on the facts and state its opinion as to whether the facts found disclose a breach by the State concerned of its obligations under the Convention. The individual opinions of all the members of the Commission on this point may be stated in the Report.

[2. . . . 3. not reproduced.]

*Article 32

(as amended by Tenth Protocol, Art. 1, 1992)

1. If the question is not referred to the Court in acordance with Article 48 of this Convention within a period of three months from the date of the transmission of the report to the Committee of Ministers, the Committee of Ministers shall decide by a majority of the members entitled to sit on the Committee whether there has been a violation of the Convention.
2. In the affirmative case the Committee of Ministers shall prescribe a period during which the High Contracting Party concerned must take the measures required by the decision of the Committee of Ministers.
3. If the High Contracting Party concerned has not taken satisfactory measures within the prescribed period, the Committee of Ministers shall decide by the majority provided for in paragraph 1 above what effect shall be given to its original decision and shall publish the report.
4. The High Contracting Parties undertake to regard as binding on them any decision which the Committee of Ministers may take in application of the preceding paragraphs.

*Article 50

If the Court finds that a decision or a measure taken by a legal authority or any other authority of a High Contracting Party is completely or partially in conflict with the obigations arising from the present Convention, and if the internal law of the said Party allows only partial reparation to be made for the consequences of this decision or measure, the decision of the Court shall, if necessary, afford just satisfaction to the injured party.

*Article 53

The High Contracting Parties undertake to abide by the decision of the Court in any case to which they are Parties.

*Article 54

The judgment of the Court shall be transmitted to the Committee of Ministers which shall supervise its execution.

Index